A FAREWELL TO FRAGMENTATION

Fragmentation has been much discussed as a threat to international law as a legal system. This book contends that the fragmentation of international law is far exceeded by its convergence, as international bodies find ways to account for each other and the interactions of emerging fields. Reasserting its role as the 'principal judicial organ of the United Nations', the International Court of Justice has ensured that the centre of international law can and does hold. This process has strengthened a trend towards the re-unification of international law. In order to explore this process, this book deals with the issues of fragmentation and convergence both from the point of view of the centre of the International Court and of the position of other courts and tribunals. Featuring contributions by leading international lawyers from a range of backgrounds, this volume proposes both a new take and the last word on the fragmentation debate in international law.

MADS ANDENAS is a Professor in the Faculty of Law at the University of Oslo, and the UN Special Rapporteur on Arbitrary Detention and the Chair of the UN Working Group on Arbitrary Detention, which reports to the UN Human Rights Council and the UN General Assembly. He has held senior academic appointments in the United Kingdom, including as Director of the British Institute of International and Comparative Law, London, and Director of the Centre of European Law at King's College, University of London.

EIRIK BJORGE is Shaw Foundation Junior Research Fellow at Jesus College, University of Oxford. Eirik has taught at Oxford and Sciences Po, Paris. He is the author of *The Evolutionary Interpretation of Treaties* (2014) and a co-editor, with Cameron Miles, of *Landmark Cases in Public International Law* (2016).

A FAREWELL TO FRAGMENTATION

Reassertion and Convergence in International Law

Edited by

MADS ANDENAS AND EIRIK BJORGE

CAMBRIDGE
UNIVERSITY PRESS

CAMBRIDGE
UNIVERSITY PRESS

University Printing House, Cambridge CB2 8BS, United Kingdom

Cambridge University Press is part of the University of Cambridge.

It furthers the University's mission by disseminating knowledge in the pursuit of education, learning and research at the highest international levels of excellence.

www.cambridge.org
Information on this title: www.cambridge.org/9781107082090

First published 2015

A catalogue record for this publication is available from the British Library

Library of Congress Cataloguing in Publication data
A farewell to fragmentation : reassertion and convergence in international law / edited by Mads Andenas, Eirik Bjorge.
pages cm. – (Studies on international courts and tribunals)
Includes bibliographical references and index.
ISBN 978-1-107-08209-0 (hardback)
1. International law. 2. International courts. I. Andenas, Mads Tonnesson, 1957– editor. II. Bjorge, Eirik, 1983– editor.
KZ3410.F37 2015
341 – dc23 2015002842

ISBN 978-1-107-08209-0 Hardback

CONTENTS

CONTRIBUTORS

MADS ANDENAS
University of Oslo; Chair-Rapporteur, UN Working Group on Arbitrary Detention

EIRIK BJORGE
Jesus College, University of Oxford

JUDGE ANTÔNIO AUGUSTO CANÇADO TRINDADE
Judge at the International Court of Justice

DR EMANUEL CASTELLARIN
Ecole de droit, University of Paris I

VERONIKA FIKFAK
Homerton College, University of Cambridge

DR MAGDALENA FOROWICZ
Senior Research Fellow, Faculty of Law, University of Zurich

PROFESSOR VERA GOWLLAND-DEBBAS
Emeritus Professor, Graduate Institute of International and Development Studies, Geneva

PROFESSOR LORENZO GRADONI
Faculty of Law, University of Bologna

SIR CHRISTOPHER GREENWOOD
Judge at the International Court of Justice

PROFESSOR JEAN-LOUIS HALPÉRIN
Humanities and Social Sciences Department, Ecole normale supérieure, Paris

DR LAWRENCE HILL-CAWTHORNE
School of Law, University of Reading

PROFESSOR ROBERT KOLB
Faculty of Law, University of Geneva

DR CAMERON A. MILES
Trinity Hall, University of Cambridge; 3 Verulam Buildings

DR ALEXANDER ORAKHELASHVILI
School of Law, University of Birmingham

PROFESSOR PAOLO PALCHETTI
Faculty of Law, Unversity of Macerata

PROFESSOR MEHRDAD PAYANDEH
Faculty of Law, University of Dusseldorf

SIR NIGEL RODLEY
School of Law, University of Essex; Chair, UN Human Rights Committee

PRESIDENT DEAN SPIELMANN
European Court of Human Rights

DR PHILIPPA WEBB
Dickson Poon School of Law, King's College, University of London

1

Introduction: from fragmentation to convergence in international law

MADS ANDENAS AND EIRIK BJORGE

I. The project

The title of this book, *A Farewell to Fragmentation: Reassertion and Convergence in International Law*, could be thought to indicate that in our view there is no fragmentation in international law. Fragmentation of international law has not, however, come to a complete end; the end of all fragmentation is not a realistic prospect. We regard fragmentation more as a part of a dynamic legal system, and fragmentation may be a fruitful perspective by which to study almost any legal system or sub-system.

The fragmentation of international law has in the last twenty years been discussed as a threat to international law as a legal system, and the extent and degree of fragmentation may have posed such a threat. There is, not surprisingly, a rich literature on the fragmentation of international law.[1]

There is less attention given to the move towards convergence. That is the focus of this volume. Convergence can be regarded as just as much a part of any legal system, together with fragmentation, in a Hegelian dialectic process.[2] Fear of fragmentation as a threat to the unity and

[1] See, e.g., M Koskenniemi, 'Fragmentation of International Law: Difficulties Arising from the Diversification and Expansion of International Law,' Report of the Study Group of the International Law Commission, finalized by Martti Koskenniemi, A/CN.4/L.682; J. Crawford, 'Chance, Order, Change: The Course of International Law' in *365 Collected Courses of The Hague Academy of International Law* (Leiden: Martinus Nijhoff Publishers, 2013), 9, 205–29; M. Andenas, 'The Centre Reasserting Itself: From Fragmentation to Transformation of International Law' in *Volume in Honor of Pär Hallström*, edited by M. Derlén and J. Lindholm (Uppsala: Iustus, 2012); P. Webb, *International Judicial Integration and Fragmentation* (Oxford University Press, 2013); and E. Benvenisti and G. W. Downs, 'The Empire's New Clothes: Political Economy and the Fragmentation of International Law' (2007) 60 *Stanford Law Review* 595, E. Benvenisti, *The Law of Global Governance* (The Hague Academy of International Law, 2014).

[2] G. W. F. Hegel, *Phenomenology of Spirit* (trans. A. V. Miller, Clarendon Press, 1977) 29–30 at [50]–[51]. See Castellarin, Chapter 12 in the present book.

coherence of international law or its future as a legal system may explain why convergence and unity are becoming more of a dominating feature of international law discourse than the claims to autonomy and specificity of different regimes and disciplines, which previously dominated more than they currently do.

Convergence is less studied in international law. Nonetheless, it plays a most important role in the current phase of what we call the reassertion of the International Court of Justice as, over and above simply being an organ that delivers 'transactional justice', being an institution worthy of the name 'the principal judicial organ of the United Nations'.[3] This is happening in a wider context; the general method and principles of international law are changing as a function of this reassertion, supported not only by the International Court but generally also by most other international courts and tribunals, treaty bodies and United Nations (UN) institutions, such as the International Law Commission (ILC) and special procedures of various kinds.

There is also convergence in the approach taken in many forms of State practice, such as government statements in international and domestic fora, and not the least in the jurisprudence of domestic supreme and constitutional courts, increasingly concerned with international law and openly taking account of and giving effect to international law in their judgments as they do. Scholarship follows in tow, slowly opening up to the extended comparative perspectives within public international law disciplines, in relation to domestic law, and the role of such scholarship in developing international law and its general method and principles.

We subscribe to the view of international law as a legal system, with the challenges that follow for the analysis of institutions, method, general principles and substantive law. A part of this challenge is the imperative of openness for general international law to place itself, and remain, at the centre as a generalist discipline with continuing relevance for the emerging specialist treaty regimes and disciplines.

For international law to be an effective legal system, the ever-increasing number of bodies with a role to play in international law must take account of one another, address possible conflicts, including those which cannot

[3] Charter of the United Nations, 26 June 1945, 892 UNTS 119, Art 92. See, on the beginnings of the development, G. Guillaume, 'Transformations du droit international et jurisprudence de la Cour Internationale de Justice' in R. Ben Achour and S. Laghmani (eds.), *Les nouveaux aspects du droit international* (Pedone, 1994) 175–92.

be resolved, and in the course of doing so, contribute to the development of general principles and forms of hierarchies of norms and institutions. Such convergence may contribute to a stabilization of the (still) rapidly expanding international legal system. Even if fragmentation, and the fear of fragmentation, is the subject of a rich literature, there is still need for empirical study to understand the impact of fragmentation on the legal system of international law. Empirical study is also required to understand the emphasis on coherence and unity in developing international law and its general method and principles, and increasingly also in finding answers to legal questions as seen in the practice of the courts.

We believe that the contributors to this book, on the whole, share this view but that the book may also have interest to scholars who do not. Much of what we see as convergence may also be seen as ways of dealing with fragmentation, and does not have to be based on, for instance, general principles or hierarchies of norms and institutions.

Since the law of human rights has become such a vector in the debates concerning fragmentation and convergence in international law,[4] and also about the role of the International Court in what we regard as a reassertion and convergence phase,[5] we have felt that this particular area merited a particular focus within the context of this book.

Against this background, this book explores convergence as a response to fragmentation. The book is organized into two parts. After this introduction follows 'Part 1: Reassertion and Convergence: 'Proliferation' of Courts and the Centre of International Law', which has two sub-parts: 'A: At the centre: The International Court' and 'B: "Regimes" of International Law'. 'Part 2: A Farewell to Fragmentation and the Sources of

[4] See, e.g., R. Jennings, 'The Proliferation of Adjudicatory Bodies: Dangers and Possible Answers' in *Implications of the Proliferation of International Adjudicatory Bodies for Dispute Resolution, ASIL Bulletin: Educational Resources on International Law* (1995) 2, 6; R. Jennings, 'The Judiciary, International and National, and the Development of International Law' (1996) 45 *ICLQ* 1, 5–6.

[5] See, for instance, Andrew Lang, 'The Role of the International Court of Justice in a Context of Fragmentation' (2013) 62 *International and Comparative Law Quarterly*, 777–812, and Ralph Wilde, 'The Extraterritorial Application of International Human Rights Law on Civil and Political Rights', Chapter 35 in Nigel Rodley and Scott Sheeran (eds.), *Routledge Handbook on Human Rights* (Routledge, 2013) 635–61, and'Human Rights Beyond Borders at the World Court: The Significance of the International Court of Justice's Jurisprudence on the Extraterritorial Application of International Human Rights Law Treaties' *Chinese Journal of International Law* (2013) 12(4) 639–77.

Law' also has two sub-parts: 'A: Custom and *jus cogens*' and 'B: Treaty interpretation'.

We would like in this introductory chapter briefly to foreshadow three themes which, in various ways, make an appearance in the chapters of this book: substantive fragmentation, institutional proliferation, and methodological fragmentation. Finally, we provide an overview of the chapters of this book and how they contribute to develop the book's theme of reassertion and convergence in international law.

II. Three forms of fragmentation

A. *Substantive fragmentation*

The first of the three themes of this book, or the first of the three forms of fragmentation, is substantive fragmentation, that is, different regimes or disciplines laying claim to autonomy and being self-contained fragmented regimes. International law, in the words of the International Court in *WHO Regional Headquarters*, 'does not operate in a vacuum'; it operates, rather, with 'relation to facts and in the context of a wider framework of legal rules of which it forms only a part'.[6] One expression of this is how international customary law, over time, may be called on to mould and even modify the content of otherwise static treaties.[7] That, as Crawford has observed,[8] was the case in *Nuclear Weapons*;[9] the International Court there took the concepts of 'proportionality' and 'necessity' from the developing customary international law concept of self-defence and read them into the concept of self-defence under Article 51 of the UN Charter.[10] Another, but related, aspect is that, as the International Court noted in the *Fisheries Jurisdiction* case, 'an international instrument must be interpreted by reference to international law'.[11] Similarly, to our mind, the International

[6] *Interpretation of the Agreement of 25 March 1951 between the WHO and Egypt* ICJ Rep 1980 73, 76 [10].

[7] J. Crawford, *Brownlie's Principles of Public International Law* (8th edn., Oxford University Press, 2012) 33.

[8] J. Crawford, *Chance, Order, Change: The Course of International Law* (2013) 365 Hague *Recueil* 1, 110.

[9] *Legality of the Threat or Use of Nuclear Weapons*, Advisory Opinion ICJ Rep 1995, 226, 244–5 [37]–[43].

[10] Charter of the United Nations, 26 June 1945, 892 UNTS 119.

[11] *Fisheries Jurisdiction (Spain* v. *Canada)*, Jurisdiction of the Court, Judgment ICJ Rep 1998, 460 [68].

Court in *Bosnian Genocide* observed, in connection with the Genocide Convention,[12] that:

> [t]he jurisdiction of the Court is founded on Article IX of the [Genocide] Convention, and the disputes subject to that jurisdiction are those 'relating to the interpretation, application or fulfillment' of the Convention, but it does not follow that the Convention stands alone. In order to determine whether the Respondent breached its obligation under the Convention . . . and, if a breach was committed, to determine its legal consequences, the Court will have recourse not only to the Convention itself, but also to the rules of general international law on treaty interpretation and on responsibility of States for internationally wrongful acts.[13]

The same approach has been taken by the European Court of Human Rights.[14] Interpreting and applying instruments which on their face provide that the tribunal having jurisdiction to interpret and apply them shall, as is the case with the UN Convention on the Law of the Sea (UNCLOS), 'apply this Convention and other rules of international law not incompatible with this Convention', international courts and tribunals have recognized that this duty is all the stronger. It is not surprising, and entirely fitting, that the International Tribunal for the Law of the Sea (ITLOS), in *Artic Sunrise* (Provisional Measures),[15] should take into account international human rights law in connection with the detention of the *Arctic Sunrise* crew, who would, absent an order for release, 'continue to be deprived of their right to liberty and security as well as their right to leave the territory and maritime areas under the jurisdiction of the Russian Federation. The settlement of such disputes between two States should not infringe upon the enjoyment of individual rights and freedoms of the crew of the vessels concerned'.[16]

In this way, through reliance on the insight that the sources of international law do not operate in a vacuum but rather in relation to a broader context of rules, fragmentation gives way to convergence.

[12] Convention on the Prevention and Punishment of the Crime of Genocide, 9 December 1948, 78 UNTS 277.

[13] *Application of the Convention on the Prevention and Punishment of the Crime of Genocide (Bosnia and Herzegovina* v. *Serbia and Montenegro)* ICJ Rep 2007, 43, 105 at [149].

[14] See, e.g., *Fogarty* v. *United Kingdom* [GC], no. 37112/97, § 35, ECHR 2001-XI; *McElhinney* v. *Ireland* [GC], no. 31253/96, ECHR 2001-XI; *Al-Adsani* v. *United Kingdom* [GC], no. 35763/97, ECHR 2001-XI.

[15] *Arctic Sunrise (Netherland* v. *Russia)* (Provisional Measures) ITLOS Case No. 22.

[16] *Arctic Sunrise (Netherland* v. *Russia)* (Provisional Measures) ITLOS Case No. 22 at [87]. See, however, the criticism in D. Guilfoye and C. Miles, 'Provisional Measures and the MV *Arctic Sunrise*' (2014) 108 *AJIL* 271, 284–6.

B. *Institutional fragmentation*

The second of the three themes of this book on the three forms of fragmentation is institutional proliferation. Despite the lack of formal hierarchy between international courts and tribunals, the pronouncements of the International Court, the only permanent tribunal of general jurisdiction, carry particular weight. The International Court provides international law with a centre of gravity.[17]

It has in later years been possible to observe a tendency according to which the International Court itself has started referring, even more than it used to do before,[18] to other types of international court and tribunal, not least the human rights courts and bodies. It was eloquent of this development when Judge Greenwood in *Diallo* (Compensation) stated that:

> International law is not a series of fragmented specialist and self-contained bodies of law, each of which functions in isolation from the others; it is a single, unified system of law and each international court can, and should, draw on the jurisprudence of other international courts and tribunals, even though it is not bound necessarily to come to the same conclusions.[19]

This seems now to have become the new orthodoxy. Special Rapporteur Sir Michael Wood has, in the context of an ILC study on the formation of customary international law,[20] observed that given the unity of international law and the fact that 'international law is a legal system', it is in principle neither helpful nor in accordance with principle to break the law up into separate specialist fields. The same basic approach to the formation and identification of customary international law, he said, applies regardless of the field of law under consideration. The Commission's work on this topic would be equally relevant to all fields of international law, including, for example, customary human rights law, customary

[17] J. Crawford, *Chance, Order, Change: The Course of International Law* (2013) 365 Hague *Recueil* 1, 216.

[18] It is important to remember that the Permanent and the International Court have on occasion referred to the decisions of other tribunals, both international and domestic: A. D. McNair, *The Development of International Justice* (New York University Press, 1954) 12–13.

[19] Declaration of Judge Greenwood, *Case Concerning Ahmadou Sadio Diallo (Republic of Guinea* v. *Democratic Republic of the Congo)*, Compensation, Judgment, ICJ Rep 2012, 324, 294 [8].

[20] 'Formation and Evidence of Customary International Law': see http://legal.un.org/ilc/guide/1_13.shtm.

international humanitarian law, and customary international criminal law.[21]

The tendency – in the literature, in the jurisprudence of international tribunals, and in the work of the ILC – seems to have gone from focusing on what is different among the different fields of international law 'to move freely over the boundaries, which seem to divide these fields of law and to bring out the underlying unities'.[22]

C. *Methodological fragmentation and a fragmented method?*

The last of the three themes of this book on the three forms of fragmentation is methodological fragmentation. The possibility of methodological fragmentation has been put forward by some commentators in connection with two aspects of the sources of law: treaty and custom. First it is true that some international courts and tribunals, perhaps especially treaty bodies, have at times insisted on regarding the treaty which they are interpreting as being in some way special. One example often referred to in this connection is that of *Mamatkulov & Askarov*.[23] There the Grand Chamber of the European Court held that, whilst on the one hand 'the Convention must be interpreted in the light of the rules set out in the Vienna Convention of 23 May 1969 on the Law of Treaties', the Court must do so 'taking into account the *special nature* of the Convention as an instrument of human rights protection (see *Golder* v. *United Kingdom*, judgment of 21 February 1975, Series A no 18, p. 14, §29)'.[24] It bears mention, however, that as is evident from the reference in *Mamatkulov & Askarov* to *Golder* above, the European Court based this statement on its finding in *Golder*, where the Court said that it would follow Articles 31–3 of the Vienna Convention, but, and even more importantly in the present connection, that for the purposes of the interpretation of the

21 M. Wood, 'Formation and Evidence of Customary International Law. Note by Michael Wood, Special Rapporteur' ILC Sixty-fourth Session Geneva, 7 May–1 June and 2 July–3 August 2012, 5 at [22] (internal references omitted).

22 A. F. Denning, 'Foreword' (1952) 1 *ICLQ* 1, 1.

23 *Mamatkulov & Askarov* v. *Turkey* (2005) 134 ILR 230. See ILC Draft Conclusions on Subsequent Agreements and Subsequent Practice in Relation to the Interpretation of Treaties 2013, ILC Report 2013, UN Doc A/68/10, 19.

24 *Mamatkulov & Askarov* v. *Turkey* (2005) 134 ILR 230, 267 [111] (emphasis added). Also: *Effect of Reservations Opinion* (1982) 67 ILR 559, 567–68; *Restrictions to the Death Penalty (Advisory Opinion OC–3/83)* (1983) 70 ILR 449, 466.

European Convention[25] account should be taken of Articles 31–3 of the Vienna Convention, but that it was also bound by Article 5 of the Vienna Convention:

> for the interpretation of the European Convention account is to be taken of those Articles subject, where appropriate to 'any relevant rules of the organization' – the Council of Europe – within which it has been adopted (Article 5 of the Vienna Convention).[26]

In other words, at any rate in the view of the European Court itself, when the Court says that the European Convention must be interpreted in accordance with Articles 31–3 but also that the Court must do so 'taking into account the *special nature* of the Convention',[27] that is nothing else than applying the scheme of the Vienna Convention, as set out in Article 5. In a sense, then, the 'special nature' approach of the European Court follows from the Vienna rules themselves. This rhymes well with the approach taken in the Vienna Convention where, apart from Article 5, no mention is made of this type of distinction in the principles of treaty interpretation. It also introduces an interesting circularity into the debate: how can a 'specialized' approach be deemed to be 'specialized' if it is mandated by the 'generalist' approach. Interstitial points such as this open up the debate; we suggest that they have, putting the point at its lowest, played a minor role in the debates as yet.

The same is the case in relation to international environmental law. It is, to take one example, possible in principle to see the evolutionary interpretations made by the International Court in environmental law cases such as *Gabcikovo–Nagymaros*,[28] *Pulp Mills*,[29] and, to some extent, also in *Whaling in the Antarctic*,[30] as evidence of a particular type of approach to treaty interpretation taken in a particular type of international law.[31] Yet,

[25] Convention for the Protection of Human Rights and Fundamental Freedoms, 4 November 1950, 213 UNTS 22.

[26] *Golder* v. *United Kingdom* (1975) 57 ILR 200, 213–14 [29].

[27] *Mamatkulov & Askarov* v. *Turkey* (2005) 134 ILR 230, 267 [111] (emphasis added).

[28] *Gabcikovo-Nagymaros Project (Hungary/Slovakia)*, Judgment ICJ Rep 1997, 7, 67–8 [112] and 78–9 [142].

[29] *Pulp Mills on the River Uruguay (Argentina* v. *Uruguay)*, Judgment ICJ Rep 2010, 14, 83 [204].

[30] *Whaling in the Antarctic (Australia* v. *Japan: New Zealand intervening)* ICJ Rep 2014 at [45] (describing the International Convention for the Regulation of Whaling, Washington, 2 December 1946, 161 UNTS 72 as 'an evolving instrument').

[31] Generally, M. Fitzmaurice, 'International Environmental Law as a Special Field' (1994) 25 *Netherlands Yearbook of International Law* 181.

the disagreement between Australia and Japan in *Whaling in the Antarctic* as to, *inter alia*, whether the terms 'conservation and development' of whale resources in the preamble as well as Articles III and V of the Whaling Convention ought to be interpreted evolutionarily or not, was plainly capable of being solved by relying upon the traditional tools of treaty interpretation. Redgwell must be right, therefore, to observe that it cannot be the case that environmental treaty-making has engendered new rules of treaty interpretation applicable only in that sphere; the dynamic development of international environmental treaties should, instead, be seen as contributing to the dynamic development of the general law of treaties.[32] In any case, as Bjorge has observed,[33] it is often the case, with what we have come to term the evolutionary interpretation of treaties, that recourse to evolution is really wholly unnecessary. There often is no need for it, as the result to which it would have led already follows from the plain meaning of the text read in good faith. This point was already made by the Permanent Court in *Employment of Women during the Night* when, in a statement of principle regarding 'provisions which are general in scope', it stated that the fact that, at the time when the treaty was concluded, certain facts or situations were not thought of, which the terms of the treaty in their ordinary meaning were wide enough to cover, 'does not justify interpreting those of its provisions which are general in scope otherwise than in accordance with their terms'.[34]

Secondly, arguments as to methodological fragmentation have been put forward in connection with customary international law. With a possible academic exception in relation to the importance of *opinio juris*,[35] the rules as to the formation of customary international law are mostly settled.[36]

[32] C. Redgwell, 'Multilateral Environmental Treaty-Making' in V Gowlland-Debbas (ed.), *Multilateral Treaty-Making: The Current Status of Challenges to and Reforms Needed in the International Legislative Process* (Martinus Nijhoff 2000) 107. Further, P. Birnie, A. Boyle and C. Redgwell, *International Law and the Environment* (Oxford University Press, 2009) 20–2.

[33] E. Bjorge, *The Evolutionary Interpretation of Treaties* (Oxford University Press, 2014) 191–3.

[34] *Convention concerning Employment of Women during the Night* PCIJ (1932) Series A/B No. 50, 377.

[35] M. Mendelson, 'The Formation of Customary International Law' (1998) 272 Hague *Recueil* 155; Final Report by the Committee on Formation of Customary Law of the International Law Association (ILA) 712, 744.

[36] See Article 38 of the Statute of the International Court of Justice, 26 June 1945, 892 UNTS 119. Special Rapporteur Sir Michael Wood, First Report on Formation and Evidence of Customary International Law ILC A/CN.4/663; Second Report on Formation and Evidence of Customary International Law ILCA/CN.4/672; P. Tomka, 'Custom and the

Judge Read in the *Fisheries* case described customary international law as 'the generalization of the practice of States'.[37] The reasons for making the generalizations involve an evaluation of whether the practice is fit to be accepted, and is in truth generally accepted as law.[38] It is in this connection that it has been argued that special problems arise in connection with human rights law.

According to Thirlway, ascertaining developments in customary international law presents particular difficulties in connection with human rights; in his view, 'there is a problem with basing human rights law on custom'.[39] This, he observes, is because in the past 'the relationship of a State with its own subjects . . . has been generally immune from the impact of developing customary law', the reason being that 'custom derives from the *de facto* adjustment of conflicting claims and interests of the subjects of international law, and it has always been – and probably still is – one of the most fundamental tenets of international law that individuals and private corporations are not subjects of international law'.[40] The traditional position, set out by Oppenheim,[41] according to which only States were considered the subject of international law, has been left behind. It is now abundantly clear, as Sir Christopher Greenwood has recently stated, that 'states can no longer be regarded as the only subjects of international law'.[42]

While admitting that the traditional position does not represent the current stage of development of international law, Thirlway observes that 'teasing intellectual problems remain'.[43] In the traditional view, he continues, the essence of custom is that its provisions have been hammered out in the resolution of conflicts of interests, or disputes, between States

International Court of Justice' (2013) 12 *The Law & Practice of International Courts and Tribunals* 195; J. Crawford, *Brownlie's Principles of Public International Law* (8th edn., Oxford University Press, 2012) 23–4.

37 *Fisheries (United Kingdom* v. *Norway)* ICJ Rep 1951, 116, 191 (Judge Read).

38 J. Crawford, *Brownlie's Principles of Public International Law* (8th edn, Oxford University Press, 2012) 23.

39 H. Thirlway, *The Sources of International Law* (Oxford University Press, 2014) Ch 2.

40 H. Thirlway, *International Customary Law and Codification* (Leiden: Brill, 1972) 7.

41 L. Oppenheim, *International Law: A Treatise* (1st edn., London: Longmans, Green & Co, 1905) 8–9.

42 C. Greenwood, 'Sovereignty: A View from the International Bench' in R. Rawlings, P. Leyland and A. Young (eds.), *Sovereignty and the Law: Domestic, European and International Perspectives* (Oxford University Press, 2013) 255. Also J. Crawford, *Chance, Order, Change: The Course of International Law* (2013) 365 Hague *Recueil* 1, 139.

43 H. Thirlway, *The Sources of International Law* (Oxford University Press, 2014) Ch 2.

in their day-to-day relations. This leads him to two problems. First, he cites Simma and Alston, who have observed that:

> An element of interaction – in a broad sense – is intrinsic to, and essential to, the kind of State practice leading to the formation of customary international law . . . The processes of customary international law can only be triggered, and continue working, in situations in which States interact, where they apportion or delimit in some tangible way. But, at least in most cases, this is not what happens when a consensus about substantive human rights obligations, to be performed domestically, grows into international law.[44]

Secondly, Thirlway draws attention to 'the striking differences between the settings in which customary law traditionally arose and the issues on which it spoke, on the one hand, and the contemporary settings in which advocates of customary international law' – particularly, one might add, in the human rights field – 'seek to employ customary norms, on the other'.[45]

It may be, however, that the types of assertions on the part of States to which one must look for the ascertainment of customary international law in connection with human rights are more manifold than the ones which Thirlway is prepared to accept. It will by definition be a more complex matrix than just statements by Ministries of Foreign Affairs. As foreshadowed above, the Special Rapporteur on the Formation of Custom, Sir Michael Wood, has observed that while:

> [t]he formation and evidence of rules of customary international law in different fields may raise particular issues and it may therefore be for consideration whether, and if so to what degree, different weight may be given to different materials depending on the field in question. At the same time it should be recalled that, in the words of Judge Greenwood, '[i]nternational law is not a series of fragmented specialist and self-contained bodies of law, each of which functions in isolation from the others; it is a single, unified system of law'.[46]

44 B. Simma and P. Alston, 'The Sources of Human Rights Law: Custom, *Jus Cogens* and General Principles' (1988) 12 *Australian Yearbook of International Law* 82, 99.

45 E. Kadens and E. Young, 'How Customary is Customary International Law?' (2013) 54 *William & Mary Law Review* 885, 914.

46 Special Rapporteur Sir Michael Wood, First Report on Formation and Evidence of Customary International Law ILC A/CN.4/663, 8 [19], citing *Ahmadou Sadio Diallo (Republic of Guinea* v. *Democratic Republic of the Congo) (Compensation Owed by the Democratic Republic of the Congo to the Republic of Guinea)*, Judgment, 19 June 2012, Declaration of Judge Greenwood [8].

The unified approach suggested by the Special Rapporteur, trending towards convergence rather than towards Thirlway's fragmentation, must be the correct one. On the view put forward in this book, there is in the method of international law more that unites than which differentiates.

It is certainly no less true to say today, than it was when, in the preface of the first published volume of *The Annual Digest of Public International Law Cases,* [47] Lauterpacht and McNair observed that they suspected 'that there is more international law already in existence and daily accumulating "than this world dreams of"'.[48] Through the process which Dame Rosalyn Higgins has called the 'widening and thickening of the context of international law',[49] public international law has developed considerably from its beginnings. It has grown from bilateral relationships, to something that is surely no more fragmented than it once was; international law has only become more diverse.[50] The more diverse international law becomes, the more important is its coherence and its integration. As the chapters of this book show, the tools needed to secure the coherence and integration of the diverse international law of today are all to hand.

III. How do the chapters contribute to the analysis of fragmentation and convergence?

Part 1: Reassertion and convergence: 'proliferation' of courts and the centre of international law

A: At the centre: the International Court

The second chapter in this book and the first in 'Part 1: Reassertion and Convergence: "Proliferation" of Courts and the Centre of International

[47] The volumes were not numbered until 1958; as R. Jennings explains, the volumes after 1958 *then* numbered 1 and 2 were edited by F. Williams and H. Lauterpacht; the present volume 3 was the first published and edited by A. McNair and H. Lauterpacht: R. Jennings, 'The Judiciary, International and National, and the Development of International Law' (1996) 45 *ICLQ* 1, 1.

[48] A. D. McNair and H. Lauterpacht, 'Preface' in H. Lauterpacht and J. Fischer Williams (eds.), *Annual Digest of Public International Law Cases 1925–26* (Cambridge University Press, 1929) ix.

[49] R. Higgins, 'A Babel of Judicial Voices: Ruminations From the Bench' (2006) 55 *ICLQ* 791, 792.

[50] J. Crawford, *Chance, Order, Change: The Course of International Law* (2013) 365 Hague *Recueil* 1, 228.

Law', under the first of its two sub-headings, 'At the Centre: The International Court', is Sir Christopher Greenwood's chapter on 'Unity and Diversity in International Law'. In his chapter, Sir Christopher Greenwood introduces many of the issues to be dealt with in the book's later chapters by drawing up the large canvas of issues thrown up by the development often referred to as the fragmentation of international law. While at the dawn of the new millennium fear of the fragmentation of international law was widespread among international lawyers, he shows how, in fact, the fear of fragmentation at the start of the present millennium appears eerily reminiscent of the panic with which the dawn of the previous millennium was greeted by those who believed that the end of the world was nigh.

Sir Christopher further shows how the degree of coherence in the treaty-making process is greater than is often supposed. Secondly, he makes the point that Article 31(3)(c) of the Vienna Convention on the Law of Treaties has been applied by a wide variety of bodies in the interpretation and application of treaties. Thirdly, he shows how the fact that those negotiating a treaty sometimes do so without considering how the provisions adopted in that treaty relate to other rules of international law, is neither surprising nor necessarily damaging. What matters, he observes, is whether international law contains – as he concludes that it does – the principles necessary for addressing that relationship and for avoiding conflict.

Chapter 3 is by Judge Antônio Augusto CançadoTrindade. In his chapter, entitled 'A Century of International Justice and Prospect for the Future', he observes that there has been a significant change in the way international lawyers have increasingly discarded euphemistic expressions such as the 'proliferation' of international tribunals and the 'fragmentation' of international law. Expressions such as these have, in his view, diverted attention to issues of delimitation of competences, away from the important issues at stake in international law, such as access to justice in international law. Talk of 'proliferation' and 'fragmentation' obscured the point of the considerable advances of the old ideal of international justice in the contemporary world.

Far from threatening the cohesion of international law, international courts and tribunals enrich and strengthen the international legal system, by asserting its aptitude to resolve disputes both as between States and between individuals and States. Contemporary international law has thereby become more responsive to the fulfilment of the basic needs of the international community, of human beings and of humankind as a whole, including the realization of justice.

CançadoTrindade also observes that international courts and tribunals have, in a development parallel to the one described above, begun to take into account and cite each other's jurisprudence. Thus, he explains, the jurisprudence of the International Court is regularly taken into account by other courts and tribunals. But the same is the case with the International Court itself, the Court having in recent years displayed considerable openness of mind; this is clear, for example, from *Diallo*.[51] In Cançado Trindade's view, such cross-fertilization between the jurisprudence of different international courts and tribunals 'exerts a constructive function in the safeguard of the rights of the *justiciables*'. This concerted reliance upon the case law of different courts and tribunals leads to a strengthening of the unity of international law and of the rule of law internationally. But it also means that international law, in Cançado Trindade's view, edges towards the creation of an *objective* law, one which goes beyond the will or consent of individual States. He gives examples of how, to his mind, the International Court recently has gone beyond an inter-State outlook. The International Court has, in recent cases, shown that the artificiality of the exclusively inter-State outlook fails to convey the complexities of international law. He takes the view that the marked rise of multiple international tribunals has been a reassuring phenomenon, filling a gap that had persisted in the international legal order. The effect has been one of widening access to justice at an international level. In this way international law has recovered the historical position of the human person as subject of the law of nations. This has gone hand-in-hand with another development – the setting of limits to State voluntarism, 'thus safeguarding the integrity of the respective human rights Conventions and the primacy of considerations of *ordre public* over the will of individual States'. Cançado Trindade finds examples of this development in the European Court of Human Rights's jurisprudence, in cases such as *Belilos*[52] and *Loizidou* (Preliminary Objections),[53] and in *Hilaire, Constantine and Benjamin*[54] in the Inter-American Court of Human Rights.

[51] *Case Concerning Ahmadou Sadio Diallo (Republic of Guinea* v. *Democratic Republic of the Congo)*, Judgment, ICJ Rep 2010, 639; *Case Concerning Ahmadou Sadio Diallo (Republic of Guinea* v. *Democratic Republic of the Congo)*, Compensation, Judgment, ICJ Rep 2012, 324.

[52] *Belilos* v. *Switzerland* (1988) 88 ILR 635.

[53] *Loizidou* v. *Turkey*, Preliminary Objections (1995) 103 ILR 622.

[54] *Hilaire, Constantine and Benjamin and Others* v. *Trinidad and Tobago* (2002) 134 ILR 293.

In dealing with the issue of jurisdiction, CançadoTrindade reverts to President Loder, the Permanent Court of Justice's first ever President (1921–4), who argued that the jurisdiction of the Court must perforce be 'compulsory'.[55] Only in this way, Trindade observes, as Loder had done in the 1920s, is it possible to achieve greater development in the realization of justice at international level. The foundation of compulsory jurisdiction lies, ultimately, in the confidence in the *rule of law* at international level. The very nature of a court of justice calls for compulsory jurisdiction. Conscience, Cançado Trindade concludes, stands above the will.

In the book's fourth chapter, entitled 'The International Court of Justice and Human Rights Treaty Bodies', Sir Nigel Rodley focuses on treaty bodies and the International Court of Justice, and their approach to each other's work. The main focus is on the reliance of the International Court on the work of treaty bodies. This is done not least through a careful case study of the *Diallo* case,[56] where the avoidance of fragmentation was at the heart of the Court's explanation of its use of their work. In doing so, Sir Nigel in his chapter analyses how the International Court in fact acted as a human rights court in the *Diallo* case, as has also been the instance in later cases such as *Belgium* v. *Senegal*.[57]

Professor Vera Gowlland-Debbas develops the argument in the book's fifth chapter, 'The ICJ and the Challenges of Human Rights Law', that one can build a construct from the Court's pronouncements on human rights law: its hierarchy, sources, content and relations to other general international law areas. The Court has also drawn the consequences of treaties with a collective interest for interpretation, application and reservations. The Court's jurisprudence on human rights has had repercussions on human rights courts and treaty bodies, as, for example, its bridging of human rights and humanitarian law. The Court has integrated human rights law into a unitary vision of the international legal system, insisting on its indivisibility, extraterritorial application and relations with other areas of international law, filling 'black holes' created in the wake of 9/11.

There are limitations of an institutional nature on the Court, established at a time when bilateral and subjective relations between States

[55] B. C. J. Loder, 'The Permanent Court of International Justice and Compulsory Jurisdiction' (1921) 2 *BYIL* 6, 11–12.

[56] *Case Concerning Ahmadou Sadio Diallo (Republic of Guinea* v. *Democratic Republic of the Congo)*, Judgment, ICJ Rep 2010, 639.

[57] *Questions Relating to the Obligation to Prosecute or Extradite (Belgium* v. *Senegal)*, Judgment, ICJ Rep 2012, 422.

based on the Lotus' golden rule prevailed. Professor Gowlland-Debbas highlights that the Court cannot always respond to expectations when faced with human rights cases. There must be a jurisdictional link; decisions bind only the parties and advisory opinions are 'advisory'. The Court has sometimes interpreted its apolitical judicial role as one of stating the law as it is, not one of developing it. The human rights community has, for example, not welcomed the Court's views on the absolute nature of State immunity. In Professor Gowlland-Debbas' view this sits uneasily alongside the development of an international public policy in which subjective interests must give way to collective values and interests.

After having set the scene in her introduction, in section II, 'The contribution of the court to the development of human rights law', Professor Gowlland-Debbas takes us back to the Permanent Court of International Justice, which, with reference to the League of Nations' minority protection regime, in its jurisprudence from the 1930s, recognized that treaties could create rights and obligations for private individuals enforceable in domestic courts. She discusses the International Court of Justice and the clarification of the hierarchical conception of human rights, drawing the parallel to the case of the regulation of the use of force where the Court has maintained a hierarchical conception of the prohibition on the use of force and related rules. She continues the exploration of the concept of collective interest treaties in the Court's jurisprudence and addresses the confirmation of *erga omnes* and then *jus cogens*. She analyses how the Court establishes the source and content of fundamental norms. She authoritatively sets out the jurisprudence on the application of human rights law in armed conflict.

In section III, 'The linkages between human rights law and general international law', she continues the analysis of how the International Court has contributed to the mainstreaming of human rights, and she analyses how the Court has determined its relationship with other areas of general international law. She also addresses the relationship between State and individual responsibility for human rights violations and the relations between the court and non-State entities. After section IV, 'Remedies for human rights violations', the final substantive section is section V, 'Limitations of the Court in dealing with human rights issues'.

Professor Gowlland-Debbas' conclusion is that the Court's findings on direct violations of human rights have been limited, but that the Court has made a significant contribution to the structural and normative framework of human rights protection. The Court has also been conscious that when acting in its contentious jurisdiction it is the principal organ of the UN, bound by the purposes and principles of the UN Charter, and a world court serving the world community.

Dr Philippa Webb in the book's sixth chapter, entitled 'Factors Influencing Fragmentation and Convergence in International Courts', seeks to identify the factors that lead to convergence or fragmentation in the international legal system. She identifies three themes: the identity of the court at issue, the substance of the law, and the procedures employed. These factors do not automatically determine whether a particular court will promote the convergence or fragmentation of international law. Instead, Webb argues, they suggest *tendencies* in a certain direction. On the basis of an analysis of these factors, in the jurisprudence of international courts and jurisprudence, she suggests that the International Court plays a central role in promoting convergence.

In common with Cançado Trindade, Webb homes in on the *permanent* nature of the International Court and its predecessor. The International Court enjoys special authority due to its status as the only court of general jurisdiction and the UN's principal judicial organ. The permanent nature of a court such as the International Court and its prominent place in an institutional system encourages stability and convergence. Multi-stage, collective decision-making processes, respect for vertical and horizontal precedent, and engagement in judicial dialogue, she argues, also promote coherence in the development of international law. On this background, Webb observes that the International Court has played – and is likely to continue to play – a central role in the promotion of convergence. It is permanent and has the ability to deal with a wide variety of topics involving both treaty and custom.

The central role in the international legal system enjoyed by the International Court could be enhanced by increased – and more transparent – participation in judicial dialogue. Until relatively recently, there was a sense that the judgments of the International Court should remain 'unsullied' by engagement with the decisions of other courts or tribunals of limited jurisdiction. Webb shows how, given overlapping jurisdictions and the similar factual scenarios that arise in multiple courts, the consideration of the decisions of other courts is central to well-reasoned judgments. Webb furthermore argues that the next step is for the International Court to provide greater transparency as to its use of the case law of other courts and tribunals. This theme is also addressed by Professor Mads Andenas in his chapter, arguing that the development of a general method is the next step in this respect, and that work on a substantive level, such as that of the ILC on the formation of customary law,[58] is already making a contribution on this more formal level.

B: 'Regimes' of international law

This part of the book turns to what has been dubbed special 'regimes' of international law, showing that their interaction, with each other and with 'general' international law, is such that one could question the whole vocabulary of 'regimes.'

In the seventh chapter in the book, 'Fragmentation or Partnership? The Reception of ICJ Case-law by the European Court of Human Rights', President Spielmann addresses how the European Court of Human Rights has used the jurisprudence of the International Court in order to contribute to the strengthening of the systemic nature of the international legal system. In his introduction he sets out the fundamental differences between the two courts, using *Loizidou* (1995) as one starting point.[59] There the European Court of Human Rights pointed out the two main differences: that the International Court is called on to examine any legal dispute between States that might occur in any part of the globe with reference to principles of international law; and that the European Court is limited to direct supervisory functions in respect of a law-making treaty such as the Convention, mainly by dealing with individual applications. President Spielmann shows how the differences can be overemphasized, by demonstrating how the Permanent Court of International Justice already ruled on individual rights issues, and how this practice continued to be present in the International Court's jurisprudence. He takes the analysis through to the most recent cases, including *Congo* v. *Uganda*, *Georgia* v. *Russia*, *Diallo* and *Belgium* v. *Senegal*. In the main parts of his chapter he then analyses the European Court of Human Rights' use of the International Court of Justice's jurisprudence, and also the recent use of European Court of Human Rights' jurisprudence by the International Court of Justice. He explicitly addresses how the fragmentation discourse has had an impact on the jurisprudence of the two courts, and their citation of one another and, on a deeper level, in the development of the law.

President Spielmann notes that the submission of the case leading to the *Danzig Advisory Opinion* (1935)[60] of the International Court's

[58] See Special Rapporteur Sir Michael Wood, First Report on Formation and Evidence of Customary International Law ILC A/CN.4/663; Second Report on Formation and Evidence of Customary International Law ILCA/CN.4/672.

[59] *Loizidou* v. *Turkey* (Preliminary Objection), 23 March 1995, § 84, Series A no. 310.

[60] *Consistency of Certain Danzig Legislative Decrees with the Constitution of the Free City*, Advisory Opinion, 1935, P.C.I.J., Series A/B, No. 65, p. 41.

predecessor, the Permanent Court of International Justice, was through an individual petition mechanism.

President Spielmann's chapter shows how the European Court of Human Rights has made use of the jurisprudence of the International Court of Justice and how the two courts are intertwined. His emphasis is on how public international law has facilitated the protection of human rights. He further points out how it has also limited them, such as in matters of jurisdictional immunities.

In his scholarly enquiry, President Spielmann cites Dame Rosalyn Higgins and reverts to the jurisprudence of the Permanent Court of International Justice, between 1922 and 1946, on 'leading' principles such as non-discrimination.[61] This is one of the principles that Strasbourg has strived to enforce in more recent years; the case-law of the Permanent Court of International Justice is still of great influence today.

The main part of President Spielmann's chapter analyses the relationship between the jurisprudence of the International Court and that of the European Court, beginning with the interpretation of treaties, before turning to questions of procedure, to the obligations of States outside their territory, to the issue of *restitutio in integrum*, and, finally, to 'the sensitive issue' of State immunities. President Spielmann shows how the European Court has applied and relied on the jurisprudence of the International Court, with express citations and sometimes extensive discussions. Among the questions of procedure, he mentions the case of *Mamatkulov &Askarov* (2005),[62] where the European Court changes its position on the binding force of interim measures and aligns it with that of the International Court with reference again to, the also in many other judgments cited, *LaGrand.*[63]

President Spielmann discusses in some depth, and again relying on Rosalyn Higgins, the approach of the two courts in matters often discussed under the heading of 'extraterritoriality'. Georgia's action against Russia before the International Court and the European Court is the starting point. He also addresses how the European Court in *Al-Jedda*v. *the United*

[61] Speech given on the occasion of the opening of the judicial year, 30 January 2009, by Rosalyn Higgins, President of the International Court of Justice, 'The International Court of Justice and the European Court of Human Rights: Partners for the Protection of Human Rights', *Dialogue between Judges*, European Court of Human Rights, Council of Europe, 2009, 42–3.

[62] *Mamatkulov & Askarov* v. *Turkey* [GC], nos. 46827/99 and 46951/99, §§ 117 et seq., ECHR 2005-I.

[63] *LaGrand (Germany* v. *United States of America)*, Judgment, ICJ Rep 2001, § 101.

Kingdom (2011)[64] and *Al-Skeini and Others* v. *the United Kingdom*[65] made use of the jurisprudence of the International Court to revert to the jurisdictional rules of international law. He does not, and not surprisingly, comment on why the European Court previously had been convinced to depart from those rules.

On what he refers to as 'the sensitive issue' of State immunities, President Spielmann points to the interaction between the International and European Courts. In the European Court's restrictive 2001 judgments in *Fogarty* v. *United Kingdom*,[66] *McElhinney* v. *Ireland*[67] and *Al-Adsani* v. *United Kingdom*,[68] both the majority relying on State immunity to block the claims and the minority relying on the *jus cogens* nature of the prohibition of torture, made reference to the jurisprudence of the International Court. In *Jurisdictional Immunities of the State* (2012)[69] the International Court placed some reliance on the *Al-Adsani* judgment and adopted the same position. The European Court subsequently applied this to the UN in *Stichting Mothers of Srebrenica and Others* v. *Netherlands*.[70]

President Spielmann makes the point that the reliance on one another's jurisprudence has prevented fragmentation. This is at the core of the argument of the European Court's judgment in *Al-Adsani*. Another observation may be that the European Court's majority in the *Al-Adsani* judgment blocked the development towards effective remedies for violations of the prohibition of torture. President Spielmann refers to 'the dissenting minority, which was composed of eminent international jurists', and, one may add, also the then President and his successor (President Wildhaber, Vice President Costa). They argued that the very concept of *jus cogens* required that such norms should prevail over any hierarchically lower rule. The minority had support in systemic arguments, and in a general practice accepted as law. There were strong dissents in the United Kingdom courts, and the majority judgments there made references to the developing restrictions on State immunity clearly leaving the way open for giving effect to Article 6 of the European Convention on Human

64 *Al-Jedda* v. *United Kingdom* [GC], no. 27021/08, ECHR 2011.

65 *Al-Skeini and Others* v. *United Kingdom* [GC], no. 55721/07, ECHR 2011.

66 *Fogarty* v. *United Kingdom* [GC], no. 37112/97, § 35, ECHR 2001-XI.

67 *McElhinney* v. *Ireland* [GC], no. 31253/96, ECHR 2001-XI.

68 *Al-Adsani* v. *United Kingdom* [GC], no. 35763/97, ECHR 2001-XI.

69 *Jurisdictional Immunities of the State (Germany* v. *Italy: Greece intervening)*, ICJ Judgment of 3 February 2012.

70 *Stichting Mothers of Srebrenica and Others* v. *Netherlands* (dec), no. 65542/12, 11 June 2013.

Rights and access to court to make a right effective. When the European Court, as a leading human rights court, did not give such weight to the human rights concerns as to let the *jus cogens* rule prevail, there was little scope left to the International Court, as the traditional inter-State court promoting State immunity, to declare that traditional arguments for State immunity had to give way to *jus cogens* human rights. It may be argued *Al-Adsani* and the later exchanges with the International Court have held back the development of the law limiting State immunity, as these judgments all make reference to allowing State immunity to block the remedies national law and international human rights law otherwise had confirmed. National courts and UN bodies have an important role in exploring how remedies can go clear of the remaining State immunity. Although this is not President Spielmann's argument, he offers no reason why asserting and expanding State immunity should lead to less fragmentation, or why a jurisprudence restricting State immunity cannot build equally on the active interchanges between the courts of the kind that President Spielmann sets out.

On the background of President Spielmann's chapter, Dr Magdalena Forowicz, in the book's eighth chapter, 'Factors Influencing the Reception of International Law in the ECtHR's Case Law: An Overiew', analyses the factors that influence the process of application of general international law by the European Court. She argues that the European Court has only reluctantly given away its self-sufficiency, and started to refer to external sources from its position as an autonomous and authoritative court exclusively charged with the application of the European Convention on Human Rights. With the proliferation of international courts and tribunals and the expansion of international law, the Court has been compelled to look beyond the Convention in its case law. Dr Forowicz explores what consequences a fragmented legal order may have for the European Court.

In her chapter, Dr Forowicz revisits the empirical assessment she previously has undertaken[71] of the Court jurisprudence and eight areas of international law: child rights, refugee rights, civil and political rights, prohibition against torture and other ill-treatment, State immunity, international humanitarian law, the law of treaties and the International Court of Justice's case law. In light of recent case law, her chapter reassesses the applications of international law and the most influential factors. She

[71] Magdalena Forowicz, *The Reception of International Law in the European Court of Human Rights* (Oxford University Press, 2010).

also explores whether, in an international legal order tending towards convergence, the European Court's approach will support and facilitate a central role for the International Court in ensuring its unity.

Dr Forowicz argues that an important reason that may have discouraged the European Court from referring to international law is that the European Convention goes further in its protection of human rights than other international instruments, granting a more extensive protection to the applicant. The international instruments have a universal reach and are not specific to the European context. Furthermore, UN Treaty bodies have a quasi-judicial nature which may have made the more fully judicial European Court, rendering binding decisions, reluctant to refer to their non-binding conclusions. Dr Forowicz takes issue with the arguments that referring to other international instruments and international case law will not contribute to the interpretation of European Convention rights, reminding us that human rights have a universal value and that they are not merely a Western creation.

In section 3, Dr Forowicz concludes her review of the European Court's jurisprudence in the eight areas of international law. She concludes that the Court's receptiveness is still to a greater extent incidental, circumstantial or even involuntary. She addresses the importance of the similarities between the European Convention on Human Rights and other international instruments and the need to improve and update the European Convention on Human Rights in receiving international law. She again points out how the European Court 'often picked up on the differences between the ECHR and general international law, as it wanted to avoid a possible weakening of the level of protection provided under the ECHR'.

In section 4, 'A self-reinforcing, but not self-sufficient regime', Dr Forowicz concludes that the European Court does not rely on an approach which is aimed at reducing fragmentation. The rationale behind the references where the Court has discretion in relying on international law 'are not grounded in the need to enhance the unity of the international legal system, but rather the need to preserve the ECHR, to improve its functioning and to ensure the protection of human rights'. Dr Forowicz concludes, however, in spite of the different approach of the European Court on refugee rights, the law of treaties and international humanitarian law, that this is outweighed by the common approach on most issues, including child rights or the prohibition on torture and other ill-treatment. In her view, where the European Court interpreted international law differently from other bodies, it has introduced uncertainty and perhaps in particular it has not sufficiently acknowledged the sources of its reasoning. The European Court has chosen those references which were aimed at reinforcing and improving the European Convention system and the protection of human rights. Dr Forowicz characterizes the European Convention system as 'a self-reinforcing, but certainly not as self-sufficient regime'.

In the final section of her chapter, Dr Forowicz asks whether the European Court will support a more central role for the International Court. While the European Court's substantive references have remained infrequent, they demonstrate that the European Court is receptive to the findings of this authoritative body. She criticizes the lack of coherency.

She chooses as her concluding example the *Behrami* case,[72] as a case where the European Court finds a solution in line with the UN Charter and general international law, by not holding States liable when acting under a UN mandate, leaving the 'ultimate' control to the UN, against which there would be no recourse before the European Court or in practice before any other instance. Mads Andenas' analysis in his concluding chapter in the present book goes the other way, and argues that the European Court departed from the clearly established doctrine of effective control in the *Behrami* case, and that it is with *Al-Jedda* v. *United Kingdom*[73] that the European Court has taken a first step towards adopting the solution that follows from the jurisprudence of the International Court and UN human rights bodies such as the Human Rights Committee and the Working Group on Arbitrary Detention.

Dr Forowicz further points to how the European Court in *Al-Jedda* avoided finding any conflict between the European Convention on Human Rights and the UN Security Council Resolution, establishing an interpretative presumption that the Security Council does not intend to impose any obligation in its Resolutions on Member States to breach fundamental principles of human rights. She criticizes how the European Court in *Nada* v. *Switzerland*[74] avoided a conflict between the European Convention on Human Rights and the UN Security Council resolutions 'through harmonious interpretation'. Dr Forowicz concludes that 'it is yet to be seen whether the *rapprochement* of the two Courts will yield

[72] *Behrami and Behrami* v. *France* and *Saramati* v. *France, Germany and Norway* (Appl. Nos. 71412/01; 78166/01), Judgment, 2 May 2007.

[73] *Al-Jedda* v. *United Kingdom*, [GC], no. 27021/08, ECHR 2011.

[74] *Nada* v. *Switzerland*, [GC], no. 10593/08, ECHR 2012.

concrete results which could ensure a greater unity of the international legal system'.

The ninth chapter is by Dr Cameron Miles, and has the title 'The Influence of the International Court of Justice on the Law of Provisional Measures. He investigates the International Court's influence in the cases before other international courts and tribunals and he asks whether there is a "uniform" approach'. While the law of provisional measures before international courts and tribunals may seem a curious topic for discussion in the context of substantive fragmentation, Cameron Miles argues that this initial reaction is flawed. After all, why cannot fragmentation be procedural? Having established that this is the case, Dr Miles demonstrates that provisional measures are a prime candidate for consideration, with most international courts and tribunals awarding interim relief in order to safeguard the effectiveness of any final award – the attendant risk of contradictory pronouncements on the 'law' of provisional measures is obvious.

In his chapter Dr Miles argues that unlike other areas of international law, there is no risk of fragmentation in the context of provisional measures, due principally to the long-standing and normative influence of the International Court of Justice. This influence takes two forms: (1) the textual influence of Article 41 of the International Court's Statute over the drafting of the constitutive instruments of later international courts and tribunals; and (2) the jurisprudential influence of the case law of the International Court, through which a number of substantive principles governing the award of interim relief have been adduced, for example the concept of prima facie jurisdiction, the need for urgency and irreparable harm, the binding nature of provisional measures, and so forth. This influence – and the relatively uniformity that it has produced – will be assessed through comparison with several other forms of international dispute settlement, namely ITLOS and Annex VII arbitration according to UNCLOS, investor-State tribunals operating under the ICSID Convention, and the European Court of Human Rights.

The tenth chapter is by Dr Lawrence Hill-Cawthorne: 'Just Another Case of Treaty Interpretation? Reconciling Humanitarian and Human Rights Law in the ICJ'. He discusses the role of the International Court of Justice in the broader project that has sought to move away from traditional conceptions of international humanitarian law and international human rights law as entirely separate normative orders, towards a more unified notion of the two as simply parts of a single, coherent international legal order. The International Court of Justice has played a key role in this project, not only by confirming that individuals do not somehow lose their rights merely because an armed conflict has come into existence, but also by offering a particular approach to the interaction between international humanitarian law and international human rights law. It is a theme of this chapter that the International Court of Justice approached the relationship between these two sets of rules as a matter of treaty interpretation, through its invocation of the principle of *lex specialis*. A number of criticisms of this approach are shown to exist and the chapter shows that, in certain cases, the International Court's approach does not necessarily yield a result reflective of State intentions. However, the chapter also argues that this is a problem that is often faced in any case of treaty interpretation, and the appropriateness of the *lex specialis* principle, as with any other interpretive maxim, can only be judged on a case-by-case basis, depending on its ability to point to relevant factors that can help approximate party intentions. The focus is on the International Court of Justice's case law. However, the cases in which the relationship between international humanitarian law and international human rights law has and will continue to be disputed will likely arise in regional and international human rights courts and other bodies. States must, therefore, take into account, in planning military operations, that they may well be held to account for certain actions before these bodies. Moreover, the jurisdictional limitations that apply to these courts will likely affect the degree to which they can take relevant rules of international humanitarian law into account. Once again, therefore, we are reminded that this 'is a continuing process' and one in which a range of different actors will continue to play a role.

Taking as his point of departure that fragmentation is not a new phenomenon, nor a pathology, but rather an endemic feature of international law, Mehrdad Payandeh in the eleventh chapter analyses the case of the *Turkish Union in Berlin/Brandenburg* v. *Germany* (*Sarrazin*)[75] decision by the Committee on the Elimination of Racial Discrimination (CERD), under the International Convention on the Elimination of all Forms of Racial Discrimination (ICERD),[76] as an illustration of the potential for conflicts of jurisprudence within international human rights law. In this way, his chapter provides a finely granulated account of how to deal with fragmentation within a field of international law, as opposed to between that field of international law and general international law.

[75] Committee on the Elimination of Racial Discrimination, Communication No. 48/2010, Decision of 26 February 2013, *TBB* v. *Germany*, UN Doc. CERD/C/82/D/48/2010.

[76] International Convention on the Elimination of all Forms of Racial Discrimination, 21 December 1965, 660 UNTS 195.

Payandeh explains how the potential for conflicts within international human rights law has increased through the proliferation of international legal regimes and institutions for the protection of human rights. On Payandeh's view that is far from being the whole picture, however. On the one hand, he shows how the operation of procedural rules can obviate the danger of conflicts of jurisdiction, and how, on the other hand, conflicts of jurisprudence pose a realistic threat to the coherence and integrity of international human rights law. This potential for conflict is caused not so much by incompatible substantive provisions of the different human rights treaties as it is caused by the different structural biases and institutional preferences that are at work within the different human rights treaty bodies.

While, as he explains, each UN human rights treaty technically constitutes an independent legal instrument, they are all part of the larger normative framework of international human rights law and are based on a common political and moral understanding of human rights. Despite the political and ideological debates about human rights, about their universality, contingency, and relativity, all human rights treaties find their deeper justification in the intersubjectively comprehensible sense of human suffering and in the vulnerability of the human person, experienced in the twentieth century through the Shoah, apartheid, and, as the preamble of the Universal Declaration of Human Rights phrases it, through other 'barbarous acts which have outraged the conscience of mankind'.

While the institutional preference of the human rights treaty bodies with regard to the human rights concern embodied in the respective treaty is, in general, not to be criticized but rather to be welcomed, this structural bias can be problematic for the coherence and inner compatibility of international human rights law, when two legitimate human rights concerns collide. Payandeh shows how this was the case in the *Sarrazin* decision, where the CERD's categorical exclusion of racist speech from the protection of freedom of expression, on his view, failed to do justice to the wording and structure of the ICERD, and also to recognize the normative and institutional embeddedness of the ICERD within a broader context of human rights law consisting of universal, regional and domestic human rights guarantees.

Dr Emanuel Castellarin in the twelfth chapter, entitled 'The European Union's Participation in International Economic Institutions: A Mutually Beneficial Reassertion of the Centre', analyses the relations between the European Union and international economic institutions as an example of centre–periphery dialectics where the centre, that is, international economic institutions, reasserts its role thanks to systemic integration with the periphery, that is, the European Union. Castellarin argues that by participating in the activity of international economic institutions the European Union obtains normative influence and social recognition, but is the subject also of considerable constraints. This, in Castellarin's view, creates a mutually beneficial institutional and normative interaction which consolidates the development of international institutional law and reinforces the legitimacy of international economic institutions as fora of global governance.

Conceptually speaking, the EU is peripheral as an international legal person, often described as a *sui generis* international organization and as the archetype of supranational organizations. The integration of the European Communities and, later, the European Union have since 1957 been a 'permanent revolution' in international law, as its basic features, such as strong integrated organs and developed external powers, are exceptional for international organizations. This institutional phenomenon corresponds to a discursive phenomenon of self-assertion aimed at strengthening the European Union's autonomy, defined both as political independence (its separate will, that is, its ability to take decisions on its own) and as institutional independence (its ability to act independently on the international scene to defend the general interest of the community of States that created it). Elaborating on a feature of all international organizations as legal persons, the Commission and the European Court of Justice, assisted by a part of European Union law doctrine, have developed a strong self-referential conception of autonomy. In particular, Castellarin argues, the Court of Justice of the European Union (CJEU) has contributed to this trend by its famous statements that 'the EEC Treaty has created its own legal system',[77] a 'new legal order of international law'.[78] For this reason, while being subjected to the principle of conferred powers like all international organization, the European Union has become a quasi-federal system, conscious and proud of its unique nature. The basic concepts for this self-assertion, such as legal personality and separate will of international organizations, Castellarin observes, came from the centre of international law, as evidenced by the jurisprudence of the International Court.[79]

[77] C-6/64, *Costa* v. *ENEL*, 15 July 1964, ECR 585, 593.

[78] C-26/62, *van Gend en Loos*, 5 February 1963, ECR 1, 12.

[79] *Reparation for Injuries Suffered in the Service of the United Nations*, Advisory Opinion, ICJ Rep 1949, 174.

Dr Veronika Fikfak's chapter thirteen, 'Reinforcing the ICJ's Central International Role? Domestic Courts' Treatment of ICJ Decisions and Opinions', investigates the role of domestic courts in the implementation of decisions of the International Court of Justice in the domestic legal order.

Scholars have argued that in the absence of a general enforcement mechanism on the international plane, domestic courts have to act as agents of the international legal order applying and enforcing decisions rendered by international institutions. Recently, many domestic courts have refused blindly to enforce such decisions. When asked to implement resolutions of the Security Council, they have, for example, asserted their power to review and proceeded to re-interpret such instruments, or at times even refused to enforce them because the protection of fundamental rights was not ensured. Dr Fikfak's chapter examines whether domestic courts have adopted a similar approach in relation to decisions and opinions of the International Court of Justice. The case law shows that the review of decisions of the International Court of Justice differs substantially. Dr Fikfak's analysis reveals that domestic courts are careful to frame their review in exclusively domestic legal terms, utilizing various distancing devices to avoid a direct challenge of the International Court of Justice's reading and interpretation of international law. In the end, domestic courts affirm the authority of the International Court of Justice as the central and ultimate maker and guardian of international law.

Part 2: A farewell to fragmentation and the sources of law

A: Custom and *jus cogens*

What do we mean when we say 'the centre', asks Professor Lorenzo Gradoni in the fourteenth chapter, 'The International Court of Justice and the International Customary Law Game of Cards', taking an article by Mads Andenas as his starting point. The centre is possibly represented by general international law as opposed to the special laws of the much despised self-contained regimes. But what if the law-applying agencies, the judicial institutions, which partake of those special regimes, have different methods of ascertaining customary law and its relationship to each special arrangement?

Possibly, then, says Professor Gradoni, the centre is a method, a method which is or should be central, which today may look somewhat encircled and in need of breaking the siege and restoring its influence. There must be – somewhere – a specialist of this method, one or more institution acting as its custodians: the most obvious candidates are the International Court of Justice and the ILC. The two totems of the 'specialists of the general'. But do these institutions have something like a method on offer? Do they not change method according to the circumstances? Are they not strategic players inclined to pick and choose among a varied repertoire of methods (in the plural)? And if their authority is relatively independent of the method they employ, can we say that they are today central decision-makers?

Dr Alexander Orakhelashvili in the fifteenth chapter, 'State Practice, Treaty Practice and State Immunity in International and English Law', argues that international law relating to State immunity does not experience any fragmentation, but merely works on the ordinary pattern of sources of law and of the hierarchy of norms, including *lex specialis* and *jus cogens*. Immunities *ratione materiae* of States and their officials rely on a single and uniform justification – to protect genuinely sovereign activities of States. State practice shows no evidence that the regimes applicable to immunities in civil and criminal proceedings are different from each other. In both types of proceedings, and in the absence of any applicable treaty provision requiring the opposite, the underlying functional test refers to acts unique to State authority.

On balance, there is no customary law obligation of one State to accord immunity to another State, but the restrictive doctrine that aspires to be customary law is quite narrow anyway, even as a matter of comity. Even if one agrees that this narrow restrictive doctrine, referring to acts unique to State authority, is part of customary law, its use in practice would still not mandate the approach adopted in *Al-Adsani*, *Jones* and *Germany* v. *Italy*.

Treaty-specific regimes can have a normative impact on immunities, requiring the denial of immunity, even if otherwise available. This concerns the finding of the right balance of underlying interests as a matter of jurisprudence of the Strasbourg Court under Article 6 of the European Convention on Human Rights. Both the European Convention on Human Rights and *jus cogens* clearly prevail over the immunity of States and their officials in both criminal and civil proceedings. The adjudication standards under the European Convention on Human Rights and *jus cogens* are flexible enough, and offer reasonable ways for balancing conflicting interests.

This contrasts to the pro-immunity view that is premised on the blanket, and thus irrational, prioritization of the interests of the impleaded State over that of its victims, thereby raising legal concerns as well as reinforcing the increasing moral disrepute of this 'traditional' school of thought.

In the sixteenth chapter, 'Historical Sketches About Custom in International Law', Professor Jean-Louis Halpérin, analyses the role of the concept of 'legal order' in legal scholarship in constructing coherence in international law.

Professor Halpérin revisits his 2001 work, where he studies the historical origins of the 'legal order' (*Rechtsordnung, ordinamento giuridico, ordre juridique*) and emphasizes the role of the doctrinal writing on international law in the apparition of this conception of an ordered legal system, from the first use of the words 'rechtliche Ordnung' by Gentz (in his 1800 work about perpetual peace) and F. J. Stahl (1830) to the developments made by von Bar (1862), Bergbohm (1892), Triepel, Anzilotti, Santi Romano, Gény and, of course, Kelsen.

As this formula could be used as well by 'dualist' theoreticians as by 'monist' ones, Professor Halpérin expresses some scepticism about a history of legal ideas (or of 'juristic thought') that is separated to too large a degree from the historical study of positive norms and from the sociological analysis of the influence of legal professionals. A positivist point of view does not require one to suspect ideological aspects in every construction of the doctrine, but it must imply a duty of cautiousness.

Through the analysis of customary law formation within the international 'legal order' (*Rechtsordnung, ordinamento giuridico, ordre juridique*) this chapter critically engages with the most important aspects of the fragmentation debate, from a theoretical vantage point.

B: Treaty interpretation

Professor Robert Kolb, in the seventeenth chapter, entitled 'Is There a Subject-Matter Ontology in Interpretation of International Legal Norms?', deals with the postulate that there are certain common and agreed rules or maxims of interpretation across the different fields of international law. By reason of the specificity of international society, the role of such agreed rules in international law takes on particular importance. The Vienna Convention on the Law of Treaties[80] has succeeded in setting out a common law of the interpretation of treaties. The regime of the Vienna Convention can be expanded by analogy to other sources and subjects in international law. The common core of the rules does not, however,

[80] Vienna Convention on the Law of Treaties, 23 May 1969, 1155 UNTS 331; (1969) 8 ILM 679.

preclude flexibility in the combination of elements to be selected in a particular context of interpretation. International practice has not as yet evidenced the need for the development of a special sub-set of rules for particular subject-matters in international law, that is, rules which would prevail over the general rules of the Vienna Convention by reason of being *lex specialis*. In Kolb's view, international practice evidences that interpretation is a complex, multifaceted process, whose reduction to unity can always only, in the final analysis, be partial. The particular interpretation will depend on many factors, among which are the person performing it, the function or goal the interpretation shall perform, and the broader legal and political context.

Professor Paolo Palchetti, in the eighteenth chapter, entitled 'Halfway Between Fragmentation and Convergence: The Role of the Rules of the Organization in the Interpretation of Constituent Treaties', deals with the role of the 'rules of the organization', and particularly rules deriving from the established practice of the organization, in the interpretation of the constituent instrument of the organization.

In dealing with the interpretation of constituent instruments one is, Palchetti argues, confronted with two different approaches. One, which emphasizes the logic of fragmentation, is to say that they are treaties of a particular nature, to which the general rules of interpretation do not entirely apply; the other, less dramatic, view is to say that the general rules apply, unless there are 'rules of the organization', the existence of which must be demonstrated, which prevail as *lex specialis* over the general rules. The latter solution, which is the one envisaged in Article 5 of the Vienna Convention, has so far been little explored.

Article 5 of the Vienna Convention provides that: 'The present Convention applies to any treaty which is the constituent instrument of an international organization and to any treaty adopted within an international organization without prejudice to any relevant rules of the organization.'

Professor Palchetti, on this background, examines the debate over this issue during the preparatory works of the Vienna Convention. A part of his chapter he dedicates to showing that an established practice of the organization may lead to the formation of particular rules of treaty interpretation; the European Union is here the main example. Another part of the chapter shows that the importance attached to the practice of the organization for the purposes of treaty interpretation may be justified by reference to the fact that such practice has given rise to rules of the organization adopting a particular interpretation of a specific provision of the constituent instrument.

Professor Palchetti concludes in this connection that there is no fragmentation; in most cases it is simply an issue of *lex specialis*, reflecting the subsidiary nature of the general rules of interpretation.

In the nineteenth and penultimate chapter, 'The Convergence of the Methods of Treaty Interpretation. Different Regimes, Different Methods of Interpretation?', Dr Eirik Bjorge, like Professor Kolb in his chapter, deals with aspects of the alleged fragmentation of the law of treaties. Firstly, the chapter deals with the notion of self-contained regimes in international law and what their alleged existence may mean for the law of treaties. In order to do so the chapter takes issue with the reliance in the literature on a 1930 article by Lord McNair, which, it is argued in the chapter, has been widely misunderstood and taken as a licence, from a distinguished author and judge, to say that the law of treaties is as fragmented as some have seen international law itself to be. The chapter then turns to the different categorizations which have been applied to treaties (focusing on the three-way split often found in the literature between human rights treaties, constitutional treaties, and contractual treaties), and the attendant arguments that some of them call for a restrictive and sovereignty-bound style of interpretation; others, for a teleologic or evolutionary one. The chapter argues that none of these distinctions is really convincing. Then the chapter, by way of an analysis of jurisprudence from the International Court, turns to that which more directly concerns the methods of treaty interpretation adopted, and ventures to show that not only does the Court use interpretation in order to dispel misgivings in the literature about the fragmentation of international law; it also, and by the same token, shows by the interpretive approaches it applies that the method of treaty interpretation itself is not fragmented but in fact unified and coherent.

Professor Mads Andenas' chapter 'Reassertion and Transformation of International Law' is the twentieth chapter and concludes the book. It has two starting points. One is the fragmentation discussion of the last two decades; the other, the International Court of Justice's development of the law, with its emphasis on the unity of international law and its method, and lesser concern with limitations of State consent.

Andenas outlines one background for the recent fragmentation discussion. In the 1990s two presidents of the International Court, Sir Robert Jennings and Gilbert Guillaume, voiced concern over the proliferation of international courts and tribunals. The International Court had achieved wider acceptance than before, and international law tied States ever tighter together, with a strengthening of compliance regimes and individual remedies. International law was given effect in domestic law by legislatures and courts and new constitutional mechanisms. New courts and other treaty bodies had compulsory jurisdiction whereas the jurisdiction of the International Court continued to rely on the consent of States. The International Court resisted the development of a hierarchy of international legal norms and although it experimented with procedural issues and working methods it often reverted to a conservative application of tradition. General international law, as applied by the International Court, could be seen to go down the road of several of the different autonomous and self-contained fragmented regimes. The conclusions of the ILC's Study Group on the fragmentation of international law 'Difficulties arising from the Diversification and Expansion of International Law' (2006) about international law as a legal system built on an analysis of the sources of international law. The International Court's jurisprudence over the last fifteen years, with some reforms of working methods and the form of judgments, and developments of both sources of law and substantive law, may be seen as a response to the fragmentation challenge.

The International Court of Justice has recently made important contributions to environmental and human rights law and the law of remedies. The Court has confirmed customary international law and *jus cogens*, and it has clarified the method of treaty interpretation, using decisions from other international tribunals and from national courts as State practice. The conclusion is that the International Court has in this way not only shown that international law is a single, unified system of law but, in doing so, reasserted its own position in this system, that is, at the centre of the international legal system. A final part of the chapter analyses how maintenance of this position may influence the International Court's contributions to the development of the law in some areas of law.

PART 1

Reassertion and convergence: 'proliferation' of courts and the centre of international law

A. At the centre: the International Court

2

Unity and diversity in international law

SIR CHRISTOPHER GREENWOOD[1]

At the dawn of the new millennium, fear of the fragmentation of international law was widespread among international lawyers.[2] International law, we were told, was in danger of breaking up into a series of isolated and largely self-contained sub-disciplines, courts and tribunals were multiplying, creating divergent bodies of jurisprudence which it would be impossible to reconcile, while new treaties were emerging at an ever-increasing rate but drafted with no consideration for developments elsewhere. The result – or so it appeared – was that international law was in danger of losing all coherence. Yet, when the matter is properly analysed, the fear of fragmentation at the start of the present millennium appears eerily reminiscent of the panic with which the dawn of the previous millennium was greeted by those who believed that the end of the world was nigh.

Of course, the fear of fragmentation rests on a rational foundation that the earlier panic lacked. International law has expanded into many new (or relatively new) areas, such as environmental protection, the regulation of world trade and the protection of human rights, which are often seen as specialisms. There is much more international law than there was only a generation ago and treaties are frequently negotiated in isolation from other developments in international law. The number of international courts and tribunals has multiplied. Yet none of that points to a fragmentation of international law any more than the omens seen by our more credulous ancestors just over a thousand years ago presaged the end of the world.

[1] Judge, International Court of Justice.

[2] M. Koskenniemi, 'Fragmentation of International Law: Difficulties Arising from the Diversification and Expansion of International Law', Report of the Study Group of the International Law Commission, finalised by Martti Koskenniemi (UN Doc. A/CN.4/L.682).

This chapter will briefly examine some aspects of the diversity of international law today and consider what it actually means for the international legal system. The term 'fragmentation' will be avoided as far as possible, partly because it has been overused in the literature but, more importantly, because implicit in that term are three assumptions, none of which is justified.

The first such assumption is that what we are witnessing is a decline from a past golden age in which international law was a single, entirely coherent system. Yet the international law of the 'pre-fragmentation era', with its attachment to regional custom[3] and the persistent objector principle,[4] not to mention its treatment of reservations to multilateral treaties[5] – all of which were well-established features of international law long before people began to tremble at the prospect of fragmentation – shows that the golden age was not so gilded after all.

The second assumption is that the increased diversity of international law must be seen as a problem – but why? That international law now regulates many areas of activity which it would once have left alone is – for the most part – a development to be welcomed. No-one who has read the Judgment of the Nuremberg Tribunal could have any doubts about the need for international protection of fundamental human rights. The emergence of a body of law on environmental protection is a response (perhaps an inadequate one) to serious problems which can only be addressed at the international level. The law on world trade has helped to prevent the latest financial crisis from tipping the world into the kind of protectionist, 'beggar-my-neighbour' policies which characterised the response to the 1929 crash.

Nor is the multiplication of international courts and tribunals a matter for concern, especially if we compare it with what went before. In 1977, the International Court of Justice had only one case on its General List,[6] although there was a small flurry of inter-State arbitrations after a dearth

[3] See *Asylum case (Colombia/Peru), I.C.J. Reports 1950*, p. 266 and *Rights of Passage (Portugal* v. *India) I.C.J. Reports 1960*, p. 6.

[4] See *Fisheries case (United Kingdom* v. *Norway) I.C.J. Reports 1951*, p. 116 and J. Charney 'The Persistent Objector Rule and the Development of Customary International Law', (1985) 56 BYIL 1.

[5] *Reservations to the Convention on Genocide, Advisory Opinion, I.C.J. Reports 1951*, p. 15; Vienna Convention on the Law of Treaties, 23 May 1969, 1155 UNTS 331; (1969) 8 ILM 679, Articles 19–22.

[6] *Aegean Sea Continental Shelf (Greece* v. *Turkey)*; the Court decided it lacked jurisdiction the following year, see *I.C.J. Reports 1978*, p. 3.

of such cases in the previous decade;[7] human rights jurisprudence was still in its infancy and applied in only one continent; there was no international criminal court in spite of the endorsement of the Nuremberg principles by the UN General Assembly thirty years earlier,[8] and the law on investment protection was enforced only by occasional instances of diplomatic protection and sporadic arbitrations derived from clauses in a particular set of oil concessions.[9] At the time of writing, the International Court had thirteen cases on the General List and there were ten further inter-State disputes pending before arbitration tribunals. The International Tribunal for the Law of the Sea (ITLOS), the criminal tribunals for Rwanda and the former Yugoslavia, the International Criminal Court and a variety of regional and global human rights courts and tribunals have all been busy in the last few years. In the field of investment arbitration, there has been an explosion in the number of cases, which now runs at something like one hundred arbitrations a year. In short, there is more scope today for the enforcement of international law than at any time in the past. It is difficult to see that development as evidence of decline.

The third assumption, encouraged by the use of the term 'fragmentation,' is that unity and diversity must be in conflict. But there is nothing inevitable about such a conflict. Diversity is inevitable in an international community characterised by decentralisation and the absence of a global legislature. It has the advantage of enabling international law to develop faster and more effectively through regional and functional groupings of States, or simply through 'coalitions of the willing' prepared to adopt and participate in a particular treaty regime. That can pose a problem for the unity and ultimate coherence of international law but it does not have to do so. What matters is that the diverse elements are bound together within a common body of principles which determine the source of legal authority and which give each diverse element its binding force, that rules and principles exist and are applied which can resolve apparent conflicts between

[7] *Channel Continental Shelf (France/United Kingdom)*, 54 ILR 6; *Beagle Channel (Argentina/Chile)* 52 ILR 93; and *Air Services (France/United States of America)* 54 ILR 303. The only major arbitration in the previous decade had been *Rann of Kutch (India/Pakistan)*, 50 ILR 2. The *Beagle Channel* case made history in another respect in that, following the failure to implement the award, the case became the subject of the first Papal mediation in over a century.

[8] General Assembly Resolution 95(I).

[9] C. Greenwood, 'State Contracts in International law – The Libyan Oil Arbitrations', (1982) 53 BYIL 27, discussing *BP* v. *Libya*, 53 ILR 297, *Texaco/Calasiatic* v. *Libya*, 53 ILR 389 and *Libyan American Oil Co.* v. *Libya*, 62 ILR 140.

different bodies of law and institutions and that the different courts and tribunals take proper account of each other's jurisprudence and practices.

This chapter will therefore explore whether such rules and principles exist; whether there is a sufficient core of unity binding together the diverse elements within international law. To that end, it is proposed to conduct what must, of necessity, be a brief and highly selective examination of diversity in the making of international law, and its application by different international courts and tribunals.

Diversity in the making of international law

It is a truism that there is no central legislature occupying in international society a position comparable to that which the national parliament occupies in most States. The result is that new law and changes to the existing body of law must emerge either from the process of States negotiating a treaty or from State practice refining the body of customary international law. Both processes are clearly decentralised and thus capable of producing diversity in the sense of different bodies of law applicable to different States and in the sense of bodies of law which emerge without any conscious design regarding their place in the overall framework of international law.

In practice, customary international law[10] creates few problems in this regard. The process by which customary international law is developed[11] is such that the emergence of a new rule or principle is usually located within the body of existing law and conflicts (real or apparent) between different customary international law norms are rare. Regional custom is very much the exception and there have been few occasions on which a State has made a serious bid to be treated as a persistent objector. For the most part, therefore, customary international law is a coherent body of rules and principles applicable to all States.

The treaty-making process is a different matter; it almost invariably leads to diversity in both senses. No State is obliged to become party to a treaty[12] and very few treaties have achieved universal, or even

[10] As to which, see the comprehensive study in the two reports prepared by Sir Michael Wood for the International Law Commission in 2013 (UN Doc. A/CN.4/663) and 2014 (UN Doc. A/CN.4/672).

[11] See M. Mendelson, 'The Process of Formation of Customary International Law' 272 Recueil des cours (1998), p. 156.

[12] Moreover, most multilateral treaties permit a State to make reservations by which that State 'when signing, ratifying, accepting, approving or acceding to a treaty . . . purports to

near-universal, participation.[13] This aspect of diversity can certainly create problems. For example, forty years after the International Committee of the Red Cross attempted to update international humanitarian law, the decision of several of the most militarily powerful States not to become party to the Additional Protocols to the Geneva Conventions means that an issue as fundamental as who is entitled to be treated as a prisoner of war is subject to two very different legal standards.[14] This problem can be even more acute in the case of those treaties which aim at the creation of an objective regime, such as that for the deep seabed, or the full effectiveness of which requires universal participation, such as some of the environmental treaties.

Yet the problem is scarcely a new one. The decision of the United States not to join the League of Nations in 1919 was arguably far more significant than its decision, decades later, not to become party to the UN Convention on the Law of the Sea[15] or the Rio Treaty.[16] Nor is the lack of universal participation in such a treaty always as damaging as might be expected. The United Nations did not achieve universal membership until the 1990s yet played a major role in international life long before then; its effectiveness at different stages of its history cannot be attributed solely, or even primarily, to how close it was to universality. Moreover, in many cases the fact that key provisions of a treaty have come to be accepted as declaratory of customary international law mitigates the failure to achieve universal participation. That has been the case, for example, with many of the provisions of the Law of the Sea Convention regarding

exclude or to modify the legal effects of certain provisions of the treaty in their application to that State' (Vienna Convention on the Law of Treaties, 1969, Article 2(d)).

13 The Charter of the United Nations, 26 June 1945, 892 UNTS 119 and the four Geneva Conventions of 1949 regarding international humanitarian law (though not the two 1977 Additional Protocols to those Conventions) are rare exceptions.

14 Contrast the test in Article 4 of the 1949 Geneva Convention on Prisoners of War, 12 August 1949, 75 UNTS 135, with that in Articles 43 and 44 of the 1977 Additional Protocol I, 8 June 1977, 1125 UNTS 3. The problem is exacerbated by the fact that even those States which are parties to Additional Protocol I on international armed conflicts are obliged to apply its provisions in a conflict in which they are engaged only if the State with which they are in conflict is also a party. Thus, in the 2003 Iraq conflict, the United Kingdom was only required to apply the provisions of the 1949 Geneva Conventions and the relevant customary international law, because although the United Kingdom was party to Additional Protocol I, Iraq was not. By contrast, in the 1999 Kosovo conflict, the Protocol was applicable between the United Kingdom and the Federal Republic of Yugoslavia, both of which were parties, but not between the Federal Republic and the United States as the latter was not party to Protocol I.

15 UN Convention on the Law of the Sea, 10 December 1982, 1833 UNTS 3.

16 Inter-American Treaty on Reciprocal Assistance (Rio Treaty), 2 September 1947, 21 UNTS 77.

the continental shelf and the exclusive economic zone,[17] as well as most of the provisions regarding methods and means of warfare and precautions in attack (though not those on entitlement to prisoner of war status) contained in Additional Protocol I to the Geneva Conventions.[18] While it would be a mistake to imagine that these developments in customary international law solve all problems created by diversity in the applicable treaty regimes, they certainly go some way towards ameliorating the situation and mean that there is a greater unity in the law than might at first appear.

The process by which treaties are made also encourages diversity in the other sense. Since most treaties are negotiated as isolated texts, a treaty can all too easily create a self-contained legal code and, even if it does not go that far, the very fact that each treaty is negotiated separately can lead to conflicts between different legal instruments and thus undermine the coherence and unity of international law. Again, this problem exists but it is not as extensive or as serious as the 'fragmenteers' suggest.

First, there is a greater degree of coherence in the treaty-making process than is often supposed. The work of the International Law Commission, the Treaty Section of the Office of Legal Affairs of the UN Secretariat and, in their specialised fields, bodies such as the International Committee of the Red Cross, the Hague Conference on Private International Law and the World Trade Organization means that many multilateral treaties are today negotiated within an overall framework that fosters greater awareness of the relationship between the draft under consideration and other international law instruments. For example, the numerous counter-terrorism treaties adopted since 1970 have clearly been negotiated in a relatively systematic way, employing what has become a standard provision on dispute settlement and with an attempt to achieve a high degree of coherence.[19]

Secondly, the principles of treaty interpretation codified in the Vienna Convention on the Law of Treaties, 1969, include the important principle that, in the interpretation of a treaty, 'there shall be taken into account,

[17] See, e.g., the treatment of this issue by the International Court of Justice in *Territorial and Maritime Dispute (Nicaragua* v. *Colombia), I.C.J. Reports 2012 (II)*, p. 624. Nicaragua was party to the Law of the Sea Convention but Colombia was not.

[18] See C. Greenwood, 'The Customary Law Status of the 1977 Additional Protocols' in C. Greenwood, *Essays on War in International Law* (London: Cameron May, 2006), p. 179. See also 'Customary International Law and the First Geneva Protocol of 1977 in the Gulf Conflict', *ibid.*, p. 555.

[19] See B. Saul, *Defining Terrorism in International Law* (Oxford: Oxford University Press, 2012).

together with the context . . . any relevant rules of international law applicable between the parties'.[20] That principle has been applied by a wide variety of bodies in the interpretation and application of treaties. For example, the European Court of Human Rights has consistently emphasised that the European Convention on Human Rights,[21] far from existing in a vacuum, is an integral part of international law and must be interpreted and applied accordingly.[22] Similarly, although the three arbitration tribunals constituted under the North American Free Trade Agreement (NAFTA)[23] that considered a Mexican argument that the imposition of a tax which allegedly violated the rights of US investors could be justified under the doctrine of counter-measures rejected that argument, none of them concluded that NAFTA created a self-contained legal regime in which doctrines of general international law such as that on counter-measures had no part.[24]

Thirdly, the fact that those negotiating a treaty sometimes do so without considering how the provisions adopted in that treaty relate to other rules of international law is neither surprising – the supposedly more coherent system for enactment of national legislation produces no shortage of examples in which one statute is in conflict with other parts of a parliament's output – nor necessarily damaging. What matters is whether international law contains the principles necessary for addressing that relationship and for avoiding conflict. That it does can be seen in the way in which different courts and tribunals have grappled with the relationship between the UN Convention against Torture, 1984,[25] together with other treaties on international criminal law, and the various rules and principles of international law regarding State and individual immunities. The records of the meetings in which the Convention was negotiated

20 Article 31(3)(c). On the importance of this provision as a unifying force in international law, see C. MacLachlan, 'The Principle of Systematic Integration and Article 31(3)(c) of the Vienna Convention' (2005) 7 ICLQ 279.

21 (European) Convention for the Protection of Human Rights and Fundamental Freedoms, 4 November 1950, 213 UNTS 222.

22 For an early example, see the Judgment in *Golder* v. *United Kingdom*, 57 ILR 200. Even more striking in this regard is the unanimous decision of the Grand Chamber in *Banković* v. *Belgium and Others*, 123 ILR 94, see also the judgment in *Hassan* v. *United Kingdom* (App. No. 29750/09), 16 September 2014; to be published in volume 161 of the *International Law Reports*. See also the chapter by President Spielmann in the present volume.

23 North American Free Trade Agreement, 17 December 1992, (1993) 32 ILM 289.

24 *ADM and Tate and Lyle Inc.* v. *Mexico*, 146 ILR 439; *Corn Products Inc* v. *Mexico*, 146 ILR 581; *Cargill Inc.* v. *Mexico*, 146 ILR 642.

25 Convention Against Torture, 10 December 1984, 1485 UNTS 85.

over a period of four years[26] show that the question of immunity was not considered, at least in any detail, and neither the text of the Convention, nor its *travaux préparatoires* gives any express guidance as to the relationship between the provisions of the Convention and the law on immunities.

That matter came before the House of Lords in the *Pinochet* case in 1998–99. The majority of the Appellate Committee considered that the Convention was not intended to dispense altogether with the immunity which the Appellate Committee found customary international law required one State to accord to the officials and former officials of another State in respect of their official acts. At the same time, the fact that the Convention defined torture in such a way that it was limited to acts committed by persons acting in an official capacity (or under colour of official authority), and that the Convention required each State Party to take action against any person accused of torture as thus defined, meant that some inroad into the normal principle of immunity must have been intended; otherwise anyone who was capable of committing torture within the meaning of the Convention would be entitled to immunity if prosecuted in a foreign State unless the State in which he or she held office chose to waive that immunity. The House of Lords thus concluded that the immunity *ratione materiae* enjoyed by all officials and former officials was incompatible with the Convention. Although most of the acts in respect of which General Pinochet's extradition was sought had been committed when he was President of Chile, by the time he was arrested he no longer held office. The conclusion, therefore, was that he was not entitled to immunity in respect of alleged violations of the Convention.[27]

Since General Pinochet had left office some years before his arrest, the House of Lords had no need to consider the immunity *ratione personae* enjoyed by a serving Head of State (as well as by certain other officials of very high rank). That matter was, however, addressed by the International Court of Justice in the *Arrest Warrant* case three years later.[28] In that case, a Belgian court had issued a warrant for the arrest of

[26] On which, see J. Burgers and H. Danelius, *The United Nations Convention against Torture* (Boston: Martinus Nijhoff, 1988).

[27] *Regina* v. *Bow Street Magistrate*, ex parte *Pinochet (No. 3)*, [2000] 1 AC 147; 119 ILR 135. The majority, however, upheld his immunity in respect of acts committed before the entry into force of the Convention between Spain (the State seeking his extradition), the United Kingdom and Chile.

[28] *Arrest Warrant (Democratic Republic of the Congo* v. *Belgium), I.C.J. Reports 2002*, p. 3.

Mr Yerodia who, at the time the case was brought before the International Court, was the serving Foreign Minister of the Democratic Republic of the Congo. The International Court held that the grant of immunity to a serving foreign minister (and, one presumes, a serving Head of State or Government) served an important purpose in making possible the conduct of relations between States and was not, therefore, overridden by the provisions requiring prosecution in a treaty unless the treaty made clear that such was its intention.[29] While the arrest warrant was for violations of the Geneva Conventions and Protocols on the laws of war, rather than for violations of the Torture Convention, it is generally considered that the reasoning of the International Court would be applicable to the latter Convention, as well as to a number of similar treaty regimes.

The House of Lords returned to the subject in 2006 in *Jones* v. *Saudi Arabia*. In contrast to both *Pinochet* and *Arrest Warrant*, which both involved criminal proceedings, *Jones* concerned a civil action against both the Kingdom of Saudi Arabia and certain of its officials[30] for acts of torture allegedly committed in violation of the 1984 Convention. The House of Lords held that there was no incompatibility between the provisions of the Convention and the immunity of the State itself, since the Convention did not require one State to provide a civil remedy against another State for violation of the Convention. It also concluded that the decision in *Pinochet* was applicable to the immunity of the official in criminal but not civil proceedings, a conclusion which has attracted some controversy but which is explicable on the ground that criminal proceedings against an official are entirely distinct from the responsibility of the State itself,[31] whereas civil proceedings for damages against an official for acts attributable to the State are in practice inseparable from the responsibility of the State.[32]

I have dwelt upon the judgments in these three cases, because they demonstrate that, in spite of the fact that the process by which the treaties

[29] As Article 27 of the Statute of the International Criminal Court does. In that respect, see the decision of the International Criminal Court in *Prosecutor* v. *Bashir*, 150 ILR 228. See also the decision of the Special Court for Sierra Leone in *Prosecutor* v. *Taylor (Immunity from Jurisdiction)*, 128 ILR 239.

[30] *Jones* v. *Saudi Arabia* [2007] 1 AC 270; 129 ILR 629. One of the officials was the Minister of the Interior.

[31] *Application of the Convention on the Prevention and Punishment of the Crime of Genocide (Bosnia and Herzegovina* v. *Serbia and Montenegro), I.C.J. Reports 2007*, p. 43 at para. 172.

[32] Not only is the State vicariously liable for the acts of the official but also damages awarded against the official (and paid to the claimant) would necessarily affect the reparation which the State itself might be required to make if its responsibility was upheld.

under consideration were adopted (a process which avoided any consideration of the law on immunities), an application of the principles of treaty interpretation, together with an analysis of the nature and purpose of the various rules on immunity removed any apparent conflict between these different bodies of law. While it would be wrong to imagine that this was an easy task,[33] the fact is that it was accomplished. Diversity in the making of the different laws did not preclude their application in a way which upheld the unity of the international legal system.

Diversity in the application of international law

It was the growth in the number of courts and tribunals that did most to spark the fear that international law was fragmenting. The scale and speed of that growth is remarkable. In the space of barely thirty years, the International Court of Justice has been joined by ITLOS, the International Criminal Court, ad hoc criminal courts or tribunals for the former Yugoslavia, Rwanda, Sierra Leone, Lebanon and Cambodia, and the dispute settlement mechanism of the World Trade Organization. The regional human rights tribunals and the global UN Human Rights Committee have become far busier and the number of arbitrations (both between States and, even more noticeably, between investors and States) has undergone a dramatic increase. With no formal hierarchy or general appeals mechanism, the risk that each court or tribunal would interpret and apply the rules of international law in its own way, disregarding or challenging the jurisprudence of other courts and tribunals became a matter of serious concern.

It was the complex machinery for dispute settlement in the 1982 Law of the Sea Convention which was the initial focus of that concern. One of the compromises which proved necessary at the Third UN Conference on the Law of the Sea in order to secure some form of compulsory settlement of disputes was the choice, embodied in Part XV of the Convention, of recourse to the International Court of Justice, the newly created ITLOS, or arbitration under Annex VII of the Convention. It was feared that, particularly in the realm of maritime delimitation, these three options would lead to very different approaches to delimitation.[34]

[33] Having been counsel in both *Pinochet* and *Jones*, I can say (most emphatically) that it was not.

[34] S. Oda, 'The ICJ Viewed from the Bench (1976–1993)' 244 Recueil des cours (1993), p. 9, 127–55; S. Oda, 'Dispute Settlement Prospects in the Law of the Sea' (1995) 44 ICLQ 863; G. Guillaume, 'The Future of International Judicial Institutions' (1995) 44 ICLQ 848.

Those fears now seem unfounded. In the years since 1982 eighteen maritime boundary disputes have been the subject of a judgment or award.[35] Far from the fragmented jurisprudence that was predicted, there has been a remarkable consistency of approach between the International Court of Justice, ITLOS and the various arbitration tribunals. Moreover, the judgments and awards given in all three fora have referred extensively to the jurisprudence of other courts and tribunals. Thus, in its 2012 judgment in the *Bay of Bengal* case, ITLOS drew heavily upon the jurisprudence of the International Court of Justice and the arbitral tribunals, both on delimitation and on more general questions of international law. Later in the same year, the International Court of Justice, in its judgment in *Nicaragua* v. *Colombia*, placed a similar reliance on the reasoning in *Bay of Bengal*, as well as that in the arbitration awards. The result has been the emergence of a coherent body of law and practice which is the stronger for having emanated from more than one institution.

A similar willingness to draw on the experience and jurisprudence of a variety of courts and tribunals is evident in the 2012 judgment of the International Court of Justice in the *Diallo* case.[36] In that judgment the Court had to determine the amount of compensation to be paid by the Democratic Republic of the Congo to Guinea in respect of the former's ill-treatment of a Guinean national. The case was only the second

[35] Eleven (many of them involving disputes over land as well as maritime territory) have gone to the International Court of Justice: *Continental Shelf (Tunisia/Libya), I.C.J. Reports 1982*, p. 18; *Gulf of Maine (Canada/United States of America) I.C.J. Reports 1984*, p. 246; *Continental Shelf (Libya/Malta), I.C.J. Reports 1985*, p.13; *Land, Island and Maritime Frontier Dispute (El Salvador/Honduras, Nicaragua intervening), I.C.J. Reports 1992*, p. 350; *Jan Mayen (Denmark* v. *Norway), I.C.J. Reports 1993*, p. 38; *Maritime Delimitation and Territorial Questions (Qatar* v. *Bahrain), I.C.J. Reports 2001*, p. 40; *Land and Maritime Boundary (Cameroon* v. *Nigeria, Equatorial Guinea intervening), I.C.J. Reports 2002*, p. 303; *Territorial and Maritime Dispute (Nicaragua* v. *Honduras), I.C.J. Reports 2007*, p. 659; *Maritime Delimitation in the Black Sea (Romania* v. *Ukraine), I.C.J. Reports 2009*, p. 61; *Territorial and Maritime Dispute (Nicaragua* v. *Colombia), I.C.J. Reports 2012*, p. 624; and *Maritime Dispute (Peru* v. *Chile)*, Judgment of 27 January 2014. ITLOS has so far decided one maritime delimitation case, *Delimitation of the Maritime Boundary in the Bay of Bengal (Bangladesh/Myanmar)*, Judgment of 14 March 2012. There have also been six arbitration awards: *Guinea-Guinea Bissau Maritime Delimitation* (1985) 77 ILR 635; *Guinea-Bissau* v. *Senegal* (1989) 83 ILR 1; *Delimitation of Maritime Areas between Canada and the French Republic (San Pierre and Miquelon)* (1992) 95 ILR 645; *Eritrea and Yemen, Phase Two (Maritime Delimitation)* (1999) 119 ILR 418; *Barbados* v. *Trinidad and Tobago* (2006) 139 ILR 449 and *Guyana* v. *Suriname* (2007)139 ILR 566. At the time of writing several further cases were pending before the International Court of Justice and various arbitration tribunals.

[36] *Ahmadou Sadio Diallo (Guinea* v. *the Democratic Republic of Congo), Compensation Judgment, I.C.J. Reports 2012*, p. 324.

occasion on which the Court had been called upon to determine the quantum of compensation.[37] By contrast, other bodies, noticeably the human rights tribunals and the Iran–United States Claims Tribunal, had extensive experience in such matters. The Court's judgment draws heavily on that experience. Although the judgment is relatively short, it referred to the practice of the European Court of Human Rights, the Inter-American Court of Human Rights, the UN Human Rights Committee, the African Commission on Human and People's Rights, the UN Compensation Commission, the Iran–United States Claims Tribunal, the Eritrea–Ethiopia Claims Commission and ITLOS, as well as the award of the umpire in the *Lusitania* claims.[38] It is difficult to see in this judgment much evidence of a fragmentation of international law; quite the contrary.

A third example of the essential unity which exists in international law, notwithstanding the diversity of the courts and tribunals which apply it, concerns an issue which has come before both international and national courts. That issue is whether international law requires a State to accord another State immunity before the courts of that State even if the wrong of which the second State is accused contravenes a fundamental rule of international law. The fact that this issue is one which comes before national courts more frequently than it does before international courts makes achieving unity markedly more difficult. That is because the courts of many, perhaps most, States are not always at liberty to apply international law in its full extent. In most national legal systems, the constitution, or other rules of law, place limitations on the extent to which the national courts may apply international law. Those limitations vary from one State to another but, at a minimum, most States require obedience to at least the fundamental rules of the national constitution irrespective of whether that entails a conflict with international law. Moreover, in some States the supremacy of parliament, concepts of binding precedent, deference to the executive on certain legal issues or the straitjacket which can sometimes be imposed by procedure constrain the courts in their ability to apply international law.

Nevertheless, the courts of several States have dealt with this question and it has also come before the International Court of Justice and the European Court of Human Rights. The precise way in which the question has presented itself has not, however, been the same. The jurisdiction of

[37] The previous occasion was the *Corfu Channel case (United Kingdom* v. *Albania), I.C.J. Reports 1949*, p. 244.

[38] VII RIAA 40.

the European Court of Human Rights is confined to the interpretation and application of the European Convention on Human Rights, although, as has already been seen, the Court has repeatedly held that the Convention forms part of international law and has to be interpreted and applied in the context of the international legal system as a whole. In 2001, the Court held that for one State to recognise the sovereign immunity of another and therefore bar an action in its courts against that State was, in principle, a denial of access to justice which could engage the responsibility of the forum State under Article 6 of the Convention. It went on to hold, however, that if international law required a State to accord immunity from the jurisdiction of its courts to another State, compliance with that obligation was a justifiable limitation on the exercise of Article 6 rights.[39] The Court has, therefore, considered whether international law requires the grant of immunity in cases where the defendant State is accused of violating fundamental rules of international law (including norms of *jus cogens*) as a prior step to determining whether a limitation on access to justice was justifiable or a violation of Article 6 of the European Convention. In *Al-Adsani* v. *United Kingdom*, the Grand Chamber of the Court decided that the status of the rule of international law a defendant State was alleged to have violated, however fundamental, did not remove the requirement for other States to accord immunity. It reached that conclusion, however, by the narrowest of margins (nine votes to eight) and with the qualification that its decision reflected the current state of international law, which might of course undergo change in the future.

It was against that background that the English courts had to consider the same question in *Jones* v. *Saudi Arabia* in 2006.[40] The facts of *Jones* were essentially the same as those of *Al-Adsani*. The claimants alleged that they had been tortured while in the defendant State. They maintained that the prohibition of torture, because of its status as a rule of *jus cogens*, prevailed over the duty under general international law to accord immunity. Since the immunity of foreign States from the jurisdiction of the English courts is governed by statute (the State Immunity Act 1978), which lays down a general rule of immunity subject to a list of defined exceptions, none of which was applicable to the facts of the *Jones* case, the position under general international law arose only in an indirect fashion. Under the Human Rights Act 1998, an English court must grant a declaration of incompatibility if a statute is inconsistent with rights under the European

[39] *Al-Adsani* v. *United Kingdom*, 123 ILR 24. See also *McElhinney* v. *Ireland*, 123 ILR 73.
[40] *Jones* v. *Saudi Arabia* [2007] 1 AC 270; 129 ILR 629.

Convention on Human Rights. The question before the English courts was, therefore, whether the State Immunity Act was inconsistent with Article 6 of the European Convention; because of the judgment of the Grand Chamber in *Al-Adsani*, that question could be answered only by first determining the present state of international law on sovereign immunity and *jus cogens*. After considering a number of international instruments and the jurisprudence of international courts, as well as the practice of several other States, the House of Lords unanimously concluded that international law still required that immunity be granted on the facts of the case and denied that there was an exception to the duty to accord immunity when a State was accused of violating a rule of *jus cogens*.

The Italian courts, however, had taken a different view in a series of cases against Germany concerning war crimes committed in the last two years of the Second World War.[41] The Supreme Court of Greece initially took the same position,[42] although this position was later reversed.[43] Those cases led Germany to institute proceedings against Italy before the International Court of Justice in 2008. Germany claimed that, by refusing to accord it immunity and entering judgment against it, Italy had violated its international law obligations to Germany.[44] This case thus raised directly the issue on which the European Court of Human Rights and the House of Lords had already had to pronounce. The judgment of the International Court of Justice, given in 2012, held that Germany had been entitled to immunity, notwithstanding the status of the rules of international law which the Italian courts had found it had violated. In reaching that conclusion, the Court considered the judgments of the European Court of Human Rights and the Court of Justice of the European Union,[45] as well as the jurisprudence of sixteen States.

Although the Court did not expressly make this point, it is clear that it examined the decisions of national courts for two distinct reasons. Those decisions were, of course, part of the State practice on which the

[41] *Ferrini* v. *Federal Republic of Germany*, 128 ILR 658. The judgment of the Italian Court of Cassation in that case was followed in several later cases.

[42] *Prefecture of Voiotia* v. *Federal Republic of Germany*, 129 ILR 513.

[43] *Margellos* v. *Federal Republic of Germany*, 129 ILR 525.

[44] *Jurisdictional Immunities (Federal Republic of Germany* v. *Italy, Greece intervening)*, *I.C.J. Reports 2012*, p. 99.

[45] That Court had ruled on a reference from a national court regarding enforcement of judgments given against Germany in the Greek courts before the latter had changed their position following the *Margellos* judgment.

customary international law of State immunity was based. As such, they were important for the Court's analysis of that practice irrespective of the quality of the reasoning on which they were based. Yet the Court also considered that reasoning in order to see what guidance it gave, in the same way as it examined the reasoning of the European Court of Human Rights in the judgments which that Court had given regarding State immunity. While the reasoning in some of those judgments was very brief, in others (particularly, *Jones*, a judgment of the Supreme Court of Poland[46] and a judgment of the Court of Appeal for the Canadian Province of Ontario[47]) there was a detailed examination of the issues on which the Court placed a degree of reliance.

The picture is thus one of a high degree of unity of approach, notwithstanding the different contexts in which the issue had been raised before the various courts. That unity has also characterised the approach of two courts in cases subsequent to the judgment in *Jurisdictional Immunities.* In 2014, the European Court of Human Rights gave judgment in *Jones* v. *United Kingdom.*[48] That case was brought by the claimants whose action against Saudi Arabia had failed because of the judgment of the House of Lords that Saudi Arabia was entitled to immunity. The claimants maintained that, by denying them access to the courts, the United Kingdom had violated their rights under Article 6 of the Convention. The Court rejected their claim and declined to reconsider its earlier judgment in *Al-Adsani.* In reaching that conclusion, the Court stated that 'the recent judgment of the International Court of Justice in *Germany* v. *Italy*... must be considered as authoritative as regards the content of customary international law'.[49] The Quebec Court of Appeal has come to a similar conclusion.[50] That judgment has now been upheld by the Supreme Court of Canada.

These three examples demonstrate that, notwithstanding the diversity of the courts and tribunals which have considered the same issues of international law and the absence of any hierarchy or provision for a final appeal to a single court, there can be, and frequently is, a high degree of consistency in their approach to those issues. Moreover, the picture which emerges is one of judges, at both the national and international level, very

46 *Natoniewski* (2010); English translation in 30 Polish Year Book of International Law, p. 299.

47 *Bouzari* v. *Iran*, DLR (4th), vol. 243, p. 406; 128 ILR 586.

48 Judgment of 14 January 2014.

49 *Ibid.*, para. 198.

50 *Hashemi* v. *Iran* (2012) QCCA 1449, 154 ILR 351 and 159 ILR 299.

much aware of one another's judgments and concerned to ensure that there is no unnecessary conflict between them.

It must, of course, be admitted that the diversity of courts and tribunals hearing questions of international law can sometimes produce conflicting views on points of law. The most notorious example is the difference between the International Court of Justice and the International Criminal Tribunal for the Former Yugoslavia regarding the responsibility of a State for the acts of a group which is not an organ of that State but with which it is in some sense allied. In its 1986 *Nicaragua* judgment, the International Court of Justice held that for an act of the '*contra*' rebels in Nicaragua to be attributed to the United States, it had to be established either that the *contras* were completely dependent upon the United States or that the specific act in question had been carried out under US direction and control.[51] However, in 1999 the Appeals Chamber of the International Criminal Tribunal, in the *Tadić* case, rejected this high standard and determined that the appropriate test was one of 'overall control'.[52] The matter came before the International Court for a second time in 2007. In its judgment in the *Bosnia* case, the Court reviewed the two conflicting authorities and reaffirmed the test laid down in *Nicaragua*, declining to alter its position on the strength of the *Tadić* decision.[53]

There is no escaping the fact that on this issue the Appeals Chamber deliberately chose to depart from the view of the law taken by the Court and that the Court then, again deliberately, rejected the view taken by the Appeals Chamber. Yet that difference between the Court and the Tribunal has to be seen in perspective. First, it is the only such difference. On a wide range of other issues, the Tribunal has been content to adopt the reasoning and rulings of the Court. Secondly, in its 2007 judgment, the Court, while declining to follow the Chamber's reasoning on attribution,[54] made clear throughout the judgment that it drew heavily on the findings of fact in the *Tadić* judgment and other judgments of the Tribunal. Indeed, this

[51] *Military and Paramilitary Activities in and against Nicaragua (Nicaragua* v. *United States), I.C.J. Reports 1986*, p. 14, paras. 110 and 115.

[52] *Prosecutor* v. *Tadić* (IT-94–1–A), 124 ILR 61, paras. 88–145.

[53] *Application of the Convention on the Prevention and Punishment of the Crime of Genocide (Bosnia and Herzegovina* v. *Serbia and Montenegro*), *I.C.J. Reports 2007*, p. 43, para. 403.

[54] The Court rightly pointed out that the question of State responsibility does not fall within the jurisdiction of the Tribunal, which is confined to the criminal responsibility of individuals. The Tribunal had discussed the question of responsibility in order to decide whether or not the conflict in Bosnia was an international armed conflict. It must be questioned, however, whether that issue really turned on the question of responsibility.

one difference between the Court and the Tribunal is the exception to a general pattern of broad consistency between the judicial institutions of international law.

More numerous differences are to be found in the jurisprudence of investment arbitration tribunals. To some extent the differences between the awards given by different tribunals is no more than a proper recognition of the differences between the bilateral investment treaties ('BITs') under which each tribunal operates. Although many BITs contain provisions on subjects like fair and equitable treatment and expropriation which are drafted in very similar language, it should always be remembered that each treaty is an agreement in its own right and that the words used have to be interpreted in the light of the context, object and purpose and, where appropriate, drafting history of *that* treaty.[55] To approach each BIT in that light is to respect a diversity that is the product of the specific wills of the parties to each BIT; it is quite wrong to treat the language of BITs simply as 'boilerplate' texts which must necessarily be given a single, unified meaning.

Nevertheless, there have been differences between arbitral tribunals which cannot be explained on this ground. The vexed question of whether a most favoured nation ('MFN') provision in a BIT is capable of expanding the scope of a provision on investor-State dispute settlement is one such example. Ever since the award in *Maffezini* v. *Spain*,[56] this question has divided the arbitration world with approximately the same number of awards accepting the theory that a MFN clause can expand the jurisdiction of the tribunal as there have been awards rejecting the same theory. This lack of a *jurisprudence constante* cannot be explained only by reference to differences between the terms of the BITs involved (although such differences can be significant). Of the four tribunals which have ruled on the effect of the MFN clause in the Argentina–Germany BIT, two have held that this clause means that an investor can circumvent the requirement in the arbitration clause of that BIT that disputes may be submitted to arbitration only after a period of eighteen months has elapsed from

[55] Vienna Convention on the Law of Treaties, 1969, Articles 31 and 32. In *Polydor* v. *Harlequin* [1982] ECR 329 the Court of Justice of the European Communities (as it then was) held that a provision in the EEC–Portugal Association Agreement had to be given a different interpretation from the identically worded provision in the EEC Treaty because the context, and object and purpose of the two agreements was different.

[56] *Maffezini* v. *Spain*, 124 ILR 1.

their submission to the local courts,[57] while two have held that the MFN clause cannot release the investor from this requirement.[58] Moreover, even where tribunals have reached the same conclusion on this issue, they have frequently done so for radically different reasons.[59]

The marked difference of views on this issue is, to say the least, unfortunate. It makes it difficult for either party to plan its approach to litigating an investment claim and places a premium on the selection of the arbitrators who will hear a case which involves (or, which may involve) this issue. But it does not indicate a hopelessly fragmented system. In spite of the fact that consistency is generally easier to achieve within, and between, institutions such as the International Court of Justice and the European Court of Human Rights, the more diverse world of international investment arbitration has achieved a far higher level of consistency than the MFN debate might suggest. The difference of views over MFN clauses and jurisdiction is best seen as one of those issues which arises from time to time in any legal system, one on which scholars as well as arbitrators or judges differ. Eventually such differences tend to be resolved and a more settled approach takes hold. That is obviously easier to achieve where there is a final court of appeal whose decision on the matter provides the last word. Yet even in the absence of such a tribunal, a settled view is generally arrived at in the end. Until that happens, the differences are regrettable but they need not be calamitous. It is worthwhile recalling that for over a decade, the French Conseil d'État and the Cour de Cassation took radically different views on the issue of the supremacy of European Community law over French legislation.[60] Neither the European legal system nor the French legal system collapsed as a result.

* * *

The international community is a decentralised society and the international legal system is a reflection of that society. One consequence of that fact is that the processes by which international law is made and applied are inevitably more diverse than those found in a national legal system.

57 *Hochtief* v. *Argentina*, ICSID Case No. ARB/07/31; *Siemens AG* v. *Argentina*, ICSID Case No. ARB/02/8.

58 *Wintershall Aktiengesellschaft* v. *Argentina*, ICSID Case No. ARB/04/14; *Daimler Financial Services* v. *Argentina*, ICSID Case No. ARB/05/01.

59 Compare the awards in *Plama Consortium Limited* v. *Bulgaria*, ICSID Case No. ARB/03/24 and *Renta 4 SVSA and others* v. *Russian Federation*, SCC Case No. 24/2007.

60 See *Société des Cafés Jacques Vabre* Cour de cassation, 24 May 1975; 93 ILR 240 and *Nicolo* Conseil d'État, 20 October 1989; 93 ILR 286.

Of late they have become more, rather than less, diverse. Yet that does not mean that international law is fragmenting. Diversity exists without, on the whole, compromising the essential unity of the legal system. That unity cannot, however, be taken for granted. It requires those involved in making and applying international law to be conscious of the place which the immediate task before them occupies in the legal system as a whole, to be aware of the work of others and to respect their efforts. Fear of fragmentation has been greatly exaggerated but a certain wariness is necessary.

3

A century of international justice and prospects for the future

ANTÔNIO AUGUSTO CANÇADO TRINDADE

I. Introduction: the emergence of international tribunals

2007 marked the centenary of the II Hague Peace Conference (of 1907), marking the centenary of the birth of international tribunals, of the judicial settlement of international disputes. By then there were already calls for the creation of permanent courts or tribunals,[1] as illustrated by two initiatives: first, to render permanent a Court of Arbitral Justice,[2] as from the model of the Permanent Court of Arbitration (PCA) envisaged in the previous I Hague Peace Conference (of 1899), and secondly, to establish an International Prize Court, with access to it granted to individuals.

The proposal for a permanent Court of Arbitral Justice as a whole was to project itself on the advent of judicial solution proper, at international level, as it became one of the sources of inspiration for the drafting of the Statute of the Permanent Court of International Justice (PCIJ) in 1920.[3] And although the projected International Prize Court, set forth in the XII Hague Convention of 1907, never saw the light of day, as the Convention did not enter into force, it presented issues of relevance for the evolution of international law, namely: first, it foresaw the establishment

[1] A. A. Cançado Trindade, 'The Presence and Participation of Latin America at the II Hague Peace Conference of 1907', in *Actualité de la Conférence de La Haye de 1907, II Conférence de la Paix (Colloque de 2007)* (ed. Y. Daudet), Leiden/La Haye, Académie de Droit International/Nijhoff, 2008, pp. 66–73, and cf. pp. 51–84, 110–12, 115–17, 122 and 205–6 (debates).

[2] Cf. D. J. Bederman, 'The Hague Peace Conferences of 1899 and 1907', in *International Courts for the Twenty-First Century* (ed. M. W. Janis), Dordrecht, Nijhoff, 1992, pp. 10–11.

[3] Cf. S. Rosenne, 'Introduction', in *The Hague Peace Conferences of 1899 and 1907 and International Arbitration – Reports and Documents* (ed. S. Rosenne), The Hague, T.M.C. Asser Press, 2001, p. XXI. And cf. also A. Eyffinger, 'A Highly Critical Moment: Role and Record of the 1907 Hague Peace Conference', 54 *Netherlands International Law Review* (2007) n. 2, pp. 217 and 227.

of a jurisdiction above national jurisdictions to decide on last appeal on maritime prizes; secondly, it provided, for example, in such circumstances, for the access of individuals directly to the international jurisdiction;[4] thirdly, it envisaged a type of international compulsory jurisdiction; and fourthly, it admitted the proposed Court's free authority to decide (the *compétence de la compétence*).[5]

The 1907 debates of the II Hague Peace Conference led to the prevailing view of granting individuals direct appeal before the projected International Prize Court. Yet, it was elsewhere, in Latin America, still in the year of 1907, that the first modern international tribunal – the Central American Court of Justice – came to operate. It did so for ten years, granting access not only to States but also to individuals;[6] in its decade of operation, the Court was seized of ten cases, five lodged with it by individuals and five inter-State cases.[7] It was in this respect truly pioneering,[8] and contributed to the gradual expansion of international legal personality. The very advent of permanent international jurisdiction at the beginning of the twentieth century, before the creation of the PCIJ, was thus *not* marked by a purely inter-State outlook of the international *contentieux*.[9]

4 It was then admitted that the individual is 'not without standing in modern international law'; J. Brown Scott, 'The Work of the Second Hague Peace Conference', 2 *American Journal of International Law* (1908) p. 22. The view prevailed that it would be in the interests of the States – particularly the small or weaker ones – to avoid giving to this kind of cases the character of inter-State disputes: 'les litiges nés des prises garderaient . . . le caractère qu'ils avaient en première instance . . . , affaires regardant d'un côté l'État capteur et de l'autre les particuliers'; S. Séfériadès, 'Le problème de l'accès des particuliers à des juridictions internationales', 51 *Recueil des Cours de l'Académie de Droit International de La Haye* (1935) pp. 38–40.

5 João Cabral, *Evolução do Direito International*, Rio de Janeiro, Typ. Rodrigues & Cia., 1908, pp. 97–8. On the evolution of this last point (the *compétence de la compétence* of international tribunals), cf., generally, I. F. I. Shihata, *The Power of the International Court to Determine Its Own Jurisdiction* (*Compétence de la Compétence)*, The Hague, Nijhoff, 1965, pp. 1–304.

6 A. A. Cançado Trindade, 'Exhaustion of Local Remedies in International Law Experiments Granting Procedural Status to Individuals in the First Half of the Twentieth Century', 24 *Netherlands International Law Review/Nederlands Tijdschrift voor international Recht* (1977) p. 376.

7 Cf. *ibid.*, pp. 376–7; and cf. F. A. von der Heydte, 'L'individu et les tribunaux internationaux', 107 *Recueil des Cours de l'Académie de Droit International de La Haye* (1962) p. 321.

8 C. J. Gutiérrez, *La Corte de Justicia Centroamericana*, San José de Costa Rica, Edit. Juricentro, 1978, pp. 42, 106 and 150–2.

9 The ideal of an international judicial instance, beyond the inter-State dimension, had already found expression in earlier experiments which granted procedural capacity to individuals, in the era of the League of Nations, such as the systems of minorities (including

II. Lessons from the past

At the time of the drafting and adoption, in 1920, of the Statute of the PCIJ, an option was, however, made for a strictly inter-State dimension for its exercise of the international judicial function in contentious matters. Yet, as I have pointed out in my Separate Opinion (paras. 76–81) in the International Court of Justice's (ICJ) Advisory Opinion (of 2012) on *a Judgment of the ILO Administrative Tribunal upon a Complaint Filed against the IFAD*, the fact that the Advisory Committee of Jurists did not find, in 1920, that the time was ripe to grant access to the PCIJ to subjects of rights other than States (such as individuals), did not mean that a definitive answer had been found to the question at issue. The fact that the same position was maintained at the time of adoption in 1945 of the Statute of the ICJ did not mean a definitive answer to the question at issue either.

The question of access of individuals to international justice, with procedural equality, continued to draw the attention of legal doctrine throughout the decades ever since. Individuals and groups of individuals began to have access to other international instances, reserving the PCIJ, and later on the ICJ, only for disputes between States. The dogmatic position taken originally in 1920, on the occasion of the preparation and adoption of its Statute, did not hinder the PCIJ to occupy itself promptly of cases pertaining to the treatment of minorities and inhabitants of cities or territories with a juridical statute of their own. In considerations developed in the examination of such matters, the PCIJ went well beyond

Upper-Silesia) and of territories under mandates, and the systems of petitions of the Islands Aaland and of the Saar and of Danzig, besides the practice of mixed arbitral tribunals and of mixed claims commissions, of the same epoch; cf. J.-C. Witenberg, 'La recevabilité des réclamations devant les juridictions internationales', 41 *Recueil des Cours de l'Académie de Droit International de La Haye [RCADI]* (1932) pp. 5–135; J. Stone, 'The Legal Nature of Minorities Petition', 12 *British Year Book of International Law* (1931) pp. 76–94; M. Sibert, 'Sur la procédure en matière de pétition dans les pays sous mandat et quelques-unes de ses insuffissances', 40 *Revue générale de droit international public* (1933) pp. 257–72; M. St. Korowicz, *Une expérience en Droit international – La protection des minorités de Haute-Silésie*, Paris, Pédone, 1946, pp. 81–174; C. A. Norgaard, *The Position of the Individual in International Law*, Copenhagen, Munksgaard, 1962, pp. 109–28; A. A. Cançado Trindade, 'Exhaustion of Local Remedies in International Law Experiments Granting Procedural Status to Individuals in the First Half of the Twentieth Century', 24 *Netherlands International Law Review* (1977) pp. 373–92. Those experiments paved the way, in the era of the United Nations, for the consolidation of the mechanisms of international individual petition; cf. J. Beauté, *Le droit de pétition dans les territoires sous tutelle*, Paris, LGDJ, 1962, pp. 1–256; M. E. Tardu, *Human Rights – The International Petition System*, binders 1–3, Dobbs Ferry N.Y., Oceana, 1979–85.

the inter-State dimension, taking into account the position of individuals themselves (as in, e.g., *inter alia*, the Advisory Opinions on *German Settlers in Poland*, 1923; on *the Jurisdiction of the Courts of Danzig*, 1928; on the *Greco-Bulgarian 'Communities'*, 1930; on *Access to German Minority Schools in Upper Silesia*, 1931; on *Treatment of Polish Nationals in Danzig*, 1932; on *Minority Schools in Albania*, 1935).[10] Ever since, the artificiality of that dimension became noticeable and acknowledged, already at an early stage of the case-law of the PCIJ.

The option in 1920 (endorsed in 1945) for an inter-State mechanism for judicial settlement of contentious cases, was made, as I have recalled:

> not by an intrinsic necessity, nor because it was the sole manner to proceed, but rather and only to give expression to the prevailing viewpoint amongst the members of the Advisory Committee of Jurists in charge of drafting the Statute of the PCIJ. Nevertheless, already at that time, some 90 years ago, International Law was not reduced to a purely inter-State paradigm, and already knew of concrete experiments of access to international instances, in search of justice, on the part of not only States but also of individuals.
>
> The fact that the Advisory Commitee of Jurists did not consider that the time was ripe for granting access, to the PCIJ to subjects of law other than the States (e.g., individuals) did not mean a definitive answer to the question... Already in the *travaux préparatoires* of the Statute of the PCIJ, the minority position marked presence, of those who favoured the access to the old Hague Court not only of States, but also of other subjects of law, including individuals. This was not the position which prevailed, but the ideal already marked presence, in that epoch, almost one century ago.[11]

The dogmatic position of the PCIJ Statute passed on to the ICJ Statute. Once again, the exclusively inter-State character of the *contentieux* before the ICJ has not appeared satisfactory at all. At least in some cases (cf. *infra*), pertaining to the condition of individuals, the presence of these latter (or of their legal representatives), in order to submit, themselves, their positions, would have enriched the proceedings and facilitated the work of the Court. The artificiality of the exclusively inter-State outlook of the procedures before the ICJ has been disclosed by the very *nature* of some of the cases submitted to it.

[10] Cf. C. Brölmann, 'The PCIJ and International Rights of Groups and Individuals', in *Legacies of the Permanent Court of International Justice* (eds. C. J. Tams, M. Fitzmaurice and P. Merkouris), Leiden, Nijhoff, 2013, pp. 123–43.

[11] A. A. Cançado Trindade, *Os Tribunais Internacionais Contemporâneos*, Brasília, FUNAG, 2013, pp. 11–12.

Such artificiality has been criticised, time and time again, in expert writing, including by a former President of the Court itself. It has been recalled that 'nowadays a very considerable part of international law' (e.g., law-making treaties) 'directly affects individuals', and the effect of Article 34(1) of the ICJ Statute has been 'to insulate' the Court 'from this great body of modern international law'. The ICJ remains thus

> trapped by Article 34(1) in the notions about international law structure of the 1920s. . . . [I]t is a matter for concern and for further thought, whether it is healthy for the World Court still to be, like the international law of the 1920s, on an entirely different plane from that of municipal courts and other tribunals.[12]

To the same effect, S. Rosenne expressed the view, already in 1967, that there was 'nothing inherent in the character of the International Court itself to justify the complete exclusion of the individual from appearing before the Court in judicial proceedings relating of direct concern to him'.[13] The current practice of exclusion of the *locus standi in judicio* of the individuals concerned from the proceedings before the ICJ, – he added, – in addition to being artificial, could also produce 'incongruous results'. It was thus highly desirable that that scheme be reconsidered, in order to grant *locus standi* to individuals in proceedings before the ICJ, as

> it is in the interests of the proper administration of international justice that in appropriate cases the International Court of Justice should take advantage of all the powers which it already possesses, and permit an individual directly concerned to present himself before the Court, . . . and give his own version of the facts and his own construction of the law.[14]

In a thoughtful International Symposium convened by the Max Planck Institute for Comparative Public Law and International Law in the early seventies, wherein the perceptions of judicial settlement of disputes were clearly disclosed, a lack of enthusiasm with judicial settlement was expressed by some participants,[15] as – in the view of one of them – 'States

12 R. Y. Jennings, 'The International Court of Justice after Fifty Years', 89 *American Journal of International Law* (1995) p. 504.

13 S. Rosenne, 'Reflections on the Position of the Individual in Inter-State Litigation in the International Court of Justice', in *International Arbitration – Liber Amicorum for M. Domke* (ed. P. Sanders), The Hague, Nijhoff, 1967, p. 249, and cf. p. 242.

14 *Ibid.*, p. 250, and cf. p. 243.

15 Cf. [Various Authors,] *Judicial Settlement of International Disputes* (International Symposium, Max Planck Institute for Comparative Public Law and International Law), Berlin/Heidelberg, Springer Verlag, 1974, pp. 165–7, 169–70 and 189.

were moving further and further away from the rule of law as the basis of their behaviour'.[16] The requirements of the rule of law, and of the unity of law, did not pass unnoticed; furthermore, the need for consistency in international case-law was pointed out.[17] Significantly, already at that time the need was acknowledged of the creation of other international tribunals, and the view was expressed that the dynamics of international relations had already long surpassed the anachronistic inter-State dimension (as by then evidenced by the rise and growth of international organizations).[18]

If we are to consider today the prospects for the future of international justice, we have also, and first, to look back in time, and grasp the lessons we can extract therefrom. The understanding that the *corpus juris gentium* applies to States and individuals alike is deeply rooted in jusinternationalist thinking, – with roots going back, through the lessons of the 'founding fathers' of international law (like F. Vitoria, F. Suárez and H. Grotius), to the classics upholding the *recta ratio*, such as the masterly *De Officis* of Cicero.

The subsequent devising of the strictly inter-State dimension (in the late nineteenth and in the twentieth centuries) represented an *involution*, with disastrous consequences. Fortunately, in the last decades, States themselves seem to have been acknowledging this, in lodging with the ICJ successive cases and matters which clearly transcend the inter-State level. And the Court has been lately responding, at the height of these new challenges and expectations, in taking into account, in its decisions, the situation not only of States, but also of peoples, of individuals or groups of individuals alike (cf. *infra*).

The gradual realization – that we witness, and have the privilege to contribute to, nowadays, – of the old ideal of justice at international level[19] has been revitalizing itself, in recent years, with the reassuring creation and operation of the multiple contemporary international tribunals. This is a theme which has definitively assumed a prominent place in the international agenda of this second decade of the twenty-first century. Since the visionary ideas and early writings, of some decades ago, – of B.C. J. Loder, André Mandelstam, Nicolas Politis, Jean Spiropoulos, Alejandro Álvarez, Raul Fernandes, Édouard Descamps, Albert de La Pradelle, René Cassin, James Brown Scott, Georges Scelle, Max Huber, Hersch Lauterpacht, John

[16] *Ibid.*, p. 168. [17] *Ibid.*, pp. 171, 173 and 187. [18] *Ibid.*, pp. 180 and 182.

[19] For a general study, cf., e.g., J. Allain, *A Century of International Adjudication – The Rule of Law and Its Limits*, The Hague, T.M.C. Asser Press, 2000, pp. 1–186.

Humphrey, among others,[20] – it was necessary to wait for some decades for the current developments in the realization of international justice to take place, not without difficulties,[21] now enriching and enhancing international law.

III. The expansion of international jurisdiction

Nowadays, the international community fortunately counts on a wide range of international tribunals, adjudicating cases that take place not only at *inter-State* level, but also at *intra-State* level. This invites us to approach their work from the correct perspective of the *justiciables* themselves,[22] and brings us closer to their common mission of securing the realization of international justice, either at *inter*-State or at *intra*-State level. From the standpoint of the needs of protection of the *justiciables*, each international tribunal has its importance, in a wider framework encompassing the most distinct situations to be adjudicated, in each respective domain of operation.[23]

In a Colloquium organized to celebrate, in 1996, the 50th anniversary of the ICJ, critical views were expressed as to the traditional features of the inter-State mechanism of adjudication of contentious cases before the ICJ, which has kept on defying the passing of time. A couple of examples were evoked as illustrations, such as the settlement of disputes on environmental issues,[24] requiring a wider range of participants in the procedure. One guest speaker, for example, recalled the manifest inadequacy of that mechanism in the handling of the case of the *Application of the*

[20] A. A. Cançado Trindade, *The Access of Individuals to International Justice*, Oxford, Oxford University Press, 2011, pp. 7–11.

[21] Cf., *inter alia*, G. Fouda, 'La justice internationale et le consentement des États', in *International Justice – Thesaurus Acroasium*, vol. XXVI (ed. K. Koufa), Thessaloniki, Sakkoulas Publs., 1997, pp. 889–91, 896 and 900.

[22] A. A. Cançado Trindade, *Évolution du Droit international au droit des gens – L'accès des particuliers à la justice internationale: le regard d'un juge*, Paris, Pédone, 2008, pp. 1–187.

[23] Cf., to this effect, A. A. Cançado Trindade, 'Contemporary International Tribunals: Their Continuing Jurisprudential Cross-Fertilization, with Special Attention to the International Safeguard of Human Rights', in *The Global Community – Yearbook of International Law and Jurisprudence* (ed. G.Z. Capaldo) Oxford University Press, 2012, vol. I, p. 188.

[24] M. Fitzmaurice, 'Equipping the Court to Deal with Developing Areas of International Law: Environmental Law – Presentation', in *Increasing the Effectiveness of the International Court of Justice* (1996 Colloquy – eds. C. Peck and R. S. Lee), The Hague, Nijhoff, 1997, pp. 398–418.

1902 Convention on the Guardianship of Infants (1958).[25] Another guest speaker was particularly critical of the handling of the *East Timor* case (1995), where the East Timorese people had no *locus standi* to request intervention in the proceedings, not even to present an *amicus curiae*, although the crucial point under consideration was that of sovereignty over their territory.

Worse still, the interests of a third State (which had not even accepted the Court's jurisdiction) were taken for granted for the purpose of protection, and promptly safeguarded by the Court, at no cost to itself, by means of the application of the so-called *Monetary Gold* 'principle'.[26] This workshop is an occasion for further reflection, rather than self-praise: the fact remains that inconsistencies of the kind have survived the passing of the century, and have now reached the centennial celebration of the Peace Palace. The aforementioned examples are far from being the only ones. They in fact abound in the ICJ's history.

In respect of situations concerning individuals or groups of individuals, reference can further be made, for example, to the *Nottebohm* case (1955) pertaining to double nationality; to the cases of the *Trial of Pakistani Prisoners of War* (1973), and of the *Hostages (U.S. Diplomatic and Consular Staff) in Teheran* case (1980); to the case of the *Application of the Convention against Genocide* (1996 and 2007); to the case of the *Frontier Dispute between Burkina Faso and Mali* (1998); to the triad of cases concerning consular assistance – namely, the cases *Breard* (1998), *LaGrand* (Germany *versus* United States, 2001), and *Avena and Others* (Mexico *versus* United States, 2004).

In respect of those cases, one cannot fail to recognise that one of their predominant elements was precisely the concrete situation of the individuals directly affected, and not merely abstract issues of exclusive interests of the litigating States in their relations *inter se.* Moreover, one may further recall that, in the case of *Armed Activities in the Territory of Congo* (D.R. Congo *versus* Uganda, 2000), the ICJ was concerned with grave violations of human rights and of international humanitarian law; and the *Land and Maritime Boundary between Cameroon and Nigeria* (1996) was likewise concerned with the victims of armed clashes.

25 S. Rosenne, 'Lessons of the Past and Needs of the Future – Presentation', in *Increasing the Effectiveness of the International Court of Justice* (1996 Colloquy – eds. C. Peck and R. S. Lee), The Hague, Nijhoff, 1997, pp. 487–8, and cf. pp. 466–92.

26 C. Chinkin, 'Increasing the Use and Appeal of the Court – Presentation', in *Increasing the Effectiveness of the International Court of Justice* (1996 Colloquy – eds. C. Peck and R. S. Lee), The Hague, Nijhoff, 1997, pp. 47–8, 53 and 55–6.

More recently, examples wherein the Court's concerns have had to go beyond the inter-State outlook have further increased in frequency. They include, for example, the case on *Questions Relating to the Obligation to Prosecute or Extradite* (2009–13) pertaining to the principle of universal jurisdiction under the UN Convention against Torture, the case of *A.S. Diallo* (Guinea *versus* D.R. Congo, 2010) on detention and expulsion of a foreigner, the case of the *Jurisdictional Immunities of the State* (2010–12), the case of the *Application of the International Convention on the Elimination of All Forms of Racial Discrimination* (2011), and the case of the *Temple of Preah Vihear* (provisional measures, 2011).

The same can be said of the last two Advisory Opinions of the Court, on the *Declaration of Independence of Kosovo* (2010), and on a *Judgment of the ILO Administrative Tribunal upon a Complaint Filed against the IFAD* (2012), respectively. The artificiality of the exclusively inter-State outlook has thus often been made manifest, and increasingly so; that outlook rests on a longstanding dogma of the past, which has survived to date as a result of mental lethargy. Those more recent contentious cases, and requests for Advisory Opinions, lodged with the Court, have asked the latter, by reason of their subject-matter, to overcome that outlook.

Even if the mechanism of dispute settlement by the ICJ remains strictly or exclusively inter-State, the *substance* of those disputes or issues brought before the Court pertains also to the human person, as the aforementioned cases and Opinions clearly show. The truth is that the strictly inter-State outlook has an ideological content, is a product of its time, a time long past. In these more recent decisions (1999–2013), the ICJ has at times rightly endeavoured to overcome that outlook, so as to face the new challenges of our times, brought before it in the contentious cases and requests of Advisory Opinions it has been seized of. I shall come back to this point in my concluding observations (*infra*).

1. *International human rights tribunals*

The United Nations era has in effect been marked by the rise of multiple international tribunals. This is, in my perception, a reassuring phenomenon, which has filled a gap which persisted in the international legal order. It has contributed to the access to justice at international level. The international procedural capacity of individuals has been exercised before international human rights tribunals, thanks to the system of international individual petitions:[27] the European Court of Human Rights (ECtHR), which celebrated its 60th anniversary in 2010, and the Inter-American Court of Human Rights (IACtHR), which celebrated its 30th anniversary in 2009, have more recently (in 2006) been followed by the African Court of Human and Peoples' Rights.

Their contribution to the historical recovery of the position of the human person as the subject of the law of nations (*droit des gens*) constitutes, in my understanding, the most important legacy of the international legal thinking of the last six decades.[28] The mechanism of the European Court has already evolved into the conferment of *jus standi* of individuals directly before the Court; that of the Inter-American Court has reached the stage of conferring *locus standi in judicio* to individuals in all stages of the procedure before the Court; each one lives its own historical moment, and operates in it, within the framework of the universality of human rights.

Another basic feature, and a remarkable contribution, of the work of the European and Inter-American Courts, is found in the position they have both firmly taken of setting limits to State voluntarism, thus safeguarding the integrity of the respective human rights conventions and the primacy of considerations of *ordre public* over the will of individual States. This is illustrated, for example, by the European Court's decisions in the cases of *Belilos* (1988), of *Loizidou* (preliminary objections, 1995), and of *Ilascu, Lesco, Ivantoc and Petrov-Popa* (2001), as well as, for example, by the Inter-American Court's decisions in the cases of the *Constitutional Tribunal* and of *Ivtcher Bronstein* (jurisdiction, 1999), as well as of *Hilaire, Benjamin and Constantine* (preliminary objection, 2001).

Both international tribunals have thus set higher standards of State behaviour and have established some degree of control over the interposition of undue restrictions by States; they have thereby reassuringly enhanced the position of individuals as subjects of international law, with full procedural capacity. By correctly resolving basic procedural issues raised in the aforementioned cases, both international tribunals have aptly made use of the techniques of public international law in order to strengthen their respective jurisdictions of protection of the human

[27] A. A. Cançado Trindade, *El Acceso Directo del Individuo a los Tribunales Internacionales de Derechos Humanos*, Bilbao, Universidad de Deusto, 2001, pp. 34–5.

[28] A. A. Cançado Trindade, *Évolution du Droit international au droit des gens – L'accès des particuliers à la justice internationale: le regard d'un juge*, Paris, Pédone, 2008, pp. 1–187; A. A. Cançado Trindade, *Le Droit international pour la personne humaine*, Paris, Pédone, 2012, pp. 45–368.

person, emancipated vis-à-vis her own State.[29] International human rights tribunals have drawn attention to the position of *centrality* of the victims, the *justiciables*.

2. *International criminal tribunals*

Contemporary international criminal tribunals saw the light of day in the 1990s, bearing in mind the precedents of the Nuremberg and the Tokyo Tribunals of the post-Second World War. Ad hoc international criminal tribunals (for the former Yugoslavia and for Rwanda) were established (in 1993 and 1994), by decision of the UN Security Council in the light of chapter VII of the UN Charter. They were followed by the permanent International Criminal Tribunal (Rome Statute of 1998), and by the so-called 'internationalized' or 'hybrid' or mixed international tribunals (for Sierra Leona, East Timor, Kosovo, Bosnia-Herzegovina, Cambodia and Lebanon).

Each of these tribunals has contributed, in its own way, to the determination of the accountability of those responsible for grave violations of human rights and of international humanitarian law. They afford yet another illustration of the rescue of the international legal personality (and responsibility) of individuals, but, ironically, first as *passive* subjects of international law (international criminal tribunals), and, only afterwards, as *active* subjects of international law (international human rights tribunals).

Such developments, due to a reaction of the conscience of humankind against crimes against peace, crimes against humanity, grave violations of human rights and of international humanitarian law, give testimony of the expansion not only of international personality (and capacity), but also of international jurisdiction and of international responsibility. This is a notable feature of our times, in this present era of international tribunals.

Their determination of responsibility, – with all its legal consequence, – has exercised a key role in the struggle against impunity. While international human rights tribunals determine the responsibility of States, international criminal tribunals determine the responsibility of individuals. Anywhere in the world, it is reckoned nowadays that the

[29] A. A. Cançado Trindade, 'The Trans-Atlantic Perspective: The Contribution of the Work of the International Human Rights Tribunals to the Development of Public International Law', in *The European Convention on Human Rights at 50 – Human Rights Information Bulletin*, n. 50 (Special Issue), Strasbourg, Council of Europe, 2000, pp. 8–9; A. A. Cançado Trindade, 'The Merits of Coordination of International Courts on Human Rights', 2 *Journal of International Criminal Justice* (2004) pp. 309–12.

perpetrators of grave violations of human rights (be they States or individuals), as well as those responsible for acts of genocide, war crimes and crimes against humanity, ought to respond judicially for the atrocities committed, irrespective of their nationality or the position held in the hierarchical scale of the public power of the State.

3. *General overview*

Thanks to the work of those international tribunals, the international community no longer accepts impunity for international crimes, for *grave* violations of human rights and of international humanitarian law.[30] The determination of the international criminal responsibility of individuals by those tribunals is a reaction of contemporary international law to *grave* violations, guided by fundamental principles, and values shared by the international community as a whole.[31] There is no more room for impunity, with the present-day configuration of a true *droit au Droit*, of the persons victimized in any circumstances, including amidst the most complete adversity.[32] International human rights tribunals as well as international criminal tribunals have operated decisively to put an end to impunity.

Their jurisprudencial advances in recent years were unforeseeable, and even unthinkable, some decades ago.[33] International human rights tribunals have helped to awaken public conscience in respect of situations of utmost adversity or even defencelessness affecting individuals, and of widespread violence victimizing vulnerable segments of the population.[34]

[30] E. Möse, 'Main Achievements of the ICTR', 3 *Journal of International Criminal Justice* (2005) pp. 932–3; E. Möse, 'The International Criminal Tribunal for Rwanda', in *International Criminal Justice – Law and Practice from the Rome Statute to Its Review* (ed. R. Bellelli), Farnham/U.K., Ashgate, 2010, p. 90. And cf. also, likewise, A. Cassese, 'The Legitimacy of International Criminal Tribunals and the Current Prospects of International Criminal Justice', 25 *Leiden Journal of International Law* (2012) p. 497.

[31] S. Zappalà, *La justice penale internationale*, Paris, Montchrestien, 2007, pp. 15, 19, 23, 29, 31, 34–5, 43, 135, 137 and 145–6.

[32] A. A. Cançado Trindade, *The Access of Individuals to International Justice*, Oxford, Oxford University Press, 2011, pp. 196–8, and cf. pp. 132–91.

[33] As to the growing importance currently devoted to the theme, cf. Y. Beigbeder, *International Justice against Impunity – Progress and New Challenges*, Leiden, Nijhoff, 2005, pp. 1–235.

[34] Cf., as to the ECtHR, e.g., M. D. Goldhaber, *A People's History of the European Court of Human Rights*, New Brunswick/London, Rutgers University Press, 2009, pp. 2, 11, 57, 123, 126–7, 149–51, 155–8 and 168; and, as to the IACtHR, e.g., A. A. Cançado Trindade, 'Die Entwicklung des interamerikanischen Systems zum Schutz der Menschenrechte', 70 *Zeitschrift für ausländisches öffentliches Recht und Völkerrecht* (2010) pp. 629–99.

They have, in effect, brought justice to those victimized, even in situations of systematic and generalized violence, and mass atrocities. They have thus contributed, considerably and decisively, to the primacy of the *rule of law* at national and international levels, demonstrating that no one is above the law, – neither the rulers, nor the ruled, nor the States themselves. International law applies directly to States, to international organizations, and to individuals.[35]

4. *The contribution of expanded advisory jurisdiction*

It was with the PCIJ that, for the first time, an international tribunal was attributed the advisory function, – surrounded as it was by much discussion. It was originally conceived to assist the Assembly and the Council of the League of Nations, but the PCIJ, making good use of it, ended up by assisting not only those organs, but States as well: among the twenty-seven Advisory Opinions it delivered, seventeen of them addressed then existing aspects of disputes between States. It thus contributed to the avoidance of full-blown contentious proceedings, and exercised a preventive function, to the benefit of judicial settlement itself of international disputes.[36] The advisory function, as exercised by the PCIJ, thus contributed also to the progressive development of international law.

Ever since, the advisory jurisdiction has expanded. While the PCIJ Statute enabled only the League Council and Assembly to request Advisory Opinions, the ICJ Statute enabled other United Nations organs (besides the General Assembly, the Security Council and the UN Economic and Social Council (ECOSOC)) and specialized agencies and others to do so, and the ICJ has issued twenty-seven Advisory Opinions to date. Other contemporary international tribunals have been endowed with the advisory jurisdiction, and there are examples of frequent use made of it, such as the advisory jurisprudential construction of the IACtHR.

Advisory Opinions of the ICJ, for their part, can also contribute, and have indeed done so, to the prevalence of the *rule of law* at national and international levels. Some of them have, likewise, contributed to the progressive development of international law (e.g., the ones on *Reparation for Injuries*, 1949; on *Namibia*, 1970; on *Immunity from Legal Process of a*

[35] A. A. Cançado Trindade, *Os Tribunais Internacionais Contemporâneos*, Brasília, FUNAG, 2013, pp. 109–10.

[36] M. G. Samson and D. Guilfoyle, 'The Permanent Court of International Justice and the "Invention" of International Advisory Jurisdiction', in *Legacies of the Permanent Court of International Justice* (eds. C. J. Tams, M. Fitzmaurice and P. Merkouris), Leiden, Nijhoff, 2013, pp. 41–5, 47, 55–7 and 63.

Special Rapporteur of the UN Commission on Human Rights, 1999; among others). The same can be said of some of the Advisory Opinions of the IACtHR (e.g., the ones on the *Right to Information on Consular Assistance in the Framework of the Guarantees of the Due Process of Law*, 1999; on the *Juridical Condition and Human Rights of the Child*, 2002; on the *Juridical Condition and Rights of Undocumented Migrants*, 2003).

IV. The move towards compulsory jurisdiction

It is not my intention in this chapter to dwell upon the bases of jurisdiction of contemporary international tribunals, as I have already done so in detail elsewhere,[37] and recently in my lengthy Dissenting Opinion (paras. 1–214) in the ICJ's Judgment (of 1 April 2011) in the case of the *Application of the Convention on the Elimination of All Forms of Racial Discrimination*; but I cannot refrain from recalling, in the centennial celebration, the difficulties experienced in the long path towards compulsory jurisdiction. Throughout the last decades, advances could here have been much greater if State practice would not have undermined or betrayed the purpose which originally inspired the creation of the mechanism of the optional clause of compulsory jurisdiction (of the PCIJ and the ICJ), that is, the submission of political interests to Law, rather than the acceptance of compulsory jurisdiction the way one freely wishes.

Only in this way would one, as originally envisaged, achieve greater development in the realization of justice at international level on the basis of compulsory jurisdiction. The foundation of compulsory jurisdiction lies, ultimately, in the confidence in the *rule of law* at international level.[38] The very nature of a court of justice (beyond traditional arbitration) calls for compulsory jurisdiction.[39] Conscience stands above the will.

[37] A. A. Cançado Trindade, 'Towards Compulsory Jurisdiction: Contemporary International Tribunals and Developments in the International Rule of Law – Part I', in XXXVII *Curso de Derecho Internacional Organizado por el Comité Jurídico Interamericano – 2010*, Washington D.C., OAS General Secretariat, 2011, pp. 233–59; A. A. Cançado Trindade, 'Towards Compulsory Jurisdiction: Contemporary International Tribunals and Developments in the International Rule of Law – Part II', in XXXVIII *Curso de Derecho Internacional Organizado por el Comité Jurídico Interamericano – 2011*, Washington D.C., OAS General Secretariat, 2012, pp. 285–366.

[38] Cf., in this sense, C. W. Jenks, *The Prospects of International Adjudication*, London, Stevens, 1964, pp. 101, 117, 757, 762 and 770.

[39] Cf., in this sense, B. C. J. Loder, 'The Permanent Court of International Justice and Compulsory Jurisdiction', 2 *British Year Book of International Law* (1921–22) pp. 11–12.

Soon renewed hopes to that effect were expressed in compromissory clauses enshrined into multilateral and bilateral treaties.[40] These hopes have grown in recent years, with the increasing recourse to compromissory clauses as basis of jurisdiction.[41] In any case, be that as it may, the ICJ retains at least the power and duty to address *motu proprio* the issue of jurisdiction.[42] The time has come to overcome definitively the regrettable lack of automatism of the international jurisdiction, which, despite all difficulties, is no longer an academic dream or utopia, but has become reality in respect of some international tribunals.

I pointed this out in my General Course on Public International Law delivered at the Hague Academy of International Law in 2005, wherein, *inter alia*, I reviewed the developments in the domain of peaceful settlement of international disputes well beyond State voluntarism, and keeping in mind the general concerns of the international community.[43] More recently, I have reiterated that:

> International jurisdiction is becoming, in our days, an imperative of the contemporary international legal order itself, and compulsory jurisdiction responds to a need of the international community in our days; although this latter has not yet been fully achieved, some advances have been made in the last decades.[44] The Court of Justice of the European Communities provides one example of supranational compulsory jurisdiction, though limited to community law or the law of integration.

And cf., earlier on, likewise, N. Politis, *La justice internationale*, Paris, Libr. Hachette, 1924, pp. 7–255, esp. pp. 193–4 and 249–50.

40 E. Hambro, 'Some Observations on the Compulsory Jurisdiction of the International Court of Justice', 25 *British Year Book of International Law* (1948) p. 153.

41 Cf. R. Szafarz, *The Compulsory Jurisdiction of the International Court of Justice*, Dordrecht, Nijhoff, 1993, pp. 4, 31–2, 83 and 86; R. P. Anand, 'Enhancing the Acceptability of Compulsory Procedures of International Dispute Settlement', 5 *Max Planck Yearbook of United Nations Law* (2001) pp. 5–7, 11, 15 and 19.

42 R. C. Lawson, 'The Problem of the Compulsory Jurisdiction of the World Court', 46 *American Journal of International Law* (1952) pp. 234 and 238, and cf. pp. 219, 224 and 227.

43 A. A. Cançado Trindade, 'International Law for Humankind: Towards a New *Jus Gentium* - General Course on Public International Law – Part II', 317 *Recueil des Cours de l'Académie de Droit International de la Haye* (2005), chapters XXIV–XXV, pp. 173–245.

44 H. Steiger, 'Plaidoyer pour une juridiction internationale obligatoire', in *Theory of International Law at the Threshold of the 21st Century – Essays in Honour of K. Skubiszewski* (ed. J. Makarczyk), The Hague, Kluwer, 1996, pp. 818, 821–2 and 832; and cf. R. St. J. MacDonald, 'The New Canadian Declaration of Acceptance of the Compulsory Jurisdiction of the International Court of Justice', 8 *Canadian Yearbook of International Law* (1970) pp. 21, 33 and 37.

The European Convention of Human Rights, after the entry into force of Protocol n. 11 on 01.11.1998, affords another conspicuous example of automatic compulsory jurisdiction. The International Criminal Court is the most recent example in this regard; although other means were contemplated throughout the *travaux préparatoires* of the 1998 Rome Statute (such as cumbersome 'opting in' and 'opting out' procedures), at the end compulsory jurisdiction prevailed, with no need for further expression of consent on the part of States Parties to the Rome Statute. This was a significant decision, enhancing international jurisdiction.

The system of the 1982 U.N. Convention on the Law of the Sea, in its own way, moves beyond the traditional regime of the optional clause of the ICJ Statute. It allows States Parties to the Convention the option between the International Tribunal for the Law of the Sea, or the ICJ, or else arbitration (Article 287); despite the exclusion of certain matters, the Convention succeeds in establishing a compulsory procedure containing coercive elements; the specified choice of procedures at least secures law-abiding settlement of disputes under the U.N. Law of the Sea Convention.[45] In addition to the advances already achieved to this effect, reference could also be made to recent endeavours in the same sense.

These illustrations suffice to disclose that compulsory jurisdiction is already a reality, – at least in some circumscribed domains of International Law, as indicated above. International compulsory jurisdiction is, by all means, a juridical possibility. If it has not yet been attained on a world-wide level, in the inter-State *contentieux*, this cannot be attributed to an absence of juridical viability, but rather to misperceptions of its role, or simply to a lack of conscience as to the need to widen its scope. Compulsory jurisdiction is a manifestation of the recognition that International Law, more than voluntary, is indeed *necessary*.[46,47]

[45] L. Caflisch, 'Cent ans de règlement pacifique des différends interétatiques', 288 *Recueil des Cours de l'Académie de Droit International de La Haye* (2001) pp. 365–6 and 448–9; J. Allain, 'The Future of International Dispute Resolution – The Continued Evolution of International Adjudication', in *Looking Ahead: International Law in the 21st Century* (Proceedings of the 29th Annual Conference of the Canadian Council of International Law, Ottawa, October 2000), The Hague, Kluwer, 2002, pp. 61–2.

[46] One such example is found in the Proposals for a Draft Protocol to the American Convention on Human Rights, which I prepared as *rapporteur* of the IACtHR, which, *inter alia*, advocates an amendment to Article 62 of the American Convention so as to render the jurisdiction of the IACtHR in contentious matters automatically compulsory upon ratification of the Convention. Cf. A. A. Cançado Trindade, *Informe: Bases para un Proyecto de Protocolo a la Convención Americana sobre Derechos Humanos, para Fortalecer Su Mecanismo de Protección*, vol. II, 2nd edn., San José of Costa Rica, Inter-American Court of Human Rights, 2003, pp. 1–64.

[47] A. A. Cançado Trindade, 'Towards Compulsory Jurisdiction: Contemporary International Tribunals and Developments in the International Rule of Law – Part II', in XXXVIII *Curso de Derecho Internacional Organizado por el Comité Jurídico Interamericano – 2011*, Washington D.C., OAS General Secretariat, 2012, pp. 310–11.

V. Emerging conceptions of the exercise of the international judicial function

With the operation of international tribunals, there have gradually emerged two basic distinct conceptions of the exercise of the international judicial function: one, – a strict one, – whereby the tribunal has to limit itself to settle the dispute at issue and to handle its resolution of it to the contending parties (a form of transactional justice), addressing only what the parties had put before it; the other, a larger one, – the one I sustain, – whereby the tribunal has to go beyond that, and say what the Law is (*jurisdictio*), thus contributing to the settlement of other like situations as well, and to the progressive development of international law. In the interpretation itself – or even in the search – of the applicable law, there is space for judicial creativity; each international tribunal is free to find the applicable law, independently of the arguments of the contending parties[48] (*juria novit curia*).

Furthermore, there are circumstances wherein the judgments of international tribunals may have repercussions beyond the States parties to a case, – as exemplified by the well-known judgments of the IACtHR (having as leading case that of *Barrios Altos*, 2001), which held amnesties leading to impunity to be incompatible with the American Convention on Human Rights.[49] Such repercussions tend to occur when the judgments succeed to give expression to the idea of an *objective* justice. In this way, they contribute to the evolution of international law itself, and to the *rule of law* at national and international levels in democratic societies.

The more international tribunals devote themselves to explaining clearly the foundations of their decisions, the greater their contribution to justice and peace is bound to be. This issue has attracted the attention of juridical circles in the last decades.[50] In my conception, in judgments of international tribunals (also at regional level, in addition to national

[48] Cf. M. Cappelletti, *Juízes Legisladores?*, Porto Alegre/Brazil, S.A. Fabris Ed., 1993, pp. 73–5 and 128–9; M. O. Hudson, *International Tribunals – Past and Future*, Washington D.C., Carnegie Endowment for International Peace/Brookings Inst., 1944, pp. 104–5.

[49] For an account, cf. A. A. Cançado Trindade, *El Ejercicio de la Función Judicial Internacional – Memorias de la Corte Interamericana de Derechos Humanos*, 3rd edn., Belo Horizonte/Brazil, Edit. Del Rey, 2013, pp. 267–8.

[50] Cf., e.g., [Various Authors,] *La Sentenza in Europa – Metodo, Tecnica e Stile*(Atti del Convegno Internazionale di Ferrara di 1985), Padova, CEDAM, 1988, pp. 101–26, 217–29 and 529–42.

tribunals as well), the *motifs* and the *dispositif* go together: one cannot separate the decision itself from its foundations, from the reasoning which upholds it. Reason and persuasion permeate the operation of justice, and this goes back to the historical origins of its conception.

VI. The relevance of general principles of law

General principles of law, enlisted among the formal sources of international law (Article 38 of the ICJ Statute), encompass those found in all national legal systems[51] (thus ineluctably linked with the very foundations of Law), and likewise the general principles of international law.[52] Such principles, in my own conception, inform and conform the norms and rules of international law, being a manifestation of the universal juridical conscience; in the *jus gentium* in evolution, basic considerations of humanity play a role of the utmost importance.[53]

The aforementioned general principles of law have always marked presence in the search for justice, despite the dictinct perceptions of this latter in distinct countries. International human rights tribunals and international criminal tribunals have ascribed great importance to such general principles of law.[54] Those principles have been reaffirmed time and time again, and retain full validity in our days. Legal positivism has always attempted, in vain, to minimize their role, but the truth is that, without those principles, there is no legal system at all, be it national or international. They give expression to the idea of an *objective justice*, paving

[51] Cf. H. Mosler, 'To What Extent Does the Variety of Legal Systems of the World Influence the Application of the General Principles of Law within the Meaning of Article 38(1)(c) of the Statute of the International Court of Justice', in *International Law and the Grotian Heritage* (Hague Colloquium of 1983), The Hague, T.M.C. Asser Instituut, 1985, pp. 173–85.

[52] It is not suprising that the heralds of absolute sovereignty of the past have resisted to the applicability to the general principles of law at international level; F. O. Raimondo, *General Principles of Law in the Decisions of International Criminal Courts and Tribunals*, Leiden, Nijhoff, 2008, pp. 59 and 41.

[53] A. A. Cançado Trindade, *International Law for Humankind – Towards a New Jus Gentium*, 2nd rev. edn., Leiden/The Hague, Nijhoff, 2013, pp. 1–726.

[54] To this effect, cf., *inter alia*, e.g., K. Grabarczyk, *Les principes généraux dans la jurisprudence de la Cour Européenne des Droits de l'Homme*, Aix-Marseille, Presses Universitaires d'Aix-Marseille, 2008, pp. 375–473; M. Shahabuddeen, *International Criminal Justice at the Yugoslav Tribunal – A Judge's Recollection*, Oxford, Oxford University Press, 2012, pp. 55, 57, 86, 88–9, 185 and 203.

the way to the application of the *universal* international law, the new *jus gentium* of our times.[55]

I have had the occasion to ponder, for example, in my Concurring Opinion in the ground-breaking Advisory Opinion no. 18 of 17 September 2003, of the IACtHR, on the *Juridical Condition and Rights of Undocumented Migrants*:

> Every legal system has fundamental principles, which inspire, inform and conform their norms. It is the principles (derived etymologically from the Latin *principium*) that, evoking the first causes, sources or origins of the norms and rules, confer cohesion, coherence and legitimacy upon the legal norms and the legal system as a whole. It is the general principles of law (*prima principia*) which confer to the legal order (both national and international) its ineluctable axiological dimension; it is they that reveal the values which inspire the whole legal order and which, ultimately, provide its foundations themselves. This is how I conceive the presence and the position of the principles in any legal order, and their role in the conceptual universe of Law. . . .
>
> From the *prima principia* the norms and rules emanate, which in them find their meaning. The principles are thus present in the origins of Law itself. The principles show us the legitimate ends to seek: the common good (of all human beings, and not of an abstract collectivity), the realization of justice (at both national and international levels), the necessary primacy of law over force, the preservation of peace. Contrary to those who attempt – in my view in vain – to minimize them, I understand that, if there are no principles, nor is there truly a legal system. Without the principles, the 'legal order' simply is not accomplished, and ceases to exist as such.
>
> (paras. 44 and 46)

An international tribunal like the ICJ has resorted to general principles of law (recognized in domestic legal system and in international law) in its *jurisprudence constante*. For their part, international human rights tribunals have always kept in mind the principle of the dignity of the human person, as well as the principle (*pro victima*) of the application of the norm most favourable to the victim. And international criminal tribunals have kept in mind the principle of humanity, as well as the principle of universal jurisdiction; and one may add, in respect of the International Criminal Court (ICC), the principle of complementarity (enshrined in its Statute), – to refer to some examples.

From this outlook, the basic posture of an international tribunal can only be *principiste*, without making undue concessions to State

[55] A. A. Cançado Trindade, *International Law for Humankind – Towards a New Jus Gentium*, 2nd rev. edn., Leiden/The Hague, Nijhoff, 2013, pp. 1–726.

voluntarism. I had the occasion of pointing this out, as guest speaker, in the opening of the judicial year of the ECtHR, on 22 January 2004, at the *Palais des Droits de l'Homme* in Strasbourg, in the following terms:

> La Cour européenne et la Cour interaméricaine ont toutes deux, à juste titre, imposé des limites au volontarisme étatique, protégé l'intégrité de leurs Conventions respectives des droits de l'homme, ainsi que la prépondérance des considérations d'*ordre public* face à la volonté de tel ou tel État, élevé les exigences relatives au comportement de l'État, instauré un certain contrôle sur l'imposition de restrictions excessives par les États, et, de façon rassurante, mis en valeur le statut des individus en tant que sujets du Droit International des Droits de l'Homme en les dotant de la pleine capacité sur le plan procédural.[56]

More recently, within the ICJ, I have likewise sustained the same position. For example, in my lengthy Separate Opinion in the ICJ's Advisory Opinion (of 22 July 2010) on the *Conformity with International Law of the Declaration of Independence of Kosovo*, I singled out, *inter alia*, the relevance of the principles of international law in the framework of the Law of the United Nations, and in relation with the *human ends* of the State (paras. 177–211), leading also to the overcoming of the strictly inter-State paradigm in contemporary international law. Subsequently, in my extensive Dissenting Opinion in the case concerning the *Application of the International Convention on the Elimination of All Forms of Racial Discrimination* (CERD, Georgia *versus* Russian Federation, Judgment of 1 April 2011), I sustained the pressing need of the realization of justice on the basis of the compromissory clause (Article 22) of the CERD Convention, discarding any yielding to State voluntarism(paras. 1–214) [cf. *supra*].

VII. The awareness of the primacy of the *jus naecessarium* over the *jus voluntarium*

As already seen, in the present era of international tribunals there have been advances towards *compulsory* international jurisdiction (cf. *supra*), seeking to secure the primacy of the *jus naecessarium* over the *jus*

[56] In 'Discours de A. A. Cançado Trindade, Président de la Cour Interaméricaine des Droits de l'Homme', Cour Européenne des Droits de l'Homme, *Rapport annuel 2003*, Strasbourg, CourEDH, 2004, pp. 41–50; A. A. Cançado Trindade, *El Desarrollo del Derecho Internacional de los Derechos Humanos mediante el Funcionamiento y la Jurisprudencia de la Corte Europea y la Corte Interamericana de Derechos Humanos*, San José de Costa Rica/Strasbourg, CtIADH, 2007, pp. 41–2, para. 13.

voluntarium. The present-day phenomenon of the multiplicity of international tribunals is indeed related to the move towards international compulsory jurisdiction.[57] As to the ICJ, the original purpose of the optional clause (Article 36(2) of the Statute) was to attract general acceptance so as to establish compulsory international jurisdiction, in the light of the principle of juridical equality of States; the subsequent practice of adding restrictions – at each State's free will – to the acceptance of the optional clause distorted the purpose originally propounded. But there is today renewed hope in the growing use of compromissory clauses, as jurisdictional basis in the *contentieux* before the ICJ; for their consideration one is, in my view, to take into account the respective conventions as a whole (including their object and purpose), in the path towards international compulsory jurisdiction.

The International Tribunal for the Law of the Sea (ITLOS) counts on a *sui generis* mechanism (*supra*), opening four alternatives for dispute settlement: if there is no agreement as to which one to select, arbitration applies. This provides another illustration that State discretion is not unlimited as in times past. The Court of Justice of the European Communities (CJEU) provides yet another illustration of the move towards international compulsory jurisdiction, in the domain of regional or subregional integration, a domain in which there is a multiplicity of international tribunals nowadays (e.g., in Latin America and in Africa). An international tribunal such as the CJEU has contributed considerably to the consolidation of the *autonomous* nature of community law, to its effectiveness and to the specificity of Community treaties, and to the identification of the essential characteristics of the Community legal order[58] (such as its primacy over the law of member States, and the direct effect of several of its provisions, applicable alike to their nationals and to member States themselves).

[57] Cf. H. Ascensio, 'La notion de juridiction internationale en question', in *La juridictionnalisation du droit international* (SFDI, Colloque de Lille de 2002), Paris, Pédone, 2003, pp. 192–4; E. McWhinney, *Judicial Settlement of International Disputes – Jurisdiction, Justiciability and Judicial Law-Making on the Contemporary International Court*, Dordrecht, Nijhoff, 1991, p. 13.

[58] Cf., e.g., P. J. G. Kapteyn, 'The Role of the Court of Justice in the Development of the Community Legal Order', in *Il Ruolo del Giudice Internazionale nell'Evoluzione del Diritto Internazionale e Comunitario – Atti del Convegno di Studi in Memoria di G. Morelli* (Università di Reggio Calabria, 1993 – ed. F. Salerno), Padova, CEDAM, 1995, pp. 161–2, 165–7 and 170–3. And cf., recently, e.g., A. von Bogdandy, *I Principi Fondamentali dell'Unione Europea – Un Contributo allo Sviluppo del Costituzionalismo Europeo*, Roma, Edit. Scientifica, 2011, pp. 63–137.

VIII. International tribunals and jurisprudential cross-fertilization

In our days, the more lucid international legal doctrine has at last discarded empty euphemistic expressions used some years ago, – such as so-called 'proliferation' of international tribunals, so-called 'fragmentation' of international law, and so-called 'forum-shopping', – which diverted attention to false issues of delimitation of competences, oblivious of the need to focus it on the imperative of an enlarged access to justice. Those expressions, narrow-minded and unelegant and derogatory, and devoid of any meaning, paid a disservice to our discipline; they missed the key point of the considerable advances of the old ideal of international justice in the contemporary world.

It has become clear today that contemporary international tribunals, rather than threatening the cohesion of international law, enrich and strengthen it, in asserting its aptitude to resolve disputes in distinct domains of international law, at both *inter*-State and *intra*-State levels. Contemporary international law has thereby become more responsive to the fulfilment of the basic needs of the international community, of human beings and of humankind as a whole, among which is that of the realization of justice. The expansion of international jurisdiction by the establishment of contemporary international tribunals is but a reflection of the way contemporary international law has evolved, no longer indifferent to human suffering, and of the current search for, and construction of, a *corpus juris* for the international community guided by the *rule of law* in democratic societies and committed to the realization of justice.

In the performance of their common mission of imparting justice, contemporary international tribunals have begun to take into account each other's case-law. The case-law of the ICJ, for example, has been regularly taken into account by other contemporary international tribunals. In addition, recently, the ICJ itself has also displayed its openness of mind and has begun to do the same, as disclosed by its Judgment (merits, of 30 November 2010) in the case of *A.S. Diallo*. For the first time in its history, the ICJ established therein violations of the two human rights treaties at issue *together*, namely, at universal level, the 1966 UN Covenant on Civil and Political Rights, and, at regional level, the 1981 African Charter on Human and Peoples' Rights, – both in the framework of the universality of human rights, – in addition to the established breach of the 1963 Vienna Convention on Consular Relations (Article 36(1)(b)).

Also in an unprecedented way, the ICJ made express cross-references to the relevant case-law of the Inter-American and European Courts of Human Rights; and again, in its subsequent Judgment (reparations, of 19 June 2012) in the same case of *A.S. Diallo*, has again referred to the pertinent case-law of other international tribunals, such as, for example, the European and Inter-American Courts of Human Rights, ITLOS, and the Iran–United States Claims Tribunal. Likewise, the handling of the *Lubanga* case (2007–12) by the ICC has been marked, from the start, by the attention dispensed by the ICC to the relevant case-law of international human rights tribunals;[59] when it came to its treatment of specific issues concerning reparations, the ICC (Trial Chamber I) has, to an even far greater extent, made express cross-references to the relevant case-law of the IACtHR in particular.

Like other contemporary international tribunals, ITLOS has also contributed to jurisprudential cross-fertilization. Thus, recently (Judgment of 14 March 2012), in the case of the *Delimitation of the Maritime Boundary between Bangladesh and Myanmar in the Bay of Bengal*, ITLOS has made several cross-references to decisions of the ICJ in distinct cases of maritime delimitation.[60] Earlier on, in its first Advisory Opinion (of 01 February 2011), on *Responsibilities and Obligations of States Sponsoring Persons and Entities with Respect to Activities in the Area*, ITLOS (Seabed Disputes Chamber) has referred to other decisions of the ICJ (paras. 57 and 169), in particular to its Judgment (of 20 April 2010) in the case of the *Pulp Mills on the River Uruguay* (paras. 57, 115, 135 and 147), as well as to the ICJ Advisory Opinion (of 22 July 2010) on the *Declaration of Independence of Kosovo* (paras. 39 and 60).

Jurisprudential cross-fertilization, furthermore, exerts a constructive function in the safeguard of the rights of the *justiciables*. It is thus to be expected that contemporary international tribunals remain increasingly aware of the case-law of each other, in their continuing performance of their common mission of imparting justice in distinct domains of international law,[61] thus preserving its basic *unity*. This is to the benefit of the international community as a whole, and of all the *justiciables*, all

[59] Pre-Trial Chamber I decision of 29.01.2007, Trial Chamber I decision of 07.08.2012.

[60] ITLOS, Judgment of 14 March 2012, paras. 90, 95, 117, 185, 191, 211, 229–30, 233, 264, 294–5 and 330.

[61] A. A. Cançado Trindade, 'Contemporary International Tribunals: Their Continuing Jurisprudential Cross-Fertilization, with Special Attention to the International Safeguard of Human Rights', in *The Global Community – Yearbook of International Law and Jurisprudence* (ed. G.Z. Capaldo) Oxford University Press, 2012, vol. I, p. 188. And cf., in general,

subjects of law around the world, – States, international organizations and individuals alike.

IX. Effects of the work of international tribunals

In the present era of multiple international tribunals, the effects of their joint work can already be perceived. These effects have been, in my perception, first, their *law-making* endeavours, not only applying but also creating an *objective* law, beyond the will or consent of individual States, on the basis of the consciousness of human values; secondly, the acknowledgment of the fundamental importance of general principles of law;[62] thirdly, the development of international legal procedure (with a blend of traditions of national legal systems around the world, and the acknowledgment of the importance for the justiciables of the holding of oral hearings); fourthly, the fostering of the *unity* of law, with the interactions between international law and domestic law; and fifthly, the aforementioned fostering of respect for the *rule of law* at national and international levels.

The assertion of an *objective* law (first point), beyond the will of individual States, is a revival of jusnaturalist thinking. Judicial settlement of international disputes is needed as a guarantee against unilateral interpretation by a State of conventional obligations. After all, the basic foundations of international law emanate ultimately from the human conscience, from the universal juridical conscience, and not from the 'will' of individual States.[63] The assertion of the *unity* of the law is intertwined with the *rule of law* at national and international levels, as access to justice takes place, and ought to be preserved, at both levels.[64]

The ICJ itself, despite its anachronistic inter-State mechanism of operation, has been attentive to developments in the domains of the

e.g., G. de Vergottini and J.-J. Pardini, *Au-delà du dialogue entre les Cours*, Paris, Dalloz, 2013, pp. 39–138.

62 A. A. Cançado Trindade, 'Foundations of International Law: The Role and Importance of Its Basic Principles', in XXX *Curso de Derecho Internacional Organizado por el Comité Jurídico Interamericano* – OAS (2003) pp. 359–415.

63 M. M. T. A. Brus, *Third Party Dispute Settlement in an Interdependent World*, Dordrecht, Nijhoff, 1995, pp. 142 and 182–3; A. A. Cançado Trindade, 'La *Recta Ratio* dans les Fondements du *Jus Gentium* comme Droit International de l'Humanité', 10 *Revista do Instituto Brasileiro de Direitos Humanos* (2010) pp. 11–26.

64 A. A. Cançado Trindade, *Os Tribunais Internacionais Contemporâneos*, Brasília, FUNAG, 2013, pp. 80–2.

international law of human rights[65] and of international humanitarian law.[66] In this respect, it should not pass unnoticed that distinct trends of protection of the *justiciables* (international law of human rights, international humanitarian law, international law of refugees, international criminal law) *converge*, rather than conflict with each other, at normative, hermeneutic and operative levels.[67]

X. Interactions between international and domestic law: the unity of the law

The work of international human rights tribunals, as well as of contemporary international criminal tribunals (cf. *supra*), bear witness to the interactions between international and domestic law in their respective domains of operation. The realization of justice becomes a common goal, and a converging one, at the domestic and international legal orders. They both testify the *unity of the Law* in the realization of justice, a sign of our times. International human rights tribunals have shown that, in the great majority of cases lodged with them, international jurisdiction is resorted to when there is no longer a possibility to find justice at domestic law level.

And there have been occasions wherein the international jurisdiction has come to support national jurisdiction (*infra*), so as to secure also within this latter the primacy of law (*préeminence du droit, rule of law*). In effect, the expansion of international jurisdiction (cf. *supra*) has counted on the co-participation of national jurisdictions.[68] After all, international

[65] Cf., *inter alia*, e.g., A. A. Cançado Trindade, 'La jurisprudence de la Cour Internationale de Justice sur les droits intangibles/The Case-Law of the International Court of Justice on Non-Derogable Rights', in *Droits intangibles et états d'exception/Non-Derogable Rights and States of Emergency* (eds. D. Prémont, C. Stenersen and I. Oseredczuk), Bruxelles, Bruylant, 1996, pp. 53–71 and 73–89.

[66] Cf., *inter alia*, e.g., G. Zyberi, *The Humanitarian Face of the International Court of Justice*, Utrecht, Intersentia, 2008, pp. 26–60 and 259–341.

[67] Cf. A. A. Cançado Trindade, *Los Tribunales Internacionales Contemporáneos y la Humanización del Derecho Internacional*, Buenos Aires, Ed. Ad-Hoc, 2013, pp. 7–185; A. A. Cançado Trindade, *Derecho Internacional de los Derechos Humanos, Derecho Internacional de los Refugiados y Derecho Internacional Humanitario – Aproximaciones y Convergencias*, Geneva, ICRC, [2000], pp. 1–66.

[68] Cf., in general, e.g., Y. Shany, *Regulating Jurisdictional Relations between National and International Courts*, Oxford, Oxford University Press, 2009, pp. 1–200. For an account of the relations between the Prosecutors' offices of the ad hoc International Tribunals for the former Yugoslavia and for Rwanda (ICTY and ICTR) and the competent national authorities, cf. V. Peskin, *International Justice in Rwanda and the Balkans – Virtual Trials*

law attributes international functions also to national tribunals.[69] These latter have a role to play also in the search for the primacy of the international *rule of law*.[70]

Among international criminal tribunals, the ICC shows, *inter alia*, that the principle of complementarity, for example, signals the call for a greater aproximation, if not interaction, between the international and national jurisdictions. And it could not be otherwise, particularly in our times, when, with growing frequency, the most diverse matters are brought before judicial control at international level.[71] Contrary to what keeps on being assumed in various legal circles, national and international jurisdictions, in our times, are not concurring or conflictive, but rather complementary, in constant interaction in the protection of the rights of the human person and in the struggle against the impunity of the violators of thoses rights.

It is not certain either, – also contrary to what is usually assumed, – that the international jurisdiction for the protection of the rights of the human person is always and only 'subsidiary' to national jurisdiction, or 'autonomous' in relation to it. The two jurisdictions interact in the present domain of protection. And, further than that, there are significant illustrations, in certain situations of extreme adversity to human beings, of the international jurisdiction having even *preceded* national jurisdiction in the protection of the rights of the victimized and in the reparations due to them.

For example, the determination, by the IACtHR, of the international responsibility of the respondent State for grave violations of human rights in the cases of the massacres of *Barrios Altos* and *La Cantuta* (Judgments of 2001[72] and 2006[73], respectively), *preceded* the condemnation, by the

and the Struggle for State Cooperation, Cambridge, Cambridge University Press, 2009 [reed.], pp. 3–257.

69 Cf. A. A. Cançado Trindade, *The Access of Individuals to International Justice*, Oxford, Oxford University Press, 2011, ch. V, pp. 76–112 (on the interaction between international law and domestic law in human rights protection).

70 A. Nollkaemper, *National Courts and the International Rule of Law*, Oxford, Oxford University Press, 2011, pp. 1–304.

71 T. Koopmans, 'Judicialization', in *Une communauté de droit – Festschrift für G.C. Rodríguez Iglesias* (eds. N. Colneric et al.), Berlin, Berliner Wissenschafts-Verlag (BWV), 2003, pp. 51–7; G. Ulfstein, 'The International Judiciary', in *The Constitutionalization of International Law* (eds. J. Klabbers, A. Peters and G. Ulfstein), Oxford, Oxford University Press, 2011 [reed.], pp. 126–52.

72 Judgments of 14.03.2001 (merits), 03.09.2001 (interpretation), and 30.11.2001 (reparations).

73 Judgment of 29.11.2006 (merits and reparations).

Special Penal Chamber of the Peruvian Supreme Court (in 2007–10), of the former President of the Republic (A. Fujimori).[74] In those two cases, in addition to the paradigmatic case of the *Constitutional Tribunal* (IACtHR's Judgment of 2001) – pertaining to the destitution of three magistrates, later reincorporated into the Tribunal – the *international jurisdiction effectively intervened in defense of the national one*, decisively contributing to the restoration of the *État de Droit*, – as it occurred, – besides having safeguarded the rights of the victimized.[75] In the history of the relations – and interactions – between national and international jurisdictions, this trilogy of cases will surely keep on being studied by the present and future generations of internationalists and constitutionalists.

XI. Concluding remarks: the tasks ahead, and prospects for the future

I now come to my concluding observations, as to the prospects for the future, keeping in mind the lessons learned along a century of experience sedimented in the domain of international justice. It is high time, in my view, to begin focusing attention constantly on the proper ways of achieving the realization of justice, rather than keeping cultivating strategies of litigation for the sake of it, making abstraction of human values. Likewise, it is high time to accompany consistently the on-going expansion of international jurisdiction, and of international legal personality and capacity, as well as international responsibility, by drawing closer attention to *all* subjects of international law, not only States, but also international organizations, peoples and individuals.

[74] For a historical account, cf. A. A. Cançado Trindade, *El Ejercicio de la Función Judicial Internacional– Memorias de la Corte Interamericana de Derechos Humanos*, 3rd edn., Belo Horizonte/Brazil, Edit. Del Rey, 2013, pp. 42–5; A. A. Cançado Trindade, *Os Tribunais Internacionais Contemporâneos*, Brasília, FUNAG, 2013, pp. 84–90.

[75] Almost three years after the IACtHR's Judgment (of 31.01.2001) in the case of the *Constitutional Tribunal*, I sent a letter to this latter (on 04.12.2003), as then President of the IACtHR, in which I expressed, *inter alia*, that 'we can appreciate this Judgment of the IACtHR in historical perspective . . . , as a landmark one not only . . . [in the] inter-American system of protection of human rights. . . . [It] constitutes an unprecedented judicial decision also at world level. It has had repercussions not only in our region but also in other continents. It has marked a starting point of a remarkable and reassuring approximation between the judicial power at national and international levels . . . ' Text of the letter reproduced in OAS, *Informe Anual de la Corte Interamericana de Derechos Humanos – 2003*, San José of Costa Rica, IACtHR, 2004, Annexo LVII, pp. 1459–60, and cf. pp. 1457–8.

In the last three years, the ICJ has given signs of its preparedness to do so. Thus, in its Order of Provisional Measures of Protection of 18 July 2011, in the case of the Temple of Preah Vihear, the ICJ, in deciding, *inter alia*, to order the establishment of a provisional demilitarized zone around the Temple (part of the world's cultural and spiritual heritage) and its vicinity, it extended protection (as I pointed out in my Separate Opinion, paras. 66–113) not only to the territory at issue, but also to the local inhabitants, in conformity with the *principle of humanity* in the framework of the new *jus gentium* of our times (paras. 114–17). Territory and people go together.

Subsequently, in the recent case of the *Frontier Dispute* (Judgment of 16 April 2013), the contending parties (Burkina Faso and Niger) themselves expressed before the Court their concern, in particular with local nomadic and semi-nomadic populations, and assured that their living conditions would not be affected by the tracing of the frontier. Once again, as I pointed out in my Separate Opinion (paras. 90, 99 and 104–5), the *principle of humanity* permeated the handling of the case by the ICJ.

In the aforementioned *A.S. Diallo* case (Judgment on reparations, of 2012), the ultimate beneficiary of the reparations ordered by the ICJ was, in my perception, the individual concerned, rather than his State of nationality. On another recent occasion, the application, by the ICJ, of the principle of *universal jurisdiction* under the 1984 UN Convention against Torture in the case of *Questions Relating to the Obligation to Prosecute or Extradite* (Judgment of 20 July 2012), has a bearing, in my understanding, on restorative justice (the realization of justice itself) for the numerous victims of the Habré regime (1982–90) in Chad, as I pointed out in my lengthy Separate Opinion (paras. 169–84).

Moving to another point, it is now time to accompany the expansion of international jurisdiction, by also fostering the dialogue and co-ordination between contemporary international tribunals. Endeavours of co-ordination already exist, but have been far from sufficient to date. There is nowadays pressing need for greater dialogue and co-ordination of contemporary international tribunals, in their common mission of imparting justice. At a conceptual level, there is pressing need of further jurisprudential developments in the matter of reparations, as well as provisional measures of protection, both still in their infancy,

I have recently pointed this out, as to reparations, in my Separate Opinion in the case of *A.S. Diallo* (ICJ Judgment on reparations, of 19 June 2012). The jurisprudential construction of the IACtHR in respect of distinct forms or reparations is surely deserving of close attention from other international tribunals. The matter discloses the relevance of the rehabilitation of victims. And as to provisional measures of protection, I have made the same point, recently, in my Dissenting Opinion in the joined cases of *Certain Activities Carried out by Nicaragua in the Border Area* and of *Construction of a Road in Costa Rica along the San Juan River* (Order of 16 July 2013), where I stressed the need to contribute to the conformation of an autonomous legal regime of those measures, beyond the traditional inter-State dimension, in the proper exercise of the international judicial function.

Likewise, the issue of compliance with judgments and decisions of international tribunals requires far greater attention and study on the part of international tribunals, – some of them being already engaged in its careful consideration currently. Here, each international tribunal counts on a mechanism of its own; yet, all of them are susceptible of improvement. May it here be recalled that, some years ago, the ECtHR, in the case Hornsby *versus* Greece (Judgment of 19 March 1997), stressed the relevance of the execution of judgments for the *effectiveness* itself of the right of access to a tribunal under Article 6(1) of the European Convention on Human Rights. In its own words,

> that right would be illusory if a Contracting State's domestic legal system allowed a final, binding judicial decision to remain inoperative to the detriment of one party. It would be inconceivable that Article 6(1) should describe in detail procedural guarantees afforded to litigants – proceedings that are fair, public and expeditious – without protecting the implementation of judicial decisions; to construe Article 6 as being concerned exclusively with access to a court and the conduct of proceedings would be likely to lead to situations incompatible with the principle of the rule of law which the Contracting States undertook to respect when they ratified the Convention.
>
> (para. 40)

This issue pertains, as pointed out by the ECtHR, to the *rule of law* itself, so as to secure 'the proper administration of justice' (para. 41). Thus, not one formal access, but also the guarantees of the due process of law, and the due compliance with the Judgment, integrate the right of access to justice *lato sensu*.[76] In the same line of thinking, the IACtHR, in its

[76] On the matter, cf. A. A. Cançado Trindade, *El Derecho de Acceso a la Justicia en Su Amplia Dimensión*, 2nd edn, Santiago de Chile, CECOH/Librotecnia, 2012, pp. 79–574.

Judgment (on jurisdiction, of 28 November 2003) in the case of Baena Ricardo and Others (270 Workers) *versus* Panama, stated that:

> The jurisdiction comprises the faculty to impart justice; it is not limited to declaring the law, but also comprises the supervision of compliance with the judgment . . . , [which is] one of the elements which integrate the jurisdiction. . . . Compliance . . . is the materialization of justice for the concrete case . . . The effectiveness of the Judgments depends on compliance with them, . . . [which is] closely linked with the right of access to justice, . . . set forth in Articles 8 (judicial guarantees) and 25 (judicial protection) of the American Convention.
>
> (paras. 72–4)

Only with the due compliance with the judgments are the proclaimed rights effectively protected; the execution of judgments, added the IACtHR lucidly,

> ought to be considered an integral part of the right of access to justice, this latter understood *lato sensu* . . . If the responsible State does not execute at national level the measures of reparation ordered by the Court, it would be denying the right of access to international justice.
>
> (paras. 82–3)

Despite all the experience accumulated so far, this remains an open issue, which – may I insist on this point – is still in its infancy, like those of reparations and of provisional measures of protection (*supra*).

It is to be hoped that the on-going reflections within some international tribunals on how to improve their respective mechanisms in this respect prove fruitful. The issue does not exhaust itself at international level. It is highly desirable that, parallel to the distinct mechanisms for the supervision of compliance with judgments of contemporary international tribunals, the States adopt procedures of *domestic* law to secure, on a *permanent* basis, the faithful compliance with the judgments of international tribunals, thus avoiding casuistic solutions.

After all, such faithful compliance with, or execution of, their judgments is a legitimate concern of all contemporary international tribunals. Such compliance ought to be integral, rather than partial or selective. This is a position of principle, in relation to an issue which pertains to the international *ordre public*, and to the *rule of law* (*préeminence du droit*) at international and national levels. In sum, the present era of international tribunals has brought about remarkable advances, and the expansion of international jurisdiction has been accompanied by the considerable increase in the number of the *justiciables*, granted access to justice, in distinct domains of international law, and in the most diverse situations, including in circumstances of the utmost adversity, and even defencelessness. Yet, there remains a long way to go.

4

The International Court of Justice and human rights treaty bodies

SIR NIGEL RODLEY

It is often forgotten that, as the preeminent judicial authority of general international law, the International Court of Justice (ICJ or World Court) is also a forum for the adjudication of international human rights law as much as any other area of international law. In fact, from its earliest days, the Court was called upon to address human rights issues, indeed consider the scope of applicability of the first post-World War II international human rights treaty: the Genocide Convention.[1] Equally rarely noted is the fact that the compromissory clauses of some human rights treaties, including a majority of the nine 'core' human rights treaties, render the Court itself as a human rights treaty body,[2]

[1] Convention on the Prevention and Punishment of the Crime of Genocide, 9 December 1948, 78 UNTS 277; *Reservations to the Convention on Genocide*, Advisory Opinion,1951 ICJ 15. See generally, Gentian Zyberi, *The Humanitarian Face of the International Court of Justice: Its Contribution to Interpreting and Developing International Human Rights and Humanitarian Rules and Principles* (Antwerp: Intersentia, 2008); Egon Schwelb, 'The International Court of Justice and the Human Rights Clauses of the Charter', *American Journal of International Law* 66 (1972): 337; Nigel Rodley, 'Human Rights and Humanitarian Intervention: The Case Law of the World Court', *International and Comparative Law Quarterly* 38 (1989): 321; Rosalyn Higgins, 'Human Rights in the ICJ', *Leiden Journal of International Law* 20 (2007): 745; and Bruno Simma, 'Mainstreaming Human Rights: The Contribution of the ICJ', *Journal of International Dispute Settlement* 3 (2012): 7.

[2] Convention against Torture and Other Cruel, Inhuman or Degrading Treament or Punishment, 10 December 1984, 1465 85, Art. 30; International Convention on the Elimination of All Forms of Racial Discrimination, 21 December 1965, 660 UNTS 195, Art. 22; Convention on the Political Rights of Women, 31 March 1953, 193 UNTS 135, Art. IX; Convention on the Elimination of All Forms of Discrimination against Women, 18 December 1979, 1249 UNTS 13, Art. 29; International Convention on the Protection of the Rights of All Migrant Workers and Members of their Families, 18 December 1990, 2220 UNTS 3, Art. 92; Convention on the Prevention and Punishment of the Crime of Genocide, 9 December 1948, 78 UNTS 277, Art. IX.

although in only one case has it acted as such, namely *Belgium* v. *Senegal.*[3]

The International Human Rights Committee of the International Law Association has considered the relationship in a recent study prepared by its Co-Rapporteur, Dr Eva Rieter, which has been of considerable assistance for the preparation of the present chapter.[4] The decision of the Committee in 2008 to undertake that study was prophetic as until then there had only been one case in which the ICJ had directly considered the practice of a treaty body, namely the *Wall* opinion in 2004.[5] Since then, there have been three others, two of them involving extensive consideration of UN treaty body practice: the *Diallo* case,[6] the *Belgium* v. *Senegal* (or *Hissène Habré*) case,[7] and the *IFAD* case.[8]

Two questions should be illuminated by our inquiry. One relates to the juridical status of the outputs of the treaty bodies. The other relates to concerns about the possible fragmentation of different fields of international law.

I. The juridical status of treaty body outputs

It is self-evident that the UN treaty bodies are not courts and, accordingly, that their outputs are not of themselves binding on States. The principal outputs of these bodies are concluding observations emitted as the outcome of the review of States' periodic reports,[9] 'views' adopted by way of findings on the validity or otherwise of individual complaints,[10] and

[3] *Questions relating to the Obligation to Prosecute or Extradite (Belgium* v. *Senegal) (Hissène Habré)*, judgment, 2012, ICJ 422.

[4] International Law Association, Washington DC Conference (2014), Draft International Human Rights Committee Final Report, available at www.ila-hq.org/en/committees/index.cfm/cid/1027.

[5] *Legal Consequences of the Construction of a Wall in the Occupied Palestinian Territory*, advisory opinion, 2004, ICJ 136.

[6] *Diallo (Republic of Guinea* v. *Democratic Republic of the Congo)*, preliminary objections, 2007, ICJ 582; *Ahmadou Sadio Diallo (Republic of Guinea* v. *Democratic Republic of the Congo)*, merits, judgment, 2010, ICJ 639; *Ahmadou Sadio Diallo (Republic of Guinea* v. *Democratic Republic of the Congo)*, compensation, judgment, 2012, ICJ 324.

[7] *Hissène Habré, supra* note 3.

[8] *Judgment No 2867 of the Administrative Tribunal of the International Labour Organization upon a Complaint Filed against the International Fund for Agricultural Development*, advisory opinion, 2012, ICJ 10.

[9] Typically, treaty bodies review reports of States parties to their treaties and issue evaluations (concluding observations) on the basis of the reviews.

[10] Most treaty bodies now have an optional procedure, whereby a State party may, either by adhering to an optional protocol or depositing a special declaration, accept the right

General Comments or recommendations addressed to all States parties reflecting the treaty body's view of the latters' obligations under the treaty in question.

For a number of reasons, *concluding observations* need to be treated with caution. They are adopted under extreme time pressure. Covering the whole range of a State party's commitments under each treaty, the treaty body typically has only a matter of hours to agree a draft text produced by one of its members. Further, the language used may leave some elements of imprecision. Thus, the 'concerns' expressed may not always be clear as to whether a violation is being found. Similarly, the recommendations flowing from these concerns may not always restrict themselves to those measures the treaty body considers to be obligatory: they may sometimes, for example, reflect 'best practice' as a means of avoiding future violations. Moreover, the observations have to be adopted by consensus, with no means of permitting individual opinions of members to be placed on record. This limits the amount of specificity that can be framed in the resulting text. So, increasingly, do word limits imposed by the General Assembly.[11] Of course, this does not mean that the contents of concluding observations are simply ad hoc propositions. Typically, a number of countries will evince similar problems and, with the support of the Secretariat, Committees are able to mine previous approaches – and even language – so that like may be treated as like. So, there may still be genuine precedential value in concluding observations. It is this writer's sense that concluding observations produced by the UN Human Rights Committee (HRC) generally represent the highest common factor, rather than the lowest common denominator.

The '*views*' in individual cases are inevitably a more reliable and authoritative guide to the opinion of the Committee. This is because on all but the most straightforward issues, the Committee will generally take as much time as it needs to finalize a 'view' that reflects a careful examination of the facts and a conscientiously arrived at application of the law.[12] As the HRC has put it in its General Comment no. 33:

of individuals to communicate complaints to the relevant treaty bodies which may then adjudicate the complaint.

11 General Assembly resolution 68/268 (2014), para. 15.

12 1.3 hours has been established by the General Assembly, based on the average time taken by the Human Rights Committee; *ibid.*, para. 26 b; evidently the average takes account of routine cases, often dismissed as inadmissible, as well as discontinued cases; many take much longer.

> While the function of the Human Rights Committee in considering individual communications is not, as such, that of a judicial body, the views issued by the Committee under the Optional Protocol exhibit some important characteristics of a judicial decision. They are arrived at in a judicial spirit, including the impartiality and independence of Committee members, the considered interpretation of the language of the Covenant, and the determinative character of the decisions . . . The views of the Committee under the Optional Protocol represent an authoritative determination by the organ established under the Covenant itself charged with the interpretation of that instrument. These views derive their character, and the importance which attaches to them, from the integral role of the Committee under both the Covenant and the Optional Protocol.[13]

This language indicates the Committee's understanding that States parties are not free simply to dismiss its findings and the remedies that it indicates. Sometimes a State party may refuse to accept the views in a specific case, for example, because of disagreement on the facts or law. The disagreement may be the result of failure to participate in the process at all, or to participate sufficiently so as to clarify its analysis of the facts of the State party's view of the law. Here the Committee reminded States that they are obliged 'to act in good faith, both in their participation in the procedures under the Optional Protocol and in relation to the Covenant itself'.[14] Implicit here is the understanding that while States may have the right to disagree with the Committee's determination of the facts and interpretation of the law, the good faith principle requires them to have fully conveyed the relevant information and legal analysis during the deliberative process and subsequently to explain the basis for their refusal to comply with the Committee's 'views'.

Of course, this is not just a matter of the respect due to a body established under the treaty in question and elected by the States parties. For the Committee, it is a duty owed to the other States parties, so that they too may arrive at an appreciation of the well-foundedness or otherwise of the position advanced by the State party in question. Again, as the Committee has put it elsewhere, States' obligations under the Covenant apply *erga omnes* and, accordingly, 'every State Party has a legal interest in the performance by every other State Party of its obligations'.[15] In any event, the Committee will treat earlier cases as precedents to be invoked

[13] *General comment no. 33, Obligations of States parties under the Optional Protocol to the International Covenant on Civil and Political Rights*, 25 June 2009, CCPR/C/GC/33 at paras. 11–13.

[14] *Ibid.*, para. 15.

[15] *General comment no. 31, The nature of the general legal obligation imposed on States Parties to the Covenant*, 26 May 2004, CCPR/C/21/Rev.1/Add.13, para. 2. Here the Committee is

in subsequent ones, in the same manner as a judicial body. Certainly the UN Secretariat classifies the 'views' as 'jurisprudence', a word that has come to mean, not only legal theory (the traditional understanding), but is now internationally used in the Civil Law sense of what is still typically called 'case law' in the Common Law system.[16]

The General Comments of treaty bodies are also intended to provide authoritative guidance on the nature of States parties' obligations under specific provisions of the treaty (or protocols). Certainly the practice of the HRC has reflected an attempt to codify its accumulated practice, often over decades.

Typically, HRC General Comments will be the result of a careful drafting process: a rapporteur will prepare a draft that will be considered, paragraph by paragraph, by the plenary body. After a 'first reading' the provisionally agreed text will be made available for 'stakeholders' (notably States parties, other international governmental organizations, other treaty bodies and civil society) to react to. A second reading will then take place to consider these contributions, as well as second thoughts of members, with a view to finalizing the text of the new General Comment. The overall drafting process may thus take some two years of deliberations.

The ensuing General Comment will then constitute an important reference source for the Committee, capable of being invoked in the context of concluding observations and in the 'views' arrived at in individual cases. The significance of the General Comments is also attested to by the intense interest of States and civil society in proposing what should be the subject of the Committee's next General Comment.[17]

II. Fragmentation?

One of the debates that have in recent years engaged international lawyers is whether international law has somehow spawned a series of sub-fields that have developed according to sub-field-specific doctrines, rather than

acknowledging a notion famously articulated in the ICJ's *Barcelona Traction Case (Belgium v. Spain)*,1970, ICJ 3, at para. 33.

16 See OHCHR treaty bodies website: www.ohchr.org/EN/HRBodies/Pages/TreatyBodies.aspx.

17 See, for example, the October 2013 interactive dialogue in the Third Committee of the General Assembly with the Chairperson of the Human Rights Committee (the present writer), where delegations suggested a new Committee General Comment on Art. 17 (right to privacy) and the Report to the Human Rights Council of the Special Rapporteur on Extrajudicial, Summary or Arbitrary Executions, UN Doc A/HRC/26/36 (2014), para. 119 (suggesting one on the right to life). The Committee chose the latter.

in accordance with the normal doctrines of general international law. This is known as the 'fragmentation debate'.[18] The various sub-fields of international law considered in this debate are mainly products of the post-World War II world. They include the law of outer space, environmental law and human rights. It is natural that human rights in particular would elicit fears of a kind of subject-specific secessionism. The very nature of human rights law required it to turn on its head fundamentally understood precepts relating to domestic jurisdiction.

The traditional mission of international law was to resolve disputes of a transnational nature. Avoidance of concern with what went on inside a State was seen as a condition *sine qua non* for such a project. For a State's system of governance to become a matter of 'international concern' was to put grit in the oil that was designed to lubricate the issue of transnational tension. Yet this is the essence of the universal human rights project that the Charter of the United Nations instigated.[19] In recent years, the potential tension between universal international law and the perceived exceptionalism of human rights has been played out in a way that reconciles the two paradigms. This was the issue of reservations to treaties.

In 1994 the HRC adopted General Comment no. 24 on reservations to treaties.[20] Not only did the Committee 'necessarily' claim the right to determine the validity of a reservation in terms of its compatibility with the Covenant: it could not discharge its functions of reviewing States' periodic reports and deciding cases under the Optional Protocol without doing so. It then controversially went on to pronounce on the legal consequences of a finding of invalidity:

[18] Martti Koskenniemi, 'Fragmentation of International Law: Difficulties Arising from the Diversification and Expansion of International Law', Report of the Study Group of the International Law Commission, finalized by Martti Koskenniemi, A/CN.4/L.682. See also: James Crawford, 'Chance, Order, Change: The Course of International Law', in 365 *Collected Courses of The Hague Academy of International Law* (Leiden: Martinus Nijhoff Publishers, 2013), 9, 205–29; Mads Andenas, 'The Centre Reasserting Itself: From Fragmentation to Transformation of International Law', in *Volume in Honor of Pär Hallström*, edited by Mattias Derlén and Johan Lindholm (Uppsala: Iustus, 2012); and Philippa Webb, *International Judicial Integration and Fragmentation* (Oxford: Oxford University Press, 2013).

[19] Nigel Rodley, 'International Human Rights Law', in *International* Law, edited by Malcolm Evans (4th edn., Oxford: Oxford University Press, 2014), 783–820. See, in particular, Charter of the United Nations, 26 June 1945, 892 UNTS 119, Arts. 1(3), 55, 56 and 68.

[20] *General Comment no. 24: Issues Relating to Reservations Made upon Ratification or Accession to the Covenant or the Optional Protocols thereto, or in Relation to Declarations under Article 41 of the Covenant*, 4 November 1994, CCPR/C/21/Rev.1/Add.6.

> In order to know the scope of its duty to examine a State's compliance under article 40 or a communication under the first Optional Protocol, the Committee has necessarily to take a view on the compatibility of a reservation with the object and purpose of the Covenant and with general international law. Because of the special character of a human rights treaty, the compatibility of a reservation with the object and purpose of the Covenant must be established objectively, by reference to legal principles, and the Committee is particularly well placed to perform this task. The normal consequence of an unacceptable reservation is not that the Covenant will not be in effect at all for a reserving party. Rather, such a reservation will generally be severable, in the sense that the Covenant will be operative for the reserving party without benefit of the reservation.[21]

In fact, in 1993 the International Law Commission (ILC) had decided to draft guidelines on reservations to treaties. In 1997, its Rapporteur, Alain Pellet, produced draft conclusions on this issue, including draft conclusion 10:

> The Commission notes also that, in the event of incompatibility of a reservation with the object and purpose of a treaty, it is primarily the reserving State that has the responsibility of taking action. This action may consist, for example, in the State either foregoing becoming a party or withdrawing its reservation, or modifying the latter so as to eliminate the incompatibility.[22]

This text was clearly intended as a refutation of the approach taken in HRC General Comment no. 24. The draft conclusion did not even refer to the possibility of severability being the result of invalidity.[23] The Special Rapporteur had taken the view that universal human rights treaty bodies (unlike regional courts) did not have the power to determine the consequences of invalidity.[24] Indeed he objected to the 'excessive pretentions of the Human Rights Committee in seeking to act as the sole judge of the permissibility of reservations'.[25]

There were a number of meetings between treaty bodies and the ILC[26] in which the treaty bodies clarified that they took the view that general

[21] *Ibid.*, para. 18. [22] UN Doc A/CN.4/L.540 (1997).

[23] 'Severability' means that, despite the reservation, the State remains bound by the treaty in question without benefit of the reservation; the other possibility is that an invalid reservation prevents the State becoming party to the treaty.

[24] UN Doc. A/52/10 (1997), paras. 82–7.

[25] *Ibid.*, para. 87; it may have been relevant that the word 'generally' is absent from the French version of General Comment no. 24, para. 18.

[26] For the last of which, see report of the meeting of the ILC with the treaty bodies intercommittee working group on reservations, 15–16 May 2007, UN Doc. A/CN.4/614 (2009);

principles of treaty interpretation applied, but that there should be a strong presumption in favour of severability in respect of human rights treaties. This was because of the non-synallagmatic nature of human rights obligations, that is, no other State suffers direct harm from one State's violation and so has no immediate interest in protesting such a violation. They did, however, accept that the presumption of severability was rebuttable and that, ultimately, it was the intention of the reserving State that determined the severability or otherwise of the reservation.[27] The ILC concluded in relation to invalid reservations that '[u]nless the author of the invalid reservation has expressed a contrary intention or such intention is otherwise established, it is considered a contracting State or a contracting organization *without the benefit of the reservation*'.[28]

Thus, the presumption in favour of severability argued for by the treaty bodies, at least as regards human rights treaties, was now accepted by the ILC in respect of *all* multilateral treaties. So, far from the treaty bodies promoting fragmentation of the normal understanding of the expected consequences of invalid reservations, general international law seemed to have embraced for the whole corpus what had been perceived as a subject-specific approach.

III. The general approach of the ICJ

The ICJ has expressed itself in terms that address both the juridical nature of treaty body outputs and the concern to avoid fragmentation. As will be seen below, the Court in the *Wall* advisory opinion referred with respect and approval to all the outputs of the treaty bodies: concluding observations of the HRC and of the Committee on Economic, Social and Cultural Rights, 'views' of the HRC in individual cases under the Optional Protocol and a General Comment of the HRC. It did this without indicating any general approach.

In the 2010 *Diallo* case, however, the ICJ gave the following exposition of its understanding of the HRC's General Comments and decisions under the Optional Protocol:

the present writer co-chaired the final segment as Chairperson/Rapporteur of the working group: *ibid.*, para. 2.

27 Report of the Working Group on Reservations, UN Doc. HRI/MC/2007/5: the State remains a party without benefit of the reservation, 'unless its contrary intention is incontrovertibly established' (page 7, recommendation 70).

28 ILC, Guide to Practice on Reservations, UN Doc. A/66/10 (2011), para. 75, Guideline 4.5.3, para. 2, emphasis added.

> Since it was created, the HRC has built up a considerable body of interpretative case law, in particular through its findings in response to the individual communications which may be submitted to it in respect of States parties to the first Optional Protocol, and in the form of its 'General Comments'.
>
> Although the Court is in no way obliged, in the exercise of its judicial functions, to model its own interpretation of the Covenant on that of the Committee, it believes that it should ascribe great weight to the interpretation adopted by this independent body that was established specifically to supervise the application of that treaty. The point here is to achieve the necessary clarity and the essential consistency of international law, as well as legal security, to which both the individuals with guaranteed rights and the State obliged to comply with treaty obligations are entitled.[29]

This passage merits close attention. The language of the first of the quoted sub-paragraphs is particularly important. First, the Court's use of the term 'case law' ('*jurisprudence*' in the French version) is noteworthy. This is a term that would normally be reserved for judgments of a court. Evidently, the ICJ is treating HRC decisions in respect of communications under the Optional Protocol as if they were judicial decisions. It may seem unexpected that it uses the same terminology in respect of the Committee's 'General Comments'. This presumably reflects the Court's awareness of the careful drafting process that precedes adoption of General Comments, including its tendency to 'codify' existing Optional Protocol decisions.[30] The use of the adjective 'interpretative' also acknowledges the necessary Committee role of interpreting the Covenant: its function is not just to make factual conclusions or offer advice in the form of recommendations.

The second of the quoted sub-paragraphs of paragraph 66 of the *Diallo* judgment is similarly illuminating. While quite rightly maintaining its independent authority to interpret the Covenant, the Court then explains why it should not lightly depart from the interpretation arrived at by the Committee. First, it feels it should 'ascribe great weight' to the Committee's interpretation, precisely because it is the 'independent body . . . established specifically to supervise the application of that treaty'. Implicit is the acknowledgement of a special status inherent in

[29] *Ahmadou Sadio Diallo*, merits, *supra* note 6, at para.66. See P. R. Ghandhi, 'Human Rights and the International Court of Justice in the *Ahmadou Sadio Diallo* Case', *Human Rights Law Review* 11, 3 (2011): 536.

[30] See Judge Cançado Trindade, address to the 100th session of the Human Rights Committee, UN Doc. CCPR/C/SR. 2772 (2010), paras. 1–17.

the HRC's creation by the Covenant and its members' election by States parties.

Secondly, the need to achieve 'clarity and the essential consistency of international law' suggests a concern to avoid the fragmentation that could arise from two conceivable interpretations: one, that suggested by a general international law approach and one suggested by a more human rights-centred approach. In fact, it is clear that the Court is aware that the requirement to interpret any treaty in the light of its object and purpose[31] will conduce to an outcome that could not be human rights neutral in respect of a human rights treaty. A third motivation of the Court is to vouchsafe the 'legal security' to which the individual rights bearers and the State party duty bearers are entitled. While located in a passage dealing with the fragmentation issue, the underlying concern, then, is that the Committee needs to be understood as speaking with determinative authority, given the role assigned to it by the Covenant. Accordingly, in *Diallo*, the ICJ laid the basis for the respect it accorded both to decisions on individual communications and to General Comments. *Diallo* itself only involved these two outputs. The *IFAD* and *Hissène Habré* cases (the latter of the Committee against Torture) only involved individual cases, while the *Wall* case alone also made use of concluding observations. As will be seen below, the concluding observations in question played a central role in the Court's reasoning.

IV. Human rights issues addressed by the ICJ

The issues that have been of concern to the World Court when referring to treaty body outputs have been of both a procedural (jurisdictional) and substantive nature. These two categories will be dealt with separately.

(i) Procedural issues

a. Extra-territorial jurisdiction

One question that was central to the Court's handling of the *Wall* case was that of whether the International Covenant on Civil and Political Rights (ICCPR) required States parties to apply the Covenant outside their territorial jurisdiction. The matter was one of interpretation of Covenant Article 2 (i) which reads:

[31] Vienna Convention on the Law of Treaties, 23 May 1969, 1155 UNTS 331; (1969) 8 ILM 679, Art. 31.

> Each State Party to the present Covenant undertakes to respect and to ensure to all individuals within its territory and subject to its jurisdiction the rights recognized in the present Covenant, without distinction of any kind, such as race, colour, sex, language, religion, political or other opinion, national or social origin, property, birth or other status.

The issue was whether this language meant that human rights guarantees contained in the Covenant benefitted only those persons who were both under the legal jurisdiction of the State and were at the same time geographically located within the territory of the State. That is, did the Covenant have extra-territorial effect?[32] The position defended on behalf of Israel and traditionally upheld by the United States of America was that this (conjunctive) reading was the correct understanding of the provision. The alternative (disjunctive) reading, consistently defended by the Committee, was that the Covenant guarantees extended to persons within the States' territories and to persons within the jurisdiction, but who may be outside the territory. The Court preferred the Committee's interpretation. Having looked to the object and purpose of the Covenant, from which it inferred that it would be 'natural' for States to be bound even when acting outside its frontiers, it immediately noted that 'the constant practice of the Human Rights Committee is consistent with this'. It referred to cases of arrests effected by Uruguay in Brazil and Argentina, as well as a case of a confiscated passport involving the same State party in Germany.[33] Then, having sought corroboration of its purposive interpretation of Article 2(i) in this case law of the Committee, it turned to the *travaux préparatoires* to corroborate the Committee's own approach.

[32] See Michael J. Dennis and Andre M. Surena, 'Application of the International Covenant on Civil and Political Rights in Times of Armed Conflict and Military Occupation: The Gap between Legal Theory and State Practice', *European Human Rights Law Review* 6 (2008): 714; and Nigel Rodley, 'The Extraterritorial Reach and Applicability in Armed Conflict of the International Covenant on Civil and Political Rights: A Rejoinder to Dennis and Surena', *European Human Rights Law Review* 6 (2009): 628. See generally, *Extraterritorial Application of Human Rights Treaties*, edited by Fons Coomans and Menno T. Kamminga (Antwerp: Intersentia, 2004); Marko Milanovic, *Extraterritorial Application of Human Rights Treaties: Law Principles, and Policy*(Oxford: Oxford University Press, 2011); and Ralph Wilde, 'Human Rights Beyond Borders at the World Court: The Significance of the International Court of Justice's Jurisprudence on the Extraterritorial Application of International Human Rights Treaties', *Chinese Journal of International Law* 12 (2013): 639.

[33] *López Burgos* v. *Uruguay*, Communication No. 52/79 (1981) UN Doc. CCPR/C/OP/1 at 88 (1984); *Celiberti de Casariego* v. *Uruguay*, Communication No. 56/79 (1981) UN Doc. CCPR/C/OP/1 at 92 (1984); *Montero* v. *Uruguay*, Communication No. 106/81, UN Doc. Supp. No. 40 (A/38/40) at 186 (1983).

Having found the necessary corroboration, it then referred to the Committee's concluding observations on Israel in 1998[34] and 2003, the latter specifically addressing the responsibility of the State party's 'authorities or agents' in the occupied territories.[35] The Court unambiguously concluded that it considered that the Covenant 'is applicable in respect of acts done by a State in the exercise of its jurisdiction outside its own territory'.[36]

b. Jurisdiction in armed conflict

In addition to the dimension of the extra-territorial applicability of the ICCPR, the case of Israel also raised the issue of its applicability in time of armed conflict. Israel has consistently maintained that international human rights law (IHRL) stops where international humanitarian law (IHL) begins. A variation on this is that, to the extent that IHRL applies, it is to be sought in the *lex specialis* of IHL.

Some credence was given to this conception in the ICJ's *Nuclear Weapons* advisory opinion.[37] There the Court addressed the argument – not unconvincing given that the human rights paradigm is one where State power is stable and the individual is relatively weak and in need of protection from it – that 'the Covenant was directed to the protection of human rights in peacetime, but that questions relating to unlawful loss of life in hostilities were governed by the law applicable in armed conflict'.[38] The Court's response was 'that the protection of the [Covenant] does not cease in times of war, except by operation of Article 4 of the Covenant whereby certain provisions may be derogated from in time of national emergency'.[39] However, it then went on to say that the content of Article 6 fell to be determined by the applicable *lex specialis*, namely, the law applicable in armed conflict.[40]

It may be noted parenthetically that the HRC had twelve years earlier adopted General Comment no. 14 on the Right to Life and Nuclear Weapons.[41] The Court ignored it. This was perhaps to the benefit of

[34] UN Doc. CCPR/C/79/Add.93 (1998), para. 10.

[35] UN Doc. CCPR/CO/78/ISR (2003), para. 11.

[36] *Wall, supra* note 5, 180 at para. 111. The Court could have cited *General comment no. 31, supra*, note 15, para. 10, but this was only adopted and made public after proceedings in the *Wall* opinion had closed.

[37] *Legality of the Threat or Use of Nuclear Weapons*, advisory opinion, 1996, ICJ 226.

[38] *Ibid.*, 239–40 at para. 24. [39] *Ibid.*, 240 at para. 25. [40] *Ibid.*

[41] UN Human Rights Committee, *CCPR General Comment no. 14: Article 6 (Right to Life) Nuclear Weapons and the Right to Life*, 9 November 1984.

the Committee which, with no substantiation, had gone as far as to opine that '[t]he production, testing, possession, deployment and use of nuclear weapons should be prohibited and recognized as crimes against humanity'.[42] This was not the sort of Committee output that an international judicial body could be expected to treat with uncritical respect.[43]

In the *Wall* opinion the Court reiterated the words quoted above from the *Nuclear Weapons* opinion. It then made clear that IHL would not always be the *lex specialis* for IHRL:

> As regards the relationship between international humanitarian law and human rights law, there are thus three possible situations: some rights may be exclusively matters of international humanitarian law; others may be exclusively matters of human rights law; yet others may be matters of both these branches of international law.[44]

In addition to the previous approval of the position of the HRC, the Court also invoked the rejection by the Committee on Economic, Social and Cultural Rights of Israel's claim that the International Covenant on Economic, Social and Cultural Rights was inapplicable to the occupied territory 'inasmuch as they are part and parcel of the context of armed conflict, as distinct from a relationship of human rights'.[45]

(ii) *Substantive issues*

a. Freedom of movement

Freedom of movement has been a central issue in two cases: the *Wall* opinion and *Diallo*. In the *Wall* opinion, the issue was whether the security barrier – that at some points took the form of a wall several metres high – was an unlawful interference with the freedom of Palestinians to move within their territory, according to the guarantee of ICCPR

42 *Ibid.*, para. 6.

43 Yet Nauru and the Solomon Islands invoked the General Comment (Nauru, at 20; Solomon Islands, at paras. 4.34–5). The United Kingdom, responding, pointed out that it was controversial and was evidently anyway clearly making a Statement *de lege ferenda*. (para. 3.107); note, the submission also supported the broader notion of IHL being the *lex specialis*, not only for the right to life, but '*a fortiori*, in respect of the protection of other human rights' (para. 3.109), accessed from the Court's website 5 May 2014: www.icj-cij.org/docket/index.php?p1=3&p2=4&k=5a&case=131&code=mwp&p3=1.

44 *Wall*, *supra* note 5, 180–1 at para. 106.

45 *Ibid.*, para. 112.

Article 12(1).[46] The Court noted that this was not an absolute right: it would, under sub-paragraph 3, be subject to restrictions for certain public purposes.[47] In determining the scope of the principle in the light of the permitted restriction, the Court specifically cited the approach of the HRC as contained in its General Comment no. 27, namely, that the restrictive measures 'must conform to the principle of proportionality' and 'must be the least intrusive instrument amongst those which might achieve the desired result'.[48] The ICJ concluded on the facts that these conditions were not met.

In *Diallo*, the pertinent issue was whether the expulsion of a Guinean national from the Democratic Republic of the Congo (DRC) had been reached in accordance with the law in conformity with Covenant Article 13.[49] The Court interpreted the paragraph as both requiring an expulsion's consistency with national law (a necessary condition) and that it be consistent with other Covenant provisions and not be arbitrary (sufficient conditions).[50] It then found that this interpretation was 'fully corroborated by the jurisprudence of the Human Rights Committee', citing an Optional Protocol case (*Maroufidou* v. *Sweden*) and Committee General Comment no. 15 (on the position of aliens under the Covenant).[51] The reference to the *Maroufidou* case, in which the Committee did not find a violation, was to the paragraph (9.3) requiring consistency of the proposed measure with both the provisions of the Covenant and the procedural and substantive aspects of national law. Paragraph 10 of General Comment no. 15 stresses the goal of avoiding arbitrariness. On the facts, the Court held that the DRC had violated Article 13 by not ensuring a prior consultation by the body established by law before an expulsion measure may be undertaken and by failing to give substantial reasons for the expulsion.[52]

[46] International Covenant on Civil and Political Rights, 16 December 1966, 999 UNTS 171, Art. 12 (1) reads: 'Everyone lawfully within the territory of a State shall, within that territory, have the right to liberty of movement and freedom to choose his residence.'

[47] *Wall*, *supra* note 5, 192–3 at para. 136.

[48] *Ibid.*

[49] Art. 13 reads: 'An alien lawfully in the territory of a State Party to the present Covenant may be expelled therefrom only in pursuance of a decision reached in accordance with law and shall, except where compelling reasons of national security otherwise require, be allowed to submit the reasons against his expulsion and to have his case reviewed by, and be represented for the purpose before, the competent authority or a person or persons especially designated by the competent authority.'

[50] *Ahmadou Sadio Diallo*, merits, *supra* note 6, at para.65; see *Maroufidou* v. *Sweden*, Communication No. 58/1979 (1981), UN Doc. CCPR/C/OP/1 at 65 (1984).

[51] *Ibid.*, 663–4 at para. 66.

[52] *Ibid.*, 665–6 at para. 72.

Two of the ICJ judges disagreed with the majority view that Article 13 contained an independent element of arbitrariness in addition to the need for lawfulness and the procedural protection it requires. They argued, not that the HRC, as quoted by the Court, had got it wrong, but that the Court had misread the HRC. They argued, with some justice, that in General Comment no. 15 all the Committee was doing was citing the avoidance of arbitrariness as a purpose of the procedures (indicating the avoidance of mass expulsions), while in *Maroufidou* the Committee had not referred to arbitrariness as an independent element.[53] The issue then was merely one of how to interpret the Committee's outputs, not about the correctness of their content.

b. Liberty and security of person

Guinea's complaints about Mr Diallo's arrests and detentions (there were two admissible phases of arrest and detention[54]) claimed that the detentions were unlawful under DRC law and that they were arbitrary, thus violating ICCPR Article 9(1).[55] There was also a claim for failure to inform him of the reasons for the arrest as required by Article 9(2). On the facts, the Court would and did have no trouble in upholding the claims, as long as detention effected for the purpose of effecting a deportation fell under Article 9 at all. On this, the Court cited HRC General Comment no. 8 dealing with Article 9 in support of its view that Article 9 would 'apply in principle to any form of arrest or detention decided upon and carried out by a public authority, whatever its legal basis and the objective being pursued'.[56] Indeed, the first paragraph of the General Comment made clear that the Committee's view that Article 9 covered 'all deprivations of liberty, whether in criminal cases or in other cases such as, for example . . . immigration control etc.'. In a separate opinion Judge Cançado Trindade examined, approvingly, the Committee's case law at length, albeit not apparently to disagree with the majority.[57]

53 Separate Opinion Judges Greenwood and Keith in *Ahmadou Sadio Diallo*, merits, *supra* note 6, 712.

54 An earlier one was inadmissible.

55 Art. 9 (1) reads: 'Everyone has the right to liberty and security of person. No one shall be subjected to arbitrary arrest or detention. No one shall be deprived of his liberty except on such grounds and in accordance with such procedure as are established by law.'

56 *Ahmadou Sadio Diallo*, merits, *supra* note 6, at para. 77.

57 *Ibid.*, 678–9 at paras. 112–16 and 687 at paras. 145–7.

c. Reparation

In *Diallo* the Court decided, without reference to but consistent with the practice of the HRC, that reparation for the violations of Articles 9 and 13 of the ICCPR should take the form of compensation for non-material and material injury. The Court noted that the HRC refrained from awarding specific sums, but rather indicated the need for 'adequate compensation'.[58] Accordingly, the Court looked to the practice of those tribunals that had previously awarded specific sums by way of compensation (especially the European and Inter-American Courts of Human Rights). Judge Cançado Trindade also referred to other forms of reparation that the HRC considered appropriate according to the nature of the violation, including restitution, rehabilitation and satisfaction.[59]

d. Ill-treatment of prisoners and universal jurisdiction regarding torture

International treaty body practice on treatment of prisoners played a minor role in the *Diallo* case. Here Guinea had argued that Mr Diallo had been ill-treated in detention. The Court dismissed the claim for want of evidence. It did not refer to treaty body practice. However, it made an *obiter dictum* apparently inconsistent with that practice. This pointed out that, contrary to the claim of Guinea, Mr Diallo was able to communicate with his lawyers and relatives 'without any great difficulty.' It continued: 'even if this had not been the case, such constraints would not *per se* have constituted treatment prohibited by Article 10, paragraph 1 of the Covenant'.[60] In fact, HRC General Comment no. 21 dealing with Article 10 refers to the relevance of contacts with the outside world (family, lawyer, social and medical services, non-governmental organizations).[61] Indeed, General Comment no. 21 on the prohibition of torture and ill-treatment noted that protection of the detainee 'requires that prompt and regular

[58] *Ahmadou Sadio Diallo*, compensation, *supra* note 6, at para. 24. The same was true for the African Commission on Human Rights, whose African Charter on Human and Peoples' Rights the Court, 17 June 1981, 1520 UNTS 323, was also applying: *ibid.*

[59] Separate Opinion Judge Cançado Trindade in *Ahmadou Sadio Diallo*, merits, *supra* note 6, 800 at paras. 208–9, but these would not be typical in Art. 9 cases.

[60] *Ahmadou Sadio Diallo*, merits, *supra* note 6, 671 at para. 88; Art. 10 (1) reads: 'All persons deprived of their liberty shall be treated with humanity and with respect for the inherent dignity of the human person.'

[61] UN Human Rights Committee, *CCPR General Comment no. 21: Article 10 (Humane Treatment of Persons Deprived of Their Liberty)*, 10 April 1992, para. 12.

access be given to doctors and lawyers'.[62] Since the Court's observation was evidently speculative and may, as suggested by Judge Cançado Trinidade, 'have taken a somewhat hurried decision on this particular point' (that is, the treatment issue),[63] the Court's dictum should not be accorded too much weight, either in respect of the substantive issue or as regards the position of the Committee.

The obligations of States under the UN Convention against Torture and Other Cruel, Inhuman or Degrading Treatment or Punishment (UNCAT) were, by contrast, central to the issues in the *Hissène Habré* case, in which two cases decided by the Committee against Torture played a significant role. The case was brought by Belgium, which was seeking extradition of former Chadean dictator Hissène Habré, in particular under the universal jurisdiction clauses ('prosecute or extradite') of UNCAT. Indeed, the failure of Senegal to submit the case to prosecution, after its *Cour de Cassation* had declared that there was no legislative basis for prosecuting Habré, and the finding by the Committee of a consequent violation in the *Guengueng* case were part of Belgium's case against Senegal.[64] The Court had no difficulty in following the *Guengueng* case in respect of the finding that the delays in adopting legislation permitting Senegalese jurisdiction violated Article 6 or UNCAT[65] and the finding that the failure to submit the case for prosecution violated Article 7.[66] There had been no extradition request at the time of *Guengueng*, but the Court found, like the Committee, that the obligation to prosecute did not depend on the existence of a prior request for extradition.[67]

However, it relied on the very first individual case of the Committee, *O.R., M.M. and M.S.* v. *Argentina*, to conclude that the Convention applied only to acts committed after Senegal became a party to the Convention. Judge Cançado Trindade was critical of this, given that *Guengueng* (and

[62] *Ibid.*, para. 11.

[63] Separate Opinion Judge Cançado Trindade in *Ahmadou Sadio Diallo*, merits, *supra* note 6, 752 at para. 72, pointing out that the burden of proof in such cases should fall on the State.

[64] *Suleymane Guengueng et al.* v. *Senegal*, Communication No. 181/2001, UN Doc. CAT/C/36/D/181/2001 (2006).

[65] *Hissène Habré*, *supra* note 3, 452–3 at para. 81. Art. 6 requires States parties to detain a person alleged to be responsible for torture, make a preliminary inquiry and inform other relevant States parties.

[66] *Ibid.*, 460–1 at para. 117. Art. 7 requires States parties to try or extradite alleged torturers on their territory.

[67] *Ibid.*, 456 at para. 94.

another case[68]) had established no such limitation.[69] On the other hand, except in respect of continuing offences, such as enforced disappearance,[70] the doctrine of non-retroactivity is traditional treaty law.[71] The Court dismissed the relevance of *Guengueng*, on the grounds that the question of the temporal scope of the obligations containing in the Convention had not been not raised, nor had the Committee itself raised that question.[72] In fact, it might have been open to the Court to conclude *ratione temporis* that, even though Senegal's obligation to prosecute could not have arisen before 26 June 1987 when the Covenant entered into force for Senegal, that obligation, once established, could have extended to acts of torture committed before that date. The Court's basic predisposition was to follow the Committee's cautious approach in its very first cases.

e. Fair hearing

The *IFAD* case[73] concerned an 'appeal' by the Director-General of the International Fund for Agricultural Development against a decision of the Administrative Tribunal of the International Labour Organization (ILOAT) upholding a staff member's claim against dismissal. The question arose whether the Court should exercise its discretion not to respond to the request in view of the anachronistic inequality of status between the employer and the employee. Under the ILOAT statute only the employing organization could refer a case to the ICJ if it disagreed with the Tribunal decision, not the employee if the case went against her. Moreover under the Statute of the ICJ, only States have standing for the Court's contentious jurisdiction and, in any event, even in advisory proceedings[74] only States and intergovernmental organizations have standing to appear personally in the proceedings. The Court decided that in the circumstances it could give the requested opinion while signalling that, if the inequality were

[68] *Bouabdallah Ltaief v. Tunisia*, Communication No. 189/2001, UN Doc. CAT/C/31/D/189/2001 (2003).

[69] Separate opinion Judge Cançado Trindade in *Hissène Habré*, *supra* note 3, 551–2 at para. 163.

[70] In fact, that first case concerned, not the typical problem of torture of prisoners, but of persons whose disappearance was argued to be a form of torture.

[71] *Hissène Habré*, *supra* note 3, 457 at para. 100.

[72] *Ibid.*, 457–8 at para. 101.

[73] *Judgment No. 2867 of the Administrative Tribunal of the International Labour Organization upon a Complaint Filed against the International Fund for Agricultural Development (IFAD)*, advisory opinion, 2012, ICJ 10.

[74] 'Appeals' from some administrative tribunals of the UN family can take place by reference to the Court for an advisory opinion, which the relevant secretariats are committed to accept.

maintained, it may not do so in future.[75] It did so having found a way at least to redress the imbalance in terms of participants in the proceedings. Since it could not permit the staff member to submit documentation or to appear personally before it, it required the IFAD Director-General to transmit all material that she wished to submit and it refused the IFAD oral proceedings, given that the staff member could not appear in person.

The cornerstone of, and so the authority for, the ICJ's reasoning in favour of the need for equality of arms is found in paragraph 39:

> To turn to the general question of the concept of equality, the development of the principle of equality of access to courts and tribunals since 1946, when the review procedure was established, may be seen in the significant differences between the two General Comments by the Human Rights Committee on Article 14, paragraph 1, of the International Covenant on Civil and Political Rights of 1966. That provision requires that '[a]ll persons shall be equal before the courts and tribunals.' The first Comment, adopted in 1984, just seven years after the Covenant came into force, did no more than repeat the terms of the provision and call on States to report more fully on steps taken to ensure equality before the courts, including equal access to the courts (HRC, General Comment No. 13: Article 14 (Administration of Justice), paras. 2–3). The later Comment, one adopted in 2007 on the basis of 30 years of experience in the application of the above-mentioned Article 14, gives detailed attention to equality before domestic courts and tribunals. According to the Committee, that right to equality guarantees equal access and equality of arms. While in non-criminal matters the right of equal access does not address the issue of the right of appeal, if procedural rights are accorded they must be provided to all the parties unless distinctions can be justified on objective and reasonable grounds (Human Rights Committee, General Comment No. 32: Right to Equality before Courts and Tribunals and to a Fair Trial, paras. 8–9, 12 and 13). In the case of the ILOAT, the Court is unable to see any such justification for the provision for review of the Tribunal's decisions which favours the employer to the disadvantage of the staff member.[76]

The passage stresses both equality of access and procedural equality. The comparison between the earlier and later General Comments is presumably intended to imply that the scope of the idea of equality may not have been so clear in 1984, but it was unmistakable nearly a quarter of a century later. The reference to the fact that under Covenant Article 14 there is no automatic right of appeal in non-criminal matters, but that where there is

[75] *IFAD*, *supra* note 73, 31 at para. 48. See also Separate Opinion of Judge Greenwood, in *ibid.*, 94.

[76] *IFAD*, *supra* note 73, 31 at para. 39.

appeal the parties should be equal – a point addressed clearly in the General Comment and reflecting the Committee's case law[77] – is presumably to offset any argument in favour of IFAD that Article 14 principles would not apply to an appeal in a non-criminal case.[78]

As it happens there were also delays in IFAD's cooperation with the procedure indicated by the Court to assist submissions by the staff member. One is tempted to conclude that, had it not been clear that its decision would be to uphold the ILOAT decision in her favour, which gave it the opportunity to deliver a withering demolition of the system and of the behaviour of IFAD before and during the ICJ proceedings, it would indeed have declined jurisdiction as requested by the staff member.[79] It was for all of this that the HRC's General Comment provided the authority.

V. Conclusion

The stars may well have been aligned when the ICJ considered the first case (after the *Genocide Convention* case) in which it had to confront human rights issues head on, that is, the *Wall* case. In that case, several of the judges had had experience of human rights work in UN bodies. Judge Al-Khasawneh had been a member of the Sub-Commission on Promotion and Protection of Human Rights and Judge Kooijmans had been the first UN Special Rapporteur on the question of torture. Meanwhile, Judges Buergenthal and Higgins had been members of the Human Rights Committee, while Judge Simma had been a member of the Committee on Economic, Social and Cultural Rights. There can be little doubt that this group brought with them a predisposition in favour of the human rights project generally and its institutional guardians specifically. This can only have been helpful in a court that had traditionally been hyper-respectful of the sovereign prerogatives of States. As has been seen, IHRL represents a substantial limitation on earlier notions of State sovereignty. These judges could educate their colleagues in both the subject-matter of IHRL and the seriousness of the institutions, especially what was perceived as the most senior treaty body, the Human Rights Committee.[80] Having been

[77] *Paul Perterer v. Austria*, Communication No. 1015/2001, UN Doc. CCPR/C/81/D/1015/2001 (2004).

[78] The only area of law in which the Covenant expressly requires provision for review of a judgment by a higher court is in the case of convictions for crimes, in Art. 14(5).

[79] *IFAD*, *supra* note 73, 27–8 at para. 40.

[80] Note CERD was adopted a year before the ICCPR, but the power of its Committee to deal with individual petitions under Article 12 came into force after the Optional Protocol to

apprised of this, it would follow that the Court would treat the outputs of the treaty bodies with respect, not just because of their official provenance and functions, but also because they had demonstrated that such respect was due in fact.

Once it was established that the treaty bodies and their outputs had to be reckoned with, it followed that it was important that there be as much coherence as possible as regards the pronouncements of the Court and the treaty bodies. This perception was highlighted by the prevalent concern about the risks of 'fragmentation' of public international law. Indeed, it is no accident that when the Court came to articulate the basis of its policy of presumptive deference to the Human Rights Committee (and other universal and regional treaty bodies) in the *Diallo* case, it particularly underlined the value of achieving 'the necessary clarity and the essential consistency of international law', in other words the value of avoiding fragmentation.

There has been a limited number of cases in which the Court has had to adjudicate human rights issues, albeit that these cases have covered a substantial number of them, including the rights to life, to liberty and security of the person and to a fair hearing, as well as some economic and social rights. The importance of the procedural or jurisdictional dimension, especially as regards the extra-territorial application of the ICCPR and the relationship with IHL should also not be underestimated.

Nevertheless, the Court has wisely reserved its own independent power of appreciation. After all, just as no single court has a monopoly of wisdom, neither does any one quasi-judicial treaty body. Indeed, it may well be that even different human rights treaty bodies may strive but fail to reach the same view of the same facts.[81]

For example, on the one hand, the Human Rights Committee has changed its practice in respect of automatic deprivation of the voting rights of people with mental disability. It now follows the view of the Committee on the Rights of Persons with Disabilities (CRPD) that any such deprivation must not be status based, but may only be on the grounds of actual individual inability. On the other hand, the Committee is unable to follow what seems to be the practice of the CRPD in determining that

the Covenant that gave the Human Rights Committee the same power. The later body soon built up a far more substantial body of case law. As to the relevance of the backgrounds of the judges, see Higgins, *supra* note 1, at 746.

[81] See Using Other Treaty Bodies' Interpretations to Construe the Covenant, Draft note prepared by the Rapporteur Mr Gerald L. Neuman, UN Doc. CCPR/C/109/R.4, discussed in public session at the 3066th meeting of the Human Rights Committee, 28 March 2014.

no mental disability whatever can justify denial of direct autonomous decision-making.[82]

It remains important for all decision-making bodies applying IHRL to seek to avoid taking positions that would place States in a situation of conflicting obligations. Consistency and coherence are inescapable demands of the rule of law. As long as the application of IHRL is not a regular feature of the World Court's docket, it is appropriate that when it does have occasion to interpret human rights treaties, it continues to apply the (inevitably rebuttable) presumption that a treaty body's interpretation of its own treaty is the appropriate one.

[82] Compare UN Human Rights Committee, General Comment no. 35 on liberty and security of person, adopted October 2014: procedures for detention 'should ensure respect for the views of the individual' (para. 19) with Committee on the Rights of Persons with Disabilities General Comment no. 1, UN Doc. CRPD/C/GC/1 (2014): 'detention [of persons with disabilities] in institutions against their will . . . constitutes arbitrary deprivation of liberty' (para. 36).

5

The ICJ and the challenges of human rights law

VERA GOWLLAND-DEBBAS

I. Introduction

Alongside the so-called fragmentation and compartmentalization of international law into separate sectorial areas of international law, we have paradoxically seen universalizing tendencies in the emergence and expansion of a domain of general or public interest – a sort of *ordre public* – based on objective community interests, which is juxtaposed alongside a network of contractual relations between atomistic States. While this development may be nebulous, it nevertheless encapsulates certain norms which undeniably have vital functions in the system ranging from maintenance of international public order and the incorporation into law of a certain universal moral or ethical foundation to the very survival of our species.[1]

In this consequent process of hierarchization of international law, human rights law has gained centre stage and its tentacles have permeated various functional fields of international law, whether international humanitarian law (IHL), international criminal law, collective security, environmental law, development or investment law, or has been internalized in the law of international institutions under external pressure and with consequent re-interpretation of mandates.

While human rights law has been acknowledged as forming part and parcel of general international law,[2] human rights treaty bodies have at the same time also upheld its special character, claiming the right, for example, to diverge from the reservations regime of the 1969 Vienna Convention

Emeritus Professor of Public International Law, Graduate Institute, Geneva.

[1] See Vera Gowlland-Debbas, 'Issues Arising from the Interplay between Different Areas of International Law', 63 *Current Legal Problems* (2010) 597–630.

[2] The ECtHR has often contended that the European Convention 'should so far as possible be interpreted in harmony with other rules of international law of which it forms a part' (see, e.g., *Al-Adsani* v. *UK*, Application no. 35763/97, judgment of 21 November 2001, para. 55).

on the Law of Treaties (VCLT) or from the rules on State succession. It is evident also that human rights law has skewed the traditional inter-State framework of international law. In relation to the sources of international law for example, human rights law, like IHL or international criminal law, has derived its binding force less from a general practice of States than from its underlying relevance for the protection of fundamental global interests.[3]

The International Court of Justice (ICJ) could not remain impervious to this increasingly individually oriented international law and has been solicited in a growing number of cases raising serious violations of human rights as well as humanitarian law: right to self-determination, racial discrimination, human rights in armed conflict, grave breaches of the Geneva Conventions, torture and genocide, among others.

A priori, of course, nothing disbars the Court from handling disputes concerning human rights since it has jurisdiction in all legal disputes over any question of international law brought to it by the parties. In addition, the Court has always been conscious that it is not only an autonomous adjudicative body with its own Statute, but that as the principal judicial organ of the United Nations, it is bound to promote the purposes and principles of the Charter in which human rights occupies a prominent place. As such it has played a non-negligible and on occasion a significant role in the development of international human rights law and the place it occupies within general international law.[4]

[3] See Anja Seibert-Fohr, 'Unity and Diversity in the Formation and Relevance of Customary International Law', in Andreas Zimmermann and Rainer Hofmann (eds.), *Unity and Diversity of International Law* (Berlin: Duncker & Humblot, 2006), pp. 257–88; and Vera Gowlland-Debbas, 'Comment', in *ibid.*, pp. 285–97, at 288.

[4] For an early treatment of the Court and human rights issues, see: Vera Gowlland-Debbas, 'Judicial Insights into the Fundamental Values and Interests of the International Community', in A. S. Muller, D. Raic and J. M. Thuranszky (eds.), *The International Court of Justice: Its Future Role After 50 Years* (Hague: Martinus Nijhoff, 1997), pp. 327–66; more recently by the same author: 'The Role of the International Court of Justice in the Formulation and Development of Fundamental Norms of International Law', in S. S. Caballero and R. A. Stoffels (eds.), *Retos de la Jurisdiccion Internacional* (Madrid: Thomson Reuters, 2012), pp. 69–95. For two contributions by Judges of the ICJ, see Rosalyn Higgins, 'Human Rights in the International Court of Justice', 20 *Leiden Journal of International Law* (2007) 745–51; Bruno Simma, 'Human Rights Before the International Court of Justice: Community Interest Coming to Life?', in Christian Tams and James Sloan (eds.), *The Development of International Law by the International Court of Justice* (Oxford University Press, 2013), pp. 301–25; and by the same author, 'Mainstreaming Human Rights: The Contribution of the International Court of Justice', 3 *Journal of International Dispute Settlement* (2012) 7–29.

It has done that notwithstanding that human rights issues in their large majority have come before it in a sporadic and incidental manner and in cases in which human rights may not even have been at the core of the dispute – the 1948–9 *Corfu Channel* case which had to do with military intervention and the 1970 *Barcelona Traction* case dealing with diplomatic protection of shareholders of corporations, or the 1996 Advisory Opinion on the Legality of Nuclear Weapons, are cases in point. Some disputes before the Court have arisen in the context of past or on-going armed conflicts (the ICJ has a role to play in peace maintenance as is underlined in the Charter). However, the bringing of inter-State disputes directly under the compromissory clauses of human rights instruments, namely, the Genocide Convention, the International Convention on the Elimination of Racial Discrimination (CERD) and the Convention against Torture (CAT) is a recent development which has meant that the Court has had to face human rights issues squarely where it has claimed jurisdiction.

In adjudicating human rights issues, the ICJ has faced a number of challenges. Not least is the fact that it is an inter-State court open only to States under its contentious jurisdiction, and reliant on State consent, while human rights as intra-State rights touch on sensitive issues of sovereignty which States may be reluctant to bring before the Court. It is, of course, less constrained in its advisory function, which may explain the important role advisory opinions have played in addressing human rights issues.

In addition, the outcome of many of these cases have depended on the vision which particular judges have had of the role the Court should play in the development of international law. Sir Hersch Lauterpacht was of the view that the Court had a duty to consciously and conscientiously further the development of international law and not just to react to existing law; it should not create the impression of ethical indifference, nor act as an 'automatic slot-machine'. He also adhered to the notion that 'behind the personified institutions called States there are in every case individual human beings to whom the precepts of international law are addressed . . . '.[5] But attitudes to the judicial function and to notions of

[5] See Shabtai Rosenne, 'Sir Hersch Lauterpacht's Concept of the Task of the International Judge' 55 *AJIL* (1961) 825, 835, 854–5. See also the views of Judge Alvarez, who as far back as 1949 would have had the Court fulfil a new mission, 'that of creating and formulating new precepts' to bring the law into harmony with the new conditions of social and international relations, founded on social interdependence, owing also 'to the predominance of the general interest' states were 'bound by many rules which have not been ordered by their will': *Corfu Channel Case (UK* v. *Albania)* (Merits), ICJ Reports 1949, Individual opinion

justice have differed. Judges like Fitzmaurice were very sensitive to the dangers of exceeding the limits of the judicial function, which explains his dissent in the *Namibia* and *SW Africa* cases,[6] while Judge Guillaume believed in transactional justice, the role of the ICJ being that of strictly addressing the dispute at hand and no more.[7]

The Court itself has stated on numerous occasions that it 'states the existing law and does not legislate. This is so even if, in stating and applying the law, the Court necessarily has to specify its scope and sometimes note its general trend.'[8]

This juxtaposition of views may probably be too simplistic an approach. As Judge Kooijmans has pointed out:

> in actual practice the situation often, be it not always, is rather nebulous. The ICJ is a collegiate body and both approaches will be reflected in its composition. And the final product of the deliberations, whether a judgment or an advisory opinion, will usually be more determined by the specificities of the case than by a contest of approaches.[9]

Nevertheless, the practice of the ICJ has illustrated at different times these different sets of views as reflected in the outcome of such cases as the 1966 *SW Africa* cases in which the Court denied legal standing to the two African States which had brought the case to it and which has classically been contrasted to the more daring 1971 Advisory Opinion in *Namibia* as well as, I should add, the recent 2004 *Wall* case.

The election to the Court of judges who had previously served in international human rights bodies – Rosalyn Higgins, Peter Kooijmans, Thomas Buergenthal, Bruno Simma and Antonio CançadoTrindade – were also, as Judge Higgins has herself written, to provide 'a "critical mass" of persons particularly versed in human rights law', thus contributing 'to human rights being viewed as in the centre of what the Court does, not

of Judge Alvarez, pp. 40 and 43; *International Status of South West Africa*, ICJ Reports 1950, Dissenting Opinion of Judge Alvarez, pp. 175–7.

6 J.G. Merrills, *Judge Sir Gerald Fitzmaurice and the Discipline of International Law: Opinions on the International Court of Justice, 1961–1973* (The Hague: Kluwer, 1998), pp. 70–4.

7 See Gilbert Guillaume, 'Transformations du droit international et jurisprudence de la Cour Internationale de Justice', in R. Ben Achour and S. Laghmani (eds.), *Les nouveaux aspects du droit international* (Paris: Pedone, 1994), pp. 175–92.

8 *Legality of the Threat or Use of Nuclear Weapons* (Advisory Opinion), ICJ Reports 1996, para. 18. See also *South West Africa (Liberia* v. *South Africa*; *Ethiopia* v. *South Africa)*, ICJ Reports 1966, para. 89.

9 P. Kooijmans, 'The ICJ in the 21st Century: Judicial Restraint, Judicial Activism, or Proactive Judicial Policy', 56 *ICLQ* (2007) 741–53 at 742.

at the margin'. She adds: '[t]he passage of time, and the change of judicial culture more generally, have played their role, too'.[10]

II. The contribution of the court to the development of human rights law

A. *Minority rights and the Permanent Court of International Justice*

Well before the development of modern human rights law, the Permanent Court of International Justice (PCIJ) had recognized that treaties could create direct rights and obligations for private individuals enforceable in domestic courts.[11] With reference to the League of Nations' minority protection regime, the PCIJ had underlined that '[e]quality in law precludes discrimination of any kind; whereas equality in fact may involve the necessity of different treatment in order to attain a result which establishes an equilibrium between different situations'.[12] This concept of affirmative action, is by now familiar to human rights lawyers.

In another classic statement, the PCIJ initiated the process of erosion of the domestic jurisdiction barrier so important in the human rights field, by pointing out that: '[t]he question whether a certain matter is or is not solely within the jurisdiction of a State is an essentially relative question: it depends upon the development of international relations' and the current state of international law.[13] The subsequent development of UN Charter Article 2(7) spearheaded by the General Assembly bears witness to the way in which human rights issues are by now unquestionably accepted as falling within international jurisdiction and concern. Yet the PCIJ was, of course, at the same time also very deferential to State sovereignty.

B. *The ICJ and a hierarchical conception of human rights*

As in the case of the regulation of the use of force, the Court has held a hierarchical conception of human rights.

10 R. Higgins 'Human Rights in the International Court of Justice', 746.

11 *Jurisdiction of the Courts of Danzig* (1928), PCIJ Series B, No. 15, pp. 20–21, concerning the 1921 Agreement between the Free City of Danzig and Poland (the *Beamtenabkommen*).

12 *Minority Schools in Albania* (1935), PCIJ Series A/B, No. 64, pp. 19 and 17 on the need for equality while at the same time preserving the special characteristics of minorities. See also, *Certain Questions Relating to Settlers of German Origin in the Territory Ceded by Germany to Poland* (1923), PCIJ Series B, No. 6; *Treatment of Polish Nationals and Other Persons of Polish Origin or Speech in the Danzig Territory* (1932), PCIJ Series A/B, No. 44, p. 28: 'the prohibition against discrimination, in order to be effective, must ensure the absence of discrimination in fact as well as in law'.

13 *Nationality Decrees issued in Tunis and Morocco* (1923), PCIJ Series B, No. 4, pp. 23–4.

1) The concept of collective interest treaties

The ICJ has given voice to the concept of collective interest embedded in multilateral treaties having a humanitarian purpose. In its 1951 Advisory Opinion on *Reservations to the Genocide Convention*, the Court stated:

> In such a convention the contracting states do not have any interests of their own; they merely have, one and all, a common interest, namely, the accomplishment of those high purposes which are the raison d'être of the convention. Consequently, in a convention of this type one cannot speak of individual advantages or disadvantages to states, or of the maintenance of a perfect contractual balance between rights and duties . . . [14]

It was because of the nature of the Genocide Convention that the Court departed from the traditional unanimity rule in acceptance of reservations. Yet, ironically, although this reservations regime, subsequently incorporated with some exception in the 1969 VCLT had its origins in a human rights treaty, the human rights treaty bodies have underlined the special nature of their own instruments in questioning the appropriateness of having individual States determine the admissibility of reservations with respect to treaties, in which '[t]he principle of inter-State reciprocity has no place'.[15]

This concept of collective interest treaties has had an impact on their interpretation, leading the ICJ to adopt a teleological, evolutionary or dynamic approach. The Mandate for South-West Africa was considered to embody 'international engagements of general interest', insofar as it 'was created, in the interest of the inhabitants of the territory, and of humanity in general, as an international institution with an international

[14] *Reservations to the Convention on Genocide*, Advisory Opinion, ICJ Reports 1951, p. 23. Interestingly, because of the origins and character of the Convention and the fact that express provisions of the Convention (Articles XI and XVI) associate the General Assembly with the life of the Convention, the Court in matters of interpretation sought to establish not only the intentions of the contracting parties but also those of the United Nations and the object and purpose which the United Nations had in mind in adopting the convention (*ibid.*, pp. 19–20, 23). For the concept of collective interest treaties, see D. N. Hutchinson, 'Solidarity and Breaches of Multilateral Treaties', 59 *BYIL* (1988) 151–215, and Vera Gowlland-Debbas, 'The Role of the International Court of Justice in the Development of the Contemporary Law of Treaties', in Christian Tams and James Sloan (eds.), *The Development of International Law by the International Court of Justice* (Oxford University Press, 2013), pp. 25–52. This concept has been implicitly reflected in the law of treaties as well as the law of State responsibility.

[15] Human Rights Committee, General Comment No. 24 (52) (CCPR/C/21/Rev.1/Add.6), para. 17.

object – a sacred trust of civilization'.[16] In the subsequent *Namibia* Opinion, the Court, in referring to the evolution of the concept of 'sacred trust' embodied in Article 22 of the League Covenant, which it considered to have contained the seeds of the contemporary right of self-determination of peoples as its ultimate objective, had stated that though '[m]indful as it is of the primary necessity of interpreting an instrument in accordance with the intentions of the parties at the time of its conclusion', where the concepts embodied in a treaty are not static but 'by definition, evolutionary', their interpretation cannot remain unaffected by the subsequent development of the law and should be 'interpreted and applied within the framework of the entire legal system prevailing at the time of the interpretation'. It nevertheless tried not to depart too much from traditional consensual views of interpretation by stating that it surely must have been the intention of the parties to have considered the terms of the treaty to be evolutionary.[17] It should be said, however, that the Court has not restricted this evolutionary approach to the case of human rights treaties.[18]

Relying in some measure on the Court's pronouncement in the *Namibia* Opinion, the human rights treaty bodies have also approached their respective treaties as 'living instrument[s] which must be interpreted in the light of present-day conditions', upholding their fundamental and non-synallagmatic nature.[19]

[16] *International Status of South West Africa*, Advisory Opinion, ICJ Reports 1950, p. 132.

[17] *Legal Consequences for States of the Continued Presence of South Africa in Namibia (South West Africa) notwithstanding Security Council Resolution 276* (1970), Advisory Opinion, ICJ Reports 1971, para. 53.

[18] See *Aegean Sea Continental Shelf*, ICJ Reports 1978, para. 77; *Gabčíkovo-Nagymaros Project* (Hungary/Slovakia), ICJ Reports 1997, paras .112 and 140; more recently, *Navigational and Related Rights (Costa Rica* v. *Nicaragua)*, ICJ Reports 2009, paras. 64–8. The Court has approached the UN Charter in similar fashion in developing the doctrine of implied powers; see *Reparation for Injuries Suffered in the Services of the United Nations*, ICJ Reports 1949; *Certain Expenses of the United Nations (Art. 17, paragraph 2, of the Charter)*, ICJ Reports 1962; *Namibia*, ICJ Reports 1971; and *Western Sahara*, ICJ Reports 1975.

[19] See e.g *Ireland* v. *UK*, ECtHR, judgment of 18 January 1978, Ser A, No. 25,90, para. 239; *Matthews* v. *United Kingdom*, ECtHR, judgment of 18 February 1999, para. 39; also Inter-American Court of Human Rights, *Effect of Reservations on the Entry into Force of the American Convention on Human Rights (Arts 74 and 77)*, Advisory Opinion OC-2/82 of 24 September 1982, Ser A, No. 2 (1982), paras. 28 and 29; *Right to Information on Consular Assistance in the Framework of the Guarantees of the Due Process of Law*, Advisory Opinion OC-16/99, 1 October 1999, Ser A, No. 16 (1999), para. 114, in which the Court stated that 'human rights treaties are living instruments, whose interpretation ought to follow the evolution of times and the current conditions of life'. Similar reference to the *Namibia* opinion was made by the WTO Appellate Body, finding that the term 'exhaustible natural

Moreover, as will be seen in the *Belgium* v. *Senegal* case, the Court identified CAT as a treaty embodying obligations *erga omnes partes*. It declared:[20]

> As stated in its Preamble, the object and purpose of the Convention is 'to make more effective the struggle against torture . . . throughout the world'. The States parties to the Convention have a common interest to ensure, in view of their shared values, that acts of torture are prevented and that, if they occur, their authors do not enjoy impunity . . . All the other States parties have a common interest in compliance with these obligations by the State in whose territory the alleged offender is present. That common interest implies that the obligations in question are owed by any State party to all the other States parties to the Convention.

Finally, while the Court did not need to go into the question of State succession to establish its jurisdiction in the *Application of the Genocide Convention*, it did say that this was '[w]ithout prejudice as to whether or not the principle of "automatic succession" applies in the case of certain types of international treaties or conventions' and recalled the non-syllagmatic nature of the Genocide Convention, which it had underlined in its Advisory Opinion of 1951.[21]

2) The enrichment of the hierarchical terminology

The ICJ has also enriched, or some may think obfuscated, the hierarchical terminology. It has distinguished bilateralist obligations such as diplomatic protection from obligations deriving from the 'principles and rules concerning the basic rights of the human person, including protection from slavery and racial discrimination' (the oft-quoted *Barcelona Traction* case[22]) and the prohibition of genocide (*Application of the Genocide*

resources' in Article XX(g) of the GATT 1994 was 'by definition evolutionary', and that it 'must be read . . . in the light of contemporary concerns of the community of nations about the protection and conservation of the environment' (WTO, *United States–Import Prohibition of Certain Shrimp and Shrimp Products*, Report of the Appellate Body (12 October 1998) WT/DS58/AB/R, paras. 129–30).

[20] *Case concerning Questions Relating to the Obligation to Prosecute or Extradite (Belgium* v. *Senegal)*, ICJ Reports 2012, para. 68.

[21] *Case concerning Application of the Convention on the Prevention and Punishment of the Crime of Genocide (Bosnia-Herzegovina* v. *Yugoslavia)* (Preliminary Objections), ICJ Reports (1996), paras. 20–4. But see Separate Opinions of Judges Parra-Aranguren and Shahabbudeen, *ibid.*, pp. 656 and 637, respectively.

[22] *Barcelona Traction, Light and Power Company, Limited (Second Phase)*, ICJ Reports 1970, para. 33. It is not clear from this passage whether the Court was referring here to all human rights or only to some.

Convention[23]) giving rise to obligations *erga omnes* in which all States had a legal interest in their protection. The Court also considered, in the *East Timor* case, as 'irreproachable' the assertion that 'the right of peoples to self-determination, as it evolved from the Charter and from United Nations practice, has an erga omnes character'.[24] This was reasserted in the *Wall* case in which the Court observed that the obligations *erga omnes* violated by Israel included 'the obligation to respect the right of the Palestinian people to self-determination, and certain of its obligations under international humanitarian law'.[25]

It has also been responsible for the proliferation of hierarchical terminology. It accepted the existence in international law of 'certain general and well-recognized principles, namely: elementary considerations of humanity even more exacting in peace than in war',[26] which has been relied on by the international criminal tribunals.[27] It referred to 'intransgressible' norms of customary international law in the *Nuclear Weapons* Opinion in relation to many of the rules of humanitarian law applicable in armed conflict, though subsequently clarifying this notion in the *Wall* case by stating that these rules incorporate obligations which are essentially of an *erga omnes* character.[28] The Genocide Convention, proscribing a crime which 'shocks the conscience of mankind', was also seen as endorsing in legal form 'elementary principles of morality'.[29] The Court also referred to the 'fundamental principles' enunciated in the Universal Declaration of Human Rights in the *Tehran Hostages* case.[30]

As for *jus cogens*, one had to wait for the *DRC* v. *Rwanda* case for its first direct endorsement by the Court, in which it referred to the prohibition of

23 ICJ Reports (1996), para. 31.

24 *East Timor (Portugal* v. *Australia)*, ICJ Reports 1995, para. 29.

25 *Legal Consequences of the Construction of a Wall in the Occupied Palestinian Territory*, Advisory Opinion, ICJ Reports 2004, paras. 155–6.

26 *Corfu Channel* (Merits), ICJ Reports 1949, para. 215; *Nicaragua* (Merits), ICJ Reports 1986, p. 14. para. 218, referring to the 'minimum yardstick' governing both internal and international armed conflicts, namely common Article 3 of the Geneva Conventions.

27 See ICTY, *Tadic*, Case IT-96–21-A, judgment of 20 January 2001, paras. 140 *et seq.*

28 *Nuclear Weapons* (Advisory Opinion), ICJ Reports 1996, para. 79; *Wall*, ICJ Reports 2004, para. 157. In the view of some of the judges, the term 'intransgressible' was to be equated with *jus cogens*, see e.g. *Nuclear Weapons*, Separate Opinion of Judge Bedjaoui, p. 273, Dissenting Opinion of Judge Weeramantry, p. 496, Judge Koroma, p. 574.

29 *Reservations to the Convention on Genocide*, Advisory Opinion, ICJ Reports 1951, p. 23.

30 *US Diplomatic Staff in Tehran*, ICJ Reports 1980, para. 91: 'Wrongfully to deprive human beings of their freedom and to subject them to physical constraint in conditions of hardship is in itself manifestly incompatible with the principles of the Charter of the United Nations, as well as with the fundamental principles enunciated in the Universal Declaration of Human Rights.'

genocide as 'assuredly' having the character of *jus cogens*.[31] It subsequently also endorsed the *jus cogens* character of the prohibition of torture in the *Belgium* v. *Senegal* case, which it considered to have assumed customary international law status.[32]

3) The source and content of fundamental norms

As to the sources of human rights law, those who attempt to escape strict positivism in the promotion of human rights law have relied on the Court's Nicaragua jurisprudence in seeming to uphold the primacy of *opinio juris* and in glossing over the inconsistencies of State practice in its examination of the customary norm on the use of force.[33] Its use of general principles as a source of human rights law, thus moving away from State consent, has also been inspirational to human rights defenders.[34] The Court has drawn on the underlying moral, ethical or constitutional foundations of the international community, on some occasions seeming to recognize a spontaneous social process generating general principles of international law whether forming part of customary law, general principles in the sense of Article 38 (lc), or a *sui generis* source.[35] In the Gulf of Maine, the Court also referred to that part of customary law which was made up of 'a limited set of norms for ensuring the co-existence and vital co-operation of the members of the international community', which it distinguished from those customary rules 'whose presence in the opinio juris of States can be

[31] *Armed Activities on the Territory of the Congo (New Application: 2002) (Democratic Republic of the Congo* v.*Rwanda)*, Jurisdiction and Admissibility, ICJ Reports 2006, para. 64.

[32] *Case concerning Questions Relating to the Obligation to Prosecute or Extradite (Belgium* v. *Senegal)*, ICJ Reports 2012, para. 99.

[33] *Military and Paramilitary Activities in and Against Nicaragua (Nicaragua* v. *United States of America)* (Merits), ICJ Reports (1986), para. 186. See e.g. *Prosecutor* v. *Tadic*, Case No. IT-94–1-AR72, ICTY Appeals Chamber, Decision on the defence motion for interlocutory appeal on jurisdiction, 2 October 1995, para. 99, emphasizing state pronouncements and military manuals over the practice of belligerents.

[34] In the *South West Africa* cases *(Liberia/Ethiopia* v. *South Africa)*, Judge Tanaka had founded the concept of human rights and of their protection in the general principles mentioned in Article 38, (lc), which did not require the consent of states as a condition of their recognition since it extended 'the concept of the source of international law beyond the limit of legal positivism according to which . . . international law is nothing but the law of the consent and auto-limitation of the State'. ICJ Reports 1966, Dissenting Opinion, p. 298.

[35] See Pierre-Marie Dupuy, 'Le juge et la règle générale', in Mélanges Michel Virally (ed.), *Le droit international au service de la paix, de la justice et du développement* (Paris : Pedone, 1991), pp. 570–97.

tested by induction based on the analysis of a sufficiently extensive and convincing practice, and not by deduction from preconceived ideas'.[36]

To avoid any accusation that it was thereby 'falling into the error of natural law dogma',[37] the Court has stated that in order that humanitarian or moral considerations generate legal rights and obligations, they 'must be given juridical expression and be clothed in legal form', and it was necessary not to confuse the moral ideal with the legal rules intended to give them effect.[38]

The ICJ has also upheld the fundamental role of General Assembly resolutions in the development of the customary law of human rights, in such cases as *Namibia*, *Western Sahara*, *Nauru* and *East Timor*, so long as these were backed by a substantial majority,[39] citing for example, the role of General Assembly (GA) Resolutions 1514 (XV) and 2625 (XXV) in the evolution among others of the principle of self-determination. The Court has also contributed to promoting and clarifying the normative basis of the United Nations purposes and principles in a number of advisory opinions.

Finally, the Court's consideration of the relationship between treaty law and customary international law – the fundamentally norm-creating character of certain provisions in a multilateral treaty in the generation of new customary law;[40] the continuing separate or parallel existence of customary law rules even as between the treaty parties;[41] or the importance of customary law as a supplement to or interpretative tool for treaty obligations[42] – have also been important in the context of the reinforcement of human rights law.

As to content and scope of human rights norms, the Court has in the *Western Sahara* case set out the basic principles governing the decolonization process as undertaken by the General Assembly. It defined the

36 *Delimitation of the Maritime Boundary in the Gulf of Maine Area*, ICJ Reports 1984, p. 299.

37 To use the words of Judge Tanaka, *South West Africa cases (Liberia/Ethiopia* v. *South Africa)*, ICJ Reports 1966, Dissenting Opinion, p. 298.

38 *South West Africa*, ICJ Reports 1966, p. 34.

39 Cf. *Nuclear Weapons* (Advisory Opinion), ICJ Reports 1996, para. 71.

40 *North Sea Continental Shelf (Germany/Denmark; Germany/Netherlands)* [1969] ICJ Rep 3, para. 71.

41 *Military and Paramilitary Activities in and against Nicaragua (Nicaragua* v. *USA)* (Merits) [1986] ICJ Rep 14, paras. 175–9.

42 *Nuclear Weapons* (Advisory Opinion), ICJ Reports 1996, paras. 28–33, in which it affirmed that the customary law dual conditions of necessity and proportionality applied to Article 51 of the UN Charter.

right to self-determination as the right of peoples, *inter alia*, 'to determine their future political status by their own freely expressed will', and through 'informed and democratic processes'; the genuinely voluntary nature of the choice being insisted on in several parts of the Opinion, as constituting an essential feature of this right.

Historic title could not be viewed as derogating from the right of peoples to decide their own destiny, but could only assist the General Assembly, which had a measure of discretion in its determination of the forms and procedures by which the right was to be realized. One will recall Judge Dillard's poetic statement that 'it is for the people to determine the destiny of the territory and not the territory the destiny of the people'.[43]

In the *Northern Cameroons*, *Namibia*, *Western Sahara*, *Nauru* and *Wall* cases, the Court upheld the competence of the General Assembly to decide on the forms and procedures by which the right was to be realized, since it considered that these Assembly resolutions had definitive legal effects.[44] Thus in the *Wall* case, it demonstrated that the question of Palestine could not be regarded as only a bilateral matter between Israel and Palestine but was the permanent responsibility of the United Nations 'until the question is resolved in all its aspects in a satisfactory manner in accordance with international legitimacy'[45] and that it should be dealt with in the framework of the United Nations 'Roadmap' set in place as early as 1948.

The right to self-determination also placed obligations on all other States in accordance with General Assembly Resolution 2625 (XXV) to promote through joint and separate action its realization and to render assistance to the United Nations in its implementation.[46]

Though recognizing that the derivative of the principle of self-determination, namely the principle of permanent sovereignty over natural resources, was a principle of customary international law, the ICJ in the *DRC* v. *Uganda* case refused to consider its applicability in time of armed conflict, or to occupied territory, preferring to remain within

[43] *Western Sahara* (Advisory Opinion), ICJ Reports 1975, para. 59; Separate Opinion of Judge Dillard, p. 122.

[44] The Court had previously determined that the supervisory functions over the administration of League of Nations mandates had devolved upon the United Nations, in particular the General Assembly (*International Status of South West Africa*, Advisory Opinion, ICJ Reports 1950, pp. 128, 133).

[45] *Wall*, ICJ Reports 2004, para. 49.

[46] *Wall*, ICJ Reports 2004, para. 156.

the confines of the *jus in bello* in finding Uganda in breach, *inter alia*, of Article 47 of the 1907 Hague Regulations on pillage in respect of the natural resources in the occupied district of Ituri.[47]

It thus departed from the African Commission of Human Rights, which had found that the illegal exploitation/looting of the natural resources of the Democratic Republic of Congo (DRC) was in contravention of Article 21 of the African Charter on permanent sovereignty over natural resources, adding that such acts also violated the right of the people of the DRC to their economic, social and cultural development.[48] Yet, curiously, the ICJ did find a violation of Article 21(2) of the African Charter relating to the right of dispossessed people to restitution and compensation for damage in case of spoliation.[49] The pronouncements of the Court on the question of natural resources are nevertheless of great importance since these were largely responsible for fuelling the war in the DRC.

The ICJ also failed altogether to invoke the principle of permanent sovereignty over natural resources in relation to the construction of a wall in the Occupied Palestininian Territory, despite pointing out with reference to IHL and the right to self-determination, that this construction had seriously affected agricultural production and annexed most of the western aquifer system supplying half of the water resources of the West Bank, and despite the reaffirmation of the principle in General Assembly Resolution 58/229 (2003) on Palestine, which had also called for restitution.

In supporting the right to self-determination of peoples, the Court, however, has been careful to channel its potentially disruptive effects. It consecrated the *uti possidetis juris* principle, recognizing not only its exceptional importance for the independence and stability of the African continent, but also its universal character.[50]

It has also been pointed out that the Court has abstained from any encouragement of the territorial claims of indigenous peoples

[47] *Armed Activities on the Territory of the Congo (Democratic Republic of the Congo* v. *Uganda)*, ICJ Reports 2005, paras. 246, 248 and 250.

[48] African Commission on Human and Peoples' Rights, Communication 227/99 – D. R. Congo / Burundi, Rwanda and Uganda, Decision of May 2003, paras. 94–5. Article 21 of the African Charter provides: '(1) All peoples shall freely dispose of their wealth and natural resources. This right shall be exercised in the exclusive interest of the people. In no case shall a people be deprived of it.'

[49] *DRC* v. *Uganda*, ICJ Reports 2005, paras. 244–5.

[50] *Frontier Dispute (Burkina Faso* v. *Mali)* (Judgement), ICJ Reports 1986, para. 20.

encapsulated within territories which have achieved independence through recognition of their rights.[51]

The views of the Court on the status of treaties concluded with non-State entities in the context of indigenous peoples on the one hand and a recognized national liberation movement fighting for self-determination on the other may be contrasted. In examining Nigeria's claim to the title to the Bakassi peninsula, in the *Land and Maritime Boundary Dispute* between Nigeria and Cameroon, the Court in considering the international legal status of an 1884 'Treaty of Protection', concluded between the Kings and Chiefs of Old Calabar and Great Britain, referred to Max Huber's pronouncement in the *Island of Palmas* case that such a treaty 'is not an agreement between equals; it is rather a form of internal organisation of a colonial territory, on the basis of autonomy of the natives ...' in rejecting the view that the treaty implied international personality.[52]

On the other hand, the Court accepted in the *Wall* case that the Israeli–Palestinian Interim Agreement on the West Bank and the Gaza Strip of 28 September 1995 created rights and obligations under international law: it imposed commitments on both Israel and the Palestine Liberation Organization (PLO) and was one more indication of the recognition of the 'legitimate rights' of the Palestinian people under international law, which included a right to self-determination, as well as recognition of the PLO as their legitimate representatives.[53] The Court thus recognized the treaty-making capacity of a national liberation movement.

But at the same time, despite the positions of several States in the *Kosovo* case, the ICJ refused to pronounce on the question of the legality of secession, considering that there was no general prohibition of

[51] See W. Michael Reisman, 'Protecting Indigenous Rights in International Adjudication', 89 *AJIL*, 1995, pp. 350–62, at pp. 355–6. Thus a chamber of the International Court in the *Gulf of Fonseca* judgment rejected the submission of El Salvador relating to methods of territorial delimitation based on historical rights of indian '*poblaciones*' or settlements. *Land, Island and Maritime Frontier Dispute (El Salvador* v. *Honduras, Nicaragua intervening)*, ICJ Reports 1992, pp. 392–3.

[52] *Land and Maritime Boundary between Cameroon and Nigeria (Cameroon* v. *Nigeria, Equatorial Guinea Intervening)*, ICJ Reports 2002, paras. 205, 207, 212. Judge Koroma dissented from this finding of the Court: in his view, it was clear from its terms that the 1884 Treaty was governed by the principle of *pacta sunt servanda*, and constituted an acknowledgement by Great Britain that the Kings and Chiefs of Old Calabar were capable of entering into a treaty relationship with a foreign power (*ibid.*, Dissenting Opinion of Judge Koroma, para. 15).

[53] Para.118.

the making of a declaration of independence; the pronouncements of illegality by the Security Council in the case of the Unilateral Declaration of Independence of Southern Rhodesia, Northern Cyprus or the Republika Srpska stemming not from their unilateral character but from the fact that they were connected with violations of *jus cogens* norms.[54] The references made to this Advisory Opinion in justifying the subsequent secession of Crimea from the Ukraine and its annexation by the Russian Federation shows the political repercussions that the Court's pronouncements may have.

In respect of another fundamental norm, the prohibition of racial discrimination, the Court has condemned the establishment and enforcement of 'distinctions, exclusions, restrictions and limitations exclusively based on grounds of race, colour, descent or national or ethnic origin' as well as apartheid as being contrary to the purposes and principles of the UN Charter.[55] It also indicated provisional measures to safeguard against racial discrimination in the *Georgia* v. *Russia* case, although it missed out on the opportunity of examining further the scope and content of racial discrimination under CERD as it subsequently upheld an objection by Russia that Georgia had failed to satisfy the procedural precondition to the seisin of the Court contained in Article 22 of the CERD.[56]

It has expounded at length on the scope and content of the prohibition of genocide, for example on the definition of the protected group and on the qualitative and quantitative aspects of the perpetration of the crime of genocide; it also distinguished physical and biological destruction from destruction of the historical, religious and cultural heritage of a group, which it considered not to fall within the scope of the Convention.[57]

Finally, to look at human rights writ large, the Court has elaborated on the 'cardinal principles' of IHL, such as the principle of distinction,

[54] *Accordance with International Law of the Unilateral Declaration of Independence in Respect of Kosovo* (Advisory Opinion), ICJ Reports 2010, para. 81.

[55] *Namibia*, ICJ Reports 1971, paras. 130–2.

[56] *Application of the International Convention on the Elimination of All Forms of Racial Discrimination (Georgia* v. *Russian Federation)* (Provisional Measures), ICJ Reports 2008; (Preliminary Objections), ICJ Reports 2011. The case arose following on the armed conflict in August 2008 and concerned the alleged breach by Russia of CERD both by its own actions as well as those of the de facto authorities in South Ossetia and Abkhazia.

[57] *Application of the Genocide Convention*, ICJ Reports 2007, e.g. paras. 193–6, 198–9, 200, 344.

the prohibition of unnecessary suffering and the Martens clause, among others.[58]

C. *Bridging human rights and IHL*

Generally speaking, as Chinkin and Boyle have pointed out, 'the case-law of the International Court of Justice suggests that where possible it prefers an integrated conception of international law to a fragmented one',[59] although it must be said that it has also given impetus to the concept of self-contained regimes in the framework of State responsibility.[60]

One valuable and innovative contribution the Court has made, subsequently followed by the human rights treaty bodies, has been its demonstration of the continuing applicability of human rights law in armed conflict, in line with the very visible trend towards permeability between different fields of law which traditionally were hermetically sealed off from each other. It has also underlined the unity and indivisibility of human rights treaties, as well as their extraterritorial reach. Unlike its holding operation in the case of the norms regulating the use of force (as, e.g, in the *Wall case* and *DRC* v. *Uganda*, in which the ICJ staunchly stood by a restrictive interpretation of Article 51 of the Charter), the Court has been at the vanguard of progressive developments in the strengthening of human rights law, particularly at a time of armed conflict; both types of approaches – restrictive and progressive – have served as bulwarks against the unravelling of international law in the context of the so-called 'war on terror' and the consequent creation of black holes in the protection of individuals.

Particularly in recent years, the ICJ has approached armed conflicts not only from the perspective of the rights and duties of States, but also from that of the rights of individuals, addressing the continuing existence of human rights in armed conflict situations, the relationship between State and individual responsibility, as well as restitution and compensation to individual persons, among other issues.

[58] For a development, see Vincent Chetail, 'The Contribution of the International Court of Justice to International Humanitarian Law', 85 *International Review of the Red Cross* (No. 850, June 2003), pp. 235–69.

[59] Alan Boyle and Christine Chinkin, *The Making of International Law* (Oxford University Press, 2007), p. 211.

[60] *United States Diplomatic and Consular Staff in Tehran (USA* v. *Iran)*, ICJ Reports 1980, para. 86.

1) The articulation of the relationship between human rights and IHL

In the *Nuclear Weapons* Advisory Opinion, the Court had to address the argument that the use of nuclear weapons would violate the right to life as guaranteed by Article 6 of the International Covenant on Civil and Political Rights (ICCPR).[61] The Court recognized the Convention's continuing application in time of armed conflict beyond that of non-derogable rights, like the right to life, with the exception of those rights which had been formally derogated from. But while acknowledging the potential of nuclear weapons 'to destroy all civilization and the entire ecosystem of the planet', it disappointingly observed that the test of what is an arbitrary deprivation of life contrary to Article 6 of the Covenant 'falls to be determined by the applicable *lex specialis*, namely, the law applicable in armed conflict . . . and not deduced from the terms of the Covenant itself', thus evincing human rights law from its consideration of the law applicable to nuclear weapons,[62] which shows the rather reductionist and exclusionary effect of this particular discretionary maxim.[63] For interpretation of the right to life under the human rights instruments cannot be made exclusively in the light of IHL since the notion of what is 'arbitrary' deprivation of life must also be interpreted in the context of the human rights treaties themselves, including their object and purpose and their constantly evolving standards in response to subsequent practice, including that of the treaty bodies, for human rights treaties have been acknowledged as living instruments.

In the subsequent *Wall* Advisory Opinion, the Court took a further leap forward in implying that the complementarity principle continued to operate alongside the *lex specialis* test:[64]

[61] See Vera Gowlland-Debbas, 'The Right to Life and Genocide: the Court and an International Public Policy', in Laurence Boisson de Chazournes and Philippe Sands, *International Law, the International Court of Justice and Nuclear Weapons* (Cambridge University Press, 1999), pp. 315–37. It will be recalled that Article 73 of the VCLT excludes from its scope the question of the continuing existence of treaties in armed conflict.

[62] ICJ Reports 1996, para. 25.

[63] The 1969 Vienna Convention on the Law of Treaties does not include this maxim in its provisions relating to successive treaties.

[64] *Wall* Advisory Opinion, ICJ Reports 2004, para. 106. The Human Rights Committee has also moved away from the *lex specialis* articulation of the relationship between international human rights law (IHRL) and IHL and adopted the complementarity not exclusivity articulation of both fields (see General Comment No. 31). The ICTY has even pointed out that with regard to certain of its aspects, international humanitarian law can be said to have fused with human rights law, although one had to take into consideration the

> As regards the relationship between international humanitarian law and human rights law, there are thus three possible situations: some rights may be exclusively matters of international humanitarian law; others may be exclusively matters of human rights law; yet others may be matters of both these branches of international law. In order to answer the question put to it, the Court will have to take into consideration both these branches of international law, namely human rights law and, as *lex specialis*, international humanitarian law.

This passage was reiterated in the *DRC* v. *Uganda* case, the Court finding in its *dispositif* that Uganda by the conduct of its armed forces on the territory of the DRC had violated human rights and international humanitarian law.[65]

The unitary nature of human rights law has likewise been upheld. In the *Wall* Advisory Opinion, the ICJ re-affirmed the application in time of armed conflict not only of the ICCPR but also of *all* human rights instruments, including the International Covenant on Economic, Social and Cultural Rights and the Convention on the Rights of the Child.[66] This insistence on the indivisibility of human rights was further confirmed by the ICJ in the *DRC* v. *Uganda* case, which also included in the list of applicable law the African Charter on Human and Peoples' Rights.[67]

The Court has further pronounced on the extraterritorial nature of international human rights instruments. By virtue of the *erga omnes* nature of the crime of genocide, it noted in the *Application of the Genocide Convention* case 'that the obligation each State has to prevent and to punish the crime of genocide is not territorially limited by the Convention'.[68] It reiterated this in its 2007 judgment, further observing that while Article VI only obliged the Contracting Parties to exercise territorial criminal jurisdiction, it did not prohibit them from exercising other bases of jurisdiction so long as these were compatible with international law.

specificities of the latter body of law (*Kunarac*, IT.96.23.T, judgment of 22 February 2001, paras. 467 and 471). See also *Serdar Mohammed* v. *Ministry of Defence* [2014] EWHC 1369 (QB) in which it was stated that 'the lex specialis cannot operate to solve a conflict between HRs and IHL' – this could only be done by applying the provisions for derogation in the human rights convention itself (at para. 284).

65 *DRC* v. *Uganda*, ICJ Reports 2005, para. 345 (3).

66 *Wall*, ICJ Reports 2004, paras.178, 106.

67 *DRC* v. *Uganda*, ICJ Reports 2005, paras. 216–17 (though curiously not CAT, despite accepting that Ugandan troops had committed acts of torture).

68 *Application of the Genocide Convention* (Preliminary Objections), ICJ Reports 1996, para. 31, ICJ Reports 2007, paras. 183–4.

The major human rights instruments were also stated to be applicable 'in respect of acts done by a State in the exercise of its jurisdiction outside its own territory', particularly in occupied territories,[69] occupation being defined as the substitution of one authority by another, although the establishment of a structured military administration of the territory occupied was not a necessary requirement.[70] Similarly, in *Georgia* v. *Russia* it found that 'these provisions of CERD generally appear to apply, *like other provisions of instruments of that nature*, to the actions of a State party when it acts beyond its territory'.[71]

2) Consequences of continuing applicability of human rights law in time of armed conflict

The convergence of human rights and IHL has now been demonstrated by the indiscriminate use of both areas of law in time of armed conflict by the political organs of the United Nations, including the Human Rights Council, the General Assembly and Security Council, as well as by human rights treaty bodies, thus including all relevant guarantees of international law for the protection of individuals. At the time of the ICJ's *Nuclear Weapons* Opinion, however, there were only a handful of such cases in the regional courts,[72] yet post-1996 such cases have proliferated. Human Rights treaty bodies have dealt with the rules relating to armed conflict under their respective treaties, in particular under the provisions protecting the right to life, either as a means of interpretation or application of IHL, or have used human rights exclusively in armed conflict situations.[73] The overlap between human rights law and IHL has been bolstered by their recognition of the extraterritorial scope of application of

[69] *Wall*, ICJ Reports 2004, paras. 107–13, 178–81.

[70] *DRC* v. *Uganda*, ICJ Reports 2005, paras. 172–3.

[71] (Provisional Measures), ICJ Reports 2008, para. 109 (emphasis added).

[72] See the European Commission on Human Rights, in the cases of *Cyprus* v. *Turkey* (No. 8007/77, European Commission on Human Rights, Decisions and Reports, vol. 13 (1977), pp. 85ff) and *Loizidou* v. *Turkey*, 23 March 1995 (*Yearbook of the European Convention of Human Rights*, vol. 38, 1995, pp. 245ff); and in the Inter-American Commission on Human Rights, the case of *Disabled Peoples' International* v. *United States*, No.8007/77.

[73] See Vera Gowlland-Debbas, 'The Relationship between IHL and Human Rights Law: the Right to Life', in Christian Tomuschat *et al.* (eds.), *The Right to Life* (Leiden: Brill, 2009), pp. 123–50; and Vera Gowlland-Debbas and Gloria Gaggioli, 'The Relationship between International Human Rights and Humanitarian Law: An Overview', in Robert Kolb and Gloria Gaggioli (eds.), *Research Handbook on Human Rights and Humanitarian Law* (Cheltenham: Edward Elgar, 2013), pp. 77–103.

human rights in certain circumstances.[74] Though they may have differed in their approach to the articulation between human rights and humanitarian law and the means of their reconciliation, their decisions have contributed to the evolution of IHL in a way that is more in keeping with contemporary mores, moving it along specific paths within the framework of their constituent instruments and their respective jurisdictions. In the notable absence of IHL mechanisms, the availability of human rights remedies is important: there is no requirement of a threshold to come into operation, the protection offered extends to both civilians and combatants alike and the conditions of proportionality are very differently assessed.

3) Human rights and the *jus ad bellum*

In view of current debates over the so-called R2P (Responsibility to Protect) doctrine, whether it acts as a fig leaf for unilateral humanitarian intervention or is confined to collective action within the Security Council (which, incidentally, has no need for the doctrine as a basis for its own action), the Court's view in *Nicaragua* that the use of force is not an appropriate method to ensure respect for human rights in another State is worth recalling:

> the protection of human rights – a strictly humanitarian objective, cannot be compatible with the mining of ports, the destruction of oil installations, or again with the training, arming and equipping of the contras.[75]

Furthermore, the Court has distinguished unlawful intervention – financial and military support such as the supply of weapons – from the provision of strictly humanitarian assistance, confined to the provision of food, clothing, medicine and other humanitarian assistance and conducted in conformity with the fundamental principles of the Red Cross, 'namely "to prevent and alleviate human suffering", and "to protect life and health and to ensure respect for the human being"; it must also, and above all, be given without discrimination to all in need'.[76]

[74] For a recent case, see *Al Skeini* v. *United Kingdom*, ECtHR, Application No. 55721/07, judgment of 7 July 2011.

[75] *Nicaragua*, ICJ Reports 1986, para. 268. See Nigel S. Rodley, 'Human Rights and Humanitarian Intervention: The Case Law of the World Court', 38 *ICLQ*(1989), pp. 321–33, at pp. 327–8.

[76] *Nicaragua*, ICJ Reports 1986, para. 243.

III. The linkages between human rights law and general international law

The ICJ has contributed to the 'mainstreaming' of human rights in examining its relationship with other areas of general international law.[77] But it has only done that in passing.

A. *Human rights and diplomatic relations and protection*

In the *LaGrand* and *Avena* cases,[78] concerning German and Mexican nationals, respectively, on death row, the ICJ examined human rights in the context of diplomatic relations. But, while finding that the obligation under Article 36 (1 (a) and (b)) of the 1963 Vienna Convention on Consular Relations to inform detained foreign nationals of their right to seek consular assistance from their home country, which had been breached in both cases, were to be read not just as State rights but also as individual rights, the Court stopped short of stating that they had a human rights status forming a part of due process rights in criminal proceedings, considering that it did not have to decide on the issue.[79] Yet a few years back the Inter-American Court on Human Rights had found the right to information under Article 36(1) of the Convention to be part of the corpus of human rights in rendering effective the right to due process of law.[80]

The ICJ also merely brushed on the relations between human rights and diplomatic protection in the *DRC* v. *Uganda* case. In its second counterclaim, Uganda had accused the Congolese armed forces, *inter alia*, of

[77] The words of Bruno Simma, 'Mainstreaming Human Rights: The Contribution of the International Court of Justice', 3 *Journal of International Dispute Settlement* (2012) 7–29.

[78] *LaGrand (Germany* v. *USA)*, ICJ Reports 2001; *Avena and other Mexican Nationals (Mexico* v. *USA)*, ICJ Reports 2004.

[79] *LaGrand*, paras. 77–8; *Avena*, para.124. Mexico had even asserted that violation of Article 36 would invalidate the entire criminal proceedings (see Simma, 'Human Rights before the International Court of Justice', p. 307).

[80] Advisory Opinion no. 16 of 1 October 1999. In the *LaGrand* judgment the ICJ had held that the United States 'by means of its own choosing, shall allow the review and reconsideration of the conviction and sentence by taking account of the violation of the rights set forth in that Convention'. However, in the *Medellin* case, the US Supreme Court refuted the contention that the United States could be 'obligated to comply with the Convention, as interpreted by the ICJ' except for 'respectful consideration'. See Carsten Hoppe, 'Implementation of *LaGrand* and *Avena* in Germany and the United States: Exploring Transatlantic Divide in Search of a Uniform Interpretation of Consular Rights', 18 *EJIL* (2007) 317–36.

maltreatment of Ugandan nationals at Ndjili International Airport in Kinshasa in August 1998, who were attempting to leave the country following the outbreak of the armed conflict.[81] The Court in finding that the DRC had violated its obligations under the international minimal standard relating to the treatment of foreign nationals, as well as 'universally recognized standards of human rights concerning the security of the human person' remained, however, within the confines of diplomatic protection, missing out on the opportunity to explore the relationship between diplomatic protection in relation to the international minimum standard and human rights law, particularly the question of direct action by a State when claiming violations of *erga omnes* obligations.[82]

In contrast, in the case of *Diallo*[83] brought by Guinea to the Court, which dealt with indirect expropriation, company and shareholder rights and the international minimum standard and was submitted in the context of diplomatic protection, the Court, following on its 2007 admissibility judgment, relied, *inter alia*, on the provisions of the ICCPR and the African Charter in finding the DRC to be in violation of unlawful expulsion of aliens, arrest and detention, thus referring to Diallo's individual human rights rather than the rights of the home State.[84] Only the reparations were placed in the context of inter-State relations. As Bruno Simma points out, this case is therefore an interesting illustration of the enforcement of human rights through the channel of diplomatic protection – an inter-State mechanism:

> In thus squaring the procedures of diplomatic protection and human rights as direct rights of the individual under international law, the Court in Diallo has made an important contribution to reconciling these two areas of the law in a progressive sense, further away from the spirit of *Mavrommatis* and in line with the recent efforts of the ILC.[85]

[81] *DRC* v. *Uganda*, Counter-Memorial of Uganda, paras. 405–7.

[82] *DRC* v. *Uganda*, ICJ Reports 2005, para. 333; *dispositif* paras. 345(11) and (12). See the Separate Opinion of Judge Simma, paras. 16 *et seq*. See also Serena Forlati, 'Protection diplomatique, droits de l'homme et réclamations "directes" devant la Cour internationale de justice. Quelques réflexions en marge de l'arrêt Congo/Uganda', 111 *RGDIP* (2007) 89–116, at 92–3 and 104 *et seq.* ; Vera Gowlland-Debbas, 'The Conflict in the Democratic Republic of the Congo and the Role of Courts', in Thomas Giegerich and Alexander Proelß (eds.), *Krisenherde der Welt im Blickwinkel des Völkerrechts* (Berlin: Duncker & Humbolt, 2010), pp. 167–200.

[83] *Ahmadou Sadio Diallo (Guinea* v. *DRC)* (Merits), ICJ Reports 2010.

[84] The Court also referred to a violation of the 1963 Vienna Convention on Consular Relations but without adding anything to its *LaGrand* and *Avena* judgments.

[85] Simma, 'Human Rights before the International Court of Justice', pp. 310–12, at 312. For a detailed examination and interpretation of the human rights concerned in this case, see Separate Opinion of Judge Cançado Trindade.

B. *Human rights and criminal jurisdiction*

The *Belgium* v. *Senegal* case, on the other hand, was not a case of diplomatic protection of nationals but a request by Belgium for Senegal to either prosecute or extradite Mr Hissen Habré under CAT. Belgium based its *jus standi* on the fact that it was both an affected State, as the matter was before its national courts, and a State other than an injured State party to CAT.

The Court considered that there was no need for it to pronounce on whether Belgium had a special interest with respect to Senegal's compliance with CAT, for, with implicit reference to the International Law Commission's (ILC) Articles on State Responsibility, 'any State party to the Convention may invoke the responsibility of another State party with a view to ascertaining the alleged failure to comply with its obligations *erga omnes partes* . . . ', and concluded that Belgium consequently had standing on that basis to invoke the responsibility of Senegal and was entitled to claim performance of the obligations concerned.[86] In Simma's view this was 'the most clean-cut, "unpolitical", as it were, human rights case so far handled by the Court. If a full-fledged "*droits de l'hommiste*"' were to express it somewhat colloquially: this is a human rights case which is almost too good to be true.'[87] And yet one based exclusively on an inter-State construction of CAT.[88]

The relationship between extradition and prosecution and the conditions applicable to them in the matter of international crimes was also touched on by the Court. Though specific to the provisions of CAT, this was an important elucidation of what have become frequent provisions in transnational conventions and necessary adjuncts to the International Criminal Court's (ICC) provisions on complementarity and inter-State cooperation. The ILC has made extensive use of the Court's pronouncements in this case in the context of its topic on the obligation to prosecute

86 *Questions relating to the Obligation to Prosecute or Extradite (Belgium* v. *Senegal)*, judgment, ICJ Reports 2012, paras. 69–70. The Court's view concerning Belgium's entitlement to bring its claims against Senegal before the Court on the basis of the *erga omnes* nature of the Convention and its refusal to dwell on the special interest of Belgium in Senegal's compliance was not shared by all the judges: see in particular the Declaration of Judge Owada and Dissenting Opinion of Judge Xue, for different reasons, the latter considering that a common interest is not the same thing as a right of any State party to invoke the responsibility of any other State party before the Court, particularly in view of the opt-out clause in the dispute settlement clauses of CAT (*ibid.* pp. 464 and 571, respectively); and the detailed arguments of Ad Hoc Judge Sur in his Dissenting Opinion (*ibid.*, p. 605).

87 Simma, 'Human Rights before the International Court of Justice', p. 313.

88 Simma, 'Mainstreaming Human Rights', pp. 22–3.

or extradite and in light of ILC discussions on potential future work on a convention on crimes against humanity.[89]

C. *The relationship between State and individual responsibility for human rights violations*

The ICJ has also examined the relationship between State and individual responsibility in the *Application of the Genocide Convention* case; this case, brought by Bosnia against Yugoslavia, dragged on from 1993 right through to the ICJ's final and crucial judgment in 2007, with some extraordinary ramifications along the way. The Court pointed out that although Article 1 of the Convention does not expressly require States to refrain from themselves committing genocide, speaking only of prevention, it would be paradoxical if the parties had an obligation to prevent acts of genocide under Article 1 but were not forbidden to commit such acts through their own organs, or persons over whom they had effective control, where such conduct may be attributable to them. In short, the obligation to prevent genocide on the State concerned necessarily implied the prohibition of the commission of genocide, as well as of all the other acts enumerated under Article III of the Convention, including complicity, by the State itself.[90] While complicity was not a notion which existed in the law of international responsibility, the Court traced it to the 'aid or assistance' furnished by one State for the commission of a wrongful act by another State embedded in Article 16 of the ILC's Articles on State Responsibility, which includes the requirement that the organ or person whose conduct is attributed to the State acted 'knowingly'.[91]

The Court moreover confirmed the possibility of duality of responsibility but also concluded that State responsibility for genocide and complicity under the Convention could arise without individual criminal responsibility being involved.[92]

This judgment has come under fire. The Court, after an extensive reading of the Convention to include State responsibility for genocide and not only a duty to prevent and to punish, first found that genocide had been committed only in Srebrenica and then proceeded to disculpate

[89] See Report of the 65th session of the ILC (UN Doc. A/68/10), Annex A: Report of the Working Group on the Obligation to extradite or prosecute (*aut dedere aut judicare*) and Annex B: Crimes against humanity (Mr Sean D. Murphy).

[90] *Application of the Genocide Convention*, ICJ Reports 2007, paras. 166–79.

[91] *Ibid.*, paras. 419–21.

[92] *Ibid.*, paras. 173, 182.

Serbia from responsibility for that genocide and from complicity for genocide. It concluded that Serbia had only breached its duty to prevent and to punish.

As seen, therefore, the Court has delved into the rules of State responsibility for human rights violations, whether they be matters of attribution, obligations of prevention or reparation, and endorsed the ILC's notion of 'complicity' as formulated in Article 16 of the Articles in terms of 'aid or assistance' in the commission of an internationally wrongful act. The latter has gained particular credence today in the context of the 'war on terror', in view of widespread accusations of complicity by States, for example, in 'rendition' cases.

D. *The tension between human rights and immunities*

The ICJ has been dragged into the debate concerning the tension between human rights and immunities in cases which concerned either individual criminal responsibility or State responsibility for war crimes or crimes against humanity committed by high-ranking officials of a State. In two relevant cases, the Court upheld immunities over human rights.

In the *Arrest Warrant* case the Court upheld the absolute immunity from the criminal jurisdiction of *national* courts of a former foreign minister, including for past official acts constituting grave crimes against humanity and even incitement to genocide.[93] It was careful to underline, however, that immunity did not imply impunity, for immunity did not apply for the court of nationality nor before international tribunals. In the case of *Jurisdictional Immunities*, Germany argued that Italy was

[93] *Arrest Warrant of 11 April 2000 (DRC* v. *Belgium)* ICJ Reports 2002. In *Certain Questions of Mutual Assistance in Criminal Matters (Djibouti* v. *France)*, ICJ Reports 2008, paras. 170–4, the Court reaffirmed its judgment considering that it was established customary international law that high-ranking officials of a State enjoyed immunity from both civil and criminal jurisdiction, in particular a Head of State who enjoyed 'full immunity from criminal jurisdiction and inviolability' protecting him or her against any *constraining act of authority* of another State, though it considered that a summons addressed to the President of the Republic of Djibouti by the French investigating judge inviting him to testify did not constitute such an infringement on immunities. This case did not involve human rights but an alleged violation by France, *inter alia*, of the Treaty of Friendship and Co-operation concluded between France and Djibouti on 27 June 1977. The case relating to immunity from alleged crimes against humanity and acts of torture of high-ranking Congolese officials brought by the Republic of Congo against France in 2003 was discontinued in 2010 (*Certain Criminal Proceedings in France (Republic of the Congo* v. *France)* (Provisional Measures), ICJ Reports 2003.

responsible for breach of sovereign immunity for the actions of its *Corte di Cassazione*, which had in a series of judgments denied immunity to Germany in relation to reparation claims involving war crimes and crimes against humanity perpetrated by the Third Reich against Italian and Greek victims. Italy countered that Germany was not entitled to immunity on account of the particular nature of its acts during World War II, which involved serious violations of peremptory norms for which no alternative means of redress was available. The Court, though declining jurisdiction in the matter of the crimes committed because of limitations *ratione temporis*, tackled the issue of immunity as a preliminary question. But it concluded that the customary international law on the absolute nature of sovereign immunity had not changed, nor was that dependent upon the peremptory nature of the substantive rules alleged to have been breached. The Court did not consider that there was any conflict between rules of *jus cogens* and the rules on State immunity for:

> the law of immunity is essentially procedural in nature. It regulates the exercise of jurisdiction in respect of particular conduct and is thus entirely distinct from the substantive law which determines whether that conduct is lawful or unlawful.[94]

Granting immunity, even when peremptory norms were at stake, did not amount, therefore, to recognizing as lawful the situation created by the breach of a *jus cogens* rule or rendering aid and assistance in maintaining that situation.

A number of judges departed from the Court's views on absolute immunity. In the *Arrest Warrant* case, Ad Hoc Judge Wyngaert considered that not only was the Court wrong on this but that

> [t]he more fundamental problem lies in its general approach, that disregards the whole recent movement in modern international criminal law towards recognition of the principle of individual accountability for international core crimes.[95]

Judges Yusuf and Trindade were also in disagreement in the *Jurisdictional Immunities* case. Judge Yusuf stated in his Dissent, that State immunity was 'as full of holes as Swiss cheese' for in the area of violations of human rights and humanitarian law, it remained an unsettled and uncertain area of law. In his view, a balance had to be struck between two sets of functions

[94] *Jurisdictional Immunities of the State (Germany* v. *Italy, Greece intervening)*, ICJ Reports 2012, para. 58.

[95] ICJ Reports 2002, p. 137, para. 27.

both valued by the international community. The law of State immunity could not be interpreted in a way which conflicted with basic rights, for

> In today's world, the use of State immunity to obstruct the right of access to justice and the right to an effective remedy for violations of fundamental human rights and humanitarian law may be seen as a misuse of such immunity.[96]

Though coming as a great disappointment to the human rights community, the ICJ's position echoed the European Court of Human Rights (ECtHR) in *Al-Adsani*, which basing itself on Article 31 (3(c)) of the VCLT had in fact failed to uphold the provisions of its own treaty relating to torture over State immunity.[97]

The Court likewise bolstered the immunities of international organizations when it upheld the immunities of UN special rapporteurs on human rights –Mazilu in 1989 and Coomaraswamy in 1999[98] – although, as Bruno Simma has pointed out, the Court's advisory opinions in these cases served paradoxically to strengthen the human rights machinery in preventing State intervention in the affairs of the United Nations.[99]

IV. Remedies for human rights violations

What, however, of the legal consequences of a violation of an obligation *erga omnes* or of a peremptory norm brought before the ICJ and what about remedies for individuals? How would the traditional Chorzow Factory principles, namely the inter-State duty to pay reparations, based on the bilateral structures of international law, be applicable in such circumstances?

Generally, the Court has called for cessation and reparations in an inter-State context, even when involving breaches of human rights.

[96] ICJ Reports 2012, p. 291, Dissenting Opinion of Judge Yusuf, paras. 26 -30. See also the Dissenting Opinion of Judge CançadoTrindade with its extensive survey of the matter (*ibid.*, p. 179), in which he rejects what he terms the assumption of a formalist lack of conflict between 'procedural' and 'substantive' rules and upholds *jus cogens* over immunity for international crimes (paras. 315–16).

[97] *Al-Adsani* v. *UK*, ECtHR (GC), 2001.

[98] *Applicability of Article VI Section 22 of the Convention on the Privileges and Immunities of the United Nations*, (Advisory Opinion), ICJ Reports 1989; *Difference Relating to Immunity from Legal Process of a Special Rapporteur of the Commission on Human Rights* (Advisory Opinion), ICJ Reports 1999. The EctHR has also done likewise in its judgments of 18 February 1999 in *Waite and Kennedy* v. *Germany* (Application No. 26083/94, judgment of 18 February 1999) and *Beer and Regan* v. *Germany* (Application No. 28934/95).

[99] Simma, 'Human Rights before the International Court of Justice', p. 305.

In the *Hostages* case, which concerned in any case diplomatic relations based on traditional reciprocal bilateral relations, the Court stated that the obligation of Iran to make reparation was due to the United States.[100]

In the *DRC* v. *Uganda* case, again remaining in the context of inter-State relations, the ICJ endorsed the DRC's claim to reparation for the 'massive war damage' caused by 'years of invasion, occupation, fundamental human rights violations and plundering of natural resources of the DRC'. It also found that the DRC was under an obligation to make reparation to Uganda for its attacks on the Ugandan Embassy in Kinshasa, but found inadmissible its claim concerning nationals injured at Ndjili airport.[101]

Despite placing itself in the context of human rights law in the *Diallo* case, the Court likewise concluded, as mentioned above, that reparation was due to Guinea in the exercise of diplomatic protection and, importantly, awarded compensation for both the material and *non-material* injury suffered by Mr Diallo flowing from his wrongful detention and expulsion. Nevertheless, it expressly indicated that the sum which was awarded was 'intended to provide reparation for the latter's injury'.[102]

Finally, in the *Application of the Genocide Convention* case, the ICJ concluded that since there was not a sufficiently direct causal nexus between Serbia's breach of the obligation to prevent genocide and the injury suffered by the acts, neither *restitutio in integrum* nor financial compensation was the appropriate form of reparation. It resorted instead to satisfaction by means of a declaration that Serbia had failed to comply with its obligations under the Genocide Convention to prevent and to punish. It thus failed to satisfy Bosnia's request for full compensation, 'in its own right and as *parens patriae* for its citizens', for the damages and losses caused.[103]

[100] ICJ Reports 1980, para. 95(5).

[101] ICJ Reports 2007, paras. 345 (5) and (13) respectively. (This raises the question of the relationship between the *jus ad bellum* and the *jus in bello* for purposes of compensation arising from armed conflict – who is to bear the burden of reparations in the face of such widespread and egregious violations of IHL and human rights? See Vera Gowlland-Debbas, 'Some Remarks on Compensation for War Damages under Jus Ad Bellum', in Andrea de Guttry *et al.* (eds.), *The 1998–2000 War between Eritrea and Ethiopia: An International Legal Perspective* (The Hague: T.M.C. Asser Instituut, 2009), pp. 435–48.)

[102] *Ahmadou Sadio Diallo (Guinea* v. *Democratic Republic of the Congo)*(Compensation), ICJ Reports 2012, para. 57, *dispositif*, para. 61 (1) and (2).

[103] *Application of the Genocide Convention*, ICJ Reports 2007, paras. 460–5.

Nevertheless, although general remedies for individual victims of violations of IHL are rare,[104] the Court has exceptionally called for restitution and compensation to individual persons. Having demonstrated in the *Wall* Opinion that Israel had engaged its responsibility through breaches of a number of fundamental obligations concerning human rights law, IHL, use of force and self-determination, and relying implicitly on the ILC Articles on State Responsibility, the ICJ declared that in the event of the impossibility of restitution, Israel was under an obligation to make reparation to all natural or legal persons having suffered 'any form of material damage' as a result of the wall's construction in the Occupied Palestinian Territory, including in and around East Jerusalem.[105] But this has been a unique situation, arising from the particular status of Palestine.

In terms of other remedies, it is interesting that the Court, in the *Georgia* v. *Russia* case ordered interim measures of protection going beyond inter-State interests and rights in the form of protection of rights under CERD, considering that the harm done to the individual rights of ethnic Ossetian and Abkhazian populations was tantamount to the 'irreparable harm or prejudice' that a request for provisional measures had to address.[106] Similarly, its efforts to protect the right to life in the interim measures it ordered in the *LaGrand* and *Avena* cases as well as its ordering of guarantees of non-repetition go beyond inter-State interests and rights.

Nevertheless, the obstacles to remedies caused by the lack of *jus standi* of individuals before the Court, despite their position as bearer of rights under international law, is illustrated by the Advisory Opinion requested by the International Fund for Agricultural Development (IFAD). The Opinion underlined the difficulties faced by the ICJ when confronted by an appeal in a case in which the real dispute was that between an official and an international organization. The Court reiterated the concern it had voiced in the past over the inequality of access to the Court arising from the review process under Article XII of the Annex to the Statute of the Administrative Tribunal of the International Labour Organization (ILOAT), for '[t]he principle of equality of the parties follows from the requirements of good administration of justice'. While that principle had

[104] But see GA Res. A/Res/60/147 of 16 December 2005 annexing the Basic Principles and Guidelines on the Right to a Remedy and Reparation for Victims of Gross Violations of International Human Rights Law and Serious Violations of International Humanitarian Law, and Article 75 of the ICC Statute which provides for reparations and the establishment of a trust fund.

[105] *Wall* Opinion, ICJ Reports 2004, paras. 151–3 and *dispositif* 163 (3C).

[106] (Provisional Measures), ICJ Reports 2008, paras. 142–5.

to be understood as including access on an equal basis to appellate remedies, the appeal system established in 1946 led to an unequal position before the Court as the complainant was prevented from appearing in hearings in accordance with the Court's Statute in contrast to the international organizations concerned.[107] In an attempt to ensure some equality in the proceedings, the Court decided in its Order of 29 April 2010, that the complainant could make representations and present documents through the Fund and that there would be no oral proceeding. This 'procedural *acrobatie*' to mitigate the Court's structural deficiencies was found unsatisfactory by both Judges Cançado Trindade and Greenwood.[108]

The Court has also underlined not a right, but a *duty*, of third States under customary international law to react to breaches of fundamental human rights and IHL norms. It recalled, for example, in the *Nicaragua* and *Wall* cases, the obligation of State parties under common Article I of the Geneva Conventions not only to 'respect' the conventions, but even 'to ensure respect for them "in all circumstances"'.

In its *Wall* Opinion it called on all States given the character and importance of the obligations breached not to recognize or to assist in maintaining the illegal situation created by the construction of the wall, with implicit reference to Article 41 of the ILC Articles on State Responsibility relating to reactions to violations of peremptory norms; as well as to bring to an end any impediment to the exercise by the Palestinian people of its right to self-determination. But the Court also underlined the responsibility of the United Nations to consider further action to bring to an end the illegal situation.[109]

[107] *Judgment No. 2867 of the Administrative Tribunal of the International Labour Organization upon a Complaint Filed against the International Fund for Agricultural Development* (Advisory Opinion), ICJ Reports 2012, paras. 41–2, 44–6. The Court pointed to its previous judgments: *Judgments of the Administrative Tribunal of the ILO upon complaints made against the UNESCO* (Advisory Opinion), ICJ Reports 1956, p. 86; *Application for Review of Judgement No.158 of the United Nations Administrative Tribunal* (Advisory Opinion), ICJ Reports 1973, paras. 34, 179–80. In the present case, Ms Saez García had obtained a judgment in her favour, ordering the IFAD to pay to her moral and material damages, which the IFAD challenged by way of a request to the ICJ for an advisory opinion.

[108] ICJ Reports 2012, p. 51, Separate Opinion of Judge Trindade, para. 52, calling for a reconsideration of the scheme in order to grant *locus standi* to individuals in proceedings before the ICJ; *ibid.*, p. 94, Declaration of Judge Greenwood, paras. 3 and 4, considering that 'The Court should not be asked to participate in a procedure whose inequality is at odds with contemporary concepts of due process and the integrity of the judicial function' and which reduced Ms Saez García 'to the role of spectator rather than a participant in proceedings whose outcome would have a direct and substantial effect upon her'.

[109] *Wall* Opinion, ICJ Reports 2004, paras. 158–60, and *dispositif.*

Finally, in the *Application of the Genocide Convention* case the Court also outlined a duty of prevention under Article I of the Convention, though one embedded in a number of other international instruments, stating that the 'obligation on each contracting State to prevent genocide is both normative and compelling'. It outlined its view on this notion of 'due diligence' – one both to prevent and punish – as an obligation of conduct not of result. In assessing whether a State had duly discharged its obligations, one had to look at its capacity to influence effectively the actions of persons likely to or already committing genocide. This depended on geographical distance and on the political links which existed between the State concerned and the main actors in the perpetration of genocide. Responsibility, however, arose only at the time of commission of genocide in accordance with Article 14(3) of the Articles on State Responsibility, and entailed knowledge of the existence of the risk of genocide being perpetrated. In so doing, the Court also distinguished the obligation to prevent genocide – mere failure to adopt and implement suitable measures – from complicity in genocide which entailed positive action in the form of aid and assistance.[110]

V. Limitations of the Court in dealing with human rights issues

A. *The bilateral nature of State disputes*

The Court has emphasized the consensual nature of its jurisdiction even where *erga omnes* obligations were involved. *Barcelona Traction* had qualified the Court's sweeping rejection in the 1966 *South West Africa* case of the existence of an '"*actio popularis*", or right resident in any member of a community to take legal action in vindication of a public interest'.[111] But it is clear that in the absence of jurisdictional links, claims relating to obligations *erga omnes* cannot be accommodated. The Court on the one hand can pronounce on the *erga omnes* nature of self-determination in the *East Timor* case and on the other dismiss it on traditional '*Monetary Gold*' *principles* because it would be pronouncing on the lawfulness of Indonesia's conduct in its absence.[112]

Yet in *DRC* v. *Uganda* – as in its *Nauru* judgment in which it considered that a State which is not a party to a case is free to apply for permission to

[110] *Application of the Genocide Convention*, ICJ Reports 2007, paras. 427–32.
[111] ICJ Reports 1966, para. 88.
[112] *East Timor (Portugal* v. *Australia)*, ICJ Reports 1995, paras. 26, 35.

intervene in accordance with Article 62 of the Statute – the Court did not consider that this principle applied, for 'the interests of Rwanda clearly do not constitute "the very subject-matter" of the decision to be rendered by the Court on the DRC's claims against Uganda'.[113]

The inadequacy of this, however, was questioned by Judge Kooijmans, who stated:

> The system of international judicial dispute settlement is premised on the existence of a series of bilateral inter-State disputes... It inadequately reflects the structural instability and insecurity in the region, the overall pattern of lawlessness and disorder and the reprehensible behaviour of all parties involved. A reading of the Judgment cannot fail to leave the impression that the dispute is first and foremost a dispute between two neighbouring States about the use of force and the ensuing excesses, perpetrated by one of them. A two-dimensional picture may correctly depict the object shown but it lacks depth and therefore does not reflect reality in full.[114]

In the case of *DRC* v. *Rwanda*, the Court reiterated its position on jurisdiction in rejecting the DRC's contention that Rwanda's reservations, which bore on the Court's jurisdiction (Article IX of the Genocide Convention and Article 22 of CERD), were contrary to the object and purpose of their respective conventions and to *jus cogens* norms (prohibition of genocide and racial discrimination).[115] The Court stated:

> The fact that a dispute relates to compliance with a norm having such a [*jus cogens*] character... cannot of itself provide a basis for the jurisdiction of the Court to entertain that dispute. Under the Court's Statute that jurisdiction is always based on the consent of the parties.

It thus confirmed its position in *Legality of Use of Force*.[116] In this it clearly departed from the views held by both the Human Rights Committee and

113 *DRC* v. *Uganda*, ICJ Reports 2005, para. 204.

114 *DRC* v. *Uganda* case, Separate Opinion of Judge Kooijmans, paras. 11 and 14.

115 *DRC* v. *Rwanda*, ICJ Reports 2006, paras. 64–70, 76–9. This view was contested by some of the judges who pointed out that the procedural nature of a treaty clause did not preclude it from being a part of the treaty's object and purpose (Joint Separate Opinion of Judges Higgins, Kooijmans, Elaraby, Owada and Simma, *ibid.*, p. 65), as well as the Dissenting Opinon of Judge Koroma, who stated that Article IX of the Genocide Convention was indeed part of the object and purpose of the treaty, its very raison d'être, which is the prevention and punishment of the crime of genocide, because 'it is the only avenue for adjudicating the responsibility of states' (*ibid.*, p. 55, paras. 11–13).

116 See e.g. *Legality of Use of Force (Yugoslavia* v. *Spain)*, (Provisional Measures), ICJ Reports 1999, paras. 32–3; *Legality of Use of Force (Yugoslavia* v. *United States of America)* (Provisional Measures), ICJ Reports 1999, paras. 24–5.

the ECtHR on the invalidity of reservations which do not accept their competence.[117]

The Court is concerned with inter-State relations and with State responsibility for non-conformity with human rights obligations, not with the relation between the individual and the State which is that of human rights law. The individual victim of human rights violations appears only through the lens of diplomatic protection,[118] though the Court recognized in *Diallo* that the scope of diplomatic protection had widened from the international minimum standard of treatment of aliens to the internationally guaranteed human rights.[119] Interestingly, this was exactly the lens adopted by the ECtHR in its most recent case involving Cyprus and Turkey, in which it established that the Convention did not preclude the possibility of claiming damages in inter-State cases similar to those filed in the context of diplomatic protection, referring to the ICJ *Diallo* case. It underlined, however, as had the ICJ, that it should always be done for the benefit of the individual victim. It may be seen therefore that the institution of diplomatic protection is not alien to a human rights court in which individuals have *locus standi*.[120]

Because of State reluctance, there have been no inter-State disputes brought under the universal human rights treaty mechanisms and very few before the ECtHR. Yet, as seen, three cases have come to the Court under the compromissory clauses of the treaties concerned: CERD (in the *Georgia* v. *Russia* case), the Genocide Convention (in the *Bosnia* v. *Yugoslavia* case) and CAT (in the *Belgium* v. *Senegal* case).[121]

The Court's 'surprisingly narrow' and 'excessively formalistic' approach to Article 22 of CERD as a precondition to the seisin of the Court in deciding in the *Georgia* v. *Russia* case that States first had to have recourse to

117 See e.g. *Loizidou* v. *Turkey* (Preliminary Objections), judgment of 23 March 1995, ECtHR, Ser. A, No. 310; Human Rights Committee, *Rawle Kennedy* v. *Trinidad and Tobago*, Communication No. 845/1999, views adopted on 26 March 2002 (UN Doc. CCPR/C/67/D/845/1999); see also International Law Commission, Alain Pellet, Special Rapporteur, Tenth Report on Reservations to Treaties, UN Doc. A/CN.4/558/Add.1, 1 June 2005, 18.

118 Simma, 'Human Rights before the International Court of Justice', p. 319.

119 ICJ Reports 2007, para. 39.

120 *Case of Cyprus* v. *Turkey* (Application no. 25781/94) (Just satisfaction (GC)), judgment of 12 May 2014, paras. 45–6. The Court made several references to the ICJ case-law on the question of the formation of customary international law, reparations and diplomatic protection.

121 Simma, 'Human Rights before the International Court of Justice', p. 318, in which it is pointed out that only two other conventions have compromissory clauses (the 1952 Convention on the Political Rights of Women and the 1979 Convention on the Elimination of Discrimination Against Women (CEDAW)).

the other means of settlement provided for in the compromissory clauses, was strongly criticized in a Joint Dissenting Opinion, which underlined the importance of a less formalistic approach to access to the Court where human rights are concerned, stressing that the Court's purpose should not be to 'erect needless and over-exacting procedural obligations liable to delay or impede the applicant's access to justice'.[122]

B. *Relations between the Court, non-State entities and human rights bodies*

Non-State actors are denied access to the Court except perhaps in a different guise under Article 50 of the Statute (for the purposes of an enquiry or expert opinion), though recently both the PLO as representatives of the Palestinian people and the Kosovar authorities who had declared the independence of Kosovo on 17 February 2008 were allowed to submit their views to the Court in the context of advisory proceedings.

Recognition of a collective interest cannot therefore imply recognition of an automatic right to protection before the Court. So long as international organizations or non-governmental organizations (NGOs) are barred from accessing the Court in contentious matters, it is left up to States to establish that they have a jurisdictional right to claim in the protection of the general interest. In the *Nuclear Weapons* Opinion the Court was clearly confronted by the mobilizing force of civil society, including the symbolic testimony of the mayors of Hiroshima and Nagasaki who appeared before the Court, yet the role played by NGOs appears to have been disparaged by Judge Oda.[123]

There has, however, been a fruitful interaction with human rights bodies, the judgments of the Court carrying considerable weight in these specialized fora, as seen above. In turn, the Court has relied on the findings of, for example, Special Rapporteurs in the *Wall* Opinion, and *DRC* v. *Uganda* case, on the Concluding Observations of the Human Rights Committee on Israel and on its General Comments on extraterritoriality in the *Wall* Opinion and on the administration of justice in its IFAD Opinion; and on CAT in the *Diallo* case; it also relied on the International Criminal Tribunal for the Former Yugoslavia (ICTY) in the *Application*

[122] *Georgia* v. *Russia* (Preliminary Objections), Joint Dissenting Opinion by President Owada, Judges Simma, Abraham, Donoghue and Judge Ad Hoc Gaja, ICJ Reports 2011, p. 142.

[123] See ICJ Reports 1996, p. 330, Dissenting Opinion of Judge Oda, para. 8.

of the Genocide Convention case.[124] The Court, however, distanced itself from the latter's 'overall control' test on the question of effective control in the context of attribution of responsibility, stating rather scathingly that it found this test 'unpersuasive' and 'unsuitable'; for the ICTY was not called upon to rule on questions of State responsibility or on issues of general international law which did not lie within its jurisdiction.[125]

It is interesting to note in the context of a sporadic debate over whether the Secretary-General, as the head of a principal organ, should be authorized to request advisory opinions that this proposal had been originally put forward by the Secretary-General himself in 1950 with respect to the Human Rights Committee.[126] This would have provided a conduit from subsidiary organs or human rights treaty bodies to the Court, where these represented the interests of non-State entities debarred from access to international – as opposed to regional – judicial fora. If it ever came to it, this would be another way of bringing collective interests to the Court's forum without necessitating vast amendments to the Court's Statute.

Conclusion

Bruno Simma points out that 'the few swallows [in the Court's contribution to human rights law] have yet to make a summer'.[127] Yet one can build a construct from the Court's scattered pronouncements on human rights law: its hierarchy, sources, content and relations to other general international law areas, i.e its 'mainstreaming' as Simma puts it.

As I have attempted to show, the ICJ has not shied away from pronouncing on fundamental norms of international law, including those of

124 For a detailed exposition of the evolving Court's approach to the case law of human rights bodies, see the latest report of the ILA Human Rights Committee, 2014, 'Interim Report on International Human Rights Law and the International Court of Justice' (www.ila-hq.org/en/committees/index.cfm/cid/102730).

125 *Application of the Genocide* Convention, ICJ Reports 2007, paras. 403–4. Challenged on its overall control test in the *Delalic* case (2001), the ICTY Appeals Chamber had stated that the Tribunal was an autonomous international judicial body entitled to reach its own conclusions and that: although the ICJ is the 'principal judicial organ' within the United Nations system to which the Tribunal belongs, there is no hierarchical relationship between the two courts (*The Prosecutor* v. *Zejnil Delalic, Zdravko Mucic, Hasim Delic and Esad Landzo,* Case No. IT-96–21-A, Appeals Chamber, Judgment of 20 February 2001, para. 24).

126 See Rosalyn Higgins, 'A Comment on the Current Health of Advisory Opinions', in Vaughan Lowe and Malgosia Fitzmaurice (eds.), *Essays in Honour of Judge Jennings* (Cambridge University Press, 2008), pp. 567–81 at pp. 569–74.

127 Simma, 'Human Rights before the International Court of Justice', p. 319.

human rights, which underlie the emergence of an international public policy, even when this has meant playing a role in on-going armed conflict situations in which there are egregious violations of the rights of the civilian population.

In the realm of treaty-making, it has been conscious of the impact of the substantive content of a treaty on its formal and procedural rules and its furtherance of the concept of treaties with a collective interest has had ramifications in the fields of interpretation, application and reservations, among others. It is also undeniable that its scattered pronouncements relating to human rights have had repercussions on human rights courts and treaty bodies, as, for example, its bridging of human rights and humanitarian law. Rosenne posits the question as to whether:

> with the political polarization of the world and the accompanying tendency towards the fragmentation of international law into some sort of regional units and specialized functional branches, a Court organized primarily as a world Court applying general international law is always the most suitable form of international judicial organization.[128]

The Court, as has been seen, has integrated human rights law into a unitary vision of the international legal system, in insisting on its indivisibility, extraterritorial application and relations with other areas of international law, thus contributing to filling the 'black holes' created in the wake of 9/11.

The ICJ, an institution established at a time when bilateral and subjective relations between States based on the golden rule in *Lotus* prevailed, cannot always respond to expectations when faced with human rights cases. The requirement of a jurisdictional link and the fact that its decisions bind only the parties and its advisory opinions are just that, sits uneasily alongside the development of an international public policy in which subjective interests must give way to collective values and interests. Conscious of its apolitical judicial role,[129] which at times it has interpreted as one of stating the law as it is, not one of developing it, the Court's judgments have not always been welcomed by the human rights community, as for example its views on the absolute nature of State immunity.

128 S. Rosenne, *The Law and Practice of the International Court, 1920–1996*, vol. 1: The Court and the United Nations (The Hague: Martinus Nijhoff, 3rd edn. 1997), p. 7.

129 Though as Rosenne points out: 'the function performed by the existence of the Court (as distinct from the performance of that function by the Court itself) is to be seen in the ultimate analysis as a political one' (*ibid.*, p. 7).

But, while certainly its findings on direct violations of human rights have been limited, it has over time and in light of the evolution of the international environment resulting in a changing 'judicial culture', made a significant contribution to the structural and normative framework of human rights protection. Though in fits and starts, in part dependent on its composition at the time, the Court has on several occasions shown that it is conscious that in interpreting or applying the law, it could not make an abstraction of the human objectives behind the rules nor of the values and finalities which impregnate the international legal system. In this, it has also been conscious that even when acting in its contentious jurisdiction it is the principal organ of the United Nations bound by the purposes and principles of the UN Charter and therefore conceived to be a world court serving the world community.[130]

[130] See Vera Gowlland-Debbas, Commentaries on 'Art. 7, UN Charter' and 'Art. 1, ICJ Statute', in Andreas Zimmermann, Christian Tomuschat and Karin Oellers-Frahm (eds.), *Commentary on the Statute of the International Court of Justice* (Oxford University Press, 2006), pp. 79–105 and 195–204, respectively.

6

Factors influencing fragmentation and convergence in international courts

PHILIPPA WEBB

I. Introduction

International courts are not only deciding cases with common factual patterns, but are also interpreting, applying, and developing the same legal principles. One example is the law on genocide. The International Court of Justice (ICJ) has jurisdiction over state responsibility for genocide pursuant to Article IX of the Genocide Convention. The provisions of the Genocide Convention have also been incorporated almost verbatim into the statutes of the international criminal courts mandated to prosecute individuals.[1] As a result, the Genocide Convention is being interpreted and applied – through the lenses of state responsibility and individual criminal responsibility – by the ICJ, International Criminal Court (ICC), International Criminal Tribunal for the former Yugoslavia (ICTY), and the International Criminal Tribunal for Rwanda (ICTR).

A study of areas of law where there is a high level of activity by multiple international courts reveals that in most cases similar factual scenarios and similar legal issues are treated in a consistent manner.[2] In other words, the trend is towards convergence, though there are some areas of 'apparent integration' where judges attempt to integrate their decisions with those of other courts, but due to differing facts or the misapplication of legal concepts, cracks appear beneath the surface.

When one steps back from the detail of specific cases and discrete legal issues, three common themes can be identified which influence the degree

This chapter is based on the findings of my book: P. Webb, *International Judicial Integration and Fragmentation* (Oxford: Oxford University Press, 2013).

[1] Statute of the International Criminal Tribunal for the former Yugoslavia, Art. 5; Statute of the International Criminal Tribunal for Rwanda Art. 2; ICC Statute, Art. 6.

[2] See Webb, *International Judicial Integration and Fragmentation*, which examines cases on genocide, immunities and the use of force as decided by the ICJ, ICC, ICTY, and ICTR.

of convergence or fragmentation.[3] First, the type of court, including its temporal nature, its function, and the institutional regime it is embedded within (whether the United Nations system or something else) appears to be an important factor in the degree to which judges seek to integrate their decisions with existing jurisprudence. Second, the area of law involved in the case and whether it is governed by treaty or custom, is regularly subject to judicial settlement, or is controversial, has an impact on the degree of flexibility judges have in interpreting and developing the law. Finally, the procedural rules and practices of a court relating to evidence, judgment drafting, and the use of existing case law also affect the degree of fragmentation or convergence.

This chapter will examine how these three themes – the identity of the court, the substance of the law and the procedures employed – explain convergence and fragmentation in the international legal system.

II. Identity of the court

A. *Permanent versus ad hoc*

A key aspect of the identity of a court – and of its tendency towards convergence or fragmentation – is its temporal nature.

The permanent nature of a court increases its tendency towards convergence. Permanence is associated with stability and authority. Although international courts exist in a horizontal arrangement, with no official hierarchy among them, the permanent nature and long history of the ICJ give its judgments a certain weight and the ability to clarify a legal issue and integrate pre-existing streams of reasoning. For example, the ICJ's *Arrest Warrant* Judgment has become the touchstone for the nature and extent of immunity *ratione personae*.[4] The Judgment has both expanded the categories of officials who enjoy this immunity and confirmed absolute immunity from criminal process. It is likely that the same phenomenon will arise with respect to the 2012 *Jurisdictional Immunities* Judgment, which rejected an exception to state immunity for violations of international law, even if they are of a *jus cogens* character.[5]

[3] Cf. the twelve factors identified in Chester Brown, *A Common Law of International Adjudication* (Oxford: Oxford University Press, 2007) ch. 7.

[4] *Arrest Warrant of 11 April 2000* (*Democratic Republic of the Congo* v. *Belgium*) (Judgment) [2002] ICJ Rep. 3.

[5] *Jurisdictional Immunities of the State*(*Germany* v. *Italy, Greece Intervening*) (Merits: Judgment) [2012] ICJ Rep.

At the same time, the permanence of the ICJ can make it act cautiously and thus refrain from integrating varied interpretations about a legal question. The long-term view of the Court may encourage it to wait for a future case that raises the question squarely on the facts with a solid basis of jurisdiction and proper pleadings, rather than passing 'through the eye of the needle' to pronounce on a question forming a tangent to the core legal issues.[6] The ICJ has a pattern of declining to pronounce on controversial legal issues that are not perceived as necessary for the resolution of the dispute between the parties.[7] This hesitancy may, however, also be a result of the lack of clear state practice on an issue.

While it is too early in the life of the ICC to reach definitive conclusions, the Court appears to possess a sense of the long-term development of a body of law. In its limited case law, the ICC has placed emphasis on its Statute, Rules and Elements of Crimes as opposed to trying to divine customary rules of international law. It also displayed a tendency towards convergence, making a conscious effort to refer to the decisions of the ICJ and ICTY and to align its reasoning accordingly.

Whereas permanence tends to promote convergence (unless caution prevents action), the ad hoc nature of an international court or tribunal seems to generate innovation, boldness, and, sometimes as a result, the fragmentation of international law. The ICTY's *Tadic Appeal* Decision is a classic example of the boldness or 'surprising temerity'[8] that may be displayed by ad hoc judicial bodies. In seeking to assert its independence in an early appeal[9] – and perhaps riding the wave of the *Tadic Jurisdiction* Decision where the Tribunal had decided upon its own legitimacy – the Appeals Chamber labelled the ICJ's *Nicaragua* 'effective control' test for the attribution of state responsibility to be 'unconvincing'[10] and

[6] This phrase was in fact used by Judge Higgins in her Separate Opinion in *Oil Platforms* (*Islamic Republic of Iran* v. *United States of America*) (Judgment) [2003] ICJ Rep. 161, para. 26, while criticizing the Court's decision to engage in analysis of the law on the use of force.

[7] See, for example, Judgments relating to the identity of the attacker in the context of an armed attack triggering the right to self-defence, and the test for State (and individual) complicity in genocide.

[8] Allison Marston Danner, 'When Courts Make Law: How the International Criminal Tribunals Recast the Laws of War' (2006) 59 *Vanderbilt Law Review* 101, 132.

[9] In another Appeals decision on the same topic, the Chamber noted that it was an 'autonomous international judicial body' that was not in a hierarchical relationship with the ICJ: *Prosecutor* v. *Delalic and others 'Celebici'* (Judgment) IT-96–21-A, A Ch (20 February 2001) para. 24.

[10] *Prosecutor* v. *Tadic* (Judgment) IT-94–1-A, A Ch (15 July 1999) para. 116.

developed its own, less stringent standard of 'overall control'.[11] However, the ICTY was deciding an issue that went beyond its jurisdiction. In the *Bosnia Genocide* Judgment, the ICJ, displaying some of the authority that flows from permanence, carefully explained how this was a situation of only apparent fragmentation; the two tests could co-exist since they addressed different issues.[12]

Ad hoc courts like the ICTY and ICTR, and the hybrid courts that they have paved the way for, may provide benefits similar to soft law in that they allow governments to 'introduce rules on a tentative basis, test political reactions to them[,] and preserve deniability if the responses are adverse'.[13] Yet, this propensity towards experimentation and innovation also carries with it the risk of fragmentation and incoherence. The incentives to take a long-term view and embed themselves in existing legal frameworks are weaker for ad hoc courts. This is vividly illustrated by the practice of arbitral tribunals on the use of force, where short-term views and the misapplication of the decisions of international courts have created uncertainty. For example, the Eritrea–Ethiopia Claims Commission (EECC) and the Guyana/Suriname arbitral tribunal have applied the law on the use of force in ways that have generated confusion rather than consistency.[14]

Arbitral tribunals usually exist only for the purposes of the specific dispute; the tribunal disbands once the case is over and the award rendered. The registries, arbitrators, and applicable rules vary from case to case. There is inconsistent publication of pleadings and reporting of awards, which hinders the accumulation of a body of jurisprudence that may be referred to by parties and arbitrators. All these factors contribute to a sense of deciding in a vacuum rather than as part of an international legal system.

Interestingly, ad hoc courts may begin to share some of the features of permanent courts over time. As an institution ages, a certain inertia may

[11] *Ibid.*, para. 120.

[12] *Application of the Convention on the Prevention and Punishment of the Crime of Genocide* (*Bosnia and Herzegovina* v. *Serbia and Montenegro*) (Judgment) [2007] ICJ Rep. 43 ('*Bosnian Genocide* Judgment').

[13] K. W. Abbott and D. Snidal, 'Pathways to International Cooperation', in Eyal Benvenisti and Moshe Hirsch (eds.), *The Impact of International Law on International Cooperation* (Cambridge: Cambridge University Press, 2004), p. 70.

[14] Eritrea–Ethiopia Claims Commission *Partial Award- Jus ad Bellum: Ethiopia's Claims 1–8* (2005) 45 ILM 430; *Guyana/Suriname* (Award of the Arbitral Tribunal) (17 September 2007) (regarding use of force and title to territory and the degree of gravity required for an 'armed attack' in the context of the right to self-defence).

set in that pushes against creative legal reasoning and solutions (which could cast doubt on previous decisions or reasoning).[15] The ICTY and ICTR have generally become less innovative in recent years. This is due in part to the fact that novel legal questions arose more frequently in the early years of the tribunals. However, it might also indicate that as the tribunals near their second decade of operation and accumulate a substantial body of case law, they see the benefits of proceeding incrementally. The time pressure generated by the completion strategy may also lead to decisions being focused on the disposition of the particular case rather than on experimenting with the substantive body of law.[16]

Finally, 'permanence' can have an important personal component along with the generalist element. Particular lawyers over their careers, wearing different hats, may provide much of the permanence in various courts, particularly if they are generalists.[17]

B. Function

The function of an international court permeates its approach, defines its goals, determines its structure, and shapes its self-perception.

The fact that a court, such as the ICJ, is concerned with inter-state dispute settlement does not automatically mean it has a tendency towards convergence or fragmentation. Rather, problems with fragmentation surface when a court steps beyond its bounds, or is perceived as having done so. For example, the ICC may be forced into deciding issues of state responsibility due to the 2010 amendments made to its Statute on the crime of aggression.[18] According to Article 8bis of the amendment adopted at the Kampala Review Conference in 2010, in order to convict an individual for the 'crime of aggression' the ICC would first need to

[15] Compare ICTY Trial Chamber II's attempt to replace joint criminal enterprise with co-perpetration in *Prosecutor* v. *Stakić* (Judgment) IT-97–24-T, T Ch II (31 July 2003), with the Appeals Chamber's decision to retain the original joint criminal enterprise structure in *Prosecutor* v. *Stakić* (Judgment) IT-97–24-A, A Ch (22 March 2006).

[16] Cf. however the controversial *Gotovina* Appeals Judgment of the ICTY (*Prosecutor* v. *Ante Gotovina and Mladen Markač*, IT-06–90-A, 16 November 2012) and the majority's implicit change in standards of review and the 'specific direction' standard for aiding and abetting that the ICTY announced in *Perišić* (IT-04–81), Appeals Chamber Judgment of 28 February 2013 and *Stanišić* (IT-03–69), Trial Chamber Judgment of 30 May 2013.

[17] I am grateful to Judge Keith for this point.

[18] Kampala Review Conference 'Resolution on the Crime of Aggression, Annex III' (11 June 2010) ICC Doc. RC/Res.6. The Assembly of States Parties may decide to alter the amendments after 2017.

make a judicial finding that an 'act of aggression' had occurred. That 'act of aggression' is defined as state conduct, recalling the words of Article 2(4) of the UN Charter. If there is a prior finding of an 'act of aggression' by a body competent to do so, such as the ICJ or the Security Council, and the ICC follows that finding, then the scenario is one of convergence. If, however, the ICC departs from such a finding, there will be fragmentation, unless the disparate results can be explained on the basis of, for example, standard of proof. If there is no prior finding and the ICC's decision constitutes the first statement on aggression, this raises the potential for fragmentation, given that this is the primary (though not exclusive) purview of another body, which is unlikely to defer to or seek to integrate with the ICC. The potential for fragmentation is heightened by the fact that in nearly all of its other tasks under the Statute,[19] the ICC acts as a court concerned with individual criminal responsibility and its procedural framework reflects this. It was not designed to be a court that deals with inter-state matters, let alone the controversial and evolving law on the use of force.

The different functions of the international courts may make it possible to 'relativize' legal rules so that, for example, 'the required intent for genocide as per the ICJ' may have different contours from 'the required intent for genocide as per the ICTY and ICTR'.[20] Since these courts are set up under different statutory regimes and, despite some important overlaps, are concerned with different spheres of behaviour (state responsibility versus individual responsibility, civil versus criminal), it would be expected for one type of court to take one position and another to take a different position in some circumstances. If these differences can be 'relativized' and justified on the basis of function, then this need not result in fragmentation. Convergence does not equate to uniformity; as long as disparities in treatment of the same or similar legal issues are explained and justified, the end result can still be convergence. The difficulty is that this 'relativization' requires precise and clear legal reasoning as well as a full awareness of the different functions of each of the courts and the context in which they are making decisions. Without this precision and awareness, 'relativization' could easily slip into fragmentation, resulting in uncertainty as to the content and applicability of legal rules.

[19] The definition of crime against humanity incorporates the ideas of a state or organizational policy to commit an attack, which may require the ICC to examine state conduct: ICC Statute, Art. 7(2)(a).

[20] I am grateful to Professor Lea Brilmayer for this suggestion.

C. *Institutional context*

The institutional context in which a court is embedded has a critical impact on its behaviour. It encompasses the relationship between the court and other international organizations or bodies (such as the UN) as well as the relationship between the court and states or individuals, expressed through its jurisdictional arrangements. The regime in which a court operates can provide incentives towards the convergence or fragmentation of international law.

The institutional context of various international courts has shaped their jurisdiction, which in turn has an impact on how they develop international law. The ICJ, ICTY, ICTR, and ICC are all reactive; their body of case law depends on which cases come before them. This already presents a challenge for developing the law in any comprehensive way. Scholarly bodies such as the International Law Commission (ILC) and the *Institut de droit international* can select the legal areas they wish progressively to develop or to codify.[21] They then have time – usually several years, or more – to study the topic in-depth, not through the factual constraints of a case. This allows such non-judicial bodies proactively to develop the law in a comprehensive manner. This ability comes, of course, at the expense of the end-product (a set of draft articles or a resolution) not possessing binding power over any state, unless it is later adopted as a treaty.

In addition to their reactive nature, each court faces distinct jurisdictional challenges. For example, each of the 193 UN member states is a party to the ICJ Statute, but that merely constitutes an *entitlement* to use the Court.[22] States cannot be compelled to bring their disputes to the ICJ – consent is required to be a party to a case. This principle of consent originates in the UN's emphasis on sovereign equality.[23] Organizations with smaller and perhaps more cohesive memberships have made resort to their regional courts compulsory in nature.[24] Only sixty-seven states have made declarations accepting the ICJ's jurisdiction under Article 36(2) of the Statute. States occasionally come to the court by joint

[21] Under its Statute, the ILC shall also consider proposals for the progressive development of international law referred by the General Assembly (Art. 16) or submitted by UN member states, the principal organs other than the General Assembly, specialized agencies or official bodies established by inter-governmental agreements to encourage the progressive development and codification of international law (Art. 17).

[22] UN Charter, Art. 93(1). [23] *Ibid.*, Art. 2(1).

[24] See, for example, the European Court of Human Rights, the European Court of Justice, and the Andean Tribunal of Justice. Consent to the jurisdiction of the Inter-American Court of Human Rights is optional and the United States, for example, has not consented.

agreement[25] or, very unusually, by simply inviting the intended respondent to accept the Court's jurisdiction for the purpose of the case.[26] The most common way of consenting to the Court's jurisdiction is by compromissory clauses contained in about three hundred treaties that refer to the Court in relation to the settlement of disputes arising from their application or interpretation.[27]

When a case comes to the ICJ by the compromissory clause in a treaty, the Court is constrained by the subject matter of that treaty. For example, in the *Bosnia Genocide* case the Court only had jurisdiction under the Genocide Convention and therefore could not examine alleged breaches of other international obligations, 'even if the alleged breaches were of obligations under peremptory norms, or of obligations which protect essential humanitarian values, and which may be owed *erga omnes*'.[28] While this allowed the ICJ to undertake a close analysis of the Genocide Convention and contribute to the convergence of law in that field, it did not allow it to consider crimes against humanity.

The requirement of party consent to jurisdiction for each case before the ICJ means that some cases that have the potential to advance the understanding of important legal areas cannot be decided by the Court. The *Congo* v. *France* case involved fascinating questions about the scope of the immunity of state officials, but it was later removed from the Court's List at the request of the Republic of the Congo.[29] Some commentators have suggested that the Court tries to encourage states to consent to its jurisdiction by reaching uncontroversial 'middle ground' decisions.[30] They cite a temptation to reach outcomes that give all parties something and appear to provide a fair basis for settlement.[31] The fact that some

[25] See, for example, *Sovereignty over Pulau Ligitan and Pulau Sipadan (Indonesia/Malaysia)*; *Sovereignty over Pedra Branca/Pulau Batu Puteh, Middle Rocks and South Ledge (Malaysia/Singapore)*; *Frontier Dispute (Benin/Niger)*; *Frontier Dispute (Burkina Faso/Niger)*.

[26] ICJ Statute, Art. 38(5). This is known as *forum prorogatum*.

[27] For example, between 1998 and 2003, three cases were brought to the Court by Paraguay, Germany, and Mexico, claiming the United States had violated the right of their arrested nationals to consular notification. Jurisdiction was based on a clause contained in the Vienna Convention on Consular Relations.

[28] *Bosnia Genocide* Judgment, para. 147.

[29] *Certain Criminal Proceedings in France (Republic of the Congo* v. *France)* (Order) [2010] ICJ Rep. 143.

[30] E. Posner and J. Yoo, 'Judicial Independence in International Tribunals' (2005) 93 *California Law Review* 1.

[31] Yuval Shany, 'Bosnia, Serbia and the Politics of International Adjudication' (2008) 45 *Justice* 21; G. Abi-Saab, 'Fragmentation or Unification: Some Concluding Remarks' (1999) 31 *New York University Journal of International Law and Politics* 919, 930.

judgments appear cautious or attempt to 'split the difference' is more attributable to factors such as the permanence of the ICJ and its collegial method of decision-making than its consensual jurisdiction. There are at the same time many judgments that are robust and go against the interests of powerful states.[32]

The jurisdictional regimes of the ICTY and ICTR set a relatively narrow frame for the tribunals to operate within. Their jurisdictions are limited to a specific conflict, a defined period of time,[33] and a list of crimes. However, two aspects of jurisdiction have given the tribunals the freedom to develop the law within these confines. First, both tribunals have primacy over national courts and may thus request that other courts defer to their competence.[34] This gives the tribunals a leadership role in shaping the law, which – when combined with the temporary nature of the tribunals – appears to provide an incentive towards innovation and possible fragmentation.[35] Second, many of the crimes within the subject-matter jurisdiction of the tribunals had not been prosecuted since the Nuremberg and Tokyo tribunals, if at all. While some treaties defined the prohibited acts in general terms, the way in which individuals could be held criminally responsible for such acts was largely left to the tribunals to develop.

The ICC's jurisdiction differs to the ICTY and ICTR in two important ways. First, its jurisdiction is governed by the principle of complementarity.[36] It may only exercise jurisdiction where the national legal system is not taking any action[37] or is 'unwilling or unable genuinely

[32] *Maritime Delimitation in the Black Sea* (*Romania* v. *Ukraine*) (Judgment) [2009] ICJ Rep. 61 was a clear victory for Romania. The ICJ has found against the United States in the *Oil Platforms*, and in the series of cases based on the Vienna Convention on Consular Relations; it also found against the Russian Federation in the provisional measures phase of the *Application of the International Convention on the Elimination of All Forms of Racial Discrimination* (*Georgia* v. *Russian Federation*) (Request for the Indication of Provisional Measures: Order) [2008] ICJ Rep. 353.

[33] The ICTY's temporal jurisdiction has a specific start date, but an open-ended end date (ICTY Statute. Art. 8).

[34] ICTY Statute, Art. 9(1), (2), and ICTR Statute, Art. 8(2).

[35] The ICJ also has a leadership role as the principal judicial organ of the UN, but the permanence of the institution tends to lead it towards convergence rather than fragmentation.

[36] ICC Statute, Art. 17.

[37] This limb of the admissibility test was clarified by the ICC Appeals Chamber in the *Prosecutor* v. *Germain Katanga and Mathieu Ngudjolo Chui* (Judgment on the appeal of Mr Germain Katanga against the Oral Decision of Trial Chamber II of 12 June 2009 on the Admissibility of the Case) ICC-01/04–01/07, A Ch (25 September 2009). See Ben Batros, 'The Judgment on the Katanga Admissibility Appeal: Judicial Restraint at the ICC' (2010) 23 *Leiden Journal of International Law* 343.

to carry out the investigation or prosecution'.[38] This feature – combined with the reactive nature of jurisdiction common to all courts – limits the types of cases that will come before the ICC, hampering its ability to develop the law in a holistic or systematic way. Second, unlike the ICTY and ICTR, the ICC is explicitly required by Article 21(3) of its Statute to interpret the crimes within its subject-matter jurisdiction in a manner 'consistent with internationally recognized human rights, and . . . without any adverse distinction founded on grounds such as gender . . . , age, race, colour, language, religion or belief, political or other opinion, national, ethnic or social origin, wealth, birth or other status'.[39] This rule of interpretation provides an incentive for judges to embed the ICC's decisions within the broader framework of existing international human rights law jurisprudence.

III. Substance of the law

A. *Treaty or custom*

If an area of law is governed by a detailed and comprehensive treaty, the potential contribution of judicial decisions is usually limited to providing specific interpretations of terms or articles and elaborating on the meaning of general provisions. On the other hand, if an area of law largely relies on customary international law and the attendant 'amorphous processes of state practice and *opinio juris*'[40] the court's contribution is greater: it can analyse existing practice, determine the general rule, consider whether contemporary developments have created exceptions to the general rule, and so on. The scope for interpretation is larger; the court is not limited to the rules in the Vienna Convention on the Law of Treaties regarding the ordinary meaning of a text and consideration of context, object and purpose, and the *travaux préparatoires*.[41] Instead, a court addressing customary international law may consider a whole range of expressions of state practice and *opinio juris*.

For example, the existence of the comprehensive, widely ratified Convention on the Prevention and Punishment of Genocide has facilitated

[38] ICC Statute, Art. 17.

[39] ICC Statute, Art. 21(3). The differences (relating to complementarity and sources) between the ICC Statute and the Statutes of the ICTY and ICTR limit the convergence that flows from the otherwise similar drafting of the constitutive instruments: cf. Brown, *A Common Law*, pp. 226–7.

[40] A. Boyle and C. Chinkin, *The Making of International Law* (Oxford: Oxford University Press, 2007), p. 268.

[41] Vienna Convention on the Law of Treaties 1969, Arts. 31 and 32.

convergence in a number of areas. There is widespread agreement among the international courts that the protected groups are restricted to the four categories of national, ethnical, racial, or religious as specified in the *chapeau* to Article II of the Convention. As the courts delved into the meaning of these terms, especially the vague notion of 'ethnical', some contradictory holdings emerged. However, after a period of time, there is consensus on most points. There is also genuine convergence on the nature of the destruction required (physical–biological). The clear phrasing of the acts listed in Article II of the Convention has also led to the common approaches to interpretation.

At the same time, the law on genocide also demonstrates how the brevity or vagueness of a provision in a treaty may increase the risk of fragmentation. The reference in Article II to 'the intent to destroy, in whole or in part, a national, ethnical, racial or religious group, as such' has led to diverging purpose-based and knowledge-based approaches in the various international courts. The ambivalence in the judicial practice has now been codified in the ICC Elements of Crimes, which refers to both purpose-based and knowledge-based approaches in its provision on the mental element for crimes within the jurisdiction of the Court.

By contrast to genocide, most of the law on immunities is customary in nature. National and international courts are therefore often engaged in a process that is much more creative and flexible than the interpretation and application of treaty law. As seen in the ICJ *Arrest Warrant* and *Jurisdictional Immunities* Judgments or the UK House of Lords Judgment in *Jones* v. *Saudi Arabia*, judges are engaged in analysing a variety of materials: national legislation, national case law, international case law, statutes of international criminal courts, unratified treaties, ILC reports, *Institut de droit international* resolutions, and doctrine.[42] The breadth of this material – much of which does not evince a clear pattern in one direction or another – contributes to the diverging interpretations that have emerged from courts on the nature and scope of immunity *ratione materiae*.

The type of law – treaty or custom – can also have broader consequences, in that it can shape the behaviour of the judicial institution itself, including the extent to which the court is inward-looking or outward-looking and whether it is concerned with fragmentation or oblivious to

[42] *Jones* v. *Minister of Interior of Kingdom of Saudi Arabia* [2006] UKHL 26, [2006] 2 WLR 70.

it. This impact is most visible with respect to the international criminal courts. The ICC, for example, operates in a heavily codified legal environment. It not only applies the detailed ICC Statute, but also the Rules of Procedure and the Elements of Crimes. The latter two documents were drafted by the political governing body, the Assembly of States Parties (ASP), and not the judges themselves, which is a departure from the practice of the ad hoc tribunals. In this context, the ICC may assume that the states undertook the work of integrating international law when drafting these instruments. Yet, the Statute, the Rules, and Elements constitute, at most, a snapshot of custom at a particular point in time; this raises the prospect for future fragmentation between the codified law and the evolution of custom on the ground. Indeed, states explicitly contemplated future fragmentation and sought to regulate the relationship between potentially divergent sources when they drafted Article 10 of the Statute:

> Nothing in this Part [on Jurisdiction, admissibility and applicable law] shall be interpreted as limiting or prejudicing in any way existing or developing rules of international law for purposes other than this Statute.

The determination of where the ICC Statute and customary international law part company, however, will not always be easy, especially as states implement the provisions in their national legal systems in keeping with the principle of complementarity.

As for the ICJ, the application of treaty or custom is contingent on the nature of the case that comes before it and the basis of jurisdiction. In one case the Court may be required to rely on customary international law,[43] whereas another case must be confined to the interpretation of a specific treaty.[44] This means that the Court's overall behaviour is influenced by more constant factors, such as its permanence and its place in the UN system, than the type of law it tends to apply.

B. *Level of development*

In a similar way to how the use of customary international law provides courts with greater scope for creativity, the relative sparseness of judicial practice on an area of law also provides space for judicial innovation. If

[43] See, e.g., *Military and Paramilitary Activities in and against Nicaragua* (*Nicaragua* v. *United States of America*) (Jurisdiction and Admissibility: Judgment) [1984] ICJ Rep. 392.

[44] See, e.g., *Bosnia Genocide* Judgment.

an area of law has been the subject of extensive judicial practice, later decisions will be easier to integrate into the existing body of jurisprudence. The amount of judicial practice on a legal area or issue depends on two factors. The first factor is the rate at which disputes on that legal area are submitted to judicial settlement. Some legal areas are usually addressed through non-legal means of dispute settlement, such as negotiation, enquiry, mediation, conciliation, resort to regional agencies or arrangements, or other peaceful means of the parties' choice.[45] Disputes regarding the use of force, for example, tend to be addressed bilaterally through diplomatic exchanges, in regional fora or in the Security Council. The second factor is the passage of time. The innovations by the ICTY and ICTR have become progressively less pronounced over the years; there are fewer novel issues confronting the judges and the focus has shifted from developing international criminal law as a whole to completing the work of the tribunals before specific deadlines and achieving internal consistency. A legal issue may arise as a result of contemporary developments, and it takes time for a corpus of court decisions to accumulate, as we can see with the question of a human rights exception to state immunity.[46]

As case law on a legal area aggregates, apparent or genuine fragmentation on a certain issue may transform into convergence. This will depend on the degree to which judges engage in dialogue because convergence requires awareness of the existing points of view.

There tends to be greater convergence on *core* legal issues and more uncertainty and fragmentation on issues at the *periphery*. This is unsurprising since most legal disputes will tend to concern the core legal issues, and such issues will attract the attention of the judges and occupy the pleadings of the parties. Core issues will also arise more frequently. Judges will be aware of a growing body of jurisprudence (at least within their own court) analysing the issue, and probably seek to locate themselves within it. In the law on immunities, for example, there is consensus on the types of immunities and which officials enjoy them, but there is disagreement on which acts are covered by immunity *ratione materiae* and the specific question of whether there is an exception to the immunity of officials for human rights violations.

[45] Based on UN Charter, Art. 33(1).

[46] See, e.g., *Jurisdictional Immunities of the State* (*Germany* v. *Italy, Greece Intervening*) (Merits: Judgment) [2012] ICJ Rep.

C. *Level of controversy and change*

Controversy and change both increase the tendency towards fragmentation, at least in the short term. Case law tends to become unsettled as judges either avoid legal issues or propose creative solutions adapted to current conditions. Convergence can, however, be achieved over time as the body of jurisprudence grows, and consensus emerges on controversial or cutting-edge points of law.

A high level of controversy may lead courts to avoid reaching decisions if not absolutely required on the facts before them. Several Judgments of the ICJ on the use of force demonstrate this tendency. It may be a matter of judges declining to decide difficult issues in the belief that political bodies – or the accretion of state practice – are better suited to resolve such questions.[47] However, judges may also see problems with pronouncing on important legal issues when the facts or the jurisdictional basis of the case do not require them to make such findings.[48]

Changing conditions, whether the impact of globalization, the development of new weapons, or the rise of non-state actors, also complicate the judging function. Assumptions underlying legal rules or underpinning an existing body of case law may need to be re-examined and adjusted. International courts face the challenge of 'modulating the contradictory demands of rule stability and flexibility'.[49]

Controversy is often associated with change, but the impact of changing conditions on judicial practice has its own distinctive features. Shifts in underlying conditions tend to promote judicial activity rather than caution. As Eskridge has argued in the domestic US context, dynamic statutory interpretation of the law is most appropriate 'when the relevant texts are old, where a single legislative purpose is not obvious, and where underlying conditions have changed'.[50] This 'evolutive' theory of interpretation suggests that international courts should adopt

[47] On a different but related point, see the Separate Opinion of Judge Keith, *Accordance with International Law of the Unilateral Declaration of Independence in Respect of Kosovo* (Advisory Opinion) [2010] ICJ Rep. 1(stating the ICJ should have exercised its discretion to refuse to answer the question which the General Assembly submitted to it because the request was essentially concerned with the actual exercise of special powers by another organ under the Charter, the Security Council).

[48] See *Oil Platforms*, para. 26 (Separate Opinion of Judge Higgins).

[49] Danner, 'When Courts Make Law', 105.

[50] W. Eskridge Jr, 'Dynamic Statutory Interpretation' (1987) 135 *University of Pennsylvania Law Review* 1479, 1483–4.

a dynamic approach and engage in 'judicial updating' of the relevant laws.[51]

IV. Procedure

A. *Fact-finding and evidence*

The procedures related to evidence influence the extent of judicial convergence or fragmentation in a manner that is perhaps less visible than the identity of the court or the substance of the area of law. Yet, the fact-finding ability of a court, its approach to proof, and its treatment of evidence shape the judicial decision-making in important ways. Two courts may reach different legal conclusion on the same legal issue as a result of disparate approaches to the facts of the case. For example, the availability of a broad range of evidence (forensic material, witness testimony, investigative reports, expert evidence) may enable one court to reach comprehensive conclusions whereas another court is dependent on what the parties present in their pleadings. In another situation, a court may reach a conclusion without specifying a standard of proof whereas another court is required to test evidence against an express and stringent standard.

The ICJ and the international criminal courts possess different fact-finding abilities as result of their functions. Findings of fact for a criminal court necessarily entail different procedures from those in a civil court. The ICC, ICTY, and ICTR have much more control over the production of evidence. Each court possesses an 'Office of the Prosecutor' that includes a large Investigations Division. Yet, the courts rely on state cooperation, especially when gathering evidence in the field.[52] The inability of international criminal courts to gather evidence – when combined with their strict rules on standard of proof – can change the outcome of a case. If the same legal issue comes before two courts, with different evidence available before each institution, the risk of fragmentation is apparent.

The differing approaches to burden of proof and standard of proof within and between the various courts may impact on convergence or fragmentation. At the ICTY, ICTR, and ICC, the burden of proof is on

[51] *Ibid.* See also Danner, 'When Courts Make Law', 151.

[52] See the reports of the ICC Prosecutor to the Security Council regarding Sudan's lack of cooperation.

the prosecution, save perhaps for defences and the proof of mitigating circumstances at sentencing.[53] For the ICJ, a party alleging a fact bears the burden of proving it. Sometimes each party will bear that burden, albeit in relation to different claims.[54] This simple rule can become quite complicated in practice, including in the way it interacts with inferences.[55]

As regards standard of proof, the law on genocide is an apt field for exploring the contrast between the ICJ and the international criminal courts. The standard at the international criminal courts is transparent: proof beyond reasonable doubt. The ICC Statute explicitly states that 'the Court must be convinced of the guilt of the accused beyond reasonable doubt'.[56] The Statutes of the ICTY and ICTR are silent as to standard of proof, but the standard of 'beyond reasonable doubt' was adopted by the judges in the Rules of Procedure without any controversy.[57]

Establishing the standard of proof for state responsibility has been more convoluted at the ICJ for two reasons. First, the Court's role in deciding disputes between states on a huge range of potential international law questions[58] has made it reluctant to specify a global standard of proof. Its prime objective appears to have been to retain freedom in evaluating evidence, relying on the facts of each case.[59] Second, the diverse composition of the bench leads to different approaches. As Former President Rosalyn Higgins has explained: '[p]art of this reluctance to be specific is caused by

[53] See, for example, ICC Statute, Art. 66(2) ('The onus is on the Prosecutor to prove the guilt of the accused') and Art. 67(1)(i) (the rights of the accused include '[n]ot to have imposed on him or her any reversal of the burden of proof or any onus of rebuttal'). See W. Schabas, 'Article 66', in Otto Triffterer (ed.), *Commentary on the Rome Statute of the International Criminal Court: Observer's Notes, Article by Article* (2nd edn., Oxford: Hart and Nomos Publishing, 2008).

[54] For example, it is incumbent on the applicant claiming diplomatic protection to prove that local remedies were exhausted or to establish that exceptional circumstances relieved the allegedly injured person whom the applicant seeks to protect of the obligation to exhaust available local remedies. It is for the respondent to show that there were effective remedies in its domestic legal system that were not exhausted. See also C. Amerasinghe, *Evidence in International Litigation* (Leiden: Brill, 2005), pp. 61–72.

[55] *Corfu Channel case* (*United Kingdom* v. *Albania*) (Merits: Judgment) [1949] ICJ Rep. 4, 18–19. See also David McKeever, 'The Contribution of the International Court of Justice to the Law on the Use of Force: Missed Opportunities or Unrealistic Expectations?' (2009) 78 *Nordic Journal of International Law*361, 390–1.

[56] ICC Statute, Art. 66(3).

[57] ICTY, Rules of Procedure and Evidence, rule 87; ICTR Rules of Procedure and Evidence, rule 87.

[58] ICJ Statute, Art. 36(2).

[59] M. Kazazi, *Burden of Proof and Related Issues: A Study of Evidence before International Tribunals* (Alphen aan den Rijn: Kluwer Law International, 1996), p. 323.

the gap between the explicit standard-setting approach of the common law and the "*intime conviction du juge*" familiar under civil law'.[60]

Nonetheless, the ICJ did establish a standard of proof for state responsibility for genocide in the *Bosnia Genocide* Judgment.[61] The Court stated that 'charges of exceptional gravity' required 'evidence that is fully conclusive'. This standard was applied to allegations that the crime of genocide or other acts in Article III of the Convention (conspiracy, incitement, attempt, complicity) had been committed as well as to the proof of attribution for such acts.[62] In respect of the claims related to the obligations to prevent and punish genocide, the Court required 'a high level of certainty appropriate to the seriousness of the allegation'.[63]

The different standards of proof employed by the ICJ and international criminal courts are rational, given the different roles and methodologies of these judicial institutions.[64] The ICJ's 'fully conclusive' standard is neither higher nor lower than 'beyond reasonable doubt'; 'it is a *comparable* standard, but using terminology more appropriate to a civil, international law case'.[65] It would seem that these different standards can co-exist. The risk of fragmentation springs *not* from the differing standards of proof, but from the tendency of the ICJ to avoid specifying a standard of proof, as it has failed to do in earlier cases.[66] This tendency has also been observed in arbitral tribunals dealing with inter-state conflicts.[67]

B. *Drafting and reasoning process*

International courts are composed of judges and staff members from a range of nationalities and legal backgrounds.[68] Judges may

60 Rosalyn Higgins, President of the ICJ, 'Speech to the Sixth Committee of the General Assembly – Judicial Determination of Facts' (2 November 2007).

61 It had also been more explicit in other recent cases, such as *Armed Activities on the Territory of the Congo* (*Democratic Republic of the Congo* v. *Uganda*) (Merits: Judgment) [2005] ICJ Rep. 168.

62 *Bosnia Genocide* Judgment, para. 209.

63 *Ibid.*, para. 210.

64 Cf. criticism of the ICJ's 'shifting standards of proof' in A. Asuncion, 'Pulling the Stops on Genocide: the State or the Individual?' (2009) 20 *European Journal of International Law*1195, 1206–9.

65 Higgins, 'Judicial Determination of Facts'(emphasis in original) cf. A. Seibert-Fohr, 'State Responsibility for Genocide under the Genocide Convention' in Paola Gaeta (ed.), *The UN Genocide Convention: A Commentary* (Oxford: Oxford University Press, 2009), p. 349.

66 See, for example, the criticisms of Judge Higgins, Judge Buergenthal, and Judge Owada in their Separate Opinions in *Oil Platforms*.

67 The EECC ignored the issue of standard of proof in the *Jus ad Bellum* Award: C. Gray, 'The Eritrea/Ethiopia Claims Commission Oversteps its Boundaries: A Partial Award?' (2006) 17 *European Journal of International Law* 699, 715.

68 See, e.g., ICJ Statute, Art. 9.

come from careers as diplomats, foreign ministers, senior officials in international organizations, academics, high-level practitioners, or as judges on national, regional, or other international courts. This diverse group of people then has to work within a legal framework that is itself a combination of legal traditions. The statutes of each international court blend aspects of common law and civil law, producing *sui generis* procedures.[69] Assessing the impact of this environment on the drafting and reasoning processes of the courts is not straightforward, given the secrecy that surrounds the preparation of judgments.[70] Nonetheless, on the basis of the limited available information, and through inferences drawn from the style and content of judgments, some conclusions may be drawn about the impact of the drafting and reasoning process on judicial convergence and fragmentation.

The ICJ has the most collegial and thorough drafting process, which reflects the nature of its cases (complex inter-state disputes) and its status as the principal judicial organ of the UN. The Court's drafting process is set out in its resolution concerning its internal judicial practice,[71] but this does not present the entire picture. Some insights into the practice may be gained from the writings of various judges and senior officials.[72] *Every* judge is involved at *every* phase of the drafting process – a practice that appears to be unique among international courts. The draft judgment, prepared by a drafting committee chaired by the President, returns to the plenary three times for comment.[73]

[69] See, e.g., Mirjan Damaška, 'Problematic Features of International Criminal Procedure', in Antonio Cassese et al. (eds.), *The Oxford Companion to International Criminal Law* (Oxford: Oxford University Press, 2009), pp. 175–186.

[70] ICJ Statute, Art. 54(3).

[71] International Court of Justice, Resolution Concerning the Internal Judicial Practice of the Court, Rules of Court (adopted 12 April 1976).

[72] See, e.g., Robert Y. Jennings, 'The Role of the International Court of Justice' (1998) 68 *British Yearbook of International Law* 1; Hugh Thirlway, 'The Drafting of ICJ Decisions: Some Personal Recollections and Observations' (2006) 5 *Chinese Journal of International Law* 15; Raymond Ranjeva, 'La Genèse d'un arrêt de la Cour internationale de Justice', in C. Apostolidis (ed.), *Les arrêts de la Cour internationale de Justice* (Dijon: Editions Universitaires de Dijon, 2005), p. 83; Rosalyn Higgins, 'Introduction to Part 9: The Judicial Years', in Rosalyn Higgins (ed.), *Themes and Theories; Selected Essays, Speeches and Writings in International Law*, 2 vols. (Oxford: Oxford University Press, 2009), vol. I, p. 1037; Kenneth J. Keith, 'Resolving International Disputes: The Role of Courts' (2009) 7 *New Zealand Yearbook of International Law* 255, 263–4.

[73] There is the written amendment stage where Judges submit written suggestions (stylistic and substantive) to the Committee; first reading in the Deliberations Chamber where the draft is considered paragraph by paragraph); second reading in the Deliberations Chamber where the draft is considered page by page.

Several features of this drafting process facilitate convergence, both with the decisions of other international courts and among the decisions of the ICJ itself. The three main collective meetings – deliberations, First Reading, and Second Reading – ensure that judges are aware of each other's views and are unlikely to pursue a tangential or idiosyncratic point.[74] The ability of each judge to participate also reinforces continuity within the ICJ where five judges come up for election every three years;[75] those judges with institutional knowledge are able to express their views even if they are not on the drafting committee. Equally, judges who have come from other courts, or who simply have knowledge of the work of other courts, are able to share relevant information with their colleagues. The drafting process, in particular the consideration paragraph by paragraph and then page by page in both French and English, also nurtures an incredible attention to detail. Few factual or linguistic errors are made and there is a heightened awareness of the meaning of words.

At the same time, the drafting process may dilute or obscure points of law in order to solidify consensus or achieve a majority, which increases the risk of fragmentation. Controversial points that are not central to the disposition of the case may be avoided, the fullness and cogency of the Court's reasoning may be sacrificed for brief statements of the law.[76] The precise source of its conclusions may be glossed over. In the *Wall* Advisory Opinion, the ICJ stated several times that on the 'material before it', it reached the conclusion that certain actions by Israel were not proportionate to the aims pursued, and thus amounted to violations of international law.[77] In his Declaration Judge Buergenthal observed that the Court did not actually provide any details about the 'material before it', let alone a detailed assessment of proportionality and necessity.[78] Judge

[74] E. W. Thomas, *The Judicial Process: Realism, Pragmatism, Practical Reasoning and Principles* (Cambridge: Cambridge University Press, 2005), p. 244.

[75] ICJ Statute, Art. 13. Often, some of these judges are re-elected to the Court so the turnover is fewer than five judges every three years.

[76] G. Schwarzenberger, *International Law as Applied by International Courts and Tribunals* (3rd edn., London: Sweet & Maxwell, 1957), p. 32. But cf. Christian Tams and Antonios Tzanakopoulos, 'Barcelona Traction at 40: The ICJ as an Agent of Legal Development' (2010) 23 *Leiden Journal of International Law* 781, who argue that even where the ICJ's pronouncements are remarkably brief or debatable, they may very well shape the law (at 796).

[77] *Legal Consequences of the Construction of a Wall in the Occupied Palestinian Territory* (Advisory Opinion) [2004] ICJ Rep. 136, paras. 135, 137, 140; McKeever, 'The Contribution of the International Court of Justice to the Law on the Use of Force', 389.

[78] *Wall* Advisory Opinion, para. 7 (Declaration of Judge Buergenthal).

Higgins has also criticized the Court's lack of clarity as to sources of evidence and standards of proof.[79]

The ICTY, ICTR, and ICC have a more streamlined and faster-paced drafting process than the ICJ. Judges may work on their own (if sitting as single judge) or in chambers of three or five judges. Unlike the ICJ, the international criminal courts rely heavily on their staff members for the drafting of motions, orders, and judgments. There is no standard drafting procedure in the ICTY or ICTR; each trial team has its own methods, working under the supervision of the Senior Legal Officer. This leads to significant differences in style and approach. What is common is that the timeframe for the drafting process is compressed due to the nature of the criminal proceedings and, more recently, the deadlines set by the completion strategies at the tribunals.

The drafting process at the international criminal courts leads to significant variation among chambers and courts in both the quality and the content of the judgments. The drafting process is not focused on consistency, precision of language or institutional knowledge. It also does not reflect a wide variety of views; often the judge will be working with one legal officer or a small team. There is less scope and time for debates with his or her judicial colleagues. This variety may nurture creativity, but the decentralized, delegated system of decision-making can also lead to fragmentation as each chamber operates in its own sphere.

C. *Precedent and dialogue*

There are two aspects of procedure that may facilitate judicial convergence and both have been applied to varying degrees by the international courts. First, a concept of precedent – or at least of striving to maintain a consistent body of jurisprudence – is vital to judicial convergence. Second, judicial dialogue and exchange among international courts raise awareness of each other's jurisprudence, clarify the reasoning process as it relates to existing case law, and has the potential to develop international law in a coherent manner.

Turning first to precedent, there is no formal system of precedent or avenue of appeal between international courts. Even *within* international courts, there is no doctrine of *stare decisis*.[80] Article 59 of the Statute of

[79] *Wall* Advisory Opinion, para. 40 (Separate Opinion of Judge Higgins). *Oil Platforms*, paras. 30–9 (Separate Opinion of Judge Higgins).

[80] The doctrine of *stare decisis* also does not exist formally in civil law systems, but it is understood that after a sufficient number of similar higher court decisions on the same legal issue,

the ICJ provides: 'The decision of the Court has no binding force except between the parties and in respect of that particular case.' The ICTY and ICTR Statutes are silent in this regard. The ICC Statute provides the non-binding instruction that '[t]he Court *may* apply principles and rules of law as interpreted in its previous decisions'.[81] However, a loose notion of vertical precedent does appear to be shared by the courts, in that they make an effort not to depart from previous decisions unless there is a compelling reason to do so.[82] The ICJ has observed: '[t]here can be no question of holding [a state] to decisions reached by the Court in previous cases... [but] [t]he real question is whether, in [the current] case, there is cause not to follow the reasoning and conclusions of earlier cases'.[83] This was echoed in a more recent case.[84] The ICJ regularly cites its own decisions and those of its predecessor, the Permanent Court of International Justice,[85] belying the 'subsidiary' status that such judicial decisions are meant to possess according to Article 38 of its Statute. Nonetheless, the ICJ does sometimes depart from previous decisions. If such departures are not carefully reasoned and placed in context, it risks serious fragmentation.[86]

The ICTY and ICTR have taken a similar approach to the ICJ on precedent, stating that previous decisions of the tribunal should only be departed from in 'exceptional circumstances'.[87] However, the more powerful factor in the use of precedent is structural in nature. The fact

the lower courts consider themselves bound by '*la jurisprudence constante*': Jonathan I. Charney, 'Is International Law Threatened by Multiple International Tribunals?'(1998) 271 *Recueil des Cours* 101, 358.

81 ICC Statute, Art. 21(2) (emphasis added).

82 It is too early to tell if the ICC will share this approach.

83 *Land and Maritime Boundary between Cameroon and Nigeria* (*Cameroon* v. *Nigeria*) (Preliminary Objections: Judgment) [1998] ICJ Rep. 275, para. 28.

84 *Application of the Convention on the Prevention and Punishment of the Crime of Genocide* (*Croatia* v. *Serbia*) (Preliminary Objections: Judgment) [2008] ICJ Rep. 412, para. 53: 'To the extent that the decisions contain findings of law, the Court will treat them as it treats all previous decisions: that is to say that, while those decisions are in no way binding on the Court, it will not depart from its settled jurisprudence unless it finds very particular reasons to do so.'

85 For an excellent study, see M. Shahabuddeen, *Precedent in the World Court* (Cambridge: Cambridge University Press, 1996).

86 See the series of cases on the Balkans involving Serbia, Bosnia and Herzegovina, Croatia, and many of the NATO states.

87 *Prosecutor* v. *Aleksovski* (Judgment) IT-95–14/1-T, T Ch I (25 June 1999) para. 97. See also *Prosecutor* v. *Semanza* (Decision of the Appeals Chamber) ICTR-97–20-A, A Ch (31 May 2000) para. 92.

that the ICTY and ICTR have a common Appeals Chamber has ensured convergence on points of law that reach that level.

Judicial dialogue involves the citation, discussion, application, or interpretation of case law from other courts, but it can also encompass informal exchanges of information, inter-court conferences, and the transfer of personnel and parties among courts. It facilitates the convergence of international law by raising awareness of the practice of other bodies and clarifying the reasoning process. The point is not for a court simply to follow the decisions of other courts; there are a variety of factors that may call for that court to reach a different decision. Rather, the benefit of dialogue is that a court can take a decision in the knowledge of existing case law, and may be able to explain and justify its reasoning more effectively.

Quite apart from the rather formal judicial dialogue that may occur in particular cases, there is also an emerging dialogue among international courts on a more personal and informal level. This dialogue is still very ad hoc, but it contains the seeds for greater linkages among international courts that may in turn enhance convergence. The ICJ, for example, has taken the lead in holding inter-court meetings on legal topics of mutual interest with judges from the international criminal courts as well as the International Tribunal for the Law of the Sea, the European Court of Justice, and the European Court of Human Rights.[88] This has been complemented by exchanges of summaries or extracts of case law among these bodies.[89] Exchanges of information also occur at the biennial meetings of the *Institut de droit international*, whose membership includes judges from a number of international courts.

Finally, there is great potential for dialogue and exchange on the level of counsel and parties. The International Bar is small and the same persons tend to appear for parties in the ICJ, arbitral tribunals, and to a lesser extent, as counsel in the international criminal courts.[90] Judges of the ICJ also serve as occasional arbitrators in inter-state matters, which provides an opportunity for convergence among the ICJ and arbitral tribunals.[91]

[88] Judge Rosalyn Higgins, President of the ICJ, 'Speech to the General Assembly of the United Nations' (30 October 2008).

[89] *Ibid.*

[90] J-P. Cot, 'Le monde de la justice internationale', in Société Francaise pour le Droit International, *Colloque de Lille: La juridictionnalisation du droit international* (2003) pp. 511, 513–4, cited in Brown, *A Common Law*, p. 230.

[91] *Iron Rhine Arbitration* (*Belgium/Netherlands*) (Award of the Arbitral Tribunal) (24 May 2005) 27 RIAA 35 (2007) (of the five arbitrators, three were ICJ Judges: Judges Higgins,

Parties are also moving among the different courts. This relates to the personal aspect of the 'permanence' of an international court referred to above.

V. Conclusion

This chapter has sought to identify the factors that lead to convergence or fragmentation in the international legal system. The three themes identified here – the identity of the court, the substance of the law, and the procedures employed – do not automatically determine whether a particular court will promote the convergence or fragmentation of international law. Instead, they suggest *tendencies* in a certain direction. The permanent nature of a court and its prominent place in an institutional system encourages stability and convergence. The fact that an area of law is governed by a comprehensive treaty, is relatively uncontroversial, and is not being affected by societal changes, will facilitate convergence. Multi-stage, collective decision-making processes, respect for vertical and horizontal precedent, and engagement in judicial dialogue also promote coherence in the development of international law. On the other hand, the temporary nature of a court increases the risk that it may decide in a vacuum. If a court oversteps its functions, this also raises the potential for fragmentation. If an area of law is governed by customary international law, is relatively underdeveloped, and is controversial, this may also result in diverging decisions in different courts. Variations in fact-finding and the assessment of evidence, lack of attention to existing case law, and decentralized and delegated judgment-drafting processes increase the tendency towards fragmentation.

Given these factors, it is suggested that the ICJ has played – and will continue to play – a central role in promoting convergence. The ICJ has special authority due its status as the only court of general jurisdiction and the UN's principal judicial organ. It is permanent and has the ability to deal with a wide variety of topics involving both treaty and custom. The ICJ has established, collegial procedures and strong judicial control over the drafting process.

The central role of the ICJ in the international legal system could be enhanced by increased – and more transparent – participation in

Simma, and Tomka); *Abyei Arbitration* (*The Government of Sudan/The Sudan People's Liberation Movement/Army*) (Award) (22 July 2009) (the arbitrators included Judge Al-Khasawneh, a sitting ICJ Judge, and Judge Schwebel, former President of the ICJ).

judicial dialogue. Until relatively recently, there was a sense that ICJ judgments should remain 'unsullied' by engagement with the decisions of other courts or tribunals of limited jurisdiction.[92] Given overlapping jurisdictions and the similar factual scenarios that arise in multiple courts, the consideration of the decisions of other courts is central to well-reasoned judgments. The endorsement or rejection of a view by the ICJ is sure to carry significance and may well enhance its standing in the world of international courts – it is a role that the Court should embrace, and recent case law indicates the Court is prepared to engage in judicial dialogue.[93] The next step is for the ICJ to provide greater transparency as to its use of the case law of other courts and tribunals. Currently, cases that may be referred to in written and oral pleadings and judicial deliberations are rarely cited in the final judgment.

The prominent role of the ICJ in the international legal system also requires the Court to grapple with difficult problems and not to avoid controversial tasks, as long as they fall within its jurisdiction.[94] In 1999 Abi-Saab urged the ICJ to 'seiz[e] all opportunities to provide an authoritative interpretation of the principles and rules of general international law, rather than always trying to base its decision on the narrowest, and, preferably, consensual, grounds'.[95] In more recent years the ICJ has had occasion to demonstrate a certain hardiness and clarity in its decision-making.[96] These are hopeful signs that the Court will embrace its important, integrative role in the international legal system. States could consider this factor during the process for the nomination and election of judges to the Court, while always aiming to elect the most highly qualified candidates. In their commentary on and monitoring of the Court,

[92] This idea is expressed but not endorsed by Charney, 'Is International Law Threatened', 372.

[93] See, e.g., *Jurisdictional Immunities of the State* (*Germany* v. *Italy, Greece Intervening*) (Merits: Judgment) [2012] ICJ Rep.; *Ahmadou Sadio Diallo* (*Republic of Guinea* v. *Democratic Republic of the Congo*) (Compensation) [2012] ICJ Rep.

[94] Abi-Saab, 'Fragmentation or Unification', 930.

[95] *Ibid.*, 930. Pierre-Marie Dupuy also calls for the Court to take every opportunity 'to advance the interpretation of the law', and not limit itself merely to resolving the dispute at hand: Pierre-Marie Dupuy, 'The Unity of Application of International Law at the Global Level and the Responsibility of Judges' (2007) 1(2) *European Journal of Legal Studies* 1, 23.

[96] Examples include the way the ICJ dealt with the *Nicaragua–Tadic* divide and in its treatment of ICTY material in the *Bosnia Genocide* Judgment. In a different field, see *Maritime Delimitation in the Black Sea* (*Romania* v. *Ukraine*) (Judgment) [2009] ICJ Rep. 61, which set out in clear terms the methodology for maritime delimitation and achieved a unanimous Judgment without any Separate or Dissenting Opinions for the first time in the ICJ's history.

non-governmental organizations and the academy could place emphasis on the extent to which the ICJ confronts and resolves difficult legal issues of relevance to other courts. States could also provide practical support to the work of the judges through granting budgetary requests for qualified legal staff and upgraded facilities.

B. 'Regimes' of international law

7

Fragmentation or partnership? The reception of ICJ case-law by the European Court of Human Rights

DEAN SPIELMANN[1]

A recent conference marking the centenary of the Peace Palace in The Hague, a building which embodies the history of public international law, has provided the opportunity to reflect on the longstanding and significant influence of the International Court of Justice (ICJ), through its case-law, on the European Court of Human Rights in Strasbourg. This chapter will address and illustrate that theme, stressing the importance of the on-going dialogue between these two courts, in spite of the differences between them, at a time when there are concerns about the increasing complexity and 'fragmentation' of international law.

The differences between the ICJ and the European Court of Human Rights are well known. First, the ICJ is the principal judicial organ of the United Nations possessing general subject-matter jurisdiction. It has the exclusive capacity to interpret the UN Charter. It only hears inter-State cases. Moreover, it is competent to entertain a dispute only if the States concerned have accepted its jurisdiction. In the leading case of *Loizidou*[2] the European Court of Human Rights pointed out the distinction between the two courts as follows:

[1] The author wishes to thank Mr Linos-Alexandre Sicilianos, Judge of the European Court of Human Rights, Mr Patrick Titiun and Mr James Brannan, for their assistance in preparing this contribution, of which an earlier version has been published in French by Wolf Legal Publishers (in *A Century of International Justice and Prospects for the Future*, A. A. Cançado Trindade and D. Spielmann, pp. 29–44). The original paper was given at a conference held by the International Court of Justice in The Hague on 23 September 2013, under the theme 'The ICJ in the Service of Peace and Justice: A Century of International Justice and Prospects for the Future'.

[2] *Loizidou* v. *Turkey* (preliminary objection), 23 March 1995, § 84, Series A, No. 310.

> the context within which the International Court of Justice operates is quite distinct from that of the Convention [European Convention on Human Rights] institutions. The International Court is called on *inter alia* to examine any legal dispute between States that might occur in any part of the globe with reference to principles of international law. The subject-matter of a dispute may relate to any area of international law. In the second place, unlike the Convention institutions, the role of the International Court is not exclusively limited to direct supervisory functions in respect of a law-making treaty such as the Convention.

Secondly, the European Court of Human Rights, for its part, has a regional vocation and deals mainly with individual applications, even though inter-State cases are also envisaged under Article 33 of the European Convention on Human Rights; its mission is thus mainly the protection of individual rights. It remains very committed to the mechanism of individual petition, whereas it is not possible for individuals to bring cases directly before the ICJ.

It is nevertheless of interest to note that, whilst the ICJ has no such mechanism, the principle has not always been excluded: suffice it to recall the Advisory Opinion of its predecessor, the Permanent Court of International Justice (PCIJ), dated 4 December 1935, concerning two decrees of 29 August 1935 amending the Danzig Penal Code and Code of Penal Procedure.[3] It was through the petition mechanism, as it then existed, that those decrees were submitted to the PCIJ. Admittedly, the right of petition was limited in scope, because the Court's intervention took the form of an Advisory Opinion, not a Judgment, but one can see here the embryo of the human rights adjudication system that was later to develop in Strasbourg. Above all – and this was the most significant point – petitions fell outside the sovereignty of States, which could neither prohibit nor hinder them. That was very modern for the time. In the specific case of the city of Danzig, the petitions came from three political parties and the question raised concerned human rights as protected under the Constitution of the Free City. Admittedly, the 'filtering' which existed at that time precluded the matter from being dealt with as a contentious case, unlike the system which ultimately emerged in Strasbourg with the Commission and the 'old' Court. Nevertheless, one can say that the petition mechanism and Strasbourg's individual applications are not unrelated.

[3] *Consistency of Certain Danzig Legislative Decrees with the Constitution of the Free City*, Advisory Opinion, 1935, P.C.I.J., Series A/B, No. 65, p. 41.

Furthermore, once the Advisory Opinion was delivered, the Senate of the City of Danzig amended the legislation at issue.

That being said, times have changed, fortunately, and the idea of restricted access to a court would today be ill-suited to human rights complaints. That is what makes the Strasbourg system strong, even though it is paying the price, so to speak, by having to deal with such a high volume of applications.

It will now be shown how the European Court of Human Rights has made use of the jurisprudence of the ICJ and how the two courts are intertwined, emphasising first and foremost how public international law has facilitated the protection of human rights, without forgetting that, on occasion, it has also limited them, as is the case, for example, in matters of jurisdictional immunities.

Before going to the heart of the subject, it is necessary to bear in mind that the commitments of States under the UN Charter go hand in hand with their commitments under the European Convention on Human Rights. The Courts of The Hague and of Strasbourg do not have the same role, but they come together in many areas and there is no watertight partition between them. The solutions adopted by the ICJ have an impact on the fundamental rights protected by international law, rights that an individual can invoke in Strasbourg. The European Court takes into account the rulings of the International Court concerning principles of international law, seldom straying from its decisions. Strasbourg has largely drawn inspiration from them when justifying its findings either in a politically sensitive international context or where there is a need to make good an omission. In addition, since human rights protection has become the cornerstone of the system of public international law, Strasbourg has on occasion turned to the ICJ to complement or fine-tune the content and protection of the rights secured by the Convention.

Moreover – and this is quite natural – parties to proceedings in Strasbourg have also relied on the case-law of the ICJ (for example, the Belgian Government in the '*Belgian linguistic*' case;[4] or the Turkish Government in the *Akdivar and Others* judgment).[5] References to ICJ jurisprudence can also be found in the separate (concurring or dissenting) opinions of

[4] *Case 'Relating to Certain Aspects of the Laws on the Use of Languages in Education in Belgium'* (preliminary objection), 9 February 1967, Series A, No. 5.

[5] *Akdivar and Others* v. *Turkey*, 16 September 1996, *Reports of Judgments and Decisions* 1996-IV.

judges. The significant number of international public law specialists on the Strasbourg bench is not unrelated to that tendency.

Whilst it examines the cases before it from the standpoint of inter-State relations, the ICJ, like its predecessor, has delivered judgments which carry considerable weight in respect of rights under international law that individuals themselves may invoke.

As the then President of the ICJ, Dame Rosalyn Higgins pointed out, in a speech given at the European Court of Human Rights in 2009, the PCIJ, between 1922 and 1946, had already ruled on 'leading' principles such as non-discrimination.[6] This is one of the principles that Strasbourg has strived to enforce in more recent years; the case-law of the PCIJ is still of great influence today.

First, in the *Polish Upper Silesia* case,[7] the PCIJ went to great lengths to clarify what was necessary to make the protection of national minorities a reality. It held that minorities were entitled to equality in fact as well as in law; and that, while the claim to be a member of a national minority should be based on fact, self-identification was the only acceptable method of association. This principle has been one of lasting importance in human rights law, particularly for the European Court of Human Rights, whose jurisprudence in the field of minority rights is abundant.[8]

The second example is *Minority Schools in Albania*,[9] where the PCIJ determined that special needs and equality in fact were 'indeed closely interlocked, for there would be no true equality between a majority and a minority if the latter were deprived of its own institutions, and were consequently compelled to renounce that which constitute[d] the very essence of its being as a minority'. Of equal importance was the finding that differentiation for objective reasons did not constitute discrimination.[10] This is another principle that is very prominent in the Strasbourg case-law.

As far as Strasbourg is concerned, even though there are relatively few decisions or judgments of the Commission and Court (less than

[6] Speech given on the occasion of the opening of the judicial year, 30 January 2009, by Rosalyn Higgins, President of the International Court of Justice, 'The International Court of Justice and the European Court of Human Rights: Partners for the Protection of Human Rights', *Dialogue between Judges*, European Court of Human Rights, Council of Europe, 2009, pp. 42–3.

[7] *Certain German Interests in Polish Upper Silesia*, Merits, Judgment No. 7, 1926, P.C.I.J, Series A, No. 7.

[8] See Higgins, note 6 above, p. 42.

[9] *Minority Schools in Albania*, Advisory Opinion, 1935, P.C.I.J., Series A/B, No. 64, p. 4.

[10] See Higgins, note 6 above, p. 43.

thirty in all) which refer expressly to the ICJ/PCIJ case-law, they are mostly decisions of some importance for the development of its own jurisprudence or for the international community as a whole. Such an influence should not be surprising: international courts, whether regional or universal, are increasingly called upon to address similar questions. A human rights court may then be obliged either to hear a case that has also been referred to another international court, or to rule on the basis of norms that another international court has developed.

Without claiming to be exhaustive, this chapter will give a few examples, starting with the question of the interpretation of treaties, before turning to questions of procedure, to the obligations of States outside their territory and to the issue of *restitutio in integrum*. It will lastly address the sensitive issue of State immunities.

First, on the question of the interpretation of treaties, the European Court of Human Rights has not hesitated to refer to the findings of the ICJ. For example, in the *Stoll* v. *Switzerland* case,[11] it was found that the two authentic texts of the Convention were not in complete harmony. The Court thus referred to Article 33 §§ 3 and 4 of the Vienna Convention on the Law of Treaties of 1969, reflecting customary international law in relation to the interpretation of treaties authenticated in two or more languages. On that basis it was able to agree with the Swiss Government that the conviction of the applicant, a journalist, pursued the legitimate aim of preventing the 'disclosure of information received in confidence'[12] within the meaning of Article 10 § 2, in the light of the broader French text. The European Court of Human Rights expressly cited the *LaGrand* judgment of 27 June 2001[13] in support of that reference.

Turning now to questions of procedure, the most significant one is that of the binding force of interim measures[14] indicated by the European Court of Human Rights to member States under Rule 39 of the Rules of Court. The case-law on this question has considerably evolved. The first major case in Strasbourg was that of *Cruz Varas and Others* v. *Sweden*[15] in 1991, when the Court observed that the Convention, unlike other international treaties or instruments (for example, Article 41 of the Statute of the ICJ), did not contain a specific provision with regard to such

[11] *Stoll* v. *Switzerland* [GC], No. 69698/01, § 59, ECHR 2007-V.

[12] The broader French text of Article 10 § 2 reads '*pour empêcher la divulgation d'informations confidentielles*'.

[13] *LaGrand* (*Germany* v. *United States of America*), Judgment, I.C.J. Reports 2001, § 101.

[14] Referred to by the ICJ as 'provisional measures'.

[15] *Cruz Varas and Others* v. *Sweden*, 20 March 1991, § 94, Series A, No. 201.

measures. It took the view that the power to order interim measures could not be derived from the Convention or other sources.

However, that decision was subsequently reversed in the case of *Mamatkulov and Askarov* of 4 February 2005,[16] with reference again to *LaGrand*, and the new approach has since been followed in many other cases. The Court quoted the ICJ's finding in *LaGrand* with regard to the above-mentioned Article 41 on provisional measures, to the effect that:

> It follows from the object and purpose of the Statute, as well as from the terms of Article 41 when read in their context, that the power to indicate provisional measures entails that such measures should be binding, inasmuch as the power in question is based on the necessity, when the circumstances call for it, to safeguard, and to avoid prejudice to, the rights of the parties as determined by the final judgment of the Court. The contention that provisional measures indicated under Article 41 might not be binding would be contrary to the object and purpose of that Article.[17]

The ICJ's judgments in *Nicaragua* v. *United States of America*,[18] and *Mexico* v. *United States of America*,[19] were also cited in that judgment.

A related factor which pointed to the binding nature of orders made under Article 41 of the ICJ's Statute, and to which the European Court of Human Rights also attached importance, was the existence of a principle which had already been recognised by the PCIJ when it referred to 'the principle universally accepted by international tribunals and likewise laid down in many conventions . . . to the effect that the parties to a case must abstain from any measure capable of exercising a prejudicial effect in regard to the execution of the decision to be given, and, in general, not allow any step of any kind to be taken which might aggravate or extend the dispute' (see *Electricity Company of Sofia and Bulgaria* (Interim measures of protection)[20]).

[16] *Mamatkulov and Askarov* v. *Turkey* [GC], Nos. 46827/99 and 46951/99, §§ 117 *et seq.*, ECHR 2005-I.

[17] *LaGrand*, note 13 above, § 102.

[18] *Military and Paramilitary Activities in and against Nicaragua* (*Nicaragua* v. *United States of America*), Merits, Judgment, I.C.J. Reports 1986, p. 14.

[19] *Avena and Other Mexican Nationals* (*Mexico* v. *United States of America*), Judgment, I.C.J. Reports 2004, p. 12.

[20] *Electricity Company of Sofia and Bulgaria*, Order of 5 December 1939, P.C.I.J., Series A/B, No. 79, p. 194, as cited in *LaGrand*, note 13 above, and in turn in *Mamatkulov and Askarov*, note 16 above, § 48.

There is another area in which the respective case-law of the two courts interacts: that of the obligations of States outside their territory – sometimes referred to as the 'territory of human rights'. The territorial scope of certain obligations in matters of human rights is a recurring question in both The Hague and Strasbourg. Before the European Court, this question generally arises where it is necessary to ascertain whether or not the obligations arising from the European Convention apply to a Contracting State outside its territory. Such a situation may occur in various circumstances.

As Dame Rosalyn Higgins has explained,[21] at the ICJ, that question has been dealt with in two contexts. First, it has upheld the general principle that the State is responsible for acts imputable to it when committed under its authority in a foreign country. Thus, in *Congo* v. *Uganda*,[22] the ICJ held that Uganda had, at all times, responsibility for all actions and omissions of its own military forces in the territory of the Democratic Republic of the Congo. Secondly, the ICJ is sometimes called upon to examine whether a State is bound, outside its territory, by its obligations under a treaty. The answer will depend on the interpretation of the treaty itself, according to its context and in the light of its object and purpose.[23] Thus, in considering the issue of the extraterritorial application of human rights treaties, the International Court observed in the *Wall* opinion that, in the light of its object and purpose, the International Covenant on Civil and Political Rights[24] was 'applicable in respect of acts done by a State in the exercise of its jurisdiction outside its own territory'.[25] In the recent case of *Georgia* v. *Russia*,[26] the parties disagreed as to the territorial scope of the obligations of a State party to the International Convention on the Elimination of All Forms of Racial Discrimination.[27] Georgia took the view that this instrument did not include any limitation

[21] See Higgins, note 6 above, pp. 44–5.

[22] *Armed Activities on the Territory of the Congo* (*Democratic Republic of the Congo* v. *Uganda*), Judgment, I.C.J. Reports 2005, p. 168.

[23] See Higgins, note 6 above, p. 44.

[24] International Covenant on Civil and Political Rights, 16 December 1966, 999 UNTS 171.

[25] *Legal Consequences of the Construction of a Wall in the Occupied Palestinian Territory*, Advisory Opinion, I.C.J. Reports 2004, pp. 136, 180 [111].

[26] *Application of the International Convention on the Elimination of all Forms of Racial Discrimination* (*Georgia* v. *Russian Federation*), Provisional Measures, Order of 15 October 2008, I.C.J. Reports 2008, p. 353.

[27] International Convention on the Elimination of All Forms of Racial Discrimination, 21 December 1965, 660 UNTS 195.

on its territorial application, whilst the Russian Federation argued that the provisions of that treaty could not govern a State's conduct outside its own borders. In its Order of October 2008 the ICJ observed that the Convention at issue did not contain any restriction of a general nature relating to its territorial application. In the Court's view, Articles 2 and 5 of the International Convention on the Elimination of All Forms of Racial Discrimination 'generally appear to apply, like other provisions of instruments of that nature, to the actions of a State party when it acts beyond its territory'.[28] As far as general international law is concerned, 'a State will', in the words of Dame Rosalyn Higgins, 'of course be responsible for the acts attributable to it, even when those occur outside of its own jurisdiction'.[29] In other words, the approach taken by the International Court is a broad one.

The *Georgia* v. *Russia* case is indicative of the phenomenon mentioned above, where parties successively raise identical or similar legal questions in different fora.

The ICJ was thus called upon to examine the dispute between Georgia and Russia in respect of the events of August 2008 in the context of a contentious case relating to the application of the above-mentioned Convention. In an Order it observed that the question could equally have been brought before the Committee on the Elimination of Racial Discrimination. Almost at the same time, Georgia lodged an inter-State application before the European Court of Human Rights alleging a violation of Articles 2 (right to life) and 3 (prohibition of inhuman or degrading treatment) of the European Convention on Human Rights and of Article 1 of Protocol No. 1 thereto.[30] Strasbourg then indicated interim measures, calling upon the parties to fulfil their obligations under the European Convention, in particular Articles 2 and 3. It has since received thousands of applications against Georgia concerning the hostilities that broke out in South Ossetia in August 2008.

Generally speaking, it is mainly in a complex international context (inter-State conflicts, terrorist threat) that Strasbourg has had occasion to examine the question of the extraterritorial application of the Convention,

[28] *Application of the International Convention on the Elimination of all Forms of Racial Discrimination*, note 26 above, p. 386 [109].

[29] R. Higgins, 'A Babel of Judicial Voices? Ruminations from the Bench' (2006) 55 *ICLQ* 791, 795.

[30] *Georgia* v. *Russia* (II), application No. 38263/08 (decision of 13 December 2011).

that is, the question whether the obligations under this treaty apply to a Contracting State acting outside its territory and therefore whether State responsibility is engaged. Here are a few examples of such cases.

In the cases concerning the status of the entity known as the 'Turkish Republic of Northern Cyprus', relying on the case-law of the ICJ, the Strasbourg Court found that the impugned events fell under Turkey's jurisdiction and it thus protected the rights of the victims (see the *Loizidou* v. *Turkey* judgment of 18 December 1996).[31]

In the cases of *Ilaşcu and Others* v. *Moldova and Russia* (8 July 2004)[32] and *Catan and Others* v. *the Republic of Moldova and Russia* (19 October 2012),[33] the European Court of Human Rights found, referring to the case-law of the ICJ, that Russia had effective control over the territory of Transdniestria. It relied in particular on the criterion applied by the ICJ in the case concerning the *Application of the Convention on the Prevention and Punishment of Genocide* (judgment of 26 February 2007).[34]

In its *Đokić* v. *Bosnia and Herzegovina* judgment of 27 May 2010,[35] the Strasbourg Court referred again to the case-law of the ICJ in finding that the acts of those who had committed genocide in Srebrenica were not attributable, as such, to the Federal Republic of Yugoslavia under the international law of State responsibility.

In the 'Iraq case' of *Al-Jedda* v. *the United Kingdom* (7 July 2011),[36] the European Court of Human Rights found, in the light of the ICJ's case-law, that the role played by the United Nations as regards security in Iraq in 2004 was completely different from its role in Kosovo in 1999. The Court thus found that the applicant's internment had been attributable to the United Kingdom.

Similarly, in the other 'Iraq case' of the same day, *Al-Skeini and Others* v. *the United Kingdom*,[37] the Court took the view that following the removal from power of the Ba'ath regime and until the accession of the Interim Government, the United Kingdom, through its soldiers engaged

[31] *Loizidou* v. *Turkey* (merits), 18 December 1996, *Reports of Judgments and Decisions* 1996-VI.

[32] *Ilaşcu and Others* v. *Moldova and Russia* [GC], No. 48787/99, ECHR 2004-VII.

[33] *Catan and Others* v. *the Republic of Moldova and Russia* [GC], Nos. 43370/04, 8252/05 and 18454/06, ECHR 2012.

[34] *Application of the Convention on the Prevention and Punishment of the Crime of Genocide* (*Bosnia and Herzegovina* v. *Serbia and Montenegro*), Judgment, I.C.J. Reports 2007, p. 43.

[35] *Đokić* v. *Bosnia and Herzegovina*, No. 6518/04, 27 May 2010.

[36] *Al-Jedda* v. *the United Kingdom* [GC], No. 27021/08, ECHR 2011.

[37] *Al-Skeini and Others* v. *the United Kingdom* [GC], No. 55721/07, ECHR 2011.

in security operations in Basra, had exercised authority and control over individuals killed in the course of such security operations, so as to establish a jurisdictional link between the deceased and the United Kingdom.

Another area in which the ICJ's case-law has had a major influence is that of the *restitutio in integrum* principle. Going back in time, it will be recalled that the PCIJ, in its 13 September 1928 judgment concerning the *Factory at Chorzów*,[38] held as follows:

> reparation must, as far as possible, wipe out all the consequences of the illegal act and reestablish the situation which would, in all probability, have existed if that act had not been committed. Restitution in kind, or, if this is not possible, payment of a sum corresponding to the value which a restitution in kind would bear; the award, if need be, of damages for loss sustained which would not be covered by restitution in kind or payment in place of it – such are the principles which should serve to determine the amount of compensation due for an act contrary to international law.

In more recent years, the *restitutio in integrum* jurisprudence has gradually been developed by the European Court of Human Rights. Even though the *Factory at Chorzów* case is not always cited as such, the Court systematically cites its own *Papamichalopoulos* judgment of 31 October 1995, which itself refers back to the 1928 finding. In *Papamichalopoulos* v. *Greece*[39] it was thus held that the return of the property in issue would be the best form of redress for the applicants' loss. In other words, and for the first time in its history, the Court found that *restitutio in integrum* constituted the most appropriate means of execution of its judgment.

International law has been used in other areas; for example, in the *Anchugov and Gladkov* v. *Russia* judgment,[40] delivered by the European Court of Human Rights on 4 July 2013. That sensitive case concerned the right of prisoners to vote in elections. It was different from *Hirst* v. *the United Kingdom*[41] in that the Russian ban on prisoner voting was enshrined in the Constitution and even in a part that could be amended only by a very complex procedure. In order to apply the *Hirst* (and *Scoppola*)[42] jurisprudence, the Court had to overcome that hurdle. To do so it relied on the principle of international law whereby a State could not invoke its domestic law, including its Constitution, to justify

[38] *Factory at Chorzów*, Merits, Judgment No. 13, 1928, P.C.I.J., Series A, No. 17, p. 47.
[39] *Papamichalopoulos and Others* v. *Greece* (Article 50), 31 October 1995, § 38, Series A, No. 330-B.
[40] *Anchugov and Gladkov* v. *Russia*, Nos. 11157/04 and 15162/05, 4 July 2013.
[41] *Hirst* v. *the United Kingdom* (*no. 2*) [GC], No. 74025/01, ECHR 2005-IX.
[42] *Scoppola* v. *Italy* (*no. 3*) [GC], No. 126/05, 22 May 2012.

a failure to perform an international legal obligation. In support of its findings, the Court referred to the recent reiteration of this principle by the International Law Commission, based on the case-law of the PCIJ.[43]

The examples given above serve to illustrate the influence of international law on human rights adjudication. However, human rights may also sometimes be limited by State sovereignty, and the delicate question of immunities will thus now be addressed.

A conflict may well arise between a State's human rights obligations and the rules of international law on immunities. The jurisdictional immunity of States is a principle of international law that is upheld by the European courts, for one State cannot be subject to the jurisdiction of another. However, such restrictions appear somewhat incompatible with the requirements of the rule of law. Whilst State immunity prevails over the right of access to a court, this can be justified only if the complainants have other remedies by which to seek protection of their rights under the European Convention on Human Rights. The opposition between the rules of customary international law on immunities and the growing idea that there can be no impunity for violations of human rights is a matter that is increasingly being raised in both Strasbourg and The Hague.[44] In three Grand Chamber judgments delivered at the end of 2001, the European Court of Human Rights found that the application of the principle of sovereign immunity, whereby proceedings could not be brought in domestic courts against foreign States, did not breach the right to a fair hearing under Article 6 of the European Convention.[45]

In the 2002 case concerning the *Arrest Warrant*,[46] the ICJ was called upon to examine the question whether, in customary international law, there could be an exception to immunity based on human rights. It concluded from its examination of the practice of regional and national courts that, in the current state of general international law, there were not yet any exceptions, in any form whatsoever, to the rule granting immunity in criminal matters to a serving Minister for Foreign Affairs, even one suspected of committing war crimes or crimes against humanity. This is, however, an area of law which is developing rapidly and which the two courts will certainly be keeping under review.[47]

[43] *Treatment of Polish Nationals and Other Persons of Polish Origin or Speech in the Danzig Territory*, Advisory Opinion, 1932, P.C.I.J., Series A/B, No. 44, p. 24.

[44] See Higgins, note 6 above, pp. 43–4. [45] See Higgins, note 6 above, p. 43.

[46] *Arrest Warrant of 11 April 2000* (*Democratic Republic of the Congo* v. *Belgium*), Judgment, I.C.J. Reports 2002, p. 3.

[47] See Higgins, note 6 above, p. 44.

To return to Strasbourg, it was found as follows in the *Fogarty* v. *the United Kingdom* judgment of 21 November 2001:[48] 'The Convention should so far as possible be interpreted in harmony with other rules of international law of which it forms part, including those relating to the grant of State immunity'. Measures taken by a State which reflect the established principles concerning immunity cannot be regarded as a disproportionate restriction to the right of access to a court. In the cases of *McElhinney* v. *Ireland*[49] and *Al-Adsani* v. *the United Kingdom*,[50] referring to the principles of general international law, the Court held that the application of the principle of sovereign immunity, preventing foreign States from being sued in domestic courts, did not breach Article 6 of the Convention.

To allay concerns about the fragmentation of international law, the approach to the question of State immunities illustrates, on the contrary, the harmony of case-law at international level. The *Al-Adsani* case, decided by the European Court of Human Rights, is a good example. It concerned the inability of the applicant, who alleged he had been tortured by security guards in Kuwait, to bring civil proceedings against Kuwait in the UK courts. He complained of a violation of his right of access to a court, as secured by Article 6 of the European Convention on Human Rights. This controversial case divided the Court's Grand Chamber, which adopted its judgment by nine votes to eight. It noted that sovereign immunity was a concept of international law, developed out of the principle *par in parem non habet imperium*, by virtue of which one State could not be subject to the jurisdiction of another. In their reasoning, the majority began by acknowledging the legitimacy of the restriction, which pursued the aim of 'complying with international law to promote comity and good relations between States through the respect of another State's sovereignty'. The Court went on to address the question of proportionality, for which it took into account the relevant rules of international law applicable between the parties. It took the view that measures which reflected generally recognised rules of public international law on State immunity could not in principle be regarded as imposing a disproportionate restriction on the right of access to a court.

However, the real question was whether those rules had to give way to a peremptory norm, namely the absolute prohibition of torture in

[48] *Fogarty* v. *the United Kingdom* [GC], No. 37112/97, § 35, ECHR 2001-XI.

[49] *McElhinney* v. *Ireland* [GC], No. 31253/96, ECHR 2001-XI.

[50] *Al-Adsani* v. *the United Kingdom* [GC], No. 35763/97, ECHR 2001-XI.

international law. The Court had no doubt that such prohibition had, at that time, attained the status of *jus cogens.* Nevertheless, there was no basis on which to conclude that a State no longer enjoyed immunity from civil suit in the courts of another State. The Court took the view that the situation in the United Kingdom was 'not inconsistent with those limitations generally accepted by the community of nations as part of the doctrine of State immunity'. By contrast, the dissenting minority, which was composed of eminent international jurists, opined that the very concept of *jus cogens* required that such norms should prevail over any hierarchically lower rule.

A certain reciprocal influence between the ICJ and the European Court of Human Rights can be observed in this area. In its judgment of 3 February 2012 on the *Jurisdictional Immunities of the State,*[51] the ICJ significantly cited the *Al-Adsani* judgment[52] and ultimately adopted the same position. More recently, Strasbourg relied on that ICJ judgment in applying the principle of jurisdictional immunity to the United Nations (in the decision *Stichting Mothers of Srebrenica and Others* v. *the Netherlands*[53]). It can again be seen here that the European Court of Human Rights has developed case-law based on that of the ICJ.

In matters of immunity, attention should be drawn to one relatively complex case heard in Strasbourg because it involved proceedings in both Greece and Germany, and later returned to the European Court of Human Rights before being taken to the ICJ. It is thus a good illustration of successive judicial intervention in this area. The first Strasbourg case was that of *Kalogeropoulou,*[54] concerning the attempt by a group of Greek nationals to obtain damages from Germany for the massacre perpetrated in Distomo in 1944.

At national level, the case of the Distomo massacre had been examined favourably by the Greek Court of Cassation,[55] which rejected Germany's argument of State immunity. However, that judgment was never enforced. Under domestic law, the power of enforcement lay with the Government, which refused to exercise that competence. It was that refusal which gave rise to an application to the European Court of Human Rights under

[51] *Jurisdictional Immunities of the State* (*Germany* v. *Italy: Greece intervening*), Judgment, I.C.J. Reports 2012, p. 99.

[52] *Al-Adsani* v. *the United Kingdom*, note 50 above.

[53] *Stichting Mothers of Srebrenica and Others* v. *the Netherlands* (dec), No. 65542/12, 11 June 2013.

[54] *Kalogeropoulou and Others* v. *Greece and Germany* (dec.), No. 59021/00, ECHR 2002-X.

[55] *Voiotia* v. *Germany* (*Distomo Massacre Case*) 129 ILR 513 (Greece (CoC) 2002).

Article 6 of the Convention, the enforcement of a judgment being regarded in Strasbourg case-law as forming an integral part of the right to a court. Applying the *Al-Adsani*[56] jurisprudence, the Chamber declared the case inadmissible on the ground that the Greek Government could not be legally required to override the rule of State immunity against their will.

The case was then taken to the German courts, where it was dismissed at all levels of jurisdiction, up to the Federal Constitutional Court, on the ground that there was no legal basis, whether domestic or international, enabling the State's responsibility to be established. The matter later returned to Strasbourg – this time in the case of *Sfountouris* v. *Germany* – leading to a decision of 2011.[57] The complaints at that stage were different – the applicants alleged that their damages claim fell under Article 1 of Protocol No. 1 (protection of property) and further complained of discrimination. The Court disposed of the case with only a brief reference to public international law. In the main, it took the view that the applicants had no 'possession' within the meaning of Article 1 of Protocol No. 1. This was clear from the detailed and comprehensive reasoning of the German courts, whose conclusions had been neither arbitrary nor unreasonable.

Lastly, the matter was brought before the ICJ in the above-cited case concerning *Jurisdictional Immunities of the State*,[58] which was decided in 2012. The time had come to provide a definitive answer. The ICJ referred to the relevant Strasbourg case-law and in particular considered the minority's view about norms of *jus cogens* in the *Al-Adsani* case.[59] It found, however, that such a view was not solidly supported by State practice and refused to recognise the existence of a conflict of norms or rules. It explained that the rules of State immunity, being procedural in nature, did not bear upon the question whether or not the conduct in respect of which the proceedings were brought was lawful or unlawful, and as the peremptory norm of prohibition of torture was of a different nature, there was no conflict between them.

The case taken to The Hague mainly concerned the position adopted by the Italian courts on the question: in the *Ferrini* judgment adopted by the Italian Court of Cassation in 2004,[60] and in a decision of the Florence

[56] *Al-Adsani* v. *the United Kingdom*, note 50 above.

[57] *Sfountouris and Others* v. *Germany* (dec), No. 24120/06, 31 May 2011.

[58] *Jurisdictional Immunities of the State* (*Germany* v. *Italy: Greece intervening*), note 51 above.

[59] *Al-Adsani* v. *the United Kingdom*, note 50 above.

[60] *Ferrini* v. *Germany* (2004) 87 RDI 539 (Corte di Cassazione, 2004).

Court of Appeal – upheld by the Court of Cassation – to the effect that the judgment in the case concerning the Distomo massacre could be enforced in Italy. In Greece, the Distomo jurisprudence was overturned in 2002 by the judgment of the Special Supreme Court in the *Margellos* case,[61] where it was held that Germany was entitled to invoke its immunity from civil suit.

That departure from precedent was to trigger another case before the European courts, concerning other atrocities perpetrated in wartime. First before the Court of Justice of the European Union, on a preliminary reference from a Greek Court of Appeal as to whether the applicants' claim against Germany fell within the Brussels Convention on jurisdiction and the enforcement of judgments in civil and commercial matters. The Luxembourg court responded in the negative,[62] and it was that decision which formed the basis of the complaint then submitted to the European Court of Human Rights.

The case in question was *Lechouritou and Others* v. *Germany and 26 other member States of the European Union*,[63] decided in 2012. The applicants alleged that the decision of the Court of Justice of the European Union had represented a denial of justice, as there had been no other basis on which they could obtain damages from Germany. The case was decided by a committee of three judges. As in the *Sfountouris* case, the European Court of Human Rights did not find anything arbitrary or unreasonable in the reasoning of the Luxembourg court, thus leading it to declare the application inadmissible.

On the subject of the term 'fragmentation', as used by the International Law Commission's Study Group in its 2006 report,[64] the European Court of Human Rights referred to that report in two recent cases before the Grand Chamber which raised a fundamental human rights issue, namely the relationship in a given situation between the obligations imposed by the United Nations system and those arising from the European Convention on Human Rights. Each of those cases produced a different response.

[61] *Germany* v. *Margellos* [A.E.D.] Special Supreme Court 6/2002 129 ILR 526 (2002).

[62] *Eirini Lechouritou and Others* v. *Dimosio tis Omospondiakis Dimokratias tis Germanias* (case C-292/05), 15 February 2007.

[63] *Lechouritou and Others* v. *Germany and 26 other member States of the European Union* (dec), No. 37937/07, 3 April 2012.

[64] *Fragmentation of International Law: Difficulties Arising from the Diversification and Expansion of International Law*, Report of the Study Group of the International Law Commission (fifty-eighth session 2006), finalised by Martti Koskenniemi.

In the above-cited case of *Al-Jedda*,[65] where the applicant had complained of his internment by British forces in Iraq, it had to be determined whether his right to physical liberty under Article 5 of the Convention was nuanced or displaced by Security Council Resolution 1546. The interpretation of that resolution was a key issue in the case. Before looking at that question, the Court noted that the mission of the United Nations was not only to maintain international peace and security but also to ensure respect for human rights. It thus concluded as follows (§ 102):

> in interpreting its resolutions, there must be a presumption that the Security Council does not intend to impose any obligation on member States to breach fundamental principles of human rights. In the event of any ambiguity in the terms of a Security Council Resolution, the Court must therefore choose the interpretation which is most in harmony with the requirements of the Convention and which avoids any conflict of obligations.

In that case, as there had been no binding obligation to use internment, there was no conflict between the United Kingdom's obligations under the UN Charter and its obligations under the Convention.

In the more recent case of *Nada* v. *Switzerland*,[66] the question of the hierarchy between UN obligations and those of the European Convention on Human Rights arose once again. The Swiss Government, supported by France and the United Kingdom, argued that their obligation to uphold the relevant Security Council resolutions against Al-Qaeda prevailed over their obligations under Article 8 of the Convention vis-à-vis the applicant. The facts of the case were rather singular, as the applicant had been confined to the tiny Italian enclave of Campione d'Italia for almost six years. Although he was an Italian national, he had been prevented from travelling within his own country during that time. He was also elderly and in poor health.

Article 103 of the UN Charter unambiguously provides that the obligations under the Charter prevail in the event of a conflict with obligations under any other international agreement. The UN Charter is thus the highest instrument in the hierarchy under the law of international treaties.

In its reasoning the Grand Chamber confirmed the presumption laid down in its *Al-Jedda* judgment, whilst observing that in *Nada*, by contrast, there was a clear and express requirement for States to take the measure in

[65] *Al-Jedda* v. *the United Kingdom* [GC], No. 27021/08, ECHR 2011.

[66] *Nada* v. *Switzerland* [GC], No. 10593/08, ECHR 2012.

question, namely to prevent the individuals on the UN Sanctions Committee's list from entering or transiting through their territory. However, that was not the end of the matter. Noting that the Security Council did not impose on States a particular model for the implementation of its resolutions, the Court found that Switzerland had enjoyed some latitude, which was admittedly limited but nevertheless real. On that basis the Court concluded that the Swiss authorities had not sufficiently taken into account the realities of the case or the applicant's very specific situation. In the Court's view it should have been possible to alleviate the very strict sanctions regime applicable to Mr Nada without circumventing the binding nature of the relevant resolutions.

It was therefore unnecessary to determine the question, raised by the respondent and intervening Governments, of the hierarchy of norms. The Court added that it had been for the Swiss authorities – which had failed to show that they had made any efforts to that end – to harmonise, as far as possible, the obligations they had regarded as divergent.

As regards the *Nada* judgment, mention should also be made of the other complaint upheld by the Court, namely the lack of an effective remedy. In a rather brief paragraph,[67] the Court espoused the reasoning of the European Court of Justice in its leading *Kadi* judgment,[68] to the effect that judicial review of the internal lawfulness – in the light of fundamental freedoms – of a measure implementing a Security Council Resolution was not to be excluded. It was thus held that Switzerland had breached Article 13 of the Convention.

The process that has just been described also serves to illustrate a related phenomenon that is prevalent in this day and age – the increasing complexity and density of international law. In her speech before the European Court of Human Rights,[69] Dame Rosalyn Higgins thus observed that 'the plethora of judicial and quasi-judicial bodies operating in the field of human rights [did] pose the risk of divergent jurisprudence'. She did not, however, find this to be a real cause for concern. As to the European human rights system, she underlined the frequent references in the Strasbourg case-law to that of the ICJ, which itself would often look to the Convention jurisprudence. In the view of Dame Rosalyn Higgins,

[67] *Nada* v. *Switzerland*, note 65 above, § 176.

[68] *Yassin Abdullah Kadi and Al Barakaat International Foundation* v. *Council of the European Union and Commission of the European Communities* (joined cases C-402/05 P and C-415/05 P), 3 September 2008.

[69] See Higgins, note 6 above, p. 45.

the Courts of The Hague and Strasbourg could 'be perceived as partners for the protection of human rights'. She further approved the growing practice among international courts of periodically holding meetings to build international judicial dialogue. Mutual observation and dialogue are absolutely essential in order to avoid fragmentation of international law, and these are without any doubt the hallmarks of the relationship between the ICJ and the European Court of Human Rights.

8

Factors influencing the reception of international law in the ECtHR's case law: an overview

MAGDALENA FOROWICZ

1. Preliminary remarks

The European Court of Human Rights (ECtHR) has established itself as one of the most experienced and efficient human rights courts onto which other bodies have looked for guidance. It has developed creative, complex and expansive case law to put flesh onto and to expand the scope of the European Convention on Human Rights (ECHR). As an autonomous and authoritative court exclusively charged with the application of the ECHR, the Court reluctantly gave away its self-sufficiency to refer to external sources. However, with the proliferation of international courts and tribunals and the expansion of international law, the Court has been compelled to look beyond the Convention in its case law. Slowly, the phenomenon of reception of international law in the case law of the ECtHR has established itself. This trend has opened the question as to the consequences that a fragmented legal order may have for the ECHR and also as to the role that the Court could play in it.

An empirical assessment of the Court's references to eight areas of international law – child rights, refugee rights, civil and political rights, prohibition against torture and other ill-treatment, State immunity, international humanitarian law (IHL), the law of treaties and the International Court of Justice's (ICJ) case law – has shown how the reception of international law in the case law of the ECtHR occurs and whether it leads to fragmentation.[1] Recent developments prompt the need to revisit this

[1] This chapter is based in part on some of the findings of my book, which was published by Oxford University Press in 2010. These findings needed to be updated and re-evaluated as part of this publication, due to the changes which have ensued since the publication of the book. See Magdalena Forowicz, *The Reception of International Law in the European Court of Human Rights*, Oxford University Press, Oxford/New York, 2010.

analysis. In light of recent case law, this chapter re-evaluates the factors which have an impact on the reception of international law under the ECHR. It further discusses which of these factors have been the most influential. This evaluation then sheds some light on the Court's approach towards the reception of international law. In the context of this edited volume, the question should also be posed whether, in an international legal order tending towards convergence, the Court's approach will support and facilitate a central role for the ICJ in ensuring its unity.

2. Factors influencing the reception of international law in the ECtHR

The case law of the ECtHR demonstrates that there are specific factors which have a bearing on the receptiveness of international law. They are the starting point which essentially determines whether references will occur in a given field. The factors listed below concern specific considerations pertaining to the nature of the relevant ECHR provision, the nature of the international instrument considered and the nature of the dispute and the circumstances of the case. They have determined to a large extent the frequency and the intensity of the references made to international sources. The reception process is never based on a single factor and different factors usually appear in various combinations in the reasoning of the judges.

2.1. International law was invoked at the domestic level

In most cases, the reception of international law is facilitated by the fact that the relevant international legal sources are either invoked by the parties at the domestic level or are applied by the domestic courts in their judgments. The Court probably felt that under such circumstances the Contracting States would not contest their use of these external sources. The fact that international instruments had been previously invoked provides a rubber stamp and gives more confidence to the Court. As these instruments are already part of the case, the Court probably considers that it would not be criticised by Contracting States if it also refers to them. Such references are treated as a legitimate reliance on international law and increase the level of receptiveness. Naturally, there are also cases with no apparent references to international law at the domestic level, where the Court relies on international law in its reasoning. It is, however, not possible to determine with certainty whether any such international law references do not occur in the earlier phases of the case, namely during the hearings at the domestic level or in Strasbourg, without conducting further research in the relevant archives.

2.2. *Case intertwined with international law*

When cases are very closely intertwined with a certain international procedure, it becomes almost impossible for the Court not to refer to international law. In those instances, the Court behaves in a receptive manner, simply because international law is already part of the legal reasoning or the parties' pleadings in the case. These references to international law are not tremendously surprising or impressive, as they are a necessary part of the reasoning. This occurred, for instance, in a specific category of cases which were intertwined with the Hague Convention on the Civil Aspects of International Child Abduction[2] and the Hague Convention on Protection of Children and Cooperation in respect of Intercountry Adoption.[3] The Hague Conventions were ratified by most ECHR Contracting States, and they have become the *modus operandi* in matters which they regulate. Thus, the Court did not have any other choice than to refer to the relevant international instruments. Thus, the Court felt confident enough to intervene in the domestic application of the Hague Convention on International Abduction, finding that the domestic courts had misinterpreted the instrument.[4]

The situation was also similar with refugee cases intertwined with domestic asylum proceedings. These proceedings were often based on the Convention relating to the Status of Refugees,[5] which *ipso facto* made its way into the decisions and judgments of the Strasbourg bodies. Moreover, the Court was also prompted by the necessity of referring to international law in the *Bosphorous*,[6] the Al-Jedda,[7] or the *Nada* cases, [8] which was

[2] *The Hague Convention on the Civil Aspects of International Child Abduction*, 1343 UNTS 89, entered into force 1 December 1993.

[3] *The Hague Convention on Protection of Children and Cooperation in Respect of Intercountry Adoption*, 32 ILM 1134 (1993), entered into force on 1 May 1995.

[4] *Monory* v. *Romania and Hungary* (Appl. No. 71099/01), judgment, 5 April 2005; *Neulinger and Shuruk* v. *Switzerland* (Appl. No. 41615/07), judgment, 6 July 2010.

[5] *United Nations Convention Relating to the Status of Refugees*, 606 UNTS 267, entered into force on 22 April 1954.

[6] *Bosphorous Hava Yolları Turizmve Ticaret Anonim Şirketi* v. *Ireland* (Appl. No. 45036/98), judgment, 30 June 2005.

[7] *Al-Jedda* v. *United Kingdom* (Appl. No. 27021/08), judgment, 7 July 2011.

[8] *Nada* v. *Switzerland* (Appl. No. 10593/08), judgment, 12 September 2012.

closely intertwined with a decision taken by the UN Security Council (UNSC) under the UN Charter.

There are also cases which require a reference as a condition for resolving the dispute at hand.[9] This occurred, for instance in some cases, closely entangled with the International Covenant on Civil and Political Rights (ICCPR),[10] which were introduced before the Human Rights Committee (HRC) and the Court. These cases concerned the co-existence of both bodies, and the Court had to refer to the procedure undertaken before the HRC in order to reach a solution in the case. Another example of this category of cases can be found in *Banković and Others* v. *Belgium and 16 Other Contracting States*[11] and *Ilascu* v. *Moldova and Russia*,[12] where the ECHR dealt with jurisdiction questions in relation to the principle of State responsibility in international law.

2.3. *Need to harmonise a provision with international law*

Another important factor having a bearing on the reception of international law at the ECHR level is the necessity to update the Convention's meaning. International instruments have been used sometimes as evidence of current human rights standards.[13] In fact, the Court has justified a particular interpretation of the ECHR by claiming that it is consistent with the treatment of the same issue under a different international treaty. This interpretation technique ensures that international human rights law develops consistently and that it constitutes a coherent branch of international law as 'human rights law' as a opposed to a number of disparate treaty provisions.[14]

Harmonisation has been used by the Court to bring the ECHR in line with current standards in the area of child rights. The ECHR contains very few explicit references to children and it lacks any firm recognition of their rights. Moreover, little guidance was provided in the ECHR as

9 Christos Rozakis, 'The European Judge as a Comparatist', 80 (1) *Tulane Law Review*, 157, 275 (2005).

10 *United Nations Covenant on Civil and Political Rights*, 99 UNTS 171, entered into force 23 March 1976.

11 *Banković and Others* v. *Belgium and 16 Other Contracting States* (Appl. No. 52207/99), secision, 12 December 2001, para. 320.

12 *Ilascu and Others* v. *Moldova and Russia* (Appl. No. 48787/99), judgment, 8 July 2004, para. 57.

13 John Graham Merrills, *The Development of International Law by the European Court of Human Rights*, Manchester University Press, Manchester/New York, 1993, p. 222.

14 *Ibid.*, p. 224.

to how these rights should be articulated. This situation has evolved over time, as the Court adapted the ECHR to the changing domestic and international standards. The ECHR became increasingly more child-friendly as a result of the update that the Strasbourg bodies performed through their receptive case law.

The harmonisation method was also used in some cases concerning civil and political rights. For instance, in the *Goppera Radio AGand Others* v. *Switzerland* case,[15] the Court attempted to harmonise Article 10 ECHR with Article 19 ICCPR. In that case, the Court held that licensing of broadcasting, authorised under Article 10 (1) ECHR, had to fulfil the conditions laid down in Article 10 (2) ECHR and could not be left entirely to a Contracting State's discretion. The Court supported this reasoning with Article 19 ICCPR and its negotiating history, which do not contain any reference to licensing. According to the Court, this view confirmed the conclusion that Article 10 (1) ECHR allowed States to control broadcasting by means of a licensing system, but it did not entail that licensing measures could be exempted from Article 10 (2) ECHR requirements.

Quite similarly, in the *Riener*[16] and the *Bartik*[17] cases, the Court attempted to harmonise Article 2 of Protocol No. 4 with Article 12 ICCPR, both guaranteeing the freedom of movement. The Court referred to the ICCPR in a fairly unhindered manner in those cases. This was due, in part, to the textual resemblance between Article 12 ICCPR and Article 2 of Protocol No. 4 and to the fact the former served as a basis to draft the latter. These references to the ICCPR served to support its reasoning and to clarify further the meaning of the requirements under Article 2 of Protocol No. 4. Further, in the recent case of *Bayatayan* v. *Armenia*[18] the ECtHR looked for developments in international law to adapt its previous position to current standards where the provisions in other instruments resembled closely the ECHR provisions. The case related to the question whether the imprisonment of a man for his refusal to perform military service on account of being a Jehovah's Witness constituted a violation of his freedom of thought, conscience and religion. The Grand Chamber stated that 'in defining the meaning of terms and notions in the text of the Convention, the Court can and must take into account elements of

[15] *Goppera Radio A.G. and Others* v. *Switzerland* (Appl. No. 10890/84), judgment, 28 March 1990, Series A, Vol. 273.

[16] *Riener* v. *Bulgaria*, (Appl. No. 46343/99), judgment, 23 May 2006.

[17] *Bartik* v. *Russia*, (Appl. No. 55565/00), judgment, 21 December 2006.

[18] *Bayatyan* v. *Armenia*, (Appl. No. 23459/03), judgment, 7 July 2011.

international law other than the Convention and the interpretation of such elements by competent organs'.[19] Departing from previous case law, the Grand Chamber found that opposition to military service where it is motivated by a serious conflict between serving in the military and deeply held beliefs is sufficient to attract the protection of Article 9 ECHR. In order to reach this conclusion, the Court relied on international instruments, including the ICCPR and the EU Charter of Fundamental Rights,[20] as well as their interpretation by competent bodies.

The notion of harmonisation has been analysed by the International Law Commission (ILC) Study Group in the context of the systemic interpretation rule contained in Article 31 (3) (c) of the Vienna Convention on the Law of Treaties (VCLT).[21] In this sense, harmonisation acquires a broader meaning which implies that treaties are part of the international legal system; they must be interpreted as being part of a whole and in accordance with the general principles of international law. Article 31 (3) (c) VCLT[22] has been read with renewed interest in the context of fragmentation and judicial interpretation of international law. It has been considered that systemic interpretation could be one of the possible ways to deal with the lack of unity and with normative conflicts in international law.

Systemic interpretation, as contained in Article 31 (3) (c) VCLT, has also been applied by the Court in its case law. These references are scarce and problematic given that the Court did not address the uncertainties inherent in this provision; it seems to have bypassed these difficulties and applied it in a mechanical manner. The Court has resorted to Article 31 (3) (c) VCLT in cases where substantive issues of great importance for the protection of human rights presented themselves, such as State immunity, reservations, access to court, jurisdiction, interim measures, child abduction, child adoption and freedom of association. It is possible that the Court needed Article 31 (3) (c) VCLT as a rubber stamp to legitimate its use of international law. However, in a landmark case, *Demir*

[19] *Ibid.*, para. 102.

[20] Charter of Fundamental Rights of the European Union, OJ C 326, 26 October 2012, p. 391.

[21] United Nations General Assembly, Fragmentation of International Law: Difficulties Arising from the Diversification and Expansion of International Law, Report of the Study Group of the International Law Commission, finalised by Martti Koskenniemi, International Law Commission, 58th session, 1 May–9 June and 3 July–11 August 2006, UN Doc. No. A/CN.4/L.682, 13 April 2006, pp. 25 and 206.

[22] Vienna Convention on the Law of Treaties, 1155 UNTS 331, entered into force 27 January 1980.

and Baykara v. *Turkey*,[23] the Court interpreted Article 31 (3) (c) VCLT more expansively than before to develop Article 11 ECHR. It asserted a broad competence to interpret the ECHR in light of a wide range of international sources. It has been accurately pointed out that this case has a transformative effect on the Court's approach to rights interpretation and that it marks a shift in its power to hold the Contracting States to legal instruments beyond their control.[24] Nevertheless, the Court's approach is weakened by the fact that it did not engage meaningfully with the components of Article 31 (3) (c) VCLT.

It is puzzling that the Court has not resorted to this provision in other cases referring to international instruments. It can be argued that, in most cases where the Court incorporated international law into its reasoning, it may have resorted to this provision indirectly.[25] However, the references to Article 31 (3) (c) VCLT do not exhibit any coherent trend in the Court's approach. The Court probably avoided citing this provision explicitly due to the interpretation problems that it presents. As a result, any deductions on the basis of the Court's case law regarding the operationalisation of this rule in the context of fragmentation seem to be difficult to make.

2.4. *Used in the drafting of the ECHR*

When a provision to be interpreted was inspired by another international treaty dealing with the topic, the Court has naturally turned to this instrument for guidance.[26] This then allowed it to expand the meaning of the Convention in a fairly uncontroversial manner. As mentioned in the preceding section, this interpretation technique was applied in the *Riener*[27] and the *Bartik*[28] cases, where the Court attempted to harmonise

23 *Demir and Baykara* v. *Turkey*, (Appl. No. 34503/97), judgment, 12 November 2008.

24 Julian Arato, 'Constitutional Transformation in the ECHR: Strasbourg's Expansive Recourse to External Rules of International Law', 37 (2) *Brooklyn Journal of International Law* 349 (2012).

25 François Ost, 'The Original Canons of Interpretation of the European Court of Human Rights', in Mireille Delmas-Marty and Christine Chodakiewicz (eds.), *The European Convention for the Protection of Human Rights: International Protection versus National Restriction*, Martinus Nijhoff, Dodrecht/Boston/London, p. 288; Alastair Mowbray, 'The Creativity of the European Court of Human Rights', 5 *Human Rights Law Review* 57, 59 (2005); Merrills, *The Development of International Law*, note 13 *supra*, p. 69.

26 *Ibid.*, p. 218. See with regard to domestic courts, Basil Markesinis and Jörg Fedtke, *Judicial Recourse to Foreign Law: A New Source of Inspiration*, University of Texas at Austin, Studies in Foreign and Transnational Law, University College London Press, London, 2006, pp. 135–7.

27 *Riener* v. *Bulgaria*, note 16 *supra*.

28 *Bartik* v. *Russia*, note 17 *supra*.

Article 2 of Protocol No. 4 with Article 12 ICCPR (guaranteeing the freedom of movement). The Court referred to the ICCPR in a fairly unhindered manner in those cases due to the textual resemblance between Article 12 ICCPR and Article 2 of Protocol No. 4 and to the fact the former served as a basis to draft the latter.

This interpretation mode was also used in the *Vander Mussele* case[29] – a representative example – where the Court analysed the meaning of 'forced or compulsory labour' which was included, albeit not defined, in Article 4 ECHR. As the *travaux préparatoires* were of little assistance, the Court turned to the International Labour Organisation (ILO) Convention No. 29. The Court considered that it was evident 'that the authors of the European Convention – following the example of the authors of Article 8 of the draft ICCPR – based themselves, to a large extent, on an earlier treaty of the International Labour Organisation, namely Convention No. 29 concerning Forced or Compulsory Labour'.[30] Noting that there was a striking similarity between Article 4 (3) ECHR and Article 2 (2) ILO Convention No. 29, the Court considered that the definition of 'forced or compulsory labour' could provide a starting point for the interpretation of Article 4 ECHR.[31]

These types of references are perhaps the most natural and most useful in seeking guidance with regard to the ECHR given that they originate from the instrument which has inspired it. As such, they are more legitimate than other references and are bound to awaken less disagreement on the part of Contracting States if used. They also play an essential role in shedding further light on the ECHR provisions. Furthermore, they constitute an important means for the development of coherent case law in areas where several instruments may overlap. It should be noted, however, that few of the instruments considered here have had a bearing on the creation of the ECHR framework, given that most of them came into force after the ECHR.

2.5. *Uncertainty regarding international law*

A factor which appears to have inhibited the Court's reception of international law is the uncertainty which pervades some of its areas. There are numerous issues which remain unsettled or which are still subject to international debate. Given the difficulties of reaching a universal agreement

[29] *Van der Mussele* v. *Belgium* (Appl. No. 8919/80), judgment, 23 November 1983, Series A, Vol. 70.

[30] *Van der Mussele* v. *Belgium*, note 29 *supra*, para. 32. [31] *Ibid.*

among non-homogenous States, international law is sometimes unable to provide precise and unequivocal answers. Further, due to the existence of divergent interpretations of certain international instruments, it may be increasingly more difficult for the Court to rely on international law. When international law is unsettled or vague, it becomes more difficult for the Court to rely on it as an aid in interpretation. In fact, reliance on international sources defeats its initial purpose if it is unable to assist the Court.

Although the Strasbourg bodies have incorporated the uncertainties of international law into some areas of their case law, there were also instances where they explicitly announced that unsettled international law could not be of assistance to them. For instance, in the *Civil Service Unions* case,[32] the Commission found that the differences in language contained in international law instruments demonstrated that there was no settled view under international law as to the position of members of the 'administration of the State' in respect of trade union rights. Thus, it was found that the international instruments invoked by the applicants could be discarded in the present case. This practice should, however, be contrasted, with the Strasbourg bodies' application of Article 31 (3) (c) VCLT, where they did not feel inhibited by the uncertainties relating to this provision. The Court and the Commission seem to have applied this provision mechanically without fully engaging with its problematic aspects. There are, nonetheless, few explicit references to this provision in the Strasbourg case law. Moreover, they seem to be grounded in the necessity of the situation and the Strasbourg bodies' selectivity in applying the required sources.

The Court's use of international instruments is often justified by their utility; if international law cannot be of assistance, then it is often set aside by the Court. Uncertainty and vagueness are not novel problems in international law. As part of its references, the Court is bound to encounter this problem on a regular basis. An important aspect to keep in mind is not to deepen the existing divides or uncertainties in international law. However, going further and attempting to resolve uncertainties in international law may be precluded, as the Court was not created for this purpose. As desirable as such a function for one of the most influential human rights courts may be, it may simply be unfeasible due to the Court's limited mandate.

32 *Civil Service Unions and Others* v. *United Kingdom* (Appl. No. 11603/85), decision, 20 January 1987, D.R. 50, p. 228.

2.6. *Need to fill in gaps*

In a number of cases, the Court was brought to address issues which were not explicitly regulated by the ECHR. Taking a bold approach, it decided on occasion to fill such gaps on its own. Further, given that the ECHR was concluded almost sixty years ago, the Court often felt compelled to update its content through evolutive interpretation in certain important areas. This approach sometimes entailed reading into or finding implied rights in the Convention. Although it contributed to the protection of human rights, the Court's methodology was met with vivid criticism, often from its own members, claiming that it was performing a legislative function.

The Court decided in *Golder* v. *United Kingdom*[33] that the right of access to court was inherent in Article 6 (1) ECHR. Using Article 31 (3) (c) VCLT, the Court referred to Article 38 (1) (c) of the ICJ Statute, which includes, among the relevant legal sources, 'general principles of law recognized by civilized nations'. The Court considered that the principle whereby a civil claim must be capable of being submitted to a judge constituted a fundamental principle of law. Further, the prohibition of denial of justice was another such principle of international law. Thus, the Court found that Article 6 (1) ECHR must be read in the light of these principles and based itself, *inter alia*, on these to include a right which was not previously contained in the ECHR.

Another representative example of gap filling occurred in the *Mamatkulov* judgment.[34] The Grand Chamber held that interim measures acquired a binding character under the ECHR. The Court relied, *inter alia*, on the change in the ICJ's case law to support its finding that interim measures had an obligatory character. Thus, it reversed previous case law on the topic,[35] which had established that interim measures were not binding on the basis of the Contracting States practice. While in 1991 the old Court found that no power to order binding interim measures could be inferred from the ECHR, the new Court decided in 2003 and 2005 that such an inference was nonetheless possible. While it seemed as a radical innovation, the remedying of such omissions was a fundamental

[33] *Golder* v. *United Kingdom* (Appl. No. 4451/70), judgment, 21 February 1975, Series A, Vol. 18.

[34] *Mamatkulov and Askarov* v. *Turkey* (Appl. Nos. 46827/99; 46951/99), judgment, 4 February 2005. See also *Mamatkulov and Abdurasulovic* v. *Turkey* (Appl. Nos. 46827/99; 46951/99), judgment, 6 February 2003.

[35] *Cruz Varas and Others* v. *Sweden* (Appl. No. 15576/89), judgment, 20 March 1991, Series A, Vol. 201.

step for the preservation and the strengthening of the ECHR machinery. The Court's approach has aided in ensuring that the provisions of the ECHR remain practical and effective.

2.7. *Textual and substantive similarities*

The ECtHR's willingness to refer to external sources is often conditioned by the similarities that exist between the ECHR and other international instruments. These similarities were conducive to the reception of international law in situations where the Court and the Commission wanted to clarify or to expand the meaning of the ECHR. Being unable to find guidance within their own jurisdiction, they turned to documents which most resembled the ECHR. The most similarities appeared among the ECHR and other international human rights regimes, given that they cover similar areas and strive for the same goals. There were few similarities between the ECHR and the two areas of general international law covered by this study.

From the substantive point of view, the ICCPR is most akin to the ECHR as it contains a similar catalogue of civil and political rights, provides for an individual complaint procedure and has analogous aims. The references to this instrument are therefore not very unusual and unduly strenuous for the Court. Further, there are several textual parallels between the ICCPR, the ILO Convention No. 29 and the ECHR framework; they have also made the reception process much easier. These textual resemblances are rooted, in part, in the fact that these instruments have served in the drafting of the ECHR and its Protocols. Thus, the Court was also compelled to consider sources that have influenced the creation of the ECHR framework.

2.8. *More specific guidelines available in international law*

The ECHR encompasses an extensive array of human rights. Its provisions are often vague and general, which naturally prompts the need on the part of the Court and the Commission to develop them. In this context, it is often necessary for the Strasbourg bodies to use international instruments, as they were more specific and provided more guidance than the ECHR. This has occurred in the past in cases where the Court wanted to harmonise the ECHR with international law, wanted to put flesh onto ECHR provisions as well as to remedy an omission. In these instances, the Court's methodology was also motivated by the specificity of the relevant international instrument. Thus, a general factor underlying many references appears to have been the lack of precision of the ECHR in certain areas and the corresponding need to seek guidance elsewhere. This occurred, for instance, in relation to the definition of torture, the adoption and abduction of children, treaty interpretation rules as well as civil and political rights. Rather curiously, the Court's references to IHL were not premised on the rule that this body of law consitutes *lex specialis* in the field of armed conflict. Several reasons could explain this state of affairs, namely the potential inadequacy of the *lex specialis* rule and the need to ensure that human rights are applied (and not suspended), or the political consideration surrounding the application of IHL to the respondent governments.

2.9. *Need to assess the human rights situation in a country*

The Court relied on reports originating from international organisations in expulsion cases under Article 3 ECHR when it needed to evaluate the situation in the country receiving the applicant to be expelled. In fact, when the Court assesses the risk of mistreatment, it considers all the material placed before it or, if necessary, material obtained on its own initiative.[36] It is in principle for the applicant to provide evidence capable of proving that he/she would be exposed to a real risk of being subjected to treatment contrary to Article 3 EHCR. Further, the Court clarified in *Saadi* v. *Italy*[37] that, in order to determine whether there is a risk of ill-treatment, it must examine the general situation in the receiving country. In the past, 'it has often attached importance to the information contained in recent reports from independent international human-rights-protection associations such as Amnesty International, or governmental sources, including the US State Department . . . '.[38] While this material is not the only evidence to be taken into consideration in such cases, it provides relevant information as to the general situation and constitutes a good basis for the Court's evaluation. Thus, the possibility of using independent international reports has recently enhanced the Court's receptiveness of external sources.

[36] *H.L.R.* v. *France* (Appl. no. 24573/94), judgment, 29 April 1997, para. 37; *Hilal* v. *United Kingdom* (Appl. no. 45276/99), judgment, 6 March 2001, para. 60; *Saadi* v. *Italy* (Appl. no. 37201/06), judgment (Grand Chamber), 28 February 2008, para. 128.

[37] *Saadi* v. *Italy*, note 36 *supra*.

[38] *Ibid.*, para. 131.

2.10. *Political issues and State interests*

The political climate has had a bearing on the level of reception of international law in certain cases. As the evaluation of the Strasbourg case law has demonstrated, the political issues as well as State interests can both enhance and inhibit the Strasbourg bodies' predisposition to consider international law. While the Court is an independent body, which cannot be swayed by political considerations, it does not function in isolation from the context which surrounds it. The Court may sometimes feel the need to ensure that its authority is preserved, which requires it to take a pragmatic approach with regard to the standards set in its case law.[39] It remains vulnerable to criticism from Contracting States that it is not taking State practice into account. This aspect is of tremendous importance as the Convention's effectiveness is based on the States' cooperation in implementing the necessary changes into domestic law following a Court ruling.[40]

The Court's approach with regard to IHL may have been influenced by the atmosphere surrounding the cases and the States' reluctance to have IHL applied to them. Initially, the ECtHR's approach was based on the exclusive application of the Convention and the indirect references to IHL. In fact, the Court appears to have borrowed the IHL vocabulary and reasoning without acknowledging the source from which they originated. In cases such as *Güleç* v. *Turkey*,[41] *Ergi* v. *Turkey*,[42] *Özkan* v. *Turkey*[43] or *Isayeva and Others* v. *Russia*,[44] it was rather unlikely that the respondent governments would have welcomed the finding that IHL applies to the confrontations occurring on their territories. Despite the legal advantages of using IHL, certain States refuse to comply with its requirements due to the political cost and stigmatisation that it could entail. Being aware of these considerations, the Court may have chosen an approach which accommodates the political climate and the Contracting States articulated interests.

The Court's approach appears to have changed following the *Korbely* v. *Hungary* case,[45] where it referred to IHL directly by making explicit

[39] Ed Bates, *The Evolution of the European Convention on Human Rights*, Oxford University Press, 2010, p. 213.

[40] *Ibid.*, p. 214.

[41] *Güleç* v. *Turkey* (Appl. No. 21593/93), judgment, 27 July 1998.

[42] *Ergi* v. *Turkey* (Appl. No. 23818/94), judgment, 28 July 1998.

[43] *Özkan* v. *Turkey* (Appl. No. 21689/93), judgment, 6 April 2004.

[44] *Isayeva and Others* v. *Russia* (Appl. Nos. 57947/00; 57948/00; 57949/00), judgment, 24 February 2005.

[45] *Korbely* v. *Hungary* (Appl. No. 9174/02), judgment, 19 September 2008, Reports 2008.

use of Common Article 3 to the Geneva Conventions as a starting point for its reasoning under Article 7 ECHR. However, the Court remained very cautious and did not provide an extensive analysis of the concepts that it relied on. In the *Kononov* v. *Latvia* case,[46] the Court appears to have confirmed that it abandoned its approach of referring to IHL *sub siletio*. The Court engaged more directly with the interpretation of IHL when it considered (reversing the Chamber judgment[47]) that the conviction of a former Soviet partisan for war crimes during World War II contravened Article 7 ECHR. The Grand Chamber found that there had been a sufficiently clear legal basis, even at the time of the events in 1944, for the crimes of which the applicant was convicted. The Court considered here sensitive historical questions and dealt with fundamental questions concerning the principle of legality and substantive justice in IHL and international criminal law (ICL). This trend continued in the *Al-Jedda* case[48] and *Al-Skeini* case,[49] where the Court interpreted the question of internment IHL directly, which generated some criticism as to the accuracy of its analysis.[50] This different approach of the ECtHR to IHL should, however, be read carefully against the background of the cases. The changed approach of the Court may be merely incidental due to the close intertwinement of the cases with IHL. Further, the reliance on IHL was in these cases less controversial, as it did not involve a possible determination as to the confrontations which occurred on the territories of the respondent governments.

As part of another political setting, the Court used a diametrically different approach to international law. With regard to the German Democratic Republic (GDR) cases concerning border policing,[51] the Court was overzealous in relying on international instruments. It has applied the ICCPR when this instrument was ratified, albeit not implemented, by the GDR. The Covenant had a rather dubious status at the national level and

[46] *Kononov* v. *Latvia* (Appl. No. 36376/04), judgment, 17 May 2010.

[47] For a criticism of the case, see Giulia Pinzauti, 'The European Court of Human Rights' Incidental Application of International Humanitarian Law and International Criminal Law: A Critical Discussion of *Kononov* v. *Latvia*', 6 *Journal of International Criminal Justice* 1043 (2008).

[48] *Al-Jedda* v. *United Kingdom*, note 7 *supra*.

[49] *Al-Skeini and Others* v. *United Kingdom* (Appl. No. 55721/07), 7 July 2011, Reports 2011.

[50] Jelena Pejic, 'The European Court of Human Rights' Al-Jedda Judgment: The Oversight of International Humanitarian Law', 93 (883) *International Review of the Red Cross* 837 (September 2011).

[51] *Streletz, Kessler and Krenz* v. *Germany* (Appl. Nos. 34044; 35532 and 44801/98), judgment, 22 March 2001; *K.-H. W.* v. *Germany* (Appl. No. 37201/97), judgment, 22 March 2001.

could hardly be interpreted as invalidating the defences invoked by the applicants that existed under the GDR law at the time. In addition, a part of the acts committed by the applicants in the cases took place before the ICCPR[52] had been ratified by the GDR. Thus, the application of the ICCPR[53] provisions was rather strained and questionable. Behaving in a very open and receptive manner, the Court simply applied the relevant ICCPR provisions without further consideration.

This approach could have also been prompted, in part, by the fact that the case was intertwined at the domestic level with ICCPR provisions and that the German courts had previously referred to them. However, it seems to be more plausible that the Court was conscious of the political climate surrounding these cases. While the first individuals to have been tried in the reunified Germany were East German border guards,[54] the Germans soon grew weary with trials of those who carried out the orders and proceeded to try the more important political figures. Given the unsatisfactory outcome of these trials, there was a strong pressure to bring remaining officials of the former GDR to trial. The attempt on the part of the German courts to convict the applicants and the ECtHR's determination to respect their findings are apparent in the artificial and strained legal arguments used.

Thus, the political climate can exert an important influence on the Court's approach to international law, either by inhibiting or prompting references. While it is difficult for ECtHR judges to ignore the context of a given case, reliance on international law must be conducted with care. A lack of justification, acknowledgement or proper interpretation of the international sources used can be detrimental to the unity of international law. Undoubtedly, the Court finds itself at the apex of a delicate balance, but the political climate or States interests should not impede it from referring to international law in a properly justified manner.

2.11. *More advantageous to use the ECHR*

Another important reason which may have discouraged the Court from referring to international law is the fact that reliance on the ECHR is sometimes more advantageous than on other international instruments.

52 *Ibid.* 53 *Ibid.*

54 Adrienne Quill, 'To Prosecute or Not To Prosecute: Problems Encountered in the Prosecution of Former Communist Officials in Germany, Czechoslovakia and the Czech Republic', 7 *Indiana International and Comparative Law Review* 165, 178–180 (1996).

The ECHR is clearly one of the most effective instruments to protect human rights at the European level; it contains an extensive catalogue of rights and has a strong enforcement mechanism. While a number of international instruments are more adapted to certain types of violations, the ECHR still contains certain provisions which grant a more extensive protection to the applicant. Further, the ECHR offers better prospects for enforcement than other international human rights instruments.

For instance, in the case of refugee rights, the Court was clearly conscious that the ECHR provides a greater protection to the applicant, running the risk of being tortured or mistreated upon his return or expulsion to a receiving country, than the one afforded by the 1951 Refugee Convention. In *Chahal* v. *United Kingdom*,[55] a representative case, the Court found that, pursuant to Article 3 ECHR, 'the activities of the individual in question, however undesirable or dangerous, cannot be a material consideration. The protection afforded by Article 3 is thus wider than that provided by Articles 32 and 33 of the United Nations 1951 Convention on the Status of Refugees . . . '.[56] It should be noted that the principle of *non-refoulement* under the 1951 Refugee Conventions is limited, as Articles 32 and 33 of the 1951 Refugee Convention provide that a refugee can be expelled on grounds of national security and public order. As underlined by the Court, Article 3 ECHR is absolute and does allow such exceptions.

This distinction between both instruments may have been prompted by the Court's wish to justify the lack of reliance on the 1951 Refugee Convention in a case which was so closely tied in with this instrument. This statement exceeds the Court's usual references in cases closely intertwined with international law. By providing further clarifications pertaining to international law on its own initiative, the Court has given greater weight to its reasoning. More importantly, however, it appears that the Court was simply attempting to distance itself from the UN High Commissioner for Refugees (UNHCR) network in order to ensure that certain human rights are better protected. The differentiation of the ECHR from the 1951 Refugee Convention[57] seems to have been prompted by the specificity

[55] *Chahal* v. *United Kingdom* (Appl. no. 22414/93), judgment, 15 November 1996.

[56] *Ibid.*, para. 80. See also *Kashiyev and Akayera* v. *Russia* (Appl. no. 57942/00 and 57948/00), judgment, 24 February 2005, para. 88, where the Court stated that '[e]ven in the most difficult circumstances, such as the fight against terrorism and organised crime, the Convention prohibits in absolute terms torture and inhuman or degrading treatment or punishment'.

[57] *Ibid.*

of the ECHR and the necessity of rendering ECHR rights practical and effective.

It is thus not surprising for the Court to differentiate the ECHR from other international instruments when these do not ensure the same level of protection or fulfil a different purpose. The Strasbourg bodies have been less receptive and have taken a divergent route when this was justified by the unique requirements of the legal regime within which they operate. For instance, with regard to the case law of the ICJ, the Court explicitly distinguished itself from that Court, finding in the *Loizidou* case[58] that '[u]nlike international treaties of the classical kind, the Convention comprises more than mere reciprocal engagements between Contracting States. It creates over and above a network of mutual bilateral undertakings, objective obligations which in the words of the preamble benefit from a "collective enforcement" '.[59] In this manner, the Court entrenched the special character of the ECHR and distanced itself from the ICJ's case law relating to the opposability of reservations. Thus, the ECtHR's assessment of reservations differs from the ICJ's case law on grounds that the Convention is a human rights treaty. Here, the Court also wished to underline that the ECHR constitutes the *lex specialis* in this case.

2.12. *Procedural and substantive law*

In the Strasbourg case law, there are differences in the level of reception of international procedural law and international substantive law. In this context, international procedural law refers to a treaty which sets up a given procedure to follow in order to resolve a dispute; international substantive law, on the other hand, refers to treaties granting concrete rights and obligations to States and individuals. By nature, procedural law is more neutral and does not usually refer to politically charged or controversial issues. Substantive law (especially human rights law) can, unfortunately, be a subject of vivid disagreement among Contracting States. The level of reception in the Strasbourg case law was higher when a case involved an international procedure than when it concerned substantive rights.

This may explain, in part, why the ECtHR may feel less inhibited when referring to the Hague Convention on the Civil Aspects of International

[58] *Loizidou* v. *Turkey* (Preliminary Objections) (Appl. no. 15318/89), judgment, 23 March 1995, Series A, Vol. 310.

[59] *Ibid.*, para. 70.

Child Abduction and the Hague Convention on Protection of Children and Cooperation in respect of Intercountry Adoption. The Court has emphasised that the Hague Convention on the Civil Aspects of International Child Abduction is 'essentially an instrument of a procedural nature and not a human rights treaty protecting individuals on an objective basis'.[60] Both the Hague Conventions set out the procedure to resolve disputes regarding child adoption and abduction. These areas are not tremendously controversial and both treaties benefit from strong support on the part of the ECHR Contracting States. In most of these cases, the Court did not examine complex family questions, but rather more practical aspects concerning the compliance with the ECtHR of decisions taken under those instruments.

Other references to international procedural law appeared in cases relating to the co-existence of the HRC and the ECtHR. Some cases were introduced before both the Committee and the Court. The Court thus felt the need to refer to the proceedings under the First Optional Protocol (OP)[61] in order to clarify its role vis-à-vis the Committee. The fact that certain cases were brought before both bodies enhanced reception, but the references which appeared in the case were not those meant to ensure that international law is harmonised and not fragmented. Rather, they were necessary in order to preserve and define further the co-existence of both bodies in order to avoid cases of litispendence.

While references to international procedural law enhance reception due to their uncontroversial nature, they are not as instructive with regard to the Court's approach to international law as the references to more substantive provisions. References to substantive international law, such as other international human rights treaties, are usually a source of greater debate at the international level. It is as part of these references that the Court's self-perception in the international legal system can be assessed most adequately. When relying on substantive rights enshrined in international instruments, the Court often has to make a deliberate choice to refer to a debated or controversial provision. This can, at times, compromise its credibility and authority among Contracting States. References to international procedural law remain, nonetheless, an important part of a comprehensive assessment of the Strasbourg case law.

[60] *Neulinger and Shuruk* v. *Switzerland* (Appl. No. 41615/07), judgment, 6 July 2010, Reports 2010.

[61] Optional Protocol to the International Covenant on Civil and Political Rights, 999 UNTS 302, entered into force 23 March 1976.

2.13. Ratification record

In cases where the Court refers to international human rights instruments, it also often notes that the relevant instrument was ratified by the Contracting State implicated in the case or by a significant number of Contracting States. In doing this, the Court may not want to appear to be imposing additional obligations contained in external documents not approved by the Contracting States. The fact that most Contracting States adhere to a given international instrument provides greater legitimacy to the Court's reference and greater authority to its reasoning. The consensus among Contracting States constitutes an important factor in maintaining the Court's institutional credibility and in ensuring that its decisions are implemented. Occasionally, however, the Court was prepared to go further and to invoke the Convention on the Civil Aspects of International Child Abduction even if the State involved did not ratify it at the time of the judgment.[62] While this reference was particularly courageous, the Court appears to have resolved the matter on the basis of the ECHR. The Court has also invoked the ICCPR when this instrument was ratified, albeit not implemented, by the GDR in border-policing cases.[63]

2.14. Universal reach of international instruments

The unwillingness of the Strasbourg Court to depart from the ECHR is also due, in part, to the fact that international instruments have a universal reach and that they are not specific to the European context. The various UN Covenants have been adapted to issues appearing in all countries, and they can bear a different meaning in different parts of the world. Further, the ECHR Contracting States only represent a minority of the State Parties to the international treaties evaluated. As a result, some decisions handed down by the UN Treaty Bodies concern issues that do not arise in Europe. Furthermore, the UN Treaty Bodies have a quasi-jurisdictional nature and the ECtHR, rendering binding decisions, may have been reluctant to refer to their non-binding conclusions. Thus, the Court has probably considered that referring to other international instruments and international case law would not necessarily contribute to the interpretation of ECtHR rights. The ECHR, a regional instrument,

[62] *Barjami* v. *Albania* (Appl. No. 35853/04), judgment, 12 December 2006.

[63] *Streletz, Kessler and Krenz* v. *Germany*, note 51 *supra*; *K.-H. W.* v. *Germany*, note 51 *supra*.

is made up of a relatively homogeneous group of States which have similar economic, social, political and legal cultures. However, the international treaties considered here apply to State Parties with very diverse backgrounds. While these considerations need to be taken into account, they should not dominate the judges' reasoning. It is important to remind that human rights have a universal value and that they are not merely a Western creation.[64]

3. Overview of the factors' influence

An analysis of the Strasbourg case law referring to the law of treaties, State immunities, child rights, refugee rights, prohibition on torture and other ill-treatment, civil and political rights and IHL,[65] taking into account the recent developments in case law, indicates that some of the factors have remained more influential than others in the reception of international law by the Strasbourg Court. These are quantitative generalisations which are deduced on the basis of the majority of the case law in these fields. Clearly, there are numerous exceptions to these findings and they may need to be qualified. They constitute an indication of the trends appearing in the reasoning of the Court, rather than its exhaustive documentation of their interpretation method. It was considered that an empirical analysis of the case law would provide a real and effective assessment of the situation concerning the reception of international law by the Court. Further, the underlying rationale of this analysis is to find out what factors prevail overall in the Court's analysis. It was considered valuable not only to focus on landmark cases containing far-reaching international law references but to reach out to all case law containing international law references to obtain a complete picture of the case law. This approach therefore includes both landmark cases and other cases with lower importance. When assessing the Strasbourg case law, it should be recalled that not all influential material is cited in the case law. For instance, some material may have been referred to in argument or may have been part of a judge's general understanding but was not cited for various reasons in the judgment or decision. The assessment of these latent influences has been left aside here, but it is important to mention that they do exist.

64 Rosalyn Higgins, 'Ten Years of the UN Human Rights Committee: Some Thoughts Upon Parting', 6 *European Human Rights Law Review* 574 (1996).

65 Forowicz, note 1 *supra*.

3.1. *Pre-existing and technical reasons*

Factors concerning pre-existing or technical reasons appear to have played a dominant role in the Strasbourg jurisprudence. The fact that international law was invoked at the domestic level, the fact that the case was intertwined with international law and the procedural character of international law are part of this category. The first two of these factors constituted in most cases the strongest basis for referring to international law concerning special or general regimes. The prevailing tendency in the Strasbourg case law is that the Court generally refers to international law once it has already been part of the legal reasoning or the parties' pleading. It is thus easier and more legitimate for it to rely on external sources which had been previously brought up by the parties or domestic courts. Further, if international law is already part of the proceedings, the Court often has no other choice than to consider it. The fact that international law has a procedural character features less prominently in the Court's case law, but appears to still constitute a valid factor conditioning these references.

Pre-existing and technical reasons have thus had one of the most important influences on the reception of international law in the Strasbourg case law. The references prompted by them did not involve a substantial amount of discretion on the part of the Court; they usually fell beyond its control, leaving little room for manoeuvre. The Court was also compelled to refer to international instruments, as this was sometimes required to reach a solution in such a case. As such, these references may say little about the Court's own initiative and approach to international law. Rather, they demonstrate that the receptiveness of the Court is still to a greater extent incidental, circumstantial or involuntary. Clearly, such a mechanical reliance on external sources, deprived of a greater and more specific purpose, cannot on its own resolve complex dilemmas concerning the fragmentation of international law.

3.2. *Need to improve and update the ECHR*

Another reason which has a dominant bearing on the Court's reception of international law is the need to improve and update the ECHR. Its influence on the Strasbourg case law is comparable to that of the pre-existing or technical reasons. The need to harmonise an ECHR provision with international law, the need to fill gaps in the ECHR and the availability of more specific guidelines in international law have played an important role in the Court's interactions with external regimes. While the first three factors have had a bearing on reception in most areas evaluated, the last factor had an impact on all of them. Given that they came under its control, these factors required the Court to use its discretion when deciding to reach beyond the ECHR confines. The references influenced by these factors were to some extent prompted by the Court's willingness to use international law.

As such, these factors are very instructive in understanding the Court's approach to international law. They reveal that the underlying motivation of the Court in referring to international law was the need to reinforce the ECHR system and the protection of human rights at the European level (and sometimes beyond). This functional approach is based on the fact that a clear benefit could be derived for the ECHR from the reliance on international law. Although the motivation behind these references could have been less self-reinforcing, this tendency is overall encouraging as it indicates that the Court uses its discretion and is not solely dependent on the circumstances of each case. This statement needs, however, to be qualified as in many regimes the need to improve and to update the ECHR often appears in combination with other technical and pre-existing reasons. It is therefore difficult to determine which category of factors has played a greater influence on the reception process in cases where they both appeared. Thus, the combination of pre-existing and technical reasons as well as the need to reinforce the ECHR would provide the main ground prompting references to international law in the Strasbourg case law.

3.3. *Common ground between the ECHR and international law*

The similarities between the ECHR and other international instruments play a crucial but less important role than the pre-existing technical reasons and the need to improve and to update the ECHR in receiving international law. The textual and substantive similarities as well as the fact that an instrument was used during the drafting of the ECHR and/or its Protocols were relevant mostly in the field of civil and political rights and child rights. When they emerged, these similarities constituted important points of reference and inspiration for the Strasbourg bodies. Their less significant influence on the reception of international law in the Strasbourg case law is grounded in the fact that few of the instruments examined as part of this analysis closely resemble the ECHR. Most of the UN Covenants considered entered into force after the ECHR and are more specialised than this instrument. Naturally, there are also few resemblances between the ECHR and the law of treaties and the ICJ case law. The Strasbourg Court often picked up on the differences between the ECHR and general international law, as it wanted to avoid a possible weakening of the level of protection provided under the ECHR. Thus, when a case involved an international treaty which substantially diverged from the ECHR, the Court explicitly tried to distance itself from this instrument and abstained from receiving it in the case law.

3.4. *Other factors*

The specificity and the greater protection of the ECHR constitute important factors in the Court's decision not to receive international law. Naturally, the Court avoids reaching beyond the confines of the ECHR when this is not clearly useful or beneficial for its own system. Further, the Court appears to be distraught by the universal reach of certain international treaties. The fact that they concern a wider spectrum of issues and a more heterogeneous group of Member States may discourage the Court's references to these instruments. However, the main motivation behind these tendencies appears to be the need to reinforce and not to weaken the ECHR system. Thus, the same reasons which have prompted the Court's references to international instruments have also influenced their tendency to disregard international law. As such, the need to better protect ECHR rights constitutes a cornerstone of the Strasbourg reception process. Interestingly, the ratification record appears not to have played a significant role in the Court's reasoning. While it is an important rubber stamp legitimating references to international law, the Court has circumvented it when it wanted to achieve a certain result or when an important issue was at stake.

4. A self-reinforcing, but not self-sufficient regime

This analysis reveals that the Court does not rely today on an approach which is aimed at reducing fragmentation. The rationale behind the references where the Court has discretion in relying on international law shows that these are not grounded in the need to enhance the unity of the international legal system, but rather the need to preserve the ECHR, to improve its functioning and to ensure for the protection of human rights. It would be unrealistic to expect the Court to behave as the central entity in Europe – or perhaps beyond – for preventing fragmentation. Such a role could be incompatible with its current function under the ECHR. The Court, as a guardian of the ECHR, remains focused to a large extent on its own system and jurisdiction.

While references to international law in the Strasbourg case law are frequent and numerous, they are usually – with a few exceptions – not very far reaching or engaged. Potential anti-fragmentation tools, such harmonisation and systemic integration, have been used by the Court with the aim of contributing to the ECHR system and to human rights protection rather than enhancing the unity of international law. The Court is also interested in maintaining and in strengthening its authority. The extent of this authority largely depends on the acceptance and good will of the Contracting States. Far-reaching references to or reliance on external sources may thus be illegitimate when they are not approved by the Contracting States. The Court's discretion in referring to international law is thus conditioned by the need to protect its institutional credibility. In addition, the Court's quasi-constitutional or constitutional features may further be a factor which contributes to self-sufficiency instead of openness towards external sources.

Despite this, the approach taken until now by the Court does not appear to have generated excessive difficulties for international law. In cases where fragmentation occurred (i.e. refugee rights, the law of treaties, IHL or ICJ case law), this was generally justified by the need to ensure that ECHR rights were protected. Further, in cases relating to special human rights regimes, such as civil and political rights, child rights or the prohibition on torture and other ill-treatment, the Court's reasoning has converged in most part with their standards. This is not a surprising finding due to the similar aims that the ECHR and other special human rights regimes share. Presumably, the references in this field can be made most easily, naturally, effectively and without weakening the ECHR system. This reason may thus explain why the Court has been most receptive to special human rights regimes. Despite this, there are still instances where Court interpreted international law differently from other bodies, introduced further uncertainty and did not acknowledge the sources of its reasoning. Overall, the rationale transcending most references to international law appears to be the necessity to refer to them. In cases, where the Court had a room for manoeuvre, it appears to have chosen those references which were aimed at reinforcing and improving the ECHR system and the protection of human rights. The ECHR regime may therefore still be portrayed as a self-reinforcing, but certainly not as self-sufficient regime.

5. *Ceterum censeo*: Will the Court support a more central role for the ICJ?

As the main UN judicial body, the ICJ could be portrayed as a central body which could reduce fragmentation at the international level.[66] The ICJ benefits from a considerable reputation which reaches beyond the UN system to the ECtHR. It is considered that the ICJ has the power to authoritatively interpret the UN Charter. Through this, it contributes to the development of UN law and to the achievement of the UN objectives. The question could be posed here whether the ECtHR would be able and willing to support the ICJ in becoming a central body for ensuring the unity of international law? Further, does the Court use the ICJ case law to strengthen the systemic nature of the international legal system?

It is important to remember that there are substantial differences between the ICJ and the ECtHR resulting from the nature of their legal systems. One fundamental difference relates to the specific human rights context of the ECHR, which aims at protecting individual applicants from their governments. However, disputes before the ICJ are of a different nature in that they concern States. Further, the ECHR grants the right to individual applicants whereas the ICJ Statute only grants rights to States. Also, the ICJ can judge any type of dispute between States that occurred in any part of the globe concerning any area of international law. Unlike the ECtHR, its role is not limited to the supervision of a single law-making treaty. Both bodies also have a very different audience and membership. Other important differences between both frameworks relate to the nature of their jurisdiction and to the nature of reservations that States are allowed to enter. In spite of these contrasts, the ICJ has been dealing increasingly more with human rights issues in its jurisprudence. Further, general international law has also become more imbued with human rights standards. These developments have led to a greater *rapprochement* between the ICJ and the ECtHR.

The Court has for many years now referred to ICJ judgments in order to interpret and to develop the ECHR. While substantive references were infrequent, they demonstrated that the Court is receptive to the findings of this authoritative body. This trend did not reveal, however, a coherent approach on the part of the Court towards the ICJ's case law. When the

[66] Pierre-Marie Dupuy, 'The Danger of Fragmentation or Unification of the International Legal System and the International Court of Justice', 31 *New York University Journal of International Law and Politics* 791, 798–801 (1999).

Court decided on occasion not to follow the judgments of the ICJ, it seems to have done so to protect the rights of the individual. Usually, the Strasbourg case law referring to the ICJ judgments has concerned crucial international policy issues or the need to fill in gaps in the ECHR system. As the case law evolved, the Court emphasised the differences that existed between the systems and drew limits to the references that it made to the ICJ framework. In this way, it distanced itself from ICJ case law and the Statute, when these did not advance the effective protection of human rights law. However, the Court reached a critical moment in the *Behrami* case,[67] where it attributed to the UN Charter and the corresponding ICJ decision a rank higher than that occupied by the ECHR. In applying the primacy principle of the UN Charter over conflicting international treaties, the Court declined to review UN actions in Kosovo in order not to tamper with the UN's mission in maintaining international peace and security. In this case, it showed deference to the ICJ and relinquished its role as human rights Court, justifiably attracting widespread criticism.

In subsequent case law, the Court refused to follow the *Behrami* route and settled for a more subtle solution. In order to avoid answering questions concerning the hierarchy between the ECHR and the UN Charter in *Al-Jedda* v. *United Kingdom*,[68] the Court simply tried to avoid situations of conflict between the ECHR and the UNSC Resolution in order to prevent the application of Article 103 UN Charter. The Court even went further on this occasion by establishing an interpretative presumption that the Security Council does not intend to impose any obligation in its Resolutions on Member States to breach fundamental principles of human rights. In case of ambiguity, the Court would rely on an ECHR conform interpretation in order to avoid conflicts of obligations. When the question of hierarchy came up again in *Nada* v. *Switzerland*,[69] the Court decided once more to avoid a conflict between the ECHR and the UNSC resolutions through harmonious interpretation. The Court's position therefore remains nebulous as to the status that it may accord to the UN Charter and to its interpretation by the ICJ.

Recently, the ECtHR has shown itself respectful of the ICJ case law and has shied away from conflict. On occasion, it was even prepared to go

[67] *Behrami and Behrami* v. *France* and *Saramati* v. *France, Germany and Norway* (Appl. Nos. 71412/01; 78166/01), judgment, 2 May 2007.

[68] *Al-Jedda* v. *United Kingdom*, note 7 *supra*.

[69] *Nada* v. *Switzerland*, note 8 *supra*.

further to ensure the protection of human rights (the *Al-Jedda* case).[70] Any central role that the ICJ may now be trying to assume with regard to the unity of the international legal system needs to be fully human rights compliant, or at least ECHR conform, if it is to be embraced by the ECtHR in the near future. It is yet to be seen whether the *rapprochement* of the two courts will yield concrete results, which could ensure a greater unity of the international legal system. This may be facilitated, if in the vein of De Scelle's *dédoublement fonctionnel*, the Court is willing 'to act on behalf of the UN legal order, aiming specifically at facilitating the realization of values stemming from that order'.[71]

[70] However, in the recent *Jones* v. *United Kingdom* case, the Court has missed a good opportunity to introduce a much needed exception to State immunity for *jus cogens* violations. In its reasoning, it relied to a great extent on the ICJ's *Jurisdictional Immunities of the State* judgment, which it considered to be 'authoritative as regards the content of customary international law' (para. 198). *Jones and Others* v. *United Kingdom* (Appl. No. 34356/03; 40528/06), judgment, 14 January 2014.

[71] Pasquale De Sena and Maria Chiara Vitucci, 'The European Courts and the Security Council: Between Dédoublement Fonctionnnel and Balancing of Values', 20 *European Journal of International Law* 193, 210 (2009).

9

The influence of the International Court of Justice on the law of provisional measures

CAMERON A. MILES

The law of provisional measures before international courts and tribunals may seem a curious topic for discussion in the context of substantive fragmentation, but closer investigation reveals this initial reaction to be flawed – after all, why cannot fragmentation be procedural? With this established, provisional measures become a prime candidate for consideration, with most international courts and tribunals awarding interim relief in order to safeguard the effectiveness of any final award – the attendant risk of contradictory pronouncements on the 'law' of provisional measures is obvious.

This chapter, however, argues that unlike other areas of international law, there is no risk of fragmentation in the context of provisional measures, due principally to the long-standing and normative influence of the International Court of Justice. This influence takes two forms: (1) the textual influence of Article 41 of the International Court of Justice Statute over the drafting of the constitutive instruments of later international courts and tribunals; and (2) the jurisprudential influence of the case law of the International Court of Justice, through which a number of substantive principles governing the award of interim relief have been adduced, for example, the concept of *prima facie* jurisdiction, the need for urgency and irreparable harm, the binding nature of provisional measures, and so forth. This influence – and the relative uniformity that it has produced – will be assessed through comparison with several other forms of international dispute settlement, namely the International Tribunal for the Law of the Sea and Annex VII arbitration according to the United Nations Convention on the Law of the Sea, investor-state tribunals operating under the Convention on the Settlement of Investment Disputes between States and Nationals of Other States (ICSID) , and the European Court of Human Rights.

I. Introduction

The purpose of this volume is, *inter alia*, to investigate the premise that the International Court of Justice (ICJ) is reasserting its position as the informal 'centre' of international law so as to avert its substantive fragmentation. In certain circumstances, this rehabilitation has taken the form of a new, more inclusive thread within its jurisprudence in areas as diverse as maritime delimitation[1] and state immunity.[2] But in other areas, such an approach has been rendered unnecessary due to the Court's omnipresence within certain substantive or procedural fields. One such field – and perhaps the example *par excellence* – is that of provisional measures.[3]

In general terms, provisional measures represent a form of relief granted *pendente lite* in order to protect rights subject to litigation and to prevent further aggravation of the dispute. Analogues in municipal systems, such as the common law interlocutory injunction, the French *ordonnance de référé* and the German *einstweilige Verfügung* are well known,[4] but the institution takes on additional importance in the context of international litigation due to the pace of proceedings, which frequently proceed on

[1] *Territorial and Maritime Dispute (Nicaragua* v. *Colombia)*, ICJ, Judgment of 19 November 2012, at ¶178, citing the decision of ITLOS in *Delimitation of the Maritime Boundary between Bangladesh and Myanmar in the Bay of Bengal (Bangladesh/Myanmar)*, ITLOS Case No. 16 (Judgment, 14 March 2012).

[2] *Jurisdictional Immunity of the State (Germany* v. *Italy; Greece intervening)*, ICJ, Judgment of 3 February 2012, at ¶90, citing the decisions of the ECtHR in *Al-Adsani* v. *United Kingdom* [2001] ECtHR 35763/97 (GC) and *Kalogeropoulou and Ors* v. *Greece and Germany* [2002] ECtHR 59021/00.

[3] Also referred to, *inter alia*, interim measures, interim measures of protection and precautionary measures. These are substantively interchangeable, and for the sake of convenience, will be referred to universally here under the rubric of 'provisional measures' – although the prophylactic function of the concept as a whole is probably best reflected in the French term *mesures conservatoires*: C. Brown, *A Common Law of International Adjudication* (Oxford: Oxford University Press, 2007) 121. The law of provisional measures, as presented here, is current as of January 2015.

[4] Earlier analogues may be detected in the Roman law institution of the *interdict*, which could be made to bear provisional characteristics when considering actions for the possession of disputed property: see W. W. Buckland and A. D. McNair, *Roman Law and Common Law: A Comparison in Outline* (Cambridge: Cambridge University Press, 2nd edn, 1965), pp. 420–3.

what appears to be a geological timescale. Consequently, international courts or tribunals must be in a position to assert themselves on an interim basis to protect the integrity of final judgment and the status quo as between the parties.[5]

Within the constellation of international courts and tribunals, the ICJ boasts the largest and most chronologically consistent corpus of jurisprudence in relation to provisional measures. Moreover, Article 41 of its Statute has become a sort of model clause for the drafters of the constituent instruments of other courts and tribunals. As a consequence, the Court's jurisprudence has proved eminently exportable, and is indeed the dominant influence on what might be seen as a 'uniform law' of provisional measures emergent in the international judicial sphere. This position is not, however, unqualified, and other courts and tribunals may see fit to retrofit the legacy of the ICJ so as to meet their particular needs. This chapter proposes to examine the extent of the inheritance and retrofitting of the ICJ's jurisprudence by four different kinds of international tribunal: the permanent International Tribunal for the Law of the Sea (ITLOS) and its associated tribunals convened according to Annex VII of the UN Convention on the Law of the Sea (UNCLOS),[6] arbitral tribunals formed under the auspices of the International Centre for the Settlement of Investment Disputes (the Centre),[7] and the European Court of Human Rights (ECtHR).

The chapter will proceed in three parts. In the first, it will examine the drafting of the relevant provisions of the constituent instruments of the relevant tribunals and the influence of Article 41 of the Statute on each (Section II). In the second, it will examine the importation of substantive principles relevant to the award of provisional measures from the ICJ into

[5] B. Oxman, 'Jurisdiction and the Power to Indicate Provisional Measures', in L. F. Damrosch (ed.), *The International Court of Justice at a Crossroads* (Dobbs Ferry: Transnational Publishers, 1987), pp. 324–6; M. H. Mendelsohn, 'Interim Measures of Protection in Cases of Contested Jurisdiction' (1972–1973) 46 BYIL 259, 259; C. Brown, *A Common Law*, p. 121.

[6] 10 December 1982, in force 16 November 1994, 1833 UNTS 3.

[7] Naturally a plethora of other international courts and tribunals also award provisional measures. In the interests of brevity these will not be considered here, but see further F. G. Jacobs, 'Interim Measures in the Law and Practice of the Court of Justice of the European Communities', in R. Bernhardt (ed.), *Interim Measures Indicated by International Courts* (Berlin: Springer-Verlag, 1994); T. Buergenthal, 'Interim Measures in the Inter-American Court of Human Rights', in *ibid.* See further the useful summary of more obscure institutions up to 1983 in J. Sztucki, *Interim Measures in the Hague Court: An Attempt at Scrutiny* (Deventer: Kluwer, 1983), pp. 4–11.

the decisions of the other courts and tribunals, notwithstanding the fact that these do not always (and indeed, most often do not) appear expressly in the text of the relevant instruments (Section III). Finally, it will situate provisional measures in the wider discussion, on-going in international law, on substantive fragmentation, and describe how the ICJ continues to exert a centralizing influence over a body of law formally unique to each individual court or tribunal (Section IV).

II. The constitutive instruments and the 'prototype' of the Permanent Court of International Justice

A. *Article 41 of the Statute of the Permanent Court of International Justice*

This enquiry begins in 1920 with the drafting of the Statute of the Permanent Court of International Justice (PCIJ). In 1920, the Council of the League of Nations established the Advisory Committee of Jurists to prepare plans for the formation of the Court.[8] A memorandum prepared by the League Secretariat requested that the Committee consider whether the Court would be competent 'to decree, as regards the subject-matter of the dispute, the fixation of the *status quo* pending its decision'.[9] The Committee was further referred to, *inter alia*, Article XVIII of the Convention establishing the Central American Court of Justice.[10] A further, unspoken, influence, was common Article 4 of the Bryan Peace Treaties between the US and China, France and Sweden.[11] A draft text was

[8] See M. O. Hudson, *The Permanent Court of International Justice* (New York: Macmillan, 1943), pp. 114–16; J. B. Elkind, *Interim Protection: A Functional Approach* (The Hague: Martinus Nijhoff, 1981), pp. 43–6; S. Rosenne, *Provisional Measures in International Law: The International Court of Justice and the International Tribunal for the Law of the Sea* (Oxford: Oxford University Press, 2005), pp. 22–6.

[9] *Documents presented to the Committee relating to the Existing Plans for the Establishment of a Permanent Court of International Justice* (London: League of Nations, 1920), p. 127.

[10] 20 December 1907, in force 20 December 1907, 206 CTS 78. Art. XVIII read as follows: 'From the moment in which any suit is instituted against one or more governments up to that in which a final decision has been pronounced, the court may at the solicitation of any one of the parties, fix the situation in which the contending parties must remain, to the end that the difficulty shall not be aggravated and that things shall be conserved in *statu quo* pending a final decision.'

[11] US–China Treaty for the Advancement of Peace, 15 September 1914, in force 15 September 1914, 10 AJIL Supp. 268; US–France Treaty for the Advancement of Peace, 15 September 1914, in force 15 September 1914, 10 AJIL Supp. 278; US–Sweden Treaty for the Advancement of Peace, 13 October 1914, in force 13 October 1914, 10 AJIL Supp. 304. Common Art. 4 of these treaties – which was not repeated in the various other Bryan Treaties –

presented to the First Assembly of the League in 1920, accompanied by a lengthy commentary noting the debt of the proposed Article 39 on provisional measures to the Bryan Treaties, and, significantly, noting that the Committee did not consider the measures granted under the provision to be binding on the parties.[12] Before a sub-committee of the Assembly's Third Committee further amendments were undertaken[13] before the provision was included as Article 41 of the PCIJ's Statute. This read:

> The Court shall have the power to indicate, if it considers that the circumstances so require, any provisional measures which ought to be taken to reserve the respective rights of the parties.
>
> Pending the final decision, notice of the measures suggested shall forthwith be given to the parties and the Council.

This provision may safely be said to provide the prototype for the modern law of provisional measures. It was invoked with what (for the PCIJ) constituted regularity, having been raised on six individual cases,[14] two of which – the *Sino-Belgian Treaty* case and *Electricity Company of Sofia and Bulgaria* – resulted in the grant of provisional measures. These cases, furthermore, produced a jurisprudence that was recognizably modern, supplementing the bare words of Article 41 with concepts drawn from the procedure of certain civil law jurisdictions – notably Germany and Switzerland – as mediated through the decisions of the post-war mixed

provided relevantly: 'In case the cause of the dispute should consist of certain acts already committed or about to be committed, the commission [of inquiry] shall as soon as possible indicate what measures to preserve the rights of each party ought in its opinion be taken provisionally and pending the delivery of its report.'

[12] *Procès-Verbaux of the Proceedings of the Committee, June 16th–July 24th 1920, with Annexes* (The Hague: van Langenhuysen Brothers, 1920), pp. 735–6.

[13] These were more than merely cosmetic. Principally, the word 'indicate' was substituted for 'suggest' in the English text to bring it in line with the French and certain introductory phrasing removed so that the omissions infringing international rights were covered as well as acts. This was earlier proposed in the Advisory Committee and rejected: *ibid.*, p. 619.

[14] *Denunciation of the Treaty of 2 November 1865 between China and Belgium (Belgium* v. *China)* (1927) PCIJ Ser. A No. 8; *Factory at Chorzów (Indemnities) (Germany* v. *Poland)* (1927) PCIJ Ser. A No. 12; *Legal Status of the South-Eastern Territory of Greenland (Denmark* v. *Norway)* (1932) PCIJ Ser. A/B No. 48; *Administration of the Prince von Pless (Germany* v. *Poland)* (1933) PCIJ Ser. A/B No. 54; *Polish Agrarian Reform and the German Minority (Germany* v. *Poland)* (1933) PCIJ Ser. A/B No. 58; *Electricity Company of Sofia and Bulgaria (Belgium* v. *Bulgaria)* (1939) PCIJ Ser. A/B No. 79. On the jurisprudence of the PCIJ and its predecessors, see now C. A. Miles, 'The Origins of Provisional Measures before International Courts and Tribunals' (2013) 73 ZaöRV 615.

arbitral tribunals established to determine investor-state claims arising from the First World War.[15] It was this corpus of jurisprudence that was inherited by the ICJ in 1947. The experience of the PCIJ vis-à-vis provisional measures is thus written into the DNA of its successor and other descendent institutions.

B. *Article 41 of the Statute of the International Court of Justice*

Having established a prologue in the PCIJ, our attention may now turn towards extant international courts and tribunals, beginning with the ICJ itself. As can be appreciated from Article 41 of the Court's Statute, the concept of provisional measures – at least insofar as they were expressed in a constitutive instrument – was not the subject of drastic alteration between 1920 and 1947.[16] Indeed, the only alterations between the Article 41 and its predecessor were (1) the correction of the printer's error 'reserve' in place of 'preserve', (2) the insertion of the adjective 'Security' in front of 'Council', and (3) the numbering of the resulting paragraphs. The conclusion of this entire section of the Statute at the San Francisco Conference proved uncontroversial, with the relevant Committee voting unanimously 'to approve, without discussion, [Articles] 39–64 *en bloc*'.[17] Article 41 remains unchanged today, notwithstanding certain deficiencies that have become apparent in its wording.[18]

[15] See e.g. *Electric Tramway Company of Sofia* v. *Bulgaria and Municipality of Sofia* (1923) 3 TAM 928, 929; *Central Agricultural Union of Poland* v. *Poland* (1925) 6 TAM 329, at 330 (relief unavailable when damages will suffice); *Tiedemann* v. *Poland* (1923) 3 TAM 596, at 599–600 (relief available before the jurisdiction of the tribunal is definitively established). On the provisional measures jurisprudence of these tribunals in general, see E. Dumbauld, *Interim Measures of Protection in International Controversies* (The Hague: Martinus Nijhoff, 1932), pp. 129–44.

[16] See Rosenne, *Provisional Measures*, pp. 30–4. Also: K. Oellers-Frahm, 'Article 41', in A. Zimmermann, C. Tomuschat and K. Oellers-Frahm (eds.), *The Statute of the International Court of Justice: A Commentary* (Oxford: Oxford University Press, 2006), pp. 926–7.

[17] *Documents of the United Nations Conference on International Organization, San Francisco 1945* (New York: UNIO, 1945) vol. 13, pp. 59, 170. Further: Oellers-Frahm, 'Article 41', p. 927.

[18] Principally over the question of whether provisional measures could be considered to be binding under Art 41. See e.g. comments by Hersch Lauterpacht as part of a wider plea for the revision of the Statute in 1955: H. Lauterpacht, 'The Revision of the Statute of the International Court of Justice' (2002) 1 LPICT 55, 94–6. The matter was eventually resolved by the Court in *LaGrand (Germany* v. *US)*, ICJ Reports 2001 p. 466.

C. *Article 290 of the UN Convention on the Law of the Sea*

The ICJ had been in operation for some 35 years prior to the conclusion of UNCLOS and had as a result established itself as the dominant model for the granting of provisional measures in international disputes. Consequently, it is unsurprising that the delegates to the Third UN Conference on the Law of the Sea (UNCLOS III) turned almost immediately to Article 41 of the Court's Statute when seeking to define the scope for provisional measures within the dispute resolution provisions of UNCLOS. The informal working group that prepared the 1975 working paper that formed the basis of UNCLOS III's deliberations, however, departed from the wording of Article 41, on the basis that, *inter alia*, the word 'indicate' as used in the provision did not clearly convey the binding nature of provisional measures.[19] A further consideration that emerged over the course of UNCLOS III was how to adapt the precedent set by the ICJ to the scheme of dispute resolution[20] contained in UNCLOS Part XI, which under UNCLOS Article 287 permits parties to submit disputes concerning the interpretation or application of UNCLOS to ITLOS, the ICJ or to two forms of ad hoc arbitration under UNCLOS Annexes VII and VIII.[21] The result is a somewhat lengthy provision available to all courts and tribunals that have jurisdiction under UNCLOS:[22]

> 1. If a dispute has been duly submitted to a court or tribunal which considers that *prima facie* it has jurisdiction under this Part or Part XI, section 5, the court or tribunal may prescribe any provisional measures

[19] S. Rosenne and L. B. Sohn (eds.), *United Nations Convention on the Law of the Sea 1982: A Commentary* (Dordrecht: Martinus Nijhoff, 1989) vol. 5, p. 53.

[20] For a useful summary, see Rosenne, *Provisional Measures*, p. 45. On dispute settlement and UNCLOS in general, see N. Klein, *Dispute Settlement in the UN Convention on the Law of the Sea* (Cambridge: Cambridge University Press, 2005).

[21] In practice Annex VIII arbitration under UNCLOS has proved to be something of a dead letter. The Annex provides for the composition of special arbitral tribunals with respect to certain technical areas and was included as a concession to the Soviet states, which wanted greater control over the selection of expert tribunal members. It has never been used: J. Crawford (ed.), *Brownlie's Principles of Public International Law* (Oxford: Oxford University Press, 8th edn, 2012), p. 735.

[22] Oxman, 'Jurisdiction', p. 179 avers to the potential that the use of UNCLOS Art. 290 could 'harmonize' the practice of the ICJ with respect to provisional measures. This has not come to pass. Under UNCLOS Art. 287(5), if the parties elect different methods of dispute resolution, the matter is to be referred to Annex VII arbitration, which together with a relatively low number of states electing the ICJ under UNCLOS Art. 287 has led to a situation in which the Court has never considered a referred matter.

which it considers appropriate under the circumstances to preserve the respective rights of the parties to the dispute or to prevent serious harm to the marine environment, pending the final decision.

2. Provisional measures may be modified or revoked as soon as the circumstances justifying them have changed or ceased to exist.

3. Provisional measures may be prescribed, modified or revoked under this article only at the request of a party to the dispute and after the parties have been given an opportunity to be heard.

4. The court or tribunal shall forthwith give notice to the parties to the dispute, and to such other States Parties as it considers appropriate, of the prescription, modification or revocation of provisional measures.

5. Pending the constitution of an arbitral tribunal to which a dispute is being submitted under this section, any court or tribunal agreed upon by the parties or, failing such agreement within two weeks from the date of the request for provisional measures, the International Tribunal for the Law of the Sea or, with respect to activities in the Area, the Seabed Disputes Chamber, may prescribe, modify or revoke provisional measures in accordance with this article if it considers that *prima facie* the tribunal which is to be constituted would have jurisdiction and that the urgency of the situation so requires. Once constituted, the tribunal to which the dispute has been submitted may modify, revoke or affirm those provisional measures, acting in conformity with paragraphs 1 to 4.

6. The parties to the dispute shall comply promptly with any provisional measures prescribed under this article.

Although more complicated than Article 41 of the Statute, UNCLOS Article 290 is still clearly descended from the former provision. Its complexity in part derives from a desire on the part of UNCLOS III to codify the practice of the ICJ and to avoid those areas of uncertainty thrown up by the Court's jurisprudence since 1947. In the first place, both UNCLOS Articles 290(1) and (5) make reference to the need for the court or tribunal seised to establish its jurisdiction on a *prima facie* basis prior to the granting of provisional measures, a point not mentioned expressly in Article 41 and which had generated considerable controversy in the ICJ's first consideration of provisional measures in the *Anglo-Iranian Oil* case.[23] In the second, UNCLOS Article 290(6) clearly provides for the automatic binding effect of provisional measures on the parties, thereby forestalling a debate that was still very much alive in relation to the ICJ

[23] *Anglo-Iranian Oil Co (UK v. Iran)*, Provisional Measures, ICJ Reports 1951 p. 89, 92–3, 96–8 (Judges Winiarski and Badawi Pasha, diss.). Further: Oxman, 'Jurisdiction'; Mendelsohn, 'Contested Jurisdiction'.

in 1982.[24] The binding nature of provisional measures under UNCLOS Article 290 is also reflected in the wording of paragraphs (1), (3), (4), (5) and (6), which refer to the 'prescription' of provisional measures, rather than their 'indication'.[25] Finally, UNCLOS Article 290(1) is phrased in similar terms to Article 41 of the Statute in that it describes the purpose of provisional measures as being to 'preserve the respective rights of the parties to the dispute'.[26]

Two further features of UNCLOS Article 290 may be pointed out. First, the provision broadens the rights with respect to which provisional measures may be ordered to include measures designed to 'prevent serious harm to the marine environment' in paragraph (1). Thus, interim relief may be ordered not in relation to rights under dispute, but 'mainly or even solely' to prevent harm to the environment.[27] Second, UNCLOS Article 290(5) provides that, absent contrary agreement by the parties, ITLOS (or its Sea-Bed Disputes Chamber as required) may order provisional measures pending the constitution of an Annex VII or VIII tribunal. The capacity to order interim relief *on behalf of* another court or tribunal is one that is not usually available to international adjudicative bodies,[28] and may be seen to raise particular issues of legitimacy when utilized.[29]

D. Article 47 of the Convention on the Settlement of Investment Disputes between States and Nationals of Other States

ICSID governs investor-state arbitration under the auspices of the Centre.[30] The Convention includes Article 47, which provides:

[24] T. Mensah, 'Provisional Measures in the International Tribunal for the Law of the Sea (ITLOS)' (2002) 62 ZaöRV 43, 44–6.

[25] See also Art. 95(1) of the ITLOS Rules, which provides that '[e]ach party shall inform the Tribunal as soon as possible as to its compliance with any provisional measures the Tribunal has prescribed': www.itlos.org/fileadmin/itlos/documents/basic_texts/Itlos_8_E_17_03_09.pdf (accessed 3 June 2013).

[26] R. Wolfrum, 'Provisional Measures of the International Tribunal for the Law of the Sea', in P. C. Rao and R. Khan (eds.), *The International Tribunal for the Law of the Sea: Law and Practice* (The Hague: Kluwer, 2001), pp. 175–8.

[27] Mensah, 'Provisional Measures in ITLOS', 45–6.

[28] Cf. the Locarno Treaties of 1925 (e.g. France–Germany Agreement, 16 October 1925, in force 16 October 1925, 54 LNTS 317), which in Art. 19 permitted the award of provisional measures by the PCIJ in place of an unconstituted conciliation commission: Dumbauld, *Interim Measures of Protection*, p. 128.

[29] Mensah, 'Provisional Measures in ITLOS', 46–7.

[30] 18 March 1965, in force 14 October 1966, 575 UNTS 159.

> Except as the parties otherwise agree, the Tribunal may, if it considers that the circumstances so require, recommend any provisional measures which should be taken to preserve the respective rights of either party.

The wording of ICSID Article 47 is much more closely referable to Article 41 of the Statute than UNCLOS Article 290, and Article 41 indeed served as a model for the Centre's procedure.[31] The fact, however, that the text of Article 41 emerged from the ICSID drafting process with what appears to be only minor alteration fails to reflect its controversial character. Early drafts of the provision reveal that much stronger wording was originally envisioned guaranteeing these measures as binding and including a power to impose sanctions for non-compliance. These proposals encountered considerable opposition and although a countervailing proposal to excise the provision entirely was dropped, the compromise position was a text that suffered from the same ambiguity as Article 41, i.e. in its use of the terms 'recommend' (similar in meaning to the term 'indicate' in Article 41) and 'should be taken' when describing the grant of interim relief.[32]

In practical terms, ICSID Article 47 differs from the other provisions considered in that much of its early use was as a variant of anti-suit injunction,[33] used to restrain parallel proceedings in national courts.[34] In this, the experience of ICSID tribunals has been similar to that of the Iran–US Claims Tribunal, which suffered from a similar problem.[35] As will be seen, this has modified how ICSID Article 47 is applied in modern proceedings. A further difference arises in relation to the capacity of ICSID tribunals to award provisional measures in circumstances where the jurisdiction of the tribunal has not been definitively established. Unlike the ICJ and dispute settlement under UNCLOS, ICSID contains a

[31] C. Schreuer, L. Malintoppi, A. Reinisch and A. Sinclair, *The ICSID Convention: A Commentary* (Cambridge: Cambridge University Press, 2nd edn, 2009), p. 759.

[32] *Ibid.*

[33] Further: R. Fentiman, *International Commercial Litigation* (Oxford: Oxford University Press, 2010), ch. 15.

[34] Collins estimates that two thirds of the early cases were directed towards the prevention of parallel proceedings: L. Collins, 'Provisional and Protective Measures in International Litigation' (1993) 234 Hague Recueil 19, 99. For an overview of the early decisions of this kind, see P. D. Friedland, 'Provisional Measures in ICSID Arbitration' (1986) 2 Arb. Int'l 335, 339–47; C. N. Brower and R. E. M. Goodman, 'Provisional Measures and the Protection of ICSID Jurisdictional Exclusivity Against Municipal Proceedings' (1991) 6 ICSID Rev. – FILJ 431. Such action was taken pursuant to ICSID Art. 26, which provides: 'Consent of the parties to arbitration under this Convention shall, unless otherwise stated, be deemed consent to such arbitration to the exclusion of any other remedy. . . '.

[35] D. D. Caron, 'Interim Measures of Protection: Theory and Practice in Light of the Iran-United States Claims Tribunal' (1986) 46 ZaöRV 465, 504–8.

mechanism by which a tribunal's jurisdiction might be reviewed through the agency of the Centre's Secretary-General. ICSID Article 36(3) provides that the Secretary-General shall register a request for arbitration unless he or she finds that the dispute is manifestly outside the Centre's jurisdiction.[36]

E. *Rule 39 of the Rules of the European Court of Human Rights*

The constituent instrument of the ECtHR is the 1950 Convention for the Protection of Human Rights and Fundamental Freedoms,[37] now known as the European Convention on Human Rights (ECHR). ECHR Section II provides for the creation of the Court, and sets out the usual questions of election, composition, jurisdiction and admissibility and further provides for the binding force of the Court's decisions. Conspicuous by its absence, however, is an express provision giving the ECtHR the capacity to award interim measures of protection, a situation that does not persist with respect to other regional human rights tribunals such as the Inter-American Court of Human Rights.[38] At the time of drafting, suggestions to include such a provision were ignored,[39] a choice that Bernhardt ascribes to 'the reluctance of States and their representatives in 1949/50 to introduce a control machinery without at the same time protecting to a certain extent the sovereign rights of States'.[40]

[36] Schreuer et al., *ICSID Commentary*, p. 772; Brower and Goodman, 'Jurisdictional Exclusivity', 452–6.

[37] 4 November 1950, in force (as amended) 1 June 2010, 213 UNTS 222.

[38] American Convention on Human Rights, 22 November 1969, in force 18 July 1978, 1144 UNTS 123, Art. 63(2): 'In cases of extreme gravity and urgency, and when necessary to avoid irreparable damage to persons, the Court shall adopt such provisional measures as it deems pertinent in matters it has under consideration. With respect to a case not yet submitted to the Court, it may act at the request of the Commission.'

[39] See e.g. Art. 35 of the Draft Statute of the European Court of Human Rights as prepared by the International Juridical Section of the European Movement, in Council of Europe, *Collected Edition of the Travaux Préparatoires of the European Convention on Human Rights* (The Hague: Martinus Nijhoff, 1975), vol. 1, p. 314.

[40] Similar suggestions were also made and discarded during the drafting of the ECHR's Protocol 11 (Restructuring the Control Machinery Established Thereby), 11 May 1994, in force 1 November 1998, ETS 155: R. Bernhardt, 'Interim Measures under the European Convention on Human Rights', in R. Bernhardt (ed.), *Interim Measures Indicated by International Courts* (Berlin: Springer-Verlag, 1994) p. 96. However, efforts to include a basis for interim relief in the ECHR itself remain on foot: Council of Europe, Steering Committee for Human Rights (CDDH), *Report on Interim Measures under Rule 39 of the Rules of Court*, CDDH(2013)R77, Addendum III (22 March 2013), ¶ 7: www.coe.int/t/dghl/standardsetting/cddh/CDDH-DOCUMENTS/CDDH(2013)R77_Addendum%20III_en.pdf (accessed 2 January 2014).

Despite this silence, the ECtHR arrogated to itself the power to award provisional measures pursuant to ECHR Article 25(d).[41] Rule 39 of its current procedural ordinance[42] (ECtHR Rules) provides:

> 1. The Chamber or, where appropriate, the President of the Section or a duty judge appointed pursuant to paragraph 4 of this Rule may, at the request of a party or of any other person concerned, or of their own motion, indicate to the parties any interim measure which they consider should be adopted in the interests of the parties or of the proper conduct of the proceedings.
> 2. Where it is considered appropriate, immediate notice of the measure adopted in a particular case may be given to the Committee of Ministers.
> 3. The Chamber or, where appropriate, the President of the Section or a duty judge appointed pursuant to paragraph 4 of this Rule may request information from the parties on any matter connected with the implementation of any interim measure indicated.
> 4. The President of the Court may appoint Vice-Presidents of Sections as duty judges to decide on requests for interim measures.

Rule 39 originally appeared as Rule 34 of the Court's 1959 procedural rules and has been subject to incremental amendment since then.[43] However, the core of the provision – paragraph 1 – has remained substantially unaltered since its introduction.[44] The wording of Rule 39(1) suffers from many of the same deficiencies as Article 41 of the ICJ Statute in that it fails to clearly state whether measures awarded under the provision are binding on the parties and indeed, the fact that the power was introduced in an instrument that did not require the consent of states that were party to the ECHR raises additional concerns of legitimacy.

As with ICSID tribunals, the fact that the ECtHR is exclusively concerned with claims between an individual and a state recontextualizes to a degree the award of interim relief. In almost all cases, the applicant is

[41] This is by no means an exceptional or exorbitant action. A number of other international tribunals have also seen fit to incorporate provisional measures into their self-generated procedure without reference to an express provision in their constituent instruments, beginning with the Mixed Arbitral Tribunals of the interwar period, e.g. the Rules of the Franco-German Mixed Arbitral Tribunal, 2 April 1920, 1 TAM 44. This may be seen as a reflection of the need on the part of these tribunals to effectively carry out their functions: Brown, *A Common Law*, pp. 125–6.

[42] Rules of the European Court of Human Rights, 1 January 2014:www.echr.coe.int/Documents/Rules_Court_ENG.pdf (accessed 2 January 2014).

[43] Most significantly, references to the European Commission of Human Rights have been removed following the abolition of that body via Protocol 11 in 1998.

[44] Bernhardt, 'Interim Measures under the ECHR', pp. 98–9.

the individual seeking redress for an alleged human rights violations.[45] Given the nature of the field, the Court's case load is unusually sensitive to political conditions within ECHR members. This is particularly the case where the application concerns protection arising under ECHR Article 3 regarding extradition or expulsion to a third state where the applicant fears torture or inhuman treatment or punishment. Between 2006 and 2010, this revealed itself in a colossal increase in the number of requests for measures of protection before the Court,[46] leading to the adoption, for a short time, of a 'quasi-systemic' approach involving a presumption in favour of the applicant.[47] This was replaced on 7 July 2011 by a revised practice direction on interim measures.[48] Requests for provisional measures are now subjected to triage by a specialized 'Rule 39 unit' within the Registry.[49] The introduction of the unit (among other measures) has largely ameliorated the crisis that prompted its creation;[50] however, at the same time it has drastically reduced the likelihood of such measures being granted.[51]

III. Substantive preconditions to the award of provisional measures

Section II above is in part intended to demonstrate a fairly elementary proposition, viz. that the centrality of the ICJ to the law of provisional

[45] On one occasion, the European Commission on Human Rights asked an applicant to discontinue a hunger strike: *Bhuyiam* v. *Sweden* [1995] ECommHR 26516/95. The Court's inter-state jurisdiction tells a different story, but there are limited examples in this field: see e.g. *Georgia* v. *Russia (II)* [2011] ECtHR 38263/08, at ¶ 5.

[46] For example, between October 2010 and January 2011 alone, the Court received 2,500 requests for interim relief concerning returns to Iraq: CDDH, *Report on Interim Measures*, ¶ 3.

[47] *Ibid.*, ¶ 3 (fn. 6).

[48] Practice Direction: Requests for Interim Measures, 7 July 2011: www.echr.coe.int/Documents/PD_interim_measures_ENG.pdf (accessed 2 January 2014).

[49] CDDH, *Report on Interim Measures*, ¶ 11; ECtHR Registry, *Article 39 of the Rules of Court: Modalities of Application and Procedure (Information Document by the Registry of the Court*, GT-GDR-C(2012)009 (7 December 2012): www.coe.int/t/dghl/standardsetting/cddh/gt-gdr-c/GT-GDR-C(2012)%20009%20Interim%20measures_Registry%20info%20doc.pdf (accessed 2 January 2014). Further: H. Keller and C. Marti, 'Interim Relief Compared: Use of Interim Measures by the UN Human Rights Committee and the European Court of Human Rights' (2013) 73 ZaöRV 325, 335.

[50] *Report on Interim Measures*, ¶ 12.

[51] For example, in 2010 the average application for interim relief had 40 per cent chance of success – by 2012 this had dropped to 5 per cent: Keller and Marti, 'Interim Relief Compared', 335–6.

measures in international law – at least insofar as the courts and tribunals under consideration are concerned – is in part by design. In 1965 and 1982, when ICSID and UNCLOS were respectively concluded, the ICJ represented the most successful tradition of provisional measures in international law, drawing not only on its own jurisprudence, but that of the PCIJ before it. Consequently, Article 41 of the Court's Statute represented a precedent that was difficult for the drafters of the relevant conventions to ignore – even if modifications were made to suit the anticipated needs of the dispute settlement systems so created, particularly in the case of UNCLOS.

It will not have escaped the reader's attention, however, that the *wording* of Article 41 and the *reality* of its application have not exactly overlapped. The provision as drafted leaves much to the discretion of the Court, with the only apparent limitations arising from the words 'if it considers that the circumstances so require', and 'to preserve the respective rights of the parties'. On plain meaning this places a fairly light yoke around the collective neck of the Bench. The Court, perhaps anticipating a crisis of legitimacy if this power were too widely used,[52] has therefore introduced a number of further limitations in its jurisprudence, an instinct evidenced even in the *Sino-Belgian Treaty* case.[53] The purpose of this section is to assess whether the courts and tribunals under consideration have moved beyond the textual inheritance of the ICJ and begun to apply concepts that have emerged in the Court's jurisprudence alone. It is here the true potential for fragmentation, at least in a substantive sense, lies. Four elements will be examined: (1) the requirement of *prima facie* jurisdiction; (2) the grant of provisional measures for certain specified purposes alone; (3) the related concepts of urgency and irreparable harm; and (4) the scope and force of provisional measures.

A. Prima facie *jurisdiction as a barrier to provisional measures*

1. The International Court of Justice

In a consent-based system of international adjudication, the power of a court or tribunal to award provisional measures without first being

[52] Early concerns of this nature can be seen in the debates between members of the Permanent Court concerning the amendment of its Rules in 1931: (1931) PCIJ Ser. D No. 2 Add. 2, at 181ff. A summary of the deliberations may be found in Elkind, *Interim Protection*, pp. 59–68.

[53] (1927) PCIJ Ser. A No. 8, at 6–7, making reference to as preservation of the rights of the parties pending resolution of the dispute, the notion that provisional relief is only available where damages would be insufficient, and the idea that the order so given was without prejudice to the merits.

wholly satisfied as to its jurisdiction has proved controversial, especially in an era where provisional measures are widely seen as binding.[54] The problem, such as it is, did not arise in any concerted way during the tenure of the PCIJ,[55] but emerged in the *Anglo-Iranian Oil* case. There, a vigorous dissent was raised by Judges Winiarski and Badawi Pasha, who argued that provisional measures could only be awarded where it was 'reasonably probable' that the Court possessed jurisdiction over the merits,[56] an approach seemingly followed by the majority in *Interhandel*.[57] In succeeding cases, a variety of formulations were proposed[58] as to the precise extent to which the Court had to be satisfied as to its jurisdiction before provisional measures could be awarded, ranging from the view that it must be established in full,[59] to the view that it did not need to be proved at all.[60] Such extremes were clearly unacceptable: on the one hand, the urgency of a *bona fide* provisional measures application risked further harm to rights *pendente lite* if a full hearing on jurisdiction was required;[61] on the other, the consent-focused character of the Court's jurisdiction rendered *some* investigation of its competence necessary to prevent the

[54] Generally: K. Oellers-Frahm, 'Expanding the Competence to Issue Provisional Measures – Strengthening the International Judicial Function', in A. von Bogdandy and I. Venzke (eds.), *International Judicial Lawmaking: On Public Authority and Democratic Legitimation in Global Governance* (Heidelberg: Springer, 2012).

[55] The issue almost arose in *Electricity Company of Sofia and Bulgaria*, where an application for provisional measures was made by Belgium in the face of a jurisdictional challenge by Bulgaria: (1938) PCIJ Ser. C No. 88, 17. This initial application was withdrawn, however, following Bulgarian assurances, and only reasserted after the Court had affirmed its jurisdiction: (1939) PCIJ Ser. A/B No. 77, 84. Further: Mendelsohn, 'Contested Jurisdiction', 266–8.

[56] *Anglo-Iranian Oil*, ICJ Reports 1951 p. 89, at 96–8.

[57] *Interhandel (Switzerland* v. *US)*, Provisional Measures, ICJ Reports 1957 p. 105, at 111.

[58] Mendelsohn, 'Contested Jurisdiction', 262–4; J. Collier and V. Lowe, *The Settlement of Disputes in International Law: Institutions and Procedures* (Oxford: Oxford University Press, 1999), pp. 169–71. Oellers-Frahm, 'Article 41', p. 935, helpfully summarizes the spectrum as follows: 'certain jurisdiction, quasi-certain jurisdiction, *prima facie* existing jurisdiction to *prima facie* lacking jurisdiction, doubtful jurisdiction, manifestly lacking jurisdiction, impossible jurisdiction, etc.'.

[59] *Nuclear Tests (Australia* v. *France)*, Provisional Measures, ICJ Reports 1973 p. 99, at 111 (Judge Forster, diss.), at 118–19 (Judge Gros, diss.); *Nuclear Tests (New Zealand* v. *France)*, Provisional Measures, ICJ Reports 1973 p. 135, at 148 (Judge Forster, diss.), at 153–4 (Judge Gros, diss.); *Aegean Sea Continental Shelf (Greece* v. *Turkey)*, Provisional Measures, ICJ Reports 1976 p. 3, at 22 (Judge Morozov).

[60] Collier and Lowe, *Settlement of Disputes*, pp. 3, 169.

[61] By way of a (slightly atypical) example, *Nicaragua* v. *Colombia* was filed on 6 December 2001, but Colombia's objections to jurisdiction were only determined on 13 December 2007: *Nicaragua* v. *Colombia*, Preliminary Objections, ICJ Reports 2007 p. 832.

violation of a state's sovereignty on the basis of a frivolous or vexatious application.

However, the question of provisional jurisdiction today is, at least in the abstract, uncontroversial, with a consensus developing within the Court based on Judge Lauterpacht's dissent in *Interhandel*, where it was said:

> The Court may properly act under the terms of Article 41 provided that there is the instrument such as a Declaration of Acceptable of the Optional Clause, emanating from the Parties to the dispute, which *prima facie* confers jurisdiction upon the Court and which incorporates no reservation obviously excluding its jurisdiction.[62]

This statement has formed the basis of a *jurisprudence constante*, and has been deployed by majorities in, *inter alia*, the *Icelandic Fisheries* cases,[63] the *Nuclear Tests* cases,[64] *Nicaragua*,[65] *Pulp Mills*[66] and *Georgia* v. *Russia*.[67] Although it sets a somewhat reduced threshold, surmounting the test is not automatic, as demonstrated by the attempted revisiting of *Nuclear Tests* by New Zealand in *Examination of the Situation*. There, an attempt to secure provisional measures on the basis of the famous paragraph 63 of the Court's 1974 decision[68] failed on the basis that the paragraph could only be invoked as a basis for jurisdiction on the basis of *atmospheric*

62 *Interhandel (Switzerland* v. *US)*, ICJ Reports 1957 p. 105, at 118–19.

63 *Fisheries Jurisdiction (UK* v. *Iceland)*, Provisional Measures, ICJ Reports 1972 p. 12, at 16; *Fisheries Jurisdiction (Germany* v. *Iceland)*, Provisional Measures, ICJ Reports 1972 p. 30, at 34.

64 *Nuclear Tests (Australia* v. *France)*, ICJ Reports 1973 p. 99, at 101; *Nuclear Tests (New Zealand* v. *France)*, ICJ Reports 1973 p. 135, at 137.

65 *Military and Paramilitary Activities in and against Nicaragua (Nicaragua* v. *US)*, Provisional Measures, ICJ Reports 1984 p. 169, at 179.

66 *Pulp Mills on the River Uruguay (Argentina* v. *Uruguay)*, Provisional Measures, ICJ Reports 2006 p. 113, at 128–9.

67 *Application of the International Convention on the Elimination of All Forms of Racial Discrimination (Georgia* v. *Russia)*, Provisional Measures, ICJ Reports 2008 p. 353, at 377.

68 *Nuclear Tests (New Zealand* v. *France)*, ICJ Reports 1974 p. 457, at 477: 'Once the Court has found that a State has entered into a commitment concerning its future conduct it is not the Court's function to contemplate that it will not comply with it. However, the Court observes that if the basis of this Judgment were to be affected, the Applicant could request an examination of the situation in accordance with the provisions of the Statute; the denunciation by France, by letter dated 2 January 1974, of the General Act for the Pacific Settlement of International Disputes, which is relied on as a basis of jurisdiction in the present case, cannot constitute by itself an obstacle to the presentation of such a request'.

nuclear testing, whereas France only persisted in conducting *underground* nuclear testing.[69]

It need hardly be added that a failure to prove *prima facie* jurisdiction (both *ratione materiae* and *ratione personae*) does not bode well for a subsequent full examination of jurisdiction, and the Court may (reluctantly) order a case removed from its General List when a request for provisional measures fails for want of jurisdiction, a fate which befell the applications against the US and Spain by Yugoslavia in the *Legality of the Use of Force* cases.[70]

2. Dispute settlement under UNCLOS

ITLOS and Annex VII tribunals have to an extent embraced the *prima facie* jurisdiction standard established by the ICJ, but this is hardly surprising – it is incorporated directly into UNCLOS Articles 290(1) and (5). It is interesting to note, however, that ITLOS has not sought to tread its own path when applying the test of *prima facie* jurisdiction.[71] In its first indication of provisional measures under UNCLOS Article 290(1) in *M/V Saiga (No. 2)*, the Tribunal expressed the test in a form of words identical to that characteristically used by the ICJ, noting that:

> *Considering* that before prescribing provisional measures the Tribunal need not finally satisfy itself that it has jurisdiction on the merits of the case and yet it may not prescribe such measures unless the provisions invoked by the applicant appear *prima facie* to afford a basis on which the jurisdiction of the Tribunal might be founded . . .[72]

[69] *Request for Examination of the Situation in Accordance with Paragraph 63 of the Court's Judgment of 20 December 1974 in the* Nuclear Tests (New Zealand *v.* France) *case (New Zealand* v. *France)*, Provisional Measures, ICJ Reports 1995 p. 288, at 306 (ironically also in ¶ 63).

[70] *Legality of the Use of Force (Yugoslavia* v. *Spain)*, Provisional Measures, ICJ Reports 1999 p. 761, at 769; *Legality of the Use of Force (Yugoslavia* v. *US)*, Provisional Measures, ICJ Reports 1999 p. 916, at 925. Cf. *Armed Activities on the Territory of the Congo (New Application: 2002) (Democratic Republic of the Congo* v. *Rwanda)*, Provisional Measures, ICJ Reports 2002 p. 219, at 223–4. Further: Rosenne, *Provisional Measures*, pp. 132–4.

[71] Cf. the extra-curial writings of Judge Ndiaye, who argues that the jurisdiction to award provisional measures only arises where 'it is reasonably probable that the arbitral tribunal would have jurisdiction on the merits': T. M. Ndiaye, 'Provisional Measures Before the International Tribunal for the Law of the Sea', in M. H. Nordquist and J. N. Moore (eds.), *Current Marine Environmental Issues and the International Tribunal for the Law of the Sea* (The Hague: Martinus Nijhoff, 2001), p. 97.

[72] *M/V Saiga (No. 2) (St. Vincent and the Grenadines* v. *Guinea)*, Provisional Measures (1998) 117 ILR 111, at 122. The connection was drawn explicitly with the jurisprudence of the ICJ in the Separate Opinion of Judge Liang: *ibid.*, at 133 (fn. 11).

This formula was also invoked – although it was credited to *M/V Saiga (No. 2)* – in *M/V Louisa*, the only other case (so far) in which provisional measures were requested of ITLOS under UNCLOS Article 290(1).[73] Such language has not been invoked in those cases in which ITLOS has considered provisional measures under UNCLOS Article 290(5), in which the Tribunal has simply contented itself with citing the provision at length or otherwise alluding to its content.[74] In the *ARA Libertad*, however, the majority adopted the passage for use in relation to its referred jurisdiction to order provisional measures.[75]

Nonetheless, there is the perception on the part of some members of ITLOS that there is a difference between provisional measures ordered in the name of the Tribunal proper and measures ordered on behalf of an Annex VII tribunal or some other nominated court. In *ARA Libertad*, Judges Wolfrum and Cot noted that:

> Whereas under article 290, paragraph 1, of the Convention, the Tribunal is called upon to decide *prima facie* on its own jurisdiction, under article 290, paragraph 5, of the Convention, it must decide on the *prima facie* jurisdiction of such other court or tribunal. Out of respect for the other court or tribunal the Tribunal has to exercise some restraint in questioning *prima facie* jurisdiction of such other court or tribunal . . . It is equally unsatisfactory if the arbitral tribunal under Annex VII denies its jurisdiction which the Tribunal has established *prima facie* as it is for the settlement of the said dispute if the Tribunal denies *prima facie* jurisdiction in a situation where the arbitral tribunal would have voted otherwise.[76]

This passage would tend to highlight, if not a reduced threshold of *prima facie* jurisdiction, then at least the notion of giving the benefit of a further doubt to the applicant in UNCLOS Article 290(5) cases.[77] But at

[73] *M/V Louisa (St. Vincent and the Grenadines* v. *Spain)*, ITLOS Case No. 18 (Provisional Measures, 23 December 2010), at ¶ 69. In *MOX Plant (Ireland* v. *UK)*, Procedural Order No. 3 (2003) 126 ILR 310, at 317, the Annex VII tribunal noted that the jurisdiction to order provisional measures exists under UNCLOS Art. 290(1) where 'there is nothing which manifestly and in terms excludes the Tribunal's jurisdiction'.

[74] *Southern Bluefin Tuna (New Zealand* v. *Japan; Australia* v. *Japan)*, Provisional Measures (1999) 117 ILR 148, at 160; *MOX Plant (Ireland* v. *UK)*, Provisional Measures (2001) 126 ILR 257, at 271; *Land Reclamation by Singapore in and around the Straits of Johor (Malaysia* v. *Singapore)*, Provisional Measures (2003) 126 ILR 487, at 497; *Arctic Sunrise (Netherlands* v. *Russia)*, ITLOS Case No. 22 (Provisional Measures, 22 November 2013), at ¶ 58.

[75] *ARA Libertad (Argentina* v. *Ghana)*, ITLOS Case No. 20 (Provisional Measures, 15 December 2012), at ¶ 60.

[76] *Ibid.*, at ¶ 5 (Judges Wolfrum and Cot).

[77] Cf. *Southern Bluefin Tuna* (2001) 117 ILR 148, at 181–5 (Judge ad hoc Shearer), arguing that the majority's inquiry into its provisional jurisdiction went far beyond a *prima facie* investigation.

the same time, the judges noted, greater jurisdictional rigour was generally required of dispute settlement bodies convened under UNCLOS as, unlike the ICJ, these operate under a narrow grant of competence *ratione materiae* covering only those disputes concerning the interpretation and application of UNCLOS.[78] Thus:

> Any attempt to broaden the jurisdictional power of the Tribunal and that of arbitral tribunals under Annex VII going beyond what is prescribed in article 288 of the Convention is not in keeping with the basic philosophy governing the dispute settlement system of the Convention [and] [u]ndermines the understanding reached at [UNCLOS III].[79]

It would appear that in *ARA Libertad* ITLOS was minded to adopt a very liberal interpretation of *prima facie* jurisdiction. The case concerned the seizure of an Argentine warship in the Ghanaian port of Tema, classified as internal waters for the purposes of the Convention. The seizure was in clear violation of the universally recognized immunity of warships under customary international law,[80] but UNCLOS only expressly incorporated this immunity with respect to the high seas per Article 95. The Tribunal found, however, that UNCLOS Article 32, providing relevantly that 'nothing in this Convention affects the immunities of warships and other government ships operated for non-commercial purposes', could form a basis for *prima facie* jurisdiction, as it could be interpreted as extending warship immunity under the Convention into internal waters. Such a reading is patently absurd, as is made clear by the subsequent analysis of Judges Wolfrum and Cot, which was argued by reference to the case law of the ICJ.[81] First, the provision is clearly a savings clause, providing only that the customary immunity is not undermined by the Convention, as opposed to establishing a positive treaty right that could be the subject of jurisdiction. Second, had the drafters of the provision intended that it have the effect contended, then a perfectly good model was available in the form of UNCLOS Article 95 concerning high seas

[78] UNCLOS Art. 288(1).

[79] *ARA Libertad*, ITLOS Case No. 20, at ¶ 6 (Judges Wolfrum and Cot).

[80] See e.g. *The Schooner Exchange* v. *M'Faddon*, (1812) 7 Cranch 116; *Chung Chi Cheung* v. *R* [1939] AC 160 (PC); *Wijsmuller Salvage BV* v. *ADM Naval Services*, District Court of Amsterdam, 19 November 1987, (1989) 20 NYIL 294. See now the UN Convention on the Jurisdictional Immunities of the State, annexed to GA Res. 59/49, 2 December 2004, Art. 21(1)(b). Further: H. Fox, *The Law of State Immunity* (Oxford: Oxford University Press, 2nd edn, 2008), p. 645.

[81] *ARA Libertad*, ITLOS Case No. 20, at ¶¶ 38–51 (Judges Wolfrum and Cot).

immunity: if UNCLOS Article 32, as contended, was intended to incorporate warship immunity wholesale into the Convention, then UNCLOS Article 95 would be superfluous.

It is too early to tell whether *ARA Libertad* signals the beginning of a move by ITLOS to reduce the threshold of *prima facie* jurisdiction in UNCLOS Article 290(5) cases. What is clear, however, is that greater efforts on the part of the Tribunal are required to define the jurisdictional requirements in such cases, as well as the differences (if any) with the approach of the ICJ.[82]

3. Investor-state arbitration under ICSID

ICSID is slightly different again in that the Convention makes express provision for an assessment of jurisdiction prior to the composition of the Tribunal. ICSID Article 36(3) provides that on receiving a request for arbitration, the Secretary-General of ICSID must register the request 'unless he finds, on the basis of the information contained in the request, that the dispute is manifestly outside the jurisdiction of the Centre'. The test of manifest lack of jurisdiction as expressed in ICSID Article 36(3) would appear to be broadly commensurate with the test of *prima facie* jurisdiction as set down by the ICJ, or may indeed be slightly lower.[83] Although the Tribunal is in no way bound by the decision of the Secretary-General in this respect in determining its jurisdiction to award provisional measures, it provides an additional basis on which such a decision may be made.[84]

This notwithstanding, the practice of most ICSID tribunals has been to attempt to establish jurisdiction to award provisional measures independently of the Secretary-General's preliminary finding. Early decisions did not set out the standard of jurisdiction to be proved in this respect, although it was recognized in the first ICSID decision on the subject, *Holiday Inns* v. *Morocco*, that any determination on jurisdiction for the purpose of awarding provisional measures was without prejudice to any later finding on jurisdiction proper, or the merits themselves.[85] Significantly, in that case the claimants were relying, *inter alia*, on the decision of the ICJ in *Anglo-Iranian Oil*.[86] The position established in that case has been followed with regularity by other ICSID tribunals and in the

[82] *Ibid.*, at ¶ 5 (Judges Wolfrum and Cot).

[83] Brower and Goodman, 'Jurisdictional Exclusivity', 452ff.

[84] Friedland, 'Provisional Measures in ICSID Arbitration', 341.

[85] *Holiday Inns* v. *Morocco*, Decision on Jurisdiction (1974) 1 ICSID Reports 658.

[86] P. Lalive, 'The First "World Bank" Arbitration (*Holiday Inns* v. *Morocco*) – Some Legal Problems' (1980) 51 BYIL 123, 153.

pleadings of the parties before them.[87] Conspicuous by its absence from the *Holiday Inns* v. *Morocco* decision on provisional measures, however, is any reference to the threshold of jurisdiction required at this stage of proceedings.

Over time, however, ICSID tribunals have come to have greater reliance on the decisions of the ICJ in elaborating on the substantive aspects of ICSID Article 47. To an extent, this has arisen out of the tendency for lawyers with established public international law credentials – including members of the ICJ – to sit on ICSID tribunals. A key example in this respect is *Casado* v. *Chile*, in which Mohammed Bedjaoui sat as arbitrator, and Pierre Lalive as President. In that case, the Tribunal's decision on provisional measures recognized the debt owed by ICSID Article 47 to Article 41 of the Statute,[88] and further recognized that it was not bound by the Secretary-General's decision to register the case per ICSID Article 36(3). It then relied on the case law of the ICJ in determining that it was under an obligation to determine 'in cases where jurisdiction is contested, the *prima facie* existence of jurisdiction or, to couch this in negative terms, the absence of a clear lack of jurisdiction'.[89] A more express formulation of this conclusion may be seen in the later decision of *Occidental* v. *Ecuador*, in which it was said that:

> Whilst the Tribunal need not definitely satisfy itself that it has jurisdiction in respect of the merits of the case at issue for purposes of ruling upon the requested provisional measures, it will not order such measures unless there is, *prima facie*, a basis upon which the Tribunal's jurisdiction might be established.[90]

4. The European Court of Human Rights

Unlike the other tribunals analysed, the question of *prima facie* jurisdiction has not arisen before the ECtHR, perhaps due to the fact that the

[87] See e.g. *Vacuum Salt Products Ltd* v. *Ghana*, Provisional Measures (1993) 4 ICSID Reports 323; *Société Générale de Surveillance SA* v. *Pakistan*, Procedural Order No 2 (2002) 8 ICSID Reports 388, at 392; *Bayinder Insaat Turizm Ticaret Ve Sanayi AS* v. *Pakistan*, ICSID Case No. ARB/03/29 (Jurisdiction, 14 November 2005), at ¶ 47.

[88] *Casado and Allende Foundation* v. *Chile*, Provisional Measures (2001) 6 ICSID Reports 373, at 377.

[89] *Ibid.*, at 379.

[90] *Occidental Petroleum Corporation and Occidental Exploration and Production Company* v. *Ecuador*, ICSID Case No. ARB/06/11 (Provisional Measures, 17 August 2007), at ¶ 55. Further: *Churchill Mining PLC* v. *Indonesia*, ICSID Case No ARB/12/14 (Procedural Order No 3, 4 March 2013), at ¶ 36: 'It is undisputed that the Tribunal has the power to recommend provisional measures prior to ruling on its jurisdiction. However, the Tribunal will not exercise such power unless it has *prima facie* jurisdiction.'

express power to award provisional measures is absent from the ECHR and orders made under Rule 39 were considered non-binding until the Court's 2003 judgment in *Mamatkulov and Abdurasulovic.*[91] But given the uniformity with which the criterion has been adopted by the other courts and tribunals considered here – and indeed by other human rights bodies both judicial and quasi-judicial – it seems likely that if such an objection were raised, the ECtHR would have to give the matter serious consideration.[92]

However, provided an application on the merits has already been lodged, an application for interim relief is met by a consideration as to whether the case is *prima facie* admissible within the meaning of ECHR Article 35.[93] The Court has in mind a reduced standard of review at this stage: 'when an interim measure is indicated, it is not for the Court to analyse the case in depth – and indeed it will often not have all the information it would need in order to do so'.[94] Under the new special procedure for screening applications under Rule 39 through the Registry, a decision to apply Rule 39 is accompanied by a notification of the case to the government in question, with a refusal to apply accompanied by a decision to declare the application inadmissible.[95]

B. *The purpose of provisional measures*

1. The International Court of Justice

The second question to be addressed is the purpose for which provisional measures may be awarded. This, characteristically, has revolved around the need to preserve the integrity of the final judgment until such time as that judgment can be given.[96] This may be seen expanded in the remarks of the Court in the *Aegean Sea Continental Shelf* case. There it was said that:

> The essential object of provisional measures is to ensure that the execution of a future judgment on the merits shall not be frustrated by the actions

[91] *Mamatkulov and Abdurasulovic* v. *Turkey* [2003] ECtHR 46827/99 and 46951/99, at ¶¶ 109–27. See also the decision of the Grand Chamber in *Mamatkulov and Askarov* v. *Turkey* [2005] ECtHR 46827/99 and 46951/99 (GC), at ¶¶ 125, 128. Further: Brown, *A Common Law*, p. 138.

[92] J. M. Pasqualucci, 'Interim Measures in International Human Rights: Evolution and Harmonization' (2005) 38 Vand. J T L 1, 38.

[93] Keller and Marti, 'Interim Relief Compared', 332.

[94] *MSS* v. *Belgium and Greece* [2011] ECtHR 30696/09 (GC), at ¶ 355.

[95] CDDH, *Report on Interim Relief*, ¶ 14.

[96] Collins, 'Provisional and Protective Measures', 10–11.

> of one party *pendente lite*... According to general principles of law recognized in municipal systems, and to the well-established jurisprudence of this Court, the essential justification for the impatience of a tribunal in granting relief before it has reached a final decision... is that the action of one party '*pendente lite*' causes or threatens a damage to the rights of another, of such a nature that it would not be possible to fully restore those rights, or remedy the infringement thereof, simply by a judgment in its favour.[97]

Simply remarking that provisional measures are intended to preserve the integrity of the judgment is to oversimplify the matter. Rather, provisional measures exist for the preservation of rights that are the subject of the dispute. This entails two further lines of enquiry pertaining to: (1) the existence of the rights in question; and (2) their relationship to the merits of the dispute.

Insofar as the first point is concerned, Rosenne argues that the Court should be prevented from any examination of the merits of the claim prior to the actual hearing of the merits proper,[98] as until jurisdiction is determined the consent of the parties to any such examination has not been given. This is formally correct, but as Oellers-Frahm points out, without any prospect of success in the case, there is no need for provisional measures as a matter of necessity.[99] To this may be added a second reason: for the Court to award provisional measures without averring to the merits of the case would be to invite abusive applications, with the award of interim relief in turn being used as a bargaining chip in negotiations.

Notwithstanding some early hints that the Court was examining the merits as part of the interim calculus,[100] this practice became far more overt in the wake of the *LaGrand* case,[101] presumably because the realization that such provisional measures are binding rendered their violation an internationally wrongful act within the law of state responsibility. In *Obligation to Prosecute or Extradite*, the Court accepted that some examination of the merits was required, stating that 'the power of the Court to indicate provisional measures should be exercised only if the Court is

[97] *Aegean Sea Continental Shelf*, ICJ Reports 1976 p. 3, at 15–16.

[98] Rosenne, *Provisional Measures*, p. 72.

[99] Oellers-Frahm, 'Article 41', p. 938.

[100] See e.g. *Nuclear Tests (Australia* v. *France)*, ICJ Reports 1973 p. 99, at 111, 114 (Judge Forster, diss.), at 124, 126 (Judge Petrén, diss.), at 128, 131 (Judge Iganacio-Pinto, diss.); *Passage through the Great Belt (Finland* v. *Denmark)*, Provisional Measures, ICJ Reports 1991 p. 12, at 36 (Judge Shahabuddeen).

[101] Y. Lee-Iwamoto, 'The Repercussions of the *LaGrand* Judgment: Recent ICJ Jurisprudence on Provisional Measures' (2012) 55 Japanese YIL 237, 247–51.

satisfied that the rights asserted by a party *are at least plausible*'.[102] This 'plausibility' formula has been repeated in other recent decisions, and now appears to be part of the accepted practice of the Court,[103] along with a requirement that the rights in question must be reasonably connected to the measures sought.[104] It does not, however, appear to be the equivalent of the 'serious question to be tried' or 'good arguable' case test which serves as a prerequisite to interim relief in some domestic jurisdictions.[105] The Court is assessing only whether the applicant *possesses* the rights in question – it pointedly does not assess whether those rights have been *breached* by the respondent, much less if said breach is *excusable*.[106]

Insofar as the second point is concerned, the rights to be protected by the imposition of provisional measures must be linked directly to the rights that are the subject of the main claim.[107] Thus, in *Arbitral Award of 31 July 1989*, the subject matter of the claim was the formal validity of an arbitral award determining the rights to certain maritime areas between Guinea-Bissau and Senegal. As part of its request, Guinea-Bissau asked the Court to order provisional measures with respect to activities in the maritime areas themselves. This was rejected on the basis that:

> [T]he Applicant . . . asks the Court to pass upon the existence and validity of the award but does not ask the Court to pass upon the respective rights of the Parties in the maritime areas in question . . . [A]ccordingly, the alleged rights sought to be made the subject of provisional measures are not the subject of proceedings before the Court on the merits of the case.[108]

As such, the key question is whether the rights protected by the measures are those that will fall to be determined in the final judgment,[109] a

102 *Questions relating to the Obligation to Prosecute or Extradite (Belgium* v. *Senegal)*, Provisional Measures, ICJ Reports 2009 p. 139, at 151 (emphasis added).

103 *Certain Activities carried out by Nicaragua in the Border Area (Costa Rica* v. *Nicaragua)*, Provisional Measures, ICJ Reports 2011 p. 6, at 18; *Request for Interpretation of the Judgment of 15 June 1962 in the* Case concerning the Temple of Preah Vihear (Cambodia *v.* Thailand) *(Cambodia* v. *Thailand)*, ICJ, Order of 18 July 2011, at ¶ 33.

104 *Activities in the Border Area*, ICJ Reports 2011 p. 6, at 20.

105 See e.g. *American Cynamid Co* v. *Ethicon Ltd* [1975] AC 396, at 407 (Lord Diplock). A similar formulation was argued in the *Great Belt* case by Denmark, but was not taken up by the Court: *Great Belt (Finland* v. *Denmark)*, ICJ Reports 1991 p. 12, 17.

106 D. Müller and A. B. Mansour, 'Procedural Developments at the International Court' (2009) 8 LPICT 459, 499; but cf. H. Sakai, 'New Developments of the Order of Provisional Measures by the International Court of Justice' (2009) 52 Japanese YIL 231, 263 (fn .112).

107 Oellers-Frahm, 'Article 41', pp. 938–9; Lee-Iwamoto, 'Repercussions of *LaGrand*', 241–7.

108 *Arbitral Award of 31 July 1989 (Guinea-Bissau* v. *Senegal)*, Provisional Measures, ICJ Reports 1990 p. 64, at 70.

109 *Application of the Convention on the Prevention and Punishment of the Crime of Genocide (Bosnia and Hezegovina* v. *Serbia and Montenegro)*, Provisional Measures, ICJ Reports

requirement that appears early on in both the *South-Eastern Greenland*[110] and *Polish Agrarian Reform*[111] cases. A feature of the recent jurisprudence has been to phrase this requirement not in terms of direct equivalence between the two rights, but rather a link of 'sufficiency' between them,[112] which perhaps explains its curious decision to award provisional measures in reinterpretation cases under Article 60 of the Court's Statute.[113]

A separate purpose for which provisional measures may be ordered within the jurisprudence of the ICJ is to prevent the further escalation of the dispute. In its decision in *Electricity Company of Sofia and Bulgaria*, the PCIJ referred to Article 41 of its Statute as reflecting the

> principle universally accepted by international tribunals . . . to the effect that the parties to a case must abstain from any measures capable of exercising a prejudicial effect in regard to the execution of the decision to be given *and, in general, not allow any step of any kind to be taken which might aggravate and extend the dispute.*[114]

This formula has been repeated in the jurisprudence of the ICJ and appears to be a valid basis on which provisional measures may be awarded.[115] The measures awarded under this category are, moreover, often quite general in nature. In *Georgia* v. *Russia*, for example, the Court provided that '[e]ach party shall refrain from any action which might prejudice the rights of the other Party in respect of whatever judgment the Court may render in the case, or which might aggravate or extend the dispute before the Court or make it more difficult to resolve'.[116] It should be noted that

1993 p. 3, at 19 ('[The Court] ought not to indicate measures for the protection of any disputed rights other than those which might ultimately form the basis of a judgment in the exercise of the jurisdiction').

110 *South-Eastern Greenland* (1932) PCIJ Ser. A/B No. 48, at 284–5.

111 *Polish Agrarian Reform* (1933) PCIJ Ser. A/B No. 58, at 177.

112 *Pulp Mills*, Provisional Measures II, ICJ Reports 2007 p. 3, at 10–11.

113 In such cases, protection was given to the subject of the principal request underpinning the original judgment, *not* the rights created by the judgment that fell to be reinterpreted: *Request for Interpretation of the Judgment of 31 March 2004 in the* Case concerning Avena and other Mexican Nationals (Mexico *v.* US) *(Mexico* v. *US)*, Provisional Measures, ICJ Reports 2008 p. 311, at 326–8; *Temple (Reinterpretation)*, ICJ, at ¶ 34.

114 *Electricity Company of Sofia and Bulgaria* (1929) PCIJ Ser. A/B No. 79, at 199 (emphasis added). Cf. H. Thirlway, *The Law and Procedure of the International Court of Justice: Fifty Years of Jurisprudence* (Oxford: Oxford University Press, 2013), vol. 1, pp. 946–53.

115 See e.g. *Fisheries Jurisdiction (Iceland* v. *UK)*, ICJ Reports 1972 p. 12, at 14; *Nuclear Tests (Australia* v. *France)*, ICJ Reports 1973 p. 99, at 106; *US Diplomatic and Consular Staff in Tehran (US* v. *Iran)*, Provisional Measures, ICJ Reports 1979 p. 7, at 21; *Frontier Dispute (Burkina Faso/Mali)*, Provisional Measures, ICJ Reports 1986 p. 3, at 9, 11–12.

116 *Georgia* v. *Russia*, ICJ Reports 2008 p. 353, at 399.

in the *Pulp Mills* case it was held that measures for the non-escalation of a dispute could not be awarded independently of measures of the protection of a right or interest: the former is dependent on and supplements the existence of the latter.[117]

2. Dispute settlement under UNCLOS

UNCLOS Article 290(1) takes a similar position to that of Article 41 of the ICJ Statute, providing expressly that provisional measures may be awarded in order to preserve the rights of the parties. At the present point in time, neither ITLOS nor an Annex VII tribunal has seen fit to expand at length as to what this requirement means in the context of UNCLOS dispute resolution, although it should be noted that no request under UNCLOS Article 290 has been rejected for a lack of a sufficient connection between the measures protected and the rights *pendente lite*. It may therefore be presumed that dispute resolution bodies under UNCLOS are following the same broad strokes established by the ICJ, although they have not yet shown an inclination to examine the strength of the claimant's case on the merits as part of this calculation. Such a discussion was expressly discarded – at least in the sense that such an inquiry must be definitive – as necessary by ITLOS in the *M/V Louisa*.[118] It is worth noting, however, that the Tribunal did not say that *no* inquiry was required into the plausibility of the rights on which an application was based. Whether this means that *some* inquiry is required is a matter, however, for a future case.

Furthermore, ITLOS appears to have endorsed the separate power to award provisional measures so as to prevent escalation or aggravation of a dispute, despite the fact that – as with Article 41 of the ICJ Statute – this capacity does not appear in the wording of UNCLOS Article 290(1). In the *Southern Bluefin Tuna* case, both Australia and New Zealand requested that 'the parties ensure that no action of any kind [be] taken which might aggravate, extend or render more difficult of solution the dispute submitted'.[119] No comment on the application was made by the majority beyond simply granting the request,[120] and the only separate opinion to address the issue did not disagree with the notion that ITLOS possessed

[117] *Pulp Mills*, ICJ Reports 2007 p. 3, at 16; cf. *ibid.* at 21 (Judge Buergenthal). Further: P. Palchetti, 'The Power of the International Court of Justice to Indicate Provisional Measures' (2008) 21 LJIL 623.

[118] *M/V Louisa*, ITLOS Case No. 18, at ¶ 69: '*Considering* that, at this stage of the proceedings, the Tribunal does not need to establish definitively the existence of the rights claimed by Saint Vincent and the Grenadines'.

[119] *Southern Bluefin Tuna* (1999) 117 ILR 148, at 158.

[120] *Ibid.*, at 165.

such a power, but only that it was inappropriate in the circumstances considered.[121] Given the lack of further evidence, it may again be presumed that ITLOS was here drawing inspiration from the ICJ.

UNCLOS Article 290(1), however, contains an elaboration not seen in Article 41 of the ICJ Statute, namely the capacity for a nominated dispute settlement body to award provisional measures specifically 'to prevent serious harm to the marine environment'.[122] As is self-evident, this does not require that a request for provisional measures be directly linked to the rights which are not the subject of the dispute. As Wolfrum notes, '[t]his reflects the change of international law from a mechanism providing for the coordination of States' activities to one which also recognizes and preserves common values of the community of States'.[123] Put another way, this elaboration reflects the same set of concerns that rendered protection of the marine environment an obligation *erga omnes*.[124]

Provisional measures for the protection of the marine environment have been regularly sought in cases under both UNCLOS Articles 290(1) and (5).[125] Analysis of the circumstances in which the need to protect the environment in the jurisprudence of ITLOS and Annex VII tribunals owes very little to the jurisprudence of the ICJ, with the various judicial bodies instead focusing on the requirement of 'seriousness' as it appears in the wording of UNCLOS Article 290(1).[126]

3. Investor-state arbitration under ICSID

Given the fact that it was directly modeled on Article 41 of the ICJ Statute, provisional measures awarded under ICSID Article 47 have tended to

[121] *Ibid.*, at 194 (Judge Eiriksson, diss.).

[122] A further elaboration may be seen in the United Nations Agreement for the Implementation of the Provisions of the United Nations Convention on the Law of the Sea of 10 December 1982 relating to the Conservation and Management of Straddling Fish Stocks and Highly Migratory Fish Stocks, 4 August 1995, in force 11 December 2001, 2167 UNTS 88, Art. 31(2): provisional measures may also be ordered in order to prevent damage to relevant fish stocks.

[123] Wolfrum, 'Provisional Measures of ITLOS', p. 176. See also *M/V Louisa*, ITLOS Case No. 18, ¶ 4 (Judge Wolfrum, diss.).

[124] See e.g. *Responsibilities and Obligations of States Sponsoring Persons and Entities with Respect to Activities in the Area*, ITLOS Case No. 17 (Advisory Opinion, 1 February 2011), at ¶ 180.

[125] *MOX Plant* (2003) 126 ILR 310, at 327–8; *MOX Plant* (2001) 126 ILR 257, at 274; *M/V Louisa*, ITLOS Case No. 18, at ¶¶ 71–7; *Southern Bluefin Tuna* (1999) 117 ILR 148, at 163–4; *Land Reclamation* (2003) 126 ILR 487, at 504–5.

[126] *MOX Plant* (2003) 126 ILR 310, at 327–8; *Land Reclamation* (2003) 126 ILR 487, at 520 (Judge Chandrasekhara Rao); *Southern Bluefin Tuna* (1999) 117 ILR 148, at 168–9 (Judge Wairoba).

require that prophylactic action be linked to rights which are related to the litigation,[127] although in so doing the tendency has been to rely on the bare words of ICSID Article 47 rather than the jurisprudence of the ICJ.[128] As a general rule, the relevant rights are defined by the claimant, a point made clear by the decision on provisional measures in *Plama* v. *Bulgaria*:

> The rights to be preserved must relate to the requesting party's ability to have its claims and requests for relief in the arbitration fairly considered and decided by the arbitral tribunal and for any arbitral decision which grants to the Claimant the relief it seeks to be effective and able to be carried out. Thus the rights to be preserved by provisional measures are circumscribed by the requesting party's claims and requests for relief. They may be general rights, such as the rights to due process or the right not to have the dispute aggravated, but those general rights must be related to the specific disputes in arbitration, which, in turn, are defined by the Claimant's claims and requests for relief to date.[129]

As such, provisional measures under ICSID follow the same broad pattern as that of the ICJ, and interim relief may be declined where the request does not relate to rights connected to the dispute. Thus, in *Amco Asia* v. *Indonesia*, the respondent complained about various newspaper articles which, it was asserted, could have a detrimental effect on its economy. The Tribunal held that '[i]t might possibly be that a large press campaign could have such an influence. However, even so, it would not be an influence on rights in dispute'.[130] Thirty years later, in *Churchill Mining* v. *Indonesia*, the respondent sought provisional measures on the basis of certain public statements made by the claimant on the content of the arbitration which it claimed prejudiced, *inter alia*, its rights to regulate and promote investments in natural resources and its rights to enforce regulations on investments in natural resources. The same reply was given: the rights in question were not related to the dispute.[131] The pattern established by the ICJ is thus perpetuated, although as a general rule ICSID tribunals tend to award relief in order to protect procedural rights such as the preservation and production of evidence, the exclusive nature of ICSID arbitration and

[127] Indeed, Rule 39(1) of the Centre's Arbitration Rules requires that a party requesting interim relief specify the right to be preserved.

[128] *Plama Consortium Ltd* v. *Bulgaria*, ICSID Case No ARB/03/24 (Order, 6 December 2005) at ¶ 40.

[129] *Ibid.* [130] *Amco Asia Corporation* v. *Indonesia* (1983) 1 ICSID Reports 410, at 411.

[131] *Churchill Mining* v. *Indonesia*, ICSID Case No. ARB/12/14, at ¶ 49.

the confidentiality of proceedings.[132] ICSID panels have also embraced the notion of measures for the non-aggravation of the dispute, despite the lack of a textual basis in ICSID Article 47.[133] In *Amco* v. *Indonesia*, the Tribunal referred to a rule 'according to which both parties to a legal dispute should refrain, in their own interest, [from doing] anything that could aggravate or exacerbate the same, thus rendering the solution possibly more difficult'.[134] This instinct was linked to the jurisprudence of the ICJ in *Casado* v. *Chile*, by way of reference to *Electricity Company of Sofia and Bulgaria*, *Anglo-Iranian Oil*,[135] and the *Armed Activities (DRC* v. *Uganda)* case.[136]

Furthermore, and unlike ITLOS and Annex VII tribunals, investor-state arbitration tribunals under ICSID have begun to look at the merits of the dispute in awarding provisional measures. In *Burlington* v. *Ecuador*, both parties agreed that a tribunal had to establish the existence of the rights with respect to which protection was sought on a *prima facie* basis, albeit without reference to the jurisprudence of the ICJ.[137] Similarly, in *Occidental* v. *Ecuador*, the Tribunal stated that at the provisional measures phase 'the right to be preserved only has to be asserted as a theoretically existing right, as opposed to proven to exist in fact' and that 'the Tribunal . . . will only deal with the nature of the right claimed, not with its existence or with the merits of the application'.[138] Most recently, in *Tethyan Copper* v. *Pakistan*, it was said that at the provisional measures stage of proceedings, it suffices that the party requesting the provisional measure 'establishes a *prima facie* case that it owns a legally protected interest'.[139] The standard in all three cases aligns – though perhaps not deliberately – with the recent jurisprudence of the ICJ, in requiring only that rights with respect to which relief is claimed be proved plausible. It

[132] Schreuer et al., *ICSID Commentary*, p. 779. On the latter, see generally Brower and Goodman, 'Jurisdictional Exclusivity'.

[133] Schreuer et al., *ICSID Commentary*, pp. 793–5.

[134] *Amco* v. *Indonesia* (1983) 1 ICSID Reports 410, at 411.

[135] *Anglo-Iranian Oil*, ICJ Reports 1951 p. 89, at 93.

[136] *Armed Activities in the Territory of the Congo (Democratic Republic of the Congo* v. *Uganda)*, Provisional Measures, ICJ Reports 2000 p. 111, at 128.

[137] *Burlington Resources Inc and Ors* v. *Ecuador and Empresa Estatal Petróleos del Ecuador (PetroEcuador)*, ICSID Case No. ARB/08/5 (Procedural Order No 1, 29 June 2009), at ¶ 53. The parties may have reached this shared conclusion based on the jurisprudence of the ICJ, but the pleadings are not publicly available. See also and earlier *Casado* v. *Chile* (2003) 6 ICSID Reports 373, at 386–7.

[138] *Occidental* v. *Ecuador*, ICSID Case No. ARB/06/11, at ¶ 117.

[139] *Tethyan Copper Company Pty Ltd* v. *Pakistan*, ICSID Case No. ARB/12/1 (Decision on Provisional Measures, 13 December 2012), at ¶ 117.

stops short of requiring that the applicant prove a prospect of success on the merits. In this, a distinction may perhaps be drawn between ICSID and the decision of the ad hoc UNCITRAL tribunal in *Paushok* v. *Mongolia*. There, it was said that 'the Tribunal need not go beyond whether a reasonable case has been made which, if the facts alleged are proven, might possibly lead the Tribunal to the conclusion that an award could be made in favour of Claimants' and that further, 'the Tribunal needs to decide only that the claims made are not, on their face, frivolous or obviously outside the competence of the Tribunal'.[140]

4. The European Court of Human Rights

Again, the ECtHR brings a different perspective to the issue. Under the approach adopted by the ECtHR, an application for interim relief may precede the application on the merits proper, so long as it discloses elements that indicate the presence of an arguable case: an essential element of the Court's procedure is therefore to examine the merits when considering interim relief. As such, the Court's Practice Direction on interim relief requires applicants to state the reasoning behind their submission, including 'grounds on which his or her particular fears are based, the nature of the alleged risks and the [ECHR] provisions alleged to have been violated'.[141] In such a case, Rule 39 is applied on the presumption that an application will follow,[142] and if it does not, then the interim measure will be lifted.[143]

In this light, it is clear that an application for interim measures must contemplate a right or interest that falls within the jurisdiction *ratione materiae* of the Court, viz. those arising under the ECHR and its Protocols. In this sense, it follows that interim measures are not autonomous, but must relate to a specific matter brought before the Court.[144] It follows *ipso facto* that interim relief cannot protect rights that are outside the

[140] The Tribunal made reference to *Casado* v. *Chile* but appears to have misconstrued the order in that case – in the relevant paragraph the Tribunal was discussing *prima facie* jurisdiction: *Casado* v. *Chile* (2003) 6 ICSID Reports 373, at ¶ 8.

[141] Practice Direction: Requests for Interim Measures, 1.

[142] This more lenient approach has on occasion served as an invitation for abuse, particularly in immigration cases, with applicants disappearing into hiding once relief has been granted: Keller and Marti, 'Interim Relief Compared', 332. See e.g. *JZ* v. *France* and *RZ* v. *France* [2012] ECtHR 43341/09 and 43342/09; *Kaderi and Ors* v. *Switzerland* [2012] ECtHR 29919/12.

[143] See e.g. *HN* v. *UK* [2011] ECtHR 56676/11.

[144] Keller and Marti, 'Interim Relief Compared', 331.

scope of the main application – an extension of the principle enunciated in *South-Eastern Greenland*.

C. *Urgency and irreparable prejudice*

1. The International Court of Justice

The related criteria of urgency and irreparable prejudice have long been determinative in the success or failure of an application for provisional measures. The requirements are judge-made, and like questions of jurisdiction or relationship to rights *pendente lite* do not appear expressly in the wording of Article 41 of the Statute. In a sense, the terminology is unfortunate: a right subject to litigation cannot be 'harmed' or 'damaged', much less irreparably. This notwithstanding, this concept was invoked with regularity before the PCIJ, with President Huber referring in the *Sino-Belgian Treaty* case to prejudice which 'could not be made good simply by the payment of an indemnity or by compensation or restitution in some other material form'.[145]

Irreparability in the jurisprudence of the ICJ has moved beyond the notion of harm per se, and is now more concerned with the risk of irreparable *prejudice* to rights that are the subject of the proceedings at hand.[146] Unsurprisingly, the adherence to a criterion of irreparability in the context of something as abstract as a 'right' has resulted in a somewhat incoherent approach to the question in the jurisprudence.[147] Whilst the question is relatively clear cut in cases such as *Breard*,[148] *LaGrand* and *Avena*,[149] it is more opaque in others – in the *Aegean Sea* case, for example, one may ask how 'exclusivity of the rights . . . to acquire information concerning the natural resources of the area of the continental shelf'[150] could be found capable of reparation.

The better view is probably that propounded by Oellers-Frahm, whereby the Court uses 'a steadily widening margin of appreciation with a view to all the circumstances of the case' to determine the need for interim

[145] *Sino-Belgian Treaty* (1927) PCIJ Ser. A No. 8, at 7. Further: *South-Eastern Greenland* (1932) PCIJ Ser. A/B No. 48, at 284, referring to the need for provisional measures where 'the damage threatening [the rights in dispute] would be irreparable in fact or in law'.

[146] *Fisheries Jurisdiction (UK* v. *Iceland)*, ICJ Reports 1972 p. 12, at 16.

[147] Oellers-Frahm, 'Article 41', p. 940.

[148] *Vienna Convention on Consular Relations (Paraguay* v. *US)*, Provisional Measures, ICJ Reports 1998 p. 248.

[149] *Avena and Other Mexican Nationals (Mexico* v. *US)*, Provisional Measures, ICJ Reports 2003 p. 77.

[150] *Aegean Sea Continental Shelf*, ICJ Reports 1976 p. 3, at 11.

relief, and is more likely to grant them where 'an obvious and flagrant violation of the rights claimed on the merits cannot be tolerated until the delivery of the final judgment'.[151] This provides some satisfaction in its flexibility, although it does run the risk of reducing the criterion of prejudice to the maxim of 'I know it when I see it'.[152]

Given the temporary nature of provisional measures, it is necessary that if it is to be granted, interim relief be required urgently.[153] The requirement is self-evidently linked to that of irreparable prejudice, such that they may often be considered as one: if there is not imminent irreparable prejudice, then provisional measures are clearly not urgent. This prejudice, moreover, must manifest itself prior to the likely or conceivable date of judgment: thus, in the *Great Belt* case, relief was denied due to the fact that the complained of obstruction of the passage would not be realized before the end of 1994, by which time proceedings could reasonably be expected to have concluded.[154] Similarly, in the *Arrest Warrant* case, the person named in the warrant, Mr Yerodia, was no longer the claimant's Foreign Minister, and thus was unlikely to be engaged in international travel prior to the determination of the case.[155] Conversely, in *LaGrand*, the eponymous Walter LaGrand was scheduled to be executed by the US state of Arizona the day after the request for provisional measures was filed: this led to the granting of provisional measures in the record time of twenty-three hours, with final judgment eventually being given over two years later.

2. Dispute settlement under UNCLOS

The instinct of both ITLOS and Annex VII tribunals has been to avoid in-depth consideration of irreparable prejudice[156] and to instead focus

151 Oellers-Frahm, 'Article 41', p. 940.

152 *Jacobellis* v. *Ohio*, 378 US 184, at 197 (1964) (Stewart J): 'I shall not today attempt further to define the kinds of material I understand to be embraced within that shorthand description; and perhaps I could never succeed in intelligibly doing so. But I know it when I see it, and the motion picture involved in this case is not that.'

153 This is an underlying presumption of Art. 72 of the Court's Rules, which provides as follows: '(1) A request for the indication of provisional measures shall have priority over all other cases. (2) The Court, if it is not sitting when the request is made, shall be convened forthwith for the purpose of proceeding to a decision on the request as a matter of urgency.'

154 *Great Belt (Finland* v. *Denmark)*, ICJ Reports 1991 p. 12, at 18.

155 *Arrest Warrant of 11 April 2000 (Democratic Republic of the Congo* v. *Belgium)*, Provisional Measures, ICJ Reports 2000 p. 182, at 201.

156 When discussed by ITLOS, the concept appears to be discussed in only a transitory sense: *M/V Louisa*, ITLOS Case No. 18, at ¶ 72; *Lana Reclamation* (2003) 126 ILR 487, at 501.

on considerations of urgency.[157] Indeed, it has been argued that the 'grave standard' of irreparability is 'inapt for application in the wide and varied range of cases that . . . are likely to come before [ITLOS]',[158] a somewhat nonsensical position given the plenary jurisdiction of the PCIJ and ICJ, which together have cheerfully applied the standard since 1927. It might plausibly be argued, however, that given the fact that UNCLOS Article 290(1) requires that harm to the marine environment be 'serious' in order to justify provisional measures, it would be inappropriate to deny provisional measures under that head of damage merely because the harm predicted was 'serious but not irreparable'.[159]

However, despite the fact that it is not mentioned in UNCLOS Article 290, it is telling that applicants for provisional measures under this provision generally phrase their requests in terms of irreparable harm. In the *Land Reclamation* case, for example, Malaysia based its application on the argument that '[t]o the extent that [Singapore's land reclamation projects] impair Malaysia's rights . . . the harm caused could not be other than irreversible or irreparable'.[160] Similarly, in *ARA Libertad*, Argentina argued that Ghana's decision to impound its training vessel was 'producing an irreparable damage to the Argentine rights in question, namely the immunity that the Frigate ARA Libertad enjoys, the exercise of its right to leave the territorial waters of Ghana, and its freedom of navigation more generally'.[161] It may be that the issue has assumed importance over time, as ITLOS and its allied tribunals have brought their jurisprudence more into line with the practice of the ICJ. Although no mention of irreparability was made in the *M/V Saiga (No. 2)* decision of 1998, by 2003 the Annex VII tribunal in *MOX Plant* considered the issue of irreparability to be key, stating that '[i]nternational judicial practice confirms that a general requirement for the prescription of provisional measures to protect the

[157] The concept is, however, discussed not infrequently in individual minority judgments: see e.g. *M/V Saiga (No. 2)* (1998) 117 ILR 111, at 142–3 (Judge Liang); *Southern Bluefin Tuna* (1999) 117 ILR 148, at 170–1 (Judge Liang), 178 (Judge Treves), *ARA Libertad*, ITLOS Case No. 20, at ¶ 1 (Judge Paik); *Land Reclamation* (2003) 126 ILR 487, at 520 (Judge Chandrasekhara Rao), at 529–30 (Judge Cot), *Arctic Sunrise*, ITLOS Case No. 22, at ¶¶ 7–8 (Judge Kulyk, diss.).

[158] *Southern Bluefin Tuna* (1999) 117 ILR 148, at 170 (Judge Liang). Also: *M/V Saiga (No. 2)* (1998) 117 ILR 111, at 143 (Judge Liang).

[159] *M/V Saiga (No. 2)* (1998) 117 ILR 111, at 143 (Judge Liang). Further: Wolfrum, 'Provisional Measures of ITLOS', pp. 174–7.

[160] *Land Reclamation*, Malaysia: Request for Provisional Measures (4 September 2003), at ¶ 15.

[161] *ARA Libertad*, Argentina: Request for Provisional Measures (14 November 2012), at ¶ 29.

rights of the Parties is that there needs to be a showing both of urgency and of irreparable harm to the claimed rights',[162] giving the decision of the ICJ in *Certain Criminal Proceedings*[163] as an example of this. Similarly, in the *M/V Louisa* case, the absence of irreparable harm was considered determinative in the denial of provisional measures.[164] But this trend is far from certain, with the concept notably absent from the orders given in *Arctic Sunrise*. This omission was the subject of lengthy comment in the dissenting opinion of Judge Kulyk.[165] The disagreement between these decisions – *M/V Louisa* and *MOX Plant* on the one hand, and *ARA Libertad* and *Arctic Sunrise* on the other – is of considerable concern, and is of very little help to parties desiring a greater level of certainty in the practice of the various UNCLOS tribunals.

As stated, however, the central textual requirement of provisional measures under UNCLOS Article 290, particularly in ITLOS jurisprudence, is urgency. Although only mentioned expressly in UNCLOS Article 290(5), urgency has also been considered relevant in proceedings under UNCLOS Article 290(1) as well, with the Annex VII tribunal in *MOX Plant* seeing the issue, as described, as a general requirement for the award of provisional measures by international courts and tribunals.[166] The wording of UNCLOS Article 290(5), however, introduces a consideration additional to the reasoning of the ICJ. Given that under that provision ITLOS is acting on behalf of an Annex VII or ad hoc arbitral tribunal, its consideration of urgency ends at the point at which that body can convene and award its own provisional measures (if required) under UNCLOS Article 290(1), a point made clear by ITLOS in the *Southern Bluefin Tuna* case.[167] The period between the awarding of interim relief and the composition of the relevant tribunal is not, however, definitive for the assessment of the

[162] *MOX Plant* (2003) 123 ILR 310, at 328.

[163] *Certain Criminal Proceedings in France (Republic of the Congo* v. *France)*, Provisional Measures, ICJ Reports 2003 p. 102, at 110.

[164] *M/V Louisa*, ITLOS Case No. 18, at ¶ 82.

[165] *Arctic Sunrise*, ITLOS Case No. 20, at ¶¶ 7–8 (Judge Kulyk, diss.).

[166] *MOX Plant* (2003) 123 ILR 310, 328. Curiously, the issue was not considered overly relevant in either of the ITLOS decisions under UNCLOS Art. 290(1). In *M/V Saiga (No. 2)* ((1999) 117 ILR 111, at 122–4) no mention of either irreparable prejudice nor urgency was made by the majority (although cf. *ibid.*, at 140–1 (Judge Liang), rejecting the concept in the context of UNCLOS Art. 290(1)) and in *M/V Louisa* (ITLOS Case No. 18, at ¶ 72), rejection of the Vincentian request was predicated on a lack of irreparable prejudice.

[167] *Southern Bluefin Tuna* (1999) 117 ILR 148, at 162–3. Further: Mensah, 'Provisional Measures in ITLOS', 47.

urgency of the situation – the urgency of the situation must be assessed taking into account the period in which the tribunal is not yet in a position to 'modify, revoke or affirm those provisional measures'.[168]

3. Investor-state arbitration under ICSID

At one point in its history, it seemed that ICSID Article 47 would make express mention of a requirement of irreparable prejudice and urgency.[169] Although a proposal to this effect was defeated during negotiations, it has nonetheless become clear through the jurisprudence of the Centre's various tribunals that provisional measures will only be awarded where a question cannot await the outcome of an award on the merits.[170]

In adopting the criteria of irreparable prejudice (referred to occasionally as the requirement of 'necessity'[171]) and urgency, a number of ICSID tribunals have relied on the jurisprudence of the ICJ. The debt in this respect may be seen clearly in *Occidental* v. *Ecuador*. In that case, it was stated that in order for interim relief to be granted 'there must exist both a right to be preserved and circumstances of urgency and necessity to prevent irreparable harm',[172] with the Tribunal invoking both the *Aegean Sea* and *Great Belt* cases as support for this proposition, before going on to find that the lack of irreparable prejudice to the rights identified by the claimant was determinative in rejecting the request.[173]

The need for prejudice of some sort has been reiterated by a large number of tribunals, such as to become a relatively uncontroversial article of faith.[174] That said, a number of tribunals have queried whether the ICJ's standard of *irreparable* harm is truly justified on the basis of ICSID Article 47, preferring instead a reduced threshold of *significant* harm. In *City Oriente* v. *Ecuador*, the Tribunal considered earlier authorities that had adopted the ICJ's stance on the subject and concluded that:

[168] *Land Reclamation* (2003) 126 ILR 487, at 501.

[169] Schreuer et al., *ICSID Commentary*, pp. 775–6.

[170] *Biwater Gauff (Tanzania) Ltd* v. *Tanzania*, ICSID Case No ARB/05/22 (Procedural Order No 1, 31 March 2006), at ¶ 68.

[171] *Churchill Mining* v. *Indonesia*, ICSID Case No. ARB/12/14, at ¶ 44.

[172] *Occidental* v. *Ecuador*, ICSID Case No. ARB/06/11, at ¶ 61.

[173] *Ibid*, at ¶¶ 87–9.

[174] See e.g. *Plama* v. *Bulgaria*, ICSID Case No. ARB/03/24, at ¶ 38; *Railroad Development Corporation* v. *Guatemala*, ICSID Case No ARB/07/23 (Decision on Provisional Measures, 15 October 2008), at ¶ 34; *Quiborax SA, Non Metallic Minerals SA and Allan Fosk Kaplún* v. *Bolivia*, ICSID Case No. ARB/06/02 (Decision on Provisional Measures, 26 February 2010), at ¶ 113; *Iona Micula and Ors* v. *Romania*, ICSID Case No. ARB/05/20 (Decision on Provisional Measures, 2 March 2011), at ¶ 12.

> [T]he Tribunal has verified that neither Article 47 of the Convention nor Rule 39 of the Arbitration Rules require that provisional measures be ordered only as a means to prevent irreparable harm... Rule 39 only refers to 'circumstances that require such measures'. It is the opinion of the Tribunal that this wording requires only that provisional measures must not be ordered lightly, but only as a last resort, after careful consideration of the interests at stake, weighing the harm spared the petitioner and the damage inflicted on the other party. It is not so essential that provisional measures be necessary to prevent irreparable harm, but that the harm spared the petitioner by such measures must be significant and that it exceed greatly the damage caused to the party affected thereby.[175]

A similar position has been adopted by other ICSID tribunals,[176] and has been defended in academic terms by Sarooshi.[177] Insofar as the source of the conflict is concerned, it might be inferred that it originates in the overlap between ICSID tribunals and tribunals convened in international commercial arbitrations, which may follow a different tradition of provisional measures. In *Burlington Resources* v. *Ecuador*, for example, the Tribunal based its adoption of the significant harm standard on Article 17A(1) of the UN Commission on International Trade Law (UNCITRAL) Model Law[178] – a mechanism used almost exclusively in the context of international commercial arbitration[179] – which provides that it 'is not so essential that provisional measures be necessary to prevent irreparable harm', but only that the potential harm must be 'significant'.[180] Questions may be asked, however, if given that the ICJ itself seems to be retreating from a strict insistence on irreparability as a precondition to interim relief and moving towards a 'steadily widening margin of appreciation' as

[175] *City Oriente Limited* v. *Ecuador and Empresa Estatal Petróleos Del Ecuador*, ICSID Case No. ARB/06/21 (Decision on Revocation of Provisional Measures, 13 May 2008), at ¶¶ 70–2.

[176] *Burlington Resources Inc and Ors* v. *Ecuador and Empresa Estatal Petróleos del Ecuador*, ICSID Case No, ARB/08/5, (Procedural Order No 1, 29 June 2009), at ¶ 51; *Perenco Ecuador Ltd* v. *Ecuador and Empresa Estatal Petróleos del Ecuador*, ICSID Case No. ARB/08/6 (Decision on Provisional Measures, 8 May 2009), at ¶ 43.

[177] D. Sarooshi, 'Provisional Measures and Investment Treaty Arbitration' (2013) 29 Arb. Int'l 361, 367–79.

[178] UNCITRAL Model Law on International Commercial Arbitration (1985, amended 2006): www.uncitral.org/pdf/english/texts/arbitration/ml-arb/07-86998_Ebook.pdf (accessed 4 January 2014]).

[179] N. Blackaby and C. Partasides (with A. Redfern and M. Hunter), *Redfern and Hunter on International Commercial Arbitration* (Oxford: Oxford University Press, 5th edn, 2009), pp. 68–81.

[180] *Burlington Resources* v. *Ecuador*, ICSID Case No. ARB/08/5, at ¶ 81.

suggested by Oellers-Frahm,[181] the difference so created by these dissident tribunals is anything more than a disagreement about labeling.[182]

Where ICSID is poised to make a unique contribution to the jurisprudence surrounding provisional measures, however, is in a procedural sense. As stated, the overtly commercial nature of these disputes and the fact that they have an increased potential to conflict with proceedings in national courts has led to requests for provisional measures in order to stay municipal proceedings, compel the preservation and production of evidence and prevent the taking of further punitive measures against the claimant.[183] To this end, certain tribunals have demonstrated willingness to permit the scope of the specific request to modify the content of the measures, and more particularly, the determination as to whether the relief requested is reasonable.[184] In *RDC* v. *Guatemala*, for example, the Tribunal was required to rule on a request by the claimant for the preservation of certain categories of documents whilst the arbitration was pending. The three categories identified were extremely broad,[185] which formed a basis for objection by the respondent. On consideration, the Tribunal concluded that the request should fail for lack of necessity or urgency: the claimant was unable to prove that there was a risk that any relevant documents would be destroyed, and in any event, the request would place an unfair burden on the respondent if compliance were required.[186] As such, the Tribunal injected (or perhaps only emphasized) an element of 'reasonableness' in the calculation of urgency and irreparable prejudice:

181 Oellers-Frahm, 'Article 41', p. 940.

182 See e.g. *CEMEX Caracas Investments BV and CEMEX Caracas II Investments BV* v. *Venezuela*, ICSID Case No ARB/08/15 (Provisional Measures, 3 March 2010), at ¶ 46.

183 Further: Schreuer et al., *ICSID Commentary*, pp. 780–93; L. Malintoppi, 'Provisional Measures in Recent ICSID Proceedings: What Parties Request and What Tribunals Order', in C. Binder, U. Kriebaum, A. Reinisch and S. Wittich (eds.), *International Investment Law for the 21st Century: Essays in Honour of Christoph Schreuer* (Oxford: Oxford University Press, 2009) pp. 172–81; C. Mouawad and E. Silbert, 'A Guide to Interim Measures in Investor-State Arbitration' (2013) 29 Arb. Int'l 381, 400–16. Cf. *Burkina Faso/Mali*, ICJ Reports 1986 p. 3, at 9, in which a Chamber of the ICJ awarded provisional measures due to the risk that 'armed actions within the territory in dispute could result in the destruction of evidence material to the Chamber's eventual decision'.

184 *Biwater Gauff* v. *Tanzania*, ICSID Case No ARB/05/22, at ¶ 76. Further: Malintoppi, 'Provisional Measures in Recent ICSID Proceedings', pp. 161–4.

185 As broken down by the respondent, the requests in their totality encompassed some sixty types of document, in most cases without a time limit: *RDC* v. *Guatemala*, ICSID Case No ARB/07/23, at ¶ 33.

186 *Ibid.*, at ¶ 36.

> Since no qualifications on the powers of an ICSID Tribunal to recommend provisional measures found their way into the text of the ICSID Convention, the standard to be applied is one of reasonableness, after consideration of all the circumstances of the request and after taking into account the rights to be protected and their susceptibility to irreversible damage should the tribunal fail to issue a recommendation.[187]

The ICSID jurisprudence surrounding the award of interim relief to protect procedural rights has resulted in a further development in this respect, namely the circumvention (or automatic satisfaction) of the urgency standard in particular cases.[188] In *Abaclat* v. *Argentina*, the respondent filed a request for provisional measures requesting, *inter alia*, an urgent hearing for the questioning of certain witnesses and an injunction to prevent the applicant from destroying certain documents. The Tribunal determined that the first request failed for lack of urgency,[189] but found that urgency existed in relation to the second. However, it declared in relation to the latter that 'even if urgency were not at stake, the Tribunal finds that it can recommend provisional measures for the preservation of Respondent's rights of defense'.[190] A slightly different emphasis was placed on the same principle by the Tribunal in *Quiborax* v. *Bolivia*, which recognized a general right to the procedural integrity of arbitral proceedings as inhering in the parties. Measures designed for the protection of this right were considered to be urgent *ipso facto*, as any prejudice to them necessarily could only occur prior to the final award – as such, urgency did not need to be independently proved. The Tribunal said:

> The Tribunal agrees with Claimants that if measures are intended to protect the procedural integrity of the arbitration, in particular with respect to access to or integrity of the evidence, they are urgent by definition. Indeed, the question of whether a Party has the opportunity to present its case or rely on the integrity of specific evidence is essential to (and therefore cannot await) the rendering of an award on the merits.[191]

An interesting corollary of this decision concerns the need for measures to protect a right *pendente lite*. Self-evidently, a right to procedural integrity is unlikely to be a subject of litigation in the same manner as a breach of state immunity might be. *Quiborax* v. *Bolivia* in particular deals with this as recognizing procedural integrity as an independent basis for the

[187] *Ibid.*, at ¶ 34. [188] Mouawad and Silbert, 'Guide to Interim Measures', 389.

[189] *Abaclat and Others* v. *Argentine Republic*, ICSID Case No ARB/07/5 (Procedural Order No 11, 27 June 2012), at ¶ 14.

[190] *Ibid.*, at ¶ 20. [191] *Quiborax* v. *Bolivia*, ICSID Case No. ARB/06/02, at ¶ 153.

award of interim relief, in much the same way as the commonly given injunction against acts or omissions likely to exacerbate or extend the dispute.[192] Another reading is that such measures are still designed to protect a right subject to litigation – but that the measure requested is procedural in nature, for example, the preservation of evidence of expropriation permits an expropriation to be proved and subsequently redressed. This itself has a further implication, namely the injection of urgency back into the calculation (as the measures are now conceived as protecting a right *pendente lite*) and thus upending the concept of urgency *ipso facto*.

4. The European Court of Human Rights

Like the ICJ, the ECtHR has read a requirement of irreparable prejudice into the wording of Rule 39, with the Grand Chamber noting that 'in practice the Court applies Rule 39 only if there is an imminent risk of irreparable damage'.[193] Furthermore, the identification of possible prejudice is rendered easier by the nature of the rights subject to consideration in this respect, with the Grand Chamber indicating that Rule 39 would only be utilized in cases concerning the right to life (ECHR Article 2), the right not to be subjected to torture or inhuman treatment (ECHR Article 3) and, exceptionally, the right to privacy and family life (ECHR Article 8). Whilst other rights under the ECHR are hypothetically capable of being prejudiced irreparably, the Court has been careful to limit the application of Rule 39 to 'limited spheres', and the prejudice caused to a right other than those identified would need to be 'exceptional' for interim relief to be awarded.[194]

[192] That said, and certainly some (though not all) procedural tactics may have the effect of extending the dispute, thereby subsuming the practice of the *Abaclat* v. *Argentina* and *Quiborax* v. *Bolivia* tribunals within a recognized category.

[193] *Mamatkulov and Askarov* [2005] ECtHR 46827/99 and 46951/99 (GC), at ¶ 104. See also *ibid.*, at ¶ 125, stating that the object of Rule 39 was to avoid 'irreversible situations that would prevent the Court from properly examining the application and, where appropriate, securing to the applicant the practical and effective benefit of the Convention rights asserted'.

[194] *Ibid.* Other rights with respect to which such 'exceptional' relief has been awarded include the right to a fair trial (ECHR Art. 6), the right to liberty and security (ECHR Art. 8), the right of individual petition (ECHR Art. 34) and the right to property (ECHR Protocol 1 (Enforcement of certain Rights and Freedoms not included in Section I of the Convention), 20 March 1952, in force 18 May 1954, ETS 9, Art. 1): ECtHR Registry, *Article 39 of the Rules of Court*, ¶¶ 24–6.

Given the similarity between the standards, it may be inferred that the ECtHR acquired the criterion of irreparability from the jurisprudence of the ICJ. However, given the particular character of the ECHR and the rights contained therein, the jurisprudence surrounding irreparability has become highly specialized, particularly in relation to immigration proceedings. When examining a request for interim relief concerning a deportation case under ECHR Article 3, the Registry – and if required, the Court – will examine:

- the general situation in the destination country;
- the existence of a personal risk for the applicant established by a substantiated account;
- the seriousness of the damage alleged in the case of return;
- the elements of proof provided and their *prima facie* authenticity (arrest/search warrant, medical certificates etc.);
- the relevant case law of the Court (judgments and decisions but also precedents relating to Rule 39); and
- reasoning of decisions of national authorities and courts.[195]

The final point represents an interesting departure from the other courts and tribunals considered, with the Registry placing particular weight to the reasoning of domestic authorities 'which it considers better placed to evaluate the evidence presented before it'.[196] Accordingly, it follows that the 'detailed and precise reasoning of national courts constitutes a solid base allowing the Court to be assured that the examination of the risks alleged by the applicant has been in conformity with the requirements of the Convention, and consequently to conclude by the possible rejection of the request for interim measures'.[197] This effectively introduces the margin of appreciation doctrine found elsewhere in the Court's jurisprudence[198] to the dictation of terms of interim relief. The fact that this is express and somewhat institutionalized is a unique contribution by the ECtHR to the comparative jurisprudence surrounding provisional measures, although it could be argued that the sheer mass of applications that the Court receives in relation to immigration forces its reliance on sufficiently detailed domestic reasoning. For the Court and

[195] *Ibid.*, ¶ 28. [196] *Ibid.*, ¶ 29. [197] *Ibid.*

[198] See e.g. Y. Arai-Takahashi, *The Margin of Appreciation Doctrine and the Principle of Proportionality in the Jurisprudence of the ECHR* (Antwerp: Intersetia, 2001); A. Legg, *The Margin of Appreciation in International Human Rights Law: Deference and Proportionality* (Oxford: Oxford University Press, 2012).

Registry to do their own assessment of every such application would be thoroughly unfeasible, making a measure of deference to national authorities unavoidable.

As with the other courts and tribunals considered, the ECtHR also employs a standard of temporal urgency as a prerequisite to interim relief, in the sense that the irreparable harm identified must be 'imminent'.[199] Imminence is obviously dependent on the particular circumstances of the case, but in the context of immigration matters, the term means that the deportation is about to take place or the person concerned can be removed without any further decisions being taken.[200] In this sense, the exhaustion of local remedies rule in ECHR Article 35 is incorporated into the provisional measures calculus, though it is confined to those local remedies with the capacity to suspend the order of deportation – as such, a right to appeal a decision to deport from the country of deportation would not modify a conclusion of urgency.[201]

D. *The scope and force of provisional measures*

1. The International Court of Justice

The question of whether provisional measures ordered under Article 41 of the PCIJ[202] and ICJ Statutes were binding proved to be a vexed question for much of their shared history, with the Court in both iterations being placed in the somewhat fortunate position of not being asked to rule on the matter directly until comparatively recently.[203] As is by now well known, the Court in the *LaGrand* case adopted a functional reading of Article 41, concluding that:

> The object and purpose of the Statute is to enable the Court to fulfil the functions provided for therein, and, in particular, the basic function

[199] *Mamatkulov and Askarov*, [2005] ECtHR 46827/99 and 46951/99 (GC), at ¶ 104.

[200] Keller and Marti, 'Interim Relief Compared', 341.

[201] Practice Direction: Requests for Interim Measures, 1.

[202] An examination of the private deliberations of the PCIJ on the amendment of its procedural rules on multiple occasions throughout the 1920s and 1930s indicates that the personal view of nearly all of the judges at that time was that provisional measures were in fact *not* binding: Miles, 'Origin of Provisional Measures', IV.2. For the view of the Registrar of the Court at the time, see Å. Hammarskjöld, 'Quelques aspects de la question des mesures conservatoires en droit international positif' (1935) 5 ZaöRV 5.

[203] Indeed, Fitzmaurice in 1958 declared it 'perhaps unlikely' that the Court would even pronounce on the question: G. Fitzmaurice, *The Law and Procedure of the International Court of Justice*, (Cambridge: Grotius Publications, 1986), vol. 2, p. 548.

> of judicial settlement of international disputes by binding decisions in accordance with Article 59 of the Statute. The context in which Article 41 has to be seen within the Statute is to prevent the Court from being hampered in the exercise of its functions because the respective rights of the parties to a dispute before the Court are not preserved. It follows from the object and purpose of the Statute, as well as from the terms of Article 41 when read in their context, that the power to indicate provisional measures entails that such measures should be binding, inasmuch as the power in question is based on the necessity, when the circumstances call for it, to safeguard, and to avoid prejudice to, the rights of the parties as determined by the final judgment of the Court. The contention that provisional measures indicated under Article 41 might not be binding would be contrary to the object and purpose of the Article.[204]

Although this interpretation of the Statute prompted some criticism[205] – especially as the wording of Article 41 is predicated on the apparently less-than-mandatory concept of the 'indication' of provisional measures – it nonetheless represents the new status quo,[206] and, as mentioned, may have contributed to recent efforts by the Court to safeguard Article 41 against frivolous applications for relief.[207]

Questions may be asked, however, as to the utility of making provisional measures binding in the context of proceedings before the ICJ.[208] Aside from the additional moral compulsion to comply with the Court's directions, the requirement of irreparable prejudice would indicate that the breach of provisional measures cannot be made good subsequently, as the execution of the LaGrand brothers made abundantly clear. Adding to this is the fact that the ICJ is only minded to award damages in extremely limited circumstances,[209] a breach of provisional measures is far more likely to be met with a simple declaration of wrongdoing rather than a

[204] *LaGrand*, ICJ Reports 2001 p. 466, at 502–3. Further: J. A. Frowein, 'Provisional Measures by the International Court of Justice – The *LaGrand* Case' (2002) 62 ZaöRV 54; R. Jennings, 'The *LaGrand* Case' (2002) 1 LPICT 13.

[205] The most articulate of these is Thirlway, *Law and Procedure*, vol. 1, pp. 956–8.

[206] *Ibid.*, vol. 2, p. 1807.

[207] Lee-Iwamoto, 'Repercussions of *LaGrand*', 247–51.

[208] Oellers-Frahm, 'Article 14', pp. 958–9.

[209] Indeed, such damages have only been issued in two cases, being *Corfu Channel (UK* v. *Albania)*, Compensation, ICJ Reports 1949 p. 224 and *Ahmadou Sadio Diallo (Guinea* v. *Democratic Republic of the Congo)*, ICJ, Compensation Judgment of 19 June 2012. The PCIJ only awarded damages once, in *SS Wimbledon (UK, France, Italy and Japan* v. *Germany; Poland intervening)* (1923) PCIJ Ser. A No. 1. Generally, damages will only be awarded where the claimant submits a claim for indemnification to prevent violation of the *non ultra petita* rule: Oellers-Frahm, 'Article 14', p. 959. Such an application for a breach of provisional measures was made in *Cameroon* v. *Nigeria*, but the Court found the allegation of breach not proved: *Land and Maritime Boundary between Cameroon and*

pecuniary penalty. The Court may choose to take the breach into account for the purposes of determining final liability,[210] but this is no more than was done by the PCIJ when the question of the binding nature of provisional measures putatively remained open. Although breach of provisional measures under such an approach may give rise to a right to countermeasures on the part of the aggrieved party,[211] this right may be limited by the general obligation of the parties not to aggravate or extend the dispute.[212]

Insofar as the scope of provisional measures is concerned, one of the cardinal rules is that the measure cannot act as an interim judgment so as to resolve the dispute. This was established by the PCIJ in the *Factory at Chorzów (Indemnities)* case, in which Germany argued that, following the ruling of the Court in the *Polish Upper Silesia* case,[213] Polish damages had been fixed at 'a certain minimum'. As such, Germany applied for provisional measures directing Poland to pay the minimum amount, with the balance to be determined at final judgment. The Court unanimously rejected the request without requesting submissions from Poland and without consulting either of the ad hoc judges.[214] The Court's reasoning was perfunctory, noting only that 'the request of the German government cannot be regarded as relating to the indication of measures of interim protection, but as designed to obtain an interim judgment in favour of a part of the [German] claim'.[215] In other words, provisional measures cannot be used as a mechanism to achieve complete or partial resolution of the main claim as an 'interim judgment'.[216]

The position in *Factory at Chorzów (Indemnities)* notwithstanding, however, the Court has on occasion issued orders for interim relief which

Nigeria (Cameroon v. *Nigeria; Equatorial Guinea intervening)*, ICJ Reports2002 p. 303, at 453. Further: Lee-Iwamoto, 'Repercussions of *LaGrand*', 251–60.

[210] See e.g. *Application of the Convention on the Prevention and Punishment of the Crime of Genocide (Bosnia and Herzegovina* v. *Servia and Montenegro)*, ICJ Reports 2007 p. 43, at 236: 'for the purpose of reparation, the Respondent's non-compliance with the provisional measures ordered is an aspect of, or merges with, its breaches of the substantive obligations of prevention and punishment laid upon it by the Convention'.

[211] See Articles on the Responsibility of States for Internationally Wrongful Acts, ILC Ybk2001/II(2) 31, Art. 49(1).

[212] *Electricity Company of Sofia and Bulgaria* (1939) PCIJ Ser. A/B No. 79, at 199.

[213] *Certain German Interests in Polish Upper Silesia (Germany* v. *Poland)* (1926) PCIJ Ser. A No. 7, 81.

[214] *Factory at Chorzów (Indemnities)* (1927) PCIJ Ser. A No. 12, at 10. [215] *Ibid.*

[216] H. Thirlway, 'Indication of Provisional Measures by the International Court of Justice', in R. Berhardt (ed.), *Interim Measures Indicated by International Courts* (Berlin: Springer-Verlag, 1994), pp. 27–8.

appear to resolve the dispute before it, at least partially.[217] The obvious example is the *Teheran Hostages* case, in which the Court ordered the release by Iran of the detained US consular personnel that were the subjects of the dispute, as well as the return of seized diplomatic premises to US control.[218] The US, moreover, was not required to provide security for the transfer. Whilst it did not render the dispute entirely moot – the question of whether Iran had breached the Vienna Convention on Diplomatic Relations[219] remained to be determined – the order certainly purported to neutralize the main points of contention. Had Iran complied with the order and then gone on to win on the merits, it seems unlikely that the US would have handed the hostages back. Whilst it may be validly argued that the failure to order such relief would have resulted in irreparable prejudice to the interests of the US, that is not an excuse for the engaging in *de facto* resolution of the dispute at the provisional measures phase, especially when other options remain available to the Court. In *Teheran Hostages*, it would have been sufficient for the Court simply to order that the hostages be returned to US consular premises in Teheran and not harmed until the Court had dispensed final judgment. This would have bought the Court's Order into line with less intrusive measures such as those ordered in the *Fisheries Jurisdiction* and *Nuclear Weapons* cases. There, the subject of the claim was a particular course of conduct undertaken by the respondent, with the substance of the relief ordered being the temporary cessation of that course of conduct. Whilst in both cases this provoked relatively caustic dissenting opinions,[220] the essential point of difference is that their reversal did not require the cooperation of a party that lost on the merits. The same cannot be said of the Court's approach in *Teheran Hostages*.

2. Dispute settlement under UNCLOS

The difficulties only recently resolved by the ICJ with respect to the binding nature of provisional measures never troubled dispute settlement

[217] S. Oda, 'Provisional Measures: The practice of the International Court of Justice', in V. Lowe and M. Fitzmaurice (eds.), *Fifty Years of the International Court of Justice: Essays in Honour of Sir Robert Jennings* (Cambridge: Cambridge University Press, 2007), pp. 553–4. An alternative reading of the situation would be that the orders, whilst not an interim judgment, were wholly disproportionate.

[218] *Teheran Hostages*, ICJ Reports 1979 p. 7, at 21.

[219] 18 April 1961, in force 24 April 1964, 500 UNTS 95.

[220] *Fisheries Jurisdiction (UK* v. *Iceland)*, ICJ Reports 1972 p. 12, at 25 (Judge Padilla-Nervo, diss.); *Fisheries Jurisdiction (FRG* v. *Iceland)*, ICJ Reports 1972 p. 30, at 42 (Judge Padilla-Nervo, diss.); *Nuclear Tests (Australia* v. *France)*, ICJ Reports 1972 p. 99, 113 (Judge Forster, diss.); *Nuclear Tests (New Zealand* v. *France)*, ICJ Reports 1973 p. 135, at 148 (Judge Forster, diss.).

bodies acting under UNCLOS Article 290, as paragraph (6) of the provision creates an obligation on the part of states to comply with measures so ordered. In addition, both UNCLOS Article 290(1) and (5) permit provisional measures to be 'prescribed', rather than merely 'indicated' or 'suggested'.[221] This has filtered down into the cases themselves: for example, in the *Land Reclamation* case, ITLOS prescribed the creation of an independent group of experts to determine the effects of Singapore's land reclamation project and directed Singapore to halt any manifestation of the project that might cause irreparable prejudice to Malaysia's rights or serious harm to the marine environment.[222]

It is possible, however, that ITLOS has reserved the right to order non-binding provisional measures: in *M/V Saiga (No. 2)*, the Tribunal *prescribed* that Guinea should refrain from taking or enforcing judicial measures against the *M/V Saiga* and its associated personnel, but only *recommended* that the parties attempt to find a negotiated solution and avoid taking any measure which might aggravate or extend the dispute.[223] Similarly, in *MOX Plant*, the Annex VII tribunal *affirmed* the previous mandatory orders issued by ITLOS, whilst only *calling on* the parties to prevent the aggravation of the dispute.[224] A possible explanation for this practice may be that whilst Article 290(1) makes express mention of the granting of measures to prevent prejudice to rights or serious harm to the marine environment, measures generally requiring non-escalation of the dispute possess no textual basis, leading to a certain coyness in the wording of provisional measures by the relevant bodies.

Beyond this, the UNCLOS Article 290 jurisprudence on the scope and effect of provisional measures is similar to that of the ICJ. Although neither ITLOS nor an Annex VII tribunal has yet to forbid the granting of an interim judgment by way of provisional measures, the principle has been reiterated extra-curially by its former President.[225] It also has a textual basis – UNCLOS Article 290(1) clearly states that the purpose of measures under the provision is preservation pending final judgment, not anticipation of that judgment.[226]

221 Mensah, 'Provisional Measures in ITLOS', 45; Wolfrum, 'Provisional Measures at ITLOS', pp. 184–7.

222 *Land Reclamation* (2003) 126 ILR 486, at 506.

223 *M/V Saiga (No. 2)* (1998) 117 ILR 111, at 124–5.

224 *MOX Plant* (2003) 126 ILR 310, at 331.

225 Wolfrum, 'Provisional Measures at ITLOS', p. 183.

226 The timeline for preservation is self-evidently even shorter with respect to measures under UNCLOS Art. 290(5).

However, like the ICJ, ITLOS has been willing to do precisely what President Wolfrum cautioned against extra-curially, and take a decision 'which *de facto* or *de jure* cannot be reversed by the final judgment'.[227] In the *ARA Libertad* case, ITLOS – acting on behalf of an Annex VII tribunal pursuant to UNCLOS Article 290(5) – directed Ghana to release the seized Argentine vessel that was the subject of the dispute.[228] Following this order, Ghana elected to settle the dispute[229] rather than pursue the matter further – however, again, if Ghana were to succeed on the merits, it is highly unlikely that Argentina would have return the vessel to the port of Tema.

However, ITLOS adopted a preferable approach in the *Arctic Sunrise* case. There the Tribunal – again acting under UNCLOS Article 290(5) – directed Russia to release a Dutch-flagged vessel operated by the environmental group Greenpeace and its crew from detention in Murmansk.[230] The ship had been involved in a protest against a Russian oilrig operating within the Russian exclusive economic zone (EEZ). The Tribunal did not precisely follow its earlier decision in *ARA Libertad*, as the ordered release was contingent on the payment of a €3.6 million bond, a measure criticized by Judge Jesus as amounting to a 'back-door prompt release procedure' analogous to that available in cases involving illegal fishing in the EEZ under UNCLOS Article 73(2).[231] The requirement of collateral – a response to an offer made by the Netherlands[232] – clearly goes a long way towards ameliorating the concerns generated by decisions such as *Teheran Hostages* and *ARA Libertad*, though it might perhaps be suggested (as indeed did Judge Kulyk[233]) that the Tribunal should not have been quite so hasty in releasing the vessel and its crew where other, less invasive options were available. This is especially the case when the release of the vessel and crew may compromise a domestic criminal investigation, as was the case in *Arctic Sunrise*.[234]

3. Investor-state arbitration under ICSID

With respect to the binding nature of provisional measures, ICSID Article 47 suffers from similar problems to Article 41 of the ICJ Statute.

[227] Wolfrum, 'Provisional Measures at ITLOS', p. 184.

[228] *ARA Libertad*, ITLOS Case No. 20, at ¶ 108. Ironically, Judge Wolfrum agreed with this decision: *ibid.*, at ¶ 70 (Judges Wolfrum and Cot).

[229] See www.pca-cpa.org/showpage.asp?pag_id=1526(accessed7November2013).

[230] *Arctic Sunrise*, ITLOS Case No. 22, at ¶ 105.

[231] *Ibid.*, at ¶ 7 (Judge Jesus).

[232] *Ibid.*, at ¶ 91–3.

[233] *Ibid.*, at ¶ 11 (Judge Kulyk, diss.)

[234] *Ibid.*, at ¶ 7(c) (Judge Jesus).

Indeed, the textual argument with respect to binding measures under ICSID Article 47 is perhaps weaker still, with the provision only allowing tribunals to 'recommend' provisional measures. Nonetheless, the question as to the binding nature of such measures has not caused any appreciable hand wringing on the part of ICSID tribunals. When the question was posed in *Maffezini* v. *Spain*, the Tribunal simply stated that it did not believe the drafters of ICSID and the Centre's Arbitral Rules to have intended any more than a semantic difference between the term 'recommend' used in ICSID Article 47 and Rule 39 of the Arbitral Rules and the term 'order' used elsewhere. Accordingly, it was said '[t]he Tribunal's authority to rule on provisional measures is no less binding than that of a final award'.[235] More substantial reasoning was provided by the Tribunal in *Casado* v. *Chile*, which had the benefit of the ICJ's decision in *LaGrand*. The Tribunal applied the reasoning of that decision to ICSID Article 47, noting that its logic seemed 'manifestly' to apply by analogy.[236]

Insofar as consequences for the breach of ICSID provisional measures are concerned, the options available are limited:[237] as a general rule, provisional measures are conceived of as orders of the relevant tribunal, not awards, and are therefore not subject to the enforcement regime of ICSID Articles 53–5.[238] As with the ICJ, there is the potential for the award of damages on the application or counterclaim of the aggrieved party – and it might be thought that the parties in investor-state arbitration will generally be more inclined to request them and to be in possession of an easily quantifiable claim. In addition, ICSID tribunals have also indicated that any breach of provisional measures may be taken into account in the final decision on the merits. In *AGIP* v. *Congo*, the respondent persistently failed to comply with provisional measures, leading the Tribunal to take into account the fact that this intransigence had deprived the claimant of the chance to access certain documents.[239] In *MINE* v. *Guinea*, the Tribunal warned the claimant that any failure to comply could have

[235] *Emilio Agustín Maffezini* v. *Spain*, Provisional Measures (1999) 5 ICSID Reports 387, at 394.

[236] *Casado* v. *Chile* (2001) 6 ICSID Reports 373, at 381. The Tribunal also drew on the case law of the US–Iran Claims Tribunal: see e.g. *Rockwell International Systems* v. *Iran* (1983-I) 2 Iran–US CTR 310, at 310–11. Further: Caron, 'Interim Measures of Protection', 508–11.

[237] A proposal to have ICSID Art. 47 include a power on the part of the Tribunal to 'fix a penalty for failure to comply with provisional measures' was defeated at the drafting table: Schreuer et al., *ICSID Commentary*, p. 768; Caron, 'Interim Measures of Protection', 511.

[238] But cf. Mouawad and Silbert, 'Guide to Interim Measures', 416–33.

[239] *AGIP SpA* v. *People's Republic of the Congo* (1979) 1 ICSID Reports 306, at 317.

adverse consequences in the final award. Tardiness in complying with the Tribunal's direction to abandon attachment proceedings in Belgium and Switzerland resulted in Guinea counterclaiming for costs and legal fees, and being awarded a portion thereof to the tune of US$210,000.[240]

The emphasis on preservation in ICSID Article 47 leads to the safe conclusion that, as with Article 41 of the ICJ Statute and Article 290 of UNCLOS, provisional measures under this provision cannot amount to an interim judgment. Moreover, unlike cases such as *Teheran Hostages* and *ARA Libertad*, no example of interim relief by an ICSID tribunal has effectively determined an element of an active dispute on either a *de facto* or *de jure* basis.

4. The European Court of Human Rights

Insofar as its relationship with the ECtHR is concerned, the influence of the ICJ has been greatest in determining the binding nature of provisional measures. The original position of the Court on the question was that interim relief awarded pursuant to the Court's Rules was not binding. In the 1991 case of *Cruz Veras*,[241] the Court was required to rule on the binding nature (*vel non*) of a provisional stay of extradition ordered by the European Commission on Human Rights, and whether Sweden's breach of this directive breached the applicant's right to petition the Court or Commission under ECHR Article 25(1). The Court held that the absence of an express provision in the ECHR granting the Commission the capacity to award interim relief meant that any attempt by that body to arrogate such a power through its procedural rules could not be binding on the parties.[242] Furthermore, it was said, it would strain the plain meaning of the words 'undertake not to hinder in any way the effective exercise of this right' as they appeared in Article 25 to read the provision as requiring compliance with a non-binding recommendation from the Commission.[243] Although at that time there had been almost total compliance with such directives, the Court preferred to view this as a matter of 'good faith co-operation' rather than evidence of a belief on the part of the contracting parties that such measures were binding.[244] The Court further said that recourse to general international law was unhelpful,

240 *Maritime International Nominees Establishment* v. *Guinea* (1988) 4 ICSID Reports 3, at 69, 77.

241 *Cruz Varas* v. *Sweden* [1991] ECtHR 15576/89. See also *Čonka* v. *Belgium* [2001] ECtHR 51564/99.

242 *Cruz Varas* [1991] ECtHR 15576/89, at ¶ 98.

243 *Ibid.*, at ¶ 99.

244 *Ibid.*, at ¶ 100.

as no uniform rule as to the binding nature of provisional measures had yet emerged.[245]

This position, however, was the subject of a startling *volte face* by the Court in *Mamatkulov and Abdurasulovic*.[246] In that case, the applicants argued, *inter alia*, that Turkey's decision to breach a Rule 39 directive staying the extradition of two Uzbek nationals back to Uzbekistan violated the applicants' right of petition, now housed in ECHR Article 34. Substantively, the case was a nearly identical reflection of the facts of *Cruz Veras*, with the only difference being that relief was ordered by the Court as opposed to the (now-defunct) Commission. The wider landscape of international law had, however, been altered by the ICJ's ruling on the binding nature of provisional measures in *LaGrand*, prompting the Court to revisit its earlier decision. It concluded that states party to the Convention were bound to comply with interim measures and refrain from any act or omission that would undermine the authority and effectiveness of the final judgment – accordingly, in breaching the Court's Rule 39 directive, Turkey had violated ECHR Article 34.[247] In reaching this conclusion the Court referred to the need for an effective and evolutive interpretation[248] of the ECHR so as to render the rights contained therein practical and effective.[249] Also cited was Article 31(3)(c) of the Vienna Convention on the Law of Treaties (VCLT),[250] requiring that relevant rules of international law applicable between the parties be taken into account in treaty interpretation.[251] The reasoning of the ICJ in *LaGrand* was key in this respect,[252] forming part of a wider review of the practice of international courts and tribunals that revealed the emergence of the

[245] *Ibid.*, at ¶ 101.

[246] Further: C. Tams, 'Interim Orders by the European Court of Human Rights: Comments on *Mamatkulov and Abdurasulovic v Turkey*' (2003) 63 ZaöRV 681; C. Brown, 'Strasbourg Follows Suit on Provisional Measures' (2003) 62 CLJ 532.

[247] *Mamatkulov and Abdurasulovic* [2003] ECtHR 46827/99 and 46951/99, at ¶¶ 110–11.

[248] See: R. Bernhardt, 'Evolutive Treaty Interpretation, especially of the European Convention on Human Rights (1999) 42 German YIL 12; M. Dawidowicz, 'The Effect of the Passage of Time on the Interpretation of Treaties: Some Reflections on *Costa Rica v Nicaragua*' (2011) 24 LJIL 201; J. Crawford, *State Responsibility: The General Part* (Cambridge: Cambridge University Press, 2013), pp. 246–50; E. Bjorge, *The Evolutionary Interpretation of Treaties* (Oxford: Oxford University Press, 2014). See also *Navigational and Related Rights (Costa Rica* v. *Nicaragua)*, ICJ Reports 2009 pp. 213, 242.

[249] *Mamatkulov and Abdurasulovic* [2003] ECtHR 46827/99 and 46951/99, at ¶¶ 93–105.

[250] 22 May 1969, in force 27 January 1980, 1155 UNTS 331.

[251] See: C. McLachlan, 'The Principle of Systematic Integration and Article 31(3)(c) of the Vienna Convention' (2005) 54 ICLQ 279.

[252] *Mamatkulov and Abdurasulovic* [2003] ECtHR 46827/99 and 46951/99, at ¶ 103.

uniform view as to the binding nature of provisional measures in general international law that was lacking at the time of *Cruz Veras*. On appeal, the Grand Chamber adopted a similar view of the relevance of *LaGrand*.[253]

IV. Provisional measures and the problem of fragmentation

A. *Substantive fragmentation and the uniformity of provisional measures*

When considering the problem of fragmentation in international law, provisional measures are not generally considered to contribute to the problem. Substantive fragmentation arises when two international courts or tribunals that are formally equal issue conflicting pronouncements on the same point of law. Several examples have arisen as between the ICJ and the International Criminal Tribunal for the former Yugoslavia, most famously in the context of state responsibility, and more particularly, in the attribution of the conduct of non-state actors to a state.[254] It may be argued that this is not a problem in the context of provisional measures, as each individual court or tribunal draws its power to award provisional measures from its own constituent instrument and procedural rules – as a result, they are not purporting to apply the same law, but a *sui generis* item of procedure unique to that particular tribunal. The ICJ applies a different law of procedural measures which is different to that applied by ITLOS, which is different to that utilized in ICSID arbitration, which differs in turn from that employed by the ECtHR and so on.

But to adopt such a view would be to miss the point. What Section III of this chapter has attempted to establish is that although the constitutional sources of the power to award provisional measures are formally separate, dispute settlement bodies under UNCLOS, ICSID and the ECHR clearly conceive of these sources as expressions of a wider general principle of international law.[255] The Annex VII tribunal in *MOX Plant* made reference to a 'general requirement' arising from 'international judicial practice'.[256] Similarly, the ICSID tribunal in *Casado* v. *Chile* made reference to requirements arising from 'international case

[253] *Mamatkulov and Askarov* [2005] ECtHR 46827/99 and 46951/99, at ¶117. Cf. *ibid.*, at ¶¶ 147–51 (Judges Caflisch, Türmen and Kovler, diss.).

[254] Crawford, *State Responsibility*, pp. 146–56. The matter appears to have been resolved by the Court in the *Bosnian Genocide* case: ICJ Reports 2007 p. 43, at 209.

[255] Further: Brown, *A Common Law*, pp. 126–7; Elkind, *Interim Protection*, pp. 3–4.

[256] *MOX Plant* (2003) 126 ILR 310, at 328.

law'.[257] In *Mamatkulov and Abdurasulovic*, the ECtHR engaged in a lengthy review of other international courts and tribunals before reinterpreting the ECHR in light of VCLT Article 31(1)(c).[258] It may therefore be hypothesized that a uniform law of provisional measures is emerging or has emerged within international law and that the tribunals discussed here are purporting to pronounce on its content. As such, the risk of substantive fragmentation in the event of inconsistent statements of law is evident.

This risk, however, has not as yet materialized – at least insofar as the tribunals considered are concerned. An examination of the substantive preconditions for the award of provisional measures – largely unwritten within the relevant treaty provisions – demonstrates uniformity in the jurisprudence. All of the tribunals considered have incorporated requirements of, *inter alia*, limited purpose, urgency and irreparability and binding force into their jurisprudence, even where such requirements are not specifically forced upon them. All but one has adopted a further limitation of requiring proof of *prima facie* jurisdiction as a prerequisite to relief. Any deviations tend to be based on the exigencies of the constitutive instrument or the particular jurisdiction of the tribunal – for example, the capacity to award provisional measures on behalf of another tribunal in the context of UNCLOS Article 290(5) has resulted in a slightly different consideration of the meaning of urgency. Likewise, the need for ICSID tribunals to make frequent awards in order to protect procedural rights has resulted in a more developed jurisprudence in that respect. The ECtHR has outsourced triage for Rule 39 applications to its Registry and with respect to certain decisions, has come to rely heavily on the earlier treatment of domestic authorities in identifying a risk of irreparable harm.

Moreover, the apparent source of these conditions is, for the most part, the jurisprudence of the ICJ,[259] both in terms of the influence of its Statute on UNCLOS and ICSID (the ECHR sitting apart in this respect), but also arguably due to its position at the informal apex of the system of international courts and tribunals. Unlike the debate with respect to

[257] *Casado* v. *Chile* (2001) 8 ICSID Reports 383, at 378.

[258] *Mamatkulov and Abdurasulovic* [2003] ECtHR 46827/99 and 46951/99, at ¶ 99–111.

[259] An exception might be identified in the case of the *prima facie* establishment of the disputed rights under ICSID, which may have developed independently of the International Court.

attribution and non-state actors, there has been no express refutation of a decision of the ICJ with respect to provisional measures. Moreover, the willingness to adopt the reasoning of the ICJ has apparently increased over time – for example, whilst the order on provisional measures in *M/V Saiga (No. 2)* was silent on the question of urgency and irreparable harm (with Judge Liang in a separate opinion rejecting both concepts as applicable), both had become central elements of the UNCLOS Article 290 jurisprudence by the time of *M/V Louisa* and *ARA Libertad* a decade later. Similarly, whilst early ICSID provisional measures decisions such as *AGIP* v. *Congo* and *MINE* v. *Guinea* made little reference to the ICJ, the Court's reasoning in *LaGrand* was central to the order in *Casado* v. *Chile*, and its case law continues to be cited with regularity in more recent decisions such as *Churchill Mining* v. *Indonesia. LaGrand* was further key in convincing the ECtHR to abandon the position established in *Cruz Varas* and determine that measures awarded under Rule 39 were binding in *Mamatkulov and Abdurasulovic.*

B. *The future of provisional measures*

The next question that might be asked is what direction the future jurisprudence of these institutions might take. In the first place, it would not be unreasonable to expect that the most recent innovation of the ICJ, the testing of the plausibility of the rights on which the claim for provisional measures is based, might find its way into the jurisprudence of UNCLOS, as it already has (perhaps independently) with ICSID. Given that the rights contained in the ECHR are self-evident, it is unlikely that the ECtHR will adopt a similar test. In the second place, and more interestingly, it might be asked whether the jurisprudence of other institutions will begin influencing the practice of the ICJ. Certainly, both ITLOS and Annex VII tribunals and ICSID tribunals possess expertise in certain areas that the ICJ lacks, as does the ECtHR. ITLOS, for example, may be able to make a contribution to the award of provisional measures when considering rights *erga omnes* through its consideration of serious harm to the marine environment under UNCLOS Article 290(1), not to mention its use of collateral in *Arctic Sunrise* to offset the release of a contested asset on a provisional basis. ICSID, more significantly, has generated a large amount of provisional measures jurisprudence suited to the protection of procedural rights such as the preservation of evidence and the exclusivity of proceedings, resulting in some tribunals recognizing a further basis for the award of provisional measures, namely the protection of procedural integrity. In an institutional sense, the ECtHR offers a potential model for dealing with a serious influx of provisional measures applications – although it is unlikely that the ICJ will ever be faced with a situation of comparable severity.

But notwithstanding the possible relevance of the jurisprudence emerging from other tribunals, it seems unlikely that the Court will refer to provisional measures decisions arising under UNCLOS, ICSID or the ECHR in the same manner as it referred to *Bangladesh* v. *Myanmar* in *Nicaragua* v. *Colombia* or *Al-Adsani* in *Germany* v. *Italy*. Unlike more substantive questions of international law – and irrespective of what other tribunals might think – the Court seems to consider provisional measures as within the Court's internal practice, and thus relatively quarantined from outside influence. In engineering terms then, the Court is presently a check valve – the flow of ideas is relatively uninhibited, but travels in only one direction. That is not to say, however, that a more unconscious influence cannot be exerted.

V. Conclusions

Provisional measures have become one of the most important tools of modern international litigation, and are invoked on a regular basis in a multiplicity of forums. Whilst it seems unlikely that a request for interim relief will become as seemingly de rigueur to every application as, for example, a preliminary objection to jurisdiction, their popularity has increased markedly over time. It is encouraging, therefore, that within the tribunals considered in this chapter a relatively uniform and unfragmented law of provisional measures appears to be in effect.

The central theme of this volume is the notion that the ICJ acts an informal hub of international law to decrease the problems inherent in a system where courts and tribunals are integrated only horizontally. A further theme is that the Court is in the midst of an effort to reassert itself in this respect, increasing its gravitational pull such that other international judicial institutions are pulled into its orbit without the need for visible ties. This chapter agrees with the first theme, but defies (to an extent) the second – the ICJ never needed to reassert itself in defining the law of provisional measures. Rather, it (and the PCIJ before it) invented the modern concept of interim relief and successfully transmitted it to the new institutions that emerged or expanded in the post-Cold War era, both through the text of its Statute and the internal logic of its decisions. Although dispute settlement bodies under UNCLOS, ICSID and the ECHR may seek to elaborate on its earlier work, the central core remains immutable.

10

Just another case of treaty interpretation? Reconciling humanitarian law and human rights law in the ICJ

LAWRENCE HILL-CAWTHORNE

1. Introduction

The second half of the twentieth century witnessed a vast expansion of regimes of individual protection under international law. This, of course, is most clearly illustrated with the emergence of international human rights law (IHRL) in the years immediately following the end of the Second World War, reflected in provisions of the UN Charter[1] and the adoption in 1948 of the Universal Declaration of Human Rights (UDHR).[2] General regional and international human rights treaties soon followed, in which States collectively bound themselves 'to respect and to ensure to all individuals' within their jurisdiction a broad set of enumerated rights.[3] Under

This chapter has benefited considerably from discussions with numerous people, but particular recognition should be given to Professor Dapo Akande and Dr Martins Paparinskis. Any errors or omissions remain the responsibility of the author alone.

[1] Art. 1(3) of the Charter of the United Nations and Statute of the International Court of Justice, 26 June 1945, in force 24 October 1945, 892 UNTS 119 (stating that included within the purposes and principles of the UN is the goal of achieving 'international cooperation . . . in promoting and encouraging respect for human rights and for fundamental freedoms for all without distinction as to race, sex, language, or religion'); H. Lauterpacht, *International Law and Human Rights* (London: Stevens & Sons Ltd, 1950), p. 61 (noting that this constituted 'individuals subjects of the law of nations').

[2] Universal Declaration of Human Rights, 10 December 1948, UN General Assembly Resolution 217 A(III). Although non-binding, the UDHR had important 'moral authority': H. Lauterpacht, 'The Universal Declaration of Human Rights' (1948) 25 *British Yearbook of International Law* 354, 370–5.

[3] Art. 2(1) of the International Covenant on Civil and Political Rights, 16 December 1966, in force 23 March 1976, 999 UNTS 171. See also Art. 1 of the Convention for the Protection of Human Rights and Fundamental Freedoms, 4 November 1950, in force 3 September 1953, ETS No. 126; Art. 1(1) of the American Convention on Human Rights, 22 November 1969, in force 18 July 1978, OAS Treaty Series No. 36.

these treaties, individuals were made direct beneficiaries of rights (in addition to the rights of the other States parties), and this was accompanied by the establishment of international courts and other supervisory organs to which individuals could complain directly about alleged breaches. What was truly novel about these developments was not the role played by individuals as such,[4] but rather the fact that the obligations under these instruments were truly intra-State, in contrast to previous developments in international law on the protection of the individual, which generally fell within the context of inter-State relations, such as the minimum standard of treatment of aliens.[5] Similar developments occurred around the same time with the emergence of international criminal law, exemplified by the prosecution at the International Military Tribunal in Nuremberg of crimes against humanity and, shortly thereafter, the adoption in 1948 of the Genocide Convention.[6] Indeed, it was with regard to the Genocide Convention that the International Court of Justice (ICJ) pronounced on the nature of these new developments, and it made clear that the obligations contained within these instruments differed profoundly from the contractual nature of obligations under classical international law:

> In such a convention the contracting States do not have any interests of their own; they merely have, one and all, a common interest, namely, the accomplishment of those high purposes which are the *raison d'être* of the convention. Consequently, in a convention of this type one cannot speak of individual advantages or disadvantages to States, or of the maintenance of a perfect contractual balance between rights and duties. The high ideals

4 Even before the emergence of IHRL, for example, individuals were given access to international tribunals: see, e.g., Convention (XII) Relative to the Creation of an International Prize Court, The Hague, 18 October 1907 (on the abortive International Prize Court); M. O. Hudson, 'The Central American Court of Justice' (1932) 26 *American Journal of International Law* 759 (on the short-lived Central American Court of Justice). Such institutions could not hear claims by individuals against their *own* State, however.

5 A. H. Roth, *The Minimum Standard of International Law Applied to Aliens* (Leiden: AW Sijthoff's Uitgeversmaatschappij NV, 1949), p. 23 ('[c]ontrary to the national, whom we have discovered to be practically at the mercy of his own State, the alien enjoys a much more favourable situation'); B. Simma, 'From Bilateralism to Community Interest in International Law' (1994) 250 *Recueil des Cours* 217, 242–3; see generally, M. Paparinskis, *The International Minimum Standard and Fair and Equitable Treatment* (Oxford: Oxford University Press, 2013), chs. 1 and 2. The present author elaborates on this point in L. Hill-Cawthorne, 'Humanitarian Law, Human Rights Law and the Bifurcation of Armed Conflict' (forthcoming, 2015) *International & Comparative Law Quarterly*.

6 Convention on the Prevention and Punishment of the Crime of Genocide, 9 December 1948, in force 12 January 1951, 78 UNTS 277.

> which inspired the convention provide, by virtue of the common will of the parties, the foundation and measure of all its provisions.[7]

Reflecting the same idea as the ICJ, in his Hague Academy lectures, Bruno Simma invoked IHRL as exemplifying the emergence of 'community interests' in international law, supplementing the historically 'bilateralist' international legal order.[8]

Alongside this post-war emergence of IHRL came important developments in international humanitarian law (IHL), the much older branch of international law that also deals, albeit in a very different manner, with individual protection. IHL experienced its most comprehensive codification and development to date in 1949, with the negotiation and adoption of the four Geneva Conventions, each addressing the protection of specific categories of persons in situations of armed conflict.[9] Some 25 years later, States once again came together to negotiate two Additional Protocols to the Geneva Conventions, the first addressing international armed conflicts and the second non-international conflicts.[10] Subsequent developments in both conventional and customary law have further developed the law applicable in armed conflict.[11]

Throughout its history, IHL has functioned as an important source of protection for individuals in situations of armed conflict. Indeed, its

[7] *Reservations to the Convention on the Prevention and Punishment of the Crime of Genocide*, Advisory Opinion [1951] ICJ Rep 15, p. 23.

[8] Simma, 'From Bilateralism to Community Interest', 242–3.

[9] Geneva Convention for the Amelioration of the Condition of the Wounded and Sick in Armed Forces in the Field, 12 August 1949, in force 21 October 1950, 75 UNTS 31; Geneva Convention for the Amelioration of the Condition of the Wounded, Sick and Shipwrecked Members of the Armed Forces at Sea, 12 August 1949, in force 21 October 1950, 75 UNTS 85; Geneva Convention Relative to the Treatment of Prisoners of War, 12 August 1949, in force 21 October 1950, 75 UNTS 135; Geneva Convention Relative to the Protection of Civilian Persons in Time of War, 12 August 1949, in force 21 October 1950, 75 UNTS 287.

[10] Protocol Additional to the Geneva Conventions of 12 August 1949, and Relating to the Protection of Victims of International Armed Conflicts (Protocol I), 8 June 1977, in force 7 December 1978, 1125 UNTS 3; Protocol Additional to the Geneva Conventions of 12 August 1949, and Relating to the Protection of Victims of Non-International Armed Conflicts (Protocol II), 8 June 1977, in force 7 December 1978, 1125 UNTS 609.

[11] Regarding conventional law, see, e.g., Convention on the Prohibition of the Development, Production and Stockpiling of Bateriological (Biological) and Toxin Weapons and on their Destruction, 10 April 1972, in force 26 March 1975, 1015 UNTS 163; Convention on the Prohibition of the Development, Production, Stockpiling and Use of Chemical Weapons and on their Destruction, 13 January 1993, in force 29 April 1997, [1997] ATS 3. Regarding customary law, the most recent, comprehensive statement of the law can found in J.-M. Henckaerts and L. Doswald-Beck (eds.), *Customary International Humanitarian Law*, 2 vols. (Cambridge: Cambridge University Press, 2005).

importance in individual protection can be seen in many of its provisions, such as the requirement in the 1907 Hague Regulations that prisoners of war 'must be humanely treated'.[12] However, although both IHL and IHRL developed considerably in the post-war era, the two were based on very different premises. Most importantly, unlike under IHRL, under IHL the protection afforded to individuals was not an end in itself. Rather, the 'law of armed conflict' or 'law of war' (the more traditional monikers), and its specific rules, was historically seen primarily as addressing the reciprocal rights of States; unlike those under human rights treaties, these obligations were not, generally, of an intra-State character.[13] A clear illustration of this could be seen in the *clausula si omnes* found in the 1907 Hague Regulations, which limited the Regulations' application to those wars where all the (States) parties thereto had ratified them.[14] This confirms that, whilst many of the rules contained in the Regulations benefited individuals indirectly, they comprised the reciprocal rights of States. The 1949 Geneva Conventions similarly reflected this inter-State conception of the law of armed conflict, albeit to a lesser extent. For example, Article 4 of the Fourth Geneva Convention limits that Convention's application to civilians that are not nationals of the Power in whose hands they fall, again reflecting the fact that these rules were primarily a matter not of individual protection but inter-State relations, in contrast to the applicability of IHRL, which binds States vis-à-vis all those within their jurisdiction.[15]

Notwithstanding the importance of both IHRL and IHL for the protection of individuals, therefore, the two represented very different conceptions of the structure of international legal obligation: whereas most IHL treaty provisions followed the more traditional bilateral structure of international law (seen, e.g., in the *si onmnes* clause), IHRL represented the epitome of 'collective' or 'integral' obligations, with each State party owing obligations to every other State party as a collective whole (and to

[12] Art. 4(2) of the Hague Convention (IV) Respecting the Laws and Customs of War on Land, with annexed Regulations respecting the laws and customs of war on land, 18 October 1907, in force 26 January 1910, 205 CTS (1907) 227–98.

[13] T. Meron, 'The Humanization of Humanitarian Law' (2000) 94 *American Journal of International Law* 239, 247–8.

[14] This is noted in Meron, 'The Humanization of Humanitarian Law'. See, e.g., Art. 2 of the 1907 Hague Convention IV. The *clausula si omnes* was abandoned in later codifications: see Art. 82 of the 1929 Geneva Convention Relative to the Treatment of Prisoners of War, 27 July 1929, in force 19 June 1931, 118 LNTS (No 2743) 343–411.

[15] See, e.g. Art. 1 of the European Convention on Human Rights.

individuals), with no role for reciprocity.[16] This arguably helps to explain why, at least initially, the parallel development of IHL and IHRL following the Second World War saw little cross-fertilisation between the two.[17] Rather, the law of war (IHL) and the law of peace (IHRL) were largely bifurcated, with the consensus being that the latter did not apply to the relationship between a State and the nationals of an enemy belligerent State (i.e. the relationship governed by IHL).[18]

It is now commonly noted, however, that this view has since been superseded by a new consensus, which views IHRL as continuing to apply in those situations that are simultaneously the subject matter of IHL.[19] Interestingly, this development has encouraged these two regimes to interact and engage in the kind of cross-fertilisation that, at least initially, did not appear possible. In particular, as Theodor Meron has stated, IHRL has had a 'humanising' effect on IHL, with the latter becoming more directly concerned with individual protection (as opposed to inter-State relations).[20] Indeed, one can see this trend in the specific rules of IHL. For example, regarding the nationality restrictions on the application of the Fourth Geneva Convention noted above, the International Criminal Tribunal for the former Yugoslavia (ICTY) has subsequently loosened this requirement, applying the Convention to the relationship between a State and its nationals where those nationals owe their allegiance not to that State but rather to a different entity (so as to account for the inter-*ethnic* nature of the conflict in the former Yugoslavia).[21] The ICTY confirmed that behind this change in the applicability criteria for the Convention was the development of IHRL, stating that '[i]t would be incongruous with

[16] The terms used here borrow from J. Pauwelyn, 'A Typology of Multilateral Treaty Obligations: Are WTO Obligations Bilateral or Collective in Nature?' (2003) 14 *European Journal of International Law* 907.

[17] See, e.g., R. Kolb, 'The Relationship between International Humanitarian Law and Human Rights Law: A Brief History of the 1948 Universal Declaration of Human Rights and the 1949 Geneva Conventions' (1998) 38 *International Review of the Red Cross* 409.

[18] See, e.g., G. I. A. D. Draper, 'The Relationship between the Human Rights Regime and the Law of Armed Conflicts' (1971) 1 *Israel Yearbook of Human Rights* 191, 191–6; K. Suter, 'An Inquiry into the Meaning of the Phrase "Human Rights in Armed Conflicts"' (1976) 15 *Revue de Droit Pénal Militaire et de Droit de la Guerre* 393.

[19] For an overview of the trend towards the consensus that IHRL continues to apply in situations of armed conflict, see C. Droege, 'Elective Affinities? Human Rights and Humanitarian Law' (2008) 90 *International Review of the Red Cross* 501, 503–9.

[20] Meron, 'The Humanization of Humanitarian Law'.

[21] *Prosecutor* v. *Zejnil Delalić* et al., Case No IT-96–21-T, Trial Judgment, 16 November 1998, paras. 263–6; *Prosecutor* v. *Duško Tadić*, Case No IT-94–1-A, Appeals Judgment, 15 July 1999, paras. 167–8.

the whole concept of human rights, which protects individuals from the excesses of their own governments, to rigidly apply the nationality requirement of article 4'.[22] Similarly, and perhaps most importantly, common Article 3 of the 1949 Geneva Conventions represented the first attempt at codifying rules applicable in non-international armed conflicts.[23] In such situations, a State is bound by certain minimum standards vis-à-vis that State's own nationals (with no necessary inter-State element). The law of non-international armed conflict and IHRL therefore share similar characteristics.[24] The traditionally bilateralist structure of obligations under IHL has thus evolved in significant part into the same collective or *erga omnes* structure that is exemplified by human rights treaties.[25]

With the erosion of the traditional law of war/law of peace dichotomy, however, new controversies have arisen. In particular, if IHRL is to apply alongside IHL in armed conflict, the question now is how these two bodies of law are to interact. This raises few problems where the particular issue under consideration is regulated in the same way by both bodies of law.[26] However, for those issues on which the two lay down very different standards, such as detention and targeting (where IHL is more permissive than IHRL), one is faced with having to determine how these regimes interact.[27] It is here that the ICJ has played a central role, offering not only the first authoritative statement of the general relationship between IHL and IHRL but, in doing so, also framing the debates that have taken

22 *Prosecutor* v. *Zejnil Delalić* et al., para. 266.

23 See, e.g., Art. 3 common to the four 1949 Geneva Conventions ('common Art. 3') and Additional Protocol II.

24 T. Meron, *The Humanization of International Law* (The Hague: Martinus Nijhoff, 2006), p. 7.

25 See, e.g., Pauwelyn, 'A Typology of Multilateral Treaty Obligations', 923. This helps to explain why obligations under IHL cannot be affected by otherwise lawful countermeasures: S. Borelli and S. Olleson, 'Obligations Relating to Human Rights and Humanitarian Law', in J. Crawford, A. Pellet, and S. Olleson (eds.), *The Law of International Responsibility* (Oxford: Oxford University Press, 2010). Acknowledging this, albeit to a limited extent, see Art. 50(1) of the International Law Commission Articles on Responsibility of States for Internationally Wrongful Acts (2001), Report of the ILC, 53rd Session (2001) 2 *Yearbook of the International Law Commission* 26, UN Doc A/56/10 (2001).

26 For an example of such a case, see the discussion of the *DRC* v. *Uganda* case in the following section.

27 For a discussion of this issue with regard to detention and targeting, see J. Pejic, 'Conflict Classification and the Law Applicable to Detention and the Use of Force', in E. Wilmshurst (ed.), *International Law and the Classification of Conflicts* (Oxford: Oxford University Press, 2012).

place in the last fifteen years on this topic. It is on this aspect of the ICJ's jurisprudence that the remainder of this chapter focuses, offering an appraisal of its approach to this complex relationship.

2. The approach of the ICJ

2.1. The case law

The ICJ has discussed the relationship between IHL and IHRL on three separate occasions, in two advisory opinions and one contentious case. The Court faced this issue for the first time in its 1996 advisory opinion on the *Legality of Nuclear Weapons*, where it was concerned specifically with the interpretation of the human right to life in situations of armed conflict.[28] Importantly, the Court began by confirming that the human rights obligations of States continue *prima facie* to apply in situations of armed conflict:

> The Court observes that the protection of the International Covenant of Civil and Political Rights does not cease in times of war, except by operation of Article 4 of the Covenant whereby certain provisions may be derogated from in a time of national emergency. Respect for the right to life is not, however, such a provision. In principle, the right not arbitrarily to be deprived of one's life applies also in hostilities.[29]

This was the first endorsement by the ICJ of the long trend in practice that rejected the historical dichotomy between the law of war and the law of peace, and this alone makes the opinion extremely important. The Court then went on to state its view of the relationship between the human right to life and the rules of IHL relating to the conduct of hostilities:

> The test of what is an arbitrary deprivation of life, however, then falls to be determined by the applicable *lex specialis*, namely, the law applicable in armed conflict which is designed to regulate the conduct of hostilities. Thus whether a particular loss of life, through the use of a certain weapon in warfare, is to be considered an arbitrary deprivation of life contrary to Article 6 of the Covenant, can only be decided by reference to the law applicable in armed conflict and not deduced from the terms of the Covenant itself.[30]

The Court thus rationalised the relationship between the IHL rules on the conduct of hostilities with the human right to life by interpreting the

[28] *Legality of the Threat or Use of Nuclear Weapons*, Advisory Opinion [1996] ICJ Rep 226.
[29] *Nuclear Weapons*, para. 25. [30] *Nuclear Weapons*, para. 25.

general standards of the latter in accordance with the more specific standards of the former, on the grounds that these were designed specifically for situations of armed conflict. Applying this model, what is an 'arbitrary' deprivation of life under the *lex generalis* of IHRL is to be judged according to the *lex specialis* rules of IHL.[31] If a particular deprivation of life is in accordance with applicable IHL, it is therefore non-arbitrary in the sense of IHRL and thus also compatible with that body of law.[32] By holding that applicable IHL did not set aside the human rights obligations of States, the Court was able to treat this as a matter of interpreting the content of the 'open' human right not arbitrarily to be deprived of one's life with reference to the IHL standards. Indeed, it may have been possible to reach the same result using Article 31(3)(c) of the Vienna Convention on the Law of Treaties (VCLT).[33]

The Court addressed the relationship between IHL and IHRL for a second time in its *Israeli Wall* advisory opinion.[34] Whilst apparently endorsing its previous jurisprudence in the *Legality of Nuclear Weapons* opinion, the Court in this case applied the *lex specialis* principle in a slightly different manner:

> the Court considers that the protection offered by human rights conventions does not cease in case of armed conflict, save through the effect of provisions for derogation of the kind to be found in Article 4 of the International Covenant on Civil and Political Rights. As regards the relationship between international humanitarian law and human rights law, there are thus three possible situations: some rights may be exclusively

31 D. Akande, 'Nuclear Weapons, Unclear Law? Deciphering the *Nuclear Weapons* Advisory Opinion of the International Court' (1998) 68 *British Yearbook of International Law* 165, 175 ('[i]n other words, though the right to life provided in the Covenant continues to subsist during war or armed conflict, the question whether that right had been violated can only be determined by looking to see whether the taking of the life is prohibited by the law of armed conflict').

32 Akande, 'Nuclear Weapons, Unclear Law?', 175 ('[t]he recognition of the applicability of the right to life during war and armed conflict did not therefore create any new substantive right which the victim would not already possess under international humanitarian law').

33 C. McLachlan, 'The Principle of Systemic Integration and Article 31(3)(c) of the Vienna Convention' (2005) 54 *International & Comparative Law Quarterly* 279. As Martins Paparinskis notes in the context of investment treaty interpretation, to invoke Article 31(3)(c) requires examining not simply what constitutes a relevant rule of international law but also what weight should be accorded to any such relevant rule: see M. Paparinskis, 'Investment Treaty Interpretation and Customary Investment Law', in C. Brown and K. Miles (eds.), *Evolution in Investment Treaty Law and Arbitration* (Cambridge: Cambridge University Press, 2011).

34 *Legal Consequences of the Construction of a Wall in the Occupied Palestinian Territory*, Advisory Opinion [2004] ICJ Rep 136.

> matters of international humanitarian law; others may be exclusively matters of human rights law; yet others may be matters of both these branches of international law. In order to answer the question put to it, the Court will have to take into consideration both these branches of international law, namely human rights law and, as *lex specialis,* international humanitarian law.[35]

There are two points to note here. First, the Court makes clear that not all circumstances will require resolving the relationship between IHL and IHRL, for certain matters are regulated by only one, and not the other, body of law. IHRL, for example, says nothing about the right of prisoners of war to elect a prisoners' representative to represent them before the military authorities, Protecting Power and International Committee of the Red Cross (ICRC). As a result, no question arises as to the relationship of IHRL to the IHL rules in this specific area.[36] Similarly, whilst IHL regulates, in various ways, the relationship between a belligerent State in an international armed conflict and nationals of the enemy State, it does not generally regulate the 'everyday' relationships (i.e. those with no nexus to the armed conflict) between a belligerent State and their own nationals within that State's territory.[37] Thus, one need not consider the impact of IHL on the IHRL rules relating to the right of a State's nationals to marry, for example.[38] In these areas, the relevant body of law applies without being affected by the other regime. In addition, even where each body of law has something to say on a particular issue, where there is no conflict, both can be applied in parallel without having to consider the relationship between the two.[39] It is only where the *two* bodies of law have something *different* to say about a particular issue that one must determine the relationship between the relevant norms.

Second, where this relationship does fall to be determined, the ICJ in the *Israeli Wall* opinion once again adopted the *lex specialis* approach.

[35] *Legal Consequences of the Construction of a Wall,* para. 106.

[36] See Arts. 79–81 of the Third Geneva Convention on prisoners' representatives.

[37] There are some exceptions to this general rule that IHL does not regulate the relationship between a State and its nationals. First, Arts. 13–26 of the Fourth Geneva Convention establish general rules protecting populations of belligerent States from certain consequences of war. Second, as noted above, the rules applicable in non-international armed conflict necessarily apply to a State's own nationals, against whom the state will often be fighting in such conflicts. Third, also stated above, the ICTY has extended the protections of the Fourth Geneva Convention even to nationals of a State, where they owe their allegiance to a different entity.

[38] See Art. 23 of the International Covenant on Civil and Political Rights.

[39] For an example of this, see the discussion below regarding the *DRC* v. *Uganda* case.

However, the manner in which the Court invoked the *lex specialis* principle in this case differs from that in *Legality of Nuclear Weapons*, for whereas there the Court spoke of the *lex specialis* nature of IHL with regard to the norm prohibiting arbitrary deprivation of life, here it suggested that IHL *as a body of law* is *lex specialis* to IHRL.[40] The consequence would be that, whenever a particular right is addressed by both IHL and IHRL, the (generally more liberal) standards of IHL will prevail over those of IHRL. This could create arbitrary results, with the IHL rules prevailing over applicable IHRL rules, regardless of the specificity or appropriateness of the particular IHL rules, and regardless of the intentions of the States parties. Indeed, favouring IHL over IHRL for the mere fact that the former applies (as a result of the existence of an armed conflict) would seem inconsistent with the consensus that IHRL continues *prima facie* to apply in armed conflict. Instead, if the *lex specialis* principle is indeed accepted as governing the relationship between IHL and IHRL, it would seem more appropriate that it be applied at the level of individual norms in specific circumstances, rather than at the level of entire legal regimes.[41]

The third time that the relationship between IHL and IHRL arose before the ICJ was in the context of the contentious proceedings in *DRC* v. *Uganda*.[42] Here, the Court referred back to its finding in the *Israeli Wall* advisory opinion and quoted the extract above but excluded the final sentence referring to the principle of *lex specialis*.[43] Based on this partial quotation, the Court 'concluded that both branches of international law, namely international human rights law and international humanitarian law, would have to be taken into consideration'.[44] It then went on to apply

[40] This has been criticised: see, e.g., M. Milanović, 'Norm Conflicts, International Humanitarian Law, and Human Rights Law', in O. Ben-Naftali (ed.), *International Humanitarian Law and International Human Rights Law* (Oxford: Oxford University Press, 2011), pp. 98–101.

[41] L. Doswald-Beck, 'International Humanitarian Law and the International Court of Justice on the Legality of the Threat or Use of Nuclear Weapons' (1997) 35 *International Review of the Red Cross* 316 (stating that, in certain cases, such as where an individual is in the power of a belligerent State, IHRL could well be the more specific norm); A. Lindroos, 'Addressing Norm Conflicts in a Fragmented Legal System: The Doctrine of *Lex Specialis*' (2005) 74 *Nordic Journal of International Law* 27, 42 ('*lex specialis* is in some sense a contextual principle. It is difficult to use when determining conflicts between two normative orders in abstracto, and is, instead, more suited to the determination of relations between two norms in a concrete case').

[42] *Case Concerning Armed Activities on the Territory of the Congo (Democratic Republic of the Congo* v. *Uganda)* (Judgment) [2005] ICJ Rep 168.

[43] *DRC* v. *Uganda*, para. 216.

instruments of both IHL and IHRL in parallel, holding that Uganda had violated its obligations under both of these branches of international law.[45] It is unclear what relevance, if any, the omission of any reference to *lex specialis* has. However, it must be borne in mind that the facts with which the Court was dealing were conducive to the full application of both IHL and IHRL without the need to consider the relationship between the two. For example, many of the issues arising under the right to life comprised systematic attacks against the civilian population.[46] It is clear that such acts constitute violations of both IHL (assuming such civilians do not directly participate in hostilities) and IHRL, and thus no question arises as to how the two bodies of law interact. The Court was consequently able to apply IHL and IHRL to the facts and conclude that provisions of both were violated (including Article 6(1) of the International Covenant on Civil and Political Rights on the right to life and Article 51 of Additional Protocol I on the obligation not to make civilians the object of attack), without suggesting that the applicability of one body of law might affect the interpretation of the other.[47]

2.2. *An appraisal of the Court's* lex specialis *approach*

The Court's invocation of the *lex specialis* principle in the *Legality of Nuclear Weapons* and *Israeli Wall* opinions paints an elegant picture of the relationship between IHL and IHRL. Indeed, the manner in which the two were reconciled in the *Legality of Nuclear Weapons* opinion (what is 'arbitrary' in IHRL is to be judged according to IHL) almost gives the impression that the Court had 'discovered' the overarching principle governing this relationship, which, until then, had proved elusive. In reality, however, the Court's approach to this relationship was simply to address it as a case of treaty interpretation, drawing on a principle that has a long historical pedigree in international law as an interpretive maxim.[48]

[44] *DRC* v. *Uganda*, para. 216. [45] *DRC* v. *Uganda*, paras. 217–20.

[46] *DRC* v. *Uganda*, para. 206. [47] *DRC* v. *Uganda*, para. 219.

[48] M. Akehurst, 'The Hierarchy of the Sources of International Law' (1974–5) 47 *British Yearbook of International Law* 273, 273 ('*lex specialis* is nothing more than a rule of interpretation'); Report of the Study Group of the International Law Commission (ILC), 'Fragmentation of International Law: Difficulties Arising from the Diversification and Expansion of International Law', finalised by Martti Koskenniemi, 13 April 2006, A/CN.4/L.682, 34–5 ('[t]he principle that special law derogates from general law is a widely accepted maxim of legal interpretation and technique for the resolution of normative conflicts'); *ibid.*, 36 ('[t]he idea that special enjoys priority over general has a long pedigree in international jurisprudence as well').

This is most clear in its *Legality of Nuclear Weapons* opinion where it used IHL as a means of interpreting an 'open' human rights standard in the context of armed conflict, relying on the *lex specialis* nature of the former. And as with any other principle of treaty interpretation, one of the key objectives sought in applying the principle of *lex specialis* is to ascertain the common (objective) intention of the States parties.[49] Joost Pauwelyn, for example, describes the policy behind invoking the principle in public international law in the following way:

> Consequently, much like *lex posterior* – which is based on the view that the 'latest expression of state consent' ought to prevail – the principle of *lex specialis* is but a consequence of the contractual freedom of states, grounded in the idea that the 'most closest, detailed, precise or strongest expression of state consent', as it relates to a particular circumstance, ought to prevail. Both Art. 30 [of the VCLT] and the *lex specialis* principle thus attempt to answer one and the same question, namely: which of the two norms in conflict is the 'current expression of state consent'?[50]

Finding the common intention – indeed, insofar as one exists – of the States parties is, of course, where most of the difficulty lies, and the *lex specialis* principle simply points us to certain factual elements that can help approximate such intention. The International Law Commission (ILC) put it well in its fragmentation report:

[49] See, e.g., A. McNair, *The Law of Treaties* (Oxford: Oxford University Press, 1961), p. 365 ('[i]n our submission that task [of interpreting treaties] can be put in a single sentence; it can be described as the duty of giving effect to the expressed intention of the parties, that is, their intention *as expressed in the words used by them in the light of the surrounding circumstances*'); M. S. McDougal, H. D. Lasswell and J. C. Miller, *The Interpretation of International Agreements and World Public Order: Principles of Content and Procedure* (New Haven: New Haven Press, 1967), p. xvi ('[t]he primary aim of a process of interpretation by an authorized and controlling decision-maker can be formulated in the following proposition: discover the shared expectations that the parties to the relevant communication succeeded in creating in each other'); Sir H. Lauterpacht, *The Development of International Law by the International Court* (Cambridge: Cambridge University Press, 1982), p. 27 ('the function of the interpretation of treaties' is to ascertain 'what was the intention of the parties'); A. Clapham, *Brierly's Law of Nations*, 7th edn. (Oxford: Oxford University Press, 2012), p. 349 ('[t]he object of interpretation is to give effect to the intention of the parties as fully and fairly as possible').

[50] J. Pauwelyn, *Conflict of Norms in Public International Law: How WTO Law Relates to Other Rules of International Law* (Cambridge: Cambridge University Press, 2003), p. 388. Also confirming that the principle of *lex specialis* seeks to give effect to the intentions of the State parties, see McNair, *The Law of Treaties*, p. 219; Akehurst, 'The Hierarchy of the Sources of International Law', 273; Lindroos, 'Addressing Norm Conflict', 36; G. Verdirame, 'Human Rights in Wartime: A Framework for Analysis' [2008] *European Human Rights Law Review* 689, 700.

> When a 'hard' case does emerge, then it is the role of *lex specialis* to point to a set of considerations with practical relevance: the immediate accessibility and contextual sensitivity of the standard. Now these may not be decisive considerations. They may be overweighed by countervailing ones. Reasoning about such considerations, though impossible to condense in determining rules or techniques, should not, however, be understood as arbitrary. The reasoning may be the object of criticism and whether it prevails will depend on how it succeeds in condensing what may be called, for instance, the 'genuine shared expectations of the parties, within the limits established by overriding community objectives.'[51]

In this sense, *lex specialis* is simply a useful description of that process of balancing numerous considerations that is at the heart of all treaty interpretation:[52] 'shared expectations' or 'common intention' is our aim, and in seeking this we are not 'finding' such common intention but rather examining a plethora of different factors in order to attempt to 'condense' or 'approximate' such agreement.[53]

To rely on the notion of *lex specialis*, therefore, was in no sense a new or revolutionary idea. Instead, the Court was invoking a well-grounded interpretive technique in attempting to resolve the relationship between IHL and IHRL. This notwithstanding, its approach has been criticised on a number of bases, a few of which will be explored here. The first line of critique takes issue with the consequences of the *lex specialis* approach as formulated by the ICJ.[54] Thus, by arguing that the applicable IHRL rule must be interpreted by a *renvoi* to IHL, the consequence of the Court's

[51] ILC, 'Fragmentation of International Law', 48–9, quoting McDougal et al., *The Interpretation of International Agreements*, p. 83.

[52] Pauwelyn, *Conflict of Norms*, p. 388 ('[i]n sum, they [*lex posterior* and *lex specialis*] are more factual/subjective elements in the assessment of contractual freedom and state consent than absolute legal norms in their own right').

[53] McNair, *The Law of Treaties*, p. 366 ('[t]he process of interpretation, rightly conceived, cannot be regarded as a mere mechanical one of drawing inevitable meanings from the words in a text, or of searching for and discovering some preexisting specific intention of the parties with respect to every situation arising under a treaty ... In most instances interpretation involves giving a meaning to a text – not just any meaning which appeals to the interpreter, to be sure, but a meaning which, in the light of the text under consideration and of all the concomitant circumstances of the particular case at hand, appears in his considered judgment to be one which is logical, reasonable, and most likely to accord with and to effectuate the larger general purpose which the parties desired the treaty to serve').

[54] The critique that follows is elaborated in V. Gowlland-Debbas, 'The Right to Life and Genocide: the Court and International Public Policy', in L. Boisson de Chazournes and P. Sands (eds.), *International Law, the International Court of Justice and Nuclear Weapons* (Cambridge: Cambridge University Press, 1999).

approach is that individuals in armed conflicts have no more substantive rights than would be the case were IHRL *a priori* inapplicable in such situations.[55] Whilst the texts of the major IHRL treaties require simply that a deprivation of life be non-arbitrary,[56] and thus certainly leave room for the Court's approach of invoking IHL to give detail to the non-arbitrariness standard, international human rights jurisprudence has developed a stringent content for this standard, which the Court has effectively set aside in favour of IHL. Importantly, this jurisprudence generally requires that any lethal force be used only as a last resort, where strictly necessary and proportionate for the accomplishment of a legitimate aim, such as to save another person from harm.[57] The rules of IHL on the conduct of hostilities, on the other hand, lay out a much more permissive regime, which, at least according to traditional interpretations, contains no requirement that lethal force against lawful targets be strictly necessary in the circumstances or a means of last resort: combatants can be targeted purely on the basis of their status, without regard to their conduct in the prevailing circumstances, whilst civilians, once directly participating in hostilities, can similarly be targeted even where not strictly necessary in the circumstances.[58] The ICJ's approach of applying the latter rules as the *lex specialis* to interpret the arbitrariness standard in IHRL (and thus excluding the standard developed in human rights jurisprudence) thus results in the more permissive rules of IHL operating as the governing standards. Whether one considers this approach desirable or not, the consequence, at least with regard to *substantive* rights, is no different than were IHRL *prima facie* to be inapplicable in armed conflict. In

[55] Akande, 'Nuclear Weapons, Unclear Law?', 175 ('[t]he recognition of the applicability of the right to life during war and armed conflict did not therefore create any new substantive right which the victim would not already possess under international humanitarian law').

[56] The exception is the European Convention on Human Rights, Art. 2 of which sets out an exhaustive list of permissible reasons for taking life.

[57] Droege, 'Elective Affinities?', 525.

[58] See, e.g., Y. Dinstein, *The Conduct of Hostilities under the Law of International Armed Conflict*, 2nd edn. (Cambridge: Cambridge University Press, 2010), p. 34; G. Solis, 'Targeted Killing and the Law of Armed Conflict' (2007) 60 *Naval War College Review* 127, 130. Hence the controversy surrounding the ICRC's suggestion that those otherwise constituting lawful targets may only be attacked where necessary in the prevailing circumstances: for the ICRC's approach, see ICRC (N. Melzer), *Interpretive Guidance on the Notion of Direct Participation in Hostilities under International Humanitarian Law* (Geneva: ICRC, 2009), section IX; for the criticism that this does not reflect the current *lex lata*, see, e.g., W. Hays Parks, 'Part IX of the ICRC's "Direct Participation in Hostilities": No Mandate, No Expertise and Legally Incorrect' (2010) 42 *NYU Journal of International Law and Politics* 769.

this sense, the Court's conclusion differs little from the views of certain States that, in armed conflict, IHL applies to the exclusion of IHRL.[59]

In the ILC report on fragmentation, this critique was acknowledged, but the ICJ's approach was defended on the grounds of realism:

> However desirable it might be to discard the difference between peace and armed conflict, the exception that war continues to be to the normality of peace could not be simply overlooked when determining what standards should be used to judge behaviour in those (exceptional) circumstances . . . *Lex specialis* did hardly more than indicate that though it might have been desirable to apply only human rights, such a solution would have been too idealistic, bearing in mind the speciality and persistence of armed conflict. So the Court created a systemic view of the law in which the two sets of rules related to each other as today's reality and tomorrow's promise . . . [60]

It must also be noted that the Court did not subordinate IHRL entirely to IHL, for under its approach, individuals do gain certain *procedural* rights which they would not have were IHRL inapplicable, as they can now utilise the enforcement mechanisms under international and regional human rights treaties effectively to enforce IHL (through the medium of the relevant human rights norms).[61] This could fill an important gap in the enforcement mechanisms available under IHL, although access to human rights bodies would need to be made more effective in order to ensure that this is realised.

A second problem that has been noted with the Court's invocation of *lex specialis* relates to the principle's unclear meaning. In this respect, Martti Koskenniemi has noted two different interpretations of the *lex specialis* principle:

> There are two ways in which law may take account of the relationship of a particular rule to general one. A particular rule may be considered an *application* of a general standard in a given circumstance. The special relates to the general as does administrative regulation to law in domestic legal order. Or it may be considered as a *modification, overruling* or a *setting aside* of the latter.[62]

[59] See, e.g., 'Reply of the Government of the United States of America to the Report of the Five UN Special Rapporteurs on Detainees in Guantanamo Bay, Cuba', 10 March 2006, available at www.state.gov/documents/organization?98969.pdf last visited 8 February 2015.

[60] ILC, 'Fragmentation of International Law', 57.

[61] Akande, 'Nuclear Weapons, Unclear Law?', 175–7.

[62] ILC, 'Fragmentation of International Law', 49 (emphasis in original).

The Court's use of the principle of *lex specialis* in the *Legality of Nuclear Weapons* opinion seems to follow the first sense above, by employing the special rule (IHL) so as to help interpret what was required of the general rule (IHRL) in the specific circumstances. However, not all inconsistencies between IHL and IHRL can be resolved in the interpretive manner adopted by the ICJ in the *Nuclear Weapons* case. A good example relates to preventive, security detention or 'internment'.[63] IHL clearly permits a State party to an international armed conflict to intern both enemy combatants and civilians, where they pose a security threat necessitating internment.[64] Most regional and international human rights treaties, on the other hand, simply state that a person may not be deprived of their liberty arbitrarily.[65] The same approach as the Court adopted in the *Nuclear Weapons* case could be applied here: what is an arbitrary deprivation of liberty in IHRL could be determined according to the rules regulating internment in IHL. However, this approach cannot reconcile IHL's permitted use of an 'administrative board' to review decisions to intern,[66] with the requirement in IHRL that those deprived of their liberty be given access to a *court* to challenge the legality of their internment.[67] Nor can it resolve the conflict between the authorisation to use internment in IHL with the finite list of permissible grounds for detention in Article 5 of the European Convention on Human Rights, which does not include preventive, security detention.[68] Applying *lex specialis* in these cases would seem to require invoking the second notion of the principle noted in the quote by Koskenniemi above, i.e. 'as a *modification, overruling* or a *setting aside*' of the *lex generalis* (IHRL), and some have doubted whether *lex specialis* can operate in this manner.[69]

However, it must be remembered that the *lex specialis* principle plays no normative role itself, in the sense of dictating which rule is special and therefore governs, but rather operates as one amongst many factual

[63] This example of an 'unresolvable norm conflict', together with those of targeting and the obligations of occupying powers, are given in Milanović, 'Norm Conflicts', pp. 116–18.

[64] Art. 21 of the Third Geneva Convention; Arts. 27(4), 41–3 and 78 of the Fourth Geneva Convention.

[65] See, e.g., Art. 9 of the International Covenant on Civil and Political Rights; Art. 7 of the American Convention on Human Rights.

[66] Arts. 43 and 78 of the Fourth Geneva Convention.

[67] See, e.g., Art. 9(4) of the International Covenant on Civil and Political Rights; Art. 7(6) of the American Convention on Human Rights; Art. 5(4) of the European Convention on Human Rights.

[68] Art. 5(1) of the European Convention on Human Rights.

[69] Milanović, 'Norm Conflicts', pp. 113–16.

elements to be taken into account in discerning the intentions of the States parties. It is to the *collective* intentions of the States parties that one must refer, therefore, to determine whether, in any given case, a provision of IHL is capable of setting aside an otherwise applicable rule under a human rights treaty. Whilst the fact that States have specifically developed a specialised IHL norm in a particular area might reasonably suggest an intention that their actions are to be judged against that norm, this is not definitive and it can be rebutted by evidence to the contrary that suggests no such *common* intention can be assumed amongst the States parties. In any case, it is important to note that, even where the *lex specialis* principle is invoked in the second sense, it does not displace IHRL as such; rather, it confirms the legal standard that is intended to prevail (e.g. IHL), with IHRL continuing to operate in the background, giving way to IHL only to the extent of the inconsistency.[70]

Finally, and related to the previous point, to invoke the *lex specialis* principle requires having the means to determine which rule is *lex specialis* and which *lex generalis*. Commentators have suggested that the difficulty in making such a determination renders the application of the *lex specialis* principle problematic in this area. Anja Lindroos, for example, demonstrates how this limitation of the *lex specialis* principle poses particular difficulties in applying it to the resolution of conflicts between normative orders in international law:

> Since the maxim of *lex specialis* is a notion strongly connected to a national legal order endowed with hierarchy and systemic relations, its applicability is dependent on the level of systematisation provided by the system, the treaty or some other reasoning. Thus, it has conceptual limitations which do not necessarily render it a suitable conflict resolution technique for the particularities of a fragmented order such as the international legal system, especially since *lex specialis* is not a substantive rule of international law that might help determine which rule is special in relation to a more general rule. It is a descriptive principle that has little independent normative force. It provides no criteria to decide whether one area of law is generally more important or special than another.[71]

It is submitted that the key difficulty with invoking the *lex specialis* principle in international law is not, as such, the absence of any hierarchy or non-systematicity (indeed, as the present volume demonstrates, this

[70] ILC, 'Fragmentation of International Law', 56.
[71] Lindroos, 'Addressing Norm Conflict', 66.

latter point is very much up for debate) but rather the differentiated treaty obligations of States. In the case of reconciling IHL and IHRL, however, this problem need not arise in many cases, given the universal ratification of the four 1949 Geneva Conventions and the considerable development of general international law in this area.[72] Lindroos does, however, correctly note what was said above: the principle of *lex specialis* has no normative content and thus cannot alone direct which rule is special and which general. Instead, it is no more than a useful descriptive tool that requires recourse to other sources for determining hierarchy. As noted above, the value of *lex specialis* will be determined by its ability to point to factors that will enable an approximation of party intentions to be reached. Marko Milanović argues, however, that this is based on a false premise:

> More fundamentally, *lex specialis* as a rule of conflict resolution rests on an unstated assumption – that for any given situation at any given point in time there is one, and there can *only* be one, expression of state consent or intent as to how that situation is to be regulated. But that assumption is manifestly unfounded.[73]

It is, indeed, the case that it may often be implausible to claim that there is a common intention amongst the States parties as to how a particular human right is to interact with a rule of IHL. However, this difficulty is not, as such, unique to the *lex specialis* principle, or indeed to the interactions between IHL and IHRL, but rather is a common difficulty faced whenever interpreting treaties, which, as has been noted time and again, is 'to some extent an art, and not an exact science'.[74] This criticism does, however, remind us of the importance of the default legal position with regard

[72] On custom in this area, see especially Henckaerts and Doswald-Beck, *Customary International Humanitarian Law.*

[73] Milanović, 'Norm Conflicts', 115.

[74] Sir H. Waldock, 'Third Report on the Law of Treaties' (1964), *Yearbook of International Law Commission*, vol. II, 54, para. 6. See also, e.g., R. A. Falk, 'On Treaty Interpretation and the New Haven Approach: Achievements and Prospects' (1968) 8 *Virginia Journal of International Law* 323, 355 ('[a]s matters now stand with treaty interpretation, for the tough cases there are rarely genuine shared expectations of dispositive significance . . . '); M. Koskenniemi, *From Apology to Utopia: The Structure of International Legal Argument* (Cambridge: Cambridge University Press, 2005), pp. 333–45 (demonstrating the confused role of party intentions in different schools of thought regarding treaty interpretation); Clapham, *Brierly's*, pp. 349–50 ('what a court really does when we say that it interprets, is that, by employing well-known methods of judicial reasoning, it says what it thinks the framers of the document must have intended to say. But they did not intend to say that;

to the relationship between IHL and IHRL. Thus, where no common intention that IHL is to operate as the *lex specialis* is demonstrated, the presumption stands that the relevant obligations under both IHL and IHRL apply, with the consequence that the same facts may be held to constitute violations of both sets of obligations.[75] This is confirmed in the ICJ's case law in which it adopts the two-step approach noted above: first, it recognised the default legal position that IHRL continues to apply in armed conflict; second, the operation of IHRL in armed conflict is subject to permissible derogation or, where indicated to be the intentions of the States parties, contextual interpretation in accordance with IHL as the *lex specialis*.[76] Where the presumption as to the default parallel applicability of both IHL and IHRL is not displaced, if the relevant State is to avoid the consequences under the law of State responsibility for violating its international obligations, it must adhere to the more protective standard (likely IHRL).

The nature of the obligations under human rights treaties creates additional burdens for those wishing to claim that a particular human rights treaty provision must give way to a humanitarian law treaty provision. This is best illustrated by considering the difficulties that could arise for future developments in IHL. For example, the current lack of conventional or customary rules of IHL relating to internment in non-international armed conflicts makes it difficult to argue that IHL operates as the *lex specialis* in this area; the relevant human rights obligations of States would seem, therefore, to continue to apply unaffected.[77] Should States decide to adopt a new IHL model for the regulation of internment in non-international armed conflicts by analogising to the rules applicable in international armed conflicts (which are more permissive than IHRL), this would need to be done by *all* States party to the relevant human rights treaty (or treaties) in order for a claim to be made that it operates

they probably had no intention at all in the matter that has arisen, almost certainly no common intention').

75 That the same facts can lead to violations of both IHL and IHRL was confirmed by the ICJ when applying the legal norms to the specific facts of each case in both *Legal Consequences of the Construction of a Wall*, para. 134 and *DRC* v. *Uganda*, paras. 217–20.

76 See, e.g., *Nuclear Weapons*, para. 25.

77 On this, see, e.g., M. Sassóli and L. M. Olson, 'The Relationship between International Humanitarian and Human Rights Law Where it Matters: Admissible Killing and Internment of Fighters in Non-International Armed Conflicts' (2008) 90 *International Review of the Red Cross* 599.

as the *lex specialis*.[78] That this is the case arises from the nature of the obligations assumed by States under human rights treaties, which, as was noted at the outset of this chapter, are of a collective or *erga omnes* character. By this is meant that these treaties cannot be broken down into a web of bilateral relationships; rather they are owed equally by each State party to every other State party (as well as to individuals within their jurisdiction). As a consequence, all States parties would need to agree on the new set of rules to regulate internment in such situations.[79] Were it otherwise the case, a small sub-set of States parties would then be able informally to 'contract out' of their obligations under the human rights treaty and apply less protective rules, violating the rights of all other States parties to the treaty.[80]

Seeking to 'distil' a shared intention amongst States parties regarding the relationship between a specific human right and relevant rules of IHL can, therefore, pose complex problems. But as with any other case of treaty interpretation, all we can do is attempt to approximate any such shared intention, and the *lex specialis* principle might, in particular cases, point us to certain relevant considerations. And, as Milanović notes, where no such shared intention can be found, both sets of obligations will apply in parallel, and there will be a potential conflict between a State's obligations under IHL and IHRL, which can be solved either by derogation or through a political decision; in the latter case, should the State choose to follow one norm but not the other, it will face the consequences under the law of State responsibility.[81] The point is that, just as the relationship between

[78] The recent Copenhagen Principles on the Handling of Detainees in International Military Operations attempt to formulate standards to apply in this area by analogising to the IHL rules applicable in international armed conflicts: see L. Hill-Cawthorne, 'The Copenhagen Principles on the Handling of Detainees: Implications for the Procedural Regulation of Internment' (2013) 18 *Journal of Conflict and Security Law* 481. It is worth noting, however, that the Copenhagen Principles are explicitly stated as not affecting the legal obligations of the States involved in their drafting.

[79] See, e.g., Art. 41(1)(b)(i) of the Vienna Convention on the Law of Treaties, Vienna, 23 May 1969, in force 27 January 1980, 1155 UNTS 331, prohibiting amendments to multilateral treaties between certain parties where such amendments affect the rights or obligations of the other parties. Similarly, see Pauwelyn, *Conflict of Norms*, pp. 436–7 (stating that so-called 'integral' obligations cannot be modified *inter se*).

[80] The issue may be different were the formalised amendment procedures that are provided for in certain human rights treaties followed, some of which permit amendment amongst a majority of States parties only: see, e.g., Art. 51(2) of the International Covenant on Civil and Political Rights; Art. 76(2) of the American Convention on Human Rights.

[81] Milanović, 'Norm Conflicts', pp. 116–23.

IHL and IHRL cannot be determined at the abstract level, so the validity of invoking the descriptive tool of *lex specialis* in this area can only be judged according to the specific facts of a case and its ability to point to considerations that will help approximate party intentions.

Finally, it must be borne in mind that the attempt to resolve the relationship between specific norms of IHL and IHRL is a continuing process, and it should not be assumed that unresolvable norm conflict is an inevitable feature of the international legal system. Vaughan Lowe has suggested that the emergence and consolidation of so-called 'interstitial principles' that govern the relations between primary norms is where the major developments in international law are now to be found.[82] Lowe suggests that such interstitial norms are based not on traditional concepts such as State practice and *opinio iuris*, but rather are 'drawn out' by a wide range of relevant actors and will depend for their validity on a number of factors, including the authority of the decision-maker and the persuasiveness of the interstitial norm itself. The discussion in this chapter suggests that the persuasiveness of the ICJ's invocation of the *lex specialis* principle in this area is yet to be confirmed, but it must be borne in mind that 'the gradual refinement of a consistent principle, tested in the crucible of a succession of concrete cases, makes possible the distillation of the detailed, carefully considered analyses spread throughout the mass of individual decisions. This is a continuing process.'[83] As part of this process, commentators will continue to play an important role in offering principled bases on which to rationalise this relationship between IHL and IHRL.[84]

It is clear from the above that the relationship between IHL and IHRL is much more complex than first appears from the concise statements of the ICJ as to the *lex specialis* nature of IHL. But this is the case with any attempt at treaty interpretation: rarely is the practice as neat as the theory. The final section will now very briefly examine certain consequences of this approach for the role of IHL in contemporary conflicts, as it is here in particular that a number of interesting points arise.

[82] A. V. Lowe, 'The Politics of Law-Making: Are the Method and Character of Norm Creation Changing?', in M Byers (ed.), *The Role of Law in International Politics: Essays in International Relations and International Law* (Oxford: Oxford University Press, 2000).

[83] Lowe, 'The Politics of Law-Making', p. 215.

[84] For a number of different proposals, see Droege, 'Elective Affinities?', 536–7; D. Kretzmer, 'Rethinking Application of IHL in Non-International Armed Conflicts' (2009) 42 *Israel Law Review* 8, 40–5; C. Garraway, '"To Kill or Not to Kill?" – Dillemas on the Use of Force' (2009) 14 *Journal of Conflict and Security Law* 499; L. Hill-Cawthorne, 'The Role of Necessity in International Humanitarian and Human Rights Law' (2014) 47 *Israel Law Review* 225.

2.3. *The role of IHL in contemporary conflicts*

In response to certain commentators who have noted the personal preferences and philosophies that often lie behind a chosen technique of treaty interpretation,[85] Koskenniemi makes the important addition that 'it is not really that the "canons", once chosen, would be determining . . . The solution seems more connected to the "philosophies" or evaluations – while reference to a canon only adds apparent neutrality to the choice.'[86] The point of this section is not to engage in the debates regarding the place of individual preference and politics in judicial decision-making,[87] but rather to consider the subsequent issue of the manner in which the ICJ's approach to the relationship between IHL and IHRL has been invoked by States and commentators as a means to give 'apparent neutrality' to highly political arguments. Thus, it has been noted that States engaged in military operations against transnational non-State armed groups increasingly rely on an IHL model to govern their conduct.[88] This is because, 'for States that are faced by a non-State armed attack, the resort to the armed conflict model offers the advantage of applying, as the *lex specialis*, a targeting and detention regime that is appreciably more permissive than that under international human rights law'.[89] States and commentators have been able to invoke the notion that IHL operates as the *lex specialis* in situations of armed conflict in order effectively to displace otherwise applicable rules of IHRL.[90] As a result, the notion that, at least in certain areas, IHL operates as the *lex specialis* places a veil of neutrality over what is, in fact, a highly political 'choice' over the governing legal regime.

The view that IHL operates as the *lex specialis*, therefore, has an important impact on the purpose for which this body of law is invoked. The

85 See, e.g., the discussion of different approaches in I. Hussain, *Dissenting and Separate Opinions at the World Court* (Dordrecht: Martinus Nijhoff, 1984), pp. 76–7.

86 Koskenniemi, *From Apology to Utopia*, p. 339 (fn. 102).

87 For an example of such an argument, see, e.g., J. Stone, 'Fictional Elements in Treaty Interpretation: A Study in the International Judicial Process' (1954) 1 *Sydney Law Review* 334.

88 See, e.g., C. Kreß, 'Some Reflections on the International Legal Framework Governing Transnational Armed Conflicts' (2010) 15 *Journal of Conflict and Security Law* 245, 258–61.

89 Kreß, 'Some Reflections', 260–1.

90 See, e.g., 'US Responses to Selected Recommendations of the Human Rights Committee', 10 October 2007, available at www.state.gov/documents/organization/100845.pdf, last visited 19 June 2013; M. J. Dennis, 'Non-Application of Civil and Political Rights Treaties Extraterritorially During Times of International Armed Conflict' (2007) 40 *Israel Law Review* 453.

notion that IHL serves the goal of humanising armed conflict hides from view this darker side, and those that historically sought the extension of the rules of IHL to as broad a set of circumstances as possible (such as internal armed conflicts) in order to protect the victims thereof have been replaced by those who seek to exploit its more permissive features.[91] This raises the important question of what role IHL should play in contemporary armed conflicts. Whereas traditionally it introduced elements of humanity into an otherwise inhumane process, it now appears to offer a set of rules that allow for far greater abuse than would otherwise be permitted.

In a world which rightly places increasing emphasis on the protection of individuals, one wonders whether a set of rules that allows, *inter alia*, for unnecessary killing and indefinite detention should not be reassessed to reflect more desirable principles. Of course, whenever the need to humanise IHL is raised, one is necessarily faced with the counter-considerations of military necessity and the need to maintain a realistic set of rules for a phenomenon as inherently unpleasant as war. And it is here, of course, that IHL and IHRL differ in the most basic sense, for whilst IHL accepts that war occurs and bases its rules on this assumption, IHRL, far from accepting such a premise, sets out a collection of rules that are simply incompatible with such a notion; in this sense, IHRL assumes a general existence of peace.[92] It is, in other words, the existence of war that is the trigger for all subsequent acts that, whilst potentially permissible under IHL, would be considered violations of human rights on a systematic scale. For so long as war continues, therefore, certain human rights will continue to be undermined and profoundly so. The consequence is that a long-term solution can only be found by addressing the root causes of war, for it is these that truly threaten the enjoyment of basic human rights.

3. Conclusions

This chapter has discussed the role of the ICJ in the much broader project that has sought to move away from traditional conceptions of IHL and IHRL as entirely separate normative orders, towards a more unified notion

[91] See generally Kretzmer, 'Rethinking Application of IHL'. The present author elaborates on such approaches in Hill-Cawthorne, 'Humanitarian Law, Human Rights Law and the Bifurcation of Armed Conflict'.

[92] See W. A. Schabas, '*Lex Specialis*? Belt and Suspenders? The Parallel Operation of Human Rights Law and the Law of Armed Conflict, and the Conundrum of *Jus Ad Bellum*' (2007) 40 *Israel Law Review* 592.

of the two as simply parts of a single, coherent international legal order. The Court has played a key role in this project, not only by confirming that individuals do not somehow lose their legal rights merely because an armed conflict has come into existence, but also by offering a particular approach to the interaction between IHL and IHRL. It has been a theme of this chapter that the Court approached the relationship between these two sets of rules as a matter of treaty interpretation, through its invocation of the principle of *lex specialis.* A number of criticisms of this approach were shown to exist and, in particular, one is faced with the difficulty of discerning a common intention amongst States parties. However, it was also argued that, in the absence of a clear common intention to the contrary, IHL and IHRL obligations will simply apply side by side, without affecting one another as such. The appropriateness of the Court's *lex specialis* approach, as with any other interpretive maxim, can only be judged on a case-by-case basis, depending on its ability to point to relevant factors that can help approximate party intentions.

The focus of this chapter has been on the ICJ's case law. The jurisprudence of the other treaty bodies on this issue has been mixed. The inter-American institutions have been encouraged by the ICJ's jurisprudence to draw on IHL as the *lex specialis* to interpret the American Convention on Human Rights.[93] Other bodies, however, have been less willing to refer to the *lex specialis* principle here. For example, the UN Human Rights Committee, whilst apparently supporting the ICJ's view that IHL might inform the interpretation of particular rules of IHRL, emphasised that 'both spheres of law are complementary, not mutually exclusive'.[94] The African Commission on Human and Peoples' Rights has avoided commenting on the general relationship between IHL and IHRL, instead simply noting violations of both in respect of the same conduct.[95] The European Court of Human Rights explicitly commented on this

[93] See, e.g., *Juan Carlos Abella* v. *Argentina*, Report No 55/97, 18 November 1997, para. 178; *Las Palmeras* v. *Colombia*, Judgment (Preliminary Objections), IACtHR (Ser C) No 67 (2000), para. 32. See generally C. M. Cerna, 'The History of the Inter-American System's Jurisprudence as Regards Situations of Armed Conflict' (2011) 2 *Journal of International Humanitarian Legal Studies* 3.

[94] UN Human Rights Committee, General Comment No 31: The Nature of the General Legal Obligation Imposed on States Parties to the Covenant, CCPR/C/21/Rev.1/Add.13, 26 May 2004, para. 11.

[95] See, e.g., *DRC* v. *Burundi, Uganda and Rwanda*, Comm No 227/99 (2003), paras. 79–80; D. L. Tehindrazanarivelo, 'The African Union and International Humanitarian Law', in R. Kolb and G. Gaggioli (eds.), *Research Handbook on Human Rights and Humanitarian Law* (Cheltenham: Edward Elgar, 2013), pp. 508–12.

relationship for the first time in its *Hassan* v. *United Kingdom* judgment in 2014.[96] Here, the Grand Chamber read into the detention provisions in Article 5 ECHR the more permissive grounds and procedures for detention applicable under IHL in international armed conflict, without requiring from States that they derogate in order to do so. In so doing, it relied not on the *lex specialis* maxim itself, but rather Articles 31(3)(b) and (c) of the VCLT, requiring treaty provisions to be interpreted in light of subsequent practice and other relevant rules of international law applicable between the parties.[97] It was noted above that the ICJ may well have reached the same conclusion in its *Legality of Nuclear Weapons* advisory opinion had it relied on Article 31(3)(c) VCLT rather than the *lex specialis* maxim. Article 31(3)(c), however, like the *lex specialis* maxim, should not be seen as an answer in itself to the relationship between IHL and IHRL; rather, one must still assess what rules are 'relevant', what weight they should be given and why.[98] The common intentions of the parties should still operate as the decisive element in the interpretive process.

The relationship between IHL and IHRL will continue to arise in regional and international human rights courts and other bodies. States must, therefore, take into account, in planning military operations, that they may well be held to account for certain actions before these bodies. Moreover, the jurisdictional limitations that apply to these courts will likely affect the degree to which they can take relevant rules of IHL into account. Once again, therefore, we are reminded that this 'is a continuing process' and one in which a range of different actors will play a role.

[96] *Hassan* v. *United Kingdom*, App No 29750/09, Judgment (Grand Chamber), 16 September 2014.

[97] *Hassan* v. *United Kingdom*, paras. 96–107.

[98] Paparinskis, 'Investment Treaty Interpretation and Customary Investment Law'.

11

Fragmentation within international human rights law

MEHRDAD PAYANDEH

I. Fragmentation between and fragmentation within international legal regimes

The dissociation of international law into 'functionally defined issue-areas',[1] into 'specialized and (relatively) autonomous rules or rule-complexes'[2] constitutes the core assumption of the academic discourse on the fragmentation of the international legal order. General international law is juxtaposed and contrasted with international trade law, international human rights law, international environmental law, the law of armed conflict, international investment law, the international law of the sea, or international criminal law. And while the Study Group of the International Law Commission rightly points out that the classification of these specific sub-systems of international law does not have, by itself, any normative implications,[3] the differentiation nevertheless shapes and, to a certain degree, restricts the discourse on fragmentation. With regard to international human rights law, for example, the fragmentation debate focuses on the interplay of human rights law with trade law,[4] with investment

[1] J. Pauwelyn, 'Fragmentation of International Law', in R. Wolfrum (ed.), *Max Planck Encyclopedia of Public International Law* (Oxford: Oxford University Press, 2006), para. 2.

[2] Report of the Study Group of the International Law Commission, 'Fragmentation of International Law: Difficulties Arising from the Diversification and Expansion of International Law', finalized by Martti Koskenniemi, 13 April 2006, UN Doc. A/CN.4/L.682, para. 8.

[3] *Ibid.*, para. 21. On the process of defining different regimes, see A. Lang, 'Legal Regimes and Professional Knowledges: The Internal Politics of Regime Definition', in M. A. Young (ed.), *Regime Interaction in International Law: Facing Fragmentation* (Cambridge: Cambridge University Press, 2012), p. 113.

[4] See, e.g., L. Bartels, 'Trade and Human Rights', in R. Wolfrum (ed.), *Max Planck Encyclopedia of Public International Law* (Oxford: Oxford University Press, 2010); M. Koskenniemi and P. Leino, 'Fragmentation of International Law? Postmodern Anxieties' (2002) 15 *Leiden Journal of International Law* 553, 570.

law,[5] or with the law of armed conflict,[6] as well as its relationship with general international law.[7] In its geographical or regional dimension, the fragmentation discourse scrutinizes the relationship between universal human rights regimes and regional mechanisms for the protection of human rights, such as the European Convention on Human Rights, the American Convention on Human Rights, or the African Charter on Human and Peoples' Rights.[8]

This concentration of the discourse on the relationship *between* functionally and geographically defined legal regimes tends to overlook or at least to neglect a potential for conflict *within* international human rights law. This potential for conflict is caused by the rise of international legal regimes and institutions, which are not mandated to protect human rights in general but focus on specific kinds of human rights violation – such as torture or racial discrimination – or on the protection of specific groups – such as women, children or people with disabilities. This tension within international human rights law is hardly ever explicitly addressed as an aspect of fragmentation.[9] The 256-page report of the Study Group of the International Law Commission on fragmentation in international law does not mention the issue, neither does it play a significant role within the general fragmentation discourse.

In this chapter, I argue that the emergence of more specialized regimes for the protection of human rights and the proliferation of treaty bodies, mandated to supervise compliance with these instruments, potentially raises similar issues as the relationship between human rights and other functionally defined areas of international law. Due to the specific normative and institutional arrangements of the universal human rights mechanisms, however, the possible tensions resulting from fragmentation

5 See, e.g., P.-M. Dupuy, E.-U. Petersmann and F. Francioni (eds.), *Human Rights in International Investment Law and Arbitration* (Oxford: Oxford University Press, 2009).

6 See, e.g., A. Orakhelashvili, 'The Interaction between Human Rights and Humanitarian Law: Fragmentation, Conflict, Parallelism, or Convergence?' (2008) 19 *European Journal of International Law* 161.

7 See, e.g., O. De Schutter, *International Human Rights Law* (Cambridge: Cambridge University Press, 2010), p. 48 et seq.

8 See, e.g., M. Pinto, 'Fragmentation or Unification Among International Institutions: Human Rights Tribunals' (1999) 31 *N.Y.U. Journal of International Law and Policy* 833.

9 But see, e.g., G. Ulfstein, 'Individual complaints', in H. Keller and G. Ulfstein (eds.), *UN Human Rights Treaty Bodies* (Cambridge: Cambridge University Press, 2012), pp. 73, 108–11; H. G. Cohen, 'From Fragmentation to Constitutionalization' (2012) 25 *Pac. McGeorge Global Bus. and Dev. L.J.* 381, 383.

within international human rights law differ from the problems that are generally discussed under the topic of fragmentation. First, within human rights law, conflicts of jurisprudence are more likely to occur than conflicts of jurisdiction. Procedural safeguards significantly mitigate the danger that different institutions make incompatible decisions with regard to the same case, and thereby prevent conflicts of jurisdiction. However, there is the realistic danger that general and specialized human rights institutions will interpret human rights guarantees in a substantially different manner, thereby provoking conflicts of jurisprudence. Second, while the general debate is mainly focused on the substantive dimension of fragmentation and on legal techniques for dealing with tensions or conflicts between legal rules or principles,[10] fragmentation in international human rights law is mainly problematic from an institutional perspective:[11] Problems are not caused by incompatible substantive provisions of human rights treaties but by colliding institutional preferences and structural biases of the different human rights treaty bodies.

In the following section, I will further develop and substantiate this argument in general (II), before I draw on a recent decision of the Committee on the Elimination of Racial Discrimination in order to explicate and exemplify the specific dimension of fragmentation within international human rights law (III). Finally, I argue that human rights treaty bodies need to take into consideration their embedment within the broader normative and institutional framework of international human rights law – not so much for the sake of an abstract concept of unity and

[10] This is the clear focus of the ILC Study Group, see Report of the Study Group of the International Law Commission, 'Fragmentation of International Law: Difficulties Arising from the Diversification and Expansion of International Law', finalized by Martti Koskenniemi, 13 April 2006, UN Doc. A/CN.4/L.682, para. 17 et seq.; for a critique of the rule-centered, formalistic approach of the report, see S. Singh, 'The Potential of International Law: Fragmentation and Ethics' (2011) 24 *Leiden Journal of International Law* 24.

[11] The institutional perspective is explicitly excluded by the ILC Study Group, see Report of the Study Group of the International Law Commission, 'Fragmentation of International Law: Difficulties Arising from the Diversification and Expansion of International Law', finalized by Martti Koskenniemi, 13 April 2006, UN Doc. A/CN.4/L.682, para. 13; but see also the reference to the 'structural bias' of regimes in para. 488. The tensions between the ILC report and the other work of its chairman, Martti Koskenniemi, have been analysed by S. Singh, 'The Potential of International Law: Fragmentation and Ethics', (2011) 24 *Leiden Journal of International Law* 24; T. Broude, 'Keep Calm and Carry On: Martti Koskenniemi and the Fragmentation of International Law' (2013) 27 *Temple International and Comparative Law Journal* 279.

coherence within international law, but in order to maintain their own institutional legitimacy and credibility (IV).

II. Potential for conflicts within international human rights law

The potential for conflicts within international human rights law has been significantly increased through the proliferation of international legal regimes and institutions for the protection of human rights (1). However, procedural rules significantly mitigate the danger of conflicts of jurisdiction (2). Conflicts of jurisprudence, on the other hand, pose a realistic threat to the coherence and integrity of international human rights law. This potential for conflict is caused not so much by incompatible substantive provisions of the different human rights treaties but rather by the different structural biases and institutional preferences that are at work within the different human rights treaty bodies (3).

1. *The proliferation of international human rights regimes and institutions*

On the universal level, international human rights law was developed mainly within the institutional context of the United Nations. The UN Charter contains a general commitment to human rights[12] and recognizes the protection and promotion of human rights as a purpose of the United Nations as a whole[13] and of the General Assembly,[14] the Economic and Social Council,[15] as well as the trusteeship system[16] in particular. Soon after the founding of the United Nations, the Commission on Human Rights prepared and the General Assembly adopted the Universal Declaration of Human Rights (UDHR).[17] Based on the Universal Declaration, the member states of the United Nations negotiated and concluded the International Covenant on Civil and Political Rights (ICCPR)[18] and the International Covenant on Economic, Social and Cultural Rights

[12] Preamble of the UN Charter.

[13] Article 1, para. 3; Article 55, para. 3, Article 56 of the UN Charter.

[14] Article 13, para. 1, lit. b) of the UN Charter.

[15] Article 62, para. 2 of the UN Charter.

[16] Article 77 lit. c) of the UN Charter.

[17] General Assembly Resolution 217 A (III), 10 December 1948, UN Doc. A/810 (1948).

[18] International Covenant on Civil and Political Rights, New York, 16 December 1966, in force 23 March 1976, 999 UNTS 171.

(ICESCR).[19] Together with seven other human rights treaties – dealing with specific forms of human rights violations or devoted to the protection of specific groups[20] – these nine treaties constitute the normative core of the UN human rights system.[21]

Each of these nine treaties establishes a treaty body, composed of independent experts.[22] These UN human rights treaty bodies are responsible for monitoring compliance with and implementation of the respective treaty by the state parties. To this purpose, all nine treaties establish an obligation of the member states to periodically submit reports to the respective committee on measures they have adopted in order to fulfill and comply with their treaty obligations.[23] All nine treaty regimes furthermore provide for a complaint procedure through which individuals can submit communications to the treaty body, claiming that a state party has

[19] International Covenant on Economic, Social and Cultural Rights, New York, 16 December 1966, in force 3 January 1976, 993 UNTS 3.

[20] International Convention on the Elimination of All Forms of Racial Discrimination (ICERD), New York, 21 December 1965, in force 4 January 1969, 660 UNTS 195; Convention on the Elimination of Discrimination Against Women (CEDAW), New York, 18 December 1979, in force 3 September 1981, 1249 UNTS 13; Convention against Torture and Other Cruel, Inhuman or Degrading Treatment or Punishment (CAT), New York, 10 December 1984, in force 26 June 1987, 1465 UNTS 85; Convention on the Rights of the Child (CRC), New York, 20 November 1989, in force 18 November 2002, 1577 UNTS 3; International Convention on the Protection of the Rights of All Migrant Workers and Members of their Families (ICMW), New York, 18 December 1990, in force 1 July 2003, 2220 UNTS 3; Convention on the Rights of Persons with Disabilities (CRPD), New York, 13 December 2006, in force 3 May 2008, 2515 UNTS 3; International Convention for the Protection of All Persons from Enforced Disappearance (ICED), New York, General Assembly Resolution 61/177, 20 December 2006, in force 23 December 2010, UN Doc. A/61/488.

[21] Numerous other universal treaties are dedicated to the protection of human beings, such as the Convention on the Prevention and Punishment of the Crime of Genocide, Paris, 9 December 1948, in force 12 January 1951, 78 UNTS 277, or the International Convention on the Suppression and Punishment of the Crime of Apartheid, New York, 30 November 1973, in force 18 July 1976, 1015 UNTS 243. However, since those treaties neither establish supervisory bodies nor individual complaints mechanisms, they do not contribute to the institutional fragmentation of international human rights law and are therefore outside of the scope of this chapter.

[22] The ICESCR does not establish a separate treaty body but determines that the UN Economic and Social Council (ECOSOC) should exercise the supervisory function. The ECOSOC, however, established the Committee on Economic, Social and Cultural Rights and delegated its supervisory functions on this Committee, which is structurally similar to the other UN human rights treaty bodies.

[23] For an overview of the reporting procedure see I. Bantekas and L. Oette, *International Human Rights, Law and Practice* (Cambridge: Cambridge University Press, 2013), pp. 187–97.

violated their treaty rights. This individual complaints procedure is, however, optional. It is only admissible with regard to violations committed by states that have explicitly accepted this mechanism.[24]

States have ratified the nine human rights treaties and accepted the individual complaints procedures to varying degrees. As Thomas Buergenthal and Daniel Thürer write, today every state is party to at least one of the nine core human rights treaties, and more than 80 per cent of all states are party to four or more.[25] The number of member states to the human rights treaties is rising constantly, with the CRC and the CEDAW having reached an almost universal level of ratification, and with the ICCPR and the ICESCR covering more than 80 per cent of all UN member states.[26] The individual complaints mechanisms have been accepted to a more varying degree, which is due partly to their relatively recent establishment, and partly to general concerns of states with regard to subjecting themselves to quasi-judicial enforcement mechanisms on the international level.[27] While the complaint mechanisms of the ICCPR and of the CEDAW have been accepted by more than 100 states each, states seem to be more reluctant with regard to the same mechanism under the ICERD and the CAT. Taking into account its relatively recent nature, the individual complaints procedure of the CRPD is already quite widespread, while the newly established complaint procedures under the ICED and the ICESCR have not yet been widely accepted. The complaint procedures under the CRC have entered into force in April 2014, and, due to the lack of a sufficient number of ratifications, the procedure under the ICMW has not yet entered into force.

The universal human rights architecture therefore consists of a number of international treaties codifying catalogues of civil and political rights

[24] The treaty regimes also establish different procedures for inter-state complaints; however, until today none of these mechanisms has ever been used in practice; see on this I. Bantekas and L. Oette, *International Human Rights, Law and Practice* (Cambridge: Cambridge University Press, 2013), pp. 201–2.

[25] T. Buergenthal and D. Thürer, *Menschenrechte* (Baden-Baden: Nomos, 2010), p. 64.

[26] As of April 2015 the ICCPR has 168 and the ICESCR 164 member states. The CRC is ratified by 194 states, the CEDAW by 188, the ICERD by 177 and the CAT by 157 states. The relatively new human rights treaties are slowly catching up, with the CRPD being ratified by 153 states, 47 states being party to the ICMW and 46 states to the ICED. The current status of ratification for each treaty is available in the online database of the United Nations Treaty Collection, at http://treaties.un.org.

[27] As of April 2015 the numbers of states that have accepted the individual complaints procedures are as follows: ICCPR 115 states; CEDAW 105 states; CRPD 86 states; CAT 67 states; ICERD 56 states; ICED 19 states; ICESCR 20 states; CRC 17 states; ICMW 4 states.

(ICCPR) and of economic, social and cultural rights (ICESCR) as well as treaties devoted to specific forms of human rights violations or to the protection of specific groups. The nine core treaties are supervised by treaty bodies that can increasingly be addressed by victims of human rights violations through individual complaints. Moreover, each treaty body contributes to the interpretation and development of its respective legal regime through the examination of state reports[28] as well as through the adoption of general comments[29] on specific provisions of the treaties and on aspects of their implementation.

The proliferation of substantive human rights guarantees, institutional supervisory bodies, and individual complaints mechanisms can potentially lead to conflicts within international human rights law. From a legal perspective, two different types of conflict have to be distinguished: conflicts of jurisdiction (2) and conflicts of jurisprudence (3).

2. *Conflicts of jurisdiction and their avoidance through procedural safeguards*

Conflicts of jurisdiction can arise when different dispute-settlement institutions decide the same case in a different manner. From the perspective of the parties to the proceedings, such a conflict of jurisdiction raises the question of which decision they have to follow, a question that is not easy to answer in the absence of a clear institutional hierarchy in the international judicial architecture. Conflicts of jurisdiction therefore can lead to incoherent or even contradictory normative commands.[30]

However, within international human rights law, the danger of conflicts of jurisdiction is significantly mitigated through the procedural principles of litispendence and *res judicata*. Litispendence is firmly established as a legal principle in international human rights law. It stipulates that a treaty

[28] See, e.g., W. Kälin, 'Examination of state reports', in H. Keller and G. Ulfstein (eds.), *UN Human Rights Treaty Bodies* (Cambridge: Cambridge University Press, 2012), p. 16 et seq.

[29] See, e.g., H. Keller and L. Grover, 'General Comments of the Human Rights Committee and their legitimacy', in H. Keller and G. Ulfstein (eds.), *UN Human Rights Treaty Bodies* (Cambridge: Cambridge University Press, 2012), p. 116 et seq.

[30] From a strictly formal point of view one might argue that conflicts of jurisdiction cannot arise within the UN human rights treaty bodies, since these treaty bodies do not have the competence to issue legally binding decisions. However, decisions of the treaty bodies entail normative expectations and create an obligation of member states to at least take them into consideration. On the legal status of decisions by the UN treaty bodies, see G. Ulfstein, 'Individual complaints', in H. Keller and G. Ulfstein (eds.), *UN Human Rights Treaty Bodies* (Cambridge: Cambridge University Press, 2012), pp. 73, 92–100.

body may not deal with a case while it is being examined under another procedure of international investigation or settlement. In general, the principle applies to all individual complaints procedures. It is explicitly codified in most human rights treaties or in the optional protocols that establish the individual complaints procedure.[31] While the ICERD does not contain such an explicit provision, numerous, in particular European, states have made reservations with the aim of making the principle of litispendence applicable when they accepted the competence of the treaty body to receive and consider individual complaints.

The principle of litispendence only prevents multiple supervisory bodies from dealing with the same case at the same time. The principle of *res judicata*, on the other hand, precludes a treaty body from dealing with a complaint when the same case has already been examined by a different treaty body. Most treaties or optional protocols contain a provision that declares complaints inadmissible if the same case has already been examined by a different procedure of international investigation or settlement.[32] Thereby they exclude examinations of and decisions in the same case by multiple treaty bodies or regional human rights courts.[33] However, the *res judicata* principle is not explicitly provided for in the regimes of the ICERD, the ICCPR, and the ICED. Again, at least with regard to individual complaints under the ICERD and the ICCPR, numerous states have made reservations with the aim of making the *res judicata* principle applicable.

In conclusion, the principles of litispendence and *res judicata* find widespread applicability with regard to the UN human rights treaty bodies' individual complaints procedures. In most cases – albeit not in every case – they prevent diverging decisions between the treaty bodies as well

[31] See, e.g., Article 5, para. 2, lit. a) of the Optional Protocol to the International Covenant on Civil and Political Rights, New York, 16 December 1966, in force 23 March 1976, 999 UNTS 171; Article 4, para. 2, lit. a) of the Optional Protocol to the Convention on the Elimination of All Forms of Discrimination against Women, New York, 6 October 1999, in force 22 December 2000, 2131 UNTS 83; Article 22, para. 5 lit. a) of the CAT.

[32] See Article 22, para. 5, lit. a) of the CAT; Article 4, para. 2, lit. a) of the Optional Protocol to the CEDAW; Article 7, lit. d) of the Optional Protocol to the Convention on the Rights of the Child on a communications procedure, New York, 19 December 2011, in force 14 April 2014. UN Doc. A/RES/66/138; Article 3, para. 2, lit. c) of the Optional Protocol to the ICESCR; Article 77, para. 3, lit. a) ICMW; Article 2, lit. c) of the Optional Protocol to the Convention on the Rights of Persons with Disabilities, New York, 13 December 2006, in force 2 May 2008, UN Doc. A/61/611.

[33] On the scope of the *res judicata* principle see O. De Schutter, *International Human Rights Law* (Cambridge: Cambridge University Press, 2010), p. 825 et seq.

as between the UN treaty bodies and regional enforcement mechanisms such as the European Court of Human Rights[34] or the Inter-American system for the protection of human rights.[35]

3. *Conflicts of jurisprudence and the danger of incoherence and incompatibility*

Conflicts of jurisprudence arise when treaty bodies give diverging interpretations to the same rules of human rights law in different cases.[36] Just like domestic constitutional rights guarantees, human rights provisions are highly open for interpretation. And while the UN human rights treaty bodies neither have a competence to make legally binding decisions, nor are explicitly provided with a mandate to interpret their respective human rights treaty in an authentic manner, their pronouncements on the interpretation of specific treaty provisions are highly authoritative and significantly influence legal discourse and human rights practice. The treaty bodies contribute to the interpretation of human rights provisions through different mechanisms: through general recommendations, through comments on state reports, or through their opinions with regard to individual complaints. And while each treaty body is mandated only to supervise its 'own' human rights treaty, there is nonetheless a potential for diverging interpretations and therefore conflicts of jurisprudence.

a. The shared normative content of the UN human rights treaties

While each UN human rights treaty technically constitutes an independent legal instrument, all nine treaties are part of the larger normative framework of international human rights law and are based on a common political and moral understanding of human rights. All human rights

[34] See Article 35, para. 2, lit. b) of the (European) Convention for the Protection of Human Rights and Fundamental Freedoms (ECHR), Rome, 4 November 1950, in force 3 September 1953, 194 CETS; European Court of Human Rights, *Decision on the Competence of the Court to give an Advisory Opinion*, 2 June 2004, paras. 29–31.

[35] See Article 46, para. 1, lit. c) and Article 47, lit. d) of the American Convention on Human Rights, 22 November 1969, in force 18 July 1978, 36 OAS Treaty Series; Inter-American Commission on Human Rights, Report No. 47/08, 4 July 2008, Petition 864–05, *Luis, Richard' Vélez et al.* v. *Colombia*, paras. 62–6.

[36] See 'The Proliferation of International Judicial Bodies: The Outlook for the International Legal Order', Speech by His Excellency Judge Gilbert Guillaume, President of the International Court of Justice, to the Sixth Committee of the General Assembly of the United Nations, 27 October 2000, available at www.icj-cij.org.

treaties refer to the principles of the UN Charter and to the UDHR. All refer to the inherent dignity and equality of the human person and of each member of the human family, concepts that form the moral foundation of human rights. Despite the political and ideological debates about human rights, about their universality, contingency, and relativity, all human rights treaties find their deeper justification in the intersubjectively comprehensible sense of human suffering and in the vulnerability of the human person, experienced in the twentieth century through the Shoah, apartheid, and, as the Preamble of the UDHR phrases it, through other 'barbarous acts which have outraged the conscience of mankind'.

The Universal Declaration therefore constitutes the shared normative basis and common point of reference for all UN human rights treaties. The two Covenants build upon the rights guaranteed in the Declaration. They substantiate them, make them legally binding and applicable in legal discourses and proceedings, and institute mechanisms for their supervision and protection. The ICERD builds upon the Universal Declaration's commitment to the equality of every human being in dignity and rights,[37] to the entitlement to all rights without distinction of race,[38] to equality and equal protection of the law without any discrimination and to protection against discrimination.[39] The CEDAW builds upon the UDHR's commitment to equal rights of men and women,[40] to equality in dignity and rights, and the entitlement to all rights without discrimination of sex. The CAT builds upon and expands the Declaration's prohibition of torture and cruel, inhuman or degrading treatment or punishment.[41] The CRC and the CRPD enunciate the UDHR's commitment to equality, dignity, and self-determination with regard to the specifically vulnerable groups of children[42] and of people with disabilities.

Against this background, the nine human rights treaties do not contain different rights but protect different aspects of the same rights: Freedom of expression, for example, is guaranteed as a human right in the UDHR[43] and in the ICCPR.[44] The ICERD aims at ensuring that every person enjoys this right without distinction as to race, colour, or national or ethnic origin.[45] Articles 12 and 13 of the CRC confirm that freedom of expression is also a right of every child and aim at realizing this right in a child-appropriate manner and in particular with regard to judicial

[37] Article 1 of the UDHR. [38] Article 2 of the UDHR. [39] Article 7 of the UDHR.
[40] Preamble of the UDHR. [41] Article 5 of the UDHR.
[42] Article 25, para. 2 of the UDHR. [43] Article 19 of the UDHR.
[44] Article 19 of the ICCPR. [45] Article 5, para. d) (viii) of the ICERD.

and administrative proceedings affecting the child. And while it is beyond doubt that people with disabilities also bear the right to freedom of expression, the CRPD aims at guaranteeing that they can actually exercise this right.[46] All these guarantees build upon a common concept of freedom of expression as a universal and inalienable right of every person.

While this shared normative content of the human rights treaties reflects the universality of human rights, it can lead to diverging or conflicting interpretations. Even though the UDHR, the ICCPR, the ICERD, the CRC, and the CRPD all refer to the same right of freedom of expression, it is not guaranteed, that the Human Rights Committee, the Committee on the Elimination of Racial Discrimination, the Committee on the Rights of the Child, and the Committee on the Rights of Persons with Disabilities will interpret this right in the same manner. The multiplication of human rights treaties, supervisory institutions, and enforcement mechanisms therefore creates the possibility that human rights bodies will advance different interpretations of the same right.

However, while such divergences in interpretation might be regarded as a challenge to the coherence of international human rights law and to the concept of the universality of human rights, they do not necessarily lead to legal conflicts in a strict sense. If, for example, one treaty body argues in favour of a more extensive understanding of freedom of expression, and another treaty body makes a more restrictive ruling, the two rulings do not lead to an incompatible legal situation. Different treaties can guarantee more far-reaching or more restrictive levels of protection to individuals and can contain more far-reaching or more restrictive levels of obligation for states. But that does not mean that the rights and obligations under these treaties are conflicting or incompatible with each other.

b. Conflicting rights, balancing rights

Human rights are not guaranteed absolutely but are subject to limitations.[47] Rights can be restricted to further public interests. And when the right of one individual collides with the right of another, one right has to retreat. In the case of racially discriminatory speech, for example, the right of freedom of expression can collide with the right to be protected against racial discrimination.[48] In general, two different approaches to

[46] Article 21 of the CRPD.

[47] See, e.g., O. De Schutter, *International Human Rights Law* (Cambridge: Cambridge University Press, 2010), p. 288 et seq.

[48] Article 26 of the ICCPR; Articles 2, 4, and 6 of the ICERD.

solving such a collision seem possible. One could either argue that the dissemination of racially discriminatory ideas is not protected by freedom of speech at all, thereby denying that there is an actual conflict between two rights. Or one could accept that freedom of expression, in general, also protects racially discriminatory speech but that restrictions on this right – for example in the form of criminal prosecution for the dissemination of racist ideas – can be justified in order to protect other rights or public interests.

When human rights treaty bodies or courts are faced with the task of solving such rights collisions, there is a potential for conflicts of jurisprudence. While one decision-making body may decide that racially discriminatory speech is not protected at all, others may regard freedom of expression as a more encompassing right that includes even forms of malign speech. Under the latter approach it becomes necessary to strike a balance[49] between freedom of speech and the legitimate concern of combating racism, and the decision-making bodies may strike the balance between those two interests in different ways, giving either more weight to freedom of expression or to the goals of anti-discrimination. As a result, conflicts between the jurisprudence of the different treaty bodies – and between the treaty bodies and regional human rights courts as well as domestic courts – can entail.

c. Dimensions of conflict: substantive conflicts and institutional conflicts

How are such interpretative conflicts, or conflicts of jurisprudence, dealt with within the UN human rights system? The procedural safeguards that, at least to a large degree, prevent international courts and treaty bodies from deciding the same case differently cannot prevent these institutions from interpreting their respective treaties in a substantively conflicting manner. Conflicts of jurisprudence do not occur through multiple institutions deciding the same case but through treaty bodies and courts interpreting rights and solving rights collisions in an incompatible manner.

[49] On balancing conflicting rights in general, see, e.g., J. Klabbers, *International Law* (Cambridge: Cambridge University Press, 2013), p. 114; on the evolution of proportionality analysis and balancing as general constitutionalist concepts, see A. Stone Sweet and J. Matthews, 'Proportionality Balancing and Global Constitutionalism' (2008) 47 *Columbia Journal of Transnational Law* 68.

Coherence between the treaty regimes is rather maintained through the substantive provisions of the treaties. As the references to the UDHR in every treaty's preamble indicates, the treaties are not to be understood as self-contained regimes but as part of a larger normative framework of international human rights law. The universality of human rights implies the lack of a hierarchy between those rights: in the abstract, no right is more important than any other right. In accordance with this understanding, even the specialized human rights treaties that are concerned with a specific kind of human rights violation (as, for example, the CAT) or with the protection of a specific group of people (as, for example, the CEDAW or the CRC) contain provisions that aim at reconciling the treaty with the general body of human rights law. The ICERD, for example, not only aims at preventing and abolishing discriminatory acts and practices but targets also the dissemination of racially discriminatory ideas and incitement to racial discrimination. To that purpose, the member states of the ICERD are obliged to declare such speech to be a criminal offence, and to prosecute instances of racially offensive speech accordingly.[50] This obligation, however, is not phrased in absolute terms. The framers of the Convention recognized the potential conflict with freedom of expression and therefore stipulated that the member states would have to pay 'due regard' to other human rights, including freedom of expression, when implementing their obligations under the ICERD.[51] Accordingly, when they ratified the ICERD, numerous states made declarations, emphasizing that the 'due regard' clause guaranteed that the ICERD did not oblige them to enact legislation that would be incompatible with the freedom of expression.[52] While the specialized human rights treaties therefore emphasize a specific aspect of human rights protection and lift it out of the general human rights discourse, they reflect awareness of the shared normative content of all human rights codifications and the intention not to conflict with other human rights guarantees.

The potential for conflicts of jurisprudence within international human rights law therefore lies not so much in the substantive provisions of the treaties as such, but rather in the institutional rationalities at work when

[50] Article 4, para. a) of the ICERD.

[51] Article 4 of the ICERD refers to the UDHR, and thereby to the guarantee of freedom of expression in Article 19 of the UDHR, as well as to the guarantee of freedom of expression in Article 5, para. d) (viii) of the ICERD.

[52] The declarations are published in the United Nations Treaty Collection database, available at http://treaties.un.org.

the supervisory bodies interpret the treaties. As Martti Koskenniemi has pointed out, 'it is anything but irrelevant to know, regardless of what the law is, which institution gets to decide'.[53] Or as the former President of the International Court of Justice, Judge Gilbert Guillaume phrased it in his address to the Sixth Committee of the General Assembly in 2000: 'specialized courts . . . are inclined to favour their own disciplines'.[54] This institutional dimension of the fragmentation debate is widely recognized today. However, it is mainly analysed with regard to the institutional relationship between the functionally defined issue-areas or sub-fields of international law that are at the heart of the fragmentation debate. Within the context of the 'human rights and trade' debate, for example, it is pointed out that it is less decisive how the substantive provisions of trade treaties or human rights treaties deal with this relationship, but rather whether the Dispute Settlement Body of the World Trade Organization or a human rights treaty body or court decides a case.[55] While both institutions may decide the case on the basis of the same or similar substantive provisions, they will look at it either through the prism of trade law or from the perspective of human rights law and they will exhibit different structural biases when deciding the case.[56]

This focus on the interaction of the generally recognized sub-systems of international law – for example human rights law and international trade law – must not conceal the fact that those sub-systems themselves do not consist of a homogenous mass of actors with a shared rationality. In the case of human rights law, for example, they may be utterly divided with regard to the content of specific human rights obligations or the 'best'

[53] M. Koskenniemi, 'The Politics of International Law – 20 Years Later' (2009) 20 *European Journal of International Law* 7, 10.

[54] 'The Proliferation of International Judicial Bodies: The Outlook for the International Legal Order', Speech by His Excellency Judge Gilbert Guillaume, President of the International Court of Justice, to the Sixth Committee of the General Assembly of the United Nations, 27 October 2000, available at www.icj-cij.org.

[55] See, e.g., M. Koskenniemi and P. Leino, 'Fragmentation of International Law? Postmodern Anxieties' (2002) 15 *Leiden Journal of International Law* 553, 570 et seq.

[56] For an extensive discussion of this point see M. Koskenniemi, 'The Politics of International Law – 20 Years Later' (2009) 20 *European Journal of International Law* 7; M. Koskenniemi, *From Apology to Utopia* (Cambridge: Cambridge University Press, 2nd edn. 2005), p. 600 et seq; A. Lang, 'Legal Regimes and Professional Knowledges: The Internal Politics of Regime Definition', in M. A. Young (ed.), *Regime Interaction in International Law: Facing Fragmentation* (Cambridge: Cambridge University Press, 2012), p. 113; S. Singh, 'The Potential of International Law: Fragmentation and Ethics' (2011) 24 *Leiden Journal of International Law* 24.

way to implement human rights.[57] Moreover, international human rights law is not only a sub-system of general international law but has itself experienced a process of further differentiation. Human rights lawyers may understand themselves not so much as human rights lawyers, but as anti-discrimination, feminist, or children's lawyers. They may not deal with human rights in general, but rather with torture, forced disappearance or with the suffering of ethnic minorities. While they may appear to be a homogenous group of human rights lawyers from an external perspective, a closer look reveals a higher degree of differentiation within the institutional architecture of international human rights law.

One may therefore not only identify a certain structural bias at work within a human rights treaty body that distinguishes that body from, for example, an international trade institution. There may also be different institutional rationalities at work within an anti-racism body as opposed to a children's rights committee or a general human rights supervisory institution. Just as the members of a human rights treaty body may, in general, display stronger preferences with regard to human rights issues in trade law cases, these more specialized human rights bodies may exhibit a structural bias with regard to 'their' human rights issue as opposed to other human rights concerns. Such a structural bias or institutional preference will prove to be relevant when different human rights concerns collide and a balance needs to be struck, as with the example of freedom of expression (as a general human rights concern) and the prevention of racist speech (as a more specific anti-discrimination concern). The human rights treaties themselves do not solve such conflicts in an abstract manner. The ICERD merely provides that 'due regard' has to be paid to freedom of expression when the member states implement their obligation to countervail the dissemination of racist ideas, thereby leaving some degree of leeway to the decision-making bodies and to the parties to the ICERD.

While such preferences of the human rights treaty bodies are not embodied in the substantive provisions of the treaties, they are empirically verifiable and can be explained in a plausible manner. Even a quick glimpse at the biographies of the current members of the different human rights treaty bodies reveals that most of them were not only involved with

57 See again M. Koskenniemi, 'The Politics of International Law – 20 Years Later' (2009) 20 *European Journal of International Law* 7, 13: 'Economists, environmentalists, and human rights experts are just as divided among themselves as Finns, Frenchmen, or Fijians about how to understand the world and what to do with it.'

human rights in general, but also with the specific sub-fields of human rights law they are now concerned with on the Committee. Of the members of the Committee established under CEDAW, for example, almost all have dealt with women's rights and gender equality before being called to the Committee, which comes as no surprise since the CEDAW requires 'competence in the field covered by the Convention'[58] in order for candidates to be eligible. A similar observation applies to the members of the Committee on the Rights of the Child,[59] and to the experts on the Committee on the Elimination of Racial Discrimination.[60] Members of the treaty bodies will regularly have a specific knowledge, interest and sympathy for the field covered by the respective convention already when they take up their office. Such an affinity will most probably be confirmed and reinforced through the work on the Committee: through the cooperation and discussion with the colleagues on the Committee, through the contact with non-governmental organizations and other representatives of civil society, and through the confrontation with cases and individuals who have been victims of such specific human rights violations. These aspects increase the probability that the members of a Committee will incrementally identify with the concern and purpose of 'their' human rights regime and will be disposed to emphasize its significance in general but also in relation to other human rights concerns.

While such an institutional preference of the human rights treaty bodies with regard to the human rights concern embodied in the respective treaty is, in general, not to be criticized but rather to be welcomed, since it guarantees that the members will be open, sympathetic and sensitive with regard to the victims of human rights violations, this structural bias can be problematic for the coherence and inner compatibility of international human rights law, when two legitimate human rights concerns collide.

III. Freedom of speech and the international Convention on the Elimination of All Forms of Racial Discrimination

The decision of the Committee on the Elimination of Racial Discrimination in the case of the *Turkish Union in Berlin/Brandenburg* v. *Germany* –

[58] Article 17, para.1 of the CEDAW. [59] See Article 43, para. 2 of the CRC.

[60] Article 8, para. 1 of the ICERD, however, does not specify whether the candidates need to have a particular professional background in the field of racial discrimination but demands, more generally, 'high moral standing and acknowledged impartiality'.

better known as the *Sarrazin* case – illustrates this potential for conflicts of jurisprudence within international human rights law.[61]

1. The Sarrazin *decision*

The case before the ICERD Committee revolved around an interview with Thilo Sarrazin, a former Finance Senator of Berlin and member of the Board of Directors of the German Central Bank, that was published in the German cultural journal *Lettre International* in September 2009.[62] During that interview Mr Sarrazin addressed the economic and social situation in Berlin as well as the topic of migration and made some highly controversial statements that caused public outrage within Germany and abroad. Mr Sarrazin advocated a general prohibition of influx, except for highly qualified individuals, and the abolishment of social welfare services for immigrants. He referred to the large and growing number of Arabs and Turks in Berlin who, according to Mr Sarrazin, had no productive function, except for the fruit and vegetable trade, to the high birthrates among Arabs and Turks, the 'constant supply' of brides from Turkey, the 'production of little headscarf girls', and the unwillingness to integrate of 70 per cent of the Turkish and 90 per cent of the Arab population. He complemented these statements with pseudo-scientific references to such 'facts' as the about 15 per cent higher IQ of East European Jews as compared to Germans and to the at least to some extent hereditary nature of human ability.

In response to this interview, the Turkish Union in Berlin/Brandenburg (TBB) filed a criminal complaint against Mr Sarrazin. The Office of Public Prosecution, however, concluded that Mr Sarrazin's statements neither amounted to incitement to hatred[63] nor to a punishable insult.[64] The

[61] Committee on the Elimination of Racial Discrimination, Communication No. 48/2010, Decision of 26 February 2013, *TBB* v. *Germany*, UN Doc. CERD/C/82/D/48/2010. Mr Carlos Manuel Vazquez has submitted an individual opinion that is appended to the decision, UN Doc. CERD/C/82/3. I have commented on the decision in more detail elsewhere, see M. Payandeh, 'Die Entscheidung des UN-Ausschusses gegen Rassendiskriminierung im Fall Sarrazin' (2013) *Juristenzeitung* 980.

[62] 'Thilo Sarrazin im Gespräch, Klasse statt Masse, Von der Hauptstadt der Transferleistungen zur Metropole der Eliten', *Lettre International*, number 86, 2009 fall edition, p. 197 et seq.

[63] Article 130, para. 1 of the German Criminal Code reads: 'Whoever, in a manner that is capable of disturbing the public peace: 1. incites hatred against segments of the population or calls for violent or arbitrary measures against them; or 2. assaults the human dignity of others by insulting, maliciously maligning, or defaming segments of the population, shall be punished with imprisonment from three months to five years.'

[64] Article 185 of the German Criminal Code reads: 'Insult shall be punished with imprisonment for not more than one year or a fine and, if the insult is committed by means of violence, with imprisonment for not more than two years or a fine.'

Office of Public Prosecution therefore terminated the proceedings, and the General Prosecutor, in its supervisory role, upheld that decision.

The TBB then filed an individual complaint against Germany to the Committee on the Elimination of Racial Discrimination, claiming that Germany had violated its obligations under the ICERD.[65] Under Article 4, para. a) of the ICERD the member states have to declare the dissemination of ideas based on racial superiority or hatred and incitement to racial discrimination as punishable offences. The Committee concluded that Mr Sarrazin's statements 'contain ideas of racial superiority, denying respect as human beings and depicting generalized negative characteristics of the Turkish population, as well as incitement to racial discrimination in order to deny them access to social welfare and speaking about a general prohibition of immigration influx except for highly qualified individuals'.[66] The Committee emphasized that Article 4 also demands that criminal provisions must be effectively implemented,[67] and that through its decision not to prosecute Mr Sarrazin, Germany had violated this obligation.[68] Since Mr Sarrazin's statements qualified as a dissemination of racist ideas, they could not be justified by freedom of speech.[69] The Committee furthermore expressed concerns whether the German Criminal Code adequately translates the obligations under the ICERD into domestic law,[70] and recommended that Germany review its policy and procedures concerning the prosecution of racially discriminatory statements.[71]

2. *Critical assessment*

The *Sarrazin* decision of the Committee on the Elimination of Racial Discrimination is highly problematic for a variety of reasons.[72] Most

[65] Germany has ratified the ICERD on 16 May 1969 and has accepted the individual complaints mechanism under Article 14 of the ICERD with a declaration of 30 August 2001.

[66] Committee on the Elimination of Racial Discrimination, Communication No. 48/2010, Decision of 26 February 2013, *TBB* v. *Germany*, UN Doc. CERD/C/82/D/48/2010, para. 12.6.

[67] *Ibid.*, para. 12.4.

[68] *Ibid.*, para. 12.6. The Committee furthermore refers to Article 2, para. d) of the ICERD, the more general obligation of member states to prohibit and bring to an end racial discrimination, and to Article 6 of the ICERD, the obligation to provide for effective protection and remedies against any acts of racial discrimination.

[69] *Ibid.*, para. 12.7. [70] *Ibid.*, para. 12.8. [71] *Ibid.*, para. 14.

[72] For a comprehensive appraisel of the decision see C. Tomuschat, 'Der "Fall Sarrazin" vor dem UN-Rassendiskriminierungsausschuss' (2013) *Europäische Grundrechte-Zeitschrift* 262; M. Payandeh, 'Die Entscheidung des UN-Ausschusses gegen Rassendiskriminierung im Fall Sarrazin' (2013) *Juristenzeitung*, 980.

problematic from the perspective of a possible fragmentation within international human rights law, however, is the Committee's dismissive treatment of freedom of expression. While the Committee pays lip-service to the 'due regard' clause that demands consideration of other human rights, it categorically declines to grant any protection under freedom of expression to racially discriminatory speech.[73] This approach is not only problematic due to the rather extensive definition of racial discrimination under the ICERD[74] that is highly open to interpretation. It also neglects the wording of Article 4 of the ICERD which leaves the relationship between the obligation to criminalize impugned speech and other human rights considerations open and does not stipulate a general priority of the former over the latter.[75] This understanding of the provision is reinforced by the drafting history of the ICERD, during which many states voiced severe concerns over the compatibility of the ICERD with the freedom of expression. The 'due regard' clause was inserted in order to accommodate those concerns.[76] Interpretative statements made by many states during the ratification process lend further support to this reading of the 'due regard' clause.[77]

Moreover, the preambular reference of the ICERD to the UDHR as well as the 'due regard' clause indicate that the framers of the ICERD did not want to contradict other human rights guarantees. And while the UDHR as well as the ICCPR recognize that freedom of expression can – and should – be restricted in order to prevent racially discriminatory speech,[78] neither of them stipulates a general priority of anti-discrimination concerns over freedom of speech. Similarly, the European Court of Human Rights has held that while severe cases of racist hate speech run counter

[73] The Committee refers to its General Recommendation XV, Organized violence based on ethnic origin (Art. 4), 23 March 1993, para. 4 and to Communcation No. 43/2008, Decision of 13 August 2010, *Saada Mohamad Adan* v. *Denmark*, UN Doc. CERD/C/77/D/43/2008, para. 7.6.

[74] See Article 1 of the ICERD.

[75] For a different reading see, e.g., D. Mahalic and J. G. Mahalic, 'The Limitation Provisions of the International Convention on the Elimination of All Forms of Racial Discrimination' (1987) 9 *Human Rights Quarterly* 74, 89.

[76] See J. Mchangama, 'The Sordid Origin of Hate-Speech Laws' (2011/2012) 170 *Policy Review* 45, 52 et seq.

[77] See above note 52 and accompanying text.

[78] Article 7 of the UDHR recognizes a right to equal protection against discrimination and against incitement to discrimination. Article 19, para. 3 of the ICCPR emphasizes that freedom of expression carries with it special duties and responsibilities and therefore allows for restrictions to this freedom. And Article 20, para. 2 of the ICCPR stipulates: 'Any advocacy of national, racial or religious hatred that constitutes incitement to discrimination, hostility or violence shall be prohibited by law.'

to the fundamental values of the European Convention and therefore fall outside of the scope of its protection,[79] racially discriminatory speech is, in general, protected under Article 10 of the European Convention on Human Rights, although restrictions may be justified in order to combat racial discrimination.[80]

The Committee's restrictive reading of freedom of expression furthermore neglects that the problem of balancing freedom of expression and anti-discrimination concerns does not only arise on the international level. While domestic constitutions and legal orders in general deal with this tension in different ways, comparative analysis reveals that most states do not categorically prohibit racist speech or exclude it from constitutional protection.[81] While international law may, of course, provide for and prescribe farther-reaching prohibitions against racist speech than domestic laws, the interpretation of international human rights provisions should, nonetheless, take domestic laws and in particular domestic constitutional guarantees into consideration. Such an interpretation of international law in light of domestic constitutional law is facilitated, first, by the open-textured nature of international human rights guarantees that leaves ample room for interpretation. It suggests itself, second, due to the shared historical background of international and domestic human rights guarantees. Constitutions that have been developed after the Second World War regularly build upon the UDHR.[82] Just like domestic provisions therefore may be interpreted in light of international human rights guarantees, international human rights guarantees should be open to interpretative impulses from constitutional rights guarantees. In this context, the UDHR functions as a communicative interface between the international and the domestic level. When a comparative analysis of the domestic legal orders reveals a general preference for balanced approaches to the relationship between freedom of expression and anti-discrimination concerns, there is at least an argumentative burden on the international legal order with regard to more restrictive approaches to freedom of expression.

[79] Article 17 of the ECHR; see, e.g., European Court of Human Rights, Application No. 35222/04, Decision of 20 February 2007, *Pavel Ivanov* v. *Russia*, para. 1.

[80] See, e.g., European Court of Human Rights, Application No. 15948/03, Decision of 10 July 2008, *Soulas et al.* v. *France*, para. 42 et seq.

[81] See, e.g., T. Webb, 'Verbal Poison – Criminalizing Hate Speech: A Comparative Analysis and a Proposal for the American System' (2011) 50 *Washburn Law Journal* 445.

[82] With regard to the German Constitution, see T. Rensmann, *Wertordnung und Verfassung* (Tübingen: Mohr Siebeck, 2007), p. 25 et seq.

In conclusion, the ICERD Committee's categorical exclusion of racist speech from the protection of freedom of expression neither does justice to the wording and structure of the ICERD, nor does it recognize the normative and institutional embedment of the ICERD within the broader context of human rights law consisting of universal, regional and domestic human rights guarantees.

IV. UN human rights treaty bodies: facing fragmentation

International legal discourse has been fascinated with the topic of fragmentation, a fascination that has been fuelled by the proliferation of international courts, tribunals, dispute-settlement and supervisory bodies that the modern international order has experienced, in particular since the end of the Cold War. And while many questions still remain unanswered, in general, skepticism has given way to acceptance. Fragmentation is not a new phenomenon,[83] nor is it a pathology. It is an endemic feature of international law,[84] of an international legal order that lacks a clear normative and institutional hierarchy.[85] Accordingly, the collapse of the international institutional architecture due to incoherent, incompatible, and colliding decisions has not yet taken place. As the former judge of the International Court of Justice, Bruno Simma, remarked: 'at least until present, and with only very few exceptions, the various judicial institutions dealing with questions of international law have displayed utmost caution in avoiding to contradict each other'.[86]

What is at stake is therefore not so much the unity and coherence of the international legal order in general[87] – the scope and existence

[83] J. Pauwelyn, 'Fragmentation of International Law', in R. Wolfrum (ed.), *Max Planck Encyclopedia of Public International Law* (Oxford: Oxford University Press, 2006), para. 7; A.-C. Martineau, 'The Rhetoric of Fragmentation: Fear and Faith in International Law' (2009) 22 *Leiden Journal of International Law* 1.

[84] Report of the Study Group of the International Law Commission, 'Fragmentation of International Law: Difficulties Arising from the Diversification and Expansion of International Law', finalized by Martti Koskenniemi, 13 April 2006, UN Doc. A/CN.4/L.682, para. 486.

[85] M. Koskenniemi and P. Leino, 'Fragmentation of International Law? Postmodern Anxieties', (2002) 15 *Leiden Journal of International Law* 553.

[86] B. Simma, 'Fragmentation in a Positive Light' (2004) 25 *Michigan Journal of International Law* 845, 846; see also M. Koskenniemi, 'Hegemonic Regimes', in M. A. Young (ed.), *Regime Interaction in International Law: Facing Fragmentation* (Cambridge: Cambridge University Press, 2012), pp. 305, 317.

[87] But see Report of the Study Group of the International Law Commission, 'Fragmentation of International Law: Difficulties Arising from the Diversification and Expansion of International Law', finalized by Martti Koskenniemi, 13 April 2006, UN Doc. A/CN.4/L.682,

of which are questionable and open for debate anyway. Fragmentation rather describes the competition of substantive interests and institutional preferences and the struggle for the prerogative of interpretation in the international legal order. It comes as no surprise that the dangers and pitfalls of the proliferation of international courts and tribunals have been emphasized most prominently by presidents of the International Court of Justice who – as Martti Koskenniemi and Päivi Leino have cogently pointed out[88] – fear a loss of influence of their institution and regard fragmentation as a challenge to the Court's distinguished status as 'the principal judicial organ of the United Nations'.[89]

Against this background, the *Sarrazin* decision can be understood as an attempt of the Committee on the Elimination of Racial Discrimination not only to advance human rights concerns in general, but also to claim a predominant role within the sub-system of international human rights law, in particular with regard to the general human rights interest of freedom of expression as it is protected under the UDHR and the ICCPR. Such a predominant role of anti-discrimination concerns, which would trump freedom of expression, does not follow from the substantive provisions of the ICERD. It is rather the result of the institutional logic at work in the specialized ICERD Committee and reflects its structural bias. Such a structural bias is, to a certain degree, not only understandable but also legitimate, since it is the basic *raison d'être* of specialized human rights regimes like the ICERD to approach the specific human rights issue they are meant to protect with particular knowledge, sensitivity, sympathy, and empathy. In the *Sarrazin* case, however, the Committee took its normative preference too far. Its decision is not supported by the substantive provisions of the ICERD, and it neglects or even conflicts with other human rights guarantees on the international, regional, and domestic level. As a result, the German government has already indicated that while it will examine 'the German legislation concerning criminal liability for racist statements in light of the Committee's views', it will also 'have to take into account the importance of freedom of speech, which is guaranteed by the German Basic Law and by international human rights law',[90] which is a

para. 15; more skeptical M. Koskenniemi and P. Leino, 'Fragmentation of International Law? Postmodern Anxieties', (2002) 15 *Leiden Journal of International Law* 553, 576–7.

88 M. Koskenniemi and P. Leino, 'Fragmentation of International Law? Postmodern Anxieties' (2002) 15 *Leiden Journal of International Law* 553, 575–6.

89 Article 92 of the UN Charter.

90 Permanent Mission of the Federal Republic of Germany to the Office of the United Nations and to other International Organizations Geneva, Note Verbale, No. 166/2013, 1 July 2013, Ref. Pol-10–504.14 SE TBB.

diplomatic way of saying that it will not fully comply with and implement the Committee's decision, a political choice that is legitimate under international law since decisions of the UN human rights treaty bodies are formally not binding.[91]

While the *Sarrazin* case therefore once again shows that international decision-making bodies have to walk the thin line between accommodating the interests of states while at the same time advancing the interests and values embodied in the treaties they are meant to supervise, it furthermore shows that they also have to consider the broader normative and institutional framework in which they operate. If UN human rights treaty bodies advance the normative and institutional preferences of the treaty regime they are meant to supervise in a manner that is incompatible with other international, regional, or domestic legal regimes, they run the risk of losing the support and acceptance not only of states and state representatives, but also of other human rights treaty bodies and courts. Singular decisions such as the *Sarrazin* decision do not pose a threat to the general unity and coherence of the international legal order. But they entail the danger of overstating one normative preference at the expense of others and of gambling away the legitimacy and credibility of an international actor.

[91] G. Ulfstein, 'Individual complaints', in H. Keller and G. Ulfstein (eds.), *UN Human Rights Treaty Bodies* (Cambridge: Cambridge University Press, 2012), pp. 73, 92–100.

12

The European Union's participation in international economic institutions: a mutually beneficial reassertion of the centre

EMANUEL CASTELLARIN

This chapter analyses the relations between the European Union (EU) and international economic institutions as an example of centre–periphery dialectics where the centre, i.e. international economic institutions, reasserts its role thanks to systemic integration with the periphery, i.e. the EU.

The chapter will argue that participating in the activity of international economic institutions, the EU obtains normative influence and social recognition, but also undergoes considerable constraints. This creates a mutually beneficial institutional and normative interaction consolidating the development of international institutional law and reinforces the legitimacy of international economic institutions as fora of global governance.

Section 1 sets the scene, presenting the EU as a conceptually peripheral international organisation and explaining why, although having developed for decades an extended concept of autonomy, it aims at a participation status in international economic institutions. Seeking social recognition by the centre of international law, the EU dilutes its specificity to play a greater role in the regulation of global economic phenomena.

Sections 2 and 3 explore the double-edged nature of participation in international institutions. Section 2 examines how the participation status obtained by the EU results from the interaction between the EU's external competences and rules of international institutional law. To be admitted, the EU accepts the conceptual and political structures of international economic institutions, shaped by classic international law, and therefore contributes to the reassertion of the centre.

Joining the community of subjects which take part in the activities of international economic institutions, the EU is subjected by the same token to international obligations and is liable for their violation. International economic institutions also control the EU's conduct both politically and by centralised dispute settlement mechanisms, which are their ultimate means of assertion, as shown in Section 3.

Section 4 concludes, submitting that different theories of international law and global governance can account for the reassertion of international economic institutions vis-à-vis the EU, as it is based at the same time on hierarchy and integration. Institutional law in not necessarily a zero-sum game and the periphery can also benefit from the reassertion of the centre.

1. The EU in multilateral international economic law: from the periphery to the centre

By trying to assert its autonomy on the international scene, the EU contributes to the reassertion of international economic institutions, classic international organisations or informal fora constituting the virtual centre of international economic law. From the institutional point of view, the EU's autonomy, more developed than in other international organisation, is a centrifuge force (1.1). Nonetheless, multilateralism is a constitutional objective for the EU, which needs to participate in international economic institutions to enhance its influence on global economic governance (1.2).

1.1. The EU's autonomy, a centrifuge force in international institutional law

Conceptually speaking, the EU is peripheral as an international legal person, often being described as a *sui generis* international organisation and as the archetype of supranational organisations as opposed to cooperation organisations.[1] Since 1957 the EC/EU integration has been a 'permanent revolution' in international law, as its basic features, such as strong integrated organs and developed external powers, are exceptional for international organisations. This institutional phenomenon corresponds to a discursive phenomenon of self-assertion aimed at strengthening the EU's autonomy, defined both as political independence (its separate will, i.e. its ability to take decisions on its own) and as institutional independence (its ability to act independently on the international scene to

[1] H. Schermers and N. Blokker, *International Institutional Law: Unity within Diversity*, 4th edition, Leiden, Martinus Nijhoff, 2003, 46–8; M. Diez de Velasco Vallejo, *Les organisations internationales*, Paris, Economica, 2002, 19–20.

defend the general interest of the community of States that created it).[2] Elaborating on a feature of all international organisations as legal persons, the Commission and the European Court of Justice (ECJ), assisted by a part of EU law doctrine, have developed a strong self-referential conception of autonomy.[3] In particular, the ECJ has contributed to this trend by its famous statements that 'the EEC Treaty has created its own legal system',[4] a 'new legal order of international law'.[5] For this reason, while being subjected to the principle of conferred powers like all international organisation, the EU has become a quasi-federal system, conscious and proud of its unique nature. Interestingly, the basic concepts for this self-assertion, such as legal personality and separate will of international organisations, came from the International Court of Justice (ICJ), the very centre of international law.[6]

Despite being authentically international, as it is the most accomplished form of union of nations, the EC/EU 'permanent revolution' became – like the Marxist concept of the same name – a 'revolution in one continent' and had initially mainly an internal effect. EC law consolidated as a special form of international law: while universal international law developed in its traditional centres (the Hague, New York, Geneva) was a law for a divided world,[7] Brussels, Luxembourg and Strasbourg became the centres of a regional integration focusing on the harmonisation of European national legal orders.[8] Indeed, acknowledgements of the EU's speciality mainly come from the inside: for example, European national constitutions and courts often distinguish the status of EU law and of international law, and academia seems to have accepted this idea

[2] J. d'Aspremont, 'The Multifaceted Concept of Autonomy', in R. Collins and N. White (eds.), *International Organizations and the Idea of Autonomy: Institutional Independence in the International Legal Order*, London, Routledge, 2011, 73–96.

[3] R. Barents, *The Autonomy of Community Law*, The Hague, Kluwer, 2004; J. Benoetxea, 'The EU as (more than) an International Organization', in J. Klabbers and A. Wallendahl (eds.), *Research Handbook on the Law of International Organizations*, Cheltenham, Edward Elgar, 2011, 448–65; N. Tsagourias, 'Conceptualizing the Autonomy of the European Union', in R. Collins and N. White (eds.), *International Organizations and the Idea of Autonomy: Institutional Independence in the International Legal Order*, London, Routledge, 2011, 339–52.

[4] ECJ, C-6/64, *Costa* v. *ENEL*, 15 July 1964, ECR 585, at 593.

[5] ECJ, C-26/62, *van Gend en Loos*, 5 February 1963, ECR 1, at 12.

[6] ICJ, *Reparation for Injuries Suffered in the Service of the United Nations*, Advisory Opinion, 11 April 1949, ICJ Reports 174.

[7] A. Cassese, *International law in a divided world*, Oxford, Clarendon, 1986.

[8] P. Pescatore, *Droit international et droit communautaire: essai de réflexion comparative*, Nancy, Centre européen universitaire, 1969.

by separating EU law from international law as an object of study and teaching.

The external implications of this conception of autonomy and integration, although not totally clear in the beginning, progressively became evident. Again inspired by the ICJ's case law,[9] the EU has gradually developed external competences and capabilities, which became particularly significant in the political context of the 1990s and the 2000s, when the end of the cold war, the completion of the internal market and the enlargement to Central and Eastern Europe opened new perspectives of assertion on the international scene. The growing research field of 'EU and international law' studies[10] is the consequence of the external projection of the EU's autonomy: the EU aims at influencing global governance, and successive modifications of its constitutive treaties have improved its powers to achieve this objective.[11] Historically and logically, economic liberalisation and regulation are the first meeting points for international law and EU law: the economic field is the core of EC/EU competences and forms an important component of the EU's external action.[12] Traditionally dwarfed by its member States in the political field, the EU

[9] *Reparation for Injuries Suffered in the Service of the United Nations*, at 178.

[10] Legal doctrine has started to concentrate on external powers in the 1960s. Among the first examples: J. Raux, *Les relations extérieures de la Communauté économique européenne*, Paris, Cujas, 1968; College of Europe, *The External Economic Policy of the Enlarged Community*, Bruges, De Tempel, 1973; K. J. Twitchett, *Europe and the World: The External Relations of the Common Market*, London, Europa, 1976. Among recent examples of 'EU and international law' studies: E. Cannizzaro, P. Palchetti and R. A. Wessel (eds.), *International Law as Law of the European Union*, Leiden, Martinus Nijhoff, 2011; L. Burgorgue-Larsen, E. Dubout, A. Maitrot de La Motte and S. Touzé (eds.), *Les interactions normatives: droit de l'Union européenne et droit international*, Paris, Pedone, 2012; M. Benlolo Carabot, U. Candas and E. Cujo (eds.), *Union européenne et droit international: en l'honneur de Patrick Daillier*, Paris, Pedone, 2012.

[11] The Lisbon treaty, following a trend in place since the Maastricht treaty, has extended the EU's external competences and conferred international legal personality to the EU (Article 47 of the Treaty of the European Union (TEU)). Thus, the EU replaces and succeeds the European Community (Article 1 TEU).

[12] Title V of TEU concerns the external action by the Union. It includes the common foreign and security policy (Articles 23–46 TEU) and other policies covered by part five of the TFEU. Among these, the common commercial policy (Articles 206–7 TFEU) and the economic, financial and technical cooperation with third countries (Articles 212–13 TFEU) are relevant to the participation in international economic institutions. Development cooperation (Articles 208–11 TFEU), humanitarian aid (Article 214 TFEU) and restrictive measures (Article 215 TFEU) complete the EU's external action. In addition, several internal policies, in particular the economic and monetary policy (Articles 119–44 TFEU), have important external consequences and are also relevant to the participation in international economic institutions.

has competences including all fields of international economic law and governs the world's first trading power and one of the biggest markets.[13]

Assertion on the international scene can be pursued unilaterally, bilaterally and multilaterally, but multilateralism is a significant objective of the EU's external action[14]: seen from Brussels, the participation in the activities of international economic institutions almost seems a manifest destiny for the EU. Although pushed to the margins of international institutional law by its centrifuge autonomy, the EU is also naturally attracted towards the centre.

1.2. *The EU's participation in international economic institutions: back to the centre*

At first sight, it is difficult to identify a single centre for international economic law, which is shaped by a complex network of unilateral acts, bilateral agreements and secondary law of international organisations. Focusing on multilateral economic institutions, the post-World War II grand design of three international organisations covering the whole area of international economic law and development in tight relation with the United Nations has evolved in a more complicated structure. The International Monetary Fund (IMF) and the World Bank group, based in Washington, are universal international organisations largely autonomous from the United Nations organisation, which is also competent for economic issues, in particular through the Second Commission of the General Assembly and the United Nations Economic and Social Council (ECOSOC). The Geneva-based World Trade Organization (WTO) is a quasi-universal international organisation, but could be created only in 1995 as an institutional upgrade of the General Agreement on Tariffs and Trade (GATT) system dating from 1947. The Organisation for Economic Cooperation and Development (OECD) is a restricted-membership

[13] In this chapter international economic law is conceived classically, as the province of public international law organising international macroeconomic relations, including commerce, investment protection, finance and currency (D. Carreau, P. Juillard, *Droit international économique*, 4th edition, Paris, Dalloz, 2010, § 8). Unlike some textbooks (A. Qureshi and A. Ziegler, *International Economic Law*, 3rd edition, London, Sweet and Maxwell, 2011), this definition does not include the regulation of all factors of production and development cooperation.

[14] The EU 'shall promote multilateral solutions to common problems' (Article 21 § 1 TEU), in particular to 'encourage the integration of all countries into the world economy, including through the progressive abolition of restrictions on international trade' (Article 21 § 2 lett. e TEU) and 'promote an international system based on stronger multilateral cooperation and good global governance' (Article 21 § 2 lett. h TEU).

international organisation, but it performs global functions of policy diffusion and surveillance of industrialised States. In addition, other institutions have become more and more important for global economic governance in the last forty years: the G-groups (G7, G8, G20), with no legal personality, and the technical fora (Bank of International Settlements, Basel Committe on Bank Control, Financial Stability Board, Financial Action Task Force, International Organisation of Securities Commission, International Association of Insurance Supervisors), each having a *sui generis* legal status.[15]

Yet, this polycentric pattern designs a virtual centre as the policies of all international economic institutions are complementary and substantially coherent. Although with different accents in Washington, Geneva, New York, Paris, Basel, etc., multilateral institutions share the same trend towards opening markets and regulating international economic phenomena to produce economic growth and development. Consequently, international economic institutions taken as a whole are the centre towards which the EU, as a peripheral international organisation, naturally turns in its quest for normative influence and social legitimacy in global economic governance. As a successful experience of integration, the EU can be seen as a frontrunner for other regional organisations, but, notwithstanding the extended competences it exercises in their normative and operational field, the EU stands as an institutional outsider vis-à-vis international economic institutions.[16] Structurally different both from those institutions and from their member States, it also differs from them for its working methods and its approach to economic integration, implying more extensive limitation of national sovereignty.

As a separate and different legal order within international law, the EU contributes to the fragmentation of the international legal order observed in the last decades.[17] Nevertheless, the EU and international economic

[15] R. Bismuth, *La coopération internationale des autorités de régulation du secteur financier et le droit international public*, Brussels, Bruylant, 2011; M. Giovanoli,'The International Financial Architecture and its Reform after the Global Crisis', in M. Giovanoli and D. Devos, *International Monetary and Financial Law: The Global Crisis*, Oxford, Oxford University Press, 2010, 3–39.

[16] F. Hoffmeister, 'Outsider or Frontrunner? Recent Developments Under International and European Law on the Status of the European Union in International Organizations and Treaty Bodies', *Common Market Law Review*, 2007, 41–68.

[17] M. Koskenniemi, Fragmentation of International Law: Difficulties Arising from the Diversification and Expansion of International Law, Report of the Study Group of the International Law Commission, UN Doc. A/CN.4/L.702 (2006). The EU is such a macroscopic example of fragmentation that, paraphrasing a well-known article on this topic (B. Simma and D. Pulkowski, 'Of Planets and the Universe: Self-contained Regimes in International

institutions share common functions, a fundamental defining element of each international institution.[18] Indeed, the progression of European internal economic integration has made clear that mutual ignorance does not help the performance of the liberalisation and regulation function and that external competences should be used to promote coordination among international institutions, including the EU and universal economic institutions.[19] After some decades of almost parallel evolution, in the last twenty years the EU's ambition to play a greater role in the international arena, the parallelism with its internal competences, and a spill-over effect inspired by the participation in the WTO in the framework of the common commercial policy have reshaped the relation between the EU and international economic institutions. Their relations used to be mainly based on external coordination shaped by administrative agreements,[20] but it has acquired a real institutional dimension including developed mutual obligations and the penetration of EU representatives within the structures of host institutions.[21]

Law', *European Journal of International Law*, 2006, 483–529), it is arguably not even a planet of the solar system, but a separate system. Yet, all systems are in the same universe, especially in times of globalisation.

[18] M. Virally, 'La notion de fonction dans la théorie de l'Organisation internationale', in *La communauté internationale: mélanges offerts à Charles Rousseau*, Paris, Pedone, 1974, 277–300.

[19] This is the most efficient way to rationalise and even 'constitutionalise' relations between international institutions (G. Ulfstein, 'Institutions and Competences', in J. Klabbers, A. Peters and G. Ulfstein (eds.), *The Constitutionalization of International Law*, Oxford, Oxford University Press, 2009, 45–80, at 71).

[20] R. J. Dupuy, 'Le droit des relations entre les organisations internationales', *Recueil des cours de l'Académie de droit international*, The Hague, 1960, vol. II, 457–589; R. Ferretti, *La coordination de l'action des organisations internationales au niveau européen*, Brussels, Bruylant, 1984.

[21] The doctrine has followed the development of the participation in international institutions since the beginning, focusing on international organisations: J.-P. Jacqué, 'La participation de la Communauté économique européenne aux organisations internationales universelles', *Annuaire Français de Droit International*, 1975, 924–48; H. Schermers, 'International Organizations as members of other International Organizations', in Völkerrecht als Rechtsordnung, internationale Gerichtsbarkeit, Menschenrechte: Festschrift für Hermann Mosler, Berlin, Springer, 1983, 823–38; J. Sack, 'The European Community's Membership of International Organizations', *Common Market Law Review*, 1995, 1227–56; R. Frid, *The Relations Between the EC and International Organizations: Legal Theory and Practice*, The Hague, Kluwer, 1995; S. Marchisio, 'EU's Membership in International Organisations', in E. Cannizzaro (ed.), *The European Union as an Actor in International Relations*, The Hague, Kluwer, 2002, 231–60; B. Corbach, Die Europäische Gemeinschaft, ihre Mitgliedstaaten und ihre Stellungin ausgewählten Internationalen Organisationen, Berlin, Logos, 2005; C. Flaesch-Mougin, 'Les relations avec les organisations internationales et la participation à celles-ci', in J.-L. Victor and M. Dony, *Le droit de la CE*

The question then arises of how the EU's participation in international economic institutions impacts on its autonomy and, on the other hand, whether international economic institutions take into account the special nature of the EU. In other words, the EU as a conceptually peripheral international organisation has to adapt to the conceptual schemes of the centre to obtain access to it, and it remains to be seen how intrusive and how reciprocal this adaptation is.

The next two sections will demonstrate that the relation between the EU and international economic institutions is dialectical but not based on conflict. On the contrary, it is mutually beneficial and results from the double nature of participation, which is a source both of social recognition and of social constraints.

2. Reassertion by integration: participation as social recognition

The participation status obtained by the EU in international economic institutions, i.e. the coherent set of rules that determine its legal condition within the institution and how it is associated to its activity, depends both on the EU's competences and on the unilateral grant of this status by each institution according to its proper law. Hence, the EU benefits from the recognition as a participant, but international economic institutions assert their institutional conceptions. The EU demands the most appropriate status it needs to exercise its external competences in the economic field, which it does extensively but never excluding its member States (2.1). Nonetheless, each host institution can accept its request or not, thereby determining to what extent the EU can participate in its activity: as the EU's admission is conditioned by constitutional specificities of each institution and by the point of view of third States within the institution, this results in a multitude of participation statuses (2.2).

2.1. Mixed participation with member States resulting from the EU's competences and self-restraint

As an international organisation, the EU is bound by the principle of conferral.[22] Therefore, the first condition to be fulfilled for the EU to become a participant in an international economic organisation is the

et de l'Union européenne: commentaire J. Mégret, Vol. 12, Relations extérieures, Brussels, Editions de l'Université de Bruxelles, 2005, 337–437.

[22] Article 5 § 1 TEU.

existence of a legal basis to do so in EU law. EU law governs what competences are conferred upon the Union and how they can be exercised – or not, as the Union can abstain from so doing. EU law also plays a major role in shaping the external representation of the EU within the concerned institution. The EU's autonomy implies that it can decide how to be represented, especially appointing the appropriate institution[23] or delegating one or several member States to exercise its competences. In this case, the organ of the State also representing the Union undergoes a *dédoublement fonctionnel*, as it is at the same time an agent of the Union.

The EU enjoys extensive economic competences, both exclusive and shared with its member States, but exercising them on the international plane to participate in an international economic institution is not as easy as exercising them internally: the nature of the targeted institution (an international organisation or an informal forum), its functions, and ultimately the willingness of EU institutions, especially the Council, must be taken into account. The EU is entitled to entertain administrative cooperation with international institutions and demand an observer status to an international organisation by Article 220 of the Treaty on the Functioning of the European Union (TFEU), which confers large discretionary power to the Commission.[24] On the contrary, becoming a member of an international organisation implies ratifying its constitutive treaty according to Article 218 TFEU or TFEU special procedures, which mainly rely on the Council and the European Parliament.

[23] The Lisbon treaty has reshaped the institutional landscape within the EU by creating a European External Action Service under the direction of the High Representative of the Union for Foreign Affairs and Security Policy (Article 27 TEU; Council decision of 26 July 2010 establishing the organisation and functioning of the European External Action Service, 2010/427/EU, OJ L 201/30). While this has an important general impact on the EU's external action, in the economic field the Commission and the ECB have maintained the most influential tasks of representation (L. Erkelens and S. Blockmans, *Setting up the European External Action Service: An institutional act of balance*, CLEER working paper 2012/1, www.asser.nl/media/1630/cleer2012-1web.pdf).

[24] The Article reads as follows:

1. The Union shall establish all appropriate forms of cooperation with the organs of the United Nations and its specialised agencies, the Council of Europe, the Organisation for Security and Cooperation in Europe and the Organisation for Economic Cooperation and Development.

The Union shall also maintain such relations as are appropriate with other international organisations.

2. The High Representative of the Union for Foreign Affairs and Security Policy and the Commission shall be instructed to implement this Article.

Moreover, EU law and practice, shaped by the ECJ case law, almost invariably requires mixed participation of the EU and its member States. In theory, the EU could participate exclusively in international economic institutions whose policies entirely correspond to exclusive policies of the EU; in practice, in the economic field the boundaries of the EU's exclusive competences do not correspond to the boundaries of the functions of each international economic institutions: international institutions have a larger mandate to facilitate international cooperation, whereas the EU's competences, conceived for regional integration, are defined more restrictively.[25] The EU's exclusive economic competences (customs union, monetary and commercial policies[26]) as defined by the TFEU are just a part of the scope of relevant international institutions, so that member States always have shared or exclusive powers in other fields covered by the same institution and cannot be totally substituted by the Union.[27]

Even if the EU had exclusive powers covering the whole scope of an international institution, member States could arguably be entitled to maintain their vested rights stemming from international agreements they entered before joining the EC/EU.[28] In case of doubt, the Council would probably prefer mixity, as it did for some commodities agreements for which the EU arguably had exclusive competence.[29] Indeed, the division of powers between the Union and its member States concerning the

[25] The situation is different for technical institutions, especially in the fields of fisheries (European Commission, COM(99) 613 final) and commodities (COM(2004) 89 final).

[26] Article 3 § 1, lett. a, c and e TFEU establishes the EU's exclusive competence in these fields.

[27] For example, in 1994 the ECJ has interpreted restrictively the scope of the common commercial policy as defined by the TEC: in consequence, intellectual property and trade in services largely came under the member States' competence, so that participation in the WTO had to be mixed (ECJ, *Opinion 1/94*, 15 November 1995, ECR 5267). Subsequent treaty amendments have extended the scope of the common commercial policy, but the harmonisation with the scope of the WTO is not complete, as the field of transport is still submitted to different rules. Similarly, the mandate of the IMF, broadly defined by Article I of the Articles of Agreement, has been extended in practice to focus not only on monetary issues, but also on macroeconomic policies, economic growth and financial stability, therefore exceeding the scope of the monetary policy as defined by Articles 127–33 TFEU.

[28] According to Article 352 TFEU, EU law does not affect the rights and obligations arising from agreements concluded with third States before the accession to the EC/EU, provided that member States 'take all appropriate steps to eliminate the incompatibilities established'.

[29] A well-known example is the interinstitutional arrangement PROBA 20 between the Commission and the Council of 27 March 1981 concerning the conclusion of commodity agreements.

participation in international institutions can also be seen as an issue of representation of the Union. As such, it can also be performed by member States benefitting from a redelegation of powers by the Union: in consequence, mixed participation would probably be always preferred in the economic field as a political compromise between the Commission (defending exclusive participation), the Council (composed by representatives of member States) and the Parliament (playing a growing role in this field since the Lisbon treaty). Therefore, the only case of substitution of European States by the EU was the participation in the GATT system before the creation of the WTO,[30] but even in that case the EU was not formally a party to the GATT, but only a *de facto* member.

Mixity is an obstacle for the self-assertion of the EU on the international scene and the ECJ has been criticised by a part of the doctrine for having shifted from its integrationist trend in the 1970s to a more States-friendly approach in the 1990s.[31] Nonetheless, mixity cannot hide that participation in international economic institutions is not only allowed, but necessary for the EU to exercise its external competences: unless they are redelegated, member States cannot exercise within the host institution the economic competences they have delegated to the Union. Seen

[30] ECJ, joined cases C-21/72, C-22/72, C-23/72, and C-24/72, *International Fruit Company*, 12 December 1972, ECR 1219, pt 14–18. The same reasoning was adopted for the 1950 Brussels Convention Establishing a Customs Cooperation Council (C-38/75, *Nederlandse Spoorwegen*, 19 November 1975, ECR 1439, pt 21), which became the World Customs Organization in 1994. However, unlike its member States, the EU is not yet a member of the WCO (its request to join the WCO was accepted in 2007, but the ratification process of the necessary amendment of the Convention is still pending). Most importantly, this reasoning has not been confirmed recently.

[31] External pre-emption, making a EU competence exclusive by its exercise (in other words, excluding members States' competences by exercise of an EU competence), is still admitted as a way of establishing the exclusivity of EU competences for policies which are not exclusive by nature: 'The Union shall also have exclusive competence for the conclusion of an international agreement when its conclusion is provided for in a legislative act of the Union or is necessary to enable the Union to exercise its internal competence, or in so far as its conclusion may affect common rules or alter their scope' (Article 3 § 2 TFEU). Initially, this way of establishing exclusivity was used extensively by the ECJ in its case law about implied powers (C-22/70, AETR, 31 March 1971, ECR 263, pt 17; joined cases C-3/76, C-4/76 and C-6/76, Cornelis Kramer, 14 July 1976, ECR 1279, pt 19, 20, 30 and 33; *Opinion 1/76*, 26 April 1977, ECR 741, pt 6–7). However, in the 1990s the ECJ interpreted its case law restrictively, almost denying its effect (*Opinion 2/91*, 19 March 1993, ECR 1061, pt 18, 22, 30 et 31; *Opinion 1/94*, above note 27, pt 96; *Opinion 2/92*, 24 March 1995, ECR 521, pt 33; *Opinion 2/94*, 28 March 1996, ECR 1759, pt 30). More recent case law has confirmed this restrictive interpretation, definitively legitimising mixed agreements (C-467/98, *Commission* v. *Denmark*, 22 November 2005, ECR 9519, pt 83–4; *Opinion 1/03*, 7 February 2006, ECR 1145; *Opinion 1/08*, 30 November 2009, ECR 11129).

from this point of view, for the EU obtaining a participation status is a way to assert its autonomy vis-à-vis its member States and to assert correspondingly its external competences on the international plane.[32] Self-restraint in this assertion is not simply a sign of political weakness of the Union, but confirms its institutional autonomy, because it is the result of its own decision-making.

Nonetheless, the respect of its proper law is just the first condition for the EU to obtain a participation status in international institutions: the autonomy of each international institution, free to accept or not the EU among its participants according to its proper law, must also be taken into account. This constitutes a considerable limit to the assertion of the EU on the international scene; on the contrary, it implies a reassertion of the centre.

2.2. Multiple participation statuses resulting from the constitutional variety of host institutions

Participation statuses in international institutions vary according to the host institution: as each one is autonomous, the statuses the EU obtains in international economic institutions is fragmented and highly dependent on the political and constitutional situation of each institution. In general, they can be divided in membership status – including the full range of rights and obligations that participants can have – and other statuses, often including several categories of non-members associated with the activity of the institution.[33]

As the will of the host institution is mainly shaped by non-EU States, the EU is faced with several difficulties. Indeed, whereas from the EU's point of view the existence of its legal order and its unique nature are constitutional axioms, third States and institutions are not bound to recognise its legal personality and competences, as they are not parties to its founding treaties. At the same time, in practice third States cannot

[32] However, case law has introduced two important limits to the link between internal and external assertion: firstly, the link is not automatic, as the parallelism between internal and external competences is not absolute; secondly, it can only be unilateral, as external competences cannot be used to create new internal powers.

[33] Indeed, the traditional division between members, observers and non-members (Schermers and Blokker, *International Institutional Law*, above note 1, 51–151) is blurred, because the statuses of members and observers are fragmented and designed on an ad hoc basis (T. Garcia, *Les observateurs auprès des organisations intergouvernementales*, Brussels, Bruylant, 2012, at 19). This is even more true within informal fora, where there are no formal rights and obligations stemming from a constitutive charter.

ignore EU law because of the political weight of the European bloc and the generally recognised EU factual capabilities in the economic field.

The institutions' proper law also has an impact on the EU's representation, although this issue is only governed by EU law: as member States can obtain a more advantageous status than the Union, the latter is pushed to entitle them to represent it until the host institution improves its participation status.[34] A similar phenomenon leads to internal competition among EU institutions: in particular, as the European Central Bank (ECB) enjoys separate legal personality, to a certain extent it can act autonomously to represent the EU within international institutions, thus excluding other EU institutions, especially the Commission and the European External Action Service, which therefore lose weight in the inter-institutional balance.[35]

As a result of political and institutional compromises between the EU, its member States, third States and the host institution, in practice the EU never gets an exclusive participation status in the economic field: it can obtain a participation status only if its member States also do and only in some recent, flexible and/or restricted institutions can it obtain a membership status.[36] In more classic international institutions, the EU cannot obtain a membership status, because only its member States are entitled to it.[37] However, even when the EU obtains a membership status,

[34] After the Lisbon treaty and the abolition of the EU Council's rotating presidency (Article 15 TEU), the EU should be represented, whenever possible, by a proper organ of the Union. Sometimes the participation status of the EU is insufficient and member States still have to represent the Union. This situation can lead to paradoxical consequences: for example, within the IMF Executive Board the EU can be represented by Spain, whose representative, elected through a system of constituencies, is normally Mexican and mainly represents non-EU States. In other cases, the EU obtains an improvement of its participation status, like it did for its observer status at the UN General Assembly (UNGA resolution, *Participation of the European Union in the work of the United Nations*, A/RES/65/276, 3 May 2011). However, even in this case the EU is represented less effectively than by a member State, because the latter can exert its full membership rights at the Assembly.

[35] C. Zilioli and M. Selmayr, 'The External Relations of the Euro Area: Legal Aspects', *Common Market Law Review*, 1999, 273–349.

[36] More precisely, at the European Reconstruction and Development Bank, at the WTO and in some informal fora (G7, G8 – although this is not reflected in the name of the group – G20, Bank of International Settlements, Financial Stability Board).

[37] This is the state of the art within the main institutions of the United Nations Organisation, most of its specialised agencies (including particularly the United Nations Conference on Trade and Development (UNCTAD) and the United Nations Commission on International Trade Law (UNCITRAL)), Bretton Woods institutions (the IMF and the World Bank group), the OECD, and some informal fora. The EU has generally obtained an observer status, at least in some organs of each institution.

it is regarded as an international organisation and needs to coordinate with its member States to exert its rights. To determine who can exert membership rights, the EU and its member States can be considered either a single entity[38] or separate entities each having their own rights.[39] In the first case, their rights are exerted alternatively by member States individually or by the Union, but the EU can act autonomously only in its fields of competence according to its proper law; similarly, if the EU is seen as a separate entity having its own rights, these rights are shaped not to exceed the conferral by member States.[40] In both cases, the EU has to respect the principle of conferral common to all international organisations. Even if the EU is the first international organisation to obtain a membership status in another international organisation, several other international organisations could theoretically obtain the same status, provided that their proper law establishes sufficient external competences. More importantly, the need to coordinate with its member States, especially when the European bloc forms a single entity for rights and obligations, is an evident limit to the EU's autonomy.

Legal norms seem to account only for a part of this phenomenon: the nature of the EU can be interpreted differently from different points of view and international institutions represent a classic point of view opposed to the EU's 'permanent revolution', as they are sociologically dominated by States.[41] Nonetheless, the progressive acceptance of the EU within international institutions, although incomplete, manifests a widespread social recognition, especially in the economic field. Hence, the grammar of this institutional relation is the one of classic international law and not its special version developed by the EU, but its content is beneficial both for the EU and for the host institution. International institutions are confirmed in their role of legitimate multilateral fora of

[38] In particular, at the WTO (Article IX § 1 of the Marrakesh Agreement).

[39] At the European Bank of Reconstruction and Development and in informal fora.

[40] This is particularly visible in old non-economic agreements and institutions such as the Montego Bay Convention on the Law of the Sea and the Food and Agriculture Organization (FAO), where a complex system of declarations of competence is required. Nonetheless, also at the WTO the fact that the EU has a number of votes equal to the number of its member States means that a coordination between the EU and its member States is necessary, and it can only respect the principle of conferral as a principle of EU law. Even if voting is rare (the practice of consensus prevails), in case of shared competence this can imply awkward solutions, like the need for a member State to abstain to allow the EU to cast its vote.

[41] This is shown, for example, by the declarations of some States during the discussion of resolution A/RES/65/276 at the UNGA (UN Doc. A/65/PV.88 (2011)).

economic governance and assert themselves by enlarging their influence; moreover, they impose their conception of institutional international law, pushing the EU to choose mixed participation with its members States and to reduce its conception of autonomy to that of a more classic international organisation.[42] At the same time, the EU consciously accepts the traditional conception underlying its status in international institutions, as it opens the access to multilateral economic liberalisation and regulation.

Once the EU has joined an international institution as a participant, it enjoys all rights and obligations conferred by its status. This implies that it can influence the decision-making within the institution, but also that it is subjected to legal obligations and surveillance.

3. Reassertion by obligation and surveillance: participation as social constraint

Participation in international economic institutions is a source not only of social recognition, but also of social constraint, as it entails mutual obligation between participants and vis-à-vis the host institution, made effective by compliance control through more or less institutionalised systems of political surveillance and dispute settlement. The impact of international obligations and surveillance on the EU is somehow paradoxical. The effect of obligations stemming from multilateral international economic law, although autonomously accepted by the EU, largely limits its discretionary power (3.1). At the same time, dispute settlement, although centralised and constituting the ultimate form of assertion of international economic institutions, reasserts the autonomy of the EU by reflecting its internal rules within the host institution (3.2).

3.1. Multilateral international economic law as a limit to the EU's discretionary power

The impact of international economic institutions on the EU legal order seems undervalued. As the pursuit of economic liberalisation and regulation is a constitutional objective for the EU, it is often seen as an endogenous phenomenon manifesting its autonomy, and the most effective way to assert itself internationally. Nonetheless, the EU legal order grants a relevant place to treaty-based international economic law,

[42] In bilateral negotiations, where the EU has a greater contractual power, it can assert its powers vis-à-vis its members and third States much more easily.

including secondary law of international economic institutions. According to Article 216 TFEU, it is a part of EU law: this facilitates the performance of the EU's international obligations by automatically introducing international law into its legal order and therefore avoiding its ad hoc transposition. Moreover, treaty-based international law prevails over secondary EU law,[43] which in consequence has to be consistent with binding acts produced by international economic organisations. True, the ECJ has consistently held that in most cases WTO law does not have direct effect and therefore cannot be invoked in front of an EU jurisdiction to review EU law,[44] but this does not affect the EU's legal obligation to perform WTO obligations.[45] Furthermore, law produced by other international economic organisations can have direct effect if it contains clear and precise obligations which do not require the adoption of any subsequent measure.[46]

In practice, EU compliance with multilateral international economic law is high. Besides, law produced by international economic institutions has contributed to shaping EU legislation in a determinant way in several

[43] ECJ, C-181/73, *Haegemann*, 30 April 1974, ECR 449, pt 2–6. This reasoning has been extended to secondary law of international institutions based on international agreements, at first implicitly (C-204/86, *Greece* v. *Council*, 27 September 1988, ECR 5323 and C-30/88, *Greece* v. *Commission*, 14 November 1989, ECR 3711, pt 14), then explicitly in the *Sevince* jurisprudence (C-192/89, 20 September 1990, ECR 3461, pt 9).

[44] This line of jurisprudence, developed for the GATT of 1947 (ECJ, *International Fruit*, above note 30; C-266/81, *SIOT*, 16 March 1983, ECR 731; joined cases C-267/81, C-268/81 and C-269/81, *SPI and SAMI*, 16 March 1983, ECR 801; C-280/93, *Germany* v. *Council*, 5 October 1994, ECR 4973) has been confirmed for the WTO (C-149/96, *Portugal* v. *Council*, 23 November 1999, ECR 8395; joined cases C- 27/00 and C-122/00, *Omega Air*, 12 March 2002, ECR 2569; C-377/02, *Van Parys*, 1 March 2005, ECR 1465). The ECJ has also denied the EU's non-contractual liability for violation of WTO law and subsequent retaliatory measures authorised by the Dispute Settlement Body (joined Cases C-120/06 P and C-121/06 P, *FIAMM*, 9 September 2008, ECR 6513). However, the ECJ reviews the consistency of EU secondary law with WTO law in actions for annulment if the former refers explicitly to the latter (C-70/87, *Fediol*, 22 June 1989, ECR 1781) or is adopted expressly to comply with a particular WTO obligation (C-69/89, *Nakajima*, 7 May 1991, ECR 2069).

[45] The direct effect of a provision only determines whether it can be invoked in a certain legal order and not its normative value in that legal order. WTO law can have indirect effect if it is transposed into secondary EU law (C-9/73, Schlüter, 24 October 1973, ECR 1135, pt 32) and also has an effect through consistent interpretation of EU law (C-53/96, *Hermès*, 16 June 1998, ECR 3603, pt 28; joined cases C-300/98 and C-92/98, *Christian Dior*, 14 December 2000, ECR 11307, pt 47; C-245/02, *Anheuser-Busch*, 16 November 2004, ECR 10989, pt 55–7).

[46] ECJ, C-104/81, *Kupfenberg*, 26 October 1982, ECR 3641, pt 17–27; C-87/75, *Bresciani*, 5 February 1976, ECR 129, pt 23; C-12/86, *Demirel*, 30 September 1987, ECR 3719, pt 14; C-18/90, *Kziber*, 31 January 1991, ECR 199, pt 15.

fields. Historically, customs harmonisation within the World Customs Organization (WCO) and tariff liberalisation within the GATT of 1947 were among the most important factors that led to the creation of a customs union between the highly integrated economies of the six founding members of the European Economic Community. Some fields of EU law are specifically designed to comply with WCO and WTO law,[47] which also largely affects the internal market and the common agricultural policy. This influence is not limited to international organisations, but is also strong, although more difficult to assess, when coming from informal fora: for example, the capital requirement packages on banking, directly inspired by the Basel Committee,[48] and the focus on regulation after the 2008 financial crisis have shed light on the extensive transposition of substantial multilateral financial law in EU law. From the institutional point of view, the reform of the EU's institutional system of financial surveillance is also largely inspired by standards and unilateral concerted acts issued within informal fora.[49]

[47] In particular, customs law (regulation 2913/92 of 12 October 1992 establishing the Community Customs Code, OJ L302/1, replaced by reg. 450/2008 of 23 April 2008 laying down the Community Customs Code (Modernised Customs Code), OJ 145/1; reg. 3287/94 of 22 December 1994 on pre-shipment inspections for exports from the Community, OJ L 349/79; reg. 3285/94 of 22 December 1994 on the common rules for imports, OJ L349/53, now replaced by reg. *260/2009* of 26 February 2009, OJ L 84/1), intellectual property (reg. 40/94 on the Community trade mark, amended by reg. 3288/94 of 22 December 1994, OJ L349/83, and by reg. 422/2004 of 9 March 2004, OJ L 70/1), antidumping law (reg. 521/94 of 7 March 1994 on the introduction of time limits for investigation procedures carried out against dumped or subsidised imports from countries not members of the European Community, OJ L 66/7, reg. 522/94 of 7 March 1994 on the streamlining of decision-making procedures for certain Community instruments of commercial defence, OJ L66/10, reg. 3283/94 of 22 December 1994 on protection against dumped imports from countries not members of the European Community, OJ L349/1, now replaced by reg. 1225/2009 of 30 November 2009, OJ L343/51), and protective measures (reg. 3284/94 of 22 December 1994 on protection against subsidised imports from countries not members of the European Community, OJ L349/22, now replaced by reg. 597/2009 of 11 June 2009, OJ 188/93).

[48] Since 2000, the EU has adopted three capital requirements packages including seven directives (2000/12/EC, 2006/48/EC, 2006/49/EC, 2009/111/EC, 2009/27/EC, 2009/83/EC, 2010/76/EU); the Commission has proposed a fourth package composed by a directive (COM(2011) 453 final, 20 July 2011) and a regulation (COM(2011) 452 final, 20 July 2011).

[49] Within the strengthening of the Lamfalussy process of financial supervision covering securities, banking, insurance and occupational pensions, the EU has created three European supervisory authorities and a European Systemic Risk Board (K. Alexander, 'Reforming European Financial Supervision: Adapting EU Institutions to Market Structures' *ERA Forum – Journal of the Academy of European Law*, 2011, 229–52).

The effect of international economic institutions on the EU legal order is not limited to their normative activity, but is also produced by their operations. The most striking example is the way the debt crisis started in 2011 has been handled: as it was decided to associate the IMF with the EU and the euro-States to fund loans for Greece, Portugal, and Ireland, the IMF, the ECB and the European Commission became part of the troika directing the rescue plan.[50] The plan is subject to political conditionality: as tensions within the troika have shown, the IMF applies a more strictly economic conditionality, whereas EU institutions (especially the Commission) tend to introduce more political considerations. Unlike in other cases of the EU's participation in operations of international economic institutions, for example the EU-World Bank development programmes, the IMF, through the troika, influences the way in which the EU exercises its economic and monetary policy, which also depends on the treatment of the rescued States.[51]

The acceptance by the EU of obligations stemming from international economic institutions, i.e. the exercise of its autonomy to limit its discretionary power, strongly contributes to the assertion of the centre. Legal resistance by the EU is minor in this field: whereas cases like *MOX*[52] and *Kadi I*[53] have proven that the ECJ is sometimes ready to let EU treaties prevail over international law (like some national courts do for their national constitution), no serious normative conflict has arisen so far between EU law and multilateral international economic law. Unlike in the Cold War decades, when the EU was still consolidating its customs union and internal market and had a rather defensive approach to international economic liberalisation, since the 1990s it has become the herald of multilateralism and liberalisation, associated with the idea of 'managed globalisation'[54] and, especially after the 2008 financial crisis, with a shift to regulation. In this context, non-compliance with multilateral international economic

[50] For an overview: *IMF, The IMF and Europe*, www.imf.org/external/np/exr/facts/europe.htm.

[51] When rescued States are members of the Euro-zone, the effect on the EU's competences is even more intrusive than in the case of EU–IMF aid plans for non Euro-zone member States (Hungary, Latvia, and Romania).

[52] ECJ, C-459/03, *Commission* v. *Ireland*, 30 May 2006, ECR 4635.

[53] ECJ, joined cases C-402/05 P and C-415/05 P, *Kadi and Al Barakaat International Foundation* v. *Council and Commission*, 3 September 2008, ECR 6351.

[54] F. De Ville, 'The Common Commercial Policy and Global Economic Governance', in J. U. Wunderlich and D. J. Bailey (eds.), *The European Union and Global Governance: A Handbook*, , London, Routledge, 2011, 140–8, at 142; W. Jacoby and S. Meunier, 'Europe and the Management of Globalization', *Journal of European Public Policy*, 2010, 299–317.

law has been relatively minor: only in some politically sensitive cases has the EU protected its legal order from what it regarded as excessive intrusion by international economic institutions, preferring to be condemned or even to undergo international sanction before settling the dispute.[55]

The general choice by the EU not to challenge, but to second international economic institutions, confirms their strong influence on the EU legal order, justified by the potential activation of dispute settlement systems, their ultimate means of assertion.

3.2. *Mutual strengthening through dispute settlement mechanisms*

Within all international institutions, the EU is under political surveillance. In informal fora, this process is based on soft law; in international organisations, it can be more or less structured, ranging from the OECD's peer review to the WTO's trade policy review, to the staff-led IMF's Article IV consultations. In addition, institutionalised dispute settlement mechanisms existing in commerce and investment protection also constrain the EU's conduct and raise issues of EU's representation and international responsibility.

Within the WTO dispute settlement system, the EU is generally represented only by the Commission and not by its member States. Even if EU member States could theoretically file disputes individually against other WTO members, as no official inter-institutional agreement between the EU Commission and the EU Council was ever adopted on this issue, they have never exerted this right. More importantly, it is rare that other WTO members file disputes against EU member States[56], and even in those

[55] In particular within the WTO in the cases about the regime for the importation, sale and distribution of bananas (DS27, DS38, DS16, DS27, DS105, DS158, DS361, and DS364), measures concerning meat and meat products (hormones) (DS26 and DS48), export subsidies on sugar (DS265, DS266, and DS283) and measures affecting the approval and marketing of biotech products (DS291, DS292, and DS293). For a political science analysis: A. R. Young, 'Less Than You Might Think: The Impact of the WTO Rules on EU Policies', in O. Costa and K. E. Jørgensen (eds.), *The Influence of International Institutions on the EU: When Multilateralism Hits Brussels*, New York, Palgrave MacMillan, 2012, 23–41.

[56] This only happened in some cases (DS80, DS127, DS210 (Belgium), DS83 (Denmark), DS131, DS173, DS316, DS347 (France), DS316, DS347 (Germany), DS125, DS129, DS452 (Greece), DS68, DS82, DS130 (Ireland), DS452 (Italy), DS128, DS408, DS409 (the Netherlands), DS37 (Portugal), DS316, DS347, DS443 (Spain), DS86 (Sweden), DS67, DS316, DS347 (UK)), and a panel was established only in a few of them. These data are to compare with the seventy-four disputes in which the EU was respondent.

cases the EU Commission acts as respondent (provided that a panel is established).[57] Concerning responsibility, in theory the EU and its member States should be subject either to international rules on attribution or to the internal repartition of competences. However, each organisation provided with an institutional dispute settlement system can have special rules of imputation of conducts. In the case of the WTO, even if these rules stem from WTO practice and not from EU law, theoretical problems are overcome practically in an advantageous way for the EU. Indeed, in WTO practice the EU is also held responsible for violations by its member States, which are therefore considered its agents.[58] The EU itself acknowledges and adopts the member States' conducts as its own and accepts responsibility for them.[59] This allows the EU to play a greater role than its member States within the WTO and therefore contributes to its assertion.

Another example of dispute settlement potentially concerning international economic institutions is the draft regulation concerning the financial responsibility of the Union and its member States in investment disputes, currently under discussion.[60] According to the draft regulation, the EU should bear financial responsibility when the treatment of the foreign investor/investment at issue is 'afforded by the institutions, bodies or agencies of the Union' or when the law or action in dispute was required by EU law, thus separating rules of imputation of conduct from rules of attribution of international responsibility as a consequence of a wrongful act. Although its adoption with this wording is uncertain and only concerns the relations between the EU and its member States and not international obligations vis-à-vis third States, the draft regulation might produce its effects in disputes settled by the International Centre for Settlement of Investment Disputes (ICSID) arbitral tribunals. The EU is a member neither of the ICSID nor of the World Bank, but in the long term it hopes to obtain a participation status and to have its

[57] E. Neframi, 'The Duty of Loyalty: Rethinking its Scope through its Application in the Field of EU External Relations', *Common Market Law Review*, 2010, 323–59, at 358.

[58] The Appellate Body has confirmed this practice (DS316, European Communities – Measures Affecting Trade in Large Civil Aircraft, Appellate Body Report, 18 May 2011), clarifying doubts cast by the panel report.

[59] P. Eeckhout, 'The EU and its Member States in the WTO – Issues of Responsibility', in L. Bartels and F. Ortino (eds.), *Regional Trade and the WTO Legal System*, Oxford, Oxford University Press, 449–64.

[60] COM(2012) 335 final, 21 June 2012.

specificities recognised, also thanks to the new generation of free trade agreements including investment protection chapters that it recently started to conclude.[61]

In both cases, bearing responsibility for violation of WTO law or of Bilateral Investment Treaties (BITs) to reflect the existence of an external competence is paradoxically an easily available way for the EU to assert itself on the international scene. As institutional dispute settlement also contributes to the assertion of international economic institutions; both the centre and the periphery are strengthened. In other words, responsibility issues in commerce and investment protection show that the EU can reconcile its needs with those of international institutions and third States. Despite the negative reaction of the European Commission to the International Law Commission's (ILC) draft articles on the responsibility of international organisations[62], such reconciliation is also possible in other fields, because a *lex specialis* of international responsibility can often allow taking into account the EU's specificities.[63]

In conclusion, the EU's participation in dispute settlement mechanisms within international economic organisations proves that the reassertion of the centre does not exclude the recognition of the periphery's specificities, and that participation as constraint is beneficial both for the EU and for international economic institutions.

4. Conclusion: a theoretical assessment

Sections 2 and 3 have shown that international economic institutions are strengthened by the EU's participation, but also that their reassertion is founded on integration and recognition of some of the EU's specificities. To explain theoretically this phenomenon in the wider context of international institutional law, several models of international law are useful. Among the very rich legal literature on global governance, and relations

[61] E. Castellarin, 'The Investment Chapters in the New Generation of the EU's Economic Agreements', *Transnational Dispute Management*, 2013, n. 2, www.transnational-dispute-management.com.

[62] UN Doc. A/CN.4/545 (2004), at 18; UN Doc. A/CN.4/637 (2011), at 7; E. Paasivirta and P. J. Kuyper, 'Does One Size Fit All? The European Community and the Responsibility of International Organizations', *Netherlands Yearbook of International Law*, 2005, 169–226.

[63] Special rules of responsibility are reserved by Article 64 of the draft articles (http://legal.un.org/ilc/texts/instruments/english/draft%20articles/9_11_2011.pdf); J. d'Aspremont, 'A European Law of International Responsibility? The Articles on the Responsibility of International Organizations and the European Union', SHARES Research Paper 22 (2013), http://ssrn.com/abstract=2236070.

between legal orders, some trends are particularly successful, as they seem to catch the zeitgeist of this research field. Although these theories and research projects are generally inspired by different issues, such as the role of private actors in international law, they can also apply to relations between the centre and the periphery of international institutional law. Indeed, they all provide for global approaches aimed, *inter alia*, at reacting to the fragmentation of the international legal order.

Actual trends include theories where relations between legal orders are seen from a constitutional angle[64], or at least from a public law perspective based on the concept of public authority.[65] Other trends account for the development of several legal orders interacting with each other and finally creating a coherent whole without being hierarchically structured: institutions – both public and private – create networks[66] to produce norms, including soft law[67], and perform administration.[68] In these theories, fragmentation is avoided not by a vertical relation between legal orders, but by interactions between integrated autonomous systems. Schematically, actual trends can be classified around two poles[69]: some of them underline the hierarchical relation between norms issued by different legal orders, thus suggesting a vertical relation between institutions; some others have a horizontal vision highlighting interactions between autonomous legal orders and institutions. Both sets of trends are compatible with a pluralistic approach to international institutional law, acknowledging the institutional and normative complexity of the international legal order and accounting for the dialectic relation between the centre and the periphery. No theory exactly accounts for the relation between the EU and international economic institutions, but both sets of trends present a compatible theoretical framework.

64 Klabbers, Peters and Ulfstein (eds.), *The Constitutionalization of International Law*, above note 19.

65 A. von Bogdandy, *The Exercise of Public Authority by International Institutions: Advancing International Institutional Law*, Heidelberg, Springer, 2010.

66 F. Ost and M. van de Kerchove, *De la pyramide au réseau? Pour une théorie dialectique du droit*, Brussels, Facultés universitaires Saint-Louis, 2002; A.-M. Slaughter, *A New World Order*, Princeton, Princeton University Press, 2005.

67 B. Kingsbury, N. Krisch and R. B. Stewart, 'The Emergence of Global Administrative Law', 2005, *Law and Contemporary Problems*, 15–61; S. Cassese, 'Administrative Law without the State? The Challenge of Global Regulation', *New York University Journal of International Law and* Politics, 2005, 663–94.

68 J. Pauwelyn, R. A. Wessel and J. Wouters (eds.), *Informal International Lawmaking*, Oxford, Oxford University press, 2012.

69 E. de Wet and J. Vidmar, 'Conflicts between International Paradigms: Hierarchy Versus Systemic Integration', http://ssrn.com/abstract_id=2269703

On the one hand, within the legal order of each international institution, the EU is – like all other participants – in a hierarchically subordinated position: even if some institutions are particularly flexible, a certain degree of hierarchy is inherent to each legal order.[70] Some examples of this phenomenon are the 'return to the centre' of the EU to obtain a participation status, the use of its autonomy to reduce its discretionary power, accept international obligations, undergo surveillance and engage its responsibility, and the consequent conceptual downgrading of its autonomy to a more classic conception of international organisation.

On the other hand, the assertion of the centre is possible because it contributes to the integration and the social recognition of the periphery, in other words to its assertion. Concerning dispute settlement and responsibility, the ultimate means of assertion of the centre, rules and practice within international economic institutions (in particular the WTO) take into account the unique internal organisation of the EU. Moreover, as EU law is deeply influenced by multilateral international economic law, its relations with international economic institutions are characterised by mutually beneficial systemic integration also from the substantial point of view.

Finally, international institutional law is not necessarily a zero-sum game between the host institution and its participants:[71] the relation between the EU and international economic institutions demonstrates that the dialectics of the centre and the periphery can lead to Hegelian *Aufhebung*.

[70] Schermers and Blokker, *International Institutional Law*, above note 1, at 1210.

[71] J. Klabbers, *An Introduction to International Institutional Law*, Cambridge, Cambridge University Press, 2009, at 309.

13

Reinforcing the ICJ's central international role? Domestic courts' enforcement of ICJ decisions and opinions

VERONIKA FIKFAK

Introduction

Compliance with judgments of the International Court of Justice (ICJ) is traditionally voluntary, states fulfilling their obligations under Article 94 of the UN Charter and Article 59 of the ICJ Statute to give force to binding and final decisions.[1] Yet, increasingly the decisions rendered by the ICJ are becoming inward looking and domestic courts are encouraged to act as the natural enforcers of international decisions. In *Avena*, for example, the ICJ having held that the US had violated the Vienna Convention on Consular Relations 1963 (VCCR) by failing to provide consular protection in criminal proceedings to foreign nationals, ordered the US to undertake 'review and reconsideration' of such criminal convictions. In this context, the ICJ stated that the obligation to review and reconsider was particularly suited to the 'judicial process'. The task was effectively one for US domestic courts.[2] In *Jurisdictional Immunities*, in which the ICJ held that the failure of Italian courts to accord jurisdictional immunities to German nationals in civil proceedings in *Ferrini*[3] was contrary

[1] Constanze Schulte, *Compliance with Decisions of the International Court of Justice* (Oxford University Press, 2004).

[2] *Avena and Other Mexican Nationals* (*Mexico* v. *United States of America*), Judgment, I.C.J. Reports 2004 (I). In *Avena II*, the Court clarified that there was no international obligation imposed on US courts to enforce this decision. In that case, the ICJ held that the manner in which the international obligation is met by the US was of its own choosing, e.g. not necessarily by courts. *Request for Interpretation of the Judgment of 31 March 2004 in the Case concerning Avena and Other Mexican Nationals* (*Mexico* v. *United States of America*) [Avena II] I.C.J. Reports 2009, 3.

[3] *Ferrini* v. *Federal Republic of Germany*, Decision No. 5044/2004 (*Rivista di diritto internazionale*, Vol. 87, 2004, p. 539; ILR, Vol. 128, p. 658).

to Italy's international obligations, the obligation imposed on Italy was to take appropriate measures to ensure Germany's immunity is enforced. In the absence of domestic legislation and until such legislation was enacted, providing for enforcement of the ICJ holding was a task particularly suited to domestic courts. They would be the ones to uphold the ICJ decision by ceasing to give effect to the *Ferrini* precedent.[4]

Even in Advisory Opinions questions have arisen as to the enforcement of the correct interpretation of international law. In *Legal Consequences of the Construction of a Wall in the Occupied Palestinian Territory*, the ICJ held that the construction of the barrier built by Israel was contrary to international law.[5] When similar claims arose before Israel's domestic courts, the question was whether the domestic courts would implement such interpretation of international law and whether they would do so in spite of contradicting domestic precedent.

Quick glances at these examples reveal that the links between domestic courts and the ICJ are closer than ever. Not only are domestic courts often sources of violations of international law; they are encouraged to also be a source for its enforcement. In this context, how domestic courts react to decisions and opinions of the ICJ is becoming increasingly important. Whilst it is often asserted that the ICJ, as the 'principal judicial organ of the United Nations' and the only court with jurisdiction to decide any question of international law, holds a position of 'primacy over other courts',[6] the question is whether such a position is recognised and upheld by other participants – and in particular by domestic courts – in the international legal order.

Although domestic courts are traditionally not considered participants in the international legal order, their role is becoming increasingly important. Due to the 'inward' looking nature of international decisions, domestic courts are increasingly identified as the obvious, natural enforcers of international decisions. In the absence of a general enforcement mechanism of international decisions, it is domestic courts who represent a

[4] *Jurisdictional Immunities of the State (Germany* v. *Italy: Greece intervening)*, Judgment, I.C.J. Reports 2012, p. 99. *Ferrini* v. *Federal Republic of Germany*, decision 5044/2004, *Rivista di diritto internazionale*, Vol. 87, 2004, p. 539; I.L.R. Vol. 128, p. 658.

[5] *Legal Consequences of the Construction of a Wall in the Occupied Palestinian Territory*, Advisory Opinion, I.C.J. Reports 2004, p. 136.

[6] UN Charter, art. 92; ICJ Statute, art. 1; Pierre-Marie Dupuy, 'The Unity of Application of International Law at the Global Level and the Responsibility of Judges', *European Journal of Legal Studies* 1, no. 2 (2007): 11, www.ejls.eu/current.php?id=2.

'reliable . . . system' for compelling compliance with international norms.[7] As 'actors of the international legal order' or its 'deputized agents',[8] domestic courts can provide support to the international institutions which lack an enforcement mechanism of their own, and thus ensure the effectiveness of their decisions. Even more, judicial implementation of international decisions gives the international law these institutions create 'full significance and vigour as a *legal* phenomenon'.[9] In the end, domestic courts act as a 'conduit' through which the role of the international institution – and thus the ICJ – can be fulfilled.

In this chapter, I seek to analyse whether domestic courts recognise they have a role to play in relation to decisions of the ICJ. In this context, I wish to address the following questions: What role do domestic courts assume for themselves? Do they act as agents of the international legal order and enforce ICJ's decisions? Do they accept the interpretations given and uphold the primacy of the ICJ as the final and ultimate interpreter of international law? Or do they second-guess the assessment of the Court and engage in review of its decisions? I seek to answer these questions by examining the enforcement of the VCCR decisions – *Breard*, *LaGrand*,[10] *Avena*, and *Avena II*, the *Israeli Wall Opinion* and the *Jurisdictional Immunities of the State* decision by domestic courts of the United States, Israel and Italy.

Enforcement of ICJ decisions by domestic courts

*The VCCR cases (*LaGrand, Avena, Avena II*)*

During the 1990s and throughout the 2000s a series of cases were brought before the ICJ relating to the interpretation of the VCCR. In these cases, Paraguay, Germany and Mexico alleged that the United States of America

[7] Eyal Benvenisti, 'Judicial Misgivings Regarding the Application of International Law: An Analysis of Attitudes of National Courts', *European Journal of International Law* 4 (1993): 160.

[8] Friedrich Kratochwil, 'The Role of Domestic Courts as Agencies of the International Legal Order', in R. Falk, F. Kratochwil and S. Mendlovitz (eds.), *International Law: A Contemporary Perspective* (Boulder, CO: Westview Press, 1985), 238.

[9] Richard B. Lillich, 'Proper Role of Domestic Courts in the International Legal Order', *Virginia Journal of International Law* 11 (1971/1970): 11 (emphasis added).

[10] *LaGrand* (Germany v. United States of America) (Merits) [2001] I.C.J. Reports 466; *LaGrand* (Germany v. United States of America) (Provisional Measures) 1999 I.C.J. Reports 9.

had failed to provide its nationals with the consular protection in criminal proceedings to which they were entitled under the VCCR. Many of the nationals in question had been convicted of serious crimes, including murder and some had been sentenced to death. These judgments were rendered by US courts without the nationals having been advised of their right to consult with their consulates and without being enabled to communicate with them.

The ICJ was seized of the matter at various points in the proceedings. In the first two cases, Paraguay and Germany sought to secure interim measures ordering the US to take all measures necessary to prevent the imposition of the death penalty. Although the provisional measures in both cases were not obeyed by the US, the ICJ held that Article 5 and 36 of the VCCR created established rights for foreign nationals to consular protection and that the US had failed to fulfil its international obligation partly by failing to advise the individuals of their rights and secondly, by informing them of this right too late. If, for example, the foreign nationals became aware of their right after they had exhausted all claims on state level, then according to the procedural default rule, they would be unable to invoke their objection in federal appeals. The ICJ held that both the failure of the US authorities to inform individuals of their consular assistance right 'without delay upon detention' as well as the operation of the procedural default rule breached US' obligations under the VCCR.

The third claim, brought by Mexico, concerned individuals who had been tried, convicted and sentenced to death in criminal proceedings. Again, the ICJ found the US in violation of the VCCR. Yet, whilst in relation to *Breard* and the *LaGrand* brothers the claims had become at least domestically moot as the individuals in questions were executed, many of the fifty-one Mexican nationals concerned by the *Avena* decisions remained in prison – either on death row or facing lengthy sentences. For these individuals, the ICJ ordered the US to 'provide, by means of its own choosing, review and reconsideration of the convictions and sentences of the Mexican nationals'.[11] When Mexico insisted that this 'review and reconsideration' should be 'meaningful and effective',[12] the ICJ held that although the 'choice of means for review and reconsideration should be left to the United States', 'it is the judicial process that is suited to this task'.[13]

[11] *Avena* (note 2 above) p. 72, para. 9.
[12] *Ibid.*, p. 47, para. 78. [13] *Ibid.*, pp. 65–6, para. 140.

The issues before US courts

In the two decades of litigation, several issues arose before US domestic courts relating to the implementation of the different ICJ decisions concerning the VCCR. The issues revolved around whether the US courts were bound to enforce the ICJ decisions, whether they were bound to follow the ICJ's interpretation of international law, and whether they were bound to provide review and reconsideration of the fifty-one individuals on the basis of the President's Memorandum with which President Bush sought to guarantee the domestic implementation of the ICJ's *Avena* decision.

The legal nature of the ICJ decision as interpretation of international law

The question of the legal nature of the ICJ decisions arose in two ways – firstly, the courts debated whether the ICJ's interpretation of the VCCR was binding and should be enforced even in disputes not relating to the *Breard* and *LaGrand* claimants and secondly, whether the ICJ judgment and its holding – whatever its interpretation of the law – was itself binding in proceedings concerning individuals considered by the ICJ in *Avena*. The first set of decisions therefore revolved around the proper interpretation of the VCCR, whilst the second concerned the interpretation of Article 94 of the UN Charter, Article 59 of the ICJ Statute and the Optional Protocol conferring jurisdiction upon the ICJ to resolve disputes concerning the VCCR.

Initially, claims raised before US courts turned on whether the ICJ's interpretation of the VCCR was binding. The Court distinguished two aspects of this question. On one side, the 'international' aspect concerned the question whether the VCCR created individual rights and on the other, the 'domestic' issue revolved around whether the VCCR was directly enforceable. On the international aspect, the US Supreme Court accepted that 'we should give respectful consideration to the interpretation of an international treaty rendered by an international court with jurisdiction to interpret such'.[14] The court was hesitant to question the ICJ's interpretation of an international agreement, which it treated as a task for the international court. In *Breard*, for example, the Court accepted the ICJ's interpretation that the VCCR 'arguably confers on an individual the right to consular assistance following arrest'.[15] In *Medellin* v. *Dretke*, after the Court of Appeal had held that the VCCR conferred no rights on

[14] *Breard* v. *Greene* (1998) 523 U.S. 371, 375. [15] *Ibid.*, 376.

individuals,[16] the Supreme Court avoided the question, repeating their position in *Breard*.[17] In her dissent, O'Connor argued that a holding of lower courts that treaties can never be enforced by private individuals was 'contrary to our precedents and, therefore, is not entitled to deference in subsequent federal proceedings'.[18] And in *Sanchez-Llamas*, when explicitly seized on the question of whether the VCCR conferred rights on individuals, the Court ruled that it is 'unnecessary to resolve the question whether the Vienna Convention grants individuals enforceable rights' and proceeded to rule in the case on the assumption that it did.[19]

On the domestic aspect, however, the Court stated that the proposition that the VCCR as interpreted by the ICJ is directly enforceable in domestic law is 'plainly incorrect'. It is the domestic – procedural – rules that govern the manner in which states implement the treaties. If the claimant – as was the case in *Breard* – failed to assert his VCCR rights in proceedings before state courts, then under domestic law he 'failed to exercise his rights under the Vienna Convention in conformity with the laws of the United States and the Commonwealth of Virginia'.[20] The implementation of the ICJ decision was impossible since even accepting its interpretation of the VCCR, the domestic procedural rules pre-empted its application.

When the ICJ came back in later cases and ruled that the application of the procedural default rule as described violated US international obligations and that as a consequence, a review and reconsideration of individuals' claims 'was required without regard to state procedural default rules',[21] the US Supreme Court held that this holding was not binding on domestic courts since, although the ICJ had given an international interpretation of Article 36 of the VCCR, it had failed to address the circumstances specific to the US adversary system, which were crucial to understand how the provision operated within the US domestic law. The ICJ 'overlooks the importance of procedural default rules in an adversary system';[22] its reasoning 'sweeps too broadly';[23] and as a consequence its conclusion and 'interpretation of Article 36 is inconsistent with the basic framework of an adversary system'.[24] The US Supreme Court insisted that the power to determine the meaning of international treaties as a matter of

16 *Medellin* v. *Dretke* 371 F. 3d 270 (CA5 2004), reaffirming its holding in *United States* v. *Jimenez-Nava* 243 F. 3d 192, 195 (CA5 2001).

17 *Medellin* v. *Dretke* (2005) 544 U.S. 660.

18 *Ibid.*, O'Connor dissenting.

19 *Sanchez-Llamas* v. *Oregon* (2006) 548 U.S. 331, 343.

20 *Breard* v. *Greene* (note 14 above) 375.

21 *Medellin* v. *Texas* (2008) 552 U.S. 491.

22 *Sanchez-Llamas* (note 19 above) 356.

23 *Ibid.*, 335, 357.

24 *Ibid.*, 357.

domestic federal law 'is emphatically the province and duty of the judicial department' headed by the 'one supreme Court'.[25] The Court proceeded to explain at length the purpose of the procedural default rule[26] and the manner in which it works in an adversary system. Justice Roberts writing for the majority stated: 'In an inquisitorial system, the failure to raise a legal error can in part be attributed to the magistrate, and thus to the state itself. In *our system*, however, the responsibility for failing to raise an issue generally rests with the parties themselves.'[27]

Looking at the approach of the Supreme Court to the two issues, it is clear that on one side, the Court recognises the ICJ's primary role in clarifying the meaning of international treaties. Whilst the Supreme Court never concludes that the VCCR in fact confers rights on individuals, it also never openly contradicts the ICJ's interpretation. It maintains this position even when faced with decisions of lower courts, which insisted that as a matter of domestic law treaties never confer rights on individuals but are only applicable between nations.[28] Repeating its holding in *Breard*, the Supreme Court asserts that 'respectful consideration' should be given to the ICJ's interpretation of an international treaty.[29]

Yet when it comes to the ascertainment of the content of domestic law and determining the effect of its interaction with international law, the Court has clearly claimed for itself the power 'to say what the law is'.[30] When determining how the procedural default rule operates in domestic law and whether its domestic effect could be suspended in light of ICJ judgments, its treatment of the ICJ decisions is most striking. In the passage referring to the adversarial character of the US criminal procedure, a passage which reminds one of a lecture a teacher would give a student, the Supreme Court rejects the ICJ's expertise in US domestic law and makes it clear that it is its own duty and power to determine the '*domestic* legal effect'[31] of international treaties in 'our system' and US 'domestic law'.[32] Whilst the Court was therefore not willing to challenge the ICJ's interpretation of international law, it is clearly willing to question its expertise in relation to the evaluation of the domestic law.

25 *Marbury* v. *Madison* (1803) 5 U.S. 137, 177.
26 *Massaro* v. *US* (2003) 538 U.S. 500, 504.
27 *Sanchez-Llamas* (note 19 above) 357, emphasis added.
28 *Medellin* v. *Dretke* (2005) 544 U.S. 660, O'Connor referring to the Texas court in Dretke.
29 *Breard* v. *Greene* (note 14 above) 375.
30 *Marbury* v. *Madison* (note 25 above), cited by *Sanchez-Llamas* v. *Oregon* (note 19 above) 334.
31 *Medellin* v. *Texas* (note 21 above) 504.
32 *Sanchez-Llamas* (note 19 above) 350, 356.

Different legal orders and their interaction In the second set of cases, the Supreme Court investigated whether the ICJ decisions were per se binding and required US courts to review and reconsider the claims of *Avena* individuals. In his claim, Medellin argued that under the UN Charter, the ICJ Statute and the Optional Protocol the 'ICJ's judgment in *Avena* constitutes a "binding" obligation on the state and federal courts of the United States' and that the decision has to be given force since it 'pre-empts contrary state limitations on successive habeas petitions'.[33] In response, the Supreme Court ruled:

> No one disputes that the Avena decision – a decision that flows from the treaties through which the United States submitted to ICJ jurisdiction with respect to Vienna Convention disputes – constitutes *an international law obligation* on the part of the United States. But not all international law obligations automatically constitute binding federal law enforceable in United States courts. The question we confront here is whether the Avena judgment has automatic *domestic legal effect* such that the judgment of its own force applies in state and federal courts.[34]

Again the Court draws a distinction between the 'international' aspects of the case and the 'domestic'. Whilst the ICJ decision 'constitutes an international law obligation on the part of the United States', for the purposes of domestic proceedings this is not determinative. Rather, the question before domestic courts is whether the UN Charter, ICJ Statute and the Optional Protocol are enforceable as a matter of domestic law or whether the Presidential Memorandum with which the United States aimed to 'discharge its international obligations under *Avena* by having State courts give effect to the decision' rendered it thus.[35]

On the issue of self-executing treaties, the Court stated that 'whether the treaties underlying a judgment are self-executing so that the judgment is directly enforceable as domestic law in our courts is, of course, *a matter for this Court to decide*'.[36] This had to be determined according to the text of the international treaty and the Executive's interpretation of the relevant provisions, interpretation which 'is entitled to great weight'. In this context, the Court noted that 'Executive Branch has unfailingly adhered to its view that the relevant treaties do not create domestically enforceable federal law'.[37] Article 94 of the UN Charter, for example, was interpreted by the Executive as 'a commitment on the part of U. N. Members to take future action through their political branches to comply

[33] *Medellin* v. *Texas* (note 21 above) 504. [34] *Ibid.*, 504, emphasis added.
[35] *Ibid.*, 498. [36] *Ibid.*, 519, emphasis added. [37] *Ibid.*, 513.

with an ICJ decision'.[38] As such, the Court found this 'non-self-executing treaty "addresses itself to the political, not the judicial department; and the legislature must execute the contract before it can become a rule for the Court"'.[39] Were the Court to depart from such a reading of the relevant provisions, this would be 'tantamount to vesting with the judiciary the power not only to interpret but also to create the law'.[40]

When the issue of the relevance of the Presidential Memorandum arose in the second part of the *Medellin* case, the Court did not accept that the Memorandum created enforceable domestic law. The Supreme Court did not hesitate to assert its power to interpret the US Constitution and ruled that the President could only act within the confines of his constitutionally conferred power or under the authorisation of Congress. Yet, in absence of both, the President did not have the power to transform a non-self-executing treaty into domestic law. In the end, the Court ruled that only Congress could render *Avena* enforceable in domestic law.

In both aspects of the *Medellin* v. *Texas* case, the Supreme Court is focused on establishing the 'domestic legal effect' of the international decisions. The Court is quick to reiterate that the shift from the international to the 'domestic' effects of the decision does not reduce the international relevance of the case. It insists that the 'judgment of an international tribunal' is not 'useless'.[41] The ICJ decision 'constitute[s] international obligations' but if it has no effect in domestic law, then it is not for the judiciary to enforce but is rather 'the proper subject of political and diplomatic negotiations'.[42] The argument the Court is making is therefore that '[i]nternational law and domestic law are distinct entities that operate in different spheres'.[43]

What is apparent therefore from the approach adopted by the Supreme Court in *Breard, Sanchez-Llamas* and *Medellin* v. *Texas* is that the decision of the ICJ is assessed through the lens of domestic law, in which the domestic court has the power and duty to determine the content of the applicable law. In fact, the moment the case becomes about the 'domestic' effect of the ICJ judgment, the concern of the court turns to the separation of powers. In such context, the judiciary needs to be careful not to interfere in another branch's domain. At the same time, it also has to act to enforce the Constitution by keeping the other branches of government within the confines of their power. On one side, the court therefore cannot

[38] *Ibid.*, 508. [39] *Ibid.*, 516. [40] *Ibid.* [41] *Ibid.*, 520. [42] *Ibid.*

[43] *Council of Canadians* v. *Canada (Attorney-General)* Case 01-CV-208141, 8 July 2005, Ontario Superior Court of Justice, Carswell Ontario Cases 2005, 2973, [41], [43].

make the provisions the Executive considers non-self-executing domestically enforceable. On the other, it cannot conclude that the President can single handedly render the decision self-executing since his constitutional powers in foreign affairs simply do not include the law-making function. In the end, it is the US Constitution, the US case law and precedents that take centre stage and the Court takes it upon itself to assess whether the ICJ decisions in question comply with the particular structure and values set out by the US Constitution.[44] Since this is not the case, the efforts to implement the *Avena* decision have to take another shape.

The Israeli Wall Opinion

In 2004, upon the request of the UN General Assembly, the ICJ delivered a legal opinion on the *Legal Consequences of the Construction of a Wall in the Occupied Palestinian Territory*. In its Opinion, the Court found that the wall being built by Israel in the Occupied Palestinian Territory, including in and around East Jerusalem, was contrary to international law. The ICJ held that both the barrier and the associated regime imposed on the Palestinian inhabitants violated a number of international norms, including the UN Charter and the rule on the prohibition of threat or use of force, as well as the Fourth Geneva Convention, applicable in those Palestinian territories which before the armed conflict of 1967 lay to the east of the 1949 Armistice demarcation line. In addition, the impact of the construction of the wall on the daily life of the inhabitants of the Occupied Palestinian Territory (destruction or requisition of private property, restrictions on freedom of movement, confiscation of agricultural land, cutting-off of access to primary water sources, etc.) was held to be contrary to the Hague Regulations of 1907, the Fourth Geneva Convention, and other human rights instruments (the International Covenant on Civil and Political Rights (ICCPR), the International Covenant on Economic, Social and Cultural Rights (ICESCR), and the Convention on Rights of the Child).

In the operative part of the opinion, the Court held that Israel was under an obligation to terminate its breaches of international law and cease the works of the construction of the wall, dismantle the current structure,

44 A constitution is a 'statement of our most important values and the vehicle through which these values are created and crystallized'. F. Schauer 'Judicial Supremacy and the Modest Constitution' *California Law Review* 92 (2004), 1045, at 1045.

and repeal or render ineffective all legislative and regulatory acts allowing for the existence of the wall. In the end, the ICJ also ruled that Israel was under an obligation to make reparation for all damage caused by the construction of the wall in the Occupied Palestinian Territory, including in and around East Jerusalem.

The issues before the Israeli Supreme Court

Concurrently with proceedings before the ICJ, the Israeli Supreme Court was also examining the issue of legality of the fence in *Beit Sourik*. The Court in principle recognised the necessity of the erection of the fence as a security reason.[45] However, it held that the court could not determine the legality of the fence as a whole. Instead, different segments of the fence had to be assessed separately in order to ensure that an appropriate balance had been struck between the specific security-military needs and the rights of the protected residents (expropriation of the land, the route chosen etc.). The discussion on the appropriate balance turned around whether the measures adopted by military commanders on the ground (and the interference with the rights of local residents) were proportionate with the security threat. In the end, some segments of the fence were found not to violate international law, whilst others were held to be disproportionate and the injury to inhabitants far too wide in scope. In these areas, parts of the fence were annulled and the military commanders had to make alterations to the fence in a manner which would ensure compliance with the *Beit Sourik* holding. These new routes were challenged again. Before their legality could be re-considered, the applicants in *Mara'abe and Ord* v. *Prime Minister of Israel*[46] asked the Israeli Supreme Court to give effect to the ICJ Advisory Opinion on the legality of the wall. The question then arose: Would the Israeli Supreme Court follow the ICJ decision, which found the construction of the barrier as a whole illegal, and amend the normative outline set out in *Beit Sourik*? Or, would it choose to follow its own decision in *Beit Sourik*, proceeding to evaluate the legality of each separate segment of the fence?

The legal nature of the Opinion In *Mara'abe*, the Israeli Supreme Court first underlines the legal nature of the ICJ Opinion, namely that it is advisory in nature. 'It does not bind the party who requested it . . . it does

[45] HCJ 2056/04, *Beit Sourik Village Council* v. *The Government of Israel*, 58(5) P.D. 807.

[46] HCJ 7957/04, *Mara'abe and Ord* v. *Prime Minister of Israel*, ILDC 157 (IL 2005).

not bind the states.'[47] The ICJ Opinion does not create a legal obligation upon Israel regardless of how clear the language of the operative part is. Although, the Israeli Supreme Court recognises, 'the opinion of the International Court of Justice is an interpretation of international law, performed by the highest judicial body in international law' and as such 'should be given its full appropriate weight', such weight can merely be persuasive. The Opinion 'is not *res judicata*'.[48]

The question then is how persuasive is the ICJ Opinion in the assessment of the Israeli Supreme Court. Barak, writing the majority opinion, first emphasises that the basic normative foundation upon which the ICJ and the Supreme Court in the *Beit Sourik* case based their decisions 'was a common one'.[49] He clarified that like the Supreme Court in *Beit Sourik*, the ICJ also held that Israel holds the West Bank (Judea and Samaria) pursuant to the law of belligerent occupation; that an occupier state is not permitted to annex the occupied territory; that in an occupied territory, the occupier state must act according to The Hague Regulations and The Fourth Geneva Convention; that as a result of the building of the wall, a number of rights of the Palestinian residents were impeded; and finally, that the harm to the Palestinian residents would not violate international law if the harm was caused as a result of military necessity, national security requirements, or public order.

Yet, despite this common normative foundation, Barak notes that the two courts reached different positions. 'The ICJ held that the building of the wall, and the regime accompanying it, are contrary to international law. In contrast, the Supreme Court in *The Beit Sourik Case* held that it is not to be sweepingly said that any route of the fence is a breach of international law.' Instead 'each segment of the route should be examined to clarify whether it impinges upon the rights of the Palestinian residents, and whether the impingement is proportional'.[50] What, asked Barak, was the reason for the difference between the outcomes? And how does this difference affect the approach the Supreme Court should take to giving effect to the ICJ's interpretation of international law in *Mara'abe*?

The factual basis and its impact on the law The difference between the two decisions was identified as stemming 'from the factual basis that was laid before the ICJ, which was different from that which was laid before the Court in the *Beit Sourik* case'.[51] The ICJ drew the factual basis for its

[47] *Ibid.*, para. 56. [48] *Ibid.* [49] *Ibid.*, para. 57.
[50] *Ibid.*, para. 58. [51] *Ibid.*, para. 73.

opinion from the Secretary-General's report, his written statement, the Dugard report, and the Zeigler report. In contrast, the Supreme Court drew the facts from the data brought before it by the Palestinian petitioners on the one hand, and the state on the other. In addition, the Supreme Court received an expert opinion by military experts who requested the opportunity to present their position as *amici curiae*.

Although the data which each court received regarded the same wall/fence,[52] the Supreme Court found that the 'difference between each set of data is deep and great'.[53] On one side is *the issue of security-military necessity* to erect the fence. This question was expansively presented and debated before the Supreme Court in *Beit Sourik*. The state was given an opportunity to explain how terrorism had plagued Israel since September 2000, how it had increased in scope and changed in nature (e.g. including 'human bombs' which explode in public places) and how thousands of individuals had been killed and injured as a result. The state explained how various military actions had been taken in order to defeat the terrorism, how these did not provide a sufficient solution to it and how against this background the state decided to construct the fence as a security measure. 'From the evidence presented before the Court, the conclusion arose that the decision to erect the fence was not the fruit of a political decision to annex occupied territory to Israel. The decision to erect the fence arose out of security-military considerations, and out of security-military necessity, as a necessary means to defend the state, its citizens, and its army against terrorist activity.'[54]

In contrast, the ICJ was not persuaded of the security-military necessity of the construction of the wall. According to the Supreme Court:

> [t]he security-military necessity is mentioned only most minimally in the sources upon which the ICJ based its opinion. Only one line is devoted to it in the Secretary-General's report, stating that the decision to erect the fence was made due to a new rise in Palestinian terrorism in the Spring of 2002. In his written statement, the security-military consideration is not mentioned at all. In the Dugard report and the Zeigler report there are no data on this issue at all. In Israel's written statement to the ICJ regarding jurisdiction and discretion, data regarding the terrorism and

[52] Note the difference in language used: the Supreme Court insists on talking about the 'fence'. It highlights that the same fence is labelled as 'barrier' in the Secretary General's report, and referred to as the 'wall' by the ICJ. The insistence of the Supreme Court on referring to the construction as a 'fence' appears to recognise and underline the security purposes for which it was erected.

[53] *Mara'abe* (note 46 above) para. 61.

[54] *Ibid.*, para. 62.

> its repercussions were presented, but these did not find their way to the opinion itself. This minimal factual basis is manifest, of course, in the opinion itself. It contains no real mention of the security-military aspect. In one of the paragraphs, the opinion notes that Israel argues that the objective of the wall is to allow an effective struggle against the terrorist attacks emanating from the West Bank. That's it.[55]

This different factual basis meant that from the material before it, the ICJ therefore concluded that it was 'not convinced' that the construction of the wall, the specific course chosen for the wall, and the destructions carried out contrary to the prohibition in Article 53 of the Fourth Geneva Convention, 'were rendered absolutely necessary by military operations' nor were they 'the only means to safeguard the interest of Israel against the peril which it has invoked as justification for the construction'.[56] This conclusion was in stark contrast to evaluation of the Supreme Court in *Beit Sourik*.

In addition to the different factual basis relating to the security-military necessity, the Supreme Court also looked at the difference between the factual basis regarding *the scope of the impingement of the local residents' rights* in the two judgments. In the *Beit Sourik* case, the petitioners brought various data regarding the scope of the impingement of their rights due to the construction of the fence on their lands. The state brought its own data. The Court examined the different positions. It examined each part of the route before it, separately. On the basis of the totality of the evidence before it, the scope of the impingement of the local residents' rights was established.

The ICJ, in contrast, based its factual findings regarding impingement upon the local residents' rights, upon the Secretary-General's report and his supplemental documents, and upon the Dugard report and the Zeigler report. The Supreme Court emphasised that in their arguments before the court, state's counsel noted that the information relayed to the ICJ in these reports 'is far from precise'.[57] For example, whilst the ICJ quoted data relayed by a special committee, according to which 100,000 dunams of agricultural land were seized for construction of the first phase of the obstacle, in *Mara'abe* the state contended that the figure was 'most exaggerated' and that the area was considerably smaller (around 8,300 dunams). Further, the Zeigler report, according to which Israel is annexing most of the western aquifer system through the construction of the barrier, was rejected as 'completely baseless', asserting that the

[55] *Ibid.*, para. 63. [56] *Ibid.* [57] *Ibid.*, para. 67.

construction of the fence 'does not affect the implementation of the water agreements' entered into with the Palestine Liberation Organization (PLO). Several other inaccuracies relating to the impact on individuals were identified.

In addition to these elements, the Supreme Court also emphasised that in its assessment the ICJ's *scope of examination* was importantly broader than in *Beit Sourik*. Whilst the Israeli Supreme Court considered five segments of the separation fence, approximately forty kilometers long, the ICJ examined the legality of the entire route of the fence (when finished, it would measure up to 700 km). The factual basis which was laid before the ICJ (the Secretary-General's report and written statement, the reports of the *special rapporteurs*) 'did not analyze the different segments of the fence in a detailed fashion, except for a few examples . . . The material submitted to the ICJ contains no specific mention of the injury to local population at each segment of the route.' Instead, the whole route is analysed, including expansive parts of the fence where there are no Palestinian or Israeli communities, nor is there agricultural land. 'Upon which rules of international law can it be said that such a route violates international law?' Similarly, what of the segments which separate Palestinian farmers and their lands? If gates built into the fence allow passage, when necessary, to the cultivated lands, '[c]an it be determined that this arrangement contradicts international law *prima facie*, without examining, in a detailed fashion, the injury to the farmers on the one hand, and the military necessity on the other?' Barak insisted that each of these situations – and segments – 'requires an exacting examination of the essence of the injury, of the various suggestions for reducing it, and of the security and military considerations. None of this was done by the ICJ, and it could not have been done with the factual basis before the ICJ.'[58]

The Israeli Supreme Court found that the main difference between the legal conclusions stems from the difference in the factual basis laid before the court. It is this factual basis that affected the different application of the law and thus led to a different outcome. As Barak puts it: 'Once again, the simple truth is proven: the facts lie at the foundation of the law, and the law arises from the facts (*ex facto jus oritur*).'[59] As a consequence of the different facts on the basis of which the two courts acted, the Supreme Court felt that it was not obligated to follow the ICJ's interpretation of international law and 'to rule that each and every segment of the fence violates international law'. Instead, the Court would 'continue to

[58] *Ibid.*, para. 70. [59] *Ibid.*, para. 61.

examine each of the segments of the fence, as they are brought for its decision and according to its customary model of proceedings' outlined in *Beit Sourik*.[60]

Different conceptions of the judicial role The Supreme Court clearly refuses to follow the ICJ Opinion and points to a different factual basis to explain its decision. Yet, Barak is careful to note that the mistakes committed in establishing the different factual basis in the *Wall* Opinion may not necessarily lie with the ICJ but rather with the evidence submitted to it. The 'circumstances' in which the World Court found itself 'cast an unbearable task upon the ICJ'.[61] The emphasis that at many points in the proceedings (e.g. examining the entirety of the wall rather than its segments) the ICJ 'could not have' undertaken a different examination from the one it did is notable. Even in relation to the ICJ's failure to consider the security-military necessity, Barak is hesitant to assign the blame onto the ICJ:

> We need not determine, nor have we a sufficient factual basis to determine, who is to blame for this severe oversight. Is it the dossier of documents submitted to the ICJ? Is it the oversight of the State of Israel itself, or was it the ICJ's unwillingness to use the data submitted to it by Israel and other data in the public domain? Or maybe it is the method of examination, which focused on the fence as a totality, without examining its various segments?[62]

It is to this last point – the method of examination undertaken by the ICJ – that Barak keeps coming back in his comparison of the procedures adopted by the Supreme Court and the ICJ. Speaking of the model of proceedings followed, Barak notes:

> In the proceedings before the ICJ, the injured parties did not participate. Israel was not party to the proceedings. There was no adversarial process, whose purpose is to establish the factual basis through a choice between contradictory factual figures. The ICJ accepted the figures in the Secretary-General's report, and in the reports of the *special rapporteurs*, as objective factual figures. The burden was not cast upon the parties to the proceedings, nor was it examined.[63]

The same, of course, cannot be said of proceedings before the Supreme Court. In *Beit Sourik*, the parties stood before the court and an 'adversarial process took place. The burden of establishing the factual basis before

[60] *Ibid.*, para. 74. [61] *Ibid.*, para. 70. [62] *Ibid.*, para. 65. [63] *Ibid.*, para. 69.

the court was cast upon the parties.' In this context, the factual figures presented were 'examined and made to confront each other, as the factual basis which would determine the decision was established'.[64] The proceedings lacked strict formalities, and allowed flexibility for the parties to alter the route during the hearings themselves.

Barak clearly underlines the importance of transparency allowed by the adversarial process, and the traditional standards of burden of proof and confrontation of evidence. It is these elements – or their lack thereof – that render the ICJ's interpretation of international law unpersuasive before the domestic court. Even more, it is the familiarity with the factual and legal issues and its flexibility of approach that renders the Supreme Court naturally competent to decide the issues of legality without deferring to the ICJ. In this context, Barak emphasises that the Supreme Court had thus far received ninety petitions relating to the construction of the separation fence and had completed forty-four petitions. In *Mara'abe*, the Court 'devoted seven sessions to the hearing of the petition',[65] in which both officers and workers who handled the details of the fence as well as respondents were heard. In light of these discussions, the route of the fence was altered in a number of locations. In contrast, the ICJ was seized of the matter only once and the proceedings did not allow for similar discussions between the military and the individuals impacted by the measures to take place.

These differences in procedure clearly affect the different factual basis, compelling the Supreme Court to depart from the Advisory Opinion. Yet, beyond the factual basis, the discussion of the differences in procedure by a domestic court also reveals a concern about the different institutional roles of the two courts and the struggle of domestic judges to reconcile the different visions of the judicial role. Whilst Barak recognises the judicial role of the ICJ as 'the highest judicial body in international law', the dissent in *Mara'abe* raises questions about the judicial nature of the ICJ. Cheshin, the Vice President of the Supreme Court, finds the decision of the ICJ 'so objectionable',[66] that he cannot 'guide myself by it to law, truth, and justice in the way a judge does'.[67] The ICJ, Cheshin asserts, 'is still a court'. 'The way in which the ICJ writes its opinion is the way of a court; the proceedings of the ICJ are, in principle, like the proceedings of a court; and the judges sitting in judgment don the robes of a judge in the way familiar to us from regular courts.'[68] Yet, '[t]he generality and

[64] *Ibid.* [65] *Ibid.*, para. 62. [66] *Ibid.*, Vice President Cheshin dissenting, para. 1.
[67] *Ibid.*, para. 4. [68] *Ibid.*, para. 2.

lack of explanation which characterize the factual aspect of the opinion are not among the distinguishing marks worthy of appearing in a legal opinion or a judgment.'[69] In fact, the statements of opinions and findings are so general and unexplained that 'it seems that it is not right to base a judgment, whether regarding an issue of little or great importance and value, upon findings such as those upon which the ICJ based its judgment.'[70]

Cheshin is directly critical of the ICJ's decision to accept the evidence submitted to it to establish the factual basis. Both he and Barak writing for the majority note that the ICJ's 'foreign and strange silence' ignoring the terrorism and security problems that have plagued Israel was rejected also by the ICJ dissenting judges. According to the Court, Judges Higgins, Kooijmans, Buergenthal, and Owada expressed concern about the ICJ's 'rather oblique reference to terrorist acts'[71] and lack of 'material explaining the Israeli side of the picture, especially in the context of why and how the construction of the wall as it is actually planned and implemented is necessary and appropriate'.[72] Is the majority of Supreme Court in referring to the ICJ dissenting judges not implying that the ICJ could have been more searching in its assessment of facts? And is Cheshin in his dissent not directly questioning the judicial nature of its decision?

The answer to the latter question is even clearer when Cheshin asserts that the 'opinion was colored by a political hue, which legal decision does best to distance itself from'.[73] Whilst the Supreme Court in *Beit Sourik* clearly rejected the proposition that the fence was the fruit of a political decision to annex occupied territory to Israel, instead accepting the state's position to act for security reasons, the ICJ was not so quick to dismiss the political annexation argument. The ICJ stated that it could not 'remain indifferent to certain fears expressed to it that . . . the construction of the wall and its associated regime create a "fait accompli" on the ground that could well become permanent, in which case, and notwithstanding the formal characterization of the wall by Israel, it would be tantamount to *de facto* annexation'.[74] Barak sought to minimize this reference to the political aspects of the construction of the wall. '[T]his statement – which expressed grave concerns – is not a positive finding that the fence is

[69] *Ibid.*, para. 4. [70] *Ibid.*

[71] *Legal Consequences of the Construction of a Wall* (note 5 above) 219, 223, para.13 (Kooijmans dissenting).

[72] *Ibid.*, 260, 268, para. 22 (Owada dissenting).

[73] *Mara'abe* (note 46 above), Vice President Cheshin dissenting, para. 4.

[74] *Legal Consequences of the Construction of a Wall* (note 5 above) 184, para. 121.

political, and that its objective is annexation.'[75] Cheshin, however, saw it as the confirmation that the Advisory Opinion was infused with 'an emotional element, which is heaped on to an extent unworthy of a legal opinion'.[76]

Jurisdictional Immunities of the State (Germany v. *Italy: Greece intervening)*

In 2012, the ICJ rendered its judgment in the case concerning *Jurisdictional Immunities of the State (Germany* v. *Italy: Greece intervening)*. The case concerned the application by Germany to find that Italy had failed to respect the jurisdictional immunity which Germany enjoys under international law by allowing civil claims to be brought against it in the Italian courts, seeking reparation for injuries caused by violations of international humanitarian law committed by the German Reich during the Second World War. Germany also alleged that Italy had violated its immunity by taking measures of constraint against German state property situated in Italian territory. The ICJ held that regardless of the substantive norms involved – for example, *jus cogens*, human rights protections – the norms on state immunity as procedural rules operated on a different level and they were therefore applicable. The Court ruled that through its failure to uphold the state immunity objections Italy had committed a breach of its international obligation to respect the immunity which the Federal Republic of Germany enjoys under international law. The Court ordered Italy to enact appropriate legislation, or resort to other methods of its choosing to ensure that the decisions of its courts and those of other judicial authorities infringing the immunity of Germany cease to have effect.

The issues before the Italian court

Germany's claim arose from a decision of the Court of Appeal of Florence in *Ferrini*,[77] in which it was held that Italian courts had jurisdiction over the claims for compensation brought against Germany by Mr Luigi Ferrini on the ground that immunity does not apply in circumstances in which the act complained of constitutes an international crime. The case was then reheard by the Court of Arezzo and the Court of Appeal

75 *Mara'abe* (note 46 above) para. 71.

76 *Ibid.*, Vice President Cheshin dissenting, para. 4.

77 *Ferrini* v. *Federal Republic of Germany*, note 3 above.

of Florence, which held that Germany should pay damages to Mr Luigi Ferrini as well as his case-related legal costs incurred in the course of the judicial proceedings in Italy. In particular, the Court of Appeal of Florence held that jurisdictional immunity is not absolute and cannot be invoked by a state in the face of acts by that state which constitute crimes under international law. Following the *Ferrini* judgment of the Italian Court of Cassation, twelve claimants brought proceedings against Germany in the Court of Turin, while another case was filed before the Court of Sciacca. In both cases, the Italian Court of Cassation confirmed that the Italian courts had jurisdiction over the claims against Germany.[78] A number of similar claims against Germany were pending before Italian courts at the time the ICJ was seised.

After the ICJ rendered its judgment, the question arose whether the Italian courts would abandon its settled case law on the existence of a 'human rights' exception to state immunity in civil claims in light of the judgment of the ICJ. Would the courts enforce the ICJ's decision, recognising Germany's jurisdictional immunity and thus depart from the *Ferrini* holding? The answer to this question was provided in *Military Prosecutor* v. *Albers*.[79] Although the Military Tribunal and the Military Court of Appeal followed the *Ferrini* decision, the Court of Cassation took time to consider the ICJ judgment. In this context, the Court considered both the legal nature of the ICJ decision and the isolated position of Italian courts in adopting the so-called 'evolutionary approach'.

The domestic legal nature of the ICJ decision Although according to the constitutional hierarchy, treaty provisions – and therefore Articles 94 of the UN Charter and Articles 59 and 60 of the ICJ Statute – prevail over domestic law,[80] the obligation to comply remains with the state. In *Albers*, the Court of Cassation declared 'complete autonomy of the

[78] *Jurisdictional Immunities* (note 4 above) 113–14, paras. 27–8.

[79] *Military Prosecutor* v. *Albers and ors and Germany* (joining), Final appeal judgment, No. 32139/2012, ILDC 1921 (IT 2012), 9th August 2012, 1st Criminal Section; the original in Italian also available at www.marinacastellaneta.it/wp-content/uploads/2012/08/2012_32139.pdf. For comment see Giuseppe Cataldi, 'The Implementation of the ICJ's Decision in the Jurisdictional Immunities of the State Case in the Italian Domestic Order: What Balance should be made between Fundamental Human Rights and International Obligations?', *ESIL Reflections* 2(2), 24 January 2013.

[80] Article 117 of the Italian Constitution. Although since *Albers* legislation has been adopted allowing for the reopening of proceedings in which the ICJ has excluded the possibility to subject a specific conduct of another state to civil jurisdiction: Cataldi (note 79 above) 3.

judicial function – including complete freedom in adjudicating cases'.[81] This assertion of independence shows that the Court of Cassation did not consider itself immediately and directly bound to comply with the ICJ's decision. In fact, the facts of the case concerned proceedings other than those examined by the ICJ, and as a consequence the decision of the ICJ was 'not directly controlling' in *Albers.* The Court of Cassation, for example, talks about a 'complete independence of the judicial function from direct and immediate constraints arising from the dictum of the International Court'.[82]

Nevertheless, the Italian court recognised that the ICJ's decision in clarifying '*stato attuale del diritto internazionale*' has 'unquestionable authority'.[83] As the ultimate authority to pronounce itself on the content and application of custom, the decision of the ICJ provided '*una soluzione giuridica dotata di elevata plausibilità*'.[84] Since the ICJ had clearly held that the immunity protections applied even in cases of violations of *jus cogens* norms, the Court of Cassation would act consistently with the obligations of the Italian Republic and with the provision of the Italian Constitution which requires consistency between domestic rules and customary international law. Since in case of conflict, the customary rule 'assumes primary' position, the Court of Cassation allowed the ICJ's holding to prevail regardless of the nature of the crimes involved.

The isolated position of Italian courts in adopting the 'evolutionary approach' What is interesting about the Court of Cassation's judgment in *Albers* is that the pronouncement on the 'existing state of international law' by the ICJ is not per se sufficient to persuade the Italian court to enforce the decision. In the course of its reasoning, the Court notes that after the *Ferrini* decision, Italian domestic judges have sat in 'substantial isolation' from the rest of the international community.[85] The Court laments the fact that no other domestic (European) court had reflected on the state of the law in the same manner as Italian courts and followed the *Ferrini* precedent. It quotes in particular a decision of the French Court of Cassation's decision in *GIE La Réunion Aérienne and ors* v. *Libya*, rendered after the ICJ's judgment.[86] This widespread rejection of the *jus cogens* exception to state immunity – the Court of Cassation found – confirms the clear decision of the Hague Court. A synthesis of a 'highest

[81] *Albers* ILDC commentary (note 79 above) para. H2.
[82] *Albers* original (note 79 above) para. 6. [83] *Ibid.*, paras. 5–6. [84] *Ibid.*, para. 6.
[85] *Ibid.* [86] Appeal judgment, Court of Cassation, ILDC 1770 (FR 2011), 9 March 2011.

judicial moment'[87] to give effect to the evolutionary approach adopted by *Ferrini* has therefore not yet taken root.

Different understanding of international law Although the Italian court implements the ICJ judgment, it does so hesitantly, asserting that the *Ferrini* approach was 'persuasive and legally sound'.[88] The Court of Cassation clearly finds the ICJ decision unconvincing. The ICJ's assessment that there is no conflict between peremptory norms protecting human rights and the customary rule of state immunity because the two sets of rules operate on different levels in the words of the Italian judges enjoys '*poca persuasiva attrazione*'.[89] The Italian court was 'perplexed' as to how the decision of the ICJ was consistent with the general principles of interpretation. Instead, the Court felt the ICJ's reasoning to confine the category of *jus cogens* to its substantive scope was 'unduly simplistic' and 'ignored' the fact that 'its real effectiveness' relies on the legal consequences flowing from their violations. If Germany is accorded immunity under international law, then *jus cogens* prohibitions remain ineffective.[90] In the end, the ICJ's artificial distinction between procedural and substantive norms 'causes nothing but the impunity of individuals'[91] by unpersuasively qualifying these acts as sovereign acts.[92]

Importantly, the Court notes that in spite of the ICJ's conservative holding, the dissenting opinions of some ICJ judges reveal that the emergence of a new future trend withdrawing immunity when actions affect individuals' rights is 'not excluded'.[93] If Italian courts had not been substantially isolated – they talk of being in a 'minority' in their approach – and had other countries 'shared' in their approach, then the Court would have followed the dissenting opinions to champion 'the evolutionary approach' in the international community.[94] Namely, to acknowledge immunity from jurisdiction of states in such cases is 'contrary to the rules protecting fundamental rights, the protection of which is essential in the international community'.[95]

Clearly, the Court of Cassation in *Albers* does not shy away from disagreeing with the ICJ. Even after the International Court has pronounced itself on the state of international law and established the current practice

[87] *Albers* original (note 79 above) para. 6. [88] *Ibid.* [89] *Ibid.*, para. 5.
[90] *Ibid.*, para. 4. [91] *Ibid.*, para. 5.
[92] *Ibid.*, para. 6; *Albers* ILDC commentary (note 79 above) para. H3.
[93] *Albers* original (note 79 above) para. 6. [94] *Ibid.* [95] *Ibid.*

of the international community, the Italian court does not hesitate to underline what is 'essential' in and for the international community – the protection of *jus cogens* norms. The Italian court's approach is in sharp contrast with that of the Israeli Supreme Court. Whilst the Israeli court critiques only the ICJ's evaluation of the factual basis, the Court of Cassation questions the ICJ's assessment and conclusions as to the content of international law.

Domestic courts as enforcers of ICJ decisions and opinions?

The analysis of the domestic decisions of US, Israel and Italian courts reveals that enforcement of ICJ judgments is not automatic. In fact, in all three jurisdictions the domestic courts are quick to assert their autonomy from the international institution, emphasising that they are not *apriori* bound by the decisions of the International Court. The US courts, for example, quickly establish that although the 'Avena decision constitutes an international law obligation of the part of United States . . . not all international law obligations automatically constitute binding . . . law enforceable in United States courts.'[96] A clear distinction is drawn between the 'international obligation' and the 'domestic legal effect' of the ICJ judgments. Whilst the ICJ has determined the 'international' question, in *domestic law* it is the domestic courts that have the authority and the expertise to determine the domestic legal effect of ICJ decisions, for example their self-executing nature or their relationship with domestic procedural rules.

In Israel, the Supreme Court also highlights that it is not bound by the ICJ opinion. The Advisory Opinion 'does not bind the party who requested it . . . it does not bind the states'.[97] Instead, the question before the Court is to what extent the interpretation of international law is controlling and therefore should be accorded appropriate weight in Israeli law. Although the two courts are seised of the same situation and are determining the legality of the same barrier based on the same common legal basis, the Supreme Court is autonomous in its evaluation of the case once it determines that the factual basis is sufficiently different.

The autonomous nature of the domestic court is also underlined in Italy. Even if the Court recognises that the ICJ has established the current state of international law which has to be given force, the Italian judges assert 'complete autonomy of the judicial function – including complete

[96] *Medellin* v. *Texas* (note 21 above) 504. [97] *Mara'abe* (note 46 above) para. 56.

freedom in adjudicating cases'.[98] The Court does not consider itself bound by the ICJ decision because there is no identity of claimants between the international ruling and the domestic case in *Albers*. Like the US and Israeli court before, the Italian court also insists it is answering a different question from the one considered by the ICJ.

These assertions of autonomy and subsequent failures by domestic courts to implement the ICJ decisions clearly show a hesitance on the part of domestic courts to act as an 'automatic' enforcement mechanism for international decisions. The domestic courts instead assert the authority to undertake their own assessment of the case and give different reasons for this action: US courts claim that they are acting on a different legal basis (i.e. domestic law); the Israeli Supreme Court asserts that it is proceeding from a different factual basis; whilst Italian courts insist that the proceedings concern a different claimant and therefore require an independent and separate assessment.

Yet in spite of this claim for 'complete freedom in adjudicating cases',[99] we should not read the domestic courts' treatment of ICJ's judgments as challenges of the World Court's authority to determine the content and application of international law or as an effort to undermine its position in the international legal order. Firstly, in comparison to other domestic cases concerning international law,[100] in these examples there is no discussion or doubts expressed as to whether the ICJ's rulings constitute 'law'[101] or indeed whether the ICJ is a court. Even Cheshin, who is strongly critical of the ICJ's handling of the legality of the wall, recognises that the ICJ 'is still a court'.[102] The domestic judges also do not express concern about their own familiarity with international law (e.g. there is no reference to international law not being 'the law we administer'[103]) nor do they make use of pejorative labels (e.g. asserting that international law is 'tommyrot'[104]). Instead, the Israeli Supreme Court explicitly accepts that the legal basis on which the two courts are deciding is a 'common one', i.e. one based on international law.

[98] *Albers* ILDC commentary (note 79 above) para. H2. [99] *Ibid.*

[100] In relation to ICJ judgments see e.g. *Committee of United States Citizens Living in Nicaragua* v. *Reagan* (1988) 859 F.2d 929; in relation to Security Council Resolutions see e.g. *Diggs* v. *Shultz* (1972) 470 F.2d 461 (DC Cir).

[101] Though note Cheshin's hesitance about how international law has developed and comments that more time is needed before it becomes a legal system of full standing. *Mara'abe* (note 46 above), Vice President Cheshin dissenting, para. 2.

[102] *Ibid.* [103] *Cook* v. *Sprigg* [1899] AC 572 (HL).

[104] *US* v. *Mitchell* (1965) 246 F Supp 874, 899.

Secondly, as can be clearly seen from the decisions, the ICJ's 'primacy in the determination of international issues throughout the international litigation'[105] is never called into question. The Israeli Court, for example, recognises that 'the opinion of the International Court of Justice is an interpretation of international law, performed by the highest judicial body in international law' and as such 'should be given its full appropriate weight'.[106] The US courts similarly grant 'respectful consideration' to the ICJ's interpretation of the VCCR and its rulings about the existence of international obligations for the US. In both examples, the domestic courts treat international law – or its interpretation in a given situation – as inextricably linked with the international institution and not open for an independent evaluation by the domestic court. Although the factual situation compels the domestic court to reject the ICJ opinion in *Mara'abe*, the High Court does not decide the legality of the relevant segment of the fence on the basis of its own understanding of international law (a move that would have directly demonstrated how the ICJ 'got the law wrong' and undermined its authority in international law). Instead, the Court explicitly argues that there is 'an additional source' of law on the basis of which it can establish the legality of the segment; 'the Israeli administrative law and the Basic Laws of the State of Israel'.[107] There is therefore no direct challenge of the ICJ's interpretation of international law.

Even the Italian court, which is openly hesitant about accepting the ICJ's interpretation that the jurisdictional state immunity rule applies in civil proceedings when *jus cogens* crimes are alleged, admits that the ICJ has established the current state of international law and that this decision has 'unquestionable authority'.[108] As the ultimate authority to pronounce itself on the content and application of custom, the decision of the ICJ provided '*una soluzione giuridica dotata di elevata plausibilità*'.[109] The Court does express concerns about the missed opportunity by the ICJ to set a new course for international law. Yet in the end, despite its concerns, the Court proceeds to enforce the international decision.

Finally, even the assertions of autonomy which may result in refusing enforcement of ICJ decisions are framed not in international, but exclusively in domestic legal language. The US courts talk of the 'domestic legal

[105] A. A. Cançado Trinidade 'Exhaustion of Local Remedies in International Law and the Role of National Courts' *Archiv des Völkerrechts* (1978) 17: 333, 335.

[106] *Mara'abe* (note 46 above) para. 56. [107] *Ibid.*, para. 91.

[108] *Albers* original (note 79 above) paras. 5–6. [109] *Ibid.*, para. 6.

effect' and underline how the domestic 'procedural default rules' operate 'in an adversary system'.[110] In Israel, the claim is in essence the same. The only element of the ICJ opinion to which the Supreme Court objects is the ICJ's failure to question the facts presented to it and to assess the evidence as would be done in an adversarial system. It is this distinction – between the international and the domestic legal process – that allows courts to claim and assert their authority and to question the ICJ's approach without undermining its position in the international legal order. In all these cases, the critique of the ICJ is limited to its understanding of the domestic adversarial system, not its understanding of international law.

What this reveals then is that if the ICJ or the international community counts on domestic courts serving as an enforcement mechanism of ICJ decisions, this role is not likely to develop automatically. Although domestic courts have been very respectful of ICJ decisions, they have thus far not accepted that they are blind enforcers of its judgments. Instead, they have insisted on an autonomous and independent role in the exercise of their judicial function. It is in this context, that they have asserted their power to say what the *domestic*, not international law is or what the *domestic*, not international effects of the ICJ judgments are. It is unlikely that they will ever surrender this role.

[110] *Sanchez-Llamas* (note 19 above) 356.

PART 2

A farewell to fragmentation and the sources of law

A. Custom and *Jus Cogens*

14

The International Court of Justice and the international customary law game of cards

LORENZO GRADONI

1. Introducing the card players

The point this chapter wishes to make is not necessarily in step with the present book's general claim to portray a 'centre' that, seemingly lost until recently in the madhouse of international law's fragmentation, is now in the process of reasserting itself. What constitutes the 'centre' and who is making a stand for it in contemporary international law is clear enough. In a recent article, Mads Andenas contended that the International Court of Justice (ICJ), sitting 'at the top of an open international law system' and providing the other courts and tribunals with a standard set of legal concepts, is contributing to the definition of 'common sources and methods and to the foundation of a level of unity or coherence of international law'.[1] General international law constitutes the centre, and the ICJ is its high priest. However, although *customary* international law is commonly regarded as an important component of this international legal 'core', Andenas concedes that the ICJ exercises caution in developing that specific kind of law, meaning that at least on this score it focuses more on dispute settlement than on systemic upkeep.[2] I wish to bring this insight a little further.

Since I am among those who think that the ICJ's case-law as well as its predecessor's did not throw much light on the mysterious ways of custom formation and identification, I am puzzled by the widely held belief in

[1] Mads Andenas, 'The Centre Reasserting Itself: From Fragmentation to Transformation of International Law', in Mattias Derlén and Johan Lindholm (eds.), *Festskrift till Pär Hallström* (Uppsala: Iustus Förlag, 2012), pp. 17–8, 29.

[2] Andenas, 'The Centre Reasserting Itself', p. 12. In the same vein see, among others, Martti Koskenniemi, *From Apology to Utopia: The Structure of International Legal Argument. Reissue with a New Epilogue* (Cambridge: Cambridge University Press, 2005), pp. 462–3: 'Even a rapid glance at the jurisprudence of the ICJ shows that it has tended to

the existence of a single, Hartian 'rule of recognition' of customary law, allegedly expressed by a 'background regime of general international law common to all special international regimes'.[3] In H. L. A. Hart's view, the rule of recognition is 'a form of judicial customary rule, existing only if it is accepted and practiced in the law-identifying and law-applying operations of the courts'.[4] The fragmented, non-hierarchical assortment of jurisdictions that characterizes the contemporary international legal landscape is not necessarily conducive to the formation of a single judicial customary rule, as the law-applying agencies of each special regime may well develop their own approach to customary law. Even the staunchest believers in the unity of the international legal order grant that, 'institutionally', such unity 'is not well safeguarded'.[5] Moreover, the ICJ has hardly ever lowered its guard about the details of its own approach. It has been pointed out in an authoritative voice that 'overall there is substantial reliance on the approach and case law of the International Court of Justice, including the constitutive role attributed to the two elements of State practice and *opinio juris*'.[6] While this claim is unassailable, the rule of recognition it describes may leave a bit too much to the imagination.[7] Jeremy Waldron is certainly right when he observes that it remains 'unclear how important it is for Hart that a legal system has a rule of recognition which is hard and fast and definitely rule-like as opposed to vague and standard-like

base obligations rather on the specific relation between the disputing States than general rules.' See also John G. Merrills, *Anatomy of International Law: A Study of the Role of International Law in the Contemporary World* (London: Sweet and Maxwell, 1976), p. 5: 'opposability of particular claims is a far more significant issue than their conformity with an uncertain customary rule'. On factors (other than custom) that may contribute to the overall coherence of the international legal edifice see Manuel Rama-Montaldo, 'Universalism and Particularisms in the Creation Process of International Law', in Sienho Yee and Jacques-Yvan Morin (eds.), *Multiculturalism and International Law. Essays in Honour of Edward McWhinney* (Leiden and Boston: Martinus Nijhoff, 2009), pp. 144–5.

3 Samantha Besson, 'Theorizing the Sources of International Law', in Samantha Besson and John Tasioulas (eds.), *The Philosophy of International Law* (Oxford: Oxford University Press, 2010), p. 183.

4 H. L. A. Hart, *The Concept of Law*, 3rd edn. (Oxford: Oxford University Press, 2012), p. 256.

5 Christian Tomuschat, 'International Law as a Coherent System: Unity or Fragmentation?', in Mahnoush H. Arsanjani, Jacob Katz Cogan, Robert D. Sloane and Siegfried Wiessner (eds.), *Looking to the Future: Essays on International Law in Honor of W. Michael Reisman* (Leiden: Martinus Nijhoff, 2011), p. 333.

6 Michael Wood, First Report on Formation and Evidence of Customary International Law, UN Doc. No. A/CN.4/663 (2013), p. 28, para. 66.

7 See Jonathan I. Charney, 'Universal International Law' (1993) 87 *American Journal of International Law*, 529, 550.

and tattered around the edges'.[8] But this does not detract from the fact that the very point of having a rule of recognition, i.e., a 'proper way of disposing of doubts' as the existence of primary rules of obligation (at least in routine cases), is not compatible with any degree of vagueness.[9] Be that as it may, it is undeniable that for international lawyers the idea of a standard way of identifying customary rules has become the lynchpin of a complex insurance scheme against fragmentation. Shortly after his designation as the International Law Commission's (ILC) Special Rapporteur on the topic of custom formation and identification, Sir Michael Wood put the idea into very clear words:

> It is the view of the Special Rapporteur that, given the unity of international law and the fact that 'international law is a legal system'... it is neither helpful nor in accordance with principle, for the purposes of the present topic, to break the law up into separate specialist fields. The same basic approach to the formation and identification of customary international law applies regardless of the field of law under consideration.[10]

According to Kenneth Keith, judge at the ICJ since 2006, 'general international law is a most important – possibly *the* most important – single vehicle of common action and understanding'.[11] The fact that Hart himself did not believe in the existence of a rule of recognition of customary *international* law does not seem to prevent such arguments from being constantly put forward, since Hart's treatment of the matter is widely regarded by contemporary international lawyers as either flawed or dated.[12] While

[8] Jeremy Waldron, 'International Law: "A Relatively Small and Unimportant" Part of Jurisprudence?', in Luís Duarte D'Almeida, James Edwards and Andrea Dolcetti (eds.), *Reading H.L.A. Hart's* The Concept of Law (Oxford and Portland: Hart, 2013), p. 219.

[9] Hart, The Concept of Law, p. 95.

[10] Formation and Evidence of Customary International Law, Note By Michael Wood, Special Rapporteur, UN Doc. No. A/CN.4/653 (2012), p. 5, para. 22. See also ILC, Report on the Work of its Sixty-fifth Session, UN Doc. No. A/68/10 (2013), p. 97, para. 86: 'Several members agreed that the Commission should aspire towards the elaboration of a common, unified approach to the identification of rules of customary international law, as such rules arise in a single, interconnected international legal system.'

[11] Kenneth J. Keith, 'The International Court of Justice: *Primus Inter Pares*?' (2008) 5 *International Organizations Law Review*, 7, 20.

[12] See, e.g., Anthony D'Amato, *The Concept of Custom in International Law* (Ithaca, NY: Cornell University Press, 1971), pp. 42–4; Godefridus J. H. van Hoof, *Rethinking the Sources of International Law* (Deventer: Kluwer, 1983), p. 53–6; Georges Abi-Saab, 'Cours général de droit international public' (1987) 207 *Recueil des cours de l'Académie de droit international de La Haye*, 9, 105; Thomas M. Franck, 'Legitimacy in the International System' (1988) 82 *American Journal of International Law*, 705, 753; Chittharanjan F. Amerasinghe, 'International Law and the Concept of Law: Why International Law is Law', in Jerzy

no explicit attempt at rehabilitating his views on international customary law is made here, I think that looking back on them remains instructive. Hart maintained that the rule of recognition was 'not a necessity, but a luxury', to be found only in 'social systems whose members not merely come to accept separate rules piecemeal, but are committed to the acceptance in advance of general classes of rule, marked out by general criteria of validity'.[13] In simpler orderings like international law, where the validity of unwritten rules cannot be established by reference to a more basic norm, nothing is left unexplained as to the validity or the binding force of rules that are, 'like the basic rule of the more advanced systems, binding if they are accepted and function as such'.[14] In Hart's opinion, this simple truth about international law is easily 'obscured by the obstinate search for unity and system'.[15] Two distinct factors may help explain why international lawyers have never ceased to engage in such an obdurate endeavour. The first factor runs deep in the history of international legal thought and has to do with the general proneness of international lawyers towards theorizing customary law as a formal, unified source of legal rules, a point superbly expounded by Peter Haggenmacher:

Makarczyk (ed.), *Theory of International Law at the Threshold of the 21st Century. Essays in Honour of Krzysztof Skubiszewski* (The Hague, Boston and London: Kluwer, 1996), p. 80; Pierre-Marie Dupuy, 'L'unité de l'ordre juridique international. Cours général de droit international public' (2002) 297 *Recueil des cours de l'Académie de droit international de La Haye*, 9, 76–7; Yuval Shany, *The Competing Jurisdictions of International Courts and Tribunals* (Oxford: Oxford University Press, 2003), p. 84; Lorenzo Gradoni, 'L'attestation du droit international pénal coutumier dans la jurisprudence du Tribunal pour l'ex-Yougoslavie: Régularités et règles', in Mireille Delmas-Marty, Emanuela Fronza and Elisabeth Lambert-Abdelgawad (eds.), *Les sources du droit international pénal* (Paris: Société de législation comparée, 2004), pp. 67–70 (affirming the existence of a rule of recognition of customary international criminal law, an idea I would no longer defend in the same way); David Lefkowitz, '(Dis)solving the Chronological Paradox in Customary International Law: A Hartian Approach' (2008) 21 *Canadian Journal of Law and Jurisprudence*, 129, 146–8; Jörg Kammerhofer, *Uncertainty in International Law. A Kelsenian Perspective* (London and New York: Routledge, 2011), pp. 227–9; Mehrdad Payandeh, 'The Concept of International Law in the Jurisprudence of H.L.A. Hart' (2011) 21 *European Journal of International Law* 967.

13 Hart, *The Concept of Law*, p. 235.

14 Hart, *The Concept of Law*, p. 235.

15 Hart, *The Concept of Law*, p. 236. See also Roberto Ago, 'Positive Law and International Law' (1957) 51 *American Journal of International Law*, 691, 723, on whom Hart explicitly relies. Ago polemicized against the idea that custom is a law-creating fact: 'in order to be able to recognize customary norms, legal science uses, and can only use, that same inductive method which it employs to establish the existence of those so-called primary or fundamental norms' (Ago called 'primary' Hart's secondary rules). For an isolated recent endorsement of Hart's view see Detlev von Daniels, *The Concept of Law from a Transnational Perspective* (Farnham: Ashgate, 2010), p. 146.

> Le fait d'inclure dans une même dénomination un ensemble de règles que lie en réalité seul leur caractère extra-législatif, engendre la représentation d'une catégorie de normes homogènes ayant une origine commune; et de là se dégage l'idée corrélative d'un mode de constitution uniforme empruntant à la législation l'apparence d'une source formelle du droit dont il imite dans son ordre le mécanisme générateur de normes... C'est donc notre manière même de concevoir le droit coutumier qui l'érige en problème; et c'est aussi ce qui suscite les diverses théories appelées à l'expliquer: elles tiennent lieu d'un mécanisme législatif par hypothèse inexistant.[16]

The second factor stems from contemporary apprehensions about international law breaking up into a wide array of specialized regimes.[17] Indeed, the idea of a common body of law of customary origin, valid across and between regimes, comes a long way towards soothing such anxieties.[18]

The two factors are mutually reinforcing. On the one hand, theorizing custom as a formal source of law makes it possible to think of it as an integrating, anti-particularistic element of the international legal order: a potential antidote to fragmentation. On the other hand, enrolling customary law in the fight against fragmentation entails the need to define as neatly as possible the contours of an orthodox conception of custom as a source of law in a formal sense, and to close ranks around it. The recent ILC's bid to establish signposts for custom formation and identification suggests that such an entrenchment has reached an advanced stage of institutionalization. But the prospects of such an exercise are highly uncertain. To begin with, the idea is not entirely novel: the International Law Association (ILA) spent fifteen years studying the subject before handing down, in 2000, a long-winded statement of principles to which practitioners have paid almost no heed.[19] Shinya Murase, a member of the ILC who also took part in the ILA Committee on custom formation, had this to say apropos of the Commission taking the baton from the ILA:

[16] Peter Haggenmacher, 'Coutume' (1990) 35 *Archives de philosophie du droit* 27, 28.

[17] But see, on the historical recursiveness of the fragmentation debate, Anne-Charlotte Martineau, 'The Rhetoric of Fragmentation: Fear and Faith in International Law' (2009) 22 *Leiden Journal of International Law* 1.

[18] The copyright for 'fragmentation anxiety' belongs to Martti Koskenniemi and Päivi Leino, 'Fragmentation of International Law? Postmodern Anxieties' (2002) *Leiden Journal of International Law* 553.

[19] ILA Committee on the Formation of Customary (General) International Law, 'Final Report: Statement of Principles Applicable to the Formation of General Customary International Law' (2000) 69 *International Law Association Conference Report* 712.

> If the [ILC's] Special Rapporteur were to use the London Statement of Principles Applicable to the Formation of General Customary International Law, which was a broad normative statement, as a model for his project, the project would be doomed to fail, because it would end up by stating the obvious or being ambiguous.[20]

Nor is it clear how the path taken by the ILC can significantly diverge from the trail already blazed by the ILA, as in all likelihood their main source of inspiration is going to be the same, that is, the case-law of the ICJ. As Special Rapporteur Michael Wood announced in his first report:

> The case law of the International Court of Justice and its predecessor . . . will be of great significance for the Commission's work on the present topic . . . Its judgments (including separate and dissenting opinions) shed much light on the general approach to the formation and evidence of customary international law . . . including on specific aspects of these processes.[21]

This statement echoes a view expressed from the Court's bench, according to which the subject-matter of the cases submitted to it 'provides rich opportunities to the Court and its members to contribute in a regular and systematic way to the body of general international law and its processes', a state of affairs that should be welcomed because the ICJ 'has much better opportunities than do other international courts and tribunals to do that and . . . to see things steadily and to see them whole'.[22] But in the potentially hostile environment created in the last couple of decades by the proliferation of international jurisdiction the ICJ cannot assert the centrality of its role without a strategy. And there cannot be strategy without method, understood here as a modicum of orderliness of thought and behaviour.[23] The ICJ may wish to make the rest of the international legal milieu believe that there is only one method for finding out custom – its own method – and that may well be its strategy. Be that as it may, one thing is clear: if the ICJ aspires, as it were, to the role of a methodological lighthouse, it has to shine like a beacon, that is, it must have a recognizable method, one that is intelligible enough to be replicated by other law-applying agencies.

The ICJ's judicial output may lead to higher degrees of overall systemic coherence by stimulating uniform application of customary international

[20] ILC, Provisional Summary Record of the 3148th Meeting, UN Doc. No. A/CN.4/SR.3148 (2012), p. 5.

[21] Wood, First Report, p. 21, para. 54.

[22] Keith, 'The International Court', 21.

[23] Let it be noted in passing that if one equates 'method' with 'fixed procedure', the converse is not true: there can be method without strategy.

law in two hypothetical 'modes-of-play'. The first one, which may be called 'structural', would consist in working out a *method* for the identification of customary rules that is detailed and unambiguous enough as to reduce the risks of divergent rulings by other courts and tribunals to a minimum. On this score one is always tempted to argue that the intrinsic indeterminacy of the customary *process* places limits on attempts at defining bright-line criteria. In the next section I try to dispel this ordinary misconception. The second mode-of-play, which may be described as 'incremental', would not commit the ICJ to go beyond a broad-brush characterization of the customary process like the one that made its judgment in the *North Sea Continenal Shelf* cases so prominent.[24] The Court's opinions about the *content* of customary law would be widely accepted not on account of the method underpinning them – which may well remain a mystery, or be just a bluff – but as a consequence of the Court's authoritativeness. In section 5 I contend that the ICJ has acted with extreme caution on both fronts, thus failing to strengthen or stabilize international law's putative 'centre'. In the tense atmosphere so typical of the international customary law poker game, the Court has been playing its cards close to its chest. And the attitude of its fellow players – the ILC, doctrine, and States – is not fundamentally different. Not blessed with a good hand, the ILC and doctrine sit nervously at the table and keep a watchful eye on States and the Court, both of which wear a poker face. In section 3 I say something about the vain search for a 'framework custom', understood as the product of a uniform practice of States concerning the identification of customary rules, taking into account, *inter alia*, the first reactions of States to the inquisitive attitude lately taken by the ILC in its work on the topic. In section 4 I try to expose the predicament of international legal doctrine, suspended as it is between a scientific outlook on the game and an emotional approach to the authority of the ICJ. In section 6 I briefly conclude by imagining what a showdown would reveal about the players' cards.

2. A clarification about the nature of the game

The austere game-theoretical analysis performed by Norman and Trachtman in 'The Customary International Law Game' strived to throw light

[24] ICJ, *North Sea Continental Shelf Cases (Federal Republic of Germany/Denmark; Federal Republic of Germany/Netherlands)*, Judgment of 20 February 1969, [1969] ICJ Rep 42–6, paras. 70–9.

on the mysterious ways of custom formation,[25] but the many lingering doubts surrounding it seem to be too serious to be puzzled out, and advise against emulating their effort.[26] Unlike Norman's and Trachtman's 'game', with its focus on custom *formation*, the customary international law game of cards is concerned with the *identification* of customary rules. A common objection against the search for rule-like parameters in this domain has it that 'customary law is *by its very nature* the result of an informal process of rule-creation'.[27] For Patrick Kelly, the idea of encasing the customary process in a rule of recognition is problematic precisely because that process admits of 'no separate form or ritual that tells us a norm is binding beyond general acceptance itself'.[28] This view erroneously conflates the study of the social processes from which customary rules emerge and the way in which given legal systems may regulate proof of custom in case of dispute: the definitional informality of those processes makes them impervious to proceduralist or algorithmic characterizations, while proof of custom may be regulated as precisely as one wishes.[29] In his *Essai sur la connaissance et la preuve des coutumes* (1910), Hippolyte Pissard told the story of how thirteenth-century French law saw the emergence 'd'ingénieux systèmes de preuve de la coutume'[30] – a variety of approaches relying on testimonies given by community members, experts' affidavits, or verdicts expressed by specially-appointed juries – a story that international lawyers should bear in mind when they set about theorizing about their 'own' customary law. Many authors believe that a rule of recognition (in Hart's sense) of customary international law does exist, and that it is broadly

[25] George Norman and Joel P. Trachtman, 'The Customary International Law Game' (2005) 99 *American Journal of International Law* 54.

[26] Clive Parry, *The Sources and Evidences of International Law* (Manchester: Manchester University Press, 1965), p. 27, who famously maintained that 'the sources of international law cannot be stated; [they] can only be discussed', has yet to be proven wrong.

[27] ILA Committee on the Formation of Customary (General) International Law, 'Final Report', 713, para. 2 (emphasis added).

[28] J. Patrick Kelly, 'The Twilight of Customary International Law' (2000) 40 *Virginia Journal of International Law*, 449, 494. See also Robert Kolb, 'Selected Problems in the Theory of Customary International Law' (2003) 50 *Netherlands International Law Review* 119: 'custom imports into the law and law-making the many uncertainties invariably linked with it'.

[29] Chaïm Perelman, 'L'usage et l'abus des notions confuses' (1978) 21 *Logique et analyse*, 4, 14, wrote that 'quand il s'agit de l'application d'une notion confuse, il n'existe pas de procédure unanimement admise concernant son maniement'. This assertion is probably true in most occasions. From a logical point of view, however, it remains a non sequitur.

[30] Hippolyte Pissard, *Essai sur la connaissance et la preuve des coutumes en justice, dans l'ancien droit français et dans le système romano-canonique* (Paris: Rousseau, 1910), p. 3 and *passim*.

descriptive of the process of custom formation.[31] An excerpt from the latest ILC annual report is extremely instructive in this respect:

> There was general agreement that the main focus of the Commission's work should be to clarify the common approach to identifying the formation and evidence of customary international law. The relative weight to be accorded to the consideration of 'formation' and 'evidence' was, however, the subject of debate. Some members were sceptical that the largely academic or theoretical questions relating to the formation of customary international law were necessary or relevant to the Commission's work on the topic. A view was expressed that formation and evidence are diametrically opposed concepts, as the former refers to dynamic processes that occur over time, while the latter refers to the state of the law at a particular moment. Several other members were of the view that it was impossible to distinguish the process of formation from the evidence required to identify the existence of a rule.[32]

From this passage it may be gleaned that even the members who stress the polarity between custom formation, a social process or family of processes, and custom identification, understood as the employment of a set of evidential techniques and decision-making rules, still tend to see the two as fundamentally connected, with the latter having to reflect the former in some way. This conviction is as widespread as it is perplexing. In his Postscript to *The Concept of Law*, Hart characterized the rule of recognition not as a mirror of the custom-creating practices of community members – States, in international law – but as 'a form of *judicial* customary rule'.[33] Hart's rule of recognition tracks the way in which judges decide about the existence of customary norms, not the social processes that bring the latter into existence, succinctly referred to as the accumulation of a general practice accepted by States as law. While the complex pattern of interactions giving rise to customary rules is necessarily indeterminate, the judicial ascertainment of such rules need not be so, and

[31] See, e.g., Besson, 'Theorizing', p. 178: 'Numerous secondary rules may be retrieved in international law nowadays. They can be of various legal origin: some are treaty-based . . . while others are customary like secondary rules pertaining to the *creation* of customary international law' (emphasis added); Jean d'Aspremont, *Formalism and the Sources of International Law: A Theory of the Ascertainment of Legal Rules* (Oxford: Oxford University Press, 2011), p. 165, who reproaches judicial practice for having been 'unable to offset the absence of formal law-ascertainment criteria by a consistent and intelligible reading of the *custom-making process*' (emphasis added).

[32] ILC, Report on the Work of its Sixty-fifth Session, p. 95, para. 77.

[33] Hart, *The Concept of Law*, p. 256.

may consist – as it historically did in other contexts – in the application of simple procedural rules.

It is submitted that one powerful reason behind the strange conflation of custom formation and custom identification, so common in international legal thought, is indirectly linked to the awkward position of the 'judiciary' in the international society of States. The fact that international adjudication remains optional acts as a powerful brake on the development of definite criteria and techniques of custom ascertainment by the law-applying agencies themselves: the more clear-cut the proposed methods, the less likely their acceptance by States and the latter's willingness to submit their disputes to adjudication. Indeed, if consensus among States on the appropriate techniques of custom ascertainment were not fundamentally lacking, we would perhaps find, in the ICJ Statute, a provision like this one:

> Article 51 *bis*
>
> Where the parties disagree on the existence of a rule of customary law, the Court shall refer the question to a Panel composed of five States selected by draw and whose identity shall be kept secret. The Panel decides by absolute majority. Abstentions shall be considered inadmissible. The Panel's decision is final and binding upon the Court in respect of that particular case.

This imagined provision may sound mocking to international lawyers but the point is that it could have been, in days of yore, the valued brainchild of a European jurist eager to help his Prince with the administration of justice. Since there is no *seigneur* from whom international lawyers could receive a comparable assignment, they do not put their minds to elaborating criteria or techniques of custom identification for purposes of dispute settlement, and have instead been absorbed in theorizing about custom-creating processes. International legal doctrine's fixation with custom formation, and its concomitant repression of questions more directly related to the recognition of customary rules, is nicely illustrated by the ILA Committee's commitment to deal 'only with the formation of rules of customary international law, not with their consolidation, invocation, application, amendment, termination, or other parts of the "constitutive process"'.[34] 'Recognition' or 'identification' as autonomous

[34] ILA Committee on the Formation of Customary (General) International Law, 'Final Report', 716, para. 8 (footnote omitted).

concepts were so absent from the authors' minds that they do not even feature in the negative list.

Although the foregoing remarks apply, *mutatis mutandis*, to scholars and judges alike, these two widely intersecting categories of people do not write about customary international law in exactly the same way. Differences, however, are more of style than substance. While the ICJ has chiselled out stylized images of custom formation, most eloquently in the *North Sea Continental Shelf* cases, scholars, unflinching in their tendency to dissect the Court's few pronouncements, have produced a vast and intricate literature on the subject. Jonathan Charney did not mean to be ironic when he wrote that '[a]n examination of the many analyses of the development of customary international law makes it clear that the process is opaque'![35] But the two discourses zero in on the same object, that is, on custom formation as opposed to custom identification. I am aware of the fact that many insist that the two are inextricably linked, so that no identification criterion might be devised without first earning a deep understanding of the social processes leading to the formation of customary rules, but this is about as absurd as thinking that one cannot recognize an apple unless one becomes familiar with the biochemical processes that makes it ripe for eating.[36] Blaming the non-existence in

[35] Charney, 'Universal International Law', 537. International lawyers' disregard for John Finnis' analysis of the concept of a 'framework custom' (see below note 39 and corresponding text) may have also been due to Finnis' scathing remark on their work on custom. Writing towards the end of the 1970s, he saw before him 'a vast and confused literature on custom as a source of international law'. John Finnis, *Natural Law and Natural Rights* (Oxford: Clarendon, 1980), p. 238. Finnis' suggestion was not perhaps utterly absurd if a commentator as clear-sighted as Jörg Kammerhofer could express himself as follows thirty-two years later: '[t]he "meta-law on law-creation"... is singularly unclear, and in discussing whether this or that proposed rule of customary law has actually become part of law we assume certain meta-laws... to apply, but have no proof that they do. We take from long legal tradition that the two ingredients are *usus* and *opinio*, but... we do not know what they mean; [or] we doubt that modern international law contains these two requirements in this form'. Jörg Kammerhofer, 'Book Review' (2012) 23 *European Journal of International Law*, 589, 593.

[36] Wood, First Report, p. 6, para. 15: 'in order to determine whether a rule of customary international law exist, it is necessary to consider both requirements for the formation or a rule of customary international law'. See also Portugal's recent and exceptionally explicit (for a State) *prise the position*: 'Although both aspects of the topic – formation and evidence – were important, particular emphasis should be given to the former. By describing the process of formation of customary law, the Commission would be better able to establish a methodology for identifying current and future norms of customary international law.' UNGA VI Committee, Summary Record of the 21st Meeting, UN Doc. No. A/C.6/67/SR.21 (2012), pp. 16–7, para. 94.

international law of a provision like fake Article 51 *bis* on the complexity and the indeterminacy of the customary process is therefore likewise absurd.

3. States' poker face and the quest for the 'framework custom'

While the ICJ confines itself to *following* the instructions imparted by Article 38(1)(*b*) of its own Statute – i.e. that 'international custom, as evidence of a general practice accepted as law', be applied – scholars have pondered heavily over the purport of that provision, occasionally equating it with a rule of recognition of customary international law,[37] something that Article 38(1)(*b*) certainly is not. The provision does no more than stating that custom is part of the international law that the ICJ is called on to apply. Apart from making the trivial point that customary law supervenes upon a generalized jurisgenerative practice of which someone will have to bring forward some (unspecified) evidence, the provision tells absolutely nothing as to how customary rules should be identified – on their distinctive marks, as it were. Legal analysis could not leave the matter at that.

Following in Hart's footsteps – according to whom, let it be recalled, rules of recognition are themselves customary rules – international lawyers and legal theorists almost unanimously agreed that the rule of recognition of international law, customary or otherwise, arises from the convergent practice of States. Not long after the publication of *The Concept of Law*, Antony D'Amato observed that 'the "rules of recognition" of international law . . . are a product of the practice of states'.[38] As early as 1980, John Finnis, writing specifically about international law

[37] Payandeh, 'The Concept of International Law', 989–90. See also Georg Schwarzenberger, *The Inductive Approach to International Law* (London: Stevens & Sons, 1965), 126, according to whom international custom is a 'law-creating process' since Article 38 of the ICJ Statute, with the characterization of customary law it offers, 'has its sheet-anchor firmly embedded in the near-universally expressed will of the organised world society'.

[38] Anthony D'Amato, 'The Neo-Positivist Concept of International Law' (1965) 59 *American Journal of International Law*, 321, 323. See also Josef L. Kunz, 'The Nature of Customary International Law' (1953) 47 *American Journal of International Law*, 662, 665; Louis B. Sohn, '"Generally Accepted" International Rules' (1986) 61 *Washington Law Review* 1073, 1079–80: 'methods of developing new rules of customary international law have greatly changed since the Second World War . . . States are free to decide at any time, by the same method by which customary law is made, i.e., by "general practice accepted as law," that the methods of formulating new rules of law which were developed in recent years are legitimate methods of law-creation'; Franck, 'Legitimacy in the International System', 757.

(but ignored by international lawyers), worked out the concept of 'framework custom':

> the requirements, pre-conditions, and forms of custom-formation are themselves determined, in large part, by custom (i.e. by a framework custom whose source is similar in form to the customs for the formation of which it itself provides the framework). [I]f custom-formation is to work at all well as an instrument of international order and community . . . there must be a sufficient degree of agreement in answering these questions, among others: (i) What actions of what persons in what context count as state practice? (ii) What degree of practice counts as 'widespread' in a given domain, and for how long? (iii) What expressions or silences, and whose, count as subscribing to the *opinio juris*[?] Answers to these and similar questions go to make up the content of the framework custom. [They] have to be *adopted* by most members of the community if they are to *count as* answers.[39]

Despite his professed indecision about the true nature of these meta-rules, the ILC's Special Rapporteur on the topic of custom identification will in all likelihood end up agreeing with Finnis, that the 'framework' is itself customary and has State practice as its main ingredient:

> as in any legal system, there must in public international law be rules for identifying the sources of law. These can be found for present purposes by examining in particular how States and courts set about the task of identifying the law.[40]

But although conventional wisdom grants the community of States a quasi-monopoly on the making of the framework custom, no one can fail to notice how unforthcoming States are when called on to specify (itself an extremely rare occurrence) the parameters of custom identification they use. As the Special Rapporteur himself recognized, there is 'relatively little publicly available material that directly addresses the attitude of States to the formation and evidence of customary international law'.[41] Notwithstanding this apparent lack of evidence, he pointed to three possible

[39] Finnis, *Natural Law*, p. 245 (emphasis original). See also David Lefkowitz, 'The Sources of International Law: Some Philosophical Reflections', in Samantha Besson and John Tasioulas (eds.), *The Philosophy of International Law* (Oxford: Oxford University Press, 2010), pp. 199–201.

[40] Wood, First Report, p. 17, para. 38, where the following caveat appears: 'It is perhaps unnecessary, at least at this stage, to enter upon the question of the nature of the rules governing the formation and identification of rules of customary international law, for example, whether such rules are themselves part of customary international law.'

[41] Wood, First Report, p. 20, para. 48.

avenues of enquiry. The ways in which States approach custom identification could be culled from their pleadings before international courts and tribunals, from their reactions to codification texts produced by the ILC or other entities, and from routine diplomatic encounters where States' representatives and legal advisers exchange views 'about rules of customary international law'.[42] One should not expect to discover a gold seam by searching in any of these directions.

As for the information that one may hope to draw from litigation practices, the problem seems to lie in the fact that in such context States are prone to avail themselves of pieces of evidence of any kind, including those whose relevance the same States would consider dubious if used not to prop up but to undermine their position. It is therefore reasonable to expect that a systematic survey of the practice of States acting as litigants – a daunting task – would lead to the unexciting finding that there is too much noise in the data and no discernible pattern or regularity.[43] Maurice Mendelson, acting as rapporteur for the ILA's Committee on the Formation of Customary International Law, allowed himself a generous sprinkle of sarcasm on this point:

> Insofar as [lawyers] are acting as advocates, or are seeking to find a way of justifying actions which their government wants to take away for political reasons, they naturally have a tendency to reach for anything at hand. They acknowledge no duty of impartiality, either *ratione personae* or *materiae*... Those with experience of advocacy will be familiar with... what we might call the "kitchen-sink" style of pleading: in concocting arguments to be presented to international tribunals... it is very common for international lawyers to throw in all the ingredients they can lay their hands upon; not just the meat, the salt and the pepper, but also the sugar and even the kitchen sink.[44]

An examination of States' reactions to codification efforts hardly yields better results. As is known, States' disagreement with ILC 'findings' is essentially driven by interest and policy consideration and is never premised on detailed arguments about the identification of custom.

[42] Wood, First Report, p. 20, paras. 51–2.

[43] A step in this direction had been taken by Pierre-Marie Dupuy, 'La pratique de l'article 38 du Statut de la Cour internationale de justice dans le cadre des plaidoiries écrites et orales', in United Nations Office of Legal Affairs (ed.), *Collection of Essays by Legal Advisers of States, Legal Advisers of International Organizations and Practitioners in the Field of International Law* (New York: United Nations Publications, 1999), p. 377.

[44] Maurice H. Mendelson, 'Formation of International Law and the Observational Standpoint. Appendix to the First Report of the Rapporteur (1986)' (1988) 63 *International Law Association Conference Report*, 941, 946–7.

Alleged discrepancies between customary law and draft articles are usually asserted without explanation, as it should be expected of subjective preferences dressed in thin lawyerly garb. As Michael Wood himself rightly pointed out, the dispute triggered by the study on customary international humanitarian law commissioned by the International Committee of the Red Cross (ICRC) 'shed *rare* light on the attitude of some States to the process of formation and evidence of rules of customary international law'.[45] But even in this isolated case not very much came to light after all. Taking for granted that a method of identifying 'rules of customary international law correctly and precisely' is indeed available, the United States of America famously accused the ICRC Study of having failed to stick to the orthodoxy, without, however, disclosing anything about the 'true doctrine' except for a couple of shallow routine prescriptions (i.e., deeds should matter more than words and State practice has to be 'sufficiently dense') and the rather unorthodox contention according to which, in the field of international humanitarian law, the privileged status of 'specially affected States' should be vouchsafed to countries that go to war more often.[46] On the other hand, while it is too soon to conclude that the current ILC's works on custom identification is *not* acting as a stimulus for States to own up to their ways of identifying custom (assuming that they have anything to declare), the evidence so far is discouraging.[47] The operation is rapidly turning into a fair of banalities or unwitting ironies, where States reaffirm their fidelity to the two-element doctrine,[48] opine that 'work on the topic should not indulge in progressive development',[49] condemn the unorthodox drifts of specialized but unspecified law enforcement agencies,[50] apprise the ILC of the

[45] Wood, First Report, p. 20, para. 52 (emphasis added).

[46] John B. Bellinger III and William J. Haynes II, 'A US Government Response to the International Committee of the Red Cross Study on Customary International Humanitarian Law' (2007) 89 *International Review of the Red Cross*, 443, 444–6.

[47] For a detailed survey see Lorenzo Gradoni, 'La Commissione di diritto internazionale riflette sulla rilevazione della consuetudine' (2014) 97 *Rivista di diritto internazionale* 667–98.

[48] See, e.g., UNGA VI Committee, Summary Record of the 20th Meeting, UN Doc. No. A/C.6/67/SR.20 (2012), p. 18, para. 107 (Canada); UNGA VI Committee, Summary Record of the 21st Meeting, UN Doc. No. A/C.6/67/SR.21 (2012), p. 7, para. 33; UNGA VI Committee, Summary Record of the 23rd Meeting, UN Doc. No. A/C.6/67/SR.23 (2012), p. 4, para. 14 (Vietnam).

[49] UNGA VI Committee, Summary Record of the 19th Meeting, UN Doc. No. A/C.6/67/SR.19 (2012), p. 15, para. 92 (France).

[50] UNGA VI Committee, Summary Record of the 21st Meeting, UN Doc. No. A/C.6/67/SR.21 (2012), p. 19, para. 110 (Poland).

importance of (again!) the *Northern Sea Continental Shelf* cases,[51] urge it to distinguish international from national jurisprudence and 'assign each its proper weight',[52] warn it against favouring 'written materials' over 'actual practice',[53] and even decry the ICJ's methodological inconsistencies.[54] Other States fear that the search for standards may compromise the 'flexibility inherent in the customary process'.[55] The meaning of all this is well captured in a statement made by the Dutch representative at the Sixth Committee of the UN General Assembly:

> States might sometimes wish not to be overly specific about which rules they consider to be rules of customary international law or how such rules had achieved that status; deliberations on the formation of a customary law rule normally took place behind closed doors and clarity was not provided unless the situation specifically called for a determination.[56]

This brings us to Michael Wood's third avenue of enquiry, that is, looking at what happens during routine diplomatic encounters, where, in his view, States' representatives 'no doubt also reflect on the way [customary] rules emerge and are identified', although 'in a confidential manner'.[57] This does not seem entirely plausible. But even if States sought to patch up their differences in the shadow of custom, '[m]uch of this', as the ILA's Committee on custom formation suggested, would take place 'on a basis of confidentiality and official secrecy',[58] while it is obvious that an act cannot count as State practice unless it is made public.[59]

51 UNGA VI Committee, Summary Record of the 20th Meeting, UN Doc. No. A/C.6/67/SR.20 (2012), p. 17, para. 102 (Norway on behalf of Nordic Countries); UNGA VI Committee, Summary Record of the 21st Meeting, UN Doc. No. A/C.6/67/SR.21 (2012), p. 16, para. 92 (Portugal); UNGA VI Committee, Summary Record of the 22nd Meeting, UN Doc. No. A/C.6/67/SR.22 (2012), p. 8, para. 52 (Slovenia).

52 UNGA VI Committee, Summary Record of the 23rd Meeting, UN Doc. No. A/C.6/67/SR.23 (2012), p. 5, para. 23 (Iran).

53 UNGA VI Committee, Summary Record of the 23rd Meeting, UN Doc. No. A/C.6/67/SR.23 (2012), p. 5, para. 18 (Israel).

54 UNGA VI Committee, Summary Record of the 21st Meeting, UN Doc. No. A/C.6/67/SR.21 (2012), p. 16, para. 92 (Portugal).

55 UNGA VI Committee, Summary Record of the 22nd Meeting, UN Doc. No.A/C.6/67/SR.22 (2012), 2012, p. 12, para. 73 (Singapore) and p. 6, para. 36 (United Kingdom).

56 UNGA VI Committee, Summary Record of the 21st Meeting, UN Doc. No. A/C.6/67/SR.21 (2012), p. 11, para. 54.

57 Wood, First Report, p. 20, paras. 51–2.

58 ILA Committee on the Formation of Customary (General) International Law, 'Final Report', 716, para. 6, note 8.

59 ILA Committee on the Formation of Customary (General) International Law, 'Final Report', 726.

If States are not willing to show their hand, what about scholars? Louis Cavaré believed that 'l'assentiment des gens qui réfléchissent' was a constitutive element in the formation of customary international law,[60] while Josef Kunz opined that '[t]he ascertainment whether the two conditions of the custom procedure (*sic*) have been fulfilled in a concrete case, is a task of the competent international authority, and, preliminarily, of the science of international law'.[61] To contemporary ears all this sounds old-fashioned. Today's scholars are superficially less assertive of their role but this self-effacing attitude does not seem to be always sincere and, more importantly, it is unclear whether their detailed analyses demystify customary law more than they revel in its mystique.

4. The invisible college of scientific players (and disgruntled believers)

Like all experts, international lawyers gain access to a recondite kind of knowledge through specialized intellectual training. As is known, in their professional environment even the experience of seeing customary rules *crystallizing* like minerals becomes possible.[62] In 1958, the French jurist Paul Reuter wrote that in the modern world:

> les juristes font figure de techniciens. Ils en ont l'aspect extérieur, le langage imperméable, les procédures secrètes. Ils en ont aussi les caractères plus essentiels: à la liberté relative de l'invention morale, à la sensibilité des consciences, le métier de juriste tend à substituer des mécanismes, des déterminismes, des formules magiques.[63]

The same aura of cold scientism, secrecy, and magic, emanates from Oscar Schachter's paean to the *invisible* college of international lawyers, a piece of writing that bespoke fragmentation angst before time:

[60] Louis Cavaré, *Le droit international public positif*, 3rd edn., 2 vols. (Paris: Pedone, 1967), vol. I, p. 217.

[61] Kunz, 'The Nature', 667.

[62] I do not remember if it was me or Fouad Zarbiev who invented the international lawyer-as-mineralogist joke, but I reminisce about writing him an SMS from Rome reporting that in the campus of 'la Sapienza' the Faculty of Law is a stone's throw away from the Faculty of Mineralogy. See, in a similar vein (but not at all joking), Kolb, 'Selected Problems', 121: customary norms 'are moulded by complex molecular forces, holding together a series of disparate acts and facts'.

[63] Paul Reuter, 'Techniciens et politiques dans l'organisation internationale', in Paul Reuter, *Le développement de l'ordre juridique international: Ecrits de droit international* (Paris: Economica, 1995), p. 157.

> Should we expect – and even encourage – a . . . development toward specialization in the study of international law? My own view is that this is not likely in the near future, nor is it desirable. Certainly those who devote themselves intensively to particular problems will make useful contributions by virtue of their specialization. But it remains both desirable and feasible to have their conclusions subjected to the judgment of international lawyers outside of the specialized field. This is so, because unlike the situation in many sciences, *conclusions in international law do not involve the use of such specialized techniques of inquiry as to be beyond the knowledge of international lawyers* . . . For example, *the empirical data of relevant state practice can be checked and evaluated without recourse to esoteric procedures of investigation.* It is therefore not necessary to defer to the authority of the specialists in regard to such data (as it often is in the natural sciences). For that reason, it is feasible for international lawyers as a class irrespective of specialization to take part in the communication and collaboration that define their invisible college.[64]

The key to this passage lies in the argument that there are no 'specialized techniques of inquiry' apart from the protocols of custom identification that the generalist international lawyer claims to master.[65] These protocols, however, remain undisclosed: after all, '[l]e technicien est l'homme du secret'.[66] Encounters between international lawyers and customary law are often depicted in a style where techno-scientific imagery meets effusive lyricism. Maurice Kamto, political activist, co-founder of the Movement for the Renaissance of Cameroun, and a long-time member of the ILC, wrote of 'technical bodies such as the ILC, where specialists of international law without any political legitimacy are working to identify, scientifically and patiently, like archaeologists of law, legal norms out of the jungle of treaties and case law or the practice of States'.[67] Even younger

[64] Oscar Schachter, 'The Invisible College of International Lawyers' (1977) 72 *Northwestern University Law Review*, 217, 221–2 (emphases added).

[65] Compare *United States* v. *Yousef*, 327 F.3d (2nd Cir. 2003): '[the] notion . . . that professors of international law enjoy a special competence to prescribe the nature of customary international law . . . is certainly without merit'.

[66] Reuter, 'Techniciens', p. 151. See also, in a slightly different way, Michael Akehurst, 'Custom as a Source of International Law' (1974–75) 47 *British Yearbook of International Law* 1: 'Saint Augustine of Hippo wrote in book eleven of his Confessions: "What, then, is time? If no one asks me, I know; if I wish to explain to him who asks, I know not." The attitude of international lawyers towards customary international law is somewhat similar.'

[67] Maurice Kamto, 'The Function of Law and the Codification of International Law in a Changing World', in Ulrich Fastenrath, Rudolf H. Geiger, Daniel-Erasmus Khan, Andreas Paulus, Sabine von Schorlemer and Christoph Vedder (eds.), *From Bilateralism to Community Interest. Essays in Honour of Judge Bruno Simma* (Oxford: Oxford University Press, 2011), p. 746.

authors are infatuated with the self-image of an austere linguist-ruler: 'it is submitted here that legal scholars come to play the role of grammarians of formal law-ascertainment who systematize the standards of distinction between law and non-law'.[68] But no such grammar has ever been released, nor was it the awesome *algorithm* invented by Antony D'Amato at the price of many sleepless nights spent at his writing-desk:

> In the past couple of years I arrived at a new approach to this age-old problem. I wrote a draft article . . . a huge amount of interaction with my word processor, with particular emphasis on the 'Delete' key. The current version is an article of 134 pages that offers an algorithm for identifying rules of customary international law.[69]

The study of the 'occult and insensible process'[70] of custom formation is a matter for sociology, as D'Amato himself perceptively felt as early as 1965.[71] In spite of this, international lawyers – and D'Amato with them – have had apparently no alternative to the perpetuation of the figment of 'a "legal scientific" or empirical investigation into the legal facts of State practice'.[72] They never felt to be in a position to turn from a

[68] D'Aspremont, *Formalism*, p. 209.

[69] Anthony D'Amato, 'Customary International Law: A Reformulation', 4(1) *International Legal Theory* (1998) 1, 2. See also David J. Bederman, *Custom as a Source of Law* (New York: Cambridge University Press, 2010), p. xi: 'As for the elements of custom, I contend that the best algorithm for the creation of customary norms is the traditional notion that there must be both proof of an objective practice within a relevant community and a subjective determination of the value of the norm, whether expressed as a sense of legal obligation or the reasonableness of the rule.' (italics omitted).

[70] Charles Rousseau, *Droit international public* (Paris: Sirey, 1953), p. 64, cited and translated by Daniel P. O'Connell, *International Law*, 2 vols. (London: Stevens & Sons, 1965), vol. I, p. 18.

[71] D'Amato, 'The Neo-Positivist Concept', 323.

[72] Anthony Carty, *The Decay of International Law? A Reappraisal of the Limits of Legal Imagination in International Affairs* (Manchester: Manchester University Press, 1986), p. 3, where he adds that, in his view, 'this task is as impossible in legal as it is in historical research, even though it may appear to be required by Article 38 of the Statute of the International Court of Justice'. Compare Peter Hulsroj, 'Three Sources – No River. A Hard Look at the Sources of Public International Law with Particular Emphasis on Custom and "General Principles of Law"' (1999) 54 *Zeitschrift für öffentliches Recht*, 219, 220: 'custom, having being defined in an impossible fashion in the first place, has moved . . . international law from the rigours of a true legal discipline in the direction of sociology with its subjective imponderabilities.' See also Amanda Perreau-Saussine, 'Three Ways of Writing a Treatise on Public International Law: Textbooks and the Nature of Customary International Law', in Amanada Perreau-Saussine and James B. Murphy (eds.), *The Nature of Customary Law* (Cambridge: Cambridge University Press, 2007), pp. 254–5: 'For noble liars like Holland or Oppenheim, arguments in terms of the continued acceptance of a rule of customary international law veil lawmaking by benign jurists and judges. [T]heir ideals need to

'pseudo-scientific analysis of State practice' to an overt espousal of the technique of judicial precedent,[73] let alone proposing hard and fast rules on custom identification like fake Article 51 *bis* of the ICJ Statute,[74] and this because their ideal ally, the international judiciary, has never mustered enough legitimacy and power to allow for such operations. O'Connell had more than a inkling of the unfolding drama:

> In theory the custom is that of States, but the theory wears more threadbare with every decade and with every citation of judicial precedent. The statements of law of the International Court, in particular, are accorded in writings a truly astonishing deference... Surprisingly they are delivered with the minimum of reference to diplomatic practice, although this is ordinarily submitted in prodigious quantities by the litigant States.[75]

Thirty-five years later the same bizarre logic was at work in the final report of the ILA Committee on the Formation of Customary International Law:

> A word on methodology. In attempting to ascertain the law relating to the formation of customary international law, an inductive approach has been used. That is to say, the Committee considered that the rules about the sources of international law, and specifically this source, are to be found in the practice of States.[76]

In the remaining part of the report, however, references to the case-law of the ICJ come up at every turn, while State practice is consistently disregarded under the pretext that its 'confidentiality and official secrecy' made it impossible 'always... to cite chapter and verse'.[77] Our image of customary international law can be usefully compared to the Blackstonian characterization of the common law as the general custom of the realm. As Buckland and McNair observed, 'as a matter of history' common law was 'nothing of the kind', since it was 'brought into existence by the

be disguised... Their "scientific" international law, they hope, will encourage a gradual transformation of discordant conventional practices and beliefs into the harmonious enlightened ones of their utopia.'

73 Carty, *The Decay*, p. 20. 74 See above, section 2.

75 O'Connell, *International Law*, p. 28. See also the sapid remark by Andrea Bianchi, 'Gazing at the Crystal Ball (Again): State Immunity and *Jus Cogens* Beyond Germany v *Italy*' (2013) 4 *Journal of International Dispute Settlement*, 475, 463: 'oftentimes, the Court prefers to lean on its own authority rather than on State practice, which – let's be honest about it – might occasionally yield undesirable and unwanted results!'

76 ILA Committee on the Formation of Customary (General) International Law, 'Final Report', 715, para. 6 (notes omitted).

77 ILA Committee on the Formation of Customary (General) International Law, 'Final Report', 716, para. 6, note 8.

King's Justices, all over the country, precisely because there was no general custom of the realm'.[78] State practice, for the purposes of defining a rule of recognition for international customary law, is as overlooked as were popular usages and traditions by the makers of the common law. However, in contrast to the institutional context that nurtured the common law, in international law adjudication is neither compulsory nor serviced by a coherent system of courts. While the burgeoning international judiciary arguably remains, in some respects, a 'weak department of power',[79] its weakest spot lies in the fact no unified power stands behind it. Although the ICJ may deserve to be revered as 'first among equals',[80] this does not detract from the fact that it has to jostle for States' approval and support in a world where, as Benedict Kingsbury wryly remarked, '[i]f the ICJ did not already exist, it is far from clear that it could now be created'.[81] If States are reticent about the features of a hypothetical 'framework custom', as John Finnis named it, one should not pin her hopes on the Court's eagerness to fill up the silence.[82] Scholars, however, do expect this from the ICJ, and this faith seems to underlie their intriguingly ambivalent attitudes towards the Court, which they glorify and despise at the same time.

If customary international law is admittedly 'a strange beast',[83] many international lawyers see the ICJ as its valiant tamer. In a recent book deceptively styled as an attempt to revitalize international legal positivism,[84] Jean d'Aspremont claimed that the Court 'is no doubt . . . the

[78] William W. Buckland and Arnold D. McNair, *Roman Law and Common Law: A Comparison in Outline*, edited by Harry Lawson, 2nd edn. (Cambridge: Cambridge University Press, 1965), p. 15.

[79] Yuval Shany, 'No Longer a Weak Department of Power? Reflections on the Emergence of a New International Judiciary' (2009) 20 *European Journal of International Law*, 90, 91.

[80] Keith, 'The International Court', 7.

[81] Benedict Kingsbury, 'International Courts: Uneven Judicialisation in Global Order', in James Crawford and Martti Koskenniemi (eds.), *The Cambridge Companion to International Law* (Cambridge: Cambridge University Press, 2012), p. 215.

[82] It remains to be seen whether the ILC (which is for some of its members the Court's antechamber) will be willing and able to say something significant about the 'framework custom', including that the latter does not in fact exist, if the evidence turns out to point in that direction.

[83] John R. Morss, 'Can a Custom Be Incorporated in Law? On the Place of the Empirical in the Identification of Norms' (2008) 53 *American Journal of Jurisprudence*, 85, 99.

[84] Despite its claimed adherence to a sociological conception of law à la H. L. A. Hart, d'Aspremont's positivism is in fact a moralistic plea for the (gradual) construction of an inclusive and pluralistic recognitional community: 'The social practice on which the rule of recognition is based *must*. . . not be restricted to strictly-defined law applying officials but must include all social actors.' D'Aspremont, *Formalism*, pp. 203–4 (emphasis added). Here he follows Brian Z. Tamanaha, *A General Jurisprudence of Law and Society* (Oxford:

central law-applying authority whose behaviour is the most instrumental in defining the standard of law-ascertainment', and that it is 'still endowed with a natural monopoly to set the tone in the international judicial arena'.[85] It is hard to tell how this appraisal can be squared with what the author maintained a few pages earlier: '[t]he uncertainty inherent in the non-formal nature of custom-ascertainment has hardly been alleviated by international judicial practice, for the latter has been unable to offset the absence of formal law-ascertainment criteria by a consistent and intelligible reading of the custom-making process'.[86] Olivier Corten called it a 'jurisprudence contrastée'.[87]

Alberto Alvarez-Jiménez is among those who believe that the ICJ plays a role of 'capital importance' in the international legal system as the purveyor of methods for identifying customary rules.[88] In his view, the Court 'has inferred', from its own Statute, 'the existence of two main and traditional methods for the recognition of international customs: the strict inductive method and the flexible deductive approach'.[89] The two contradictions in terms ('strict inductive' and 'flexible deductive') and the naïve assumption that the Court 'inferred' the two corresponding methods from the vapid formula of Article 38(1)(b) can be safely overlooked. However, one cannot help being taken aback by the author's assertion that in the last few years the ICJ has been able to devise two further 'methods',[90] one of which appears to be a watered down version of the judicial technique of precedent, while the other is said to consist in making implicit findings of customary status, a technique that the author himself regards as careless and inadequate.[91] But he still calls it a 'method'! Birgit Schlütter's dry statement, that the ICJ 'has no single approach to the formation of customary international law', seems more reliable.[92]

Oxford University Press, 2001), pp. 142, 159–66. On the concept of recognitional communities see Matthew D. Adler, 'Popular Constitutionalism and the Rule of Recognition: Whose Practices Ground U.S. Law?' (2006) 100 *Northwestern University Law Review* 719.

85 D'Aspremont, *Formalism*, p. 205.

86 D'Aspremont, *Formalism*, p. 165.

87 Olivier Corten, *Méthodologie du droit international public* (Brussels: Editions de l'Université de Bruxelles, 2009), p. 175.

88 Alberto Alvarez-Jiménez, 'Methods for the Identification of Customary International Law in the International Court of Justice's Jurisprudence: 2000–2009' (2011) 60 *International and Comparative Law Quarterly*, 681, 685.

89 Alvarez-Jiménez, 'Methods', 686.

90 Alvarez-Jiménez, 'Methods', 698–703.

91 Alvarez-Jiménez, 'Methods', 709.

92 Birgit Schlütter, *Developments in Customary International Law: Theory and the Practice of the International Court of Justice and the International Ad Hoc Criminal Tribunals for Rwanda and Yugoslavia* (Leiden and Boston: Martinus Nijhoff, 2010), p. 168.

According to Alan Boyle and Christine Chinkin, the ICJ did develop a methodology for spotting customary rules but then failed to implement it:

> While the ICJ has identified a methodology for identifying rules of customary international law it follows it neither consistently not rigorously. Nor has it clarified the 'mysteries' of customary international law expounded by academics . . . or attempted to reconcile its own inconsistencies. It is hard to reach any conclusion except that where the Court's own requirements present an obstacle it will discount them in order to find custom – or not – where it wishes to do so and to find supporting evidence in either case as it seems fit.[93]

The authors' exasperated tone is that of a disgruntled believer. As already noted, the premise according to which the Court ever devised a method for identifying customary rules is doubtful. But even if there were some truth in it, Boyle and Chinkin now accept that the many inconsistencies in the Court's case-law 'dispel any pretence at an objective methodology'.[94] They are not alone in recognizing that the way in which the ICJ deals with customary law is rather casual and even tainted by dissimulation. According to Jonathan Charney, the evidence used by the Court 'to establish new norms of international law is considerably less comprehensive and persuasive than some theory would suggest and substantially less than is necessary to establish that all states actually or tacitly consent to all new rules of customary international law'.[95] Alain Pellet readily concedes that although 'it is virtually impossible to objectively determine whether a particular rule applied by the World Court is customary or results from a progressive development . . . , in all cases the Court will take great care to present it as being customary if only to avoid being blamed for legislating'.[96] Rudolf Geiger and Daniel Bodansky believe that the Court's professed method for identifying customary rule is a façade overlaying a modus operandi that is not necessarily less creditable. Using Michael

[93] Alan Boyle and Christine Chinkin, *The Making of International Law* (Oxford: Oxford University Press, 2007), pp. 284–5.

[94] Boyle and Chinkin, *The Making*, p. 281.

[95] Charney, 'Universal International Law', 538. See also Pierre-Marie Dupuy, 'Le juge et la règle générale' (1989) 93 *Revue générale de droit international public*, 569, 596: 'les libertés que la Cour peut être amenée à prendre avec la pratique comme preuve de l'assentiment des Etats ne peuvent aller jusqu'à la licence.'

[96] Alain Pellet, 'Shaping the Future of International Law: The Role of the World Court in Law-Making', in Arsanjani *et al.* (eds.), *Looking to the Future: Essays on International Law in Honor of W. Michael Reisman* (Leiden: Martinus Nijhoff, 2011), p. 1076.

Reisman's vocabulary, Bodansky distinguished between the Court's myth system, where State practice and *opinio juris* feature prominently, and its operational code, i.e. the way cases are actually decided, which, in his view, 'reflects a norm of precedent'.[97] Geiger's nonfictional description of the Court's actual method is more elaborate:

> This method of detecting customary international law norms – that is, looking for legal principles and interpreting these principles to find specifying rules suitable for deciding the case, and making use of law-making treaties and resolutions of international organs as guidelines – seems to be the law-finding method which the Court *really* applies.[98]

But to argue, as the author does, that the ICJ's *real* method, as he describes it, satisfies reasonable criteria of certainty and predictability means reinstating the fiction shortly after having successfully called the Court's bluff.

5. The International Court of Justice's soft play

In the game of poker, the expression 'soft play' means failing to bet or raise to the advantage of a friend in situations which would (but for the friend) justify the opposite course of action. This, I contend, is the game the ICJ has been playing with custom in the last fifteen years or so, that is, in the age of fragmentation. As to the identity of the beneficiaries of the Court's soft play, I leave it to the reader's imagination. The Court has been extremely cautious in both the structural and the incremental modes-of-play (as defined in section 1). Not only has the ICJ been lukewarm about developing a standard approach to the identification of customary rules, it has also systematically failed to seize on the opportunity to clarify the content of customary international law and put it to use as a possible remedy against fragmentation.

To be fair to the Court, the present survey opens with the decision singled out by Sir Michael Wood as being among the very few in which a fairly detailed analysis of State practice appears,[99] namely the Judgment

[97] Daniel Bodansky, 'Prologue to a Theory of Non-Treaty Norms', in Arsanjani *et al.* (eds.), *Looking to the Future: Essays on International Law in Honor of W. Michael Reisman* (Leiden: Martinus Nijhoff, 2011), p. 127.

[98] Rudolf H. Geiger, 'Customary International Law in the Jurisprudence of the International Court of Justice: A Critical Appraisal', in Fastenrath *et al.*, *From Bilateralism to Community Interest*, p. 694.

[99] Wood, First Report, p. 25, para. 62.

rendered in the *Jurisdictional Immunities of the State* case.[100] Those who think that international lawyers share a relatively solid conception of how customary law is to be identified should be puzzled by the diversity of the reactions to the way in which the ICJ 'found the law' in that case. The Judgment is for some the product of a sustained effort to reflect actual State practice and *opinio juris* and deserves to be remembered as a vindication of the traditional method of custom identification.[101] For others, State practice was 'either contradictory or non-existent', making the Court's decision stand on shaky ground.[102] The Court's approach to the identification of customary law is indeed disputable but in order to locate its weak spot, two aspects of the decision should be distinguished. To begin with, the decision features some abstract statements about the constituent elements of custom and an inventory of categories of pertinent evidence of State practice. At this level, the Court's reasoning is unobjectionable and there can be no doubt that it will be extensively quoted by handbook writers. The Court recalls that 'it must apply the criteria which it has repeatedly laid down for identifying a rule of customary international law', it then quotes the usual excerpts from its own *North Sea Continental Shelf* Judgment, before announcing that:

> In the present context, State practice of particular significance is to be found in the judgments of national courts faced with the question whether a foreign State is immune, the legislation of those States which have enacted statutes dealing with immunity, the claims to immunity advanced by States before foreign courts and the statements made by States, first in the course of the extensive study of the subject by the International Law Commission and then in the context of the adoption of the United Nations Convention.[103]

100 ICJ, *Jurisdictional Immunities of the State (Germany* v. *Italy: Greece Intervening)*, Judgment of 3 February 2012, [2012] ICJ Rep 99.

101 See, e.g., J. Craig Baker, 'International Court of Justice: Jurisdictional Immunities of the State (Germany v Italy) Judgment of 3 February 2012' (2013) 62 *International and Comparative Law Quarterly*, 741, 750: '[t]he Court has undertaken a detailed scientific analysis of the primary sources of international law, including treaties and customary international law'. See, for another positive appraisal, Stefan Talmon, '*Jus Cogens* after *Germany* v. *Italy*: Substantive and Procedural Rules Distinguished' (2012) 25 *Leiden Journal of International Law* 979, 1002.

102 Benedetto Conforti, 'The Judgment of the International Court of Justice on the Immunity of Foreign States: A Missed Opportunity' (2011) 21 *Italian Yearbook of International Law* 135, 137. See also Kimberley N. Trapp and Alex Mills, 'Smooth Runs the Water Where the Brook is Deep: The Obscured Complexities of *Germany* v. *Italy*' (2012) 1 *Cambridge Journal of International and Comparative Law*, 153, 156–8.

103 [2012] ICJ Rep 122–3, para. 55.

All this is neither surprising nor particularly illuminating (even though some will surely regard the passage as a full-blown statement on method). Much more interesting, at least for those who take the trouble to look at the matter more closely, is the unprincipled way in which the ICJ applied its stated 'criteria'.

In a passage containing a heart-warming recognition of the ICJ's authority in matters of general international law, a section of the European Court of Human Rights held, in the *Jones* case, that it was unnecessary for it to examine State practice in detail because the ICJ's Judgment in the *Jurisdictional Immunities of the State* case had 'clearly establishe[d] that... no *jus cogens* exception to State immunity had yet crystallised', and a finding that 'must be considered... as authoritative as regards the content of customary international law'.[104] The United Kingdom, acting as respondent in the *Jones* case, maintained that the ICJ's decision is 'carefully reasoned and based on an extensive review and analysis of State practice', to which it added that the 'case-law in the United States where jurisdiction had been asserted over major violations of international law perpetrated by non-nationals overseas did not express principles widely shared and observed among other nations'.[105] In fact, the ICJ did not even refer to that case-law and has accordingly been blamed for its selectiveness.[106] But this negligence pales in comparison to the way in which the ICJ treated the cases it selected. As is known, in the Court's opinion there exist in international law a customary rule according to which a foreign State enjoys immunity against civil suits filed by victims of *crimina juris gentium* perpetrated by the armed forces of that State on the territory of the forum State, even in cases where the victims have no other remedy at their disposal. The Court maintained that this finding is warranted by a long string of national and international judgments, but it is not, because, as I tried to show elsewhere,[107] the judicial decisions actually expressing the

[104] European Court of Human Rights (Fourth Section), *Jones and Others* v. *The United Kingdom*, Applications nos. 34356/06 and 40528/06, Judgment of 14 January 2014, p. 52, para. 198.

[105] European Court of Human Rights (Fourth Section), *Jones and Others* v. *The United Kingdom*, p. 45, para. 176.

[106] See Riccardo Pavoni, 'An American Anomaly? On the ICJ's Selective Reading of United States Practice in Jurisdictional Immunities of the State' (2011) 21 *Italian Yearbook of International Law* 143.

[107] For a detailed analysis and critique see Lorenzo Gradoni and Attila Tanzi, 'Immunità dello Stato e crimini internazionali tra consuetudine e bilanciamento: note critiche a margine della sentenza della Corte internazionale di giustizia del 3 febbraio 2012' (2012) 67 *La Comunità internazionale* 203.

opinio juris that the ICJ wished to see in them[108] begin to look rather scant as soon as one takes away from the lot not only the national cases which, like *Allianz*,[109] *Littrell*,[110] or *Holland*,[111] have nothing to do with the commission of war crimes or crimes against humanity, but also, and most importantly, the decisions in *Natoniewski*,[112] *A.A.*,[113] and *Margellos*[114] – on which the ICJ relied heavily – where national courts of last instance recognized the foreign State immunity not least because, to borrow a phrase from the Polish Supreme Court's Judgment in *Natoniewski*, the applicants had 'reasonable alternative means to protect effectively their rights'.[115] Sweeping such fundamental qualifications under the carpet, as the ICJ did, is not an example of methodological probity.[116] Surely the Court cannot be criticized for having uncreatively indulged in a 'formalistic, positivist approach'.[117]

[108] [2012] ICJ Rep 135, para. 77.

[109] Court of Appeal of Aix-en-Provence, *Allianz Via Insurance* v. *United States of America* (1999), 127 ILR, 152–3.

[110] House of Lords, *Littrell v. United States of America* (1993), 100 ILR 453, 464.

[111] House of Lords, *Holland* v. *Lampen-Wolfe* (2000), 119 ILR, 372, 376, 383–4.

[112] Polish Supreme Court, Decision of 29 October 2010, *Winicjusz N.* v. *Federal Republic of Germany*, Case No. IV CSK 465/09 (2010) 30 *Polish Yearbook of International Law* 299.

[113] Constitutional Court of Slovenia, Decision of 8 March 2001, Case No. Up-13/99, paras. 6, 21 (on file with author).

[114] *Margellos and others* v. *Federal Republic of Germany* (2002), 129 ILR, 532–3.

[115] Polish Supreme Court, Decision of 29 October 2010, 303.

[116] This seems to be the thrust of Judge Yusuf's dissenting opinion: 'There is indeed considerable divergence in the manner in which the scope and extent of such immunity is interpreted and applied in the practice of States, and particularly in the judicial decisions of their courts. It is not therefore very persuasive to characterize some of the exceptions to immunity as part of customary international law, despite the continued existence of conflicting domestic judicial decisions on their application, while interpreting other exceptions, similarly based on divergent domestic courts' decisions, as supporting the non-existence of customary norms. This may give the impression of cherry-picking, particularly where the number of cases invoked is rather limited on both sides of the equation'. [2012] ICJ Rep 297, para. 23. See, in a similar vein, Alexander Orakhelashvili, 'Jurisdictional Immunities of the State (Germany v. Italy; Greece Intervening), International Court of Justice, February 3, 2012' (2012) 106 *American Journal of International Law* 609. See also, in praise of the 'balancing approach' recommended by Judge Yusuf, Francesco Francioni, 'From Utopia to Disenchantment: The Ill Fate of "Moderate Monism" in the ICJ Judgment on *The Jurisdictional Immunities of the State*' (2012) 23 *European Journal of International Law*, 1125, 1129; Lorenzo Gradoni, 'Consuetudine internazionale e caso inconsueto' (2012) 95 *Rivista di diritto internazionale* 704.

[117] Carlos Espósito, 'Of Plumbers and Social Architects: Elements and Problems of the Judgment of the International Court of Justice in Jurisdictional Immunities of States' (2013) 4 *Journal of International Dispute Settlement* 439, 450, 455–6.

Another example of the Court's casual approach to evidence is to be found in its *Genocide (Bosnia and Herzegovina* v. *Serbia and Montenegro)* Judgment. Here the Court began by stating, without further ado, that 'the applicable rule, which is one of customary law of international responsibility, is laid down in Article 8 of the ILC Articles on State Responsibility'.[118] As is known, under Article 8 the conduct of a person or group is considered an act of a State if the person or group is in fact acting under the control of that State. Whether or not it reflects customary law, the meaning of this provision – in particular the concept of 'control' – is highly controversial and the ILC's commentary leaves it largely unexplained. The Court might have wished to clarify it by probing State practice but it took an entirely different route, namely, that of *its own* case-law:

> This provision must be understood in the light of the Court's jurisprudence on the subject, particularly that of the 1986 Judgment in the case concerning *Military and Paramilitary Activities in and against Nicaragua*... It must... be shown that this 'effective control' was exercised... in respect of each operation in which the alleged violations occurred, not generally in respect of the overall actions taken by the persons or groups of persons having committed the violations.[119]

The ICJ then wrapped it all up with an argumentative sleight of hand: 'This is the state of customary law, as reflected in the ILC Articles on State Responsibility.'[120] But it is in fact the Court that makes the opaque mirror of the Articles on State Responsibility send back the image of *Nicaragua*, while State practice is not even sought for, and the International Criminal Tribunal for the former Yugoslavia is rebuked for its deviant behaviour.[121]

In the *Case Concerning Pulp Mills on the River Uruguay*, the approach to the identification of customary rules is so cavalier as to justify the suspect that the Court did not wish its conclusions to be taken seriously. The Court started by alluding to 'a practice, which in recent years has gained so much acceptance among States that it may now be considered a requirement under general international law to undertake an environmental impact assessment where there is a risk that the proposed industrial

[118] ICJ, *Case Concerning Application of the Convention on the Prevention and Punishment of the Crime of Genocide (Bosnia and Herzegovina* v. *Serbia and Montenegro)*, Judgment of 26 February 2007, [2007] ICJ Rep 207, para. 398.

[119] [2007] ICJ Rep 207, paras. 399–400.

[120] [2007] ICJ Rep 209, para. 401.

[121] [2007] ICJ Rep 209, paras. 403–6.

activity may have a significant adverse impact in a transboundary context, in particular, on a shared resource'.[122] Shortly after, the Court opines that 'general international law' does not 'specify the scope and content of an environmental impact assessment', so that, by way of consequence, it falls upon each State 'to determine in its domestic legislation or in the authorization process for the project, the specific content of the environmental impact assessment required in each case',[123] it being understood that 'once operations have started and, where necessary, throughout the life of the project, continuous monitoring of its effects on the environment shall be undertaken'.[124] No evidence whatsoever is offered to prove the existence of such an ill-defined rule or principle, which has the dubious quality of looking airy and burdensome at the same time.

In not a few cases, the Court has taken the existence of a customary rule for granted.[125] This is not necessarily blameworthy – there is no shortage of unwritten rules whose existence is unquestioned – but is hardly informative about the Court's modus operandi. In other instances the Court 'blackboxed' both the reasoning and the evidence (if any) linking the premises to its conclusion. In the *Case Concerning Maritime Delimitation in the Black Sea*, the ICJ confined itself to noticing that '[d]iverse techniques have in the past been used for assessing coastal lengths, with no clear requirement of international law having been shown as to whether the real coastline should be followed, or baselines used, or whether or not coasts relating to internal waters should be excluded'.[126] In the *Case Concerning Sovereignty over Pedra Blanca/Palau Batu Puteh, Middle Rocks and South Ledge*, the Court, gauging the relationship between symbolic acts of appropriation and the acquisition of territory by States, had only this to say:

[122] ICJ, *Case Concerning Pulp Mills on the River Uruguay (Argentina* v. *Uruguay)*, Judgment of 20 April 2010, [2010] ICJ Rep 83, para. 204.

[123] [2010] ICJ Rep 83, para. 205.

[124] [2010] ICJ Rep 84, para. 205.

[125] See, e.g., ICJ, *Case Concerning Maritime Delimitation and Territorial Questions Between Qatar and Bahrain (Qatar* v. *Bahrain)*, Judgment of 16 March 2001, [2001] ICJ Rep 97,100, paras. 185, 201; ICJ, *Case Concerning Armed Activities on the Territory of the Congo (Democratic Republic of the Congo* v. *Uganda)*, Judgment of 19 December 2005, [2005] ICJ Rep 242, para. 214; ICJ, *Legal Consequences of the Construction of a Wall in the Occupied Palestinian Territory*, Advisory Opinion of 9 July 2004, [2004] ICJ Rep 171–2, 174, paras. 87, 89, 94; ICJ, *Questions Relating to the Obligation to Prosecute or Extradite (Belgium* v. *Senegal)*, Judgment of 20 July 2012, [2012] ICJ Rep 460, para. 113.

[126] ICJ, *Case Concerning Maritime Delimitation in the Black Sea (Romania* v. *Ukraine)*, Judgment of 3 February 2009, [2009] ICJ Rep 129, para. 212.

> Symbolic acts accompanying the acquisition of territory are very common both generally and in British practice. They are not however always present. The Court does not consider that the practice demonstrates a requirement that there be a symbolic act.[127]

In a preliminary judgment concerning the *Diallo* case, the Court asked the audience to rely on its assurances of 'having carefully examined State practice and decisions of international courts and tribunals in respect of diplomatic protection of *associés* and shareholders', before concluding that those elements did not 'reveal . . . an exception in customary international law allowing for protection by substitution'.[128] The Court further explained that the fact that 'various international agreements, such as agreements for the promotion and protection of foreign investments and the Washington Convention, have established special legal régimes governing investment protection, or that provisions in this regard are commonly included in contracts entered into directly between States and foreign investors, is not sufficient to show that there has been a change in the customary rules of diplomatic protection; it could equally show the contrary'.[129] Here the Court, as always extremely ungenerous with methodological cues, possibly implied that although conventional, contractual and arbitral practice in the field of investment law is copious and fairly homogeneous, it will not bring about a new rule of general international law until a properly articulated *opinio juris* supervenes upon it.

In the *Dispute Regarding Navigational and Related Right*, the Court missed the opportunity to throw light on the identity of the subjects entitled to contribute to the formation of customary international law. The idea that States exercise a legal monopoly on the customary process is so entrenched that the question is seldom asked as to whose practice counts in this context. In the *Case Concerning Sovereignty over Pulau Ligitan and Pulau Sipadan*, the ICJ had maintained, in so many words, that 'activities by private persons cannot be seen as *effectivités* if they do not take place on the basis of official regulations or under governmental authority'.[130] The Court's later pronouncement muddles things up rather than clarifying the

[127] *Case Concerning Sovereignty over Pedra Blanca/Palau Batu Puteh, Middle Rocks and South Ledge* (*Malaysia* v. *Singapore*), Judgment of 23 May 2008, [2008] ICJ Rep 61, para. 149.

[128] ICJ, *Case Concerning Ahmadou Sadio Diallo (Republic of Guinea* v. *Democratic Republic of the Congo)*, Preliminary Objections, Judgment of 24 May 2007, [2007] ICJ Rep 615, para. 89.

[129] [2007] ICJ Rep 615, para. 90.

[130] ICJ, *Case Concerning Sovereignty over Pulau Ligitan and Pulau Sipadan (Indonesia/Malaysia)*, Judgment of 17 December 2002, [2002] ICJ Rep 683, para. 140.

law on this subject. As is known, the ICJ was asked to rule on whether there existed a bilateral custom between Costa Rica and Nicaragua requiring the latter to tolerate subsistence fishing as traditionally practised by Costa Rican subjects along the south bank of the San Juan, a river whose waters fall under Nicaraguan sovereignty. The Court answered affirmatively:

> the Parties agree that the practice of subsistence fishing is long established. They disagree however whether the practice has become binding on Nicaragua thereby entitling the riparians as a matter of customary right to engage in subsistence fishing from the bank. The Court observes that the practice, by its very nature, especially given the remoteness of the area and the small, thinly spread population, is not likely to be documented in any formal way in any official record. For the Court, the failure of Nicaragua to deny the existence of a right arising from the practice which had continued undisturbed and unquestioned over a very long period, is particularly significant. The Court accordingly concludes that Costa Rica has a customary right.[131]

This passage raises more questions that it answers. Did the fishermen play a direct role in the process that brought Costa Rica's customary right into existence? Or was Costa Rica's *implicit* espousal of their claim decisive to that effect? If the population's contribution to the emergence of the customary right was direct, then the Court failed to explain why the right accrued to Costa Rica and not to the population itself, nor did it specify whether international law, given the nature of the right involved, would leave Costa Rica free to relinquish that right unilaterally or by concluding a treaty with Nicaragua. If, on the contrary, Costa Rica's non-interference with the fishermen's age-old practice, together with Nicaragua's acquiescence, was formally required, then the Court failed to explain under which evidentiary rule it could be assumed that Nicaragua was aware of Costa Rica's phantom claim. Be that as it may, shyness about method for identifying custom is certainly not atypical for the Court.

In its advisory opinion of 22 July 2010, the ICJ rejected the allegation according to which Kosovo's declaration of independence was illegal under customary international law. Before coming to this conclusion, the Court had to go out of its way in order to put into perspective a string of resolutions by which the UN Security Council outlawed the declarations of independence of, respectively, Southern Rhodesia, Northern Cyprus

[131] ICJ, *Dispute Regarding Navigational and Related Right (Costa Rica v. Nicaragua)*, Judgment of 13 July 2009, [2009] ICJ Rep 265–6, para. 141.

and the Republika Srpska. In the Court's opinion, the case of Kosovo was clearly distinguishable:

> in all of those instances the Security Council was making a determination as regards the concrete situation existing at the time that those declarations of independence were made; the illegality attached to the declarations of independence thus stemmed not from the unilateral character of these declarations as such, but from the fact that they were, or would have been, connected with the unlawful use of force or other egregious violations of norms of general international law, in particular those of a peremptory character *(jus cogens)*. In the context of Kosovo, the Security Council has never taken this position. The exceptional character of the resolutions enumerated above appears to the Court to confirm that no general prohibition against unilateral declarations of independence may be inferred from the practice of the Security Council.[132]

The Court's hypothetical and casuistic approach leaves the audience wondering about the existence of a customary rule under which any declaration of independence pronounced in connection to a grave breach of general international law (or *jus cogens* only) would be proscribed. If from the Security Council's practice no conclusion can be drawn to the effect that unilateral declarations of independence are unlawful under international customary law, the very same practice may authorize speculations about the existence of a customary prohibition that is narrower in scope, i.e., applicable in situations where a grave breach of a peremptory norm was committed. But the Court's restraint is hardly encouraging, not least in view of the fact that it also waived the opportunity to clarify a methodological point of considerable importance concerning the value that should be ascribed to the acts and practices of the Security Council for the purposes of custom identification.

In the *Diallo* case, the Court preferred not to trespass the *obiter dictum* line instead of seizing the chance of ratifying the opinion, expressed by the ILC in its 2006 Articles on Diplomatic Protection, that customary international law permits protection by substitution of a company whose incorporation in the wrongdoer State was required by the latter 'as a precondition for doing business there'.[133] In the *Case Concerning the Arrest*

[132] ICJ, *Accordance with International Law of the Unilateral Declaration of Independence in Respect of Kosovo*, Advisory Opinion of 22 July 2010, [2010] ICJ Rep 437–8, para. 81.

[133] As the Court explained, 'the companies, Africom-Zaire and Africontainers-Zaire, were not incorporated in such a way that they would fall within the scope of protection by substitution in the sense of Article 11, paragraph *(b)*, of the ILC draft Articles on Diplomatic Protection referred to by Guinea. Therefore, the question of whether or not

Warrant of 11 April 2000, the ICJ famously gave priority to the issue of the immunity of Congo's (former) Minister of Foreign Affairs in order to steer clear of the preliminary, but highly controversial, question as to whether customary international law prevented Belgian courts from exercising universal jurisdiction over crimes of war or crimes against humanity.[134] The Court's approach is unobjectionable but nonetheless symptomatic of its unwillingness to encroach on areas of general international law, especially if unexplored or contested. More difficult to accept, and all the more indicative of the Court's restraint, is the decision it took in *Questions Relating to the Obligation to Prosecute or Extradite* to dismiss Belgium's claim according to which Senegal had *aut dedere aut judicare* obligations with respect to the former Chad's ruler, Hissène Habré, not only on the basis of the UN Convention against Torture, but also under customary international law, in relation to other crimes against humanity. In the Court's view, no such dispute existed between the parties when the application was filed.[135] As Judge Abraham rightly pointed out in his separate opinion, the Court's decision was hardly explicable on the basis of its previous case-law:

> this is the first time in the Court's entire jurisprudence that it has declined to hear one part of a case on the basis of the lack of a dispute between the Parties, even though the dispute clearly exists on the date of the Court's Judgment and was apparent in the proceedings before the Court. One may wonder what the extent now is [*quelle est encore la portée*] of the position of principle set out by the Court in the Judgment on Preliminary Objections in the *Croatia* v. *Serbia* case. I regret to note that the series of recent Judgment does not convey a great impression of consistency.[136]

As is known, in *Application of the Convention on the Prevention and Punishment of the Crime of Genocide*, the Court maintained that what matters is normally not the existence of a dispute at the date on which the application was filed but the fact 'at the latest by the date when the Court decides on its jurisdiction, the applicant [is] entitled, if it so wishes, to bring fresh proceedings in which the initially unmet condition would be fulfilled', because it would not be 'in the interest of the sound administration of justice to compel the applicant to begin the proceedings

this paragraph of Article 11 reflects customary international law does not arise in this case.' [2007] ICJ Rep 616, para. 93. See Art. 11(*b*) of the Articles on Diplomatic Protection, in ILC, Report on the Work of its Fifty-eighth Session, UN Doc. A/61/10 (2006), p. 19.

134 ICJ, *Case Concerning the Arrest Warrant of 11 April 2000 (Democratic Republic of the Congo* v. *Belgium)*, Judgment of 14 February 2002, [2002] ICJ Rep 20, para. 46.

135 [2012] ICJ Rep 444–5, para. 54–5.

136 [2012] ICJ Rep 475, para. 18.

anew ... except in special circumstances'.[137] The Court did not explain what special circumstances, if any, compelled it to declare Belgium's claim based in customary international law inadmissible. Anxiety about custom was probably a factor.

In the abovementioned case concerning the legal regime of the San Juan River, a watercourse which marks a section of the Costa Rica–Nicaragua border, the Court was invited to take a position on the existence, in customary international law, of a universal or regional regime applicable to navigation on international rivers. The Court felt entitled to turn down the offer, because – it explained – 'even if categorization as an "international river" would be legally relevant in respect of navigation, in that it would entail the application of rules of customary international law to that question, *such rules could only be operative, at the very most, in the absence of any treaty provisions that had the effect of excluding them*, in particular because those provisions were intended to define completely the régime applicable to navigation, by the riparian States on a specific river or a section of it'.[138] The Court quickly assumed that the treaty concluded between Costa Rica and Nicaragua in 1858 created a special regime so tightly self-contained as to make any enquiry about the existence of external customary rules irrelevant. This is indeed surprising of a Court which, judging from the way it made use of Article 31(3)(c) of the Vienna Convention on the Law of Treaties,[139] has been thinking highly of the so-called principle of systemic integration,[140] and is hardly in line with

[137] ICJ, *Application of the Convention on the Prevention and Punishment of the Crime of Genocide (Croatia* v. *Serbia)*, Preliminary Objections, Judgment of 18 November 2008, [2008] ICJ Rep 441, para. 85.

[138] ICJ, *Dispute Regarding Navigational and Related Rights (Costa Rica v. Nicaragua)*, Judgment of 13 July 2009, [2009] ICJ Rep 233, para. 35 (emphasis added).

[139] The ICJ regards Article 31(3)(c), according to which, in interpreting a treaty account must be taken of 'any relevant rules of international law applicable in the relations between the parties', as 'a codification of customary international law'. (see, e.g., ICJ, *Case Concerning Certain Questions of Mutual Assistance in Criminal Matters (Djibouti* v. *France)*, Judgment of 4 June 2008, [2008] ICJ Rep 219, para. 112; ICJ, *Case Concerning Kasikili/Sedudu Island (Botswana/Namibia)*, Judgment of 13 December 1999, [1999] ICJ Rep 1059, para. 18). As is well known, the ICJ capitalized spectacularly on Article 31(3)(c) in the *Case Concerning Oil Platforms (Islamic Republic of Iran* v. *United States of America)*, Judgment of 6 November 2003, [2003] ICJ Rep 182, para. 41.

[140] As the ILC Study Group on Fragmentation of International Law explained, '[t]he rationale for such principle is understandable. All treaty provisions receive their force and validity from general law, and set up rights and obligations that exist alongside rights and obligations established by other treaty provisions and rules of customary international law'. Fragmentation of International Law: Difficulties Arising from the Diversification and Expansion of International Law, Report of the Study Group of the International

the Conclusions drawn by the Study Group on the Fragmentation of International Law and endorsed by the ILC.[141] Were it not so apparent that the Court wanted to keep away from customary law, one might have thought that the Hague Headquarters of the anti-fragmentation forces had been infiltrated by the enemy. Similarly, in *Questions Relating to the Obligation to Prosecute or Extradite* the Court held that 'the issue whether there exists an obligation for a State to prosecute crimes under customary international law that were allegedly committed by a foreign national abroad is clearly distinct', hence could be treated separately, 'from any question of compliance with that State's obligation under the Convention against Torture'.[142]

In other cases the Court has been less shy in expounding its views about the content of customary international law, as it felt that a definite conclusion could be reached by way of analogical reasoning. In the *Case Concerning the Arrest Warrant of 11 April 2000*, the Court famously held that 'the *functions* of a Minister of Foreign Affairs are such that, throughout the duration of his or her office, he or she when abroad enjoys full immunity from criminal jurisdiction and inviolability'.[143] Similarly, in the *Case Concerning Certain Questions of Mutual Assistance in Criminal Matters*, the Court maintained 'the rule of customary international law reflected in Article 29 of the Vienna Convention on Diplomatic Relations, while addressed to diplomatic agents, is *necessarily* applicable to Heads of State'.[144] Recourse to analogy is not in itself reproachable but it has nothing to do with induction of customary rules from particular instances of State practice. Since the kind of analogical reasoning performed by the Court in the abovementioned cases proceeds *deductively*, it cannot in the least be regarded as informative about a supposed method for sifting through and evaluating evidence of State practice.[145] In fact, the foregoing survey strongly suggests that the Court has no method for

Law Commission Finalized by Martti Koskenniemi, UN Doc. No. A/CN.4/L.682 (2006), p. 208, para. 414.

141 Conclusions of the Work of the Study Group on the Fragmentation of International Law: Difficulties Arising from the Diversification and Expansion of International Law, in ILC, Report on the Work of its Fifty-eighth Session, UN Doc. No. A/61/10 (2006), pp. 407–23.

142 [2012] ICJ Rep 445, para. 54.

143 [2002] ICJ Rep 23, para. 54 (emphasis added).

144 [2008] ICJ Rep 238, para. 174 (emphasis added).

145 The ICJ proceeds syllogistically, as follows: i) there are *n* reasons to extend the application of customary rule *x* to case *c*; ii) there are no reasons advising against the application of customary rule *x* to case *c*; therefore, *x* applies to *c*. If the Court had (inductively) inferred proposition i) and ii) from State practice, its reasoning could have been informative. It did not.

identifying custom and that its strategy consists in striving to keep up appearances of rigour and judiciousness on a case-by-case basis.

6. The showdown

If the customary international law game were really like poker, our players – States, doctrine, the ILC, and the ICJ – would not be allowed to postpone the showdown at will. Were they compelled to show their hands, we would see two sets of cards falling face up on the green table. The faces of each custom-formation card would carry an abstract or symbolic painting – Pollock, Kandinsky, a mystical Rothko or a paradoxical Magritte for the representatives of doctrine, an orderly Mondrian for the ILC, a soothing Poliakoff for the Court, and a playful Miró for States – while the face of all custom-identification cards would be blank. But the customary international law game is not like poker in every respect, and our players can keep playing it indefinitely.

15

State practice, treaty practice and State immunity in international and English law

ALEXANDER ORAKHELASHVILI

1. Introduction: State immunity at the crossroads of the fragmentation discourse

Approaching State immunity from the perspective of the fragmentation versus convergence debate requires concentrating on whether, under international law, there is one single legal regime applicable to immunities or a multitude of normative regimes. This relates, in the first place, to the relationship between the immunity of States and of their officials. In principle, State officials can claim immunity abroad solely because their own State would be entitled to a coterminous immunity. If the official's immunity were different and invocable on a separate basis, the State would have no claim to raise if immunity were to be denied, nor could it waive that immunity for the official. In such case it would not be the State's immunity in the first place, but instead represent a kind of individual right. There is, anyway, no evidence in practice that such separate official immunity is recognised as a free-standing category.[1]

The next issue relates to immunities in civil and criminal proceedings. In relation to criminal proceedings, the International Law Commission (ILC) Special Rapporteur, Kolodkin, has suggested that 'State officials enjoy immunity *ratione materiae* from foreign criminal jurisdiction,

[1] This issue arises in relation to particular treaty regimes as well. Article 1(b)(iv) of the 2004 UN Convention on Jurisdictional Immunities of States and Their Property equates State representatives acting in that capacity to the State, though it may be open to question whether 'acting in that capacity' means being *de facto* at the service of the State or carrying out the function that is inherently and uniquely associated with the sovereign authority of that State. This point is generically similar to that arising under CAT 1984, on which see section 4 below.

i.e. immunity in respect of acts performed in an official capacity, since these acts are acts of the State which they serve itself.'[2] Again, such multiple terminology confuses the matter, for it becomes unclear whether, for the purposes of immunity, we need to focus on the nature of the act as such, the capacity in which that act was performed, or the broader purpose and interests served by the performance of that act; whether the acts in question should be 'acts of the State which they serve', or acts that fall within the sovereign authority of the State. This question is crucial for immunities in both criminal and civil proceedings (apart from the limited category of *ratione personae* immunities of a very limited number of high-ranking officials, premised on the constitutional position of those officials, as opposed to the nature of the act immunity is claimed for).

The difference between civil and criminal immunities has been maintained by the European Court of Human Rights in *Al-Adsani* v. *UK*,[3] the UK House of Lords in *Jones* v. *Saudi Arabia*,[4] subsequently approved by the Fourth Section of the European Court of Human Rights,[5] and the International Court of Justice (ICJ) in *Germany* v. *Italy*,[6] which have all upheld State immunity for serious human rights violations and for international crimes. Moses LJ has similarly suggested in the case of *Khurts Bat* that '[i]t does not follow that because there is immunity from civil suit, an individual, acting as an official on behalf of his State, is immune from criminal liability'.[7]

Courts have not worked any uniform rationale for this projected distinction. In some cases it is put forward at the level of the scope of acts *jure imperii*, while in other cases, notably in *Al-Adsani*, it is argued at the level of the effect of *jus cogens*. The distinction is certainly popular in some doctrinal circles, but is by no means generally accepted. The Second Report of the ILC Special Rapporteur falls short of subscribing to such distinction. From the other end of the doctrinal spectrum, the Institute of International Law has emphasised in the 2009 Naples Resolution that

[2] *Second Report*, RA Kolodkin, A/CN.4/631, 10 June 2010, para. 94.

[3] *Al-Adsani* v. *UK*, 34 EHRR 11(2002).

[4] *Jones* v. *Saudi Arabia* [2006] UKHL 16, 14 June 2006.

[5] *Jones and Others* v. *The United Kingdom*, Nos. 34356/06 and 40528/06, Fourth Section, 14 January 2014.

[6] *Jurisdictional Immunities of the State* (*Germany* v. *Italy: Greece Intervening*), International Court of Justice, Judgment of 3 February 2012, General List No. 143, esp. para. 87.

[7] *Khurts Bat* v. *Mongolia*, High Court [2011] EWHC 2029 (Admin), 29 July 2011, para. 74.

the criminality of the conduct of a State official should lead to the denial of their immunities in civil proceedings.[8]

A further relevant issue touches upon the sources of law on the basis of which particular judicial decisions are adopted. It may be empirically true that various sources of law can establish different regimes for criminal and civil immunities of States and their officials. For instance, as US Supreme Court has clarified in *Samantar*, that the 1976 US Foreign Sovereign Immunities Act (FSIA) does not apply to State officials.[9] It only covers situations where the foreign State is directly impleaded before American courts. The FSIA and the 1978 UK State Immunity Act (SIA) do not extend to criminal proceedings either. The same holds true for the 1972 European Convention on State Immunity (ECSI) and the above 2004 UN Convention, if and when it enters into force.

But these are merely *situational* and *empirical* differences that do not go to the underlying rationale of immunities, whether that of a State or of an official, whether civil or criminal. In common law systems, legislation displaces the pre-existing common law that incorporates international law. Cases not covered by the statute are subjected to substantially different criteria, as was the case in the decisions of English courts in *Lampen-Wolfe* and *Littrell.*[10] Similarly, *Samantar* would be differently decided by American courts whether it were based on the FSIA, or on common law as the Supreme Court said it should be.

Internationally, if the relevant treaty in force applies *in casu* and *inter se*, it will apply as *lex specialis*. If it is not in force, or the case falls outside its reach *ratione personae* or *ratione materiae*, general international law will apply – again with the possibility of furnishing the outcomes substantially different from ones that could be maintained under the treaties.

With these considerations in mind, the present chapter will first examine the merit of the restrictive doctrine of immunities, its application in criminal and civil proceedings, and its place in customary international law (Section 2). Section 3 will examine the existing or nascent treaty regimes on immunities. Section 4 will focus on the impact of human rights treaties on immunities, notably the 1950 European Convention on Human Rights (ECHR) and the 1984 UN Convention against Torture

[8] *Immunity from Jurisdiction of the State and of Persons Who Act on Behalf of the State in case of International Crimes*, IDI, Naples Session, 2009.

[9] *Samantar* v. *Yousuf*, No. 08–1555, 1 June 2010.

[10] *Holland* v. *Lampen-Wolfe* [2000] 3 All ER 845–6; *Littrell* v. *USA* [1995] 1 WLR 182.

(CAT). Section 5 will focus on the impact of normative hierarchy examining, in turn, jurisdictional arrangements under Articles 5, 7 and 14 CAT, and *jus cogens*. Section 6 will examine the extent to which the legal position under the international law on immunities could be received and given effect in English law. Section 7 will offer general conclusions.

The methodology chosen here relies on consensual positivism, premised on ordinary sources of international law, whether or not they reflect the political naturalist perspective as to the sensibility or desirability of granting or denying immunity, or to fears as to some adverse consequences that the denial of immunities is likely to entail. But as the debate is, informally at least, influenced by clichés and pre-conceptions that the pro-immunity position should be privileged as *the* right and correct one in maintaining stability and avoiding chaos, section 6 will also examine how English courts are supposed to deal with the relevant policy considerations.

2. The place of the restrictive doctrine of immunities in international law

A. *Statement of the problem*

First and foremost, we need to understand what shape of the immunity doctrine is exactly deemed or pretended to be part of customary international law. Both the House of Lords in *Jones* and the ICJ in *Germany* v. *Italy* have asserted this to be the 'restrictive' doctrine that excludes commercial acts but immunises violations of human rights and humanitarian law. This section will demonstrate that the position that such general rule of immunity exists under international law, from which a specific exception related to human rights or international crimes must then be identified, constitutes a fallacy. This is a view that can help reach some politically desirable outcomes, but not one that reflects the actual state of current positive international law.

The ICJ acknowledged in *Germany* v. *Italy* that the existence of *opinio juris* in the area of State immunity requires 'the acknowledgment, by States granting immunity, that international law imposes upon them an obligation to do so'. The Court further asserted that 'States generally proceed on the basis that there is a right to immunity under international law, together with a corresponding obligation on the part of other States to respect and give effect to that immunity.'[11] This is, as we shall see below,

[11] *Germany* v. *Italy*, para. 56.

a questionable thesis, because there is plenty of practice through which States deny the existence of customary rule on immunities, whether of foreign States or of their officials.

B. *The scope of the relevant practice*

What is the evidence that the 'restrictive' immunity along the above lines is part of customary international law? Without this being the case, any doctrine of immunities could only be an analytical rationalisation at the level of *lex ferenda*, on which phenomenon the International Court has clearly, and repeatedly, maintained the position that it cannot serve as the basis of its decisions.[12]

The issue could only be clarified through the focus on the relevant State practice. Moses LJ suggested in *Khurts Bat* that the practice through which 'States have not claimed immunity is just as much evidence of the absence of State practice as those cases where immunity is claimed but denied by the forum state.'[13] But cases in which States do not claim immunity contribute hardly anything to the development of State practice on immunities and must, for that reason, be excluded from the focus. It is in the essence of immunities that States can freely choose whether or not to claim them; not claiming immunities in a particular case does not prejudice the possibility of doing so in a later case. Only State practice that positively addresses the rationale and scope of immunities must count for ascertaining what the applicable international law is.

To illustrate, and despite suggestions in writings,[14] State practice regarding the prosecution of individuals for espionage, acting at the service of their States, contributes precious little to the practice on State immunity, unless it were to be demonstrated that the relevant agent was tried domestically even if its State of nationality claimed their immunity. The ILC Special Rapporteur suggested that it is difficult for the State to assert immunity for acts of espionage, kidnapping and sabotage committed on the territory of another State.[15] But this is not because there is any firm rule of international law preventing States from doing so, but because doing so would publicly and effectively associate the State with

[12] *Fisheries Jurisdiction* (*UK* v. *Iceland*) Merits, ICJ Reports 1974, 23–4; *Libya* v. *Malta*, ICJ Reports, 1982, 38.

[13] *Khurts Bat*, para. 99.

[14] See, e.g., A. Sanger, 'Immunity of State Officials from the Criminal Jurisdiction of a Foreign State', (2013) 62 *ICLQ*, 193, 212–13.

[15] *Second Report*, para. 85.

those activities,[16] especially in cases where the prosecution can support its case with the plausible evidence.

C. *The general essence of the restrictive doctrine*

It is generally established in international law that, to identify a customary rule on any subject-matter, we have to identify a point in time by which this rule has crystallised through practice. The rights and obligations of States on the relevant subject-matter would, then, be different before and after that point of time.[17] It must be emphasised that neither the House of Lords in *Jones* nor the ICJ in *Germany* v. *Italy* have concentrated on this temporal element to show as of which point in time the 'restrictive' approach they upheld has become part of customary law and thus binding on the relevant States.

Historically, the restrictive doctrine was first developed in relation to civil proceedings. By the time State practice took up the criminal proceedings aspect, the legal position as to the scope of *jure imperii* acts was relatively well established as covering only acts unique to State authority. The public policy dimension based on *jus cogens* or international criminality of the underlying conduct has come to State practice considerably later, with the American cases of *Letelier* and *Marcos* and the English case of *Pinochet*. This latter sub-area does not offer any alternative or a qualitatively new test. It brings moral and ethical dimension to what is already obvious – these acts are anyway of such nature that they do not require the exercise of State authority for their perpetration.

The absolute immunity doctrine, that was deemed to be in force for a long time right up to the mid-twentieth century, enabled States and their officials to evade foreign proceedings merely on the basis of their identity.[18] Lord Wright suggested in the *Cristina* case in the House of Lords that, pursuant to the absolute immunity rule the State:

> renounces *pro tanto* the competence of its Courts to exercise their jurisdiction even over matters occurring within its territorial limits, though to do so is prima facie an integral part of sovereignty. The rule may be said

[16] Cf., *France* v. *Djibouti*, ICJ Reports 2008, para. 196.

[17] For the ICJ's jurisprudence on this point see *Anglo-Norwegian Fisheries* (*UK* v. *Norway*), ICJ Reports, 1951, 116; *The Minquiers and Echrehos Case* (*France* v. *UK*), ICJ Reports, 1953, 47.

[18] Sometimes this has assumed anecdotal dimensions. See, e.g. *Mighell* v. *Sultan of Johore* [1894] QB 149, to the effect that immunities could preclude litigation as to the breach of the promise to marry. The outcome was 'a consequence of the absolute independence of every sovereign authority'.

> to be based on the principle 'par in parem non habet imperium,' no State can claim jurisdiction over another sovereign State. . . . Or it may be taken to flow from reciprocity, each sovereign State within the community of nations accepting some subtraction from its full sovereignty in return for similar concessions on the side of the others.[19]

Each State was thus expected to give as much as it would receive. The rule that went by the identity of the defendant rather than the nature of the act made this easier. The *par in parem* rule, denying jurisdiction of an equal over an equal was therefore an essential premise for the absolute immunity rule.

The restrictive doctrine of immunity requires that the defendant State and its officials additionally demonstrate that their conduct was performed in the exercise of their governmental authority. The judicial endorsement of the restrictive doctrine took place in the *Empire of Iran* case by the German Constitutional Court, suggesting that the distinction between sovereign and non-sovereign acts does not depend 'on whether the State has acted commercially. Commercial activities of States are not different in their nature from other non-sovereign State activities.' What mattered was the nature of the transaction rather than its underlying motive and policy, whether the State acted in the exercise of its sovereign authority or in a private capacity the way that any private person could act.[20]

This approach was later on more comprehensively adopted by the House of Lords in the cases of *Trendtex*[21] and *Congreso*. The House of Lords held in the latter case that the conduct of a State is not a sovereign act and attracts no immunity if it is an act which could be performed by any private actor, even if the situation related to a highly contingent political context.[22] A similar approach was voiced by the US Judiciary in the aftermath of the 1952 Tate Letter that inaugurated the restrictive doctrine in the US. In the *Victory Transport* case, the Court of Appeals for the Second Circuit clearly observed that:

> Sovereign immunity is a derogation from the normal exercise of jurisdiction by the courts and should be accorded only in clear cases . . . fall[ing] within one of the categories of strictly political or public acts . . . :

[19] *Cristina* [1938] *AC* 485 at 502–503; Lord Maugham also approved 'insisting as a condition of immunity on the adherence of other foreign Governments to the same rule as to immunity', *ibid.*, 518.

[20] *Empire of Iran, Bundesverfassungsgericht*, 30 April 1963, 45 ILR 57 at 80.

[21] *Trendtex Trading* v. *Bank of Nigeria* [1977] 1 QB 529, 552–3.

[22] *I Congreso del Partido* (HL) [1983] I AC 268.

> (1) internal administrative acts, such as expulsion of an alien.
> (2) legislative acts, such as nationalization.
> (3) acts concerning the armed forces.
> (4) acts concerning diplomatic activity.
> (5) public loans
> We do not think that the restrictive theory adopted by the State Department requires sacrificing the interests of private litigants to international comity in other than these limited categories.[23]

A comparable list of sovereign activities was included in the resolution of the Institute of International Law adopted at the proposal of the Special Rapporteur Ian Brownlie.[24]

The further application of the restrictive doctrine by English courts, such as in cases of *Lampen-Wolfe* and *Littrell*,[25] was concerned with the activities of foreign armed forces, has followed the *Congreso* approach, and focused on the nature of the relevant act in the underlying context, rather than it having been authored by armed forces as such, in determining whether immunity should be accorded. The *Congreso* approach was also carefully followed in *Kuwait Air Co* where the governmental authority test was applied to the sequence of acts that were undertaken by public bodies of the foreign State.[26] By and large, then, various jurisdictions have been uniform in applying that pattern of the restrictive doctrine. Its basic essence is that an act that anyone can perform is not one that is unique to State authority (*jure imperii*).

Overall, the restrictive doctrine does not require identifying an exception from the generally applicable immunity. Instead, it requires a careful focus on the nature of each and every relevant act. Rather clear ways of articulating the merit of the restrictive doctrine have been suggested in various areas. In relation to acts of armed forces, the authorship of those acts by armed forces is not sufficient; their nature and relationship must be further assessed. There is a clear distinction between activities within the foreign military base, directly serving the need to maintain the base and, say, their use as a contract workforce or a tool for atrocities (as was the case in *Germany* v. *Italy* below). There is a difference between ownership and control of natural resources by the State and trade in the very

[23] *Victory Transport Inc.* v. *Comisaria General* 336 F.2d 354 (1964), para. 10.

[24] *Contemporary Problems Concerning the Immunity of States in Relation to Questions of Jurisdiction and Enforcement*, IDI Basel Session, 1991, Article 2(3).

[25] *Lampen-Wolfe* [2000] 3 All ER 845–6; *Littrell* v. *USA* [1995] 1 WLR 182.

[26] *Kuwait Air Co*, Court of Appeal [1995] WLR 1147, 1162–3 (per Lord Goff).

same resources.[27] There is, similarly, a difference between the organisational policy underlying the arrangement of a foreign embassy that falls within the area of sovereignty and may attract sovereign immunity, and a more specific issue of the Embassy's compliance with the employee's contractual rights, which may not.[28]

If this approach is followed, it becomes obvious that serious human rights violations do not fall into the category of sovereign acts, and there is nothing that affiliates them with the essence of sovereign power. Human rights violations meet the criteria repeatedly articulated in jurisprudence that anyone could commit those acts.[29] This runs into Lord Hope's point in *Pinochet* about 'criminal acts which the head of State did under the colour of his authority as head of State but which were in reality for his own pleasure or benefit' not being immune.[30] These acts may be committed by public authorities, often in pursuing what they perceive as public and political interest. But the inherent nature of these acts remains the same: whether a single instance or on a mass scale, their performance does not inevitably require the use of public authority. The crucial distinction is, again, between *performance of the act by the State and its officials* and the same act *being performed as an exercise of public authority*. There is no absolute overlap between the two.

Moreover, in *Letelier*, Chile contended that assassination of a former ambassador by a car bomb, even if committed or ordered by the Chilean government, was an act *jure imperii*, as an act of 'policy judgment and decision', and immunised under the US legislation. The court responded that 'whatever policy options may exist for a foreign country, it has no "discretion" to perpetrate conduct designated to result in the assassination of an individual or individuals, action that is clearly contrary to the precepts recognised in both national and international law'.[31]

Obviously, cases decided by English and American courts on the basis of the SIA and the FSIA could not apply this restrictive doctrine because

[27] For the overview of the American jurisprudence, see G. R. Delaume, 'Economic Development and Sovereign Immunity', 79 *AJIL* (1985), 319 at 325, 327.

[28] *Fogarty* v. *UK*, 37112/97, 21 November 2001, paras. 22, 30, 38.

[29] For criminal proceedings see Joint Separate Opinion of Judges Higgins, Kooijmans and Burgenthal, *Arrest Warrant*, ICJ Reports 2002, paras. 74 and 85; for civil litigation see *Hilao* v. *Marcos*, US Court of Appeals (Ninth Circuit), 104 ILR 122–5; these violations were 'as adjudicable and redressable as would be a dictator's act of rape'.

[30] [2000] 1 AC 242.

[31] *Letelier*, 63 ILR 378 at 388. Chile considered that the act involved was immune under section 1605 of the US Foreign Sovereign Immunities Act (FSIA) of 1976.

the latter, as embodied in common law that incorporates international law, was displaced, in those jurisdictions, by the statute that prescribes that a general immunity persists unless a specific exception from it is identified.[32] The distinction between the sources of national and international law is indeed cardinal, yet not always properly understood or acknowledged in the relevant jurisprudence. Thus the Fourth Chamber of the European Court in *Jones* v. *UK* has referred to national court pronouncements to the effect that a general rule of international law according immunity to State officials for torture – the same way as to States – can be identified because the national legislation extends such immunity to them.[33] On other occasions, this elementary distinction between national and international law has been more properly grasped. To illustrate, American courts accept that 'as a matter of international and domestic law, *jus cogens* violations are, by definition, acts that are not officially authorized by the Sovereign',[34] even if the letter of domestic legislation can prevent them from applying this position domestically. This way, the position in *Siderman* reaching out to international law directly can be a valid instance of State practice the way that several other decisions constrained by national statutes could never be.

This is, however, a purely domestic legal position adopted by the national legislator; there is no evidence whatsoever that it is reflected in customary international law agreed upon as between States. This is the case, contrary to the perception expressed in writings that, after the adoption of the SIA in the UK, the jurisprudence that relies on the restrictive doctrine as part of common (and of international) law could now be accorded only historical significance.[35] In practice, when English and American courts get a chance to adjudicate outside the SIA, they follow a limited functional approach referring to the uniqueness of the act to

[32] As reflected in the argument put forward by J. Crawford, 'A Foreign State Immunities Act for Australia?' (1983) *Australian YIL* 71, 105–6. See further notes 122 and 130 and the accompanying text below.

[33] *Jones* v. *UK*, paras. 203, 210; moreover, the US, British and Dutch practice (*Samantar*, *Pinochet* and *Bouterse*) referred to in paras. 211–12 indicated that the pro-immunity position was not sustainable, yet the Court chose to disregard this practice on the basis of the House of Lords' decision in *Jones* v. *Saudi Arabia* – the very decision that was being appealed.

[34] *Siderman de Blake*, 965 F.2d at 718, as followed in *Samantar*, No. 11-1479, 2 November 2012, 19.

[35] As put forward earlier on by F. A. Mann, 'The State Immunity Act 1978', (1980) 51 *BYIL*, 43; and later on in Martin Dixon, Robert McCorquodale and Sarah Williams, *Cases and Materials on International Law* (2nd edn., Oxford: Oxford University Press 2009), 318.

sovereign authority as per *Congreso*, further applied in *Kuwait Air Co*, *Littrell* and *Lampen-Wolfe*, and by the US Supreme Court and the Fourth Circuit Appeals Court in *Samantar*, as well as earlier in *Marcos* and *Letelier*.

The flipside is that the practice of national courts based on the SIA and the FSIA that require adjudication on immunity issues solely on the basis of national (as opposed to international) law, and regardless of the examination of the nature of underlying acts,[36] cannot validly constitute State practice that could build customary law on the subject. That which excludes international law from the consideration by national courts, cannot feasibly contribute to the development of the very same international law.

D. *Restrictive doctrine and criminal proceedings*

In this area, the decision by the House of Lords in *Pinochet* was the first major material case. The acts of torture as prohibited by CAT, by a *jus cogens* norm, and as constituting an international crime, did not amount to the sovereign function of any public official.[37] It is important to understand that the House of Lords did not establish the lack of criminal immunity by focusing on the previous practice of domestic criminal prosecutions of foreign officials, because that previous practice was not concerned with immunity and its restrictive doctrine. There was no pre-existing law applicable to criminal immunities alone and such was not identified. The lack of immunity was established through the application of pre-existing functional restrictive doctrine, now to criminal cases.

The importance of this approach for getting the right result was demonstrated by the way immunities were handled in the *Khurts Bat* case later on. Moses LJ referred to the ILC Special Rapporteur to deny that immunity was available in criminal proceedings.[38] However, on a general plane, the Special Rapporteur was of the view that: 'various rationales for exceptions to the immunity of officials from foreign criminal jurisdiction prove upon close scrutiny to be insufficiently convincing. These rationales continue to be discussed in the doctrine. The practice of States is also far from being uniform in this respect'; and that: '[i]t is difficult to talk of exceptions to immunity as a norm of international law that has developed, in the

[36] As happened in the cases at note 126 below.

[37] *Pinochet III*, (HL), [2000] 1 AC 147.

[38] *Khurts Bat*, para. 99.

same way as it cannot definitively be asserted that a trend towards the establishment of such a norm exists'.[39]

And in relation to criminal immunities alone, the Special Rapporteur is perfectly right. There is, quite simply, not enough State practice out there to demonstrate the rule that confers immunity to foreign officials or denies that immunity in relation to criminal proceedings specifically. Nor can it be reinforced by practice of prosecution and exercise of jurisdiction over individuals serving the State where immunity was neither invoked nor denied. But the Special Rapporteur's approach is methodologically erroneous for taking criminal immunities as a separate area and thus only focusing on the part of the area in which State practice regarding immunities is displayed. The Special Rapporteur did not properly focus on the general rationale of immunities that derives from the nature of sovereign authority of States and the scope of this authority – which is by definition the same for both criminal and civil proceedings, in principle as well as in practice.

E. Upholding State immunity through the misapplication of the restrictive doctrine

Courts that have upheld State immunity for serious violations of human rights and humanitarian law have initially professed to follow the restrictive doctrine. But its treatment differs in each particular case. The European Court in *Al-Adsani* has provided no explanation as to the nature of the relevant acts of torture. It merely referred to the immunity that Kuwait enjoyed due to the maxim *par in parem non habet imperium*, and considered this sufficient to prevent the victims from invoking their right to the access to a court under Article 6 ECHR. This way, the European Court has effectively used the absolute immunity approach that does not properly query into and distinguish between the sovereign and non-sovereign acts.

Twelve years later, in *Jones* v. *UK*, the Fourth Chamber of the European Court has not provided any more substantiated explanation of the rationale and basis of State immunity than its derivation from the sovereignty of States either.[40] The issue of how the rule of immunity propagated in *Al-Adsani* and *Jones* has emerged and achieved binding force through State practice still remains unclarified.

[39] *Second Report*, at 30, para. 96.
[40] *Jones* v. *UK*, para. 188.

In *Jones* v. *Saudi Arabia*, the House of Lords have specified that the individual defendants allegedly responsible for the acts of torture were public officials, and torture took place in police or on prison premises. Lord Bingham and Lord Hoffmann also referred to Articles 4 and 7 of the 2001 ILC's Articles on State Responsibility, according to which the conduct of whatever organ of the State, including the ones committed in the excess of instructions or authority, are attributable to the State.[41] This has confused State responsibility with State immunity. In reality, there is some way between the act being performed through the exercise of State authority or facilities, and the same act being by its nature a sovereign act. For, if the mere fact of the involvement of public officials and premises were to be enough, the absolute immunity doctrine would be re-introduced through the backdoor, making it impossible to exclude even commercial acts from the scope of immunities if they are perpetrated by State officials or through the use of State premises or facilities.

The ICJ in *Germany* v. *Italy* has queried 'whether the [war crimes] in question fall to be assessed by reference to the law governing the exercise of sovereign power (*jus imperii*) or the law concerning non-sovereign activities of a State, especially private and commercial activities (*jus gestionis*)'.[42] Obviously that has to be international law, not national law. Otherwise each State will be able to unilaterally determine the scope of its own internationally opposable immunities. The Court did not explain what the 'law governing the exercise of sovereign power' was, whether it meant the Third Reich law or international law, or how war crimes in international law could attract immunity as valid exercises of public authority.[43] Instead, the Court relied on the concession made by the Italian government that these acts were *jure imperii* acts. As the judgment did not properly examine the reasons for or against this position, its continuing value for the development of the law on this matter is doubtful. Effectively, as Xiaodong Yang has demonstrated, the Court's reasoning has upheld the absolute immunity doctrine in relation to underlying war crimes.[44]

The International Court's analysis focused on three separate, albeit somewhat interdependent questions: torts committed within the forum's

[41] *Jones* (HL), paras. 11–12 (per Lord Bingham), 76 (per Lord Hoffmann).

[42] *Germany* v. *Italy*, para. 60.

[43] Which obviously is not the same as being lawful, but that is far from being crucial. Legality of the act and its reflection of public authority can be two separate substantial tests that may at times overlap in content, but do not have to do so.

[44] X. Yang, 'Absolute Immunity of Foreign Armed Forces from Tort Proceedings', (2012) 71 *CLJ*, 282.

territory; acts committed by armed forces; and the scope of acts *jure imperii.* When focusing on the practice related to acts of armed forces, the Court's inference was that these attract immunity as far as they are *jure imperii.*[45] Having essentially acknowledged the two-tiered nature of the problem – acts of armed forces *and* their performance as part of sovereign authority – the Court did not really address the second aspect, relying instead on the Italian concession.

When confronted with the reality that most of the national practices deny immunity for territorial torts, either generally or in conjunction with the acts of armed forces, the Court simply pleaded its unawareness that those statutory provisions have been applied by national courts to that effect; and has then recast the issue of tort immunity into that of armed forces immunity.[46] This is a rather curious way of excluding from the focus the practice that stood in the way of the desired outcome.

The Court then turned to another part of – rather limited – practice that dealt with the conduct of armed forces during an armed conflict.[47] What makes this odd is the inference, on the basis of judicial decisions adopted in a small number of States,[48] that the conduct performed during an armed conflict provides, under customary international law, a separate basis, distinct from the territorial tort issue, on which immunities can be accorded or denied; and that anything armed forces do during an armed conflict is immune.[49] The restrictive doctrine to which the Court initially alluded was supposed to apply, making immunities dependent on the sovereign nature of the relevant act in each pertinent case. If the context of the occurrence of the act, not the nature of the act, were crucial, then anything committed during an armed conflict – or for that matter in prisons or other official facilities – would be a sovereign act and immune. We call that the absolute immunity doctrine.

To compare, both the *Lampen-Wolfe* and *Littrell* cases drew on the relevant acts as part undertaken within the military base and solely for

[45] *Germany* v. *Italy*, para. 72. [46] *Germany* v. *Italy*, paras. 70–7. [47] *Ibid.*, paras. 73–4.

[48] It should be noted that in *Jones* v. *UK* the same range of limited State practice was alluded to for demonstrating the shape of a generally binding rule on immunity, see *Jones* v. *UK*, paras. 112–49. The Court does not seem to be using this practice to actually justify its own position in the operative reasoning of its Judgment.

[49] A related point could be that even if the International Court's approach on acts committed in war are *ipso jure* immune, that would still not affect the position that the bulk of cases not dealing with acts committed in an armed conflict should still be excluded from immunity. From the national courts' perspective, the reasoning in *Germany* v. *Italy* cannot be a direct legitimation of *Al-Adsani* or *Jones*.

the purpose of organising and maintaining armed forces, as opposed to more far-reaching activities affecting the civilian population. By contrast, the International Court in *Germany* v. *Italy* merely relied on the fact that the relevant acts were authored by German armed forces, as opposed to these acts validly serving their organising and maintenance purposes. Only the State can perform acts related to organising its own armed forces, which is a sovereign affair. The use of armed forces to commit crimes for which sovereign authority is not inherently needed does not, however, transform these crimes into sovereign acts. This becomes obvious if we bear in mind the above-mentioned rationale of the restrictive doctrine: the task is not to clarify whether human rights claims fall within a predetermined – commercial or other – exception, but to assess each act on its own merit to see whether it was undertaken in the genuine exercise of sovereign authority in the first place.

To summarise, the three above cases did not properly address the actual State practice, or have engaged in voluntarist reclassification of what practice was needed and what was not. Apart from the lack of the uniform approach, these three cases convey the impression as if there were two different standards to identify acts *jure imperii*, one applying to human rights claims and the other to the rest of the cases. This position does not represent the restrictive doctrine and thus the current legal position. The only remaining alternative that could reflect the proper legal position consists in carefully and accurately examining the nature of underlying acts and transactions in every pertinent case, to see whether – over and above having been perpetrated by State agents, in public interest or through the use of State facilities – they constitute valid exercises of sovereignty and public authority, instead of relying on the outdated *par in parem* maxim.

Relying on the principle of sovereign equality and on the maxim *par in parem non habet imperium* in *Germany* v. *Italy*, *Jones* v. *UK* and *Al-Adsani* essentially misconstrues the restrictive theory and misdirect the reasoning as to how the parameters of the restrictive immunity rule must be identified. If the broad range of commercial, tort and employment matters is considered, one State could indeed, and frequently, exercise its *imperium* over another. The principle of sovereign equality does precious little to upset this result. Two States would be equal if they can be impleaded before each other's courts just as they would be if they cannot be so impleaded, as long as the underlying legal position applies to them equally.

F. *State practice and customary law in the balance*

The question now arising is whether and to what extent the restrictive rule in general, or in the shape as propagated in *Al-Adsani*, *Jones* (HL), *Germany* v. *Italy* or *Jones* v. *UK* could be said to be part of positive customary international law. The rule thus construed is too nuanced. It refers to certain kinds of acts being included and others being excluded from the scope of sovereign immunity. Its conceptual justification is not as uniform or straightforward as was the case with the absolute immunity rule. Asserting the customary law status of such a rule thus presumes a substantially more complex legal position than would be presumed with regard to the older absolute immunity rule. It therefore requires a higher threshold of evidence to be cleared in order to identify that the rule of immunity thus shaped is what has been accepted as part of positive international law, being backed by State practice that is sufficiently uniform and consistent, and further supplemented by the requisite *opinio juris*.[50]

This requirement of a higher threshold is further dictated by the aspect of normativity. Under the restrictive doctrine, immunity could only be granted or denied under reference rules, not by substantive rules of conduct. Substantive rules prescribe, clearly and straightforwardly, the relevant right or obligation. Reference rules merely specify the criteria, the application of which will ultimately determine what the relevant rights and obligations are. Given that the requirement of the restrictive doctrine is to further look at the precise nature of the relevant act and transaction, the conclusion follows that immunities could at most be seen to be governed by reference rules.

Therefore, in terms of customary law, the higher burden of proof requires answering the question in relation to what element of that reference rule should the uniform or consistent State practice be identified: the general existence of the immunity rule; a particular conception of the sovereign act; or specific individual acts covered by immunity? And as it happens, States are not to the least agreed in relation to any of those criteria. The ICJ decision in *Germany* v. *Italy* only demonstrates that State practice supporting any aspect of the putative rule – sovereign nature of the act, act by armed forces or the territorial tort aspect – is very limited and thus qualitatively insufficient.

[50] See generally Article 38 of the International Court's Statute; and *North Sea Continental Shelf*, ICJ Reports, 1969, 3.

Concerns this insufficiency of evidence raises are further corroborated by further State practice. To illustrate, the United States of America does not subscribe to such version of the 'restrictive' theory as has been expounded in the cases of *Al-Adsani*, *Jones* and *Germany* v. *Italy*. The US Congress has repeatedly amended the FSIA to enable the victims of terrorist attacks to recover damages from the relevant States;[51] and, more recently, Canada followed suit after the International Court delivered its judgment in *Germany* v. *Italy*.[52] This confirms that these two States do not feel internationally bound to grant immunity to foreign States, let alone subscribe to a particular vision of immunities that has been upheld in the *Al-Adsani/Jones/Germany* v. *Italy* stream of litigation. More broadly, American courts have emphasised that 'the grant of immunity is a privilege which the United States may withhold from any claimant'.[53] On the other hand, China still adheres to the doctrine of absolute immunity, as was demonstrated in a recent litigation.[54] There is room for viewing the Chinese position as that of persistent objection. If so, then in any case dealing with China national courts would first have to query whether there is a well-established customary rule on immunities in the first place (which, as we already saw, would be a difficult task); and then accord immunity to China on the basis of its persistent objection to such rule if the latter could be identified. If China is a persistent objector, it can obtain immunity for all its acts, including commercial ones; if not, then its every pertinent act must be looked at through the prism of the restrictive doctrine *Congreso*-style. If either of these two possibilities were to be displayed within British or American jurisdictions, then in both cases, the international legal requirement in relation to the UK or the USA would be to accord or deny immunity to China in disregard of the 'general immunity versus specific exceptions' pattern to which both the SIA and the FSIA subscribe as sources of domestic law in these two jurisdictions.

[51] See, for an overview, R. Bettauer, 'Germany Sues Italy at the International Court of Justice on Foreign Sovereign Immunity – Legal Underpinnings and Implications for US Law', *ASIL Insight*, 19 November 2009.

[52] See the amendments to the Canadian State Immunity Act (R.S.C. 1985, c. S-18), 13 March 2012.

[53] *Lafontant* v. *Aristide*, 103 ILR 586; see also *United States* v. *Noriega*, 99 ILR 162–3, to the effect that the US does not consider itself bound under international law to accord immunity to foreign States and their agents. See, to the same effect, the Judgment of the US Supreme Court in *Republic of Austria* v. *Altmann*, (2004) 541 US 677.

[54] *Democratic Republic of the Congo* v. *FG Hemisphere Associates*, 8 June 2011, Hong Kong Court of Final Appeal.

Given the absence of a general agreement as to the acts covered by the restrictive immunity rule, and the *Al-Adsani* and *Jones* pretence to the contrary effect notwithstanding, Lord Denning's point that 'there is no consensus whatever' as to the customary law status of immunities still stands.[55] The lack of customary law on immunities compellingly suggests that the restrictive doctrine is at most an interpretative guide for the pre-existing jurisdictional entitlements of States and that they do not have to defer jurisdiction, unless some compelling considerations pointing to the uniquely sovereign activities requires that. And then, this is only a matter of comity, not a strict legal requirement.

In such circumstances, the only legally defensible approach, as a matter of international law, is to grant State immunity for a rather narrow category of official acts that undoubtedly constitute exercises of governmental authority, as specified in the above-examined jurisprudence on the restrictive doctrine of immunities that most prominently includes *Congreso*, and in the scholarly analysis of this area of law.[56] Otherwise, a valid human rights claim could be denied without the forum State actually owing the obligation to the relevant foreign State to accord immunity. As shown above, there is sufficient evidence that this position applies both to criminal and civil proceedings. It would, moreover, stand to no reason to classify an act or transaction as a sovereign act in relation to one kind of proceedings but not in relation to another. The issue of the nature of relevant acts is essentially a pre-proceeding issue. The nature of the act depends on its own merit and characteristics. The initiation of the particular form of proceedings is the victim's choice. It would be absurd to suggest that due to the victim's particular choice as to which proceedings should be used, the nature of an already perpetrated act should change from X to Y.

3. The (IR)relevance of treaties on State immunity

It is generally admitted that treaties can either codify the pre-existing customary law, or embody treaty-specific rules and principles that will subsequently find broader appeal among States, so that they could be seen as part of customary law as well. However, the threshold of proof on

[55] *Trendtex* [1977] 1 QB 552–3; Lord Wilberforce in *Congreso* also disapproved the option of viewing certain national legislation and international treaties as evidence of general customary law.

[56] D. P. O'Connell, *International Law* (London: Stevens & Sons, 1970), 846; R. Higgins, *Problems and Process* (Oxford: Oxford University Press, 1994), 81, 84.

demonstrating this much is quite high, as was the case both in the ICJ's *North Sea* judgment and, with regard to State immunity specifically, in *Congreso.* The relevant treaties on State immunity are unlikely to meet these requirements.

The ECSI is in force as between eight States only and falls short of representing any generally accepted legal position. The 2004 UN Convention could not reflect any pre-existing customary law either, as we already saw through the above focus on State practice. As for the potential generating customary rules anew, the Convention's low ratification status and its prioritisation of the 'general immunity versus specific exceptions' approach makes this highly unlikely.

The judicial treatment of these conventions is not free of problems. In *Al-Adsani* v. *UK*, the Strasbourg Court relied on the ECSI to support the government's position,[57] even though Kuwait was not only not party to it, but not even eligible to become such. Similarly, the House of Lords in *Jones* placed reliance on the 2004 Convention as the 'most authoritative' statement of law in this area,[58] to support the government's position, even though it was not in force. In none of those cases was any effort made to compare the terms of these conventions to the actual state of State practice.

The International Court in *Germany* v. *Italy* pronounced that both the 1972 and 2004 conventions were inapplicable to acts of armed forces. The ECSI includes a saving clause on armed forces, while the 2004 Convention was understood to have been prevailingly interpreted the same way through State practice. The Court also suggested that Article 12 of the 2004 Convention, denying immunity for territorial torts, does not represent customary law.[59] The reason why this could be the case is solely because State practice that matters for identifying any possible customary law in this area – that is practice relating to immunities specifically and that performed against the background of international, not national, law – does not take the locus of the act as the principal point of departure; it merely refers to a simple and straightforward distinction between acts that are unique to public authority and those that are not.

Furthermore, even if Article 12 of the 2004 Convention does not apply to armed forces and acts of the latter are supposedly governed by customary law, this should revert us to the restrictive doctrine theat focuses on acts unique to State authority, *not* on the 'general immunity

[57] *Al-Adsani*, paras. 22, 57–78.

[58] *Jones*, paras. 26 and47 (Lords Bingham and Hoffmann).

[59] As indicated in *Germany* v. *Italy*, para. 64.

versus specific exceptions' approach. Cases on the immunity of armed forces clearly articulate such version of the restrictive doctrine, as is clear from *Littrell* and *Lampen-Wolfe*, decided directly on the basis of English common law that incorporates international law. The International Court was also aware of Norwegian and Swedish positions regarding the scope of the 2004 Convention and used this as one of the justifications for dis-applying the territorial tort principle that Article 12 embodies.[60] But this does not quite represent the overall position of the Nordic States, which is a more pro-accountability one and might as well require denying immunity.[61] Nor, in the same problematic spirit, did the Court address the implications of the Swiss position and that of the ILC's Working Group that the 2004 Convention was not meant to apply to serious violations of human rights and breaches of *jus cogens*.[62]

Therefore, the Court's overall position to the relevant treaties is falsely premised on there being, somewhere in the background, a fall-back customary rule that obliges States to grant immunity pursuant to the approach that the Court's judgment has prioritised.

4. Immunities and human rights treaties

A. *Immunities and the European Convention on Human Rights*

The context in which State immunity has been discussed in the practice of the European Court of Human Rights relates to the right to access

[60] *Germany* v. *Italy*, para. 69.

[61] In fact, as the Norwegian Government put it to the Sixth Committee in 2011 on behalf of the Five Nordic Countries, developments including the adoption of the 1946 Nuremberg Principles have made it clear that 'no State official could have been in any doubt about his or her potential personal responsibility if participating in acts regarded by international law as crimes of concern to the international community as a whole'; and that these 'developments relating to international criminal justice as having contributed significantly to the normative production and clarification of rules pertaining to the scope for invocation of immunities. Consequentially, international criminal justice has a bearing on the general state of the law of immunities, which ought to be recognized.' Nordic Statement Delivered to the Sixth Committee of the General Assembly, Ms Margit Tveiten, Deputy Director General, 11 January 2011.

[62] Switzerland 'considers that article 12 does not govern the question of pecuniary compensation for serious human rights violations which are alleged to be attributable to a State and are committed outside the State of the forum. Consequently, this Convention is without prejudice to developments in international law in this regard.' The position of the ILC Working Group is that 'the Convention does not address questions concerning immunity arising from civil claims in relation to acts of a State in violation of human rights norms having the character of *jus cogens*, particularly the prohibition of torture'. Immunity of State Officials, Memorandum by the Secretariat, A/CN/4/596, 31 March 2008, 31–2 (para. 46); for the position of Swiss courts see note 98 below.

to a court under Article 6 ECHR, and whether the grant of immunity to the State impleaded in domestic proceedings will prejudice this right. The three initial immunity cases decided by the Strasbourg Court in 2002 did not offer any uniform approach on this matter. In *Al-Adsani* v. *UK*, the Court justified granting immunity for torture to Kuwait without any proper enquiry into the nature of relevant acts. Two other decisions – *Fogarty* v. *UK*[63] and *McElhinney* v. *Ireland*[64] – adopted a more functional and less blanket approach, offering a more nuanced application of the restrictive doctrine of immunity, to evaluate whether the relevant conduct of the State amounted to acts *jure imperii*.

Later on, the Strasbourg Court has delivered four other decisions on State immunity,[65] in which some questions are posed in a way that was not the case in *Al-Adsani*. In *Sabeh El Leil* v. *France*, the Strasbourg Court explained that:

> It would not be consistent with the rule of law in a democratic society or with the basic principle underlying Article 6§1 – namely that civil claims must be capable of being submitted to a judge for adjudication – if a State could, without restraint or control by the Convention enforcement bodies, remove from the jurisdiction of the courts a whole range of civil claims or confer immunities from civil liability on categories of persons.[66]

Such statement did not appear in *Al-Adsani*. The *Sabeh El Leil* approach is further in accordance with the European Court's general priority that ECHR rights must be secured to individuals in a way that is effective, not illusory.[67]

From here, the text step is to identify whether the grant of immunity would be a proportionate restriction on Article 6 rights. The justification in *Al-Adsani* was that 'measures taken by a High Contracting Party which reflect generally recognised rules of public international law on State immunity cannot in principle be regarded as imposing a disproportionate restriction on the right of access to a court as embodied in Article 6§1'. This was because the ECHR had to be interpreted in line with other principles of international law pursuant to Article 31(3)(c) of the Vienna Convention on the Law of Treaties 1969 (VCLT).[68] This approach to restrict the application of Article 6 in order to comply with

[63] *Fogarty* v. *UK*, 34 EHRR 12 (2002). [64] *McElhinney* v. *Ireland*, 34 EHRR 13 (2002).

[65] *Cudak* v. *Lithuania*, 15869/02, 23 March 2010; *Sabeh El Leil* v. *France*, 34869/05, 29 June 2011; *Wallishauser* v. *Austria*, 156/04; *Oleynikov* v. *Russia*, 36703/04, 14 March 2013.

[66] *Sabeh El Leil*, para. 50.

[67] *Soering*, 14038/88, 7 July 1989, paras. 87–8; *Artico*, 6694/74, 13 May 1980, para. 33.

[68] *Al-Adsani*, para. 56.

other international obligations is not what is required under the VCLT, because the VCLT admits that treaties prevail over custom as *lex specialis*. The Court's approach also conflicts with the priority stated in other cases of the Strasbourg Court that wherever States-parties undertake other international obligations, they should still implement those under the ECHR.[69] It seems that in its practice relating to State immunity the Court adopts the 'deference to other rules' approach, while in all other cases it prioritises the primacy of the ECHR.

Then, under *Al-Adsani*, once a competing obligation under another source of international law is identified, it becomes automatically necessary and proportionate under the ECHR to grant immunity. Contrary to the priorities stated elsewhere in the Strasbourg jurisprudence, no proper examination was undertaken in *Al-Adsani* as to the nature of the relevant measure, available alternatives or the balance of competing interests. In *Jones* v. *UK* in 2014, no further clarification was provided to this issue and the precise nature of the relevant acts of torture was not enquired into either.

In the subsequent jurisprudence that includes *Cudak* v. *Lithuania* and *Sabeh El Leil* v. *France*, things seem to be somewhat different. As *Sabeh El Leil* suggests, 'the grant of immunity to a State in civil proceedings pursues the legitimate aim of complying with international law to promote comity and good relations between States'. But a further requirement is then stated that 'the impugned restriction must also be proportionate to the aim pursued', to which end the restrictive immunity doctrine should be used as a point of reference.[70]

The unclear point here – compromising the ability of this projected position to be applicable on a continuous basis – is whether the grant of immunity is legitimate *because* this would ordinarily be done on the basis of the restrictive doctrine; or whether, alternatively, the legitimacy under the ECHR of the grant of immunity, even if allegedly justified under general international law, would *further depend* on the ECHR-specific requirement that such grant of immunity should be proportionate to the 'legitimate aim' pursued. The question thus is thus one of normative

[69] *M & Co* v. *FRG*, Application No. 13258/87, 9 February 1990, 33 *YB ECHR* 1990, 51–2; *Waite & Kennedy* v. *Germany*, 18 February 1999, para. 67; *Matthews* v. *UK*, ECHR 24833/94, 18 February 1999, paras. 26–35; *Bosphorus Hava Yollari Turizm* v. *Ireland*, 45036/98, paras. 155–6; *Soering* v. *UK*, No. 14038/88, Judgment of 7 July 1989; *Al-Saadoon & Mufdhi* v. *UK*, Judgment (4th Chamber), No. 61498/08, 2 March 2010; *Capital Bank* v. *Bulgaria*, 49429/99, 24 November 2005, paras. 38, 43, 110–11.

[70] *Sabeh El Leil*, paras. 52–3.

hierarchy, namely whether the ECHR-specific requirements should be applied subject to the (putative) customary law on immunities; or whether the Convention would apply as *lex specialis* and accommodate the position under that customary law only if it were compatible to those ECHR-specific requirements.

The judgment in *Cudak* v. *Lithuania* suggests that 'in cases where the application of the principle of State immunity from jurisdiction restricts the exercise of the right of access to a court [under Article 6], the Court must ascertain whether the circumstances of the case justify such restriction'.[71]

If this approach is pursued, the relevance of general international law on immunities matters for the Strasbourg Court only for identifying whether immunities pursue a legitimate aim, but does not pre-determine the further issue of whether immunities thus become a proportionate and legitimate restriction on Article 6. This latter issue must be gone into separately, contrary to the above-described deference approach in *Al-Adsani* and *Jones* v. *UK*. Article 6 would, then, prevail as *lex specialis*, and allow the grant of immunities only when these would be proportionate under the ECHR specifically, no matter whether they are mandated or required under general international law. If this is the current approach then, at the level of applicable principles at least, the Strasbourg Court's approach to immunities seems to have shifted towards a more pro-accountability stance. However, the *Jones* v. *UK* Judgment pressingly prompts the question as to whether, regarding the relationship between Article 6 and immunities, the European Court has one single approach or two separate approaches, each of which could be used through the voluntary selection at the relevant opportunity.

A separate issue, pursued in the Strasbourg jurisprudence, relates to the use, in a number of cases, of un-ratified treaties and the ones inapplicable *inter se*, to determine whether the respondent State was bound to grant immunity.[72] As we saw above, the 2004 Convention is not applicable law; it is not in force even for States that have ratified it. The reliance on it in several cases places the European Court on a rather slippery

[71] *Cudak*, para. 59.

[72] *Cudak*, para. 66 ('As to the 2004 Convention, Lithuania has admittedly not ratified it but did not vote against its adoption either'); *Sabeh El Leil*, para. 57; *Wallishauser*, para. 31; *Oleynikov*, para. 66 ('Russia has not ratified [the 2004 Convention] but has not opposed it: on the contrary, it signed the convention on 1 December 2006.') See, in this regard, Article 14 VCLT 1969.

slope. In those cases the outcome was withholding immunity and vindicating Convention rights. But would the European Court accept the relevance of un-ratified treaties if their requirement will be to cut down the scope of ECHR rights, as opposed to enforcing these rights effectively not illusorily? How would the European Court face the claim that the 2004 Convention, not ratified by one or both States involved, and not in force anyway, requires according immunity but the result thus obtained is not a necessary and proportionate restriction of Article 6 rights? This would take matters even further than *Al-Adsani* did under the pretence of applying Article 31(3)(c) VCLT, for un-ratified treaties could hardly represent 'any relevant rules of international law applicable in the relations between the parties'. On a more general plane, would the Court deem all 2004 Convention provisions to be part of customary law and adopt the approach of the absolute deference to the 2004 Convention; and if so, how would it explain it against the background of other cases that the ECHR prevails over other treaties?

B. *Immunities and Article 1 of the 1984 Convention against Torture*

Article 1 CAT defines torture, specifically for its own purposes, as:

> any act by which severe pain or suffering, whether physical or mental, is intentionally inflicted on a person . . . by or at the instigation of or with the consent or acquiescence of a public official or other person acting in an official capacity.

The question raised in jurisprudence is whether such definition has any bearing on whether torture could be a sovereign act protected by immunity. Lord Browne-Wilkinson suggested in *Pinochet* that CAT applied Pinochet's activities precisely because he had acted as a public official, namely Head of State.[73] Lord Millett observed that '[t]he official or governmental nature of the act, which forms the basis of the immunity, is an essential ingredient of the offence [under CAT]. No rational system of criminal justice can allow an immunity which is co-extensive with the offence.'[74]

It seems that, under either of these approaches, Article 1 hardly touches upon the issue of immunities. Article 1 mentions the 'act', 'public official' and 'official capacity' as separate categories. The meaning of one cannot pre-empt or pre-determine that of another. The fact that Pinochet

[73] [2000] 1 AC 200. [74] [2000] 1 AC 277.

acted as a public official does not answer the question as to the nature of his acts. Capacity means 'ability or power to do something' and 'a specified role or position'.[75] The adjective 'official' means 'relating to an authority' and 'permitted or done by a person or group in a position of authority'.[76] Therefore, for the purposes of CAT, 'official capacity' should be understood as the use of that potential, resource or facility that the fact of being public official uniquely enables one to possess or use. 'Official capacity' can at most mean acts committed 'while in office' or 'when on duty'. The nature of the 'act' perpetrated in that 'capacity' remains a separate issue.

Lord Hoffmann suggested in *Jones* v. *Saudi Arabia* that if torture was 'official enough' to fall within Article 1 CAT, then it was 'official enough' to attract immunity.[77] But would a breach of contract or another act relating to commercial relations by the official while in office be also 'official enough'? How about withholding salary payment to an embassy employee hired by an employment contract?

Even if a public official acting in official capacity is a requirement for application of CAT to the particular act of torture, this is immaterial for State immunity. Immunities focus on the nature of particular acts, not on what 'capacity' has been used to perpetrate them. A breach of contract can be committed by a person in 'a specified role or position', indeed through the use of 'position of authority' that may distinctively enable that person to commit that breach of contract. That breach will not thereby become an official act, even if 'official capacity' would be used to perpetrate it.

The restrictive doctrine of immunity requires, instead, focusing on the nature of the specific act, in this case 'act by which severe pain' is inflicted on a person, which can be perpetrated by anyone, whether or not acting in official capacity. It is merely the case that, for the purposes of CAT specifically, only 'acts' perpetrated by an official or in official capacity will be covered by other provisions of the Convention, for the purposes of prosecution and accountability. Article 1 CAT is not about immunity, but merely about description and determination of the scope of acts to which the Convention applies, and thus the scope of CAT *ratione materiae*.

That Article 1 does not envisage that torture attracts immunity as an exercise of public or official authority, or act *jure imperii*, is also confirmed by aspects of the drafting history of CAT which were not properly addressed in the relevant cases including *Jones*. The term 'official

[75] *Compact Oxford English Dictionary* (3rd edn., 2005), 139.

[76] *Compact OED*, 703. [77] *Jones*, para. 83.

capacity' was introduced into Article 1 in order to bring non-State actors into the scope of that provision. As this demonstrates, Article 1 refers to torture committed by (a) a 'public official' and (b) an 'other person acting in an official capacity'. The latter was inserted into the Convention's text to cover torture by certain non-State actors, such as rebels, guerrillas or insurgents, rather than limit the State official's responsibility to whatever is done in a strictly official capacity.[78] If this approach is followed, a public official would be liable for any act or torture while other individuals would be liable only for torture committed in that peculiar 'official capacity'. And there still would be no relation between Article 1 and immunities.

5. Immunities and normative hierarchy

A. *Conventional rules on the accountability for, jurisdiction over, and prosecution of, international crimes*

(i) Criminal jurisdiction and duty to prosecute under CAT

Articles 5 and 7 CAT establish a network of jurisdictional obligations to prosecute acts of torture. Lord Browne-Wilkinson suggested in *Pinochet* that, before the adoption of CAT, *jus cogens* alone was insufficient to remove immunity of officials engaging in torture, for 'not until there was some form of universal jurisdiction for the punishment of the crime of torture could it really be talked about as a fully constituted international crime'.[79]

On the other hand, as Lord Hope observed, 'it would be wrong to regard the Torture Convention as having by necessary implication removed the immunity *ratione materiae* from former heads of state in regard to every act of torture of any kind which might be alleged against him falling within the scope of Article 1'. Immunity for torture should be denied on the alternative basis of criminality pursuant to the developments under customary international law. Contrary to Lord Browne-Wilkinson's view, Lord Hope observed that the denial of immunity was due to the *jus cogens* prohibition of torture, which status was already achieved by the time the Convention became binding in England.[80] Under this view, CAT alone does not make the required difference.

[78] Manfred Nowak and Elizabeth McArthur, *UNCAT – A Commentary* (Oxford: Oxford University Press, 2008), 78–9.

[79] [2000] 1 AC 204–5. [80] [2000] 1 AC 246.

It is indeed doubtful whether the international criminalisation of torture is due solely and exclusively to CAT, which does not mention the word 'crime' and creates obligations that States have to implement within and through their national legal systems. Obligations are international, while the area to which they apply is national. That torture is an international crime may be due to elements arising under other sources of international law.

One possible argument is that of the primacy of CAT jurisdictional requirements over general international law. But the relative flexibility of CAT prosecution and extradition arrangements and the logical antecedence of jurisdiction to immunities could still leave room for the argument that all CAT requires is to find the place where the torturer can be tried when requirements of its Article 7 are met, not necessarily that they can be tried anywhere within the Convention's spatial remit even if they can invoke immunity in the forum.

Overall, their Lordship's treatment of CAT leaves plenty to guess on what basis CAT can override immunities in criminal proceedings: because it relates to torture committed in 'official capacity', because it establishes extra-territorial jurisdiction over torture, alone or together with customary law and *jus cogens*, or because it is complemented by the alternative basis that international law regards torture as a crime that no longer fits within official authority of the State. *Pinochet* offers no uniform *ratio decidendi* on this point and more Law Lords adopted the view of complementation and convergence as between CAT and *jus cogens* than those who saw the effect of CAT alone as crucial. Most of the Law Lords in favour of the denial of immunity have not subscribed to the exclusively CAT-centred view.

Moreover, the existence of jurisdiction under CAT does not dispose of the immunity issue, because jurisdiction is antecedent to, and essentially different from, immunities, the latter to be additionally gone into once the former is duly established. As the ILC Special Rapporteur suggested in relation to treaties such as CAT: 'If it is argued that immunity is not compatible with universal jurisdiction, then it is not fully clear why this should not relate not only to functional but also to personal immunity.'[81]

Thus, the 'jurisdictional' line of argument[82] effectively puts the cart before the horse. That there is jurisdiction established speaks merely of the entitlement of the State to prosecute a crime or adjudicate on a

[81] *Second Report*, paras. 74–7. [82] Sanger, 'Immunity of State Officials', 223–4.

tort; it does not directly relate to the nature of the act which is being subjected to that State's jurisdiction, nor to the status of the defendant. As the International Court has observed in *Arrest Warrant*, jurisdiction is essentially antecedent to immunities.[83]

And the bulk of the opinion – carrying greater weight than academic writings, even if not any inherently binding force – is still unconvinced by the argument that CAT qua treaty displaces immunities. Both the ILC Analytical Group and Special Rapporteur on immunities were quite sceptical regarding the immunities being displaced by extra-territorial jurisdiction.[84] The 2005 Institut de droit international (IDI) Resolution did not exclude immunities for crimes falling under universal jurisdiction either.[85] The same approach was adopted by the ICJ in the *Arrest Warrant* case, where it did not admit that treaties such as CAT displace immunities, even though the particular focus was on immunities *ratione personae*.[86]

But surely, as a matter of treaty interpretation pure and simple, if a treaty such as CAT impliedly incorporates one immunity exception, or defers to it hierarchy-wise, there is no reason to assert that it does not similarly accommodate other kinds of immunities. The argument on CAT versus immunity is essentially that of normative hierarchy, whether acknowledged by its proponents or not; its essence is that rules under one source of international law can and must override those under another. What matters for normative hierarchy is not the conferral of jurisdiction, which is anyway permissive. In relation to CAT specifically, the crucial factor could be the overall framework under Articles 5 and 7 that imposes on States-parties a duty to prosecute and brings together multiple elements of State jurisdiction (territorial, nationality and universal).

Unfortunately, the national and international practice is divided on this aspect of normative hierarchy. In *Germany* v. *Italy*, the International Court attempted to *a posteriori* recast the reasoning in *Pinochet* (in its turn divided on its point) as based primarily on CAT.[87] This puts *Germany* v. *Italy* in conflict with *Arrest Warrant*, where such impact of treaties like CAT was not admitted.

On the one hand, CAT has no immunity reservation in it and cannot have been intended to defer to it. It could prevail over immunities as *lex*

[83] *Arrest Warrant*, ICJ Reports 2002, para. 59.

[84] Immunity of State Officials, Memorandum by the Secretariat, A/CN/4/596, 31 March 2008, paras. 204–7; *Second Report*, 50–1.

[85] IDI Resolution on Universal Jurisdiction, Krakow Session, 2005.

[86] *Arrest Warrant*, para. 59.

[87] *Germany* v. *Italy*, para. 87.

posterior. But then, immunities might be seen as *lex specialis*, referring to a particular class of torture suspects that could claim immunities, which not all torture suspects can. While the International Court's approach is not entirely satisfactory, the evidence for viable alternatives is not straightforwardly available either. This may explain why most fora are unconvinced about extra-territorial jurisdiction displacing immunities, for immunities *ratione personae* would also be at risk.

It has to be concluded that the position that CAT (a) classes torture as an official act whereby it (b) ranks it as an act *jure imperii* and then (c) removes immunity for that very same act through establishing extra-territorial criminal jurisdiction over it is a too nuanced and complex rule, the straightforward support for which cannot be found in the *ratio decidendi* of *Pinochet*. It moreover stands to no reason why the Convention would pronounce on the issue of the scope of immunity, if it does not on its face, and was never intended to, deal with the subject-matter of immunities. Or alternatively, if jurisdiction established under CAT displaces applicable immunities, why could it not displace *ratione personae* immunities of acting heads of State and government?

The proper approach for the *ratione materiae* immunities would, therefore, be to revert, after establishing that jurisdiction over the person under CAT exists, to the above-examined restrictive doctrine of immunity under international law to see whether the act of torture involved could be classed as a sovereign act. CAT does not address, let alone provide the answer to, this latter question.

(ii) Universal civil jurisdiction under Article 14 CAT

According to Article 14(1) CAT: 'Each State Party shall ensure in its legal system that the victim of an act of torture obtains redress and has an enforceable right to fair and adequate compensation.' This clause includes no restriction *ratione loci*. Redress should be made available to any victim of torture, regardless of the locus of the act.

In *Bouzari* and *Jones* this extra-territorial effect was not accepted, not because the relevant national courts denied the inherent potential of Article 14 to displace immunities, but because Article 14 was seen to relate only to torture committed within the forum State's territory.[88] But the UN Committee against Torture has confirmed, in the aftermath of

[88] *Bouzari* v. *Islamic Republic or Iran* (Court of Appeal for Ontario), 30 June 2004, Docket: C38295, paras. 72–82, (per Goudge JA); *Jones* (HL), paras. 20 (*per* Lord Bingham), 46 (per Lord Hoffmann).

Bouzari, that the scope of Article 14 is not limited to torture committed within the forum's territory.[89]

More recently, the Committee's General Comment No. 3 specified that 'the application of Article 14 is not limited to victims who were harmed in the territory of the State party or by or against nationals of the State party'.[90] The duty to implement Article 14 in line with General Comment No. 3 has then been reiterated in relation to the UK specifically.[91]

National courts in *Bouzari* and *Jones* have, therefore, effectively engaged in a unilateral interpretation of Article 14, reading in the limitation that is not there. That the Committee's views are not inherently binding is, quite simply, immaterial. The Committee has been set up through the agreement of all States-parties to CAT and is, on that basis, in charge of implementing the Convention. Its views as to its content are supposed to be better than those of States-parties put forward unilaterally. This is all the more obvious if all the Committee has done, both in relation to Canada and the UK, is to reaffirm the duty of both States to act in line with the plain and ordinary meaning of the obligation contained in Article 14.

B. *State immunity and* jus cogens

The essence of peremptory norms of international law (*jus cogens*) is their hierarchical superiority over conflicting rules of international law. Consequently, if and to the extent international law includes a rule on State immunity, it should be disapplied whenever the enforcement of a peremptory norm is at stake. A general statement of incompatibility between *jus cogens* and immunities has been given by Lord Millett in *Pinochet* to the effect that:

> The international community had created an offence for which immunity ratione materiae could not possibly be available. International law cannot be supposed to have established a crime having the character of a *jus cogens* and at the same time to have provided an immunity which is co-extensive with the obligation it seeks to impose.[92]

[89] UN Committee against Torture, Observations of the Report of Canada, CAT/C/CO/34/CAN, paras. 4(g) and 5(f).

[90] General Comment No. 3 (2012), para. 22.

[91] Concluding observations on the fifth periodic report of the United Kingdom, adopted by the Committee at its fiftieth session (6–31 May 2013), para. 17.

[92] [2000] 1 AC 278.

One way in which immunities are impacted upon by *jus cogens* is that the acts prohibited by *jus cogens* offend against the public policy of the international legal system and therefore cannot count as sovereign acts that attract immunity. This reasoning fits perfectly with the overall rationale of the restrictive doctrine of immunity, as discussed above, as relating to acts not unique to State authority. Instead, these acts can be committed by anyone, whether or not in a position of authority, for which reason they should not attract immunity.

Another way *jus cogens* impacts immunities is the direct hierarchical primacy. This line of reasoning was put forward by the minority in *Al-Adsani*, to the effect that the rules of *jus cogens* prevail over all conflicting rules. Therefore:

> The prohibition of torture, being a rule of *jus cogens*, acts in the international sphere and deprives the rule of sovereign immunity of all its legal effects in that sphere. The criminal or civil nature of the domestic proceedings is immaterial. The jurisdictional [and procedural] bar is lifted by the very interaction of the international rules involved, and the national judge cannot admit a plea of immunity.[93]

Courts that have denied the primacy of *jus cogens* over immunities have not advocated any coherent basis for such approach. The European Court in *Al-Adsani* has adopted an evidentiary approach that while in relation to criminal proceedings the impact of *jus cogens* on immunities was recognised in international practice, the same was not the case in relation to civil proceedings. The House of Lords in *Jones*, and the ICJ in *Germany* v. *Italy*, have considered that immunities are of procedural character and not affected by substantive rules of *jus cogens*. All three courts have, however, distinguished the criminal proceedings aspect as per *Pinochet* rather than contradicting it. But their reasoning rang hollow, given that criminal immunities are just as 'procedural' as civil immunities, and if *jus cogens* can bite on the former, there is no reason why it cannot bite on the latter. This runs, then, into the issue that the (non)sovereign nature of acts for the purposes of the restrictive doctrine is a pre-proceeding issue and that if an act contradicting *jus cogens* is not *jure imperii* in one type of proceedings, it cannot be so in other kind of proceedings either.

The approach in *Arrest Warrant* that immunities are of a procedural nature was premised on the availability of alternative remedies to which condition the subsequent pro-immunity judicial practice did not adhere.

[93] Joint Dissenting Opinion, *Al-Adsani*, paras. 1, 3–4.

Lords Bingham and Hoffmann suggested in *Jones* that State immunity does not really contradict the *jus cogens* prohibition of torture but merely diverts its enforcement to other fora.[94] In the same spirit, criminal immunities would be no less procedural and jurisdictional so as to merely divert, in the language of pro-immunity proponents, the issue to another forum. That is pretty much the Special Rapporteur's position.[95] This is one more instance evidencing that the frequently repeated civil/criminal distinction does not work.

The reality is, moreover, that no diversion of the issue to another mode of settlement ever takes place in practice in cases where immunity is upheld. The outcome of the upholding of immunity in the cases of *Al-Adsani* v *UK*, *Bouzari*, *Jones* and *Germany* v. *Italy* is that the victims were left without any available remedy. This position leads precisely to the condonation and encouragement of the initial act of torture and total legal security for future acts of torture. If the grant of immunity to the State establishes the legal position that – as between the forum State and the perpetrating State – there are no legal consequences for the relevant act of torture, then this position automatically entails the position that in the mutual relations of those two States the prohibition of torture does not operate as a legal prohibition and takes no effect as a legal rule. The overall essence of the substance-jurisdiction divide is, therefore, conceptually incoherent, ethically controversial and practically unsound.[96]

The principal and mainline effect of *jus cogens* norms is always consequential, that is relates to facts, situations, rights and entitlements established, or purported to be established, after a substantive peremptory rule has been breached. In all areas where *jus cogens* applies, it deals with situations arising after the wrongful act. In addition to the VCLT, the areas of State responsibility, statehood and recognition, unilateral acts, waiver and acquiescence, or acts of international organisations, are virtually

[94] *Jones* (HL), paras. 24 and 44 (both referring to H. Fox, *The Law of State Immunity* (1st edn., Oxford: Oxford University Press, 2001)).

[95] The Special Rapporteur suggests that 'Peremptory norms criminalizing international crimes lie within the sphere of substantive law. The norm concerning immunity is, as noted above, procedural in character, does not affect criminalization of the acts under discussion, *does not abrogate liability for them* and does not even fully exclude criminal jurisdiction in respect of these acts', at 39, para. 64 (emphasis original).

[96] This view is also developed in cases and in writings without properly addressing the underlying issues of normativity, normative hierarchy and normative conflict. On which see A. Orakhelashvili, 'The Classification of International Legal Rules: A Reply to Stefan Talmon', (2013) 26 *LJIL*, 89.

unanimous in recognising the effect of *jus cogens* in relation to situations produced after the violation of the relevant peremptory norm.[97] The principal effect of *jus cogens* is to consequentially deny the rights, privileges and qualifications the relevant State action would command but for the peremptory status of the rule that the conduct in question violates. Indeed, Article 41 of the Articles on State Responsibility refers to a 'situation created by the breach' of *jus cogens*, which is impunity and lack of remedies as an immediate consequence of the denial of immunities in comparable situations. The whole approach in *Jones*, as well as *Germany* v. *Italy*, recognises precisely that situation as lawful, and is essentially aimed at perpetuating that situation.

This runs precisely into the issue of derogation from *jus cogens* through the grant of immunities. The non-derogability of peremptory norms is not limited to the ambit of Article 53 VCLT. Instead, Article 53 is one specific expression of non-derogability that operates throughout the international legal system covering the areas highlighted above. Derogation can be initiated through unilateral acts or practice, formally or informally.

Derogation is inherently a phenomenon that intends to preserve, on a general plane, the validity of the rule derogated from, yet prevent its applicability to a case, or class of cases, to which the derogation in question relates. Immunities attempt doing to relevant peremptory norms just that. For our purposes, derogation from *jus cogens* norms through the grant of immunity to the defendant projects – *inter se* and *in casu* – the putative legal position that the prohibition under the relevant *jus cogens* norm shall take no legal effect and an act committed in contravention with that norm shall operate as a lawful act attracting privileges and rights that lawful acts could ordinarily attract. If *jus cogens* norms were merely substantive prohibitions, it could be argued with the same effect that a treaty contrary to *jus cogens* could be upheld as valid because it does not go to the primary norm containing prohibition of the relevant act but merely prevents the rule that outlaws that act from being invocable and enforceable in mutual relations between States-parties to that treaty. Or that an entity established through the aggressive war could be recognised as a State, much as the prohibition of the use of force remains intact on a general plane.

[97] ILC's Articles 40–1 on State Responsibility, ILC Report (2001), GAOR, Fifty-sixth session, Supplement No. 10 (A/56/10). States shall not 'recognise as lawful a situation created by a serious breach' of *jus cogens* (Article 41). ILC Guide on Unilateral Acts, A/61/10, Article 8; Articles 41–2, ILC Articles on the Responsibility of International Organisations, 2nd reading, 2011, A/66/10.

If, as was the case with *Al-Adsani* and *Jones*, the UK gives Kuwait or Saudi Arabia total legal security for their acts of torture as far as UK–Saudi and UK–Kuwaiti bilateral relations are concerned, the effect is the same as would be if a treaty with Saudi Arabia and Kuwait were to be concluded to the effect that the international prohibition of torture has no effect in UK–Saudi and UK–Kuwaiti relations. The only difference would be one of form, consisting in a written agreement as opposed to the agreement through State practice. If the outcome in question could be lawfully secured through informal practice, it could also be secured through a written agreement. In either case, and in both criminal and civil proceedings, liability for the breach of a *jus cogens* rule would be abrogated, in a way opposite to the ILC Special Rapporteur's above thesis.

Furthermore, if it were correct that peremptory norms are merely substantive rules incapable of affecting the immunity, it has to invariably apply to civil and criminal proceedings, and State and official immunity alike. Yet, the position of several courts as well as the Institute of International Law demonstrates that such generalised assumption is unsustainable.

Apart from misreading the impact of *jus cogens* in *Pinochet*, the ICJ in *Germany* v. *Italy* did not address the 2009 Naples IDI Resolution, which upholds the lifting of immunity in civil proceedings for conduct that constitutes international crime (Article III). It relies on 'the underlying conflict between immunity from jurisdiction of States and their agents and claims arising from international crimes', and intends to contribute to 'a resolution of that conflict' (preamble). The Resolution thus refers to the existence of normative conflict between the two sets of rules. On what basis other than *jus cogens* would, one wonders, the criminality of a relevant act prevail in this normative conflict? And the Resolution specifies no such alternative basis, speaking instead of the normative hierarchy pure and simple.

After *Germany* v. *Italy* judicial practice has continued confirming the incompatibility between immunities and *jus cogens*, and the latter's primacy over the former. The Swiss Federal Tribunal reiterated the same view.[98] The US Court of Appeals for the Fourth Circuit likewise confirmed in *Samantar* that: 'Because this case involves acts that violated *jus cogens norms*, including torture, extrajudicial killings and prolonged arbitrary imprisonment of politically and ethnically disfavored groups,

[98] Judgment of 25 July 2012 (case no. BB.2011.140), paras. 5.3.5 and 5.4.3.

we conclude that Samantar is not entitled to conduct based official immunity under the common law, which in this area incorporates international law.'[99]

The assertion of substance versus jurisdiction dichotomy is, therefore, premised on a *political choice* made by a court or by a writer to support the grant of immunity that is *politically desirable* under the circumstances. The view that requires denying immunity on the basis of *jus cogens* is, on the other hand, premised solely on the continuation of the normative effect that *jus cogens* already has in other areas of international law.

There are further advantages of the *jus cogens* approach over the above-examined 'jurisdictional' approach, in that the latter focuses on exercising jurisdiction then and there, while the former focuses on the normative integrity of the relevant peremptory norm. As we saw above, the jurisdiction-based treaty primacy over immunities could be too blanket, and set at risk the *ratione personae* immunities of an acting Head of State. On the other hand, the impact of *jus cogens* is not that blanket, for it only requires preventing immunity rules from derogating from *jus cogens* rules, and thus fits comfortably with the approach developed in paragraph 61 of the *Arrest Warrant* case, preserving *ratione personae* immunities of acting high-level officials intact, not as a permanent state of affairs perpetuating impunity, but only preventing prosecution in particular jurisdictions, and then only while the official's term of office lasts. The whole question is not about whether the State in question should exercise jurisdiction over the relevant person in the particular place and time, but whether the exercise or decline of that jurisdiction will prevent the operation of the relevant *jus cogens* rules as legal rules, undermine their normative content and effect, and make them inoperable in relation to the relevant internationally wrongful act. Immunities *ratione personae* could thus be preserved without causing a derogation from *jus cogens*.

Overall, whether immunities are admitted for a violation of *jus cogens* on a permanent and general, or temporary and special, basis cannot be without importance to the question whether a derogation from the relevant *jus cogens* rule takes place. Immunities *ratione personae* do not inevitably derogate from *jus cogens* because they: (a) do not require that the relevant acts are official functions, as they are not premised on that basis at all; (b) they inherently admit the possibility of prosecution in other jurisdictions or in the same jurisdiction after the official ceases to be in office; and (c) they do not entail impunity. On the other hand,

[99] *Bashe Abdi Yousuf* v. *Mohamed Ali Samantar*, No. 11-1479, 2 November 2012, at 23.

immunities *ratione personae* do derogate from *jus cogens* because they: (a) project the relevant crimes and violations as official and sovereign acts; (b) project a permanently opposable legal position that the act of the State in question could never be adjudicated upon abroad; and (c) invariably entail impunity and the lack of remedies.

This way *jus cogens* offers a compromised view further compatible with developments in judicial practice, because both *Pinochet* and *Arrest Warrant* did single out *ratione personae* immunities as a special category. *Jus cogens* can accommodate and preserve *ratione personae* immunities of a limited number of high-level officials, while displacing *ratione materiae* immunities of both States and their officials.

C. Convergence between CAT and jus cogens

The above analysis still leaves one aspect of CAT to be gone into because, as we saw above, the ordinary meaning of Articles 5 and 7 CAT establish the duty to prosecute torturers and should, in principle, require displacing any applicable immunity, much as this was not straightforwardly accepted in judicial practice. The principal dilemma produced by the divergent practice is that while CAT as a treaty should prevail over immunities, the latter could in principle be seen as *lex specialis*, in relation to which the primacy of treaties over other rules may not necessarily help.

On the other hand, if we view Articles 5 and 7 CAT as expressive of the general doctrine of *jus cogens* in relation to prosecution of core international crimes, they could, then, secure the outcome that a treaty qua treaty is unlikely to achieve. This general doctrine was mirrored in Lord Hope's observation in *Pinochet* that:

> the prohibition of [torture] which has acquired the status under international law of jus cogens . . . compels all states to refrain from such conduct under any circumstances and imposes an obligation erga omnes to punish such conduct.[100]

And as it happens, Articles 5 and 7 CAT do very much the same thing.

There is increasing recognition in practice of the growing and sustained convergence as between normative regimes under CAT and under *jus cogens*, and their interchangeable use. The European Court in *Othman* specified that 'UNCAT reflects the clear will of the international community to further entrench the ius cogens prohibition on torture by

[100] [2000] 1 AC 242.

taking a series of measures to eradicate torture and remove all incentive for its practice'.[101] This point further undermines the argument that the denial of the immunity of a former head of State by the House of Lords in *Pinochet* was undertaken on the basis of CAT as completely separate from *jus cogens*. CAT and *jus cogens* were also interchangeably used by the House of Lords in *A* v. *Secretary of State*.[102]

Under this approach, the effect on immunities under Articles 5 and 7 CAT is merely to reflect and reinforce whatever consequences obtain from the fact that torture is a wrongful act and crime outlawed under a rule of *jus cogens*. Once jurisdiction under CAT would be established over the case, the denial of immunity would be justified only if doing otherwise would entail impunity for the underlying crime or atrocity, which in terms of normative hierarchy would amount to a derogation from the underlying rule of *jus cogens* the way that makes that rule unenforceable and imapplicable in relation to that relevant case. *Ratione personae* immunities would be preserved as per *Arrest Warrant*, unlike *ratione materiae* immunities.

6. The position at English law

The outcome obtained through the above analysis of international law applicable to immunities needs now to be applied to the position under the ordinary sources of English law. In relation to common law, we need to see how far the international legal position is incorporated into the English common law. In relation to statutory law, we need to ascertain the impact of the SIA. As we are also addressing the continuing effect of previous court decisions, we need to examine the doctrine of precedent for that purpose.

A. *State immunity and policy considerations before English courts*

When focusing on the decisions of English courts regarding State immunity, it is not easy to ascertain to what extent the political risks thought to be involved in the relevant case are among those that enter the minds of those who adjudicate. Yet it is undeniable that transnational human rights claims inevitably look different from ordinary torts, in terms of the remoteness from the forum, identity of perpetrators and applicable law.

[101] *Othman* v. *UK*, 8139/09, 17 January 2012, para. 266.

[102] *A* v. *Secretary of State* [2005] UKHL 71, 8 December 2005.

All this cannot fail to generate fears as to possible adverse consequences of the relevant litigation that both decision-makers and commentators would, subconsciously at least, be concerned with. The treatment on these issues would therefore be incomplete without addressing these policy considerations.

This process could also involve a complex balance of interests entailing morally controversial outcomes, for instance by prioritising political factors over humanitarian considerations. It is, among others, for this reason, that the express articulation of policy argument in judicial reasoning is considerably rare; where it appears it is mostly used as part of applying already established legal principles[103] and in relation to the foreign State immunities it is practically absent. Ordinarily, English courts are expected to separate law from politics and not to enter into assessing the political merits of the issues underlying the relevant litigation. They are expected to leave political considerations to other branches of the government, and only apply the existing law to underlying facts.[104] In relation to international law specifically, the use of policy arguments could not suitably happen in English courts. Unlike areas of English law such as tort law, English courts do not create and develop public international law the way they do with common law. They merely reflect the law consensually adopted at the inter-State level, which the national authority cannot unilaterally curtail or modify.[105]

As for the specific risks, it may be suggested that allowing civil claims against foreign sovereigns could lead to the deterioration of inter-State relations. But it is far from obvious how far it could be a judicial task to draw the balance on complex issues of the dynamics of international relations on which the Judiciary possesses no obvious expertise. More generally, there is no clear evidence to suggest that any serious deterioration of inter-State relations is likely if immunity is denied. In some other contexts, the possibility of the deterioration of UK-Saudi relations *might* have motivated the outcome in the *BAE* case before the House of Lords, but the outcome of the House of Lords decision was framed, however unsustainably, in legal terms, namely through reading the national security exception in the relevant international agreement that, quite simply,

[103] See *McLoughlin* v. *O'Brian* [1983] 1 AC 410 at 430 (per Lord Scarman); see more generally John Bell, *Policy Arguments in Judicial Decisions* (Oxford: Oxford University Press, 1983).

[104] See Lord Templemann in *Nottinghamshire County Council* v. *Secretary State for the Environment* [1986] AC 240 at 265–6.

[105] See more specifically subsection B below.

was not there.[106] If policy considerations were used here as premise, then the outcome of the case was based not just on the use of those policy considerations but on letting them bend the applicable law.

On a broader plane, not every irritant could inevitably entail a deterioration of inter-State relations. As deterioration is a bilateral matter, it must also be queried whether the outcome of cases like *Al-Adsani* and *Jones* and the payment of the – rather modest if the income and revenues of the relevant States are considered – compensation to victims would amount to grounds sufficient for Kuwait and Saudi Arabia to revise their traditionally good relations with the UK. Fears like these are based on no more than speculation. The deterioration of bilateral relations, or interference with the defendant State's sovereignty in relation to its resources, is not more likely than in the case of litigation drawing on the relevant State's commercial interests and resulting in much higher expense and damages, yet falling within the letter of the SIA, such as commercial, territorial tort or employment-related exceptions. A more recent instance of Gary McKinnon not being extradited to the United States, having been wanted there for the allegations of the unlawful access to sensitive military computers of the US government, could be just as irritating at the inter-State level as would be the transnational human rights litigation involving the United States as defendant. For, McKinnon was wanted in the United States in the public interest, while granting compensation to Al-Adsani and Jones would never have gone as far as impeding Kuwait and Saudi Arabia in pursuing the line of their foreign and domestic policies that they determine in the exercise of their sovereignty.[107]

The projected risk of the multiplication of claims known as litigation flood is, too, merely theoretical. The denial of immunity would in practice have the preventive impact on the governments engaging in torture whose assets abroad would be exposed, and could lead to reforms in the relevant State's domestic law and practice that will reduce the occurrence of torture by the same State in the future.[108] Less torture means less litigation abroad. Moreover, English courts have been generally sceptical about such fears as

[106] *BAE* (HL), [2008] UKHL 60, 30 July 2008, para. 46 (per Lord Bingham).

[107] More recently, the UK seems to have accepted the risk of irritation in bilateral relations as a consequence of domestic judicial proceedings in the UK, in relation to Mongolia and Nepal, as in *Khurts Bat*. See also the report regarding the prosecution of a Nepalese official for torture: www.guardian.co.uk/law/2013/jan/06/uk-defends-prosecute-nepalese-colonel?INTCMP=SRCH.

[108] To illustrate other related contexts, proceedings in the *Pinochet* case before English courts played the role of the catalyst towards altering the domestic perception to accountability

to floods of litigation. As Lord Edmund-Davies observed in *McLoughlin* v. *O'Brian*, concerned with the extension of tortuous liability, he was 'unconvinced that the number and area of claims in "shock" cases would be substantially increased or enlarged were the respondents here held liable'. He had 'often seen [the floodgates argument] disproved by later events'. Lord Scarman seconded that '[t]he "floodgates" argument may be exaggerated'.[109]

Ordinarily, thus, English courts refuse letting policy reasons affect the outcome of the case so as to modify the applicability of the established sources of law. In *Dorset Yacht*, Lord Reid referred to the American case-law that exempted prison officials from civil liability because of the heavy risky nature of their jobs, but observed that 'Her Majesty's servants are made of sterner stuff', and had 'no hesitation in rejecting this argument' seeing 'no good ground in public policy for giving this immunity to a government department'.[110]

B. *Common law and the doctrine of incorporation*

From the eighteenth century onwards, the view championed by Sir William Blackstone and accepted in the English legal system has been that international law as such and as a whole forms part of English law. The doctrine of incorporation served as the basis on which English courts initially applied the absolute doctrine of State immunity.[111] Subsequently, in the *Trendtex* and *Congreso* litigation, the incorporation approach has been applied to the newer restrictive doctrine as part of international, and now of English, law.

Dealing with the older rule of absolute immunity in *Cristina*, Lord Atkin referred to the 'propositions of international law engrafted into our domestic law which seem to me to be well established and to be beyond dispute'. That position applied both to the sovereign's person and to their property, both to *in rem* and *in personam* claims.[112] Lord Macmillan similarly entertained no doubt as to the direct effect of international

in Latin American countries, see generally N. Roht-Ariazza, *The Pinochet Effect: Transnational Justice in the Age of Human Rights* (Philidelphia, PA: University of Pennsylvania Press, 2005). More recently, the litigation saga concerning Abu-Qatada caused the Jordanian Government to amend the Constitution and ban the use in courts of the evidence obtained through torture: www.bbc.co.uk/news/uk-20295754.

[109] *McLoughlin*, 425 (per Lord Edmund-Davies), 431 (per Lord Scarman).

[110] *Dorset Yacht* [1970] AC 1004, 1032–3.

[111] See, e.g.,*Gagara* [1919] P 95; *Porto Alexandre* [1920] P 30.

[112] *Cristina* [1938] AC 485, 490–1.

law in the English legal system, with the implication that the domestic effect should be given to international legal rules to the extent that they have been agreed upon as between sovereign States. For, 'such a principle must be an importation from international law'. The position was more complicated when 'there is no proved consensus of international opinion or practice to this effect' and when 'the subject is one on which divergent views exist and have been expressed among the nations'.[113]

In *Cristina*, their Lordships have managed to avoid resolving the conflict as between the earlier cases of *Parlement Belge*, where the outcome as to immunities had been differentiated in terms of the function of a ship involved in the relevant proceedings,[114] and *Porto Alexandre*, where a more absolute approach was adopted; for the ship involved in *Cristina* had been requisitioned by the Spanish government for public purposes.[115]

The signs of the acceptance of the restrictive doctrine were already shown by English courts in the nineteenth century, considerably earlier than the absolute immunity rule was definitely abandoned. In the *Charkieh* case, Sir Robert Phillimore – adjudicating, again, from the perspective of the incorporation doctrine – considered that:

> I am not prevented from holding, what it appears to me the justice of the case, would otherwise require, that proceedings of this kind, *in rem*, may in some cases at least be instituted without any violation of international law, though the owner of the *res* be in the category of persons privileged from personal suit . . . [however] a proceeding *in rem* cannot be instituted against the property of a sovereign or ambassador if the *res* can in any fair sense be said to be connected with the *jus coronae* of the sovereign.[116]

This provided at least an initial inference that sovereign activity is what the sovereign is ordinarily meant to be doing, not what he in fact does. Most importantly, Sir Robert Phillimore specified that:

> No principle of international law, and no decided case, and no dictum of jurists of which I am aware, has gone so far as to authorize a sovereign to

113 *Ibid.*, 497–8; the incorporation approach was also upheld by Lord Wright, *ibid.*, 502.

114 On which the House of Lords has subsequently observed in *Philippine Admiral* that 'the judgment of the Court of Appeal [in *Parlement Belge*] – delivered by Brett LJ. – has sometimes been taken as saying that a sovereign can claim immunity for vessels owned by him even if they are admittedly being used wholly or substantially for trading purposes. In their Lordships' view the judgment does not lay down that wide proposition at all', *Philippine Admiral* [1977] AC 373, 392 (*per* Lord Cross).

115 *Cristina*, 496, 498 (per Lords Thankerton and Macmillan); but see *Philippine Admiral*, 394, for drawing the contrast between those two earlier cases. Therefore, *Porto Alexandre* was not followed.

116 *Charkieh* [1872–75] 4 LR 59, 93.

> assume the character of a trader, when it is for his benefit; and when he incurs an obligation to a private subject to throw off, if I may so speak, his disguise, and appear as a sovereign, claiming for his own benefit, and to the injury of a private person, for the first time, all the attributes of his character; while it would be easy to accumulate authorities for the contrary position.[117]

This reasoning leads to the consideration of the issue of how, in the first place, the sovereign enters the marketplace, or more generally private relations. In whichever way you enter it, so you carry on. This approach got further developed in *Congreso* where Lord Wilberforce emphasised that if an act can be performed by private persons it is no longer a sovereign act. Applying this test to serious human rights violations would also exclude them from the scope of *jure imperii* acts.

The 2006 House of Lords decision in *Jones, Milling & Pritchard* has suggested some qualifications to the doctrine of incorporation. The principal findings were that the international crime of aggression was not automatically criminalised under English law to enable domestic prosecutions to take place; and, more generally, international law was not part of English law, but one of its sources.[118] However, the judgment has not explained the difference between the two options. It is indeed difficult to see how international law could be a source of English law without being its part, and vice versa. This obscurity in reasoning compromises the potential of *Jones, Milling & Pritchard* to impact our continuous understanding of the doctrine of incorporation. Even assuming, for the sake of argument, that the approach in this case was correct, it is only about the specific issue of criminalisation. Therefore *Jones* must be seen as being constrained to its context and as having little legal relevance for other areas of public international law including the law of immunities.

On a broader plane, English courts are unlikely to abandon the incorporation doctrine, even in the face of some of the current thinking that the 'dualistic' approach should be used to separate the domestic application of international law from the accountability of the United Kingdom for the breaches of international law on the inter-State plane and before international courts and tribunals.[119] The abandonment of the fuller version of the doctrine of incorporation would entail two negative implications. In the first place, declining to apply the relevant international law

[117] *Ibid.*, 99–100.

[118] *R* v. *Jones, Milling et al.*, House of Lords [2006] UKHL 16, 29 March 2006.

[119] See, for instance, P. Sales and J. Clement, 'International Law in Domestic Courts: A Developing Framework', (2008) 124 *LQR*, 388.

domestically could, under circumstances, constitute the evidence that a breach of international law has been committed and that domestic courts have essentially ratified it.[120] In the second place, such 'dualism' could potentially lead to isolationism, diminishing the potential of English courts to contribute to the development of State practice internationally. For, as Brierly has wisely reminded us, 'international law is a customary law and it is developed by agencies which include, but are not limited to, the English Courts'.[121] Evading the domestic effect of customary international law, whether through the *Jones, Pritchard & Milling* route, or through the application of the SIA,[122] essentially evidences the unwillingness of domestic courts to apply international law to underlying facts. It is highly presumptive, to say the least, that the cases decided on the basis of that which excludes international law from the judicial focus could validly amount to State practice as part of custom-generation internationally.

Dualism, on its valid version, relates to the origin and sources of relevant rules. For the purposes of English law dualism only means that international law is not produced by the same sources of English law as are domestic legislation and common law. It is produced elsewhere, internationally, and then incorporated into English law. The traditional version of the incorporation doctrine is essentially premised on the dualist tradition, which means that English courts give domestic effect to the set of rules that has not been produced by the domestic law-giver, and make it part of English law.[123] This is different from the domestic transformation of international treaties where, unlike the common law incorporation of customary international law, the domestic legislator creates a new domestic legislative rule to reflect that which has been internationally enacted on a separate basis.

C. *The impact of the 1978 State Immunity Act*

When the selection as between common and statutory law is conducted in terms of which of them should be applied to the underlying claims

120 According to Article 4 of the ILC's Draft on State responsibility, a breach of international law can be committed by any State organ, including judicial organs. See 2 *ILC Yearbook* (2001), 40 (Article 4 and its commentary).

121 J. L. Brierly, 'International Law in England', (1935) 51 *LQR*, 24 at 34'.

122 See the next sub-section for the SIA more generally.

123 This is further reflected in the principle, expounded by Dicey, that English law is not necessarily limited to rules produced exclusively by domestic authorities but includes all rules that English courts apply, regardless of their origin. A. V. Dicey, *A Digest of the Law of England with the Reference to the Conflict of Laws* (London: Steven & Sons, 1896), 6ff.

relating to sovereign immunity, two important issues are at stake. In the first place, as we already saw, the common law standard that incorporates general international law requires the application of the functional approach to immunities under which the acts that constitute the proper exercises of governmental authority do attract immunity and the ones that do not fall within such category do not. The SIA eschews such classification and instead turns to the 'general rule versus specific exceptions' approach, under which all that does not fall within the specified statutory exceptions, and whatever the underlying nature of the relevant act or transaction, will attract immunity under the general statutory rule of immunity. Results could then be substantially different depending on which of these approaches is taken.

In the second place, the adherence to the SIA could entail the legitimation, through the backdoor, of the domestic standing and applicability of some international conventions that may not be apt for the use in domestic courts, given that internationally they do not constitute the applicable law as between the UK and the relevant foreign States. This concerns, in the first place, the ECSI. This also applies to the 2004 Convention, which, despite some enthusiastic references in judicial practice,[124] is neither signed nor ratified by the substantial number of States to turn it into the applicable law. Even if it were to gather the required thirty ratifications, it would only be applicable law *inter se*.

Apart from these treaties that are either not in force or have a rather limited scope of application *ratione personae*, there is no evidence whatsoever that the general, or customary, international law – which still, and inevitably, prevails apart from the narrow scope of inter-State relations where the relevant convention could prevail as *lex specialis* – subscribes to any version of that 'general immunity versus specific exceptions' approach that the two conventions uphold. Again, this may lead foreign States being accorded immunity where applicable international law does not require doing so or, alternatively, denying such immunities as may be due to be accorded. In fact, Article 24 of the ECSI effectively recognises that the Convention regime is the special one that purports to derogate from the general international law that applies in relation to non-parties and would, but for the Convention regime, apply *inter se* as well. The possibility is thus provided for to part, for the purposes of the relevant case, with the 'general immunity versus specific exceptions' approach and revert to the fall-back position under general international law that focuses on the

[124] E.g. by Lords Bingham and Hoffmann in *Jones* (HL), paras. 27 and 46.

sovereign and non-sovereign acts. As Sir Ian Sinclair has suggested: 'This optional regime was included because certain States already applying the rule of relative immunity were afraid that some acts *jure gestionis* might fall outside the catalogue of cases of non-immunity, thereby restricting the jurisdiction of their courts',[125] and thus manifesting the understanding that the underlying regimes of immunity are dual.

Ways for resolving the dilemma within the English legal system have been suggested. As Lord Phillips has pointed out in *NML* v. *Argentina*, the SIA was enacted to give domestic effect to the ECSI. However, '[t]he ECSI does not give effect to the restrictive doctrine of sovereign immunity'.[126] As Lord Goff had earlier observed in *Kuwait Air Co*, the overall impact of Article 24 ECSI, which enables States-parties to declare accordingly, entails the 'inapplicability in English law of the principle of sovereign immunity in cases in which the sovereign was not acting *jure imperii*'.[127]

The SIA is obviously the outcome of Parliament's exercise of its legislative supremacy. However, the ascertainment of the content of legislation, and the impact thereof on common law, is an entirely judicial task. In the English legal system, legislative supremacy operates subject to the requirements of the rule of law,[128] and law is what courts say it is.[129]

In order not to let domestic proceedings distort the outcomes required under international law, the proper interpretation of the SIA assumes a major importance. Purely as a matter of statutory construction, the underlying classical rules – literal, mischief and golden – are not arranged in a hierarchical manner. The literal approach seems to have prevailed in some previous cases before English courts, to the effect that the SIA was deemed to be a 'comprehensive code' on State immunity, precluding domestic courts from addressing the distinction between sovereign and non-sovereign acts as international law requires to be taken into account.[130] On the other hand, other means of statutory interpretation

125 I. Sinclair, 'The European Convention on State Immunity', (1973) 22 *ICLQ*, 254 at 268.

126 *NML* v. *Argentina* [2011] UKSC 31, 6 July 2011, para. 37 (per Lord Phillips).

127 *Kuwait Air Co* [1995] 1 WLR 1147 at 1158 (per Lord Goff).

128 *Jackson* v. *Attorney General* [2005] UKHL 56, para. 107 (per Lord Hope).

129 H. R. W. Wade and C. F. Forsyth, *Administrative Law* (10th edn., Oxford: Oxford University Press, 2009), 26.

130 See the following British and American cases: *Siderman de Blake* v. *Argentina*, 103 ILR 455; *Princz* v. *Federal Republic of Germany*, 33 ILM (1994), 1483; *Smith et al.* v. *Libyan Arab Jamahiriya*, 36 ILM (1997), 100; *Al-Adsani* v. *Kuwait*, 107 ILR 536. The point made here is the same as above in note 118 and the accompanying text.

could be helpful to understand what options are available to apply or not to apply the SIA to the relevant immunity claim.

When the SIA was being enacted and deliberated upon in Parliament, Lord Wilberforce and Lord Denning expressed some misgivings about it. Both their Lordships spoke against universalising the regional regime of the ECSI and making it applicable to all States.[131] Lord Denning went further and suggested that the State immunity bill had to be put on hold because (a) it did not reflect international law as it then stood (along with the distinction between functional and statutory tests as detailed above); and (b) it aimed at conserving the legal position which was in a constant state of development.[132]

The key question for the construction of the SIA should thus be to ascertain whether the legislator would have intended to universalise the very restricted regime of the ECSI, that is make it internationally opposable to States that neither signed nor ratified it, with the far-reaching implications contradicting the *pacta tertiis* principle. What militates against this assumption is that there is no entitlement to impose, through the sources of domestic law, on foreign States the law that is not internationally opposable to them. In the *WHO-Egypt* case, the ICJ applied this approach to the relationship between the World Health Organization (WHO) and Egypt in terms of relocating the WHO regional office from Alexandria. Neither the WHO nor Egypt could externalise their unilaterally produced law on each other, and the matter of the relocation of the WHO office could only be governed by international law that bound the two entities together, not by Egyptian law, nor by the WHO's internal rules.[133] This pattern is even more pressing with inter-State relations. The law applicable between the UK and foreign States impleaded before English courts is that which binds the UK and those foreign States together: those rules of public international law to which both relevant States have given their consent. The persistence with the application, through the domestic legislation, to foreign States of the rules to which they may not have consented could prove counter-productive. Despite the dogma of 'dualism', when applying the SIA, English courts effectively pronounce on international and inter-State relations, which are governed by public international law in the first

[131] It will be noted that the ECSI has only eight States-parties and thus it was not applicable to the major controversies focused upon in this chapter.

[132] See, generally, the Hansard (HL) volume 388 cc51–78, 17 January 1978; and volume 949 cc405–20, 3 May 1978 (interventions by Lords Wilberforce and Denning).

[133] Interpretation of the Agreement of 25 March 1951 between the WHO and Egypt, Advisory Opinion of 20 December 1980, ICJ Reports, 1980, 73.

place, and which may not always overlap with the position that the SIA purports to establish.

To illustrate, China, which adheres to absolute immunity, would grant the requisite protection to the United Kingdom while in its turn it could be subjected in English courts to inconvenience, expense and possibly embarrassment when some of its acts would come within one of the exceptions that the SIA admits. The same could possibly apply to Kuwait: it was granted immunity by the Court of Appeal in *Al-Adsani* on the basis of the SIA, but if it came to the application to Kuwait to one of the SIA's statutory exceptions, it would be far from certain that English courts would be conducting adjudication in accordance with the law in force as between the UK and Kuwait; for there is no clear-cut evidence that Kuwait consents to the international law of immunities in the shape identical to that regulated under the SIA.

It has to be made clear that the present reasoning does *not* advocate the interpretative use of *Hansard* the way its relevance has been admitted in the House of Lords' decision in *Pepper* v. *Hart*.[134] It is obvious that the legislative purpose of the SIA could not be validly identified through this approach, for the interventions by Lords Wilberforce and Denning do not fit within the *Pepper* v. *Hart* requirements in that they were not presented in the capacity of the sponsor of the legislation, nor could these interventions be used, in any straightforward manner, to identify the ambiguity or obscurity in the terms of the Act. Their Lordships were concerned with the overall rationale of the Act, rather than the clarity of the meaning to be attributed to its specific provisions.

The essence of statutory construction goes precisely to the overall rationale of the SIA and to the construction of the legislator's intention accordingly. The sponsoring statement by the Lord Chancellor during the House of Lords meeting on 17 January 1978 contained the observation that the purpose of the State immunity bill was to secure immunity to sovereign States when acting in their sovereign capacity and exclude it in relation to non-sovereign acts.[135] This approach differs from and contradicts the subsequent assertion by the Court of Appeal in *Al-Adsani* that the SIA constitutes a 'comprehensive code' on immunities, precluding courts from inquiring into whether the relevant act or transaction possesses the sovereign character. There is, thus, at least the possibility to make a prima facie case that the initial rationale behind the SIA does not completely overlap with its subsequent use in courts.

[134] *Pepper* v. *Hart* [1993] AC 593. [135] See, for the record of the meeting, above note 132.

This approach is further supported by more specific considerations. While the SIA has been enacted by Parliament to give domestic effect to the ECSI, Parliament must be deemed to have been aware of the two material considerations. Firstly, the enactment of the SIA could have the effect of generalising the particular regime designed to apply to a few States only. Secondly, given that the ECSI has itself acknowledged that the general law of immunities was not being prejudiced by its special regime, the enactment of the SIA to give effect to the ECSI could justify viewing, for the purposes of statutory interpretation, the legislative purpose behind the SIA as not prejudicing the applicability of the restrictive doctrine recognised under common law and general international law.

Therefore there is a legal and judicial option that, in relation to non-signatory States at least, the SIA can be treated as a sort of codifying statute that reflects existing common law,[136] rather than universalising an effectively sub-regional legal framework of the ECSI. Its content could then be applied to be somewhat reflective of the restrictive doctrine as accepted under customary international law and correspondingly under the pre-SIA common law in England. One example of this approach is *NML* v. *Argentina*, which has essentially approved this vision by interpreting the 'commercial exception' under section 3 of the SIA in the light of the broader context of the restrictive immunity doctrine. This way, common law may provide a background that could inform the meaning of statutory provisions to make them operate as part of the broader legal context.[137]

D. The doctrine of precedent

Historically, the English common law has been premised on the two underlying – constitutional if you wish – principles: securing the continuity and predictability of legal regulation and protecting individual freedom. The doctrine of precedent has provided a major tool to serve these aims. As has been sufficiently detailed above, the application of State immunity to human rights in English (and other) courts has produced a fairly inconsistent, at times obscure, picture. Some decisions have relied on common law while others have relied on statutory law, advancing different functional and normative justifications for immunities. This

[136] Cf. Francis Bennion, *Statutory Interpretation* (London: Butterworth, 1997), 465–6 (section 212).

[137] *NML* v. *Argentina*, para. 39 (per Lord Phillips).

militates against applying the doctrine of precedent to those previous decisions in any straightforward manner.

There are a number of options available to English courts to deal with the previous inconsistent case-law. A superior court can select between the two inconsistent decisions of the lower courts. For instance, the Court of Appeal can choose which of the two conflicting High Court decisions to apply.[138] More broadly, the doctrine of precedent does not cover previous decisions reached without argument, when a superior court merely assumes the correctness of a particular approach to the relevant legal position without addressing and examining it, even if the proposition in question was essential to the previous case.[139] The precedential force of *Jones* v. *Saudi Arabia* (having in its turn relied on *Al-Adsani* that offered no meaningful analysis of the relevant issues) is compromised by the fact that, as we saw above, on the two crucial issues – the scope of the acts *jure imperii* and the state of customary international law on immunities – it has not backed up its conclusions with the analysis of the evidence or engagement of the opposite approach. This applies, *a fortiori*, to the International Court's decision in *Germany* v. *Italy*, relying on Italian concessions both in relation to *jure imperii* acts and to the customary law status of immunities.

In *Young* v. *Bristol Aeroplane*,[140] the Court of Appeal has examined the matter of conflicting judicial decisions, and has, among others, singled out the cases which conflict with each other and those that were delivered *per incuriam*. As for the former case, it was 'beyond question that the previous decision is open to examination', and 'the court is unquestionably entitled to choose between the two conflicting decisions'.[141] More specifically:

> Where the court has construed a statute or a rule having the force of a statute its decision stands on the same footing as any other decision on a question of law, but where the court is satisfied that an earlier decision was given in ignorance of the terms of a statute or a rule having the force of a statute the position is very different.[142]

This approach has been applied to the law of State immunity especially, as we saw above, at the stages when the issue of State-owned ships was

[138] Cf. S. H. Bailey, J. P. L. Ching and N. W. Taylor, *The Modern English Legal System* (London: Sweet & Maxwell, 2007), 484–5, 493.

[139] R. Cross and J. W. Harris, *Precedent in English Law* (Oxford: Oxford University Press, 1991), 158–9, 161.

[140] *Young* v. *Bristol Aeroplane* [1944] KB 718. [141] *Ibid.*, 725, 729–30. [142] *Ibid.*, 729.

being addressed in the context of the then applicable absolute immunity doctrine, and subsequently when English courts had to address the transition, as a matter of English common law, from absolute towards restrictive State immunity. In a manner somewhat at odds with *Bristol Aeroplanes*, it has thus been possible to prioritise a Court of Appeal decision over a prior inconsistent House of Lords decision,[143] and effectively state the preference for the restrictive as opposed to the absolute doctrine of immunities.

This process also demonstrates that the selection between conflicting decisions is entirely a judicial choice, there being no binding statutory or other regulation of this matter; and also that the duty to observe past precedents is not as strict in relation to international legal issues as it is with purely domestic cases.[144] As also has been demonstrated through some detailed evidence,[145] English courts are divided on several other issues regarding the scope and customary law status of sovereign immunities. Therefore, the issue of prioritising some and disregarding other judicial decisions is not unlikely to arise before English courts in the future.

In future cases courts could either exclude international law (in which case they need to find the proper English law on immunities which does not exist, unless the SIA is used on exclusive terms); or they have to examine anew, *de novo* as it were, the state of State practice and *opinio juris* that would help properly ascertain the position under international law, and then apply it as part of English law. The latter option would, on the whole, be more suitable for reflecting the international legal position in English law, being at the same time compatible with the ordinary patterns in which the sources of English law operate.

The House of Lords in *Jones* has granted immunity to Saudi Arabia for torture, even though the law as identified in *Pinochet* would not justify this approach. In *Bat*, Moses LJ was not inclined to see himself bound by the majority in *Pinochet* regarding the point 'that the former Head of State would have immunity from prosecution for murder and conspiracy to murder in Spain'.[146] Could it be argued that subsequent English cases have upset the effect of *Pinochet*?

[143] Cf., R. Higgins, 'The Death Throes of Absolute Immunity: The Government of Uganda before the English Courts', (1979) 73 *AJIL*, 465 at 469 (focusing, among others, on *Tapioca* [1974] 1 WLR 1485 and *Trendtex* cases).

[144] As also confirmed in *Trendtex*.

[145] R. Higgins, 'Recent Developments in the Law of Sovereign Immunity in the United Kingdom', (1977) 71 *AJIL*, 423.

[146] *Khurts Bat*, para. 99.

Familiarity with the elementary principles of English common law can easily demonstrate this is not the case. In relation to the way in which common law operates, Lord Reid has observed in *Dorset Yacht* that 'when a new point emerges [in a subsequent case], one should ask not whether it is covered by authority but whether recognised principles apply to it'.[147] The question to be asked is whether *Jones* and *Bat* have contradicted the principles on which the *ratio decidendi* in *Pinochet* has turned.

The reason why *Jones* cannot override *Pinochet* is that it has expressly distinguished it and has not contradicted the principles underlying the latter's *ratio decidendi.* Both *Jones* and *Bat* are clear that they adhere to the civil/criminal divide, and therefore show no intention to overrule *Pinochet*, either on the matter of the scope of acts *jure imperii*, or in relation to the effect of *jus cogens.* The elementary distinction between overruling and distinguishing past cases will inevitably make it clear that the fact that in *Pinochet* immunity was denied while in *Jones* it was upheld is not what English common law would ordinarily place emphasis on.

Principles of law that matter for the doctrine of precedent apply not to facts and situations involved in a particular case, but to issues that could arise, over and over again, in multiple cases involving facts and situations of that kind. If the subsequent court pronounces over the issue that is different from the issue confronted on its head in the previous case, then the subsequent case could not be reasonably seen to have overruled that previous case. Nor could the ordinary pattern of overruling apply to the issues of international law which, as we saw above, is created through agreement between States, independently of English law, and then incorporated into it, as opposed to having been created unilaterally by courts as they do with ordinary rules of common law. All *Pinochet* has done, as we saw above, was to follow the restrictive doctrine and impact of *jus cogens* already accepted in international, and in common, law. It would be plainly beyond the House of Lords' gift in *Jones* to overrule this position, even if it had an inclination to do so.

7. Conclusion

The above analysis can lead us to the conclusion that international law relating to State immunity does not experience any fragmentation, but merely works on the ordinary pattern of sources of law and of the hierarchy of norms, including *lex specialis* and *jus cogens.* Immunities *ratione*

[147] *Dorset Yacht*, at 1026–7 (per Lord Reid).

materiae of States and their officials rely on a single and uniform justification – to protect genuinely sovereign activities of States. State practice shows no evidence that the regime applicable to immunities in civil and criminal proceedings is different from each other. In both types of proceedings, and in the absence of any applicable treaty provision requiring the opposite, the underlying functional test refers to acts unique to State authority. On balance, there is no customary law obligation of one State to accord immunity to another State, but the restrictive doctrine that aspires to be customary law is quite narrow anyway, even as a matter of comity. Even if one agrees that this narrow restrictive doctrine, referring to acts unique to State authority, is part of customary law, its use in practice would still not mandate the approach adopted in *Al-Adsani*, *Jones* and *Germany* v. *Italy*. The absence of fragmentation is obvious at the level of actual State practice, where the outcome obtains that State immunity is not available for human rights violations. The imitation of the opposite position in the decisions of national and international courts cannot substantiate such a position in relation to immunities when such has not been agreed in practice as between States.

Treaty-specific regimes can have normative impact on immunities, requiring the denial of immunity, even if otherwise available. This concerns the finding of the right balance of underlying interests as a matter of jurisprudence of the Strasbourg Court under Article 6 ECHR. Both ECHR and *jus cogens* clearly prevail over the immunity of States and their officials in both criminal and civil proceedings. The adjudication standards under ECHR and *jus cogens* are flexible enough, and offer reasonable ways for balancing conflicting interests. This contrasts to the pro-immunity view that is premised on the blanket, and thus irrational, prioritisation of the interests of the impleaded State over that of its victims, thereby raising legal concerns as well as reinforcing the increasing moral disrepute of this 'traditional' school of thought.

16

Historical sketches about custom in international law

JEAN-LOUIS HALPÉRIN

The historical origins of the expression 'legal order' (*Rechtsordnung, ordinamento giuridico, ordre juridique*) have a long history, and must be seen in connection with the role of the doctrinal writing upon international law in the apparition of this conception of an ordered legal system. This goes back to the first usages of the words '*rechtliche Ordnung*' by Gentz (in his 1800 work about perpetual peace) and F. J. Stahl (1830) until the developments made by von Bar (1862), Bergbohm (1892), Triepel, Anzilotti, Santi Romano, Gény and of course Kelsen.[1] As this formula could be used as easily by 'dualist' theoreticians as by 'monist' ones, I could express some scepticism about a history of legal ideas (or of 'juristic thought') too much separated from the contextual study of positive norms and from the sociological analysis of the influence of legal professionals. Not only a positivist point of view leads me to suspect – as Kelsen has clearly shown – ideological aspects in every construction of the *doctrine*, but it must imply a duty of cautiousness – which Kelsen has not always respected because of his strong commitment in favour of international law – towards the idea that international law and the international legal order were old phenomena, located in the remotest times of Antiquity.

The well-known histories of international law begin with treaties, arbiters awards and 'rules of customary law' that are supposed to constitute the lineaments of international law since the antique civilizations of Egypt, Mesopotamia, Greece and Rome.[2] Would a stage of development

[1] Jean-Louis Halpérin, 'L'apparition et la portée de la notion d'ordre juridique dans la doctrine internationaliste du XIXe siècle', *Droits* 33 (2001) 41–52.

[2] Arthur Nussbaum, *A Concise History of the Law of Nations* (Macmillan, New York, 1954); Karl-Heinz Ziegler, *Völkerrechts geschichte: ein Studienbuch* (C. H. Beck Verlag, München, 1994 and 2007); Antonio Truyol y Serra, *Histoire du droit international public* (Economica,

for international law have corresponded at every level of civilization? These approaches risk making an anachronistic assimilation between 'international' relations – more strictly, relations with foreign powers or between different 'polities' that were not national States – and the notion of international law. If we take the example, one of the best documented through different kinds of texts, of the conventions (or 'treaties') between Greek cities inside Hellenistic kingdoms, we find clauses concerning the exercise of justice (in private litigation) between citizens from different cities, but there is no evidence that these treaties have created legal rules (about the procedure or the substantive law to apply) to which the arbiters or judges were submitted.[3] For modern periods, several works, especially those of Peter Haggenmacher, have shown how the Roman concept of *ius gentium*, which has practically no connection with our modern international law (it deals with rules of private law that were considered by the Roman lawyers as common to different peoples), was reconfigured by the theologians and jurists of the Spanish School of Salamanca (Vitoria, and his expression of *jus inter gentes*, and Suarez), whose doctrinal interpretations were 'mysterious' and fragile hypotheses,[4] before being combined, in a masterly but purely doctrinal work, by Grotius in the category of *jus belli* extended to all 'extra-national' relations without any common judge.[5]

Briefly, for a legal historian with positivist convictions, the first binding rules of international law appear with multilateral treaties in the second half of the nineteenth century (the 1864 Geneva Convention about the Red Cross and humanitarian law, the 1865 Paris treaty about the International Telegraph, the 1874 Berne treaty about the General Postal Union, the 1883 Paris convention for the protection of intellectual property, the 1886 Berne convention about literary property, The Hague conventions about international law, then about the law of war, etc.) and the first arbiter awards decided according to conventional rules of international

Paris, 1995); Wilhelm Georg Grewe, *Epochen der Völkerrechts geschichte* (Nomos, Baden-Baden, 1984) and, from the same author, *Fontes Historiae Iuris Gentium: Quellen zur Geschichte der Völkerrechts* (Berlin: W. de Gruyter, 1995), vol. I.

3 Aude Cassayre, *La Justice dans les cités grecques: De la formation des royaumes hellénistiques au legs d'Attale* (Presses Universitaires, Rennes, 2010).

4 Marie-France Renoux-Zagamé, 'La disparition du droit des gens classique', *Revue d'histoire des facultés de droitet de la science juridique* (1987), 23–53.

5 Peter Haggenmacher, *Grotius et la doctrine de la guerre juste* (Presses Universitaires, Paris, 1983) and 'Grotius et le droit international – Le texte et la légende', in *Grotius et l'ordre juridique international: Travaux du colloque Hugo Grotius, Genève, 10–11 novembre 1983* (Payot, Lausanne, 1985, Alfred Dufour, Peter Haggenmacher, Jirí Toman eds.) 115–43.

law (the 1872 Geneva arbitration in the *Alabama* claims). The 'positivization' of international law has, of course, progressed through the creation of international courts, especially the Permanent Court of Arbitration (since 1899), the Permanent Court of International Justice (PCIJ, created in 1921) and its successor, the actual International Court of Justice (ICJ).

Such a positivist point of view does not mean that international law has to be considered only in a State-centred, 'voluntaristic' and 'sovereignist' perspective. Even, if one follows Kelsen's conceptions for identifying national legal orders with States, there is room (that Kelsen wanted to develop more than many of his contemporaries) for an international legal order, whose rules (or at least, one part of them) are not created by States and under their control. Saying that States are yet powerful and that many rules of international law are still dependant on the will of States (affirmed through treaties) does not imply that international law has not acquired a kind of autonomy and self-development which can evade the consent of State authorities. For this reason, I do not think that positivists can be disqualified from studying customary rules in international law (as inside national orders in a 'pluralistic' perspective), on the sole argument that they would be unable to understand the creation of legal norms outside the State. Positivists are only thinking that there is no natural or 'spontaneous' law, that legal rules are always the product of human conventions, supposing the intervention of an authority (or of several authorities) to recognize these rules (possibly, to change them) or to make an adjudication according to these rules (one has recognized the 'secondary rules' of Hart's *Concept of Law*). Consequently, one needs a competent authority to transform regularities in (international) conduct or conventional agreements without sanctions into 'customary rules', i.e. into legal components of a legal system.

With the positivist axiom that only the law can create legal rules, it is logically impossible to admit the spontaneous creation of a customary international law that would have constituted the first basis of international law before the recognition of 'legal' authorities, because only these authorities were competent to recognize this international law as law. There is no doubt, today, that this authority is mainly the one of international judges, acting independently from the States. What I would say, in these historical sketches, is that this rather recent recognition of customary rules in international law has been prepared (and largely influenced) – as the whole system of 'international legal order' – by a doctrinal theorization of custom as a major source of law. As the science of international law has preceded positive rules of international laws, customary rules postulated by the legal writers have 'anteceded' customary rules recognized by international judges and the question is: in which range has this historical scheme left its mark on international customary law?

Customary law as postulated by legal writers

The works of Martti Koskenniemi have shown how the construction of international law was, from the 1870s to the 1960s (a period finishing with Kelsen's books about international law, which would remain faithful to this doctrinal frame), dependent on the collective action of a rather small group of specialists, generally law professors in Europe and in America, who tried to stimulate (by an action of lobbying) the development of international conferences, treaties, conventions about uniform laws, arbitration and the creation of international courts.[6] The landmark in this history was the creation in 1873 of the *Institut de droit international* by Rollin, Mancini and Bluntschli. The creation happened just after the German–French war of 1870–71 (which symbolized the force of nationalist claims and influenced the book of Adolf Lasson, *Prinzip und Zukunft des Völkerrechts*, often considered as the 'negation' of international law) and the success of the *Alabama* arbitration in Geneva. The creators of the *Institut de droit international* – and many French, German, British or American professors who adhered to this learned association – wanted to be the 'organs of the legal consciousness of the civilized world' and to encourage a peaceful resolution of international conflicts.

Debates about customary rules were central in the doctrinal writing of these law professors and in the collective action of the *Institut de droit international*. They were all influenced by Savigny and the Historical School of Law; they thus shared the conviction that law has appeared and could develop, from the legal consciousness of peoples, through customs (and, in some configurations, better than through written and codified rules). They were also struck by the arguments of John Austin, *The Province of Jurisprudence determined* (1832), denying that the 'law of nations' was more than a set of moral duties. Some of these law professors thought that it was possible (and desirable) that lawyers (as representatives and interpreters of the popular consciousness, as said by Savigny) could elaborate 'customary rules' of international law. If an agreement could be

[6] Martti Koskenniemi, *The Gentle Civilizer of Nations: The Rise and Fall of International Law 1870–1960* (Cambridge University Press, 2012).

found between professors from different nationalities (often separated by national antagonisms such as those between France and Germany), the governments could follow this way (through international conventions, such as those concerning international private law and uniform resolution of conflict of laws; a good example of the outcomes of the expertise of international lawyers being The Hague conventions since 1893–94) and, possibly, the international arbiters, even without the agreement of governments.

This approach is clearly explained in the title and the content of Bluntschli's 1868 book, *Das modern Völkerrecht der zivilisierten Staaten als Rechtsbuch dargestellt*. The goal was to create a 'modern' (that supposed a break with the past situation, where in fact there was no international law properly said) law of civilized nations (not only the opposition between Western countries with Christian values and the savage peoples of Asia or Africa likely to be colonized, but also the idea that 'civil' law was a model to develop social relations based on the rights of the individuals) through a law book, as a kind of code, constructed (in the form of a set of performative sentences) by a law professor. Bluntschli imagined rules of natural (and humanitarian) law that he had transformed (under his own authority of 'jurisconsult') into 862 articles (like the sections of a Code; one has to remember that Bluntschli was the main drafter of the Civil Code of Zurich) which he proposed to be 'positivized'. Bluntschli did not explain how to transform (or to confirm the transformation of) his doctrinal opinions into binding rules, but one can presume that the theory of custom based on the repetition of facts combined with the *opinio necessitatis* was, for him, the means (in the absence of treaties) to create customary rules.

Against the objections made by Austin (there could not be customary rules of international law without the existence of an international authority and of international courts), the members of the *Institut de droit international* felt themselves competent ('habilitated') to enounce the general principles of international law (and even detailed rules, if one considers the 862 articles of Bluntschli's Code), hoping that this *opinio juris* (in fact the *communis opinio doctorum* of the international society of lawyers) would precede (and provoke) the factual repetition of State practice that was necessary to create a custom. Would not the States be interested in appearing 'civilized' and in showing that they were respecting these humanitarian rules? The structure of the *Institut de droit international*, as a transnational association of influential jurisconsults (often designated to be the representatives of States at the international conferences) was likely, first to develop consensually this *opinio juris*, then to influence State practice in favour of the respect of the postulated customary rule.

Fifty years later, the works of Kelsen about the sources of international law showed, at the same time, the keeping of these conceptions and the logical faults of such a doctrine. In his 1926 study about the relations between domestic law and international law, Kelsen placed the customary rule '*pacta sunt servanda*' as the fundamental norm, which was necessary according to him to explain the binding force of international law. As his predecessors, he has thus continued to postulate a customary rule (as a constitution of the whole international order), that doctrinal writing could alone establish, with the observation (or the hope) that the current practice of States will confirm to it.[7] In 1932, Kelsen considered that, in absence of any central organ of legislation in the international legal order, there is no other method of formation and development of international norms 'at a primary stage' than recourse to customary law.[8] One can say that Kelsen adopted, at this moment in the development of his theory, a classical conception of customary law, at least the position of those who refused the purely 'voluntaristic' interpretation of positivism (considering that only the will of States could be binding through an auto-limitation of their sovereignty, notably by the means of treaties, but also by practices establishing customary rules). The advocates of international rules, which could be analysed as objectively external and superior to the States, still needed to suppose that customary rules were independent from the will of the States, so that State practice could be consistent (or inconsistent) with a prior rule.[9]

One has to wait until the 1945 *General Theory of Law and State* until Kelsen develops his fundamental criticism, which he endowed with a great force of conviction, of the traditional theory of the formation of customary rules through the two stages of material repetition of practices and intellectual *opinio necessitatis*. Writing generally about the law-creating process (in the dynamic conception of the legal order), Kelsen underlined the contradiction of the current doctrine of custom: law subjects cannot be determined (and felt determined) in their conduct by a rule they are

[7] Hans Kelsen, 'Les rapports de système entre le droit interne et le droit international public' (transl. Charles Eisenmann), *RCADI* 14 (1926) 231–331.

[8] Hans Kelsen, 'Théorie générale du droit international public, problèmes choisis' (transl. Charles Eisenmann), *RCADI* 42 (1932) 116–351 and 'Théorie du droit international coutumier', *Revue internationale de la théorie du droit* (1939) 262–74.

[9] Serge Sur, 'La coutume', *Jurisclasseur de droit international*, 13/3 (1989) 5.

going to create through this conduct; the same fact cannot be simultaneously the application and the formation of the rule. There are, of course, possible arguments to oppose Kelsen's conception: judge-made law can be, in the same time, creation and application of a new rule, without link with a legislative frame. But the judge is not only a competent authority to say what is law (an argument that could also be used for the national authorities in charge of international affairs), but the judge has to settle a legal dispute and is obliged to find a rule for ending the case. For these reasons, the judge can create a rule he/she feels obliged to follow. The situation of other law subjects is different: not only individuals, but also State authorities, cannot be obliged by a rule that is not prior to their conduct. These law subjects, said Kelsen, make an erroneous (and probably ideological in order to legitimize their conduct) analysis of the situation if they feel themselves bound by a rule that does not pre-exist. The reasoning is much more striking for States (assimilated with domestic legal orders through Kelsen's analysis), which cannot have 'opinions'; the objective practice of State authorities being subjected to the respect of 'legal' norms (according to the principle of 'legality', or rule of law, used to explain the functioning of administrative law).[10] Furthermore, from a normativist point of view, a rule of law cannot be generated only through facts, according to the 'law of Hume' (an 'ought to' cannot be derived from an 'is').

To finish with Kelsen's theory, it is noteworthy that the recourse to customary law is not abandoned as the fundamental norm of international law. The rule *pacta sunt servanda* is now based on a rule that gives to custom the role of a source of international law: States have to act as they are accustomed to act.[11] Can this presentation from Kelsen be considered as a defeat of the legal theory towards a realist (but perhaps naïve) observation of inter-State relations, international law being unable to find a basis outside the current practice of States? It is possible, of course, to defend this point of view: international law cannot exist without the acceptance of international rules by the States and it is the reason why international law has only existed as law since the nineteenth century. This acceptance can also mean that some authorities are habilitated by the State to create customary rules: the question remain whether these authorities are legislative, judicial or doctrinal ones, as if they depend on the State (as

[10] Hans Kelsen, *Théorie générale du droit et de l'État*, French transl. Bétarice Laroce, Valérie Faure (Presses Universitaires, Paris, 1997) 168.

[11] *Ibid.*, 415.

authorities in charge of foreign affairs), or if they are independent of the State (as international organizations). Kelsen has not proposed a complete theory of the sources of international law: on one hand, it can be said that he has excluded (as in other parts of the legal order) that legal science can create legal norms;[12] on the other hand, his refusal to choose (inside a monist theory, that supposes that there are international norms) between the primacy of the international law and the primacy of domestic law, did not close the door to the idea of a customary law-creating process inside or outside the States, especially through judicial norms.

Although he continued to be an 'idealist' about the subjection of States to international law (for this reason he hoped that the creation of the United Nations Organization would change the status of international law),[13] Kelsen was aware of the failure of the League of Nations system and of the difficulties encountered by the advocates of customary rules before the PCIJ. The 1920 PCIJ Statute could be considered, of course, with its Article 38 about the rules that the Court has to apply (including 'international custom, as evidence of a general practice accepted as law'), as a treaty by which the States have recognized custom as a source of international law and empowered a World Court to apply (and implicitly, to recognize) it.

About the well-known *Lotus* case, it has been rarely noticed that the Court rejected the argumentation of the representative of the French State, Jules Basdevant, in favour of the recognition of an international customary rule. Jules Basdevant has followed exactly the programme of the *Institut de droit international* to recognize, through a doctrinal analysis, the existence of a customary rule of international general law. He has tried to show that some decisions of national courts have furnished 'precedents' of the practice of governments in their mutual relationships in favour of a customary international rule – the one that would have prohibited the extension of penal law from a country to offences committed outside its territory – and these precedents were more conclusive than legislative texts (such as the Turkish Penal Code), which were not always applied (a lesson also of realism proposing to make the judicial custom prevail on the legal statements 'on the paper'). Basdevant has also used the 'doctrine of legal writers' – according to Article 38.4 of the PCIJ Statute ('judicial decisions and the teachings of the most highly qualified publicists of the

[12] Hans Kelsen, 'Préface' to Charles Eisenmann, *La justice constitutionnelle et la Haute Cour constitutionnelle d'Autriche* (Economica, Paris, 1928) VII.

[13] Martti Koskenniemi, *The Gentle Civilizer of Nations*, 246.

various nations') – in order to produce some evidence of the customary rule, hoping to confirm the role of law professors in the establishment of such a custom.[14] To this argument, the Court responded that, even if these precedents could produce any evidence they would prove only an abstention (of penal proceedings against foreigners for offences committed outside the territory) from the State, and not the consciousness of a binding rule. The customary rule was thus not recognized and it seemed more difficult, after this decision, to prove a customary rule limiting the sovereign powers of the State.[15] Did not the international judges ring the knell of a customary rule postulated only by legal writers?

Customary law recognized by international judges: a new age for customary law?

Before some historical considerations about the conception of custom through the case law, especially of the ICJ since 1945, some trivial remarks about the sea changes of international law in the second half of the twentieth century are necessary to understand how the context of this question has been radically transformed. First, the 1945 treaty of San Francisco has annexed the Status of the ICJ with the UN Charter: all United Nations members (in 2013, 193 States) have accepted the Statute of the World Court (even if they do not accept its jurisdiction in one case or another) and have thus confirmed Article 38 of this Statute about the sources of international law. This text can be considered as a 'fundamental' norm, recognized in all the world, that has established the possibility of binding customary rules of international law and has (at least indirectly) habilitated the ICJ to 'legalize' any custom that the Court deems proved. Second, a great number of multilateral conventions have been signed, among which some of them can appear as a 'universal law' approved by the (quasi-) unanimity of States. This is the case of the 1966 International Covenant on Civil and Political Rights, which has been ratified by 167 States, of the International Covenant on Economic, Social and Cultural Rights (ratified by 160 States), of the 1948 Convention on the Prevention and Punishment of the Crime of Genocide (ratified by 142 States), of

[14] Cour permanente de justice internationale, *Actes et documents relatifs aux arrêts et aux avis consultatifs de la Cour* (Leyden, 1929), no. 13.II ('The *Lotus* Case') 194 and 196.

[15] Alain Pellet, 'Lotus que de sottises on profère en ton nom: Remarque sur le concept de souveraineté dans la jurisprudence de la Cour Mondiale', in *Mélanges en l'honneur de Jean-Pierre Puissochet* (Pedone, Paris, 2008) 215–30.

the 1966 International Convention on the Elimination of All Forms of Racial Discrimination (ratified by 175 States), of the 1984 Convention against Torture (ratified by 150 States), or on the 1989 Convention on the Rights of the Child (ratified by 193 States, including all the States of the United Nations Organization, with the exception of Somalia and the United States). Furthermore, 194 States (including the Holy See and the Cook Islands) have ratified the 1949 Geneva Conventions about humanitarian law. One can say that international general law now exists on the basis of these treaties and it has necessary consequences about customary international law. On one hand, it could be argued that customary rules are no longer useful to fill the gaps of international law and that they suffer a kind of inferiority towards universal treaties, in the absence of written statements likely to furnish the basis for norms (through an interpretative process). On the other hand, these universal or quasi-universal treaties prove the existence of converging practices of the States and do not exclude the possibility of extension of international general norms through customs.

It is well known that the ICJ has chosen the second way and has evoked, especially since the 1969 *North Sea Continental Shelf* cases, the possibility (even if this argument was rejected in the case) that a customary rule could develop quickly after the signature of a multilateral treaty and could bind some States which have not ratified this treaty.[16] In the 1984 case concerning *Military and Paramilitary Activities In and Against Nicaragua* and in the 1985 *Continental Shelf (Libyan Arab Jamahiriya/Malta)* case, the ICJ confirmed this idea of a parallel development (with the same content, which is in some way 'doubled') of multilateral treaties and customary rules.[17] Is there not room for new developments of 'savage customs', according to the well-known expression of René-Jean Dupuy,[18] renewing the traditional (and 'wise') customs accepted by old (Western) States through progressive customs wanted by Third World States?

The historical comparison with the precedent stage (the one of custom postulated by legal writers) leads to more cautious conclusions. There is

[16] *North Sea Continental Shelf* cases, § 76, in *Bréviaire de jurisprudence internationale* (Bruxelles, 2005, Giovanni Distefano and Gionata P. Buzzini eds.) 433.

[17] *Case Concerning Military and Paramilitary Activities In and Against Nicaragua*, § 73; *Continental Shelf (Libyan Arab Jamahiriya/Malta)* case, § 27, in *Bréviaire de jurisprudence internationale* (Bruxelles, 2005, Giovanni Distefano and Gionata P. Buzzini eds.) 614 and 628.

[18] René-Jean Dupuy, 'Coutume sage et coutume sauvage', in *La Communauté internationale: Mélanges offerts à Charles Rousseau* (Pedone, Paris, 1974) 75–89.

no doubt that the continuous development of the case law of the ICJ since 1948 has given to customary rules a normative basis – the 'recognition' of the customary rule through an adjudicating authority which is habilitated to say 'what the law is' according to John Austin's old scheme – they lacked in the precedent period. The international judiciary has become a 'machinery' whose control escapes the State and which is likely to develop independently judge-made law. But there are also elements of continuity with the previous status of customary rules. Since the *North Sea Continental Shelf* cases, the ICJ has decided to adopt the *ratio decidendi* of the *Lotus* case and to confirm the traditional theory (transposed by doctrinal writers of the nineteenth century from domestic law, on the basis of Roman law) of custom and *opinio juris.*[19] If this theory allows the Court to keep the complete mastery of the recognition of customary rules – the subjective criterion of *opinio juris* is let to the arbitrary judgment of the Court – it proves a fidelity (through the principle of *stare decicis*) to what one can call a 'doctrinal interpretation'. Furthermore, such a method can induce a restrictive point of view (as in the *Lotus* case) towards customs limiting the sovereignty of the State (the *opinio juris* being more difficult to presume). In the *Gulf of Maine* case the Court conceded that the customary rules were not so numerous and that they lacked details. In the same perspective, the 1951 decision in the *Anglo-Norwegian Fisheries* case recognized, with some nuances, the 'persistent objector' rule, which allows any State to contest a customary rule. For these reasons, one can doubt that customary law has become a powerful weapon in the hands of the ICJ, even if recent decisions (such as the 2012 *Jurisdictional Immunities of the State, (Germany* v. *Italy)*), have used national case law (reinforcing the idea of a tighter set of international norms through the dialogue between national judges) as a means to establish a custom (but that was already the method used by Basdevant in his argumentation in the *Lotus* case).

If one adds the links that continue to exist between the judges of the ICJ and the doctrinal writers and the fact that only the legal writers can construct (in their didactic works) international law as a unified system based on determined general rules (the ICJ and other international courts can only recognize such or such custom in a case by a casuistic approach,

[19] *North Sea Continental Shelf* cases, § 78; *Gulf of Maine* case, § 111; *Continental Shelf (Libyan Arab Jamahiriya/Malta)* case, § 27; *Nuclear Weapons* case, § 64, in *Bréviaire de jurisprudence internationale* (Bruxelles, 2005, Giovanni Distefano and Gionata P. Buzzini eds.), 434, 582, 628 and 789.

with relatively few decisions), the idea of a new age for custom can be doubted. The readers of these historical sketches could say that my rather sceptical conclusion was already pre-determined by positivist prejudice about (but not against) customary rules. But to say that the traditional theory of custom has been 'legalized' (and erected as a judicial norm) by international judges does not mean that this doctrinal construction is more coherent and more likely to support important developments of international law.[20]

[20] As shown by Peter Haggenmacher: 'La doctrine des deux éléments du droit coutumier', *Revue générale de droit international public* (1986) 6–125.

B. Treaty Interpretation

17

Is there a subject-matter ontology in interpretation of international legal norms?

ROBERT KOLB

I. Introduction

The title of this short chapter may be viewed either as being thought-provoking or rather as being obscure. In any event, it will not be very appealing for the lawyer, who tends to have a sort of inherent repulsing reaction against the speculations of philosophy. However, the meaning intended to be given to this title is quite simple (and the philosophical twist of it allows us to start this chapter on interpretation by an interpretation): Are there areas or questions of international law where special rules of interpretation, at variance with the general rules enshrined in the Vienna Convention on the Law of Treaties (VCLT) of 1969 (Articles 31–3), shall prevail? Are there subject-matters where the object and purpose of the regulation is such that a set of special rules, or at least a distinctive combination of the general elements of interpretation, tends to impose itself?

These not wholly unimportant questions will be pursued here in a quite short and limited compass. The point is not to vainly attempt to produce a monographic or exhaustive approach within the four narrow corners of a chapter, but rather to shed some preliminary light on this question.[1]

II. General considerations on the legal regime of interpretation

One of the greatest conundrums in interpretative theory is the necessity to balance the 'rule-orientedness' of the whole process with its inevitable

[1] For more detailed references on many aspects discussed here, see R. Kolb, *Interprétation et creation du droit international*, Bruylant, Brussels, 2006. The question of the 'regional ontology' is addressed there at pp. 202–19, in terms different than in the present short chapter. For a recent general overview over interpretation, see also R. Gardiner, *Treaty Interpretation*, Oxford University Press, 2008. See also E. Bjorge, *The Evolutionary Interpretation of Treaties*, Oxford University Press, 2014.

'open-endedness'. There must be constraint and freedom at once in interpretation; it is not easy to see exactly what parts each of these necessary ingredients shall hold, nor how exactly to reconcile them. On the one hand, it is now common wisdom that interpretation is an 'art' more than a 'science'; that experience plays a greater role in it than sheer knowledge; that the relevant considerations are too manifold as to be able to be pressed into a rigid straightjacket of more or less automatically applicable legal rules. On the other hand, the practical lawyer and even more intensely the legal order as such, need a certain degree of certainty and direction as to the process of interpretation. Constant and inevitable interpretative processes indeed permeate all the life of the law. They are the daily occurrence *par excellence* of the lawyer. If that process were completely open-ended and accommodated indifferently all types of argumentative combinations, there would be a sort of 'anything goes'-reality, which in turn would turn the whole legal order with its normative pretence into illusion and delusion.

Thus, we end up in some form of lenient paradox with two branches. First, theoretical enquiry (legal hermeneutics) and practical observation show us that interpretative processes are difficult to encapsulate in rigid norms. These could not fulfil their function since they would not be able to reflect all the complex reality of understanding of norms and/or social reality. Therefore the lawyers would flout them by hiding the true processes of interpretation behind the cloak of rules which they would only lexically claim to abide by. But, second, such an open-ended approach puts into vital jeopardy the legal norm itself, since that norm will be realized only through interpretations. Legal certainty and previsibility, which are cornerstones of the modern constitutional and legal systems (contrary to the legal approaches of the Middle Ages[2]), would become simple words, without a distinctive reality. Unlimited subjectivism could and probably would reign. Observation of reality seems to buttress the impossibility of 'rules' on interpretation; legal policy suggests that a certain degree of these rules is indispensable. This conflict has to be somehow mediated.

This necessity is all the more present in international law. There is no centralized legislator in international society. The law is created in a decentralized way, by agreements and by practices of the legal subjects.

[2] On the crisis and replacement of the Middle Ages pluralistic approach by modern codification, see, e.g., A. Cavanna, *Storia del diritto moderno in Europa, Le fonti e il pensiero giuridico*, vol. I, Giũffrè, Milan, 1982, p. 194ff.

These norms are hence already fragmented; they tend to be often vague or unclear; they are meant to last for long time spans (consider the difficulty in modifying treaties), a fact which increases interpretative problems; they are much more than municipal norms prone to fluctuations and power policy twists, or at least to a quite interested if not biased interpretation in self-interest by the plurality of sovereign States. International law is much more rarely than municipal law interpreted by an independent and impartial third party, vested with adjudication powers. The general rule is here rather self-interpretation by each subject of the law.[3] In such a system, open-ended rules of interpretation (like those that had been proposed by the New Haven School[4]) lead easily to a loss of all certainty of the norms, which are indeed literally dissolved. In effect, this is then leading back to the prevalence of the interpretations of the stronger States over those of the weaker. If modern legal theory and some demands of reality commend flexibility in interpretation, another aspect of reality and sound policy aspects of international law demand some clear guidance as to how the norms shall be interpreted in order not to induce their progressive dissolution and manipulation.

The attempt to square that circle is to be found in Articles 31–3 of the VCLT of 1969. By giving some prevalence to the ordinary meaning and by pushing back the true but unexpressed (and hence to some degree speculative) will of the parties or *travaux préparatoires*, the Convention has operated policy choices in favour of security and equality of States. At the same time, by combining flexibly a whole series of main or secondary means of interpretation, the Convention returns back to accommodating a multiple reality, which cannot be reduced to the rigid sway of one or two generally prevailing elements. Moreover, the Convention does not purport to codify all rules or canons of interpretation, and even less all arguments the lawyer constantly uses in that process (analogy, *a contrario*, *a fortiori*, *ejusdem generis*, *in dubio pro libertate*, etc.) The success of the VCLT articles in the case-law mainly stems from the fact that the drafters seem to have succeeded in finding a viable balance between, on the one hand, the imposition, by way of legal norms, of a degree of certainty and of

[3] See, e.g., P. Klein, 'Les prétentions des Etats à la mise en œuvre "unilatérale" du droit international', *Revue belge de droit international*, vol. 43, 2010, p. 163ff.

[4] M. McDougal, H. Lasswell and J. C. Miller, *The Interpretation of International Agreements and World Public Order*, M. Nijhoff, Dordrecht/Boston/London, 1994. In the same vein, see T. H. Cheng, *When International Law Works – Realistic Idealism after 9 /11 and the Global Recession*, Oxford University Press, 2012 (and most markedly on p. 302, where it is bluntly said that international law is just the sum of decisions of policymakers).

order in the interpretive process, and, on the other hand, of a appreciable leeway for flexibility, combination of elements and adaptation.

Even under the VCLT (and the practice which first nourished it and later stemmed from it, with its stress laid on plain meaning of the text), there remain several other elements which allow the interpreter to go far beyond a seemingly clear text if that is felt as being necessary in context. Hence, the interpretation process remains to some extent a set of keys, where one or the other (or a combination of them) may open the door, and where the exercised eye may more easily recognize which keys or combinations thereof may open a particular lock.

If that is true, one easily understands that most different international actors can easily refer themselves to the set of general rules of the VCLT of 1969 in the most differing subject-matters: for example, the World Trade Organization (WTO) appellate bodies in their jurisprudence, or the International Centre for Settlement of Investment Disputes (ICSID) tribunals in theirs. There is enough flexibility in these general VCLT rules to be able to refer to them in the most diverse areas. Hence, at first sight, no 'secessionist' claims for special rules of interpretation needed to arise. It did not prove necessary to fragment the regime of interpretation in a set of general rules (VCLT) and in different sets of special rules prevailing in this or that area of international law as *leges speciales*. At best, one could find distinctive molecular-interpretative combinations in certain areas of the law, i.e. particularly significant recourse to some elements or a combination of elements of interpretation.

III. Factors for the modulation of interpretations

The general regime of the VCLT – which can easily be also applied by analogy to non-State entities as the ICSID case-law shows – leaves sufficiently ample room for modulation in the interpretative process. What factors may here play a role for inducing different interpretative approaches? There are many such factors and, by large, not only subject-matter specificities, to which we shall revert later.

1) One such factor is the *subject* of interpretation (who interprets?). The 'who' is clearly a crucial element in the realm of interpretation. It is not the same if the International Court of Justice (ICJ), or say the US or Russia, interpret this or that norm of inter-State conduct. The eternal question '*quis judicabit*?' leads back to the not less eternal maxim '*le qui l'emporte souvent sur le comment*'. This is clearly also true for subject-matters where it is claimed that there exists some

specificity in the interpretative rules applicable. One such area is the law of international institutions (see below, section IV). The organs of the organization, especially those that are not composed of State delegates, tend to develop a particular faithfulness to the aims and objectives of the organization. They will hence often privilege teleological, dynamic and purposive interpretations, able to overcome technical difficulties in the accomplishment of the organization's mission in order to keep it on the path of new demands and new necessities of its life. This process is particularly accentuated in times where there is some political faith in international organizations and when international cooperation is gaining momentum. It is possible to find such interpretations, for example, in the advisory opinions of the ICJ (the principal judicial organ of the UN, Article 92 of the UN Charter), from 1949 (*Reparation of Injuries*[5]) to 1962 (*Certain Expenses*[6]). It is sufficient to shift to the member States in order to be confronted by a different approach. Some of them will follow or indulge in the dynamic and expansive approaches mentioned. But others will rather stress the principle of specialty of powers; will insist on textuality of the constitutive instrument; and will underscore the necessity of an agreed subsequent practice or rather the need for formal modification of the constitutive instrument, etc. Consider the position of the socialist block in the UN during the Cold War, or even the position of France on peacekeeping operations during the 1960s. Particular interests dictate here quite different interpretation approaches. Stress will thus be laid by each actor on different aspects of interpretation. Or, as a last example: the interpretations by the League of Nations mandate commissions differed significantly from those of the mandated States. They were much bolder and much more evolutive than those of the latter, which tended to stress only the rights and powers they thought to be able to derive from the mandates agreement, turning down the duties towards the League or later the UN.[7]

2) Second, the *goal* of a particular interpretation will influence the choice of interpretative means. In situation 1) there is a bilateral treaty. The obvious aim of the interpretation by an impartial judge must be to maintain (or at least to avoid upsetting) the equilibrium the parties had reached through the articulated agreement framed on a *do ut des* basis. By so acting, the point is also to maintain the equality between them. It is quite clear that a court of justice will in this context tend to favour

[5] ICJ, *Reports*, 1949, p. 174ff. [6] ICJ, *Reports*, 1962, p. 151ff.

[7] See, e.g., the *Audition of Petitioners Advisory Opinion*, ICJ, *Reports*, 1956, p. 23ff.

textual and conservative purpose-oriented interpretations (what did the parties intend, what was their aim?), as well as contextual interpretations situated within the four corners of the treaty. The *Application of the Interim Accord of 13 September 1995* (*FYROM* v. *Greece*) (2011) decision by the ICJ (on 5 December 2011) is a case in point.[8] In situation 2), there are important new social evolutions or threats which the law must face; or there are rather vague principles, but no detailed rules, a situation which may call for some development of the law. This may be true in environmental matters (one may think of the famous *Trail Smelter Arbitration*, of 1941[9]). Or consider the very generic Truman Proclamation of the Continental Shelf. Two parties were asking a Court to declare the principles and rules applicable to the delimitation of the continental shelf (ICJ, *North Sea Continental Shelf Cases*, 1969[10]). The law was uncertain; it must be first determined, then to some extent interpreted, and hence also developed. The interpretation-limb is here placed in a completely different context. Arguments of equilibrium between States have not disappeared, but the policy issues are now considerably broader. The interpretation (to the extent that it will take place at all) will shift towards considerations of a legislative nature, where the judge will try to complete a legal regime the parties have not been able to complete themselves. Or, another example: Article 103 of the UN Charter will perhaps need to be interpreted in new ways when 'authorized' enforcement actions by member States (in substitution to Article 42 of the UN Charter enforcement actions) were invented in order to overcome the obstacle of non-implementation of Article 43ff of the Charter.[11] The term 'obligations' contained in Article 103 has then perhaps to be functionally reshaped in order to fit 'authorized' operations.[12]

3) A last example for reasons of modulation may be the policy divide between *judicial activism* and *caution*.[13] The institutional strength or weakness of the judge (the place of the judge in a society; permanent

[8] It can be consulted on www.icj-cij.org. [9] RIAA, vol. III, p. 1905ff.

[10] ICJ, *Reports*, 1969, p. 3ff.

[11] On this authorized action, see the Hague lecture of L. A. Sicilianos, 'Entre multilatéralisme et unilatéralisme: l'autorisation par le Conseil de sécurité de recourir à la force', *RCADI*, vol. 339, 2008, p. 25ff.

[12] This is suggested in R. Kolb, 'Does Article 103 of the Charter of the United Nations Apply only to Decisions or also to Authorisations Adopted by the Security Council?', Zeitschrift für ausländisches öffentliches Recht und Völkerrecht *(*ZaöRV*)*, vol. 64, 2004, p. 21ff.

[13] A classical reading on that question in international law is still H. Lauterpacht, *The Development of International by the International Court*, Stevens & Sons, London, 1958.

judge or simple arbitrator; compulsory jurisdiction or optional one; strong or weak court?); his or her relations with the parties (relations of confidence or not?); the relations of the parties between themselves (confidence or tension?); the time in which the adjudication takes place (times of international confidence and cooperation or times of tension and crisis; crisis or good relations universally or in the relevant region?); these factors, among others, will determine whether the judge chooses more conservative or more progressive elements of interpretation, for example stricter text-orientation or more relaxed purpose-orientation. Consider, for example, the US Supreme Court's jurisprudence in the 1950s and 1960s, and then since the 1980s. It shifted from a phase of judicial activism and 'equal rights' to a phase of conservativism and 'originalist' interpretations.[14] At the ICJ, too, such dividing lines can be felt, for example the phase between 1947 and 1962 (judicial expansion), and the one thereafter up to at least 1986 (judicial caution).[15]

IV. Salient particular subject-matters in the realm of interpretation of international law

Again, the aim of this short chapter cannot be to offer a monographic treatment x-raying all possible areas of international law from the standpoint of interpretation. Only some short examples can be discussed, and even this rather cursorily. Three categories of subject-matter influence shall here be addressed, all quite different in nature, function and treatment.

First, there are some subject-matters which are classically pinpointed as eliciting some particular *bouquets* of interpretative elements. These are international human rights law[16] and international institutional law.[17] It

[14] See D. L. Hudson, *The Handy Supreme Court Answer Book*, Detroit/Canton, 2008.

[15] For these phases, see Kolb (*supra* note. 1), p. 349ff.

[16] See e.g. W. Kälin and J. Künzli, *The Law of International Human Rights Protection*, Oxford University Press, 2009, p. 38; R. Bernhardt, 'Thoughts on the Interpretation of Human Rights Treaties', in F. Matscher and H. Petzold (eds.), *Protecting Human Rights: The European Dimension, Essays in Honor of G. Wiarda*, Carl Heymanns, Cologne, 1988, p. 65. See also G. Letsas, *A Theory of Interpretation of the European Convention on Human Rights*, Oxford University Press, 2007.

[17] See, e.g., J. Klabbers, *An Introduction to International Institutional Law*, 2nd edn., Cambridge University Press, 2009, p. 86ff; S. Kadelbach, 'Interpretation of the Charter', in B. Simma (ed.), *The Charter of the United Nations – A Commentary*, 3rd edn., vol. I, Oxford University Press, 2012, p. 71ff. See also C. Brölmann, 'Specialized Rules of Treaty Interpretation: International Organizations', in D. Hollis (ed.), *Oxford Guide to Treaties*, Oxford, 2012, p. 507ff.

is stressed that these subject-matters are encapsulated in 'living instruments' and that they both have a constitutional function (institutions and human rights are indeed the main contents of our modern Constitutions), which requires them to keep pace with quickly changing social and political environments. Hence, dynamic-evolutive, teleological and effectiveness-oriented interpretations should prevail over static, textual or *travaux préparatoires*-oriented ones. As has already been stressed, truth is less monolithic, all depending on the subjects, the aims and functions of a particular interpretation. There is here a divide: on the one side general perspectives on the issue and, on the other, particular exercises of interpretation which may or may not fit the general scheme. There are, however, clearly also distinctive features. Thus, in the field of human rights law, there is the tendency by the international bodies to insist on interpretations giving the rights enshrined in the instruments 'practical and concrete effects' or a sort of 'maximum effectiveness' (by adding, for example, positive obligations). The European Court of Human Rights (ECtHR) and the Inter-American Court of Human Rights (IACtHR) constantly referred to this principle[18], as did the European Court of Justice (ECJ)[19] in the realm of European Union law. There is here a distinctive attempt at effectiveness of the law to the benefit of protected individuals. The protection and humanization idea induces these particular features in the interpretation of these instruments by international protection organs – but not necessarily by all States parties to those conventions. Thus, it can be recalled that States like Saudi Arabia display a different stance with regard to conventions such as those of discrimination against women or for the rights of the child. Sweeping reservations do a lot to weaken the text, rather than to strengthen the practical effects of its rights.[20] Reservations are obviously not in themselves an issue of interpretation, but they show quite clearly how the conventional norms are interpreted by the State having formulated them. Hence, the interpretation of such conventions by States like Saudi Arabia will hardly be of the type commended by the international bodies, when laying stress on the practical effects of those rights. And as far as international institutional law is concerned, all the interpretations are by far not purposive and

[18] See, e.g., *Sannino* v. *Italy* (2006), no. 30961/03, § 39.

[19] See, e.g., *Konstantinos Adeneler and others* v. *Ellinikos Organismos Galaktos* (2006), no. C-212/04, § 111.

[20] See, e.g., the discussion in K. Zemanek, 'The Legal Foundations of the International System', *RCADI*, vol. 266, 1997, p. 175ff.

teleological, as the restrictive interpretation of the ICJ in the *IMCO Committee* opinion of 1960 shows.[21] In this opinion, the Court furthered the intention of the parties-argument to have in the relevant Committee of that organization the nations with the greatest commercial ship tonnage, whichever they were. There was thus, according to the Court, no room for interpreting this provision in a progressive and dynamic way, so as to take account of the growing concern against flag-of-convenience States.

Second, there are interpretation-sensitive *sub-subject-matters* within a general subject-matter. An example is criminal international law. In criminal law, the main principle of interpretation (intertwined with substantive principles permeating that area of the law) is its strictness and the prohibition of analogies. However, these principles apply only to the material law and only in the context of interpretations unfavourable to the accused. On the contrary, when an interpretation is in its favour, it can be elastic or even rest on an analogy. Retroactivity in favour of the accused is possible: *lex mitior*. To procedural criminal law, the principles just mentioned do not apply at all. Hence, for example, the International Criminal Tribunal for the former Yugoslavia (ICTY) could indulge in a 'general-principles' approach, based on analogies with municipal law and policy considerations, in the context of the question as to the extent to which a criminal charge could be altered by the prosecution at a late stage of the procedure, when it is to the detriment of the accused (evidence had shown that he committed the more serious crime rather than the more lenient one).[22] The case-law of the same tribunal also shows that when the definition of a crime is unclear, like for rape in the 1990s, the same approach may be followed, even to the detriment of the accused (penetration of the penis into the mouth of the victim, rape or not?).[23] The preceding considerations show that the particularity of the interpretative approach in criminal matters breaks down in sub-areas (procedural law) and that there are also exceptions in substantive law.

Third, it has been suggested (but practice does not bear that out) that there are different interpretative approaches in international law as far as *treaty law* is concerned, on the one side, and as far as *customary international law* is concerned, on the other.[24] The basis for the distinction

[21] ICJ, *Reports*, 1960, p. 150ff.

[22] *Kupreskic*, ICTY, TC, Judgment of 14 January 2000, § 728ff.

[23] For the definition of rape: *Furundzija*, ICTY, TC, Judgment of 10 December 1998, § 174ff.

[24] G. Schwarzenberger, *A Manual of International Law*, 5th edn., Professional Books, London, 1967, pp. 12–14, 29, 148. Generally on the question of customary international law and its interpretation, see Kolb (*supra* note 1), p. 219ff.

is that in the context of treaties, the States have given a common pledge and thus entered voluntarily in a mutual or reciprocal enterprise. Hence, their relationship becomes permeated by considerations of mutuality, reasonableness, reciprocity, cooperation, confidence, non-unilaterality, etc. This is a type of *jus aequum*. On the other side, within the realm of customary international law, the States utter or perform acts of practice essentially under the guise of self-interest. They do not enter into close bonds with other States but consider their own interests. Hence, the whole area remains engrafted upon selfishness, power-policies and unilateralism. This is a sort of *jus strictum*. If one follows this classification, it would follow that the principles of interpretation for the two bodies of the law would significantly differ. Considerations of good faith, reciprocity and purpose would have a great importance in treaty law, besides the eternal reference to the text of the agreement. Considerations flowing from the presumption of State freedom (minimum obligation), of restriction of duties and of judicial caution would dominate the field of international customary law. Thus, treaty rights would have to be interpreted as 'relative' rights, i.e. with due regard clauses for the treaty partners, whereas customary international law would have to be interpreted as giving rise to 'absolute' rights, freedoms of States, where even abuse is not prohibited (and should not necessarily be ruled out by interpretation). Abuse here simply amounts to an unfriendly act. As already suggested, international practice does not show such a sharp and indeed highly impractical dichotomy. It could in any event not be followed as international customary and international conventional law is today closely intertwined (see, for example, the area of international humanitarian law[25]). However, this does not mean that the treaty-interpreter will not look more carefully for the equilibria reached by the parties in their common undertaking, whereas he might inspire himself more of policy considerations and exigencies of the international society as a whole when called to interpret general international law. An example for the latter is the *Jurisdictional Immunities* case (*Germany* v. *Italy*) at the ICJ.[26] Clearly, at the level of general international law, the Court will not be able to stress the textual element: unwritten law is not written law. Apart from this truism, there is certainly a slight shift of perspective when moving from an inter-party *do ut des* undertaking to general norms of the international society, not to

[25] J. M. Henckaerts and L. Doswald-Beck, *Customary International Humanitarian Law*, vols. I-III, Cambridge University Press, 2005.

[26] To be consulted on: www.icj-cij.org.

speak of community-oriented norms of *erga omnes* complexion.[27] It may be added that in the context of customary international law, the first issue may be the one of determining the existence and scope of the rule with regard to practice and *opinio juris*. An interpretation of the rule could come only in the second stage. This peculiarity explains that in practice elements of ascertainment of the rule and elements of interpretation tend to merge into one another in this particular context.

When it comes to the interpretation of *unilateral acts*, it is often claimed that the will of the declaring subject has a greater strength than in the case of bilateral acts.[28] Sometimes, resolutions of the Security Council are quoted to that effect, as also are classical unilateral acts by States.[29] Practice bears this position out, even if the text of such declarations is also of prime importance. Moreover, an intention not compatible with the text will need to be established by extremely conclusive evidence in order to prevail (questions of legitimate expectations created by the text may here heavily interfere). To some extent the same can be said of *bilateral treaties*. In their context, the intention of the parties can more often be concretely grasped than in the context of multilateral treaties, which are a form of 'international legislation'. Arbitral practice[30] shows that reliance on the intention of the parties-argument had in the past a better standing and could more easily yield results in the context of treaties with a small number of treaty parties than in treaties open to all the States of the world.[31] It may well be that this remains to some extent true today. Moreover, in the multilateral treaties, the intentions of the original parties could not prevail over the ones of the States acceding later, since that would entail inequality between the original States and the ones acceding later. It would, however, be in most cases highly fictional to elicit a common

27 For the latter ones, see, e.g., B. Simma, 'From Bilateralism to Community Interest in International Law', *RCADI*, vol. 250, 1994-VI, p. 229ff.

28 Kolb (*supra* note 1), p. 243ff. The ICJ has stressed this point in the context of the interpretation of optional declarations of compulsory jurisdiction under Article 36, § 2, of the Statute: cf., e.g., the *Fisheries Jurisdiction* (*Spain v. Canada*) case, ICJ, *Reports*, 1998, p. 454, § 48. But this is not the only utterance of the Court on that matter, and not all of these utterances have been so much subjectively bent. See the strong dissent of Judge ad hoc Torres Bernardez on this point: *ibid.*, pp. 666–9, § 224, 226, 230.

29 On the greater importance of the will- or intention-element, see M. C. Wood, 'The Interpretation of Security Council Resolutions', *Max Planck Yearbook of United Nations Law*, vol. 2, 1998, p. 73ff.

30 See, e.g., the *Timor Island* arbitration (1914), *RIAA*, vol. XI, p. 497.

31 But there is no true difference in interpretation in different types of treaties, as is sometimes claimed. Cf. for example J. H. Weiler, 'The Interpretation of Treaties, A Re-Examination', *EJIL*, vol. 21, 2010, p. 507ff.

intention of all the original and later acceding parties. These were not present at the conference adopting the treaty and original intentions could only be known through the text or, possibly, a study of preparatory work, if available. In any event, such a common intention would be a shifting and mobile one, a sort of unfolding intention, since with every new State acceding to the convention it would have to be, if not redefined, at least ascertained again. In such cases, in order to avoid manifest conundrums, the text of the treaty obtains a greater share in the interpretive process with regard to an often quite elusive common intention (which should not become a *tabula in naufragio* for the interpreter). All these minor aspects do not detract from the fact that the VCLT regime is flexible enough to accommodate such variations within the classes and types of treaties. Each one remains open to a case-by-case approach. In other words, in not all bilateral treaty disputes will the intention of the parties have a greater weight than the text; conversely in not all multilateral treaty disputes will the text be more important than a whole array of other arguments, among which could also figure the intention of the parties and preparatory work. And the regime of the VCLT is flexible enough to also be extended by analogy to other legal norms than conventional ones, even if the particular interpretative bouquets to be used may slightly shift to take account of the specific nature or purpose of the act in question (e.g., unilateral legal acts). In a certain sense, this is the miracle of Articles 31–3: to be considered at once to be sufficiently directive to cast the interpretive process out of the quagmire of boundless subjectivism and ad hoc-manipulation; and yet to remain sufficiently flexible to be able to maintain the process relevant for so many different contexts, typologies and acts. In a sense, this exercise is a squaring of the circle at its best.

V. Conclusion

The short considerations presented in this chapter have tended to show that:

1) It is a postulate of reason and of policy (concerning the importance of legal certainty) that there shall be certain common and agreed rules or maxims of interpretation.
2) Because of the specificity of international society deprived of centralized organs, the role of such agreed rules is particularly important in international law.

3) The VCLT of 1969 has succeeded in setting out a fairly articulated and common-law regime for the interpretation of treaties.
4) The regime of the VCLT can be expanded by analogy to other sources and subjects in international law, i.e. to non-State entities, to unilateral acts, to customary rules, etc., always *mutatis mutandis*.
5) The common core rules do not preclude flexibility in the combination of elements to be selected in a particular context of interpretation.
6) International practice has not as yet evidenced the need for the development of a special sub-set of rules for particular subject-matters in international law, that is rules which would prevail over the general rules of the VCLT on account of the *lex specialis* rule.
7) International practice does show that interpretation, as a high manifestation of human spirit, is and remains a complex and multifaceted process, whose reduction to unity can always be only very partial. The particular interpretation exercises will depend heavily on many factors, among which are the person performing it (*quis judicabit?*), the function or goal the interpretation shall perform, and the broader legal and political context.
8) *Unitas in varietate, ex pluribus una* or *res mutandis?* The question may here just be posed, as a sort of end and new starting point, that is: as a sort of 'shut down and restart'.

18

Halfway between fragmentation and convergence: the role of the rules of the organization in the interpretation of constituent treaties

PAOLO PALCHETTI

1. Introduction

When considering whether the general rules of treaty interpretation set forth in Articles 31 and 32 of the Vienna Convention on the Law of Treaties apply to every category of treaty or whether, to the contrary, different rules of interpretation apply depending on the nature or content of the treaty, the reference to treaties establishing international organizations becomes unavoidable.[1] This category of treaties has frequently been regarded as having a special status.[2] Those who support the view that the method of treaty interpretation is fragmented usually rely on the practice relating to the interpretation of these treaties in order to find confirmation of their view.

The debate on the suitability of the general rules set forth in Articles 31 and 32 to regulate the interpretation of constituent treaties is an old one and clearly predates the recent debate over the fragmentation of international law. When working on the codification of the law

[1] Vienna Convention on the Law of Treaties, Vienna, 23 May 1969, in force 27 January 1980, 1155 UNTS 331.

[2] See, among others, C. Brölmann, 'Specialized Rules of Treaty Interpretation: International Organizations', in D. Hollis (ed.), *Oxford Guide to Treaties* (Oxford: Oxford University Press, 2012), pp. 507–24; T. Sato, *Evolving Constitutions of International Organizations* (Dordrecht: Brill, 1996); E. Lauterpacht, 'The Development of the Law of International Organizations by the Decisions of International Tribunals' (1976) 152 *Recueil des Cours de l'Académie de Droit International de la Haye* 381–478. As is well known, the International Court of Justice also referred to the fact that treaties establishing international organizations 'can raise specific problems of interpretation'. See *Legality of the Use by a State of Nuclear Weapons in Armed Conflict (Request by WHO), Advisory Opinion*, ICJ Rep 1996, p. 66, para. 19.

of treaties, the International Law Commission was aware of the debate surrounding these treaties. Within the Commission, some eminent members forcefully stressed the need to distinguish constituent treaties from the other treaties, arguing that the rules generally applicable to 'ordinary' treaties do not necessarily apply to constitutive treaties.[3] In the end, the Commission recognized, at least indirectly, the special position of constituent treaties, as it took care to address in a specific provision, which later became Article 5 of the Convention, the question of whether the general rules of the law of treaties also cover this special category of treaties.[4] However, far from taking refuge behind a more neutral 'without-prejudice clause', the Commission, and later the Vienna Conference, took a clear stance on this issue: in principle, the general rules of the law of treaties, including the general rules on treaty interpretation, apply to any treaty 'which is the constituent instrument of an international organization'. In this respect, Article 5 provides support to the view that there is a unitary method of treaty interpretation which also applies to constituent treaties. Yet, under the Vienna Convention the recognition that the general rules of the law of treaties also apply to this category of treaty is not without qualification. As Article 5 makes clear, the application of the general rules must be 'without prejudice to any relevant rules of the organization'.

The reference to the rules of the organization contained in Article 5 may be relevant when it comes to determine whether there exists a derogatory regime of interpretation which is applicable to a given organization. Indeed, such derogatory regime may find its legal basis in the rules of the organization rather that in a *lex specialis* regulating the interpretation of all constitutive treaties. Moreover, in certain cases the interpretation of a specific provision of the constituent treaty may be explained by reference to rules of the organization which embody an agreed interpretation of the provision at issue. The reference to the rules of the organization is all the more interesting since, as we will see,[5] this notion does not encompass

[3] See, for instance, the intervention of Rosenne, in *Yearbook of the International Law Commission*, 1964, vol. I, at 278. For a review of the different positions within the International Law Commission, see W. Lang, 'Les règles d'interprétation codifies par la Convention de Vienne sur le droit des traits et les divers types de traités' (1973) 24 *Österreichische Zeitschrift für öffentliches Recht* 113–73, at 116–24.

[4] Article 5 provides that '[t]he present Convention applies to any treaty which is the constituent instrument of an international organization and to any treaty adopted within an international organization without prejudice to any relevant rules of the organization'.

[5] See Section 2 of this chapter.

only written rules embodied in the constitutive treaty or in subsequent agreements of the parties, but it also includes the established practice of the organization.

Given the potential impact of the rules of the organization on the interpretation of the constituent instruments, it is somewhat surprising that this issue has so far attracted little attention in international legal literature.[6] In fact, one may wonder whether, at least under certain circumstances, resort to a specific method for the purposes of interpreting a constituent treaty may be better justified by regarding it as an application of rules of the organization rather than by relying on the idea that there exists a *lex specialis* applying to all constituent treaties. It is the purpose of the present chapter to shed some light on this specific question.

2. Rules of the organization and treaty interpretation in the preparatory works of the 1969 Vienna Convention

A perusal of the preparatory works of the Vienna Convention on the Law of Treaties reveals that the drafters were aware of the possible impact of the rules of the organization in the context of treaty interpretation. They were also aware of the fact that the established practice of an organization forms part of the rules of the organization and that such practice has a fundamental role in the interpretation of the constituent instrument.

When it was first formulated, the provision which later became Article 5 of the 1969 Convention only concerned the applicability of the general rules on termination of treaties to treaties establishing international organizations. Draft Article 48, provisionally adopted in 1963, provided

[6] But see, most recently, Ch. Peters, 'Subsequent Practice and Established Practice of International Organizations: Two Sides of the Same Coin?' (2011) 3 *Goettingen Journal of International Law* 617–42. Explicit references to Article 5 for the purposes of treaty interpretation are quite rare in the case law of international tribunals. In *Golder* v. *United Kingdom* the European Court of Human Rights recognized that 'for the interpretation of the European Convention account is to be taken of those Articles [Articles 31 and 32 of the Vienna Convention] subject, where appropriate, to "any relevant rules of the organization" – the Council of Europe – within which it has been adopted (Article 5 of the Vienna Convention)' (Application No. 4451/70, judgment 21 February 1975, para. 29). In *Mamatkulov and Askarov* v. *Turkey* the Court referred to this passage in *Golder* as a relevant precedent supporting the recognition of 'the special nature of the Convention as an instrument of human rights protection' (Applications Nos. 46827/99 and 46951/99, Judgment [GC] 4 February 2005, para. 111 of the Judgment). However, while the European Court alluded to the possibility of special rules of interpretation which are applicable to conventions adopted within the Council of Europe, it did not clarify whether any such rule in fact existed or what its content was. I am indebted to Eirik Bjorge for having drawn my attention to these two Judgments.

that, 'where a treaty is the constituent instrument of an international organization', the application of the general rules dealing with the termination of treaties 'shall be subject to the established rules of the organization'.[7] However, when addressing other aspects of the law of treaties, the International Law Commission soon realized that the scope of application of this clause was too limited. Significantly, this issue also emerged during the discussion over the content of the rules of treaty interpretation, particularly, as we will see, in relation to the question of the weight to be given to the subsequent practice of the organization as an element of the interpretation of the constituent treaty. During the Vienna Conference, the debate over the relationship between the general rules of the law of treaties and the rules of the organization was animated by the proposal made by some delegations to delete Article 5. Several delegations defended its retention by referring, *inter alia*, to the impact that the rules of the organization may have on the interpretation of the constituent treaty.[8] The observer of the International Labour Organization, Wilfred Jenks, went so far as to suggest that the method of interpretation applied in the practice of that organization differed in some respect from that codified in the draft convention.[9]

Rules of the organization which are at variance with the general rules of the law of treaties may be contained in the constituent treaty itself. The President of the 1968–69 Vienna Conference, Roberto Ago, referred to this situation when he observed that '[t]he constituent instrument of an international organization might conceivably contain rules of interpretation which were at variance with those laid down in the convention, and the last phrase of article 4 ("without prejudice to any relevant rules of the organization") would then apply to the constituent instrument'.[10] This kind of situation appears unproblematic. As most of the rules of the law of treaties, including those on treaty interpretation, may be derogated by special rules, States are free to subject the constituent treaty to a special regime. The main element of interest in Article 5 lies in the fact that the rules of the organization are not only those contained in the constituent instrument but also include rules resulting from the established

[7] *Yearbook of the International Law Commission*, 1964, vol. II, p. 213. For the history of Article 5 see H. Anderson, 'Article 5', in O. Corten and P. Klein (eds.), *The Vienna Conventions on the Law of Treaties: A Commentary* (Oxford: Oxford University Press, 2011), vol. I, pp. 89–92.

[8] See, for instance, the interventions of the delegations of France and Ghana, *United Nations Conference on the Law of Treaties, Official records, 1st session*, respectively p. 46 and p. 55.

[9] *Ibid.*, p. 37.

[10] *United Nations Conference on the Law of Treaties, Official records, 2nd session*, p. 5.

practice of the organization. Unlike the 1986 Vienna Convention on the Law of Treaties between States and International Organizations and between International Organizations, the 1969 text does not expressly state this point. However, the drafting history of Article 5 clearly confirms that the notion of rules of the organization also includes the established practice of the organization.[11] At the Vienna Conference, the President of the drafting committee made clear that 'the term "rules" in article 4 [later Article 5 of the Convention] applied both to written rules and to unwritten customary rules'.[12] Some delegations even stressed that it was precisely because of the fundamental role played by the practice of the organization that draft Article 5 had to be included in the text of the Convention. Most revealing in this respect is the view expressed by the French representative, Michel Virally:

> At the conclusion stage it [a treaty which was the constituent instrument of an organization] was comparable to any other treaty, but the position changed when it entered into force. Ordinary treaties were applied by the States parties to them through their executive, legislative and judicial organs. A treaty which was the constituent instrument of an organization was applied both by the parties as members of the organization and by the organs of the organization. That produced a whole series of consequences which the draft convention could not cover. The inclusion of constituent instruments of international organizations in article 4 [later Article 5 of the Convention] was therefore justified.[13]

The relevance of the practice of the organization was also discussed by the Special Rapporteur, Waldock, in relation to the issue of treaty interpretation. His view, which was widely shared by the Commission, is extremely interesting for the purposes of the present study as it raises the question of the interplay between the general rules on treaty interpretation and the rules of the organization. When considering the role of the subsequent practice of the parties for the purposes of treaty interpretation, Waldock observed:

> The problem of the effect of the practice of organs of an international organization upon the interpretation of its constituent instrument raises an important constitutional issue as to how far individual Member States are bound by the practice. Although the practice of the organ as such may be consistent, it may have been opposed by individual Members or by a group of Members which have been outvoted. This special problem

[11] Anderson, 'Article 5', p. 92.

[12] *United Nations Conference on the Law of Treaties, Official records, 1st session*, p. 147.

[13] *Ibid.*, pp. 45–46.

appears to relate to the law of international organizations rather than to the general law of treaties, and the Special Rapporteur suggests that it would not be appropriate to attempt to deal with it in the present articles.[14]

This view is highly significant for a number of reasons. First, by referring to the existence of special problems raised in connection to the practice of the organs of an international organization, Waldock appears to recognize that the notion of 'practice of the organization' must be kept distinct from the notion of 'subsequent conduct of the parties' which is provided by Article 31, paragraph 3 (b).[15] Secondly, the weight to be given to the practice of the organization for the purposes of interpreting the constituent treaty is regarded as a question which has to be addressed in the light of the 'law of international organizations' and which cannot be answered on the basis of the general rules of interpretation. Finally, while Waldock appears to refer to the practice of the organization simply as a means of interpretation, the distinction he draws between the practice of the organization and the subsequent conduct of the parties, and the importance assigned in this context to the law of international organizations seem to suggest that the practice of the organization may play a greater role than that of a possible means of interpretation. His view comes close to the idea that such practice may amount to a rule of the organization and, as such, it may interfere with the ordinary application of the general rules of interpretation. This would imply that, at least with respect to established practice amounting to a rule of the organization, Article 5, and not Article 31, provides the legal basis for assessing the role of the practice of the organization in the interpretation of the constituent instrument.[16]

3. Rules of the organization establishing a *lex specialis* on the interpretation of the constituent treaty

While constituent treaties can contain specific rules of interpretation, this is certainly a rare occurrence. Some constituent treaties confer on

[14] *Yearbook of the International Law Commission*, 1964, vol. II, pp. 59–60.

[15] On this issue, see the classical studies of F. Capotorti, 'Sul valore della prassi applicative dei trattati secondo la Convenzione di Vienna', in *International Law at the Time of Its Codification: Essays in Honour of Roberto Ago*, 3 vols. (Milan: Giuffrè, 1987), pp. 213–18, and P. Reuter, 'Quelques réflexions sur la notion de "pratique internationale", specialement en matière d'organisations internationales', in *Studi in onore di Giuseppe Sperduti* (Milan: Giuffrè, 1983), pp. 198–207.

[16] For a thorough assessment of the interplay between these two provisions, see Peters, 'Subsequent Practice and Established Practice', pp. 617–42.

specific organs the power of authoritative interpretations of their terms.[17] Even in these cases, however, no indication is offered as to the method of interpretation to be employed to resolve interpretative disputes.

The fact that constituent treaties are generally silent on the matter of interpretation does not rule out the possibility that the established practice of the organization may lead to the emergence of a rule of the organization providing for the application of a specific method of interpretation. As we have seen, this possibility was expressly acknowledged by some delegations during the debate over draft Article 5. At the Vienna Conference the representative of the International Labour Organization appeared to refer to a special rule of interpretation applicable to that organization when he observed that 'ILO practice on interpretation had involved greater recourse to preparatory work than was envisaged in article 28'.[18]

This kind of situation is more likely to arise when the constituent treaty assigns the power of authoritative interpretation to a specific organ and this organ develops a consistent practice supporting the recourse to a method of interpretation which differs from that envisaged under Articles 31 and 32 of the Vienna Convention. A possible example in this respect may be offered by the practice of the European Union. In the context of this organization, the European Court of Justice has stated some general guidelines on the interpretation of EU law, including EU Treaties. In *CILFIT* the European Court of Justice observed that 'every provision of Community law must be placed in its context and interpreted in the light of the provisions of Community law as a whole, regard being had to the objectives thereof and to its state of evolution at the date on which the provision in question is to be applied'.[19] As this method of interpretation does not entirely conform to the method set forth under the general rules of interpretation, particularly because of the importance attached to the consideration of the objectives of EU law and the emphasis placed on dynamic interpretation, one may wonder whether the case law of the European judicial body on this issue could be regarded as amounting to a rule of the organization which establishes a special rules of interpretation. While this issue would deserve a more thorough assessment, it is sufficient to note here that this characterization of the case law of the

[17] See the examples mentioned by C. E. Amerasinghe, *Principles of the International Law of International Organizations* (2nd edn., Cambridge: Cambridge University Press, 2005), pp. 25–33.

[18] *United Nations Conference on the Law of Treaties, Official records, 1st session*, p. 37.

[19] C-283/81, *Srl CILFIT and Lanificio di Gavardo SpA* v. *Ministry of Health* [1982] ECR 3430.

European Court of Justice as a rule of the organization cannot be ruled out. The case law of a judicial body operating within the framework of an international organization can be regarded as a form of practice of the organization and, as such, it may give rise to a rule of the organization within the meaning of Article 5 of the 1969 Convention. This is the more so in the case of the European Court of Justice, an organ to which the Treaty on the European Union assigns the function to 'ensure that in the interpretation and the application of the Treaties the law is observed'.[20] Significantly, this view would find some support in the position expressed by the European Commission with regard to the meaning to be given to the notion of 'rules of the organization' in the context of the draft articles on the responsibility of international organizations. In the comments send to the International Law Commission, the European Commission observed that 'the notion of "established practice of the organization" must be understood broadly as encompassing the case law of the courts of an organization'.[21] It also noted that, in the case of the European Union, 'the case law of the European Court of Justice and the Court of First Instance is of particular importance', thereby clearly suggesting that, within the context of that organization, the case law of the European Court of Justice may be regarded as amounting, at least under certain circumstances, to a rule of the organization.

When the practice of the organization leads to the emergence of a special rule of interpretation, a question which may be raised is whether this special rule should only apply to the interpretation of the constituent treaty and of the acts adopted on its basis or whether it could also be applied to the interpretation of agreements concluded by the organization with States or other international organizations. The problem was raised in some cases before the European Court of Justice but the European Court did not take a clear stand on it.[22] However, as the rules of the organization do not have legal effects in relation to third subjects, there is little doubt that any special rules of interpretation, which are provided

[20] Article 19 (1) of the Treaty on the European Union, OJ C83/13, 30 March 2010. On the importance of this provision for the purpose of determining which EU organ has the power to render an authoritative interpretation of the constituent treaties, see J. Klabbers, *An Introduction to International Institutional Law* (2nd edn., Cambridge: Cambridge University Press, 2009), p. 101.

[21] UN doc. A/CN.4/545, p. 15.

[22] See C-270/80, *Polydor Ltd.* v. *Harlequin Record Shops Ltd* [1982] ECR 333; C-104/81; *Hauptzollamt Mainz* v. *C.A. Kufpferberg & Cie. KG a.A.* [1982] ECR 3664.

under the rules of the organization, should not in principle be applied to agreements concluded between the organization and a third subject.

4. Rules of the organization establishing the interpretation to be given to a provision of the constituent treaty

Apart from the case in which rules of the organization establish a special rule of interpretation which applies to the constituent treaty and, more comprehensively, to the law of that organization, the interplay between the rules of the organization and the general rules of interpretation may take a different form. Rules of the organization may directly incorporate the interpretation to be given to a certain provision of the constituent treaty. As a consequence, instead of having recourse to the general rules of interpretation set forth in the Vienna Convention, one could rely on the rules of the organization in order to determine the meaning to be attached to the provisions concerned.

Rules of the organization providing an authoritative interpretation of certain provisions of the constituent treaty may result from the established practice of the organization. It is a trite observation that the practice of the organization has a fundamental role when the interpretation of constituent treaties is at stake. The case law of the International Court of Justice, particularly those pronouncements dealing with the interpretation of the United Nations Charter, provides ample confirmation of that. It suffices here to recall that in the *Namibia* case the Court based its interpretation of Article 27 of the Charter on the practice of the organization; in particular, it observed that the 'procedure followed by the Security Council . . . has been generally accepted by Members of the United Nations and evidences a *general practice* of that Organization'.[23] In the *Wall* case, it approached the interpretation of Article 12 of the Charter moving from the premise that it was 'appropriate for it to examine the significance of that Article, having regard to the relevant texts and the practice of the United Nations';[24] it then concluded that 'the *accepted practice* of the General Assembly, as it has evolved, is consistent with Article 12, paragraph 1, of the Charter'.[25] The importance thus assigned to the element

[23] *Legal Consequences for States of the Continued Presence of South Africa in Namibia (South West Africa) notwithstanding Security Council Resolution 276 (1970)*, ICJ Rep 1971, p. 22 (italics added).

[24] *Legal Consequences of the Construction of a Wall in the Occupied Palestinian Territory*, ICJ Rep 2004, p. 148.

[25] *Ibid.*, p. 150 (italics added).

of practice has frequently been regarded as an application of the rule of interpretation set forth in Article 31 (3) (c) of the Vienna Convention.[26] However, it may be argued that, while the Court never referred in this context to Article 5 of the Vienna Convention, the weight given to the 'general' or 'accepted' practice of the organization is to be regarded as a recognition that such practice amounted to a rule of the organization and was therefore decisive for the purposes of determining the meaning of the provision concerned. In other words, one may suggest that what was at stake in these cases was not the subsequent practice of the parties under the meaning of Article 31 but the established practice of the organization under Article 5.[27] Such view finds support in the fact that the Court only gave relevance to the practice of the organization, without taking care to verify whether such practice also 'establishes the agreement of the parties regarding its interpretation', as required by Article 31. Another significant aspect is that such practice was substantially the only element which the Court took into account for the purposes of interpreting the provisions concerned.

While reference is here made only to rules of the organization establishing the agreed interpretation of certain provisions of the constituent instrument, it must be admitted that in some cases it will not be easy to draw a clear distinction between these rules and rules of the organization amending the treaty. Once it is accepted that the established practice of the organization can be decisive for the purposes of determining the meaning of a certain treaty provision, the line separating the interpretation of the treaty from its modification may become extremely thin.[28] Significantly, this aspect appears to be reflected in the definition of 'rules of the organization' contained in the 1986 Vienna Convention. While Article 2 (1) (j)

[26] See, for instance, I. Sinclair, *The Vienna Convention on the Law of Treaties* (2nd edn., Manchester: Manchester University Press, 1984), p. 137.

[27] Peters, 'Subsequent Practice and Established Practice', p. 625, fn. 30, observed that, while the International Court of Justice never referred expressly to Article 5, 'there are several cases in which the basic thought of this provision might have been applied'.

[28] As observed by the Special Rapporteur, Waldock, 'if the interpretation adopted by the parties diverges, as sometimes happens, from the natural and ordinary meaning of the terms, there may be a blurring of the line between the interpretation and the amendment of a treaty by subsequent practice'. *Yearbook of the International Law Commission*, 1964, vol. II, p. 60. In the same vein, according to G. Ress, 'The Interpretation of the Charter', in B. Simma (ed.), *The Charter of the United Nations: A Commentary* (2nd edn., Oxford: Oxford University Press, 2002), p. 30, in its advisory opinion on *Namibia*, 'the ICJ clearly went beyond the ordinary meaning of the term and gave broad consideration to the practice to determine the meaning of Art. 27(3). This exceeds the scope of treaty interpretation and enters the field of implied modification.'

requires that decisions and resolutions of the organization, in order to fall within that definition, be adopted in accordance with the constituent instrument, the same condition is not extended in respect to the established practice.[29] This suggests that rules of the organization based on the established practice may informally modify provisions contained in the constituent treaty.

5. Concluding remarks

Widely divergent views were expressed at the Vienna Conference about the impact on the integrity of the law of the treaties of the provision which later became Article 5 of the Vienna Convention. Some delegations regarded it as a factor of fragmentation of the legal regime governing treaties and proposed its deletion;[30] for others, to the contrary, it acted as a factor of convergence. The latter view was defended, in particular, by the expert consultant, Humphrey Waldock, who observed:

> [S]ome representatives had interpreted article 4 [later Article 5 of the Convention] as though the International Law Commission had intended to make a general reservation in favour of international organizations and relegate the provisions of the convention to the background. That had not been the intention of the Commission, which, on the contrary, had proceeded on the assumption that the provisions of the convention would be generally applicable to all treaties.[31]

Waldock's view seems to better capture the real significance of Article 5. While it certainly introduces a certain degree of flexibility in the legal regime applicable to treaties establishing international organizations, particularly because of the importance attached to the established practice of the organization, it can hardly be denied that this provision acts as a factor of convergence rather than as one of fragmentation.

[29] Article 2 (1) (j) provides that '"rules of the organization" means, in particular, the constituent instruments, decisions and resolutions adopted in accordance with them, and established practice of the organization'. G. Gaja, 'A New Vienna Convention on Treaties between States and International Organizations or between International Organizations: A Critical Commentary', (1987) 58 *British Yearbook of International Law*, 253–69 at 262, observed that 'the wording makes clear that . . . the reference to established practice is not conditional on the constituent instrument of the international organization being respected'. The same solution was retained in Article 2 (b) of the 2011 Articles on the responsibility of international organizations.

[30] See, in particular, the intervention of the United States, *United Nations Conference on the Law of Treaties, Official records, 1st session*, p. 43.

[31] *Ibid.*, pp. 56–7.

With regard to the interpretation of treaties establishing international organizations, Article 5 reaffirms the unity of the method of treaty interpretation while at the same time leaving open the possibility that, in respect to the interpretation of the law governing a given organization, a special rule applies. By attaching importance to the rules of the organization, this provision does not afford any support to the view that constituent treaties constitute a special category which invariably requires a special rule of interpretation. The focus is on the specificities of each organization and no concession is made to the idea of a special rule of interpretation which applies indistinctly to every constituent instrument. This solution has much to be praised. It takes due account of the fact that the approach to the interpretation of the constituent instrument may vary considerably depending on the structure and the institutional dynamics of the organization concerned.[32] Thus, it is for the interpreter, in each case, to establish the existence of rules of the organization which are controlling on matters of interpretation. If no such rule is proven to exist, the general rules of interpretation will provide guidance as to how the constituent treaty shall be interpreted.

[32] A case-by-case approach to the problem of the interpretation of constituent treaties was recently advocated by J. Arato, 'Treaty Interpretation and Constitutional Transformation: Informal Change in International Organizations', (2013) 38 *Yale Journal of International Law*, 289–357, and by J. E. Alvarez, *International Organizations as Law-makers*, (Oxford: Oxford University Press, 2005), p. 89.

19

The convergence of the methods of treaty interpretation: Different regimes, different methods of interpretation?

EIRIK BJORGE

1. Introduction

If there was some decades ago a tendency in international law to say that different fields of international law were divided by boundaries with regard to their content – but also with regard to the method used to unearth what is contained in the sources of law[1] – then surely it is possible now to say that that tendency has been reversed. This development should be seen as a positive one, as it strengthens the coherence of the international legal system.[2]

This chapter deals with the question of whether one may conclude from the debate on the fragmentation of law that the method of treaty interpretation is fragmented. In the upshot, the answer which this chapter provides to that question is 'no'.

First the chapter deals with the notion of self-contained regimes in international law and what their alleged existence may mean for the law of treaties. In order to do so the chapter takes issue with the reliance in the

[1] M. Koskenniemi, 'Fragmentation of International Law: Difficulties Arising from the Diversification and Expansion of International Law' Report of the Study Group of the International Law Commission, finalized by Martti Koskenniemi A/CN.4/L.682, e.g. [130], [159]–[171].

[2] See M. Andenas, 'The Centre Reasserting Itself – From Fragmentation to Transformation of International Law', in M. Derlén and J. Lindholm (eds), *Volume in Honor of Pär Hallström* (Uppsala: Iustus 2012); A. A. Cançado Trindade, 'A Century of International Justice and Prospects for the Future' Chapter 3 in this volume, p. 56; P. Webb, 'Factors Influencing Fragmentation and Convergence in International Courts' Chapter 6 in this volume, p. 146; J. Crawford, 'Chance, Order, Change: The Course of International Law' (2013) 365 *Hague Recueil* 1, pp. 205–29; F. Berman, 'Community Law and International Law: How Far Does Either Belong to the Other?', in B. S. Markesinis (ed.), *The Clifford Chance Lectures Volume I: Bridging the Channel* (Oxford: Oxford University Press 1996), p. 277.

literature on a 1930 article by McNair which, it is argued here, has been widely misunderstood and taken as a licence, from a distinguished author and judge, to say that the *law of treaties* is as fragmented as some have seen international law itself to be. The chapter then turns to the different categorizations which have been applied to treaties (focusing on the three-way split often found in the literature between human rights treaties, constitutional treaties and contractual treaties), and the attendant arguments that some of them call for a restrictive and sovereignty-bound style of interpretation; others, for a teleologic or evolutionary one. The chapter argues that none of these distinctions is really convincing. Then the chapter, by way of an analysis of jurisprudence from the, turns to that which more directly concerns the methods of treaty interpretation adopted, and ventures to show that not only does the Court use interpretation in order to dispel misgivings in the literature about the fragmentation of international law; it also, and by the same token, shows by the interpretive approaches it applies that the method of treaty interpretation itself is not fragmented but in fact unified and coherent.[3]

In particular, two classic judgments have been seen as setting out the classical parameters of the debate on 'self-contained regimes' in international law.[4] In *Case of the SS 'Wimbledon'* the Permanent Court held that the provisions relating to the Kiel Canal in the Treaty of Versailles were 'self-contained',[5] and in *United States Diplomatic and Consular Staff in Tehran* the International Court concluded that 'the rules of diplomatic law, in short, constitute a self-contained regime'.[6]

The Report of the Study Group of the International Law Commission (ILC) made the point that conflict-resolution and interpretation cannot

[3] R. Gardiner, *Treaty Interpretation* (Oxford: Oxford University Press 2008), p. 142; N. Matz-Lück, 'Norm Interpretation across International Regimes: Competences and Legitimacy', in M. A. Young (ed.), *Regime Interaction in International Law: Facing Fragmentation* (Cambridge: Cambridge University Press 2012), pp. 211–27.

[4] See, for example, B. Simma, 'Self-Contained Regimes' (1985) 16 *Netherlands Yearbook of International Law* 111, pp. 115–17; B. Simma and D. Pulkowski, 'Of Planets and the Universe: Self-Contained Regimes in International Law' (2006) 17 *EJIL* 483, pp. 491–2; B. Simma and D. Pulkowski, '*Leges speciales* and Self-Contained Regimes', in J. Crawford and others (eds.), *The Law of International Responsibility* (Oxford: Oxford University Press 2010) pp. 140–50; Koskenniemi, 'Fragmenation Report', note 1 above, [123]–[127]; J. Crawford and P. Nevill, 'Relations between International Courts and Tribunals: The "Regime Problem"', in M. A. Young (ed.), *Regime Interaction in International Law: Facing Fragmentation* (Cambridge: Cambridge University Press 2012) pp. 257–9.

[5] *Case of the SS 'Wimbledon'* (1923) PCIJ Series A No. 1, pp. 15, 23–4. Also: *Exchange of Greek and Turkish Populations*, Advisory opinion (1925) PCIJ Series A No. 10, pp. 6, 20.

[6] *United States Diplomatic and Consular Staff in Tehran (United States of America* v. *Iran)*, Judgment ICJ Rep 1980 pp. 3, 40 [86].

be distinguished from each other; whether there is a conflict and what can be done to it prima facie depends upon the way in which the relevant rules are interpreted. The ILC pointed to Article 31(3)(c) of the Vienna Convention as the 'master key' to the house of international law, but it also stressed that there is no need for formal reference to Article 31(3)(c) as 'other techniques provide sufficiently the need to take into account the normative environment' of a treaty.[7]

The principles of systemic integration, to which the ILC pointed with approval, have a long pedigree in international law. McNair pointed out how treaties must be 'applied and interpreted against the background of the general principles of international law'.[8] The arbitral tribunal in *Georges Pinson* even held that a treaty must be seen as referring 'tacitement au droit international commun, pour toutes les questions qu'elle ne résout pas elle-même en termes exprès et d'une façon différente'.[9] Not only has international law for many decades demanded that general international law has a role to play in treaty interpretation; it has also pointed to a need to take into account the normative environment more widely.[10] This point was made by the tribunal in *Tardieu-Jaspard*: 'il faut tenir compte du fait qu'il faut placer et interpréter l'accord Tardieu-Jaspar dans le cadre des accords de La Haye de janvier 1930, c'est-à-dire dans le cadre du Plan Young qui détermine soigneusement par quelle méthode les "paiements allemands" et les "transferts allemand" s'effectueront'.[11] The same point had been made even earlier, in the 1905 case *Muscat Dhows*,[12] where the tribunal set up by the Permanent Court of Arbitration had been asked to interpret the treaty term '*protégés*' in the Act of the Brussels Conference of 1890. The tribunal held that the interpretation must correspond to the intentions of the parties, as well as to 'principes du droit international tels qu'ils ont été exprimés dans les conventions en vigueur à cette époque, dans la législation nationale en tant qu'elle a obtenu une reconnaissance internationale et dans la pratique du droit des gens'.[13] In no way have these insights been expressed only in the diverse jurisprudence of arbitral tribunals, however. The International Court gave expression to much the same rule when it held in *Right of Passage* that 'it

[7] Koskenniemi, 'Fragmenation Report', note 1 above, [420]–[421].

[8] A. D. McNair, *The Law of Treaties* (2nd edn., Oxford: Oxford University Press 1961), p. 466.

[9] *Georges Pinson (France/United Mexican States)* (1928) 5 RIAA 327, 422.

[10] Koskenniemi, 'Fragmenation Report', note 1 above, [414].

[11] *Différend concernant l'accord Tardieu-Jaspard (Belgium/France)* (1930) 3 RIAA 1701, 1713.

[12] *Affaire des boutres de Mascate (France c Grande-Bretagne)* (1905) 11 RIAA 83.

[13] *Ibid.*, 93–4.

is a rule of interpretation that a text emanating from a Government must, in principle, be interpreted as producing and intended to produce effects in accordance with existing law and not in violation of it'.[14] That overarching debate is important for the argument which is attempted here but its relevance is primarily as a background to the question of whether a fragmentation is prevalent in terms of the methods of interpretation applied in the different fields of international law.

The proliferation, already in 1930, both of international treaties and international tribunals convinced McNair that our understanding of treaties 'will be made easier if we free ourselves from the traditional notion that the instrument known as the treaty is governed by a single set of rules, however inadequate, and set ourselves to study the greatly differing legal character of the several kinds of treaties and to frame rules appropriate to the character of each kind'.[15] It is difficult to take issue with this proposition if it is taken at face value.

McNair's article has, however, been seen as a call for a fragmented approach to the interpretation of different types of treaty. Thus, for example, Brölmann takes it for granted that different types of treaty ought to be interpreted differently, and explicitly cites McNair's 1930 article as evidence for it, when she states that 'not all interpretive rules are the same for all treaties'. As mentioned above, she sees the interpretation of treaties constituting international organizations as being different from other types of treaty interpretation, as it to her mind is more of a teleologic approach which focuses on the object and purpose of the instrument.[16] Weiler, too, has argued that different rules of treaty interpretation apply to different types of treaty. As was discussed above, he sees treaty interpretation as a wide-ranging set of practices; the general rule of interpretation, to his mind, is 'both descriptively and prescriptively an "unreal" signpost of contemporary treaty interpretation'.[17]

[14] *Case concerning Right of Passage over Indian Territory*, Preliminary Objections ICJ Rep 1957 p. 142.

[15] A. D. McNair, 'The Functions and Differing Legal Character of Treaties' (1930) 11 *BYIL* 100, p. 118; McNair, *The Law of Treaties*, note 8 above, pp. 739–54. Also: J. Crawford, *Brownlie's Principles of Public International Law* (8th edn., Oxford: Oxford University Press 2012), pp. 369–70.

[16] C. Brölmann, 'Specialized Rules of Treaty Interpretation: International Organizations', in D. Hollis (ed.), *Oxford Guide to Treaties* (Oxford: Oxford University Press 2012), pp. 507–12.

[17] J. H. H. Weiler, 'The Interpretation of Treaties – A Re-Examination' (2010) 21 *EJIL* 507, p. 507; J. H. H. Weiler, 'Prolegomena to a Meso-Theory of Treaty Interpretation at the Turn of the Century' IILJ International Legal Theory Colloquium: Interpretation and Judgment in International Law (NYU Law School, 14 February 2008), p. 14.

Andenas has argued that many of the arguments of autonomy or separateness – both regarding the substance of the law and the method applied by different organs of international law – evaporate when international courts and tribunals apply an open method taking account of sources from other jurisdictions.[18]

It is argued here that it would be a misconstruction to interpret McNair's by now classic article as saying that different methods of interpretation ought to be applied to different types of treaty. It is clear enough, as Crawford has pointed out in this regard,[19] that it is fruitful to contemplate the different features of different kinds of treaties and even to expect the development of specialized rules, such as for example how the effect of war between parties varies according to the type of treaty involved,[20] or how the fundamental change of circumstances rule is inapplicable to boundary treaties.[21] But when McNair said that the task of deciding treaty disputes would be made easier if 'we free ourselves from the traditional notion that the instrument known as the treaty is governed by a single set of rules' and exhorted us to 'study the greatly differing legal character of the several kinds of treaties and to frame rules appropriate to the character of each kind'[22] what he meant, I would argue, was not that different rules *of interpretation* were ever supposed to enter into the frame. Not only is it difficult to find evidence in the article that interpretation is what he had in mind when he spoke of 'a single set of rules', McNair's later writings on the issue – especially the part on interpretation and application of treaties in his 1961 treatise *The Law of Treaties*,[23] but also his judgments as an international judge and arbitrator,[24] seem to bear the reading for which this chapter argues.

At the time, one contemporary commentator saw McNair's article on the different types of treaty in international law as mainly a plea for the recognition of the special character of law-making treaties, or treaties which bring into existence new international entities such as

[18] Andenas, 'The Centre Reasserting Itself', note 2 above; Andenas.' Reassertion and Transformation of International Law', Chapter 20 in this volume, p. 536.

[19] Crawford, *Brownlie's Principles of Public International Law*, note 15 above, p. 14.

[20] See First Report on the Effects of Armed Conflicts on Treaties, 57th Session, A/CN.4/552, 21 April 2005.

[21] Vienna Convention on the Law of Treaties (VCLT) Article 62(2).

[22] McNair, 'The Functions and Differing Legal Character of Treaties', note 15 above, p. 118.

[23] McNair, *The Law of Treaties*, note 8 above, chs. 19–29.

[24] See for two examples of cases in which McNair sat and in which the same approach was taken to the interpretation of two very different treaties, the first a bilateral treaty; the other, a multilateral one: *Argentina/Chile Frontier Case (Palena)* (1966) 16 RIAA 109, 174; *Reservations to the Convention on Genocide*, Advisory Opinion ICJ Rep 1951 pp. 15, 20–3.

international organizations.[25] This seems to be the better understanding of the purpose of McNair's classic article. From this we can probably surmise that rather than arguing that the business of treaty interpretation was a fragmented enterprise, McNair wanted to underline that different types of treaty should be seen as having a very different impact upon general international law. In this sense, McNair's 1930 article ought surely to be seen as a forerunner to his later work on so-called objective regimes; McNair was an early advocate of so-called objective regimes. He would go on to argue, in 1957, that as an exception to the rule *pacta tertiis nec prosunt nec nocent* treaties establishing objective regimes were capable of producing effects *erga omnes*, and most prominently among the treaties capable of such effects he included treaties which bring into existence new international entities such as international organizations.[26]

Thus it can only scarcely be correct to base on McNair's 1930 article the notion that different types of treaty ought to be interpreted differently. We could, however, see it as an early example of the debate about how different treaty regimes to some extent were fragmenting in the sense that different types of treaty regime were already at that time, rather unsurprisingly, manifesting themselves in international law.

Both the impression that international law was fragmenting and the (unfounded, on the argument here propounded) proposition that this ought to suggest different interpretive methods would grow in the years to come.[27] Brownlie, in 1987, saw the phenomenon of various types of international lawyer losing the sense of their subject-matter within the matrix of rules of general international law. This, to his mind, was to the international legal order 'a threat at least as serious as any presented by political or cultural divisions'.[28] It was (as it still is presently) discussed in

[25] T. Gihl, *International Legislation: An Essay on Changes in International Law and in International Legal Situations* (Oxford: Oxford University Press 1937), p. 49.

[26] A. D. McNair, 'Treaties Producing Effects *Erga Omnes*', in *Scritti di diritto internazionale in onore di Tomaso Perassi II* (Milan: Giuffrè 1957), pp. 23–36. Also: A. A. Cançado Trindade, 'Jus Cogens: The Determination and the Gradual Expansion of Its Material Content in Contemporary International Case-Law' (2008) 35 *Curso de Derecho Internacional Organizado por el Comité Jurídico Interamericano* 3, p. 7.

[27] See, for some early examples, C. Rosseau, 'De la compatibilité des normes juridiques contradictoires dans l'ordre international' (1932) 39 13 *Revue générale de droit international public* 133, pp. 150–3; G. Scelle, *Cours de droit international public* (Paris: Domat-Montchrestien 1948) p. 642; J. Combacau, 'Le droit international: bric-à-brac ou système ?' (1986) 31 *Archives de philosophie du droit* 85, p. 86.

[28] I. Brownlie, 'Problems Concerning the Unity of International Law', in *Le droit international à l'heure de sa codification: Études en l'honneur de Roberto Ago vol I* (Milan: Giuffrè 1987), p. 160.

the literature whether, or the exact extent to which, fields such as international human rights,[29] international humanitarian law,[30] environmental law,[31] the law of the sea,[32] EU law,[33] and the law of the World Trade Organization (WTO)[34] were self-contained regimes. Perhaps the most extreme expression of the fragmented approach argued for by some was the statement by the International Criminal Tribunal for the former Yugoslavia in *Tadic* that in international law 'every tribunal is a self-contained system (unless otherwise provided)'.[35]

If we think today that this statement seems to be beyond the pale, we ought perhaps to remember that it represented the very culmination of this type of approach to international law by an international tribunal, and was thus what made the pendulum begin to swing back. Swing back it certainly did. President Sir Robert Jennings, in the same year as *Tadic* was handed down, identified rather resoundingly what he saw as 'the tendency of particular tribunals to regard themselves as different, as separate little empires which must as far as possible be augmented'.[36] This happy

[29] E. W. Vierdag, 'Some Remarks about Special Features of Human Rights Treaties' (1994) 25 *Netherlands Yearbook of International Law* 119; C. Greenwood, 'Using Human Rights Law in English Courts' (1998) 114 *LQR* 523, p. 525; C. Greenwood, 'Jurisdiction, NATO and the Kosovo Conflict', in P. Capps, M. Evans, and S. Konstadinidis (eds.), *Asserting Jurisdiction: International and European Legal Perspectives* (Oxford: Hart 2003), pp. 166–7.

[30] C. Greenwood, 'The Law of War (International Humanitarian Law)', in M. D. Evans (ed.), *International Law* (Oxford: Oxford University Press 2003), pp. 790–1; A. Orakhelashvili, 'The Interaction between Human Rights and Humanitarian Law: Fragmentation, Conflict, Parallelism, or Convergence?' (2008) 19 *EJIL* 161; V. Gowlland-Debbas, 'Issues Arising from the Interplay between Different Areas of International Law' (2010) 63 *Current Legal Problems* 597, pp. 612–30.

[31] M. Fitzmaurice, 'International Environmental Law as a Special Field' (1994) 25 *Netherlands Yearbook of International Law* 181.

[32] S. Oda, 'Dispute Settlement Prospects in the Law of the Sea' (1995) 44 *ICLQ* 44; R. R. Churchill and A. V. Lowe, *The Law of the Sea* (3rd edn., Manchester: Manchester University Press 1999), p. 461.

[33] F. Berman, 'Community Law and International Law', note 2 above.

[34] P. J. Kuyper, 'The Law of GATT as a Special Field of International Law' (1994) 25 *Netherlands Yearbook of International Law* 227; J. Pauwelyn, *Conflict of Norms in Public International Law: How WTO Law Relates to Other Rules of International Law* (Cambridge: Cambridge University Press 2003); J. Neumann, *Die Koordination des WTO-Rechts mit anderen völkerrechtlichen Ordnungen: Konflikte des materiellen Rechts und Konkurrenzen der Streitbeilegung* (Berlin: Duncker & Humblot 2002).

[35] *Prosecutor* v. *Tadic* (1995) 105 ILR 419, 458 (Jurisdiction). See the criticism of this passage in J. Crawford, *Brownlie's Principles of International Law* (8th edn., Oxford: Oxford University Press 2012), p. 41.

[36] R. Jennings, 'The Proliferation of Adjudicatory Bodies: Dangers and Possible Answers', in *Implications of the Proliferation of International Adjudicatory Bodies for Dispute Resolution,*

coinage, by a President of the International Court of Justice, was later reproduced, both in the jurisprudence of international tribunals and in the literature, in order to temper what was seen by some as especially human rights tribunals being out of line. Thus, for example, Greenwood, in an analysis of the interpretation given by the Grand Chamber of the European Court of Human Rights of Article 1 of the European Convention in *Bankovic*, observed with approval the meticulous care which the European Court showed in ensuring that it took full account of other relevant rules of international law in establishing the terms of 'jurisdiction' in Article 1. This included the citation of a long list of juristic writings on international law and other materials from outside the specialist literature of human rights, which was on his view a welcome recognition on the European Court's part that international human rights law and agreements are themselves part of international law as a whole: 'The Court did not succumb to what Sir Robert Jennings has described as "the tendency of particular tribunals to regard themselves as different, as separate little empires which must as far as possible be augmented"'.[37]

Greenwood had earlier made a point which went along much the same lines. In a criticism of how some writers in the field of human rights disregard the principles of general international law, he had made the point that international human rights law is part of international law and should be seen as such. In order to understand it, he continued, it is necessary to understand the principles of treaty interpretation and application as well as the approach to sources which form an integral part of international law:

> All too often, however, human rights lawyers – and sometimes human rights tribunals – fail to do this and treat human rights conventions and the jurisprudence which has grown up around them as though they constitute self-contained legal regimes.[38]

These warnings did not go unheeded. Not least human rights tribunals were alive to this type of criticism from general international lawyers, but these insights were taken seriously in all fields of international law. Lowe and Churchill, for example, in 1999 argued in the field of international maritime law that 'an understanding of the principles of international

ASIL Bulletin: Educational Resources on International Law (1995) 92, p. 6; R. Jennings, 'The Judiciary, International and National, and the Development of International Law' (1996) 45 *ICLQ* 1, pp. 5–6.

37 Greenwood, 'Jurisdiction', note 29 above, pp. 166–7.

38 C. Greenwood, 'Using Human Rights Law in English Courts' (1998) 114 *LQR* 523, p. 525.

law concerning nationality, international claims, State responsibility and so on is essential for a proper understanding of the law of the sea'.[39] And Judges Pellonpää and Sir Nicholas Bratza, in the 2001 Grand Chamber ruling in *Al-Adsani* v. *United Kingdom*, where the European Court was at pains not to go against the grain of what was seen as the demands of international customary law, ended their concurring opinion by quoting the former President of the International Court, 'who some years ago expressed concern about "the tendency of particular tribunals to regard themselves as different, as separate little empires which must as far as possible be augmented"'.[40] They stated in closing that they believed that in this case the European Court had avoided the kind of development of which Jennings had warned.

It is nonetheless true that some international courts and tribunals have, at times, insisted on regarding the treaty which they are interpreting as being special. This seems mostly to be the case with treaty bodies whose function it is to be the authoritative interpreter of a particular treaty, such as the European Court of Justice.[41] The tribunal in *Case Concerning the Air Services Agreement of 27 March 1946* thus took into account, in its interpretation of the treaty, 'the overall context of international civil aviation in which the Agreement was negotiated'.[42] Nonetheless, it is courts such as the European Court of Human Rights which have been the most associated with this type of approach,[43] and perhaps the most striking example is *Mamatkulov & Askarov*.[44] In that case the Grand Chamber of the European Court held that, while on the one hand 'the Convention must be interpreted in the light of the rules set out in the Vienna Convention of 23 May 1969 on the Law of Treaties', the Court must do so 'taking into account the special nature of the Convention as

39 R. R. Churchill and A. V. Lowe, *The Law of the Sea* (3rd edn., Manchester: Manchester University Press 1999) p. 461.

40 *Al-Adsani* v. *United Kingdom* App no. 35763/97 judgment [GC] 21 November 2001 (internal references omitted).

41 See P. Palchetti, 'Halfway between Fragmentation and Convergence: The Role of the Rules of the Organization in the Interpretation of Constituent Treaties' Chapter 18 in this volume, p. 486.

42 *Case Concerning the Air Services Agreement of 27 March 1946 (United States* v. *France)* (1978) 54 ILR 303, 326 [44]. Also: P. Daillier, M. Forteau and A Pellet, *Droit international public* (8th edn., Paris: LGDJ 2009), p. 290.

43 R. Bernhardt, 'Evolutive Treaty Interpretation – Especially of the European Convention on Human Rights' (1999) 42 *German Yearbook of International Law* 11; G. Letsas, 'Strasbourg's Interpretive Ethic: Lessons for the International Lawyer' (2010) 21 *EJIL* 509.

44 *Mamatkulov & Askarov* v. *Turkey* (2005) 134 ILR 230. See ILC Draft Conclusions on Subsequent Agreements and Subsequent Practice in Relation to the Interpretation of Treaties 2013, ILC Report 2013 UN Doc A/68/10, 19.

an instrument of human rights protection (see *Golder* v. *United Kingdom*, judgment of 21 February 1975, Series A no. 18, p. 14, § 29)'.[45] It is, on the face of it, difficult to imagine a clearer statement of the matter.

Nonetheless, as is evident from the reference in *Mamatkulov & Askarov* to *Golder* above, the European Court based this statement on what it had said in paragraph 29 of *Golder*. There the Court said that it was prepared to consider that it should be guided by the Vienna Convention, although at the time that convention had not entered into force, that for the purposes of the interpretation of the European Convention[46] account should be taken of Articles 31–3 of the Vienna Convention, but that it was also bound by Article 5 of the Vienna Convention:

> for the interpretation of the European Convention account is to be taken of those Articles subject, where appropriate to 'any relevant rules of the organization' – the Council of Europe – within which it has been adopted (Article 5 of the Vienna Convention).[47]

In other words, at any rate in the view of the European Court itself, when the Court says that the European Convention must be interpreted in accordance with Articles 31–3 but also that the Court must do so 'taking into account the special nature of the Convention',[48] that is nothing else than applying the scheme of the Vienna Convention, as set out in Article 5. In a sense, then, the 'special nature' approach of the European Court follows from the Vienna rules themselves.

This rhymes well with the approach taken in the Vienna Convention, where, apart from Article 5, no mention is made of this type of distinction in the principles of treaty interpretation. The ILC and later the Vienna Convention saw the law of treaties as essentially a unity.[49] More recently, the ILC has debated whether it would be appropriate to refer 'to the "nature" of the treaty as a factor which would typically be relevant to determining whether more or less weight should be given to certain means of interpretation'.[50] The ILC ultimately decided to leave the question open and for the time being to make no reference to the nature of the treaty.

[45] *Mamatkulov & Askarov* v. *Turkey* (2005) 134 ILR 230, 267 [111]. Also: *Effect of Reservations Opinion* (1982) 67 ILR 559, 567–8; *Restrictions to the Death Penalty* (Advisory Opinion OC–3/83) (1983) 70 ILR 449, 466.

[46] Convention for the Protection of Human Rights and Fundamental Freedoms, 4 November 1950, 213 UNTS 22.

[47] *Golder* v. *United Kingdom* (1975) 57 ILR 200, 213–4 [29].

[48] *Mamatkulov & Askarov* v. *Turkey* (2005) 134 ILR 230, 267 [111].

[49] Crawford, *Brownlie's Principles of Public International Law*, note 15 above, p. 370.

[50] ILC Draft Conclusions on Subsequent Agreements and Subsequent Practice in Relation to the Interpretation of Treaties 2013, ILC Report 2013 UN Doc A/68/10, 19–20.

Of interest here, however, is really only the extent to which these debates have influenced the question of whether different types of interpretation apply to different types of treaty. As we shall see in the next sections this has very much been the case. The approach taken by international tribunals to these two discrete but closely intertwined issues, however, commands the conclusion that not only have the fears of fragmentation in terms of 'self-contained regimes' been exaggerated; the same is the case with the proposition that the law of treaties is fragmented.

2. Constitutional treaties, human rights treaties, 'ordinary treaties'

Historically, the debate turned on a different taxonomy, partly inspired by national law. The theory is old according to which treaties ought to be divided into subcategories according to their contents, and that those subcategories, because of their different nature, ought to be interpreted differently. As was foreshadowed above, McNair in 1930 gave expression to the misgiving that 'inadequate attention has been given by students of International Law to the widely differing functions and legal character under the term "treaty"'.[51] He felt that the law of treaties would be in a more advanced state if more writers on the subject would study these essential differences and endeavour to provide for them instead of attempting to lay down rules applicable to treaties in general.[52] In this vein he suggested a taxonomy consisting of four types of treaty, all of which possessed different characteristics and must therefore be regulated by different rules of interpretation. The types of treaty he suggested were, first, treaties having the character of conveyances (treaties whereby one State creates in favour of another, or transfers to another, real rights); second, treaties having the character of contracts (a treaty as a compact, a bargain); third, law-making treaties (legislative treaties); and, fourth, treaties akin to charters of incorporation (treaties created by international bodies, creating at the same time more than mere contractual

[51] McNair, 'The Functions and Differing Legal Character of Treaties', note 15 above, p. 100. Also: Gihl, 'International Legislation', note 25 above, pp. 46–53; Brölmann, 'Specialized Rules of Treaty Interpretation', note 16 above, p. 507; J. Klabbers, *An Introduction to International Institutional Law* (2nd edn., Cambridge: Cambridge University Press 2009), p. 55; E. Lauterpacht, 'The Development of the Law of International Organizations by the Decisions of International Tribunals' (1976) 152 *Hague Recueil* p. 381; C. F. Amerashinge, *Principles of the Institutional Law of International Organizations* (2nd edn., Cambridge: Cambridge University Press 2005), pp. 24–65.

[52] McNair, 'The Functions and Differing Legal Character of Treaties', note 15 above, p. 100.

relationships and more than mere legislative rules). Today, this distinction, built to a very large degree upon a common law approach, may seem somewhat dated.

Perhaps a more sophisticated taxonomy as to not only different types of treaties but also different styles of treaty interpretation is the one advanced by Kolb.[53] It is not, according to Kolb, only because of the particular nature of human rights treaties,[54] constitutional treaties,[55] treaties concerned with the protection of minorities,[56] treaties concerned with international mandates,[57] and treaties concerned with the law of international waterways[58] that they have, on his view, been interpreted

[53] R. Kolb, *Interprétation et création du droit international: Esquisse d'une herméneutique juridique moderne pour le droit international public* (Brussels: Bruylant 2006), pp. 202–3.

[54] *Tyrer* v. *United Kingdom* (1978) 58 ILR 339, 353; *Interpretation of the Inter-American Declaration of Human Rights and Duties*, Advisory Opinion, Inter-American Court of Human Right (1989) 96 ILR 37 [37].

[55] *Delimitation of Polish–Czechoslovak Frontier (Question of Jaworzina)* (1923) PCIJ Series B No. 8, p. 37; *Interpretation of the Greco–Turkish Agreement of December 1, 1926* (1928) PCIJ Series B No. 16, p. 15; *Territorial Jurisdiction of the International Commission of the River Oder* (1929) PCIJ Series A, p. 5; *German Settlers in Poland* (1923) PCIJ Series B No. 6, p. 19; *Acquisition of Polish Nationality* (1923) PCIJ Series B No. 7, p. 17; *Delimitation of the Serbo–Albanian Frontier (Monastery of Saint-Naoum)* (1924) Series B No. 9, p. 6; *Competence of the International Labour Organisation to Regulate, Incidentally, the Personal Work of the Employer* (1926) PCIJ Series B No. 13, p. 6; *Jurisdiction of the European Commission of the Danube* (1927) PCIJ Series B No. 14, p. 6; *Electricity Company of Sofia and Bulgaria (Belgium* v. *Bulgaria)* (1939) PCIJ Rep Series A/B No. 77, p. 64; *Conditions for Admission of a State Membership in the United Nations (Article 4 of the Charter)* ICJ Rep 1948 p. 62; *Reparations for Injuries Suffered in the Service of the United Nations* Advisory Opinion ICJ Rep 1949 p. 174; *Effect of Award Made by the United Nations Administrative Tribunal* ICJ Rep 1954 p. 47; *Certain Expenses of the United Nations (Article 17, paragraph 2 of the Charter)* Advisory Opinion ICJ Rep 1962 p. 151; *Judgment No. 2867 of the Administrative Tribunal of the International Labour Organization upon a Complaint Filed against the International Fund for Agricultural Development*, Advisory Opinion 1 February 2012.

[56] *Rights of Minorities in Upper Silesia (Minority Schools)* (1928) PCIJ Series A No. 15, pp. 4, 31–3; *German Settlers in Poland* (1923) PCIJ Series B No 6, p. 19; *Acquisition of Polish Nationality* (1923) PCIJ Series B No. 7, p. 17; Greco–Bulgarian Communities (1930) PCIJ Series B No 17, pp. 19–23; *Minority Schools in Albania* (1935) PCIJ Series A/B, No. 64, p. 14.

[57] *Status of South-West Africa* ICJ Rep 1950 p. 132; *South-West Africa – Voting Procedure*, Advisory Opinion ICJ Rep 1955 p. 67; *Admissibility of Hearings of Petitioners by the Committee on South West Africa*, Advisory Opinion ICJ Rep 1956 p. 23; *South-West Africa Cases (Ethiopia and Liberia* v. *South Africa)*, Preliminary Objections ICJ Rep 1962 p. 319; *Legal Consequences for States of the Continued Presence of South Africa in Namibia (South West Africa) notwithstanding Security Council Resolution 276 (1970)*, Advisory Opinion ICJ Rep 1971 p. 16.

[58] *Territorial Jurisdiction of the International Commission of the River Oder* (1929) PCIJ Series A, p. 5; *Dispute regarding Navigational and Related Rights (Costa Rica* v. *Nicaragua)*

differently. On his understanding, what is important is not whether the treaty belongs to one (or more) of these categories or not. The pertinent question here is what is the principle according to which the tribunal has been acting when, according to this view, it has interpreted treaties according to different methods in these cases?

Kolb has suggested the following reply: the more a treaty is seen to protect what he refers to as *utilitas singulorum*, the more it will tend to be interpreted strictly and within the strict limits of the text, and the more a treaty protects an international *utilitas publica*, the more it will tend to be interpreted effectively, evolutionarily, and teleologically.[59] It is on his view the degree of 'internationalization' of the treaty matter that is decisive. While to some degree all treaties bear on shared interests, there are synallagmatic treaties according to which the parties keep their interests, which will be more or less contrary to one another, depending on the case.[60] As will be seen, this chapter propounds a slightly different solution.

It seems, however, that the distinction that has had the most success in the literature is a simpler one. This distinction discriminates only between treaties whose essential juridical character is that of the contract and treaties whose essential juridical character is that of law-making or legislation. This distinction has been known in the French-language literature as that between *traités-lois* (law-making treaties) and *traités-contrats* (contractual treaties),[61] and in the German-language

Judgment ICJ Rep 2009 p. 213; *Pulp Mills on the River Uruguay (Argentina* v. *Uruguay)*, Judgment ICJ Rep 2010 p. 14.

59 Kolb, *Interprétation et création du droit international*, note 53 above, pp. 202–3.

60 J. H. H. Weiler, 'The Geology of International Law – Governance, Democracy and Legitimacy' (2005) 64 *Zeitschrift für ausländisches öffentliches Recht und Völkerrecht* 547, p. 556, expresses the same idea, using instead of Kolb's term 'common assets': 'Materially, the hallmark of Community may, in my view, be found in the appropriation or definition of common assets. The common assets could be material such as the deep sea bed of the high sea, or territorial such as certain areas of space. They can be functional such as certain aspects of collective security and they can even be spiritual: Internationally defined Human Rights or ecological norms represent common spiritual assets where States can no more assert their exclusive sovereignty, even within their territory, than they could over areas of space which extend above their air-space.' Also: A. Clapham, *Brierly's Law of Nations: An Introduction to the Role of International Law in International Relations* (7th edn., Oxford: Oxford University Press 2012), pp. 112–14.

61 P. Reuter, *Introduction au droit des traités* (3rd edn., Paris: Presses Universitaires de France 1995), p. 23. Also: R. Cassin, *De l'exception tirée de l'inexécution dans les rapports synallagmatiques: exception non adimpleti contractus* (Paris: Sirey 1914) I–VI.

literature, from whence it originates, as between *Vereinbarung* and *Vertrag*.[62] Traditionally the term *traités-lois* was used of the treaties which set out the first conventional rules of international society.

As international society began by degrees to increase in complexity and density from circa 1815, treaties began to perform a social function closely analogous to legislation in national legal systems. The Vienna *Règlement* on diplomatic representation of 19 March 1815 was thus a striking example, and one could say the same of the whole of the Congress of Vienna, as it was nothing if not legislative in character.[63]

The term *traités-contrats* was used of treaties the content of which was of a contractual or synallagmatic or reciprocal kind. It was in other words a material, as opposed to formal, concept. For the purposes of interpretation, it was felt that *traités-contrats* called for a restrictive style of interpretation, while *traités-lois*were more amenable to styles of interpretation which were purposive and constitutional.[64]

The distinction between the two seems to be more a source of confusion than of assistance. This is the case not least because all treaties are contractual as between their parties; it is true also of those treaties which have been referred to as law-making 'that the legal basis of these conventions, and the essential thing that brings them into force, is the common consent of the parties'.[65] The distinction between law and contract in modern international law has, according to Reuter, lost such obvious character as it might have possessed in the past:

> Les grands actes collectifs de la société économique moderne, conventions collectives du travail, statuts syndicaux et professionnels, grandes société de capitaux ne sont plus des contrats au sens primitif du terme et une grande convention multilatérale ouverte évoque davantage les statuts d'une société anonyme dans laquelle on entre et on sort indépendamment des autres parties qu'une loi au sens du droit public.[66]

62 H. Triepel, *Völkerrecht und Landesrecht* (Leipzig: Verlag von CL Hirschfeld 1899), pp. 49–62; H. Lauterpacht, *Private Law Sources and Analogies in International Law* (London: Longman's 1927) [70].

63 P. Allot, 'The Concept of International Law' (1999) 10 *EJIL* 31, p. 43.

64 C. Rousseau, *Droit international public* (5th edn., Paris: Dalloz 1970), pp. 292–305.

65 Jointly Dissenting Opinion Judges Guerrero, McNair, Read, and Hsu Mo in *Reservations to the Convention on Genocide*, Advisory Opinion ICJ Rep 1951 pp. 15, 32; G. Fitzmaurice, 'Some Problems Regarding the Formal Sources of International Law', in *Symbolae Verzijl: Présentées au Professeur JHW Verzijl à l'occasion de son LXX-ième anniversaire* (Leiden: Martinus Nijhoff 1958), p. 157.

66 P. Reuter, *Introduction au droit des traités* note 61 above, p. 23.

Reuter concludes by saying that it is in reality very difficult to keep such distinctions according to which treaties are to be discriminated by reason of their subject-matter. This is not least because the content of treaties is in fact not homogenous; rather a treaty may contain provisions which are very different in character. The over four hundred articles of the Treaty of Versailles of 1919, for example, regulated matters as variegated as constitutive charters of international organizations, questions of territorial status as well as several other types of issue. This is illustrated by the many and varied cases on the Versailles Treaty handed down by the Permanent Court in the 1920s.[67] In the face of such realities, distinctions such as the one between *traités-lois* and *traités-contrats* simply break down. It would therefore, he concludes, be wrong to conclude that the principles of interpretation vary according to whether one is dealing with a bilateral or multilateral treaty, with *traités-lois* or *traités-contrats*; the principles necessarily remain the same.[68]

This seems to rhyme well with the approach taken in the Vienna Convention, where no mention is made of this type of distinction in the principles of treaty interpretation. The ILC and later the Vienna Convention saw the law of treaties as essentially a unity.[69] It is clear, however, that the distinction between statutory and contractual treaties, or cognate distinctions, continues to find an echo both in doctrine and in the practice of international tribunals.

In the modern literature, however, the two types of treaty that are the most contrasted with 'ordinary' or contractual treaties are human rights treaties and constitutional or constitutive treaties.[70] If we compare to the two-way split between '*traités-contrats*' and '*traités-lois*' above we could say that the latter category has been split into two elements: human rights treaties and constitutional treaties. The analysis now turns to these

[67] *Acquisition of Polish Nationality* (1923) PCIJ Series B No. 7, p. 17; *German Settlers in Poland* (1923) PCIJ Series B No. 6, p. 19; *Case of the SS 'Wimbledon'* (1923) PCIJ Series A No. 1, pp. 15, 25; *Polish Postal Service in Danzig* (1925) PCIJ Series B No. 11, pp. 6, 39; *Rights of Minorities in Upper Silesia (Minority Schools)* (1928) PCIJ Series A No. 15, pp. 4, 31–3.

[68] P. Reuter, *Introduction au droit des traités* note 61 above, p. 91.

[69] Crawford, *Brownlie's Principles of Public International Law*, note 15 above, p. 370.

[70] G. Letsas, 'Strasbourg's Interpretive Ethic: Lessons for the International Lawyer' (2010) 21 *EJIL* 509; R. Bernhardt, 'Thoughts on the Interpretation of Human Rights Treaties', in F. Matscher and H. Petzold (eds.), *Protecting Human Rights: The European Dimension. Studies in Honour of Gérard J Wiarda* (Cologne: Carl Heymann 1988); Bernhardt, 'Evolutive Treaty Interpretation', note 43 above; Brölmann, 'Specialized Rules of Treaty Interpretation', note 16 above; Lauterpacht, 'The Development of the Law of International Organizations', note 51 above.

three categories in order to see whether it is correct to say that they are interpreted according to special methods.

2.1 *Human rights treaties*

Bernhardt has stated that since the object and purpose of human rights treaties is different from those of other treaties, the interpretation of human rights treaties must be different from that of other types of treaty: a much stronger accent must in this type of treaty interpretation, so goes the argument, be placed on the object and purpose than is otherwise usual.[71] As the object and purpose of human rights treaties is different from those of many other treaties, the interpretation of human rights treaties must in the final analysis be different from that of other types of treaty. The arbitral tribunal in *La Bretagne*, in perhaps the same vein, stated that 'the emphasis placed by any interpreter on the purpose of a treaty is extremely variable and must depend to a large extent on the nature of the treaty in question'.[72] If, however, the context in which the provisions of a treaty are located and a full application of the principles of treaty interpretation lead to the conclusion that a particular approach or doctrine is the right one to use then that is quite consistent with the rules of the Vienna Convention.[73]

A more apt way of putting it, however, might be that the object and purpose of a treaty is as important in any type of treaty as it is in a human rights treaty. It may be worth pointing out that when an international tribunal, in conformity with Article 31(1) of the Vienna Convention, takes into consideration the object and purpose of a treaty then this factor is one among others taken into account in order to establish the common intention of the parties.[74] Reuter, one of the leading drafters of the Vienna Convention, put the matter in the following way: on the one

71 Bernhardt, 'Thoughts on the Interpretation of Human Rights Treaties', note 70 above, p. 65.

72 *Dispute concerning Filleting within the Gulf of St. Lawrence ('La Bretagne') (Canada/France)* (1986) 82 ILR 591, 615.

73 R. Gardiner, 'The Vienna Convention Rules on Treaty Interpretation', in D Hollis (ed.), *The Oxford Guide to Treaties* (Oxford: Oxford University Press 2012).

74 *Award in the Arbitration regarding the Iron Rhine ('Ijzeren Rijn') (Belgium* v. *Netherlands)* (2005) 27 RIAA 35, 65 ('The object and purpose of a treaty, taken together with the intentions of the parties, are the prevailing elements for interpretation'); Separate Opinion of Judge Fitzmaurice, *National Union of Belgian Police* (1980) 57 ILR 262, 293 ('The object and purpose of a treaty are not something that exist *in abstracto:* they follow from and are closely bound up with the intentions of the parties').

hand, the purpose of treaty interpretation is 'to ascertain the intention of the parties by reference to the form, the final clauses and especially the object and purpose of the treaty';[75] on the other hand, in addition to having been manifested, the intentions 'must concur to form the object and purpose of the agreement, both of which play so prominent a part in the whole law of treaties'.[76] According to Reuter the important role played by the object and purpose within the Vienna rules should not be seen as an exception to the principle of the autonomy of the will of the State. Rather it is the objective reinforcement of that very principle. The object and the purpose of a treaty are the essential elements of the intention of the parties: we must assume, therefore, that the parties would not wish for that object and purpose, freely chosen by them as their common good, to be frustrated.[77]

International tribunals in general go far in their reliance upon the object and purpose of treaties; this is not something that is more prevalent among human rights bodies.[78] It must surely be wrong, therefore, to say that because of the importance of the object and purpose of human rights treaties this particular element of interpretation should take on greater importance when one is interpreting human rights treaties than when one is interpreting other types of treaty. If one were to take the position of Bernhardt on this question – and say that because the object and purpose of human rights treaties is different from that of other treaties the interpretation of human rights treaties must be different from that of other types of treaty[79] – then one would be comparing the object and purpose of different treaties, rather than comparing and weighing different factors

[75] P. Reuter, *Introduction to the Law of Treaties* (J. Mico and P. Haggenmacher tr, London: Paul Kegan International 1995) p. 24.

[76] *Ibid.*, p. 30.

[77] P. Reuter, *La Convention de Vienne du droit des traités* (Paris: Armand Colin 1971) p. 17.

[78] *Rights of Minorities in Upper Silesia (Minority Schools)* (1928) PCIJ Series A No. 15, at p. 33; *Reservations to the Convention on Genocide*, Advisory Opinion ICJ Rep 1951 pp. 15, 23. Also: *Ambatielos case (jurisdiction)*, Judgment ICJ Rep 1952 pp. 28, 45; *Case of Certain Norwegian Loans*, Judgment ICJ Rep 1957 pp. 9, 23, 27; *Constitution of the Maritime Safety Committee of the Inter-Governmental Maritime Consultative Organization*, Advisory Opinion ICJ Rep 1960 pp. 150, 170–1; *Case Concerning US Diplomatic and Consular Staff in Tehran (USA* v. *Iran)* ICJ Rep 1980 p. 3 [54]; *Military and Paramilitary Activities in and against Nicaragua* ICJ Rep 1986 p. 14 [273]; *Oil Platforms (Islamic Republic of Iran* v. *United States of America)*, Preliminary Objection, Judgment ICJ Rep 1996 pp. 803, 820 [52]; *LaGrand (Germany* v. *United States of America)*, Judgment ICJ Rep 2001 pp. 466, 501–3 [99]–[104]; *Questions Relating to the Obligation to Prosecute or Extradite (Belgium* v. *Senegal)*, Judgment ICJ 20 July 2012 [74], [86].

[79] Bernhardt, 'Thoughts on the Interpretation of Human Rights Treaties', note 70 above, p. 65.

of interpretation against one another. The correct comparator would not be the object and purpose of other types of treaty but the other factors of interpretation in every treaty; in this regard it is clear that the object and purpose of *all treaties*, in principle, is of equal importance – in relation to the other factors of interpretation which have a bearing on the treaty in issue. It would be wrong to say that because the safeguarding of human dignity is so important (which it is not the point here to say that it is not), object and purpose as an interpretive factor ought to be more important in the interpretation of human rights treaties than that factor ought to be in tax treaties. It is thus difficult to agree with this proposition in normative terms, and in descriptive terms tribunals have not followed this, either in the sense that the object and purpose is, together with the intentions of the parties, the prevailing element for interpretation in *any* type of treaty.[80]

2.2 *Constitutional or constitutive treaties*

The International Court in *Nuclear Weapons Advisory Opinion* stated that: '[f]rom a formal standpoint, the constituent instruments of international organizations are multilateral treaties, to which the well-established rules of treaty interpretation apply'.[81] As we shall see, some authors have expended much energy on downplaying this point, choosing instead to underline that such instruments have 'certain special characteristics'[82] as well as the possible ramifications for treaty interpretations in statements by the International Court, also in *Nuclear Weapons Advisory Opinion*, such as:

> The constituent instruments are also treaties of a particular character; their object is to create new subjects of law endowed with a certain autonomy, to

[80] *Award in the Arbitration regarding the Iron Rhine ('Ijzeren Rijn') (Belgium* v. *Netherlands)* (2005) 27 RIAA 35, 65; *Territorial Dispute between Libya and Chad* ICJ Rep 1994 p. 6 [52]; *LaGrand (Germany* v. *United States of America)*, Judgment ICJ Rep 2001 pp. 466, 501–3 [99]–[104]; *Oil Platforms (Islamic Republic of Iran* v. *United States of America)*, Preliminary Objection, Judgment ICJ Rep 1996 pp. 803, 820 [52]; *South-West Africa Cases (Ethiopia and Liberia* v. *South Africa)*, Preliminary Objections ICJ Rep 1962 pp. 319, 335–6; *Case of Certain Norwegian Loans*, Judgment ICJ Rep 1957 pp. 9, 23 and 27; *Reservations to the Convention on Genocide*, Advisory Opinion ICJ Rep 1951 pp. 15, 23. Also: M. Sørensen, *Les sources du droit international: Étude sur la jurisprudence de la Cour permanente* (Copenhagen: Einar Munksgaard 1946) p. 230; R. Higgins, 'Time and the Law: International Perspectives on an Old Problem' (1997) 46 *ICLQ* 501, p. 519.

[81] *Legality of the Use by a State of Nuclear Weapons in Armed Conflict (Request by WHO)*, Advisory Opinion ICJ Rep 1996 p. 66 [19].

[82] *Certain Expenses of the United Nations (Article 17, paragraph 2 of the Charter)* Advisory Opinion ICJ Rep 1962 pp. 151, 157.

> which the parties entrust the task of realizing common goals. Such treaties can raise specific problems of interpretation, owing, *inter alia*, to their character which is conventional and at the same time institutional; the very nature of the organization created, the objectives which have been assigned to it by its founders, the imperatives associated with the effective performance of its functions, as well as its own practice, are all elements which may deserve special attention when the time comes to interpret these constituent treaties.[83]

Thus Elihu Lauterpacht in a celebrated study of the interpretation of constitutive treaties concluded that this type of treaty must be interpreted differently from regular treaties. He held that the reliance was greater in this type of interpretation on the objects and purposes of the treaty than in ordinary types of treaty, and that the intentions of the parties were rejected as a controlling element in the interpretation.[84] Akande has stated that the UN Charter is among the type of treaty which 'must be regarded as living instruments and be interpreted in an evolutionary manner, permitting the organization to fulfil its purposes in changing circumstances'.[85] Relying for his conclusions particularly upon analyses of *Reparation for Injuries*[86] and *Namibia*,[87] Akande concludes that the interpretation of constitutional treaties is by its nature different from interpretation of regular treaties.[88]

The same conclusions have been drawn with respect to the European Union. Weiler, in his analysis of *ERTA*,[89] drew a line between, on the one hand, what he saw as the traditional approach of the law of treaties and, on the other, the approach of the European Court of Justice:

> the critical point was the willingness of the Court to sidestep the presumptive rule of interpretation typical in international law, that treaties must be interpreted in a manner that minimizes encroachment on state

[83] *Legality of the Use by a State of Nuclear Weapons in Armed Conflict (Request by WHO)*, Advisory Opinion ICJ Rep 1996 p. 66 [19].

[84] Lauterpacht, 'The Development of the Law of International Organizations', note 51 above, p. 420.

[85] D. Akande, 'International Organizations', in M. D. Evans, *International Law* (3rd edn., Oxford: Oxford University Press 2010) p. 263.

[86] *Reparation for Injuries Suffered in the Service of the United Nations*, Advisory Opinion ICJ Rep 1949 pp. 174, 179.

[87] *Legal Consequences for States of the Continued Presence of South Africa in Namibia (South West Africa) notwithstanding Security Council Resolution 276 (1970)* ICJ Rep 1971 pp. 16, 21–2 [20]–[22].

[88] Akande, 'International Organizations', note 85 above, p. 263.

[89] C–22/70 *Commission of the European Communities* v. *Council of the European Communities* 1971 ECR 263.

> sovereignty. The Court favored a teleological, purposive rule drawn from the book of constitutional interpretation.[90]

Other leading authors have taken the same approach with respect to the European Union, though perhaps in an even more balanced way. Klabbers concludes in his analysis of *Van Gend & Loos*[91] and *Costa* v. *ENEL*,[92] where the Court of Justice established that the European Community was to be regarded as a new and unique legal order (directly effective in the law of the member States and enjoying superiority vis-à-vis the law of the member States) that in European Union law 'interpretation may be a little more teleological than with regular treaties'.[93] These conclusions, even the more balanced one reached by Klabbers, seem to be open to question.

We may begin by ascertaining, as former Advocate General Tesauro has done, that it would be wrong to see the approach of the European Court of Justice as wholly out of touch with the general rule of interpretation, or as much more teleologic than that which follows from that approach or the approach traditionally taken by the Permanent or International Court.[94] Furthermore it must be true, as Gardiner has pointed out, that absence of reference to particular elements of the Vienna rules does not necessarily mean that they are not being applied.[95] In the Court's first Opinion on the compatibility with the Treaty on the draft agreement establishing a European Economic area (EEA) the Court cited Article 31 of the Vienna Convention and showed that its approach in this case was in line with the general rule of interpretation:

> The fact that the provisions of the agreement and the corresponding Community provisions are identically worded does not mean that they must necessarily be interpreted identically. An international treaty is to be interpreted not only on the basis of its wording, but also in the light of its objectives. Article 31 of the Vienna Convention of 23 May 1969 on the law of treaties stipulates in this respect that a treaty is to be interpreted in good

90 J. H. H. Weiler, 'The Transformation of Europe', (1991) 100 *Yale Law Journal* 2401, 2416. Also: H. P. Ipsen, *Europäsiches Gemeinschaftsrecht* (Tübingen: JCB Mohr 1972), pp. 131–4.

91 C–26/62 *Van Gend and Loos* v. *Nederlanse Administatie der Belastingen* [1963] ECR 1.

92 C–6/64 *Flaminio Costa* v. *ENEL* [1964] ECR 585.

93 J. Klabbers, *An Introduction to International Institutional Law* (2nd edn., Cambridge: Cambridge University Press 2009), pp. 87–8.

94 Gardiner, *Treaty Interpretation*, note 3 above, pp. 120–5; G. Tesauro, *Diritto comunitario* (3rd edn., Padua: CEDAM 2003) pp. 90–1.

95 Gardiner, 'The Vienna Convention Rules', note 73 above, p. 494.

> faith in accordance with the ordinary meaning to be given to its terms in their context and in the light of its object and purpose.[96]

Dupuy has seen this type of recourse to, and explicit citation of, the Vienna Convention rules on treaty interpretation as an express manifestation by international tribunals of their attachment to general international law and to distance themselves, by the same token, from the thesis according to which one ought to see such systems as being self-contained and owing their authority to their own autonomy only.[97]

In *Van Gend & Loos*[98] the European Court of Justice held that it must consider the 'spirit, the general scheme and the wording of' the provisions under consideration. Berman has said that the European Court of Justice, in keeping with this dictum, has shied away from tying itself down to the intricacies of a complex or hierarchical system of interpretive norms; it prefers instead to keep its hand free to find the proper interpretive approach to the problem before it. He continues to say that in this approach the European Court seems remarkably similar to the International Court of Justice.[99] This must be the correct view of the jurisprudence of the European Court of Justice as compared to the 'general' law of treaties.

Postulates as to the specialness of the approach taken by the European Court of Justice are more impressive at a distance than on close examination.[100] This is not least so as in many cases the European Court of Justice has felt itself bound to a very large degree by the treaty text, and explicitly shied away from adopting an interpretation which would conform with the idea that the interpretations of the European Court of Justice are always teleologic.[101] It is, however, difficult entirely to avoid the

[96] Opinion 1/91 [1991] ECR I–6079 [14]. See also *Metalsa* [1993] ECR I–3751 [10]; *El-Yassini* v. *Secretary of State* C–416/96 [1999] ECR I–01209 [47]; *Jany* v. *Staatssecretaris van Justitie* [2001] ECR I–8615 [35]; C–386/08 *Brita GmbH* v. *Hauptzollamt Hamburg Hafen* judgment of 25 February 2010 [41]–[43].

[97] J. M. Dupuy, *Droit international public* (Paris: Dalloz 2008) pp. 335–6.

[98] C–26/62 *Van Gend and Loos* v. *Nederlanse Administatie der Belastingen* [1963] ECR 1, 12; see also C–283/81 *CILFIT* v. *Ministry of Health* [1982] ECR 3415 [17]–[20].

[99] Berman, 'Community Law and International Law', note 2 above, p. 269.

[100] A. Arnull, *The European Union and its Court of Justice* (2nd edn., Oxford: Oxford University Press 2006), pp. 607–21; G. Slynn, 'They Call It "Teleological"' (1992) 7 *Denning Law Journal* 225; *Buchanan* v. *Babco* [1977] 2 WLR 107, 112 (Lord Denning).

[101] C–152/84 *Marshall* v. *Southampton and South-West Hampshire Area Health Authority* [1986] ECR 723; C–91/92 *Faccini Dori* v. *Recreb* [1994] ECR I–3325; C–192/94 *El Corte Inglés* v. *Blázquez Rivero* [1996] ECR I–1281; C–59/85 *Netherlands* v. *Reed* [1986] ECR 1283.

impression that the European Court of Justice to some extent has taken an approach which focuses more upon teleology than other tribunals, inclusive of the European Court of Human Rights. Perhaps the closest thing to a conclusion one can reach in this regard is to extend to interpretive self-containedness that which Crawford has said about self-contained regimes in general: there are hardly any entirely self-contained regimes at all, with the European Union as the only possible candidate.[102]

It seems pertinent to conclude on this point by taking a step back. A useful perspective was provided by Hambro, who took the view that the interpretation of constitutive multilateral treaties, such as the UN Charter, plainly followed the same approach as other types of treaty interpretation.[103] He said of the approach to the interpretation of different types of treaty that:

> Rights originating from a contract may be divided, *inter alia*, into personal rights and real rights but, whether personal or real, such rights can never embrace anything not included in the common intention of the parties. A treaty or convention may create an international institution or it may define the status of a territory but its meaning and effect depend primarily on the intention of the parties thereto. The rule may therefore be stated to be that the existence, the measure, and the meaning of treaty rights and obligations are determined in accordance with the common intention of the parties to the instrument in question and, in determining this common intention, the Court invokes the aid of the accepted rules of construction.[104]

While the interpretation of multilateral treaties, on Hambro's view, gives rise to even more complicated questions than the interpretation of bilateral treaties, the same method applied to the former as to the latter: the

[102] J. Crawford, *International Law as an Open System: Selected Essays* (London: Cameron May 2002), p. 37.

[103] E. Hambro, 'The Interpretation of Multilateral Treaties by the International Court of Justice' (1953) 39 *Transactions of the Grotius Society* 235, pp. 235–7; E. Hambro, L. M. Goodrich and A. P. Simons, *Charter of the United Nations: Commentary and Documents* (3rd edn., New York: Columbia University Press 1969), p. 13. Also: E. Hambro, *The Case Law of the International Court: A Repertoire of the Judgments, Advisory Opinions and Orders of the Permanent Court of International Justice and of the International Court of Justice* (Leiden: AS Sijthoff 1958), p. 15 (where Hambro analyses *Reservations to the Convention on Genocide*, Advisory Opinion ICJ Rep 1951 pp. 15, 23, observing that the ICJ applied nothing else than the ordinary method of establishing the will of the parties: 'The origins and character of that Convention, the objects pursued by the General Assembly and the contracting parties, the relations which exist between those provisions and these objects, furnish elements of interpretation of the will of the General Assembly and the parties'.)

[104] Hambro, *A Repertoire of the Judgments*, note 103 above, p. 133.

establishment of what he called the objective intention of the parties, an imputed intention, 'because it may often be very difficult indeed to find any common purpose for the particular stipulation in question'.[105]

2.3 *'Ordinary treaties'*

Weiler contrasts the interpretation of the Community Treaties with that which he terms 'the presumptive rule of interpretation typical in international law, that treaties must be interpreted in a manner that minimizes encroachment on state sovereignty'.[106] The alleged presumption to which Weiler is referring is the principle of restrictive interpretation, or *in dubio mitius*.[107] The notion that treaties must be interpreted in a manner that minimizes encroachment upon State sovereignty was, however, at the time when Weiler was writing a 'rule' only in the most dubious sense of the term. This is nevertheless an assumption that seems to have underlain much of the debates in the literature, and not least, as in Weiler's example, debates on other types of international law, which are seen by the authors to be free of the shackles of *in dubio mitius*, which is then seen still to be controlling in general international law or the traditional law of treaties.

This is, for example, very clear in Brölmann's discussion of what, on her reading, are the differences between interpretation of constitutional treaties and of ordinary treaties. The principle of *in dubio mitius*, she says, 'is familiar from the context of "contractual treaties" (*traités-contrats*)'.[108] This principle is followed, Brölmann continues, when the contractual aspect of the international compound to be interpreted is the most striking one. When it comes to constitutive treaties, however, *in dubio mitius* plays only a small role, she concludes.[109]

The number of writers who today still believe in the principle is certainly on the wane.[110] Even the most distinguished writers, such as Jennings and

[105] Hambro, 'Interpretation of Multilateral Treaties', note 103 above, p. 237.

[106] Weiler, 'The Transformation of Europe', note 90 above, p. 2416.

[107] H. Lauterpacht, *Oppenheim's International Law* (8th edn., London: Longmans 1955) p. 953.

[108] Brölmann, 'Specialized Rules of Treaty Interpretation' note 16 above, p. 513.

[109] J. Kokott, 'States, Sovereign Equality', in R Wolfrum (ed.), *Max Planck Encyclopedia of Public International Law* (Oxford: Oxford University Press 2012), p. 571.

[110] R. E. Fife, 'L'objet et le but du traité de Spitsberg (Svalbard) et le droit de la mer', in *La mer et son droit: mélanges offerts à Laurent Lucchini et Jean-Pierre Quéneudec* (Paris: Pedone 2003), pp. 253–4.

Watts, have until relatively recently claimed that 'the principle of *in dubio mitius* applies in interpreting treaties, in deference to the sovereignty of states'; 'if the meaning of a term is ambiguous, that meaning is to be preferred which is less onerous to the party assuming an obligation, or which interferes less with the territorial and personal supremacy of a party, or involves less general restrictions upon the parties'.[111] Crawford has, while being very critical of the principles in some of his work,[112] also said of the principle of *in dubio mitius*that while he sees it as question-begging and while the International Court in *Navigational Rights* gave less scope to it than the Permanent Court did in some cases, 'the principle may operate in cases concerning regulation of core territorial privileges'; 'in these instances it is not an "aid to interpretation" but an independent principle'.[113]

We may, however, confidently say that this is wrong, and moreover that it has been wrong for many decades. Lauterpacht concluded already in 1927 that such a rule only scarcely existed: 'it is only a subsidiary means of interpretation'; 'neither the science of international law nor international tribunals can, in the long run, act upon such doctrine without seriously jeopardizing the work of interpretation'.[114] The Permanent Court had then held in *Polish Postal Service in Danzig* that the principle could be relied on 'only in cases where ordinary methods of interpretation have failed'.[115]

At the present stage of the development of international law, however, the rejection of this principle in the jurisprudence of international tribunals is very clear.[116] Such outliers as presently emerge are very few.[117]

[111] R. Jennings and A. Watts, *Oppenheim's International Law* (9th edn., London: Longman 1992), p. 1278.

[112] J. Crawford, 'Sovereignty as a Legal Value', in J. Crawford, M. Koskenniemi and S. Ranganathan (eds.), *The Cambridge Companion to International Law* (Cambridge: Cambridge University Press 2011), pp. 122–3; J. Crawford, 'Treaty and Contract in Investment Arbitration' (2008) 24 *Arbitration International* 351, p. 353.

[113] Crawford, *Brownlie's Principles of Public International Law*, note 15 above, p. 379.

[114] Lauterpacht, *Private Law Sources and Analogies*, note 62 above, pp. 179–80.

[115] *Polish Postal Service in Danzig* (1925) PCIJ Series B No. 11, pp. 6, 39.

[116] See R. Churchill and G. Ulfstein, 'The Disputed Maritime Zones Around Svalbard', in M. H. Nordquist, T. H. Heidar and J. N. Moore (eds.), *Changes in the Arctic Environment and the Law of the Sea* (Leiden: Martinus Nijhoff 2010).

[117] *SGS Société Générale de Surveillance SA* v. *Islamic Republic of Pakistan* (Procedural Order of 16 October 2002) [171] ('The appropriate interpretive approach is the prudential one summed up in the literature as *in dubio pars mitior est sequenda*, or more tersely, *in dubio mitius*') and Appellate Body Report, EC Measures Concerning Meat and Meat Products (Hormones), WT/DS26/AB/R; WT/DS48/AB/R, adopted 16 January 1998 [163]–[165]

The tribunal in *Lac Lanoux*, where the interpretation of a contractual treaty between France and Spain was in issue, said to the contention by the French government that the terms of the treaty must be 'strictly construed because they are in derogation of sovereignty' that it: 'could not recognize such an absolute rule of construction. Territorial sovereignty plays the part of a presumption. It must bend before all international obligations, whatever their origin, but only before such obligations'; 'the question is therefore to determine the obligations of the French Government in this case'.[118] In *Iron Rhine*, regarding the interpretation of a contractual treaty between Belgium and the Netherlands, the tribunal composed under the aegis of the Permanent Court of Arbitration held that 'the doctrine of restrictive interpretation never had a hierarchical supremacy, but was a technique to ensure a proper balance of the distribution of rights within a treaty system'. The principle of restrictive interpretation, it went on to explain, is not in fact mentioned in the provisions of the Vienna Convention. The object and purpose of a treaty, taken together with the intentions of the parties, is the prevailing element for interpretation. Indeed, concluded the tribunal, it had also been noted in the literature that too rigorous an application of the principle of restrictive interpretation might be inconsistent with the primary purpose of the treaty. The treaty provisions under consideration were therefore interpreted 'not by invocation of the principle of restrictive interpretation, but rather by examining – using the normal rules of interpretation identified in Articles 31 and 32 of the Vienna Convention'.[119]

The principle has in fact never been accepted by the International Court, and in *Navigational Rights*, bearing on the interpretation of a contractual treaty between Costa Rica and Nicaragua as to, among other things, navigation on the San Juan river,the International Court rejected an argument in favour of Nicaragua's sovereignty, stating that it was not convinced that Costa Rica's right to free navigation on the San Juan river should be interpreted narrowly because it represents a limitation of the sovereignty over the river conferred by the treaty on Nicaragua:

> While it is certainly true that limitations of the sovereignty of a State over its territory are not to be presumed, this does not mean that treaty provisions

(where the Appellate Body refers to 'the interpretative principle of *in dubio mitius* [as] widely recognized in international law').

118 *Lac Lanoux Arbitration* (1957) 24 ILR 101, 119–20.

119 *Award in the Arbitration regarding the Iron Rhine ('Ijzeren Rijn') (Belgium* v. *Netherlands)* (2005) 27 RIAA 35, 64–5.

> establishing such limitations, such as those that are in issue in the present case, should for this reason be interpreted *a priori* in a restrictive way.[120]

The language of treaties is therefore, as Crawford has put it in the context of the International Court's judgment in *Navigational Rights*, 'not subject to any particular presumption but will be read so as to give effect to the object and purpose of the treaty in its context'.[121] This focus in connection with a contractual treaty on object and purpose ties in with what was said above about how it is not in any way a particularity of human rights or constitutional interpretation to focus on teleology, or a treaty's object and purpose.

In *Navigational Rights* it was not just the sovereignty of one state that was in issue; the sovereignty of Costa Rica was no less important than that of Nicaragua. This is an important point which seems sometimes to be forgotten by those who have argued for the existence of the principle of *in dubio mitius*. 'International law and justice are based upon the principle of equality between states' the tribunal held in *Arbitration between the United States of America and the Kingdom of Norway under the Special Agreement of June 30*;[122] 'No principle of law is more universally acknowledged than the perfect equality of nations' the US Supreme Court stated in *The Antelope*.[123] This point has been made in the literature too: 'An international tribunal, or a municipal tribunal when giving effect to the international obligations of the State to which it belongs, pays the same attention to the rights of France as it does to the rights of Costa Rica', as McNair put it in 1937.[124] This is exactly what may be concluded from *Lac Lanoux* (where, as it happened, France in effect argued that its sovereignty was more important than that of Spain) and *Navigational Rights* (where conversely Nicaragua had in effect argued that its sovereignty was more important than that of Costa Rica). The principle of sovereign equality is codified in Article 2(1) of the Charter of the Untied Nations: 'The

[120] *Dispute regarding Navigational and Related Rights (Costa Rica* v. *Nicaragua)* Judgment ICJ Rep 2009 pp. 213, 237.

[121] J. Crawford, 'Sovereignty as a Legal Value', in J. Crawford, M. Koskenniemi and S. Ranganathan (eds.), *The Cambridge Companion to International Law* (Cambridge: Cambridge University Press 2011), p. 123.

[122] *Award of the Tribunal of Arbitration between the United States of America and the Kingdom of Norway under the Special Agreement of June 30, 1921* (1923) 17 *AJIL* 362, p. 392.

[123] *The Antelope* 10 Wheat 66; J. B. Scott, *Cases on International Law* (Boston: Boston Book Company 1902), p. 10.

[124] A. D. McNair, 'Equality in International Law' (1937) 26 *Michigan Law Review* 131, p. 136; McNair, *The Law of Treaties*, note 8 above, pp. 765–6. Also: C. Rousseau, *Droit international public I* (Paris: Sirey 1970), p. 273.

Organization is based on the principle of the sovereign equality of all its Members'.[125]

If we are to take this seriously, then surely it must mean that it cannot be right that the sovereignty of one State is to trump that of another; in a sense this argument from sovereignty also contributes to undermine the sovereignty-based principle of *in dubio mitius*. This problem with *in dubio mitius* was perhaps brought out the most clearly in *Iron Rhine*: 'the sovereignty reserved to the Netherlands under Article XII of the 1839 Treaty of Separation cannot be understood save by first determining Belgium's rights, and the Netherlands' obligations in relation thereto'.[126]

There is also a second argument from sovereignty that undercuts the alleged principle of *in dubio mitius*. It too becomes obvious once it is stated. In fact it was relied upon already in *The Wimbledon*.[127] The Permanent Court declined to see in the conclusion of any treaty by which a State undertakes to perform a particular act an abandonment of its sovereignty: 'No doubt any convention creating an obligation of this kind places a restriction upon the exercise of the sovereign rights of the State, in the sense that it requires them to be exercised in a certain way. But the right of entering into international engagements is an attribute of State sovereignty.'[128] Thus, as Crawford has stated, an argument from sovereignty is evaded by an appeal to sovereignty; if States could not enter into binding international obligations, they would lack an attribute of statehood.[129]

The unacceptability in international law of the principle of *in dubio mitius* was, in general terms, underlined by Franck when he said that: 'Sovereignty has historically been a factor greatly overrated in international relations. Among the overraters have been prominent practitioners of international law, dazzled by their status as, or aspiring to be, high officials of their national foreign offices.'[130] Huber, who in 1928 had given the

[125] *Jurisdictional Immunities of the State (Germany* v. *Italy: Greece Intervening)* Judgment ICJ Rep 2012 pp. 99, 123–4 [57]; *Questions Relating to the Seizure and Detention of Certain Documents and Data (Timor-Leste* v. *Australia)* Order ICJ 3 March 2014 [27].

[126] *Award in the Arbitration regarding the Iron Rhine ('Ijzeren Rijn') (Belgium* v. *Netherlands)* (2005) 27 RIAA 35, 65.

[127] *Case of the SS 'Wimbledon'* (1923) PCIJ Series A No. 1, p. 15.

[128] *Ibid.*, p. 25.

[129] J. Crawford, 'Treaty and Contract in Investment Arbitration' (2008) 24 *Arbitration International* 351, 353. Also: Lauterpacht, *Private Law Sources and Analogies*, note 62 above, pp. 179–80.

[130] T. Franck, *Fairness in International Law and Institutions* (Oxford: Oxford University Press 1998), p. 3.

famous definition of sovereignty in *Island of Palmas*, where he stated that 'sovereignty in the relations between States signifies independence',[131] in 1958 held that notions of sovereignty would have to give way. Huber, in common with Franck, underlined how in the chancelleries of the world exaggerated ideas of sovereignty have outlived themselves, at the expense of international cooperation:

> Nobody will venture to assert that the international law of today, in spite of new directions in 1920 and 1946, is able to cope with the present world situation. The responsibility of all concerned with international law in the widest sense of the term, whether as politicians or scientists, is all the heavier. There is only one way to a new solution: coexistence and the idea of sovereignty, which flattered and served the sense of power in big states and the desire for independence in small ones, must make way for an efficient and active community of nations.[132]

We should therefore join the conclusion of Ulfstein, who has consigned to history the principle that contractual treaties are to be interpreted restrictively in deference to State sovereignty: 'the principle is to be regarded to be of more historical than official interest'.[133] What we may conclude from this is that, while not least some of the writers who focus on other types of treaty than 'ordinary' or contractual treaties have gone very far, even in the present age, in claiming that contractual treaties are to be interpreted according to *in dubio mitius*, their contentions lack a sound basis both in the modern and classic law of treaties.[134] It must therefore be right, both normatively and descriptively, to say that whatever may have been true of old judicial authorities one is most unlikely today *ever* to see an international tribunal of repute deciding a disputed point of interpretation by reference to supposedly special doctrines thought to be specially applicable to particular types of case, such as a 'restrictive' doctrine of interpretation.[135]

131 *Island of Palmas (Netherlands* v. *United States of America)* (1928) 2 RIAA 829, 838.

132 M. Huber, 'On the Place of the Law of Nations in the History of Mankind', in *Symbolae Verzijl: Présentées au Professeur JHW Verzijl à l'occasion de son LXX-ième anniversaire* (Leiden: Martinus Nijhoff 1958), pp. 194–5.

133 G. Ulfstein, *The Svalbard Treaty* (Oslo: Scandinavian University Press 1995), p. 94. Also: L Crema, 'Disappearance and New Sightings of Restrictive Interpretation(s)' (2010) 21 *EJIL* 681, pp. 686–8.

134 See H. Lauterpacht, 'Restrictive Interpretation and the Principle of Effectiveness in the Interpretation of Treaties' (1949) 26 *BYIL* 48.

135 Berman, 'Community Law and International Law', note 2 above, p. 250.

3. Systemic coherence in both content and method

This leads us to that which more directly concerns the methods of treaty interpretation adopted. As was said in the introduction to this chapter, there is a connection between fragmentation with respect to the content of rules and fragmentation with respect to the law of treaties, that is to say fragmentation in the method of treaty interpretation. Thus Dupuy has stated that 'the techniques of treaty interpretation must not be seen only from the formal point of view'; 'they also have material consequences – that is to say consequences for the substance or contents of norms – which are of the greatest importance'.[136]

3.1. Coherence in content

The analysis here goes back to what was said in the introduction to this chapter about self-contained regimes and their relation to whether it is a tenable claim to say that the law of treaties is fragmented. The analysis will in the main turn around *Pulp Mills on the River Uruguay*[137] and *Case Concerning Ahmadou Sadio Diallo*.[138] This is not least because these two case complexes turn on the same two areas (or alleged 'self-contained regimes') that were in issue in the two classic cases with which this chapter began, *Case of the SS 'Wimbledon'*[139] and in *United States Diplomatic and Consular Staff in Tehran*[140] – namely the law of international waterways and consular protection.

In *Pulp Mills on the River Uruguay*, a case bearing on the law of international waterways and international environmental law, the International Court held that the treaty, the so-called Statute of the River Uruguay, must 'be interpreted in accordance with a practice, which in recent years

[136] J. M. Dupuy, *Droit international public* (Paris: Dalloz 2008), p. 336; H. Ruiz Fabri, 'La contribution de l'Organisation mondiale du commerce à la gestion de l'espace juridique mondial', in E. Loquin and C. Kessedjian (eds.), *La mondialisation du droit* (Paris: Litec 2000), p. 369.

[137] *Pulp Mills on the River Uruguay (Argentina* v. *Uruguay)*, Judgment ICJ Rep 2010 p. 14.

[138] *Diallo (Republic of Guinea* v. *Democratic Republic of the Congo)*, Preliminary Objections ICJ Rep 2007 p. 582; *Case Concerning Ahmadou Sadio Diallo (Republic of Guinea* v. *Democratic Republic of the Congo)*, Judgment 30 November 2010; *Ahmadou Sadio Diallo (Republic of Guinea* v. *Democratic Republic of the Congo) (Compensation owed by the Democratic Republic of the Congo to the Republic of Guinea)*, Judgment 19 June 2012.

[139] *Case of the SS 'Wimbledon'* (1923) PCIJ Series A No. 1, pp. 15, 23–4.

[140] *United States Diplomatic and Consular Staff in Tehran (United States of America* v. *Iran)*, Judgment ICJ Rep 1980 pp. 3, 40 [86].

has gained so much acceptance among States that it may now be considered a requirement under general international law to undertake an environmental impact assessment where there is a risk that the proposed industrial activity may have a significant adverse impact in a transboundary context, in particular, on a shared resource'.[141] The Court struck the same note when, in *Case Concerning Ahmadou Sadio Diallo* it did not treat consular protection as a self-contained regime, but instead relied on human rights law in its establishment of what level of protection ought to be accorded in the case.[142] This was made explicit in the concurring opinion of Judge Cançado Trindade, who stated that while the procedure for the claim for the vindication of the claim originally utilized was that of diplomatic protection, the substantive law applied by the Court was 'the International Law of Human Rights'.[143] The International Court made it clear that it was thus no longer the case that, to use the formula from *United States Diplomatic and Consular Staff in Tehran*, 'the rules of diplomatic law, in short, constitute a self-contained regime'.[144] This seemed to be in step with the criticism that had been levelled at *Tehran Hostages*, for example by Simma and Pulkowski, who have argued that while the rules of diplomatic law, due to the dictum in *Tehran Hostages*, had become the rules of international law most commonly associated with the notion of self-containment, in fact they were 'the least convincing example of a closed system of secondary rules'.[145] In fact the International Court in *Diallo* went so far, in bringing human rights norms to bear upon the law of diplomatic protection, as to cite jurisprudence from the African Commission on Human and Peoples' Rights, the Inter-American Court of Human Rights, and the European Court of Human Rights.[146] To some extent the

141 *Pulp Mills on the River Uruguay (Argentina* v. *Uruguay)*, Judgment ICJ Rep 2010 pp. 14, 83 [204].

142 *Case Concerning Ahmadou Sadio Diallo (Republic of Guinea* v. *Democratic Republic of the Congo)*, Judgment ICJ Rep 2010 pp. 639, 662–73 [63]–[98]; *Diallo (Republic of Guinea* v. *Democratic Republic of the Congo)*, Preliminary Objections ICJ Rep 2007 p. 582 [39]. Also: Clapham, *Brierly's Law of Nations*, note 60 above, pp. 259–64.

143 Concurring Opinion of Judge Cançado Trindade in *Case Concerning Ahmadou Sadio Diallo (Republic of Guinea* v. *Democratic Republic of the Congo)*, Judgment ICJ Rep 2010 pp. 639, 804 [220].

144 *United States Diplomatic and Consular Staff in Tehran (United States of America* v. *Iran)*, Judgment ICJ Rep 1980 pp. 3, 40 [86].

145 Simma and Pulkowski, '*Leges speciales* and Self-Contained Regimes', note 4 above, p. 150.

146 M. Andenas, 'International Court of Justice, Case Concerning Ahmadou Sadio Diallo (Republic of Guinea v Democratic Republic of the Congo) Judgment of 30 November 2010' (2011) 60 *ICLQ* 810, pp. 816–17. Also: Andenas, 'The Centre Reasserting Itself', note 2 above.

same could be said of *LaGrand* – a case concerned with a synallagmatic, inter-State convention, the Vienna Convention on Consular Relations.[147] In his analysis of this case, Crawford asked: in what respect is the category of 'human rights' special? The answer, he says, is that it may not be. That is why, he continues, the International Court in *LaGrand* saw the Vienna Convention on Consular Relations as giving rise to individual rights.[148]

It has in later years been possible to observe a tendency according to which the International Court itself has started referring, even more than it used to do before,[149] to other types of international court and tribunal, not least the human rights courts and bodies. It was eloquent of this development when Judge Sir Christopher Greenwood, in the 2012 ruling by the International Court in *Diallo (Compensation)*, stated that:

> International law is not a series of fragmented specialist and self-contained bodies of law, each of which functions in isolation from the others; it is a single, unified system of law and each international court can, and should, draw on the jurisprudence of other international courts and tribunals, even though it is not bound necessarily to come to the same conclusions.[150]

This seems now to have become the new orthodoxy. As referred to above, Crawford, who sees international law not only as a system, but specifically as an *open* system, said that there are hardly any entirely self-contained regimes at all; he mentions the European Union as the only possible candidate.[151] Special Rapporteur Sir Michael Wood has, in the context of an ILC study on the formation of customary international law,[152] stated that given the unity of international law and the fact that 'international law is a legal system', it is neither helpful nor in accordance with principle to break the law up into separate specialist fields. The same basic approach to the formation and identification of customary international law, he said, applies regardless of the field of law under consideration. The

147 *LaGrand (Germany* v. *United States of America)*, Judgment ICJ Rep 2001 p. 466.

148 Crawford, *International Law as an Open System*, note 102 above, pp. 28–9.

149 The Permanent and the International Court have on many occasions referred to the decisions of other tribunals: A. D. McNair, *The Development of International Justice* (New York: New York University Press 1954), pp. 12–13; Crawford, *Brownlie's Principles of Public International Law*, note 15 above, pp. 39–40.

150 Declaration of Judge Greenwood, *Case Concerning Ahmadou Sadio Diallo (Republic of Guinea* v. *Democratic Republic of the Congo)*, Compensation, Judgment ICJ Rep 2012 pp. 324, 294 [8].

151 Crawford, *International Law as an Open System*, note 102 above, p. 37.

152 M. Wood, 'Formation and Evidence of Customary International Law'.

Commission's work on this topic would be equally relevant to all fields of international law, including, for example, customary human rights law, customary international humanitarian law, and customary international criminal law.[153]

The tendency – in the literature, in the jurisprudence of international tribunals, and in the work of the ILC – seems to have gone from focusing on what is different among the different fields of international law 'to move freely over the boundaries, which seem to divide these fields of law and to bring out the underlying unities'.[154]

3.2. *Coherence in method*

It is interesting to point out that in the cases where the International Court has confirmed the coherence of international law as a system, the Court has also confirmed the coherence in the law of treaties with respect to interpretation. This shows the connection between the material substance of the rules in issue and of the methods used in order to establish that rule substance. As was said above, it was in cases bearing on the law of international waterways and consular protection that the Permanent Court and the International Court set out the classical parameters for the debate on the existence in international law of self-contained regimes.[155] This approach could be contrasted with the approach taken by the International Court more recently in especially two cases from the same two areas of international law: *Pulp Mills*[156] and *Diallo*.[157]

In *Pulp Mills* and *Diallo* the International Court refused to see the area in issue as a self-contained regime – and specifically showed this by the styles of interpretation chosen. The International Court in *Pulp Mills* adopted an evolutionary interpretation,[158] where the bilateral treaty was seen by the Court as having been intended by the parties to be capable

[153] M. Wood, 'Formation and Evidence of Customary International Law. Note by Michael Wood, Special Rapporteur' ILC Sixty-fourth Session Geneva, 7 May–1 June and 2 July–3 August 2012 5 [22] (internal references omitted).

[154] A. F. Denning, 'Foreword' (1952) 1 *ICLQ* 1, p. 1.

[155] *Case of the SS 'Wimbledon'* (1923) PCIJ Series A No. 1, pp. 15, 23–4; *United States Diplomatic and Consular Staff in Tehran (United States of America* v. *Iran)*, Judgment ICJ Rep 1980 pp. 3, 40 [86].

[156] *Pulp Mills on the River Uruguay (Argentina* v. *Uruguay)*, Judgment ICJ Rep 2010 p. 14.

[157] *Case Concerning Ahmadou Sadio Diallo (Republic of Guinea* v. *Democratic Republic of the Congo)*, Judgment ICJ Rep 2012 p. 639.

[158] See M. Dawidowicz, 'The Effect of the Passage of Time on the Interpretation of Treaties: Some Reflections on *Costa Rica* v. *Nicaragua*' (2011) 24 *LJIL* 201; G. Nolte, 'Report 1 for

of evolution, so that the provisions of the treaty were interpreted in accordance with a general practice, which in recent years had gained so much acceptance that it must be considered a requirement under general international law.[159] Coherence with respect to the content of the rules and coherence with respect to method in this way were made to go hand in hand: it was by way of evolutionary interpretation that the Court made sure that the bilateral environmental treaty was in conformity with general international law. This approach to interpretation has been seen as being alien to general international law, and particularly synallagmatic, bilateral treaties, but here the International Court applies such an approach to just such a treaty, and it did so with reference to what it had said about evolutionary interpretation in *Navigational Rights*, another example of the Court applying such an approach to a synallagmatic treaty.[160]

In *Diallo* the same mechanism may be observed.[161] Yet in this case it was not an interpretation of an evolutionary character that was adopted; what was in issue here was, I would argue, effective interpretation. The case bore on diplomatic protection, a field which, as we saw above, had been described in *Tehran Hostages* as a self-contained regime.[162] It should be noted here that the approach of the International Court in *Tehran Hostages* has been criticized in the literature, and this criticism has not only centred on the idea of a '*self-contained* regime' but the idea of a '*regime*' itself. Crawford and Nevill have held that 'the institutions of diplomatic protection cannot be usefully described as a regime'. On their view it was both unfortunate and unnecessary that the International Court used the word 'regime':

> The Court was seeking to make the point that diplomatic relations is a self-contained system insofar as the arrangement for sanctions or taking measures against diplomats is set out in diplomatic law rather than any

the ILC Study Group on Treaties over Time', in G Nolte (ed.), *Treaties and Subsequent Practice* (Oxford: Oxford University Press 2013), p. 188.

159 *Pulp Mills on the River Uruguay (Argentina* v. *Uruguay)*, Judgment ICJ Rep 2010 pp. 14, 82–3 [204].

160 *Pulp Mills on the River Uruguay (Argentina* v. *Uruguay)*, Judgment ICJ Rep 2010 pp. 14, 83 [204]: 'As the Court has observed in the case concerning the *Dispute Regarding Navigational and Related Rights*, "there are situations in which the parties' intent upon conclusion of the treaty was, or may be presumed to have been, to give the terms used – or some of them – a meaning or content capable of evolving, not one fixed once and for all, so as to make allowance for, among other things, developments in international law"'.

161 Andenas, 'Case Concerning Ahmadou Sadio Diallo', note 146 above, p. 813.

162 *United States Diplomatic and Consular Staff in Tehran (United States of America* v. *Iran)*, Judgment ICJ Rep 1980 pp. 3, 40 [86].

> other part of general international law. But the specific rules sit within general international law, to which we resort alongside and in the absence of specific subject-matter rules.[163]

It would be better, therefore, if the word regime was used in a more discriminating way, and in particular was not used to describe branches of general international law. *Diallo* is an example of this type of argument prevailing. The International Court, in considering the provisions on the expulsion of an alien lawfully in the territory of a State, made clear that the expulsion of Diallo could be effected only in accordance with the law, but that 'in accordance with the law' was not sufficient in itself. In addition, the applicable domestic law must be compatible with the other requirements of the relevant international law and the expulsion must not be arbitrary:

> it is clear that while 'accordance with law' as thus defined is a necessary condition for compliance with the above-mentioned provisions, it is not the sufficient condition. First, the applicable domestic law must itself be compatible with the other requirements of the Covenant and the African Charter; second, an expulsion must not be arbitrary in nature, since protection against arbitrary treatment lies at the heart of the rights guaranteed by the international norms protecting human rights.[164]

To focus in this way on the protection against arbitrary treatment, and to use that as a guiding principle in the interpretation of the provisions in issue, seems to be to take seriously the principle of effectiveness.[165] In fact, by concluding this way, the International Court in *Diallo* took more seriously than the European Court had done in similar cases the general exhortation, from *Airey* v. *United Kingdom*, that human rights conventions such as the European Convention are 'intended to guarantee not rights that are theoretical or illusory but rights that are practical and effective'.[166] For it does seem to have been the case that the International Court went further than the human rights bodies have done in this regard, thus following that which has been seen to be the method of the

[163] Crawford and Nevill, 'The "Regime Problem"', note 4 above, p. 259.

[164] *Case Concerning Ahmadou Sadio Diallo (Republic of Guinea* v. *Democratic Republic of the Congo)*, Judgment ICJ Rep 2010 pp. 639, 663 [65].

[165] *Dispute between Argentina and Chile concerning the Beagle Channel* (1977) 11 RIAA 53, 231; *Award in the Arbitration regarding the Iron Rhine ('Ijzeren Rijn') (Belgium* v. *Netherlands)* (2005) 27 RIAA 35, 64.

[166] *Airey* v. *United Kingdom* App No. 6289/73 Judgment 9 October 1979 [24]; *Demir and Baykara* v. *Turkey* App no 34503/97 Judgment [GC] 12 November 2008 [61].

human rights tribunals more scrupulously than those tribunals have done themselves. This will be explained in the following.

As was said above, the International Court in *Diallo*relied directly on jurisprudence from other international and regional bodies, such as the United Nations Human Rights Committee[167] and the African Commission on Human and Peoples' Rights.[168] Moreover, it noted that the interpretation by the European Court of Human Rights and the Inter-American Court of Human Rights, respectively, of Article 1 of protocol 7 to the European Convention and Article 22(6) of the American Convention – the said provisions being close in substance to those of the Covenant and the African Charter, which the Court was applying in the present case – was consistent with what had been found in respect of the latter provisions.[169]

Judges Greenwood and Keith, however, pointed out that the cited jurisprudence on the expulsion provisions in issue did not, in point of fact, confer protection on substance, only on procedure.[170] This is borne out both by the jurisprudence of the European Court and of the Inter-American Commission.[171] The leading commentaries on the European Convention also seem to bear out this proposition. One commentary tersely states that the procedural guarantees of the pertinent provision provide no protection of substance, that is, relating to the grounds on which expulsion might be sought.[172] As a result, and as Judges Greenwood and Keith show, the International Court in effect went further in its

[167] *Maroufidou* v. *Sweden* No. 58/1979 [9.3]; Human Rights Committee, General Comment No. 15: The position of aliens under the Covenant.

[168] *Kenneth Good* v. *Republic of Botswana*, No. 313/05 [204]; World Organization against Torture and International Association of Democratic Lawyers, International Commission of Jurists, *Inter-African Union for Human Rights* v. *Rwanda*, No. 27/89, 46/91, 49/91, 99/93.

[169] *Case Concerning Ahmadou Sadio Diallo (Republic of Guinea* v. *Democratic Republic of the Congo)*, Judgment ICJ Rep 2010 pp. 639, 664 [68].

[170] Separate Opinion Judges Greenwood and Keith *Case Concerning Ahmadou Sadio Diallo (Republic of Guinea* v. *Democratic Republic of the Congo)*, Judgment ICJ Rep 2010 pp. 639, 716–19 [11]–[14].

[171] *Bolat* v. *Russia*, App No. 14139/03 Judgment 5 October 2006 [81]–[83]; *Lupsa* v. *Romania*, App No. 10337/04 Judgment 8 June 2006 [54]–[61]; *Situations of Haitians in the Dominican Republic*, Inter-American Commission on Human Rights, Ann Rep 1991, 14 February 1992, ch V.

[172] R. C. A. White and C. Ovey, *Jacobs, White, and Ovey: The European Convention on Human Rights* (5th edn., Oxford: Oxford University Press 2010), pp. 544–5. Also: D. Harris, M. O'Boyle, E. Bates and C. Buckley, *Harris, O'Boyle and Warbrick: Law of the European Convention on Human Rights* (2nd edn., Oxford: Oxford University Press 2009), pp. 747–8.

effective interpretation of the human rights provisions at issue than the human rights bodies have gone.[173]

Again *LaGrand* may be of interest.[174] Crawford, in his analysis of *LaGrand*, has stated that when the International Court reached its conclusion that the Vienna Convention on Consular Relations gave rise to individual rights, it did so using that which he terms the 'principle of ordinary interpretation'.[175] It must be right therefore to say, as Crawford has done in another context, of the techniques of treaty interpretation that 'these techniques seem to have a general character, whether they arise in the International Court of Justice, in the dispute system of the WTO, in the European Court of Justice or elsewhere'.[176]

4. Conclusion

International law is indeed a legal system. It is not a series of fragmented specialist and self-contained bodies of law; it is a single, unified system of law.[177] And the techniques that the ILC invoked and recommended are simply 'techniques of general international law'.[178] It is, as Koskenniemi has observed, evident by now that 'fragmentation' did not turn out to create the chaos that was feared ten to fifteen years ago.[179] It may indeed be that we are in this regard seeing the contours of what has been called 'a process of gradual learning'.[180] This is, as this chapter has argued, also the case with the method used in treaty interpretation. The method is not fragmented; the law of treaties, the method used by various types of international tribunal in treaty interpretation, is a single, unified method of law.

173 E. Bjorge, 'Ahmadou Sadio Diallo (Republic of Guinea v Democratic Republic of the Congo)' (2011) 105 *AJIL* 534, pp. 539–40.

174 *LaGrand (Germany* v. *United States of America)*, Judgment ICJ Rep 2001 p. 466.

175 Crawford, *International Law as an Open System*, note 102 above, pp. 28–9; Crawford and Nevill, 'The "Regime Problem"', note 4 above, p. 235.

176 Crawford, *International Law as an Open System*, note 102 above, p. 37.

177 Declaration of Judge Greenwood, *Case Concerning Ahmadou Sadio Diallo (Republic of Guinea* v. *Democratic Republic of the Congo)*, Compensation, Judgment ICJ Rep 2012 pp. 324, 294 [8].

178 Crawford and Nevill, 'The "Regime Problem"', note 4 above, p. 236.

179 M. Koskenniemi, 'The Case for Comparative International Law' (2009) 20 *Finnish Yearbook of International Law* 5.

180 I. J. Sand, 'The Fragmentation of Law on the Global Level: Conflicts of Law or Processes of Learning?', in O. K. Fauchald and others (eds.), *Liber Amicorum Carl August Fleischer* (Oslo: Universitetsforlaget 2006), p. 496.

Berman has argued that the Vienna Convention rules, when they were adopted in 1969, 'swept away at the same time all the supposed special tenets of interpretation that had enveloped the subject like cobwebs'. Thus one is today most unlikely to see an international tribunal of repute deciding a disputed point of interpretation by reference to special styles of interpretation, such as a 'restrictive' doctrine of interpretation, or any other supposed special doctrine thought to be specially applicable to particular types of case.[181]

Lauterpacht and McNair in the preface of the first published volume of *The Annual Digest of Public International Law Cases*[182] famously said that '[t]he work of which this book is the first-fruits was prompted by the suspicion that there is more international law already in existence and daily accumulating "than this world dreams of"'.[183] Jennings, who, as was shown above, saw international law as being fragmented to a very large extent, in the mid-1990s, felt that the 'tendencies to fragmentation in international adjudication threaten to give an ironic modern twist to McNair's belief that there is more international law in existence "than this world dreams of"'.[184]

Jennings's fears were in the final analysis exaggerated. We should not forget what Lauterpacht and McNair added after they had stated their suspicion that there was more international law already in existence and accumulating daily than this world dreams of: they added that 'it is more international law that this world wants'.[185] That last point has indeed proved to be correct. As one commentator recently put it in an analysis of developments in the law of treaties: 'the more international law, the better'.[186] And given the development during the last few years, this

[181] Berman, 'Community Law and International Law', note 2 above, p. 250.

[182] The volumes were not numbered until 1958; as R. Jennings explains, the volumes after 1958 *then* numbered 1 and 2 were edited by F. Williams and H. Lauterpacht; the present volume 3 was the first published and edited by A. McNair and H. Lauterpacht: Jennings, 'The Judiciary', note 36 above, p. 1.

[183] A. D. McNair and H. Lauterpacht, 'Preface', in H. Lauterpacht and J. Fischer Williams (eds.), *Annual Digest of Public International Law Cases 1925–26* (Cambridge: Cambridge University Press 1929), p. ix.

[184] Jennings, 'The Judiciary', note 36 above, pp. 5–6 (Jennings claims that the citation was cast in words 'redolent of McNair'; this is why he leaves Lauterpacht out here: *Ibid.*, p. 1).

[185] A. D. McNair and H. Lauterpacht, 'Preface', note 183 above, p. ix.

[186] M. Waibel, 'Demystifying the Art of Interpretation' (2010) 22 *EJIL* 571, p. 573: Waibel adds a caveat, however, with regard to whether the accretion of international law is necessarily a good thing in the more general sense: 'it is no longer possible (if it ever was) to say that the maturing system of international law is invariably a "progressive" force, necessarily leading to an improvement of the human condition'.

accretion and accumulation of international law have not, as we have seen, meant more fragmentation but arguably less.[187] It is on this basis tempting to conclude that the more international law that has come into existence, the clearer the converging character of the international legal system has become. The extension of the development to which Lauterpacht and McNair pointed in 1929 has only continued but the problems to which one could have imagined the development would give rise have not in fact materialized.

Crawford and Nevill have argued that there is no 'meta-system' that underlies international law and that is able to safeguard its coherence.[188] Yet it must be possible to say that while the mass of international law is greater now than ever before, the extent to which international law can be said to be a coherent system is quite striking. And, on the argument presented in this chapter, this also seems to be true of the method applied in the law of treaties. Never have international tribunals produced so much treaty analysis as now; the law of treaty interpretation is indeed, and despite having been codified more then forty years ago, one of the most dynamic fields of international law.[189] Yet the convergence which the method displays is little short of striking.

The analysis in this chapter of the jurisprudence especially of the International Court has ventured to bear out the proposition that there is in international law *one* method, and that, even where tribunals insist that they are applying a particular style of interpretation, they seem in fact to be applying the same method.

[187] Weiler, 'The Geology of International Law', note 60 above, p. 549.
[188] Crawford and Nevill, 'The "Regime Problem"', note 4 above, p. 252.
[189] Waibel, 'Demystifying the Art of Interpretation', note 186 above, p. 572.

20

Reassertion and transformation of international law

MADS ANDENAS

I. The International Court and the pressing problems of fragmentation

This chapter analyses the case law of the International Court of Justice (ICJ) and the discourse about the fragmentation of international law. Different international courts and tribunals, as well as central international institutions such as the International Law Commission (ILC) and other UN bodies, have made contributions to entrench the coherence of international law as a unitary legal system. Such contributions to clarify and strengthen 'the systemic nature of international law'[1] counter a threat of fragmentation. It will not surprise that fear of fragmentation could influence the development of international law. Nonetheless, it may be difficult to show such influence empirically by way of express statements to this effect in judgments. In light of the developments in the jurisprudence of the International Court, and the responses from central international institutions and different courts and tribunals, one conclusion in this book is that even if the problems of fragmentation may remain pressing in different ways, they are not a threat to international law as a legal system.[2] The focus in this chapter is the jurisprudence of the International Court.

[1] Special Rapporteur Sir Michael Wood, Second Report on Identification of Customary International Law ILC A/CN.4/672 p. 14 at [28].

[2] James Crawford, *International Law as an Open System: Selected Essays* (Cameron May, London, 2002) and his 2014 Hague lectures; Campbell McLachlan, 'The Principle of Systemic Integration and Article 31 (3)(c) of the Vienna Convention' (2005) 54 *International and Comparative Law Quarterly* 279–320; Martti Koskenniemi, 'The Fate of Public International Law: Between Technique and Politics' (2007) 70 *The Modern Law Review* 1–30; Eyal Benvenisti and George W. Downs, 'The Empire's New Clothes: Political Economy and the Fragmentation of International Law' (2007) 60 *Stanford Law Review* 595; Eyal Benvenisti, *The Law of Global Governance* (The Hague Academy of International Law, 2014);

Twenty years of expansion of international law with new courts and enforcement mechanisms sparked concern over fragmentation among academics and judges. Institutional reforms to strengthen international law as a unitary legal system were never likely to come about via the treaty route. The chapter explores whether the developments in procedure and substantive law can be seen as an alternative response. On one level the responses are incremental and limited; on another, it is argued in this chapter, together they contribute to fundamental changes of a transformational character, as the authors of several chapters in the book argue, including both the justices of the International Court, Antônio Augusto CançadoTrindade and Sir Christopher Greenwood, in their very characteristically different ways. There is a transformation of international law taking place with changing concepts of State sovereignty, individual rights, jurisdiction, procedure and evidence incrementally remedying limitations of traditional doctrine. Support for the strengthening of international law as a legal system is found in the Vienna Convention on the Law of Treaties, Article 31(3)(c) on the application of 'any relevant rules of international law applicable in the relations between the parties'.[3] The International Court contributes to customary international law and resolving pressing problems of human rights and environmental law, moving away from the strictly inter-State perspective and non-hierarchical view of international law where State consent has put extreme restrictions on jurisdiction, obligations of States and the development of the law.

Pierre-Marie Dupuy in 1999 suggested that the International Court as a matter of 'judicial policy' should revitalise its role as the central judicial body of the international community.[4] Similarly Georges Abi-Saab observed that there can be 'a "judicial system" without a centralized "judicial power" invested in it, and with the jurisdiction of its components remaining in general ultimately consensual'. Such a system can develop

and Mads Andenas, 'Reassertion and Transformation: from Fragmentation to Convergence in International Law' (2015) 46 *Georgetown Journal of International Law* 685–734.

3 The Vienna Convention on the Law of Treaties (VCLT) Article 31(3)(c) provides that when interpreting treaties, '[t]here shall be taken into account, together with the context . . . any relevant rules of international law applicable in the relations between the parties.' See in particular, Campbell McLachlan, 'The Principle of Systemic Integration, and Article 31 (3)(c) of the Vienna Convention' (2005) 54 *International and Comparative Law Quarterly* 279–320, who pointed out that 'until very recently, Article 31(3)(c) languished in . . . obscurity', and comments on the role of *Oil Platforms (Islamic Republic of Iran* v. *United States of America)*, Judgment, ICJ Reports 2003, 4 in its revival.

4 Pierre-Marie Dupuy, 'The Danger of Fragmentation or Unification of the International Legal System and the International Court of Justice' (1999) 31 *N.Y.U. Journal of International Law and Politics* 701, 801.

through the cumulative process of international law, of which custom is the most visible, but not the only, example. Abi-Saab added that this process depends on the behaviour of the relevant legal actors, not only States but also the courts and tribunals themselves.[5]

In this chapter it is argued that the roles of the International Court, the 'principal judicial organ of the United Nations',[6] and other UN organs such as the ILC, tasked with 'encouraging the progressive development of international law and it codification',[7] are increasingly important in a more complex international law system with a multiplication of treaty regimes and enforcement mechanisms. The International Court and other UN organs not limited to a single treaty regime can rely on their own experience from other fields, and a wider body of law, and also a general legal method.

Ralph Wilde has suggested for the human rights field that the International Court 'might "add value" when compared to treatment by a specialist tribunal'.[8] The International Court has a long-standing practice and experience ranging across all areas of law and in applying multiple fields of law simultaneously, including more than one area of human rights law and multiple human rights treaties and other areas of law in addition to human rights law. The argument in this chapter is that this proposition applies not only to human rights law; rather it obtains across all of international law and its different disciplines.

Article 92 of the UN Charter establishes the International Court as 'the principal judicial organ of the United Nations', and the Court's position is strengthened not only by the extensive jurisprudence, clarifying treaty obligations and customary international law, but by the quality and respect for that jurisprudence which legal communities interact with in so many ways. Specialist bodies may have specialist competence, both in terms of expertise and authority, and the International Court has, as will be discussed in the chapter, paid respect to that in different contexts. The

[5] Georges Abi-Saab, 'Fragmentation or Unification: Some Concluding Remarks', 31 *N.Y.U. Journal of International Law and Politics* 919, 926.

[6] Article 92, Charter of the United Nations, 26 June 1945, 892 UNTS 119.

[7] Article 13(1)(a), Charter of the United Nations. See for example Peter Tomka, 'Major Complexities Encountered in Contemporary International Law-Making' (1998) 1 *Making Better International Law: The International Law Commission at 50: Proceedings of the United Nations on Progressive Development and Codification of Law* 209, 210.

[8] Ralph Wilde, 'Human Rights Beyond Borders at the World Court: The Significance of the International Court of Justice's Jurisprudence on the Extraterritorial Application of International Human Rights Law Treaties', (2013) 12 *Chinese Journal of International Law* 639 at [93].

International Court's authority is particularly strong on general international law, its principles and method.[9] The interaction between the International Court and the ILC on the formation of customary international law in the context of the ILC study on that topic,[10] is interesting. The Special Rapporteur Sir Michael Wood rationalizes and closely follows the methodological approaches developed by the International Court, which is what other UN bodies attempt to do when they address such issues.[11]

This chapter ends the book and starts the further inquiry into whether, and to what extent, the case law of the International Court has reasserted the Court's place at the summit of the international legal order. Parallel inquiries into the practice of other international courts and tribunals and their reception and application of the jurisprudence of the International Court, and other forms of 'dialogues', are important for an understanding of international law as a legal system, and also the fragmentation and convergence issues discussed in this chapter. There are valuable studies of different sectors or treaty regimes, but gaps remain and there is a need to consolidate relevant scholarship and compare across sectors and regimes. Institutional and procedural issues are important and so is the development of substantive law through the clarification of issues that are

[9] See in connection with customary international law, for example, *Continental Shelf (Tunisia/Libyan Arab Jamahiriya)*, Judgment, ICJ Reports 1982, 18, at 46, para. 43; *Military and Paramilitary Activities in and against Nicaragua (Nicaragua v. United States of America)*, Merits, Judgment, ICJ Reports 1986, 14, at 98, para. 186; *Jurisdictional Immunities of the State (Germany v. Italy: Greece intervening)*, Judgment, ICJ Reports 2012, 99, at 143, para. 101. Further: Peter Tomka, 'Custom and the International Court of Justice' (2013) 12 *The Law & Practice of International Courts and Tribunals* 195. See in connection with treaty interpretation, for example, *Territorial Dispute(Libya/Chad)*, Judgment ICJ Reports 1994, 21, 23; *Territorial Dispute(Libya/Chad)*, Judgment, ICJ Reports 1994, 21, 23; *Certain Questions of Mutual Assistance in Criminal Matters (Djibouti* v. *France)*, Judgment, ICJ Reports 2008, 177, 218; *Dispute regarding Navigational and Related Rights (Costa Rica* v. *Nicaragua)* Judgment, ICJ Reports 2009, 213. Further: G. Guillaume, 'Methods and Practice of Treaty Interpretation by the International Court of Justice', in G. Sacerdoti, A. Yanovich and J. Bohanes (eds.), *The WTO at Ten: The Contribution of the Dispute Settlement System* (Cambridge University Press 2006) 472–73; E. Bjorge, *The Evolutionary Interpretation of Treaties* (Oxford University Press 2014) 56–141.

[10] A/CN.4/663: *First Report on Formation and Evidence of Customary International Law*: see http://untreaty.un.org/ilc/guide/1_13.htm. A/CN.4/672 *Second Report on Formation and Evidence of Customary International Law.*

[11] See, for instance, UN Working Group on Arbitrary Detention, 'Deliberation No. 9 concerning the definition and scope of arbitrary deprivation of liberty under customary international law', Human Rights Council Report of the WGAD (24 December 2012), A/HRC/22/44, para. 43.

brought before the International Court and other international courts and tribunals.

II. An autonomous regime among others

Most of this chapter is concerned with the developments in the case law of the International Court. Having left behind some of the exaggerated strictures of State consent in the doctrines of the 1960s to 1990s, the International Court is now in a better position to resolve pressing problems of the expansion of international law and the multiplication of international courts and enforcement mechanisms. The different mechanisms for making new treaty regimes more effective of the 1990s could have different consequences for the International Court. They would strengthen the effectiveness of international law or at least the treaty obligations in question. Their consequences for the International Court and international law as a legal system were less clear.

Theodor Meron, President of the International Criminal Tribunal for the former Yugoslavia, in 2013 reiterated Antonio Cassese's claim to autonomy for every international court or tribunal.[12] The boundaries that divide international law increasingly came to divide it into different disciplines with claims to autonomy. Such claims were made not only by international criminal lawyers or human rights lawyers, but on behalf of international trade law, European Union law, investment law, humanitarian law and several other disciplines, by practitioners and scholars who see themselves belonging to that autonomous discipline. Sovereignty claims in relation to domestic law would be followed by claims in relation to the general discipline of international law. Such claims have served different purposes. One consequence for academic scholarship has been increased specialization: few scholars continued to undertake research in more than one of the emerging international law disciplines; very few in combination with research in general public international law, national constitutional law or comparative law in any of its many forms.

When many of the proponents of the new treaty regimes laid claim to autonomy, this would often entail a 'self-contained' status. There would be a discussion if general international law, including the general law

[12] In his speech at the Solemn Hearing at the opening of the year at the European Court of Human Rights on 25 January 2013, available at www.echr.coe.int. Antonio Cassese was the first President of International Criminal Tribunal for the former Yugoslavia.

on treaties and interpretation, could be disregarded, thus leaving the treaty regime 'self-contained'. The International Court's emphasis on State sovereignty not only in matters of jurisdiction but in interpretation, evidence and procedure narrowed down its ability to contribute to the different new treaty regimes. Its approach to individual rights exacerbated this, and also its narrow focus on the relationship between States. Finally, caution in developing international customary law and resistance to *erga omnes* and peremptory norms (*jus cogens*) focused on a role for the International Court in resolving disputes brought before it, and not in developing international law and its coherence as a legal system. There was also the concern that courts with compulsory jurisdiction, such as the World Trade Organization (WTO) Appellate Body, the European Union's Court of Justice, regional human rights courts, and international criminal courts in their different ways, would get the volume of cases, not only giving them the opportunity to develop international law but to take over as the judicial fora for developing international law. General international law as developed in the International Court could have been increasingly marginalized.

Sir Robert Jennings identified in 1995 what he saw as 'the tendency of particular tribunals to regard themselves as different, as separate little empires which must as far as possible be augmented'.[13] His concern seemed primarily to be the European Court of Human Rights and the emergence of international criminal tribunals.

Another judge and subsequent President of the International Court, Gilbert Guillaume, had voiced concern over the proliferation of international courts and tribunals more generally. He suggested that references on points of international law may be made from other international courts to the International Court.[14] This proposal, which was particularly not well received among the Anglo-American lawyers, illustrated Guillaume's concern shared by some other international lawyers that the International Court may be side-lined by the WTO Appellate Body, and other trade and human rights bodies, usually sharing a compulsory

[13] Robert Jennings, 'The Proliferation of Adjudicatory Bodies: Dangers and Possible Answers', in *Implications of the Proliferation of International Adjudicatory Bodies for Dispute Resolution, ASIL Bulletin: Educational Resources on International Law* (1995) 2, 6. See also, Robert Jennings, 'The Judiciary, International and National, and the Development of International Law' (1996) 45 *ICLQ* 11.

[14] Gilbert Guillaume, 'The Future of International Judicial Institutions' (1995) 44 *ICLQ* 848.

jurisdiction setting them apart from the International Court with its reliance on State consent and the threat of its withdrawal.[15]

Gilbert Guillaume was also a clear opponent of developing international law beyond a system of State consent and treaty obligations all at the same level. He opposed the development of peremptory norms (*jus cogens*) with a higher place in a hierarchy of norms that would prevail over norms below in the hierarchy. Gilbert Guillaume set out his views in a 2008 article the title of which points to his line of argument, 'Jus cogens et souveraineté'.[16]

A different view on international law, and a strong emphasis on international law as a system with a hierarchy of norms, is provided by 'The Report of the Study Group on the Fragmentation of International Law', finalized by Martti Koskenniemi at the 58th session of the ILC in 2006. As foreshadowed above, Special Rapporteur on the Formation of Custom, Sir Michael Wood, has observed that while:

> [t]he formation and evidence of rules of customary international law in different fields may raise particular issues and it may therefore be for consideration whether, and if so to what degree, different weight may be given to different materials depending on the field in question[,] at the same time it should be recalled that, in the words of Judge Greenwood, '[i]nternational law is not a series of fragmented specialist and self-contained bodies of law, each of which functions in isolation from the others; it is a single, unified system of law.'[17]

The unified approach suggested by the Special Rapporteur, trending towards convergence rather than to Thirlway's fragmentation, must be the correct one. On the view put forward in this book, there is

[15] Gilbert Guillaume, 'The Use of Precedent by International Judges and Arbitrators.' (2011) *Journal of International Dispute Settlement* 5–23.

[16] Gilbert Guillaume, 'Jus cogens et souveraineté', in *Mélanges à Jean-Pierre Puissochet* (Paris: Pedone 2008). Another perspective on international law and individual rights is set out by Ronny Abraham, Guillaume's successor as judge at the ICJ, in an article where he explains how the traditional perspective of reciprocity and in treaty law does not apply to the European Convention on Human Rights, with consequences for the application of the convention in French law. Lack of reciprocity cannot limit the application of a convention right. See R. Abraham, 'Les incidences de la Convention européenne des droits de l'homme sur le contentieux administratif francais' (1990) *Rev fr Droit adm.* 1053, at 1055.

[17] Special Rapporteur Sir Michael Wood, First Report on Formation and Evidence of Customary International Law ILC A/CN.4/663 p. 8 [19], citing *Ahmadou Sadio Diallo (Republic of Guinea* v. *Democratic Republic of the Congo) (Compensation owed by the Democratic Republic of the Congo to the Republic of Guinea)*, Judgment, 19 June 2012, Declaration of Judge Greenwood [8].

in the method of international law more that unites than what differentiates.

Sir Robert Jennings' 1995 statement about 'separate little empires' has later often been revisited, and in the context of courts not acting according to his prediction. Sir Christopher Greenwood, in an analysis of the interpretation given by the Grand Chamber of the European Court of Human Rights of Article 1 of the European Convention in *Bankovic*, observed with approval:

> the meticulous care which the Court showed in ensuring that it took full account of other relevant rules of international law in establishing the terms of 'jurisdiction' in Article 1 – which included the citation of a long list of juristic writings on international law and other materials from outside the specialist literature of human rights – is a welcome recognition on its part that international human rights law and agreements are themselves part of international law as a whole. The Court did not succumb to what Sir Robert Jennings has described as 'the tendency of particular tribunals to regard themselves as different, as separate little empires which must as far as possible be augmented'.[18]

However, Sir Christopher Greenwood had earlier made a point which went much along the same lines as Sir Robert Jennings' as set out above:

> International human rights law is part of international law and should be seen as such. To understand it, it is necessary to understand the principles of treaty interpretation and application and the approach to sources which form an integral part of international law. All too often, however, human rights lawyers – and sometimes human rights tribunals – fail to do this and treat human rights conventions and the jurisprudence which has grown up around them as though they constitute self-contained legal regimes.[19]

His and Sir Robert Jennings' warnings did not go unheeded. Judges Sir Nicholas Bratza and Pellonpää in *Al-Adsaniv. United Kingdom*, where the European Court was at pains not to go against the grain of what was seen as the demands of international customary law, ended their concurring opinion by quoting the eminent jurist, Sir Robert Jennings, who some years ago expressed concern about 'the tendency of particular tribunals to regard themselves as different, as separate little empires which must

[18] C. Greenwood, 'Jurisdiction, NATO and the Kosovo Conflict', in P. Capps, M. Evand and S. Konstadinidis (eds.), *Asserting Jurisdiction: International and European Legal Perspectives* (Oxford: Hart 2003) 166–7.

[19] C. Greenwood, 'Using Human Rights Law in English Courts' (1998) 114 *LQR* 523, 525.

as far as possible be augmented'. I believe that in this case the Court has avoided the kind of development of which Sir Robert warned.[20]

In this chapter, I will mainly use the ICJ's recent case law on a State's rights of consular protection for its citizens to support the argument that a transformation of international law is taking place, with a development of international law as a system with a hierarchy of norms as one central feature.

One feature is the International Court's confirmation of customary international law in different areas of law, also outside the traditional core public international law discipline. The ICJ has made important contributions to customary international law on human rights and, in another case I will briefly refer to, environmental law, moving away from the strictly inter-State perspective and non-hierarchical view of international law where State consent has put extreme restrictions on jurisdiction, obligations of States and the development of the law.

The recognition and development of *erga omnes*, and peremptory norms (*jus cogens*) are another aspects of this transformation.[21] The provisions about peremptory norms in the 1969 Vienna Convention (in Articles 53 and 64) have played a role in some States withholding their ratification. The provisions about *erga omnes* and peremptory norms (*jus cogens*) in the ILC Draft Articles on the Responsibility of States for Internationally Wrongful Acts bring the gradual development of the law further forward. The recognition of peremptory norms (*jus cogens*) by arbitral tribunals and international courts, before the ICJ itself did so in *Congo* v. *Rwanda*, is yet another.[22] The ICJ clarified and developed further its doctrine in *Diallo*[23] and *Belgium* v. *Senegal*.[24] The objections against peremptory norms (*jus cogens*) by countries such as France and Norway have in practice been withdrawn, in recognition of the Court's decisions.[25]

[20] *Al-Adsani* v. *United Kingdom* App no. 35763/97 Judgment [GC] 21 November 2001.

[21] Spurring a considerable literature, see, in particular, A. Orakhelashvili, *Peremptory Norms in International Law* (Oxford Univeristy Press 2006), and among the articles in E. Cannizzaro (ed.), *The Law of Treaties Beyond the Vienna Convention* (Oxford Univeristy Press 2011): P. Picone, 'The Distinction between Jus Cogens and Obligations Erga Omnes', at 411, and E. Cannizzaro, 'A Higher Law for Treaties?' at 425. See also the precise analysis in P. Daillier, M. Forteau and A. Pellet, *Droit International Public* (Paris: LGDJ 2009).

[22] *Armed Activities on the Territory of the Congo (New Application: 2002) (Democratic Republic of the Congo* v. *Rwanda)*, Jurisdiction and Admissibility, Judgment, ICJ Reports 2006, 6.

[23] *Ahmadou Sadio Diallo, (Republic of Guinea* v. *Democratic Republic of the Congo)*, Merits, Judgment, ICJ Reports 2010, 639 (para. 87).

[24] *Questions Relating to the Obligation to Prosecute or Extradite (Belgium* v. *Senegal)*, 20 July 2012.

[25] M. Andenas, 'International Court of Justice, Case Concerning Ahmadou Sadio Diallo' (2011) 60 *ICLQ* 810, 817.

The acknowledgment, conformation and development of customary international law and a hierarchy of norms are incrementally remedying the limitations of traditional doctrine. This is both reflecting and influencing the changing concepts in the ICJ's jurisprudence on State sovereignty, individual rights, jurisdiction, procedure and evidence.

The ICJ itself has started referring to other international courts and tribunals, not least the human rights courts and bodies. In *Diallo (Compensation)* Sir Christopher Greenwood said that:

> International law is not a series of fragmented specialist and self-contained bodies of law, each of which functions in isolation from the others; it is a single, unified system of law and each international court can, and should, draw on the jurisprudence of other international courts and tribunals, even though it is not bound necessarily to come to the same conclusions.[26]

In this chapter the relaxation of a number of restrictive doctrines and practices in the case law of the ICJ will be analysed in the context of the discourses on 'fragmentation of international law' and 'proliferation of international courts' and the loss of axiological direction of public international law.

The ICJ has in a short period of time developed a rather powerful jurisprudence on human rights, environmental law, and remedies. In the same period, the ICJ has developed the rights of individuals and confirmed the constitutionally fundamental doctrines of peremptory norms (*jus cogens*) and *erga omnes* effects. Also the opening up of the closed system of legal sources by allowing for cross citation to, and taking account of, other courts, and the lesser emphasis on jurisdictional limitations, places the Court in a new position, closer to the summit of the international legal system.

Here in this chapter it is argued that the relaxation of these restrictive doctrines and practices in the case law of the ICJ may best be understood as a response to the fragmentation and proliferation discourses, and it is asked whether the centre is not now in this way reasserting itself.

A. *Diplomatic protection and the* Nottebohm *case*

One beginning for this analysis may be found in the *Nottebohm* case of 1955.[27] Liechtenstein claimed to exercise diplomatic protection for a

[26] *Ahmadou Sadio Diallo (Republic of Guinea* v. *Democratic Republic of the Congo) (Compensation owed by the Democratic Republic of the Congo to the Republic of Guinea)*, Judgment 19 June 2012 [8].

[27] *Liechtenstein* v. *Guatemala*, ICJ Reports 1955, 4. See K. Lipstein and E. H. Loewenfeld, 'Liechtenstein gegen Guatemala: Der Nottebohm–Fall', *Gedächtnisschrift Ludwig Marxer*

naturalized citizen. The ICJ however did not recognize the Liechtenstein citizenship. To recognize a naturalization giving the right to grant diplomatic protection, the ICJ required 'effective nationality', and 'a meaningful connection' to the State.

One question for us could be whether the case could have been decided this way today. In 1955 the ICJ invented and then relied upon the requirements of 'effective nationality' and 'a meaningful connection' to the relevant State. There would have been strong pressure from the victors of the Second World War. These countries had strong economic interests in not opening up international law fora of review for many war–time confiscations. In *Nottebohm*, the majority on the ICJ used all the tools at hand for such a task. State sovereignty was given a new twist; while States themselves decided on the law of citizenship, other States' sovereignty give them the right to refuse recognition if there was no 'effective nationality' or 'meaningful connection'. The majority on the ICJ also used evidence as a limiting mechanism; they applied a high evidential threshold that allowed a finding against Liechtenstein. The majority kept its considerations at the inter-State level; their focus was not the consequences for the individual in this case, or the many other individuals in similar cases. It was the interests of States not wanting review of their confiscations that was given weight.

This was an example of 'dynamic interpretation'; there was only tenuous support for the two requirements.[28] Judge Owada has pointed out that the genuine-link theory had never been mentioned in the textbooks before the *Nottebohm* case was decided. He added, 'now, it is accepted that a genuine link has to exist in order to exercise the right of diplomatic

(Schulthess, Zurich 1963) 275–325. K. Lipstein, 'The Nottebohm Case–Reflections by Counsel', (1981) 2 Wig and Gavel 6, and K. Lipstein, 'Acta et Agenda', (1977) 36 *Cambridge LJ* 47. Mr Nottebohm fell victim to the measures taken against enemy nationals or individuals with suspected allegiance to enemy states after the United States entered the Second World War. The US measures extended beyond the US borders. Mr Nottebohm was deported by the Guatemalan authorities to the US where he spent several years in camps for enemy aliens. He was not allowed to return to Guatemala after his release and could not raise any effective challenge before the Guatemalan courts against the confiscation of his considerable property. Only in the 1990s did certain US citizens of Japanese origin get official rehabilitation and reparation through US federal legislation for their internment and confiscation of property in this period.

28 There are other views on the judgment, which is often cited and relied upon, and which has established a legal doctrine of 'effective nationality' or 'meaningful connection' also further developed in treaty law. See J. Crawford, *Brownlie's Principles of Public International Law* (8th edn., Oxford University Press 2012), 40 nn. 128–9 at 510 stating *inter alia* that 'the approach of ICJ in Nottebohm would seem to be perfectly logical in this respect'.

protection. But that was, in a sense, judicial legislation, if you like to call it.'[29]

The three judges in the minority had a very different emphasis from the majority. This is clearly brought out by the passage from Judge Read's dissent: 'justice would not be done on any plane, national or international'.[30] The three dissenting judges included the International Court's subsequent President, Helge Klaestad, and they all three made clear and unconditional findings also on the factual issues. They did not accept the requirements of 'effective nationality' or 'meaningful connection', and then went on to make findings of facts in favour of Liechtenstein, which would satisfy even these higher requirements that the majority claimed.

Judge Read's dissent powerfully sums up the argument:

> There is another aspect of this case which I cannot overlook. Mr. Nottebohm was arrested on October 19, 1943, by the Guatemalan authorities, who were acting not for reasons of their own but at the instance of the United States Government. He was turned over to the armed forces of the United States on the same day. Three days later he was deported to the United States and interned there for two years and three months. There was no trial or inquiry in either country and he was not given the opportunity of confronting his accusers or defending himself, or giving evidence on his own behalf.
>
> In 1944 a series of fifty-seven legal proceedings was commenced against Mr. Nottebohm, designed to expropriate, without compensation to him, all of his properties, whether movable or immovable. The proceedings involved more than one hundred and seventy one appeals of various kinds. Counsel for Guatemala has demonstrated, in a fair and competent manner, the existence of a network of litigation, which could not be dealt with effectively in the absence of the principally interested party. Further, all of the cases involved, as a central and vital issue, the charge against Mr. Nottebohm of treasonable conduct.
>
> It is common ground that Mr. Nottebohm was not permitted to return to Guatemala. He was thus prevented from assuming the personal direction of the complex network of litigation. He was allowed no opportunity to give evidence of the charges made against him, or to confront his accusers in open court. In such circumstances I am bound to proceed on the assumption that Liechtenstein might be entitled to a finding of denial of justice, if the case should be considered on the merits.

[29] 'To Be an International Court Judge: A Conversation with Hisashi Owada, Judge at the ICJ. Conversation with J. H. H. Weiler in the Hauser Global Law School Program, New York University School of Law, 9 November 2005. See www.law.nyu.edu/global/eventsandnews/distinguishedfellowslectureseries/ECM_DLV_015735.

[30] *Liechtenstein* v. *Guatemala*, ICJ Reports 1955, 4 at 35, dissenting opinion of Judge Read.

> In view of this situation, I cannot overlook the fact that the allowance of the plea in bar would ensure that justice would not be done on any plane, national or international. I do not think that a plea in bar, which would have such an effect, should be granted, unless the grounds on which it is based are beyond doubt.[31]

Courts were not strong on upholding individual rights, in any jurisdiction, in the 1940s or 1950s. The majority in the ICJ reflected a general view on the role of courts in restricting rights of the individual against the State, rather than in upholding them, and it did so through doctrines of State sovereignty, jurisdiction and State intent, and rules of procedure and evidence. As we shall see, it is only recently that the ICJ has opened up for diplomatic protection as a more effective tool in the protection of individual rights. Individual rights were previously just not the business of the ICJ. It took time for the human rights protection set out in the Universal Declaration of Human Rights of 1948 to take effect through recognition as customary international law and human rights treaties giving weight to individual rights, and in the application of international law more generally.

B. Congo *v.* Uganda *and* Diallo *in the ICJ*

The ICJ had an opportunity to revisit its restrictive practices on diplomatic protection and individual rights in *Congo* v. *Uganda*.[32] The majority of the Court used evidential issues relating to citizenship as an effective limiting mechanism. In his separate dissent, Judge Simma took another approach: humanitarian and human rights law are obligations *erga omnes* which by their very nature are the concern of all States.[33]

In *Diallo (Merits)*,[34] the Guinean nationality of Mr Diallo was not in question, and the Court could then consider the human rights violations.

1 Facts and findings in *Diallo*

Mr Diallo, a Guinean citizen resident in the Congo for thirty-two years, founded two companies: an import-export company and a company

[31] *Ibid.*

[32] *Armed Activities on the Territory of the Congo (Democratic Republic of the Congo* v. *Uganda)*, Judgment, ICJ Reports 2005, 168.

[33] See separate opinion by Judge Simma in *Armed Activities on the Territory of the Congo (Democratic Republic of the Congo* v. *Uganda)*, Judgment, ICJ Reports 2005, 168, 334.

[34] *Ahmadou Sadio Diallo (Republic of Guinea* v *Democratic Republic of the Congo)*, Judgment on the Merits, ICJ Reports 2010.

specializing in container transport of goods. Mr Diallo was the managing director and, in the end, the sole member of these private limited liability companies. As the managing director of the two companies, Mr Diallo initiated various steps, including judicial ones, to recover alleged debts from the State and several companies. He was arrested and imprisoned on 25 January 1988. More than a year later the public prosecutor in Kinshasa ordered his release. On 31 October 1995 the Prime Minister issued an expulsion order against Mr Diallo, who was again detained, and on 31 January 1996, deported to Guinea.

Only States may be parties to cases before the International Court, and Mr Diallo's case came before the Court by virtue of Guinea seeking to exercise diplomatic protection of his rights. The Court ruled in its 2007 Judgment on Preliminary Objections that Guinea could exercise diplomatic protection for Mr Diallo's direct rights as a member of the private limited liability companies, and rejected the Congolese objections on grounds of failure to exhaust local remedies.

In the 2010 Judgment on Merits, all the claims failed that were based on Mr Diallo's direct rights as a member or as managing director of the private limited liability companies. Congolese restrictions on these rights did not constitute a violation of any protected right to property. Claims concerning the 1988–89 arrest were submitted too late and rejected.

But the 1995–96 detention and expulsion were arbitrary and in violation of the International Covenant on Civil and Political Rights (ICCPR) and the African Charter, and gave rise to a right of compensation. There was, however, no violation of the prohibition of degrading or inhumane treatment.

2 Developing consular protection and human rights

Already in the 2007 Judgment on Preliminary Objections, the ICJ had moved away from the formalistic and traditional limitations[35] on diplomatic protection:

[35] See the discussion in G. Gaja, 'The Position of Individuals in International Law: An ILC Perspective' (2010) 21 *EJIL* 11; C. Amerasinghe, *Diplomatic Protection* (Oxford University Press, 2008) 329–33; L. Condorelli, 'La protection diplomatique et l'évolution de son domaine d'application actuelle' (2003) 86 *Rivista di diritto internazionale* 5; G. Gaja, 'Droit des Etats et droits des individus dans le cadre de la protection diplomatique', in J-F Flauss (ed.), *La Protection Diplomatique: Mutations Contemporaines et Pratiques Nationales* (Brussels: Bruylant 2003) 64; A. Verdross and B. Simma, *Universelles Völkerrecht: Theorie und Praxis* (Berlin: Duncker & Humbolt 1984) 801–2.

> Owing to the substantive development of international law over recent decades in respect of the rights it accords to individuals, the scope *ratione materiae* of diplomatic protection, originally limited to alleged violations of the minimum standard of treatment of aliens, has subsequently widened to include, *inter alia*, internationally guaranteed human rights.[36]

In his Separate Opinion to the Judgment of 2010 (on the merits), Judge Cançado Trindade explained the new approach:

> The subject of the rights that the Court has found to have been breached by the respondent State in the present case, is not the applicant State: the subject of those rights is Mr A S Diallo, an individual. The procedure for the vindication of the claim originally utilized (by the applicant State) was that of diplomatic protection, but the substantive law applicable in the present case, – as clarified after the Court's Judgment of 2007 on Preliminary Objections, in the course of the proceedings (written and oral phases) as to the merits, – is the International Law of Human Rights.
>
> (para. 223)

In *Congo* v. *Uganda*,[37] as already mentioned, Uganda could not satisfy the Court about the Ugandan nationality of the victims of human rights abuses. So in that case the traditional application of diplomatic protection became an effective limiting mechanism. In his Separate Opinion in *Congo* v. *Uganda*, Judge Simma argued for the application of humanitarian and human rights law as obligations *erga omnes* which by their very nature are the concern of all States.[38] In *Diallo*, the Guinean nationality of Mr Diallo was not in question, and the Court could then consider the human rights violations.

Mr Diallo had not been informed at the time of his arrest of his right to request consular assistance from his country. The ICJ held that the Congo was in breach of Article 36(1)(b) of the Vienna Convention on Consular Relations of 1963, to which both Guinea and the Democratic Republic of Congo (DRC) were parties (paras. 90–8).

3 Arbitrary expulsion and detention, and degrading and inhuman treatment in *Diallo* and in *Belgium* v. *Senegal*

In *Diallo (Merits)* the ICJ provided an extensive analysis of the alleged violation of international human rights obligations, first addressing Mr Diallo's rights as an individual (paras. 21–98), and then his rights as a

[36] *Diallo* (Preliminary Objections), para. 39.

[37] *Armed Activities on the Territory of the Congo (Democratic Republic of the Congo* v. *Uganda)*, Judgment, ICJ Reports 2005, 168.

[38] See separate opinion by Judge Simma in *Armed Activities on the Territory of the Congo (Democratic Republic of the Congo* v. *Uganda)*, Judgment, ICJ Reports 2005, 168, 334.

member or as managing director of the private limited liability companies (paras. 99–159).

The Court discussed the legality requirement, not accepting the claim for a national security exception, and taking the opportunity to clarify that the prohibition against arbitrary expulsion does not only provide procedural rights but a substantive right, requiring the Court to review whether the expulsion was justified on its merits.

Article 13 ICCPR and the Article 12 of the African Charter require that an expulsion of an alien can only take place 'in accordance with the law'. The Court set out three conditions that follow from this requirement of legality. First, compliance with national law is a necessary condition but not a sufficient one. Second, domestic law must also be compatible with the other requirements of the Covenant and the African Charter. Third, an expulsion must not be arbitrary in nature (para. 65).

The Court relied on the jurisprudence of other international and regional human rights bodies, such as the United Nations Human Rights Committee (HRC) and the African Commission on Human and Peoples' Rights. It also found support in the interpretation by the European Court of Human Rights and the Inter-American Court of Human Rights of their respective human rights conventions (para. 68). Judges Sir Christopher Greenwood and Sir Kenneth Keith in their Joint Declaration argued that this jurisprudence did not go beyond procedural guarantees.[39] In the case note on *Diallo* in *The American Journal of International Law*, Eirik Bjorge agrees with Greenwood and Keith that the Court goes further than the international and regional human rights bodies. He concludes that 'by developing international human rights in this way, the Court in *Diallo* forcefully has staked its claim as an arbiter of human rights to be reckoned with'.[40] It is not surprising that members and staff of human rights bodies have already given *Diallo* much attention, and it is difficult to imagine that any of these human rights bodies would do anything but gratefully adopt the view of the Court.

[39] Judge Cançado Trindade in his Separate Opinion provides an extensive discussion of the prohibition of arbitrariness in the international law of human rights (paras. 26–36). He advances a general prohibition of arbitrariness when rights are restricted, following from the legality requirement. A closer reading for instance of the case law of the European Court goes far to bearing this out. First, the due process requirements under Protocol 7 to the European Convention are set so high that there is no need for further substantive protection in any of the cases. Secondly, there is no limitation to procedural rights under the prohibition of arbitrary detention under Article 5 of the European Convention, which practically always will come into play in the expulsion cases.

[40] E. Bjorge, 'Case Concerning Ahmadou Sadio Diallo' (2011) 105 *The American Journal of International Law* 534.

The Court held that there had been violations of both procedural and substantive guarantees. There was breach of the domestic law requirements of consultation and the provision of reasons (para. 73), and of the right to be heard (para. 74). The Court did not accept that there were 'compelling reasons of national security' for an exception (para. 74).

The Court also held there was a violation of Article 9 of the Covenant and of Article 6 of the African Charter against arbitrary detention. Again there were breaches of domestic procedures (including the forty-eight hours before going before a judge). Account had to be taken of the 'number and seriousness of irregularities' tainting them. Mr Diallo had been 'held for a particularly long time'. The Government had 'made no attempt to ascertain whether his detention was necessary', and the decisions had not been 'reasoned in a sufficiently precise way' (para. 82). The proceedings against Mr Diallo were not criminal but he still had a right to be notified of reasons for arrest, and the burden was on the State to show that this had been done (paras. 72 and 84).

The Court, in the aftermath of the decade of 'anti-terror' measures, then took this opportunity to state that 'there is no doubt, moreover, that the prohibition of inhuman and degrading treatment is among the rules of general international law which are binding on States in all circumstances, even apart from any treaty commitments'. The Court's use of the words 'even apart' is a useful reminder that we are dealing with a rule of customary international law. The use of words of 'in all circumstances' can refer to a rule's peremptory or *jus cogens* status in the sense of its unconditional applicability and lack of reciprocity, even if other States breach the rule in question, or if a contrary rule or instrument is invoked to bypass the rule. But in *Diallo* there was no normative conflict that would require the Court to address further the peremptory or *jus cogens* status or nature of the prohibition of inhuman and degrading treatment. This was left to further elaboration by the Court at some later occasion, and by the human rights bodies the Court otherwise relied so expressly on for its development of this part of international law.[41] In 2012, the ICJ clarified and developed further its doctrine in *Belgium* v. *Senegal*.[42]

The Court in *Diallo (Merits)* discussed the provisions of Article 7 ICCPR (against torture and degrading treatment), Article 10 (treatment

[41] Neither did it, strictly speaking, require the Court to deal with the customary international law status of the prohibition.

[42] *Questions Relating to the Obligation to Prosecute or Extradite (Belgium* v. *Senegal)*, 20 July 2012. See the discussion below.

of detainees: with humanity and respect for dignity) and Article 5 of the African Charter ('dignity inherent in a human being'). In the event, the Court held that no breach of the prohibition of inhuman and degrading treatment 'had been demonstrated'.

The Court also established a new evidentiary position for claims to succeed in human rights cases. The burden of proof was placed on the claimant in *Pulp Mills*,[43] but this could not apply to human rights cases in general, in particular not when a party claims not to have been afforded procedural guarantees (para. 55).

The Court referred to the limits on its review of a State's interpretation of its own domestic law (para. 70). It is for each State, in the first instance, to interpret its own domestic law and the ICJ will 'not substitute its own interpretation for that of the national authorities, especially when that interpretation is given by the highest national courts'. The threshold for the review is that 'a State puts forward a manifestly incorrect interpretation of its domestic law, particularly for the purpose of gaining an advantage in a pending case'. The ICJ could provide convincing support for breach of domestic law (no consultation and not sufficient reasons (para. 73), and breach of the right to be heard (para. 74)).

In *Diallo (Merits)* the ICJ also stated that the prohibition of inhuman and degrading treatment was binding on States 'in all circumstances', clearly assuming that the prohibition of torture would be no less binding:

> There is no doubt, moreover, that the prohibition of inhuman and degrading treatment is among the rules of general international law which are binding on States in all circumstances, even apart from any treaty commitments.[44]

Here the ICJ was unanimous, and this gives the statement particular authority. It may sometimes be difficult for all judges to agree on the reasons, which were not set out in the 2010 Judgment in *Diallo (Merits)*. In the 2012 Judgment in *Belgium* v. *Senegal* the reasons are set out, and the Court is equally unanimous on this point, with the exception of Judge ad hoc Sur. In addressing torture, the ICJ in *Belgium* v. *Senegal* revisited the

[43] *Pulp Mills on the River Uruguay (Argentina* v. *Uruguay)*, Judgment of 20 April 2010, para. 162.

[44] *Ahmadou Sadio Diallo* (*Republic of Guinea* v. *Democratic Republic of the Congo*), Merits, Judgment, ICJ Reports 2010, 639 (para. 87), see M. Andenas, 'Ahmadou Sadio Diallo (Republic of Guinea v Democratic Republic of the Congo), Merits, Judgment' (2011) 60 *ICLQ* 810-19, indicating room for 'further elaboration by the Court at some later occasion' (at 814).

2010 Judgment in *Diallo (Merits)* on inhuman and degrading treatment, and provided full reasons for the classification of the prohibition of torture as *jus cogens*. The ICJ could readily have listed many further authorities, in the UN system, and in the regional human rights systems. This was simply not called for. Judge ad hoc Sur's statement about 'a disputed notion, whose substance has yet to be established' is clearly wrong in law and unfortunate as a matter of policy. None of the permanent judges shared his view, which is otherwise reduced from the minority position to become an expression of eccentricity.

The ICJ for some period of time appeared most comfortable in the realm of obligations *erga omnes*. The concept of *erga omnes* – obligations owed to the international community as a whole, in the performance of which all States have a legal interest –was first articulated by the Court in *Barcelona Traction(Second Phase)* and has since been revisited on numerous occasions.[45] In *Belgium* v. *Senegal* the ICJ for the first time pronounced on one legal effect of obligations *erga omnes* for third parties. The Court determined that the existence of a common interest in the performance of an *erga omnes* obligation was, alone, sufficient to grant legal standing to third-party States with respect to breaches of the obligation.[46] In the Draft Articles on State Responsibility (2001), the ILC indicated that the general legal interest in the fulfilment of obligations *erga omnes*, which is to say obligations owed to the international community as a whole, entitles any State to whom the obligation is owed to invoke the responsibility of the State in breach.[47] The reasoning of the ILC in this respect was clear:

[45] *Barcelona Traction, Light and Power Company, Limited (Belgium* v. *Spain)*, Second Phase, Judgment, ICJ Reports 1970, 3, 32 (paras. 33–4); *East Timor (Portugal* v. *Australia)*, Judgment, ICJ Reports 1995, 90, 102 (para. 29); *Legal Consequences of the Construction of a Wall in the Occupied Palestinian Territory*, Advisory Opinion, ICJ Reports 2004, 136, 172, 199 (paras. 88, 155–7); *Armed Activities on the Territory of the Congo (New Application: 2002) (Democratic Republic of the Congo* v. *Rwanda)*, Jurisdiction and Admissibility, Judgment, ICJ Reports 2006, 6, 32, 51–2 (paras. 64 and 125); *Case Concerning the Application of the Convention on the Prevention and Punishment of the Crime of Genocide (Bosnia and Herzegovina* v. *Serbia and Montenegro)*, Judgment of 26 February 2007, ICJ Reports 2007, 43, 104, 111 (paras. 147 and 162).

[46] *Belgium* v. *Senegal* (paras. 67–70); see Dissenting Opinion, Xue (para. 16).

[47] [2001] II *YbILC* (part ii), Article 48:

Article 48. Invocation of responsibility by a State other than an injured State

1. Any State other than an injured State is entitled to invoke the responsibility of another State in accordance with paragraph 2 if:
   (a) the obligation breached is owed to a group of States including that State, and is established for the protection of a collective interest of the group; or
   (b) the obligation breached is owed to the international community as a whole.

> In case of breaches of obligations under article 48, it may well be that there is no State which is individually injured by the breach, yet it is highly desirable that some State or States be in a position to claim reparation, in particular restitution. In accordance with paragraph 2(b), such a claim must be made in the interest of the injured State, if any, or of the beneficiaries of the obligation breached.[48]

In *Belgium* v. *Senegal*, the common interest of States parties to obligations arising under the Torture Convention – as obligations *erga omnes partes*– was sufficient to establish the standing of Belgium before the ICJ:

> The obligations of a State party to conduct a preliminary inquiry into the facts and to submit the case to its competent authorities for prosecution are triggered by the presence of the alleged offender in its territory, regardless of the nationality of the offender or the victims, or of the place where the alleged offences occurred. All the other States parties have a common interest in compliance with these obligations by the State in whose territory the alleged offender is present. That common interest implies that the obligations in question are owed by any State party to all the other States parties to the Convention. All the States parties 'have a legal interest' in the protection of the rights involved.[49]

The 'common interest in compliance with the relevant obligations' under the Torture Convention, particularly those arising under Article 6 (para. 2) and Article 7 (para. 1) of the instrument, was sufficient to establish the admissibility of Belgium's claims, apart from whatever special interest Belgium might have with respect to Senegal's compliance.[50] In this respect, the ICJ took a significant step in recognizing this procedural effect arising from obligations of an *erga omnes* nature and, in doing so, gives weight to the ILC's codification of the invocation of State responsibility by third-States for obligations *erga omnes*.

The ICJ's basis of admissibility upon obligations *erga omnes partes* was heavily criticized by several members of the Court[51] and reveals an underlying tension in the ICJ's formalistic approach to obligations under the Torture Convention and the way in which these conventional obligations codify general international law. Certain members of the ICJ felt that the Judgment went beyond the scope of the Torture Convention in its *erga omnes partes* finding, suggesting the absence of such obligations in the

[48] *Ibid.*, Commentary to Article 48.

[49] *Ibid.* (para. 68), citing *Barcelona Traction, Light and Power Company, Limited*, Judgment, ICJ Reports 1970, 32, (para. 33).

[50] *Ibid.* (paras. 67–70).

[51] See Dissenting Opinion, Xue (para. 12); Dissenting Opinion, Judge ad hoc Sur (para. 28).

realm of customary international law.[52] From a purely functional standpoint, such a finding was likely necessary to preserve the admissibility of Belgium's claim. However it is conceivable that there was something more fundamental at play in the decision of the Court. The Torture Convention, which entered into force only in 1987, codified a long-standing prohibition against torture that is widely accepted today as a peremptory norm belonging to *jus cogens*.[53] This very matter arose in oral proceedings before the Court regarding the issue of provisional measures in 2009:

> Judge Simma also asks if this is an obligation *erga omnes*. Belgium thinks it possible to reply in the affirmative. Moreover, Senegal appears to share that view, since . . . if one reads the statement of grounds for the Senegalese law which brings the main crimes under international humanitarian law within the Senegalese Penal Code, it states that this represents the 'incorporation of international rules of conventional and customary origin' . . . The customary rules to which Senegal is referring are general customary rules, not local or regional ones.
>
> Even better, by stating that these rules have 'the character of *jus cogens*', still in the statement of grounds for its law, Senegal too implicitly acknowledges their *erga omnes* character . . . So, even though some may debate the meaning and scope of custom, it is in any event clear that, as regards the customary and *erga omnes* character of the rule *aut dedere aut judicare* or *judicare vel dedere*, Belgium is pleased to note that in fact it shares the same belief as Senegal.[54]

52 Separate Opinion, Abraham (paras. 21, 31–2); Dissenting Opinion, Judge ad hoc Sur (para. 28).

53 *Filartiga* v. *Pena-Irala*, 630 F 2d 876, § 878; *Siderman de Blake* v. *Argentina*, 965 F 2d 699, §§ 714–19; *Prosecutor* v. *Furundžija*, IT-95–17/1-T (paras. 153–4); *Prosecutor* v. *Delalić et al*, IT-96–21-T (para. 454); *Regina* v. *Street Metropolitan Stipendiary Magistrate, ex parte Pinochet Urgarte (No. 3)*, House of Lords, 119 ILR 136 (1999), 260 (para. 153); *Prosecutor* v. *Kunarac et al*, IT-96–23-T & IT-96–23/1-T (para. 466); *Al-Adsani* v. *The United Kingdom*, ECtHR, 35763/97, Judgment (paras. 60–1); *Bouzari and Others* v. *Islamic Republic of Iran*, Canada, Ontario Superior Court of Justice, 128 ILR 586 (2002) (para. 94), 243 DLR (4th) 406 § 429; *Prosecutor* v. *Milan Simić*, IT-95–9/2-S (para. 34); *Brothers Gomez Paquiyauri* v. *Peru*, IACtHR, Judgment of 8 July 2004 (paras. 111–12); *Tibi* v. *Ecuador*, IACtHR, Judgment of 7 September 2004 (para. 143); *Ceaser* v. *Trinidad and Tobago*, IACtHR, Judgment of 11 March 2005 (para. 100); *Baldeón García* v. *Peru*, IACtHR, Judgment of 6 April 2006 (para. 117); *Jones* v. *Ministry of Interior Al-Mamlaka Al-Arabiya AS Saudiya (the Kingdom of Saudi Arabia)*, Judgment, [2006] UKHL 26 (para. 43, per Lord Hoffmann); *Demir and Baykara* v. *Turkey*, ECtHR, 34503/97, Judgment (para. 73); *Questions Relating to the Obligation to Prosecute or Extradite (Belgium* v. *Senegal)*, Judgment of 20 July 2012, 33 (para. 99).

54 Public sitting held 7 April 2009, CR 2009/10, 8 (para. 14, footnotes omitted) in *Questions Relating to the Obligations to Prosecute or Extradite (Belgium* v. *Senegal)*.

Judge Cançado Trindade notes in his Separate Opinion that Senegal, 'much to its credit, acknowledged the importance of the obligations, "binding on all States"', and in particular that the obligation to extradite or prosecute arising from the prohibition against torture was binding on Senegal before the Torture Convention entered into force.[55]

In his Separate Opinion, Judge CançadoTrindade rightly identified the source of the *erga omnes* status of the obligations under consideration: it arises from the *jus cogens* nature of the prohibition against torture.[56] It is certainly not the case that all obligations under multilateral conventions constitute obligations *erga omnes* (*partes*) conferring standing to all States parties, and the Court makes no such claim; however the demarcation of conventional obligations that are *erga omnes* from those that are not requires a principled distinction. In distinguishing the obligations in question from other multilateral convention obligations, the Court invokes its prior rulings in *Reservations to the Convention on the Prevention and Punishment of the Crime of Genocide* (1951) and *Barcelona Traction* (1970).[57] The most pertinent passage in the ICJ's jurisprudence, which accounts for this distinction, is found in *Military and Paramilitary Activities in and against Nicaragua* (1986), where the Court found that 'simply because' principles of general international law, 'recognized as such, have been codified or embodied in multilateral conventions does not mean that they cease to exist and to apply as principles of customary law, even as regards countries that are parties to such conventions'.[58] In effect, obligations in the Torture Convention which parallel obligations *erga omnes* have, at a minimum, a legal effect commensurate to the obligations *erga omnes* they codify, which for present purposes permit any State to which the obligation is owed to invoke the international responsibility of a State in breach.[59] To maintain otherwise would be to suggest that obligations to prevent and punish articulated by instruments codifying peremptory norms, such as the Torture Convention, do not go so far as the *erga omnes* obligations to which they give expression. The perverse effect of such reasoning in this instance would be to deny Belgium standing to invoke Senegal's responsibility for breaching an obligation *erga omnes* because the specific obligation invoked, to punish violations of the prohibition against torture, is articulated in a convention established to remove barriers to the performance of the obligation in question.

[55] Separate Opinion, Cançado Trindade (para. 164).

[56] Separate Opinion, Cançado Trindade (paras. 43, 123).

[57] 2012 Judgment (para. 68).

[58] ICJ Reports 1986 (para. 73).

[59] [2001] II *YbILC* (part ii), Article 48.

The ICJ was right to reject such a regressive understanding of the conventional expression of obligations arising from a peremptory norm in this instance.[60] The *erga omnes* character of obligations to prevent (through necessary legislative means) and punish (through extradition or prosecution) violations of the prohibition against torture codified by the Torture Convention is clearly identified by the Court, so too the legal effects arising from a breach of these obligations, namely standing of any party to which the obligation is owed to bring a claim against the offending State. This finding, as indicated below, was integral to the standing of Belgium before the Court and arises as a consequence of the *jus cogens* status of the prohibition against torture. What this further indicates is that, contrary to the position of some of its members, the Court's pronouncement on the *jus cogens* status of the prohibition against torture was not mere dicta; it is, rather, central to both the substance and procedure of the case in question.

4 Companies and investor rights in *Diallo*: *Barcelona traction* and legal personality

Guinea could exercise diplomatic protection for Mr Diallo's direct rights as a member of the private limited liability companies, and ICJ rejected the Congolese objections on grounds of failure to exhaust local remedies. The Court rejected in its 2007 *Judgment on Preliminary Objections* the claims held by companies owned by Mr Diallo or where he held a controlling position. The Court did not allow Guinea's claim to extend its protection to the two limited liability companies. They were legal persons, formed and established in the Congo, and separate from their shareholder and manager, Mr Diallo. The Court based this on *Barcelona Traction.*[61] In *Elettronica Sicula*[62] the Chamber of the Court had applied the treaty protection developed in bilateral investment treaties for protection of shareholder claims for compensation for violations against a company (protection by substitution). Guinea also referred to the ILC's draft Articles on Diplomatic Protection and case law from various human rights bodies. But in *Diallo* the Court did not extend protection by substitution to a rule of customary international law.

[60] See Separate Opinion, Cançado Trindade (para. 135).

[61] *Barcelona Traction, Light and Power Company, Limited (Belgium* v. *Spain)*, Second Phase, Judgment, ICJ Reports 1970, 33–4, para. 38.

[62] *Elettronica Sicula SPA (ELSI) (United States of America* v. *Italy)*, Order of 20 December 1988, ICJ Reports 1988, 158.

This left Mr Diallo's direct rights as a member or as managing director of the private limited liability companies. In the 2010 Judgment on Merits, all the claims based on Mr Diallo's direct claims failed.[63]

The Joint dissenting opinion of Judges Al-Khasawneh and Yusuf revisited the Court's reading of *Barcelona Traction*. They first of all pointed out that the Court in *Barcelona Traction* saw the need to attribute the diplomatic protection to one state. With one country of incorporation or establishment determining the nationality of the company, and shareholders from many countries, there could be good reasons to choose the former over the latter. In the present case, shareholders of different nationalities were not a concern, as there was a single owner in Mr Diallo.

Judges Al-Khasawneh and Yusuf pointed out that the developments in the field of foreign investments have abandoned the distinction between the corporate personality of the company on the one hand, and that of the shareholders on the other, leading to a discrepancy between the customary international law standard and the standard contained in most investment treaties.

5 Remedies

In *Diallo (Merits)* of 2010, remedies were discussed under the heading 'reparation' (the term used in the text is 'compensation', paras. 160–4). With the findings in the judgment these were limited to the detention and expulsion. The parties were given a short deadline to reach a settlement which was not complied with, opening for the final set of proceedings before the ICJ.

The ICJ awarded damages in *Diallo (Compensation)* in 2012,[64] the third and final judgment in the *Diallo* case. The judgment was also the Court's first on damages in a human rights case.[65]

63 In both the 2007 judgment on preliminary objections and the 2010 judgment on merits there is discussion of the managing director, the sole member, and the private limited liability company in the company law of the Congo. See M. Andenas and F. Wooldridge, *European Comparative Company Law* (Cambridge University Press 2009) on the French (p. 111) and Belgian (p. 124) private companies that the Congolese system and terminology of company law builds upon.

64 *Ahmadou Sadio Diallo (Guinea* v. *Democratic Republic Congo), Compensation Owed by the Democratic Republic of the Congo to the Republic of Guinea*, 19 June 2012.

65 *Corfu Channel (UK* v. *Albania)*, Assessment of Amount of Compensation, ICJ Reports 1949, 244 concerned compensation for loss suffered by a state. *Factory of Chorzów (Germany* v. *Poland)*, Merits, 1928 PCIJ Series A No. 17, in the Permanent Court of International Justice concerned compensation to two companies. But neither court had awarded damages in a human rights case.

The ICJ made the point that it had determined an amount of compensation once before, in the *Corfu Channel* case (para. 13).[66] But that case involved injury by one state to another. The *Diallo* judgment is different. As Judge Greenwood noted in his separate declaration to the judgment in *Diallo (Compensation)* of 2012, although Guinea had brought the action in the exercise of its right of diplomatic protection, 'the case is in substance about the human rights of Mr. Diallo'.[67]

In *Diallo (Merits)* of 2010, the ICJ had established that the 1995–96 detention and expulsion of Diallo were arbitrary and thus obligated the DRC 'to make appropriate reparation, in the form of compensation, to the Republic of Guinea for the injurious consequences of the violations of international obligations' under the Covenant and the African Charter.[68] In the subsequent proceedings of *Diallo (Compensation)*, Guinea sought compensation for non-material injury as well as three heads of material damage: alleged loss of personal property, alleged loss of professional remuneration during Diallo's detentions and after his expulsion, and alleged deprivation of 'potential earnings'. In the following the precise amounts are stated; it becomes obvious why. The total amount of its claim exceeded US$ 11.5 million. The DRC offered US$ 30,000 for non-pecuniary injury and nothing for material damage.

In its judgment on compensation, the ICJ first addressed the non-material injury. It recalled its earlier finding that Diallo had been arrested without being informed of the reasons for that action or being given the possibility of seeking a remedy; that he had been detained for an unjustifiably long period pending expulsion; that he had been made the object of accusations that were not substantiated; and that he was wrongfully expelled from the country where he had resided for thirty-two years and engaged in significant business activity (para. 21). Noting that 'non-material injury can be established even without specific evidence', the ICJ said it was 'reasonable to conclude that the DRC's wrongful conduct caused Mr. Diallo significant psychological suffering and loss of reputation' (*ibid.*). The ICJ took into account the duration of Mr Diallo's

[66] See preceding footnote.

[67] Declaration of Greenwood, J., para. 1. The Court itself emphasized the point when it stated 'that the sum awarded to Guinea in the exercise of diplomatic protection of Mr. Diallo is intended to provide reparation for the latter's injury'. Compensation Judgment, para. 57.

[68] *Ibid*, para. 165(7). The Court cited, in para. 165, the International Covenant on Civil and Political Rights, Articles 9(1), (2), and 13, 16 December 1966, 99 UNTS 171, and African (Banjul) Charter on Human and Peoples' Rights, Articles 6, 12(4), 27 June 1981, 1520 UNTS 217, (1982) 21 ILM 58.

detention and certain aggravating factors, including the link between the expulsions and Mr Diallo's attempts to recover debts from the state or state-owned companies (paras. 22–3). Turning to quantification, the ICJ stated that compensation for non-material injury necessarily rests on equitable considerations (para. 24). It fixed on the amount of US$ 85,000 as 'provid[ing] appropriate compensation' for the non-material injury suffered by Mr Diallo (para. 25).

The ICJ then addressed the issue of material damage. Guinea's claim for the loss to Mr Diallo of his personal property included the furnishings of his apartment listed on an inventory prepared after his expulsion, certain high-value items not on that inventory, and assets in bank accounts. Holding that Guinea had failed to prove the loss of any specific item, the Court was nevertheless satisfied that the DRC's unlawful conduct had caused some material injury, that 'at a minimum Mr. Diallo would have had to transport his personal property to Guinea or to arrange for its disposition in the DRC' (para. 33). The Court therefore awarded compensation on the basis of equitable considerations for US$ 10,000 (para. 36).

The ICJ pointed to additional evidentiary deficiencies in rejecting Guinea's claims for alleged loss of professional remuneration during the detention of Mr Diallo and as a result of his expulsion. While 'in general, a claim for income lost as a result of unlawful detention is cognizable as a component of compensation', the ICJ observed (para. 40), Guinea had failed to submit evidence capable of establishing its claims in this regard (paras. 41–6). For the same reasons, the ICJ rejected the claims based on loss of remuneration as a result of the unlawful expulsion, which it also dismissed as 'highly speculative' (para. 49). Finally, the ICJ rejected claims for loss of 'potential earnings' as essentially based on the loss in value of Mr Diallo's companies and therefore 'beyond the scope of these proceedings, given this Court's prior decision that Guinea's claims relating to the injuries alleged to have been caused to the companies are inadmissible' (para. 53).

As noted, Guinea had sought more than US$ 11.5 million. The ICJ, however, ordered the DRC to pay a total of US$ 95,000 or less than 1 per cent of that claim. There were two reasons for the lower amount. First, Guinea was unsuccessful in convincing the Court to reconsider its restrictive rulings in the two earlier judgments. As discussed above, in its judgment on preliminary objections, the ICJ had held that Guinea could not claim for alleged infringements of the rights of Mr Diallo's two companies, Africom-Zaire and Africontainers-Zaire. In the 2010 judgment on the merits, the ICJ had rejected Guinea's claims for the violation of Mr Diallo's rights as a shareholder of the companies. The ICJ did not extend protection by substitution to a rule of customary international law in the judgment on the merits of 2010, and did not reconsider the matter in the judgment on compensation in 2012.

The second reason for the ICJ's award of less than 1 per cent of Guinea's claim was the lack of supporting evidence. The award of US$ 95,000 was wholly based on 'equitable considerations'.

In *Diallo (Merits)* of 2010, the ICJ brought up the length of proceedings. The application before the ICJ was first lodged in 1998. With such delay, remedies can hardly be effective in a human rights case as this. There is all reason to undertake reforms of different kinds to reduce delay, some of which is due to the deference ICJ procedures show to State parties, and which are less appropriate where the fundamental rights of a private individual is involved. It must on the other hand be recalled that both national and other international courts have considerable delays in human rights cases, although the twenty-two years in the International Court, starting some ten years after the end of the detention with the final expulsion, must be at the extreme end.

6 Sources of authority

Courts follow different practices when it comes to citation of other courts. International Court judgments[69] have traditionally not referred to decisions by other courts, national or international, or for that matter to academic scholarship.[70] It has for some time cited and relied on arbitral decisions.[71]

In the *Wall Case* (2004)[72] the ICJ for the first time cited the UN HRC, both its decisions in individual cases, its 'constant practice' on

[69] Individual judges have more freedom in their opinions that are appended to the judgments.

[70] The European Court of Human Rights has an open practice, whereas the EU Court of Justice has been most closed and restrictive in this respect but now openly relies on judgments from the Human Rights Court. Many national courts have treated law as a closed system and not cited international or foreign courts, and in some countries this remains a contested issue. But most national, and international, courts have increasing rates of citation of decisions by courts from other jurisdictions. See for a discussion of this development, M. Andenas and D. Fairgrieve, '"There is a World Elsewhere" – Lord Bingham and Comparative Law', in M. Andenas and D. Fairgrieve (eds.), *Tom Bingham and the Transformation of the Law – A Liber Amicorum*, (Oxford University Press 2009) 831.

[71] See the discussion in G. Guillaume, 'The Use of Precedent by International Courts and Arbitrators', (2011) *Journal of International Dispute Settlement* 5–23.

[72] *Legal Consequences of the Construction of a Wall in the Occupied Palestinian Territory*, Advisory Opinion, ICJ Reports 2004, 13.

extraterritorial application, and its statements on the interpretation of the ICCPR at issue (paras. 109–10). The ICJ also cited the Committee on Economic, Social and Cultural Rights (CESCR, para, 112) and the UN Special Human Rights Mandates or Rapporteurs. The ICJ placed clear reliance on the statements of the two UN committees in the interpretation of their respective 1966 UN Covenant, and relied in the determination of factual matters on the CESCR and the UN Special Human Rights Mandates or Rapporteurs.

In its 2007 judgment in *Bosnia and Herzegovina* v. *Serbia and Montenegro*, the ICJ cited both the trial chamber of the International Criminal Tribunal for the former Yugoslavia and the International Criminal Tribunal for Rwanda.[73] While declining to embrace the Yugoslav Tribunal's views on state responsibility, the ICJ did rely on its findings of fact and on both ad hoc Tribunals for the elements of international criminal offences. In *Former Yugoslav Republic of Macedonia* v. *Greece*,[74] *Judgment No 2867 of the Administrative Tribunal of the International Labour Organization*,[75] *Belgium* v. *Senegal*,[76] and *Germany* v. *Italy*,[77] the ICJ continued to develop the use of decisions of other courts and tribunals, even broadening its consideration in the latter case to an extensive review of the case law of national courts.

The *Diallo* case occupies an important place in this development and the multiplicity of sources reflects the nature of public international law as an open system.[78] In the 2010 judgment on the merits, for example, the ICJ relied explicitly on the HRC's jurisprudence, including *Maroufidou* v. *Sweden* and General Comment No 15.[79] It justified this step on

[73] *Application of the Convention on the Prevention and Punishment of the Crime of Genocide (Bosnia and Herzegovinia* v. *Serbia and Montenegro)*, ICJ Reports 2007, 43, paras. 188, 198.

[74] *Application of the Interim Accord of 13 September 1995 (Former Yugoslavian Republic of Macedonia* v. *Greece)*, ICJ, 5 December 2011.

[75] *Judgment No. 2867 of the Administrative Tribunal of the International Labour Organization upon a Complaint Filed Against the International Fund for Agricultural Development*, Advisory Opinion, ICJ, 1 February 2012.

[76] *Questions Relating to the Obligation to Prosecute or Extradite* (*Belgium* v. *Senegal*) 20 July 2012.

[77] *Jurisdictional Immunities of the State (Germany* v. *Italy: Greece Intervening)* 3 February 2012, reported by A. Orakhelashvili at (2012) 106 *AJIL* 609.

[78] See the issues formulated in J. Crawford's opening essay 'International Law as an Open System' in his collected essays *International Law as an Open System* (London: CMP 2002).

[79] *Maroufidou* v. *Sweden*, Communication No. 58/1979, para. 9.3, in Human Rights Committee, Selected Decisions Under the Optional Protocol 80, UN Doc. CCPR/C/OP/1, UN Sales No. E.84.XIV.2 (1985); Human Rights Committee, General Comment No. 15: The Position of Aliens Under the Covenant (11 April 1986), www.unhcr.org/refworld/docid/45139acfc.html.

the importance of achieving 'the necessary clarity and the essential consistency of international law, as well as legal security, to which both the individuals with guaranteed rights and the States obliged to comply with treaty obligations are entitled.'[80] While in no way obliged to model its own interpretation of the Covenant on that of the committee, the ICJ said, it believed that 'it should ascribe great weight to the interpretation adopted by this independent body that was established specifically to supervise the application of that treaty'.[81]

Referring to the decisions of regional courts and bodies presents a different set of considerations from the perspective of the 'regime problem' in international adjudication. Because the DRC (a party to the proceeding) had ratified the African Charter on Human and Peoples' Rights, it followed that the ICJ would find some relevance in the practice of the African Commission on Human and Peoples' Rights, and indeed in its 2010 judgment on the merits the ICJ did cite two of its cases, *Kenneth Good* and *World Organization Against Torture* v. *Rwanda*.[82] It did not necessarily follow, however, that the ICJ should make use of the jurisprudence of other regional bodies, such as the Inter-American Court of Human Rights and the European Court of Human Rights.[83] But, in fact, the ICJ took the opposite approach and found additional support in the case law of both the Inter-American and the European Courts, which was 'consistent' with the ICJ's own findings.[84]

Gilbert Guillaume was a proponent of autonomy and not citing other bodies, stating that the ICJ 'always abstained itself from the smallest reference to the rationales employed by the regional jurisdictions'.[85] Previously, the Court's registrar would informally advise judges that the Court does not cite regional courts in its judgments.[86]

[80] Merits Judgment, para. 66. [81] *Ibid.*

[82] *Ibid.*, para. 67 (citing *Good* v. *Republic of Botswana*, Communication No. 313/05, para. 204, African Commission on Human and Peoples' Rights, 28th Annual Activity Report 66 (2010); *World Organization Against Torture* v. *Rwanda*, Communication Nos. 27/89, 46/91, 49/91, 99/93 (joined), *ibid.*, 10th Annual Activity Report 49 (1996)).

[83] See J. Crawford and P. Nevill, 'Relations Between International Courts and Tribunals: The "Regime Problem"', in M. Young (ed.), *Regime Interaction in International Law: Facing Fragmentation* (Cambridge University Press 2012), 235.

[84] Merits Judgment, para. 68.

[85] G. Guillaume, 'The Use of Precedent by International Judges and Arbitrators' (2011) *Journal of International Dispute Settlement* 5, 19–20.

[86] As discussed by M. Andenas, 'International Court of Justice, Case Concerning Ahmadou Sadio Diallo' (2011) 60 *ICLQ* 810, 817 n. 26.

In the secretariats of the different UN human rights bodies, different views have been taken on this, which is reflected in their decisions and general comments. But here, too, the system of citations is opening up. There is an interesting discussion in the UN Human Rights Committee, reflected in the view in *Yevdokimov* v. *Russia* where the dissenting views clarify the breach with established practice that the majority's reliance on the European Court of Human Rights in this case represented.[87]

The 2012 *Diallo* judgment on compensation further developed the ICJ's use of judgments by other international courts and tribunals. In reaching its decision, the Court (in para. 13) consciously took into account

> the practice in other international courts, tribunals and commissions (such as the International Tribunal for the Law of the Sea, the European Court of Human Rights (ECHR), the Inter-American Court of Human Rights (IACHR), the Iran–United States Claims Tribunal, the Eritrea-Ethiopia Claims Commission, and the United Nations Compensation Commission), which have applied general principles governing compensation when fixing its amount, including in respect of injury resulting from unlawful detention and expulsion.

Judge Cançado Trindade highlighted this important issue in his separate opinion by noting that 'the ICJ has rightly taken into account the experience of other contemporary international tribunals in the matter of reparations for damages' (separate opinion, Cançado Trindade, J, para. 1). Judge Greenwood elaborated the point in his declaration, observing that:

> it is entirely appropriate that the Court, recognizing that there is very little in its own jurisprudence on which it can draw, has made a thorough examination of the practice of other international courts and tribunals, especially the main human rights jurisdictions, which have extensive experience of assessing damages in cases with facts very similar to those of the present case.[88]

However, Judge Greenwood argued that the US$ 85,000 for Diallo's non-material injury far exceeded the level awarded by the European and Inter-American Courts of Human Rights. Interestingly, in the judgment on the merits, Judges Greenwood and Keith had pointed out that the jurisprudence cited by the Court on the human rights treaty provisions

87 *Yevdokimov* v. *Russia*, Communication No. 1410/2005, [2011–12] 1 Report of the Human Rights Committee 127, UN Doc. A/67/40 (Vol. I).

88 Declaration, Greenwood, J, (para. 8).

on arbitrary expulsion did not confer protection on substance, only on procedure.[89]

III. Conclusions: incremental transformation

Nottebohm and *Diallo* are good paradigm cases for studying the incremental transformation. This has not been linear, and certain periods have seen more of a hardening of conservative doctrine than others. Currently the development is going the other way. This incremental transformation promises to be a fruitful perspective on the jurisprudence of the ICJ, and more recently in the light of the fragmentation and multiplication discourses.

In this chapter I argue that the ICJ today may not have invented the requirements of 'effective nationality' and 'a meaningful connection' to the relevant state as it did in *Nottebohm* under strong pressure from the victors of the Second World War. Judge Read's dissent points to issues and rights that the current ICJ would find difficult to neglect: from the statement that 'justice would not be done on any plane, national or international', with the lack of any trial or inquiry in Guatemala or the United States, denying Mr Nottebohm the opportunity of confronting his accusers or defending himself, or giving evidence on his own behalf, and the many (fifty-seven) legal proceedings that were commenced against Mr Nottebohm, designed to expropriate, without compensation to him, all of his properties, which could not be dealt with effectively in the absence of the principally interested party.[90] The three dissenting judges did not accept the requirements of 'effective nationality' or 'meaningful connection', but then went on to make findings of facts in favour of Liechtenstein, which would satisfy even these higher requirements.

Before *Diallo* had reached the ICJ, the Universal Declaration of Human Rights of 1948 had taken effect through human rights treaties, and a new system of international human rights protection included a number of courts and other international bodies.

Returning to Sir Robert Jennings and Gilbert Guillaume and their concern over the proliferation of international courts and tribunals, it is interesting to consider the aims of the latter's proposal that references on points of international law may be made from other international

[89] Merits Judgment, ICJ Reports 2010, at 716–19 (paras. 11–14), Joint Declaration, Greenwood and Keith, JJ.

[90] *Liechtenstein* v. *Guatemala*, ICJ Reports 1955, 4 at 35, dissenting opinion of Judge Read.

courts to the International Court.[91] The reference mechanism was to prevent a side-lining by the WTO Appellate Body, other trade bodies, human rights courts and treaty bodies, and international criminal courts, many of which have a compulsory jurisdiction. Gilbert Guillaume has on several occasions expressed his critical views on the relaxation of previous restrictive doctrine, typically asking if there is State consent for the developments.[92] The question raised in this chapter is whether the ICJ relaxing its doctrines as discussed promotes these aims.

In *Diallo*, it becomes much clearer how the open method the ICJ has adopted puts it at the top of the international law system. The development of customary international law by the ICJ is now more likely to include human rights law, international trade law, environmental law and other fields of international law, which until recently seemed to fragment into autonomous regimes. The ICJ has provided itself with the tools to contribute to some level of unity and coherence of international law.

The first feature of this transformation of public international law is in the relaxation of the restrictions of State consent. The law of the ICJ is no longer predominantly concerned with the jurisdictional issues: it is concerned with substantive law. *Diallo* in 2010 and *Georgia* v. *Russia*[93] in 2011 illustrate a gradual development. In the latter case the majority of the Court rejected the claim with reference to the requirement of exhausting the treaty procedures that Georgia had not followed. But the argument in the latter case, both by a strong minority and also a cautious majority, also points towards further lowering of the barriers of State consent when jurisdictional clauses are interpreted. In both *Bosnia and Herzegovina* v.

91 G. Guillaume, 'The Future of International Judicial Institutions' (1995) 44 *ICLQ* 848.

92 G. Guillaume, 'The Use of Precedent by International Courts and Arbitrators' (2011) *Journal of International Dispute Settlement* 5–23.

93 The Judgment on the preliminary objections to jurisdiction raised by the Russian Federation on 1 April 2011 on the *Application of the International Convention on the Elimination of All Forms of Racial Discrimination (Georgia* v. *Russian Federation)* shows how the current disagreement in international law divides ICJ judges, and the limits to the transformation in the International Court's approach to jurisdiction this far. The ICJ concluded that it lacked jurisdiction under Article 22 of the International Convention on the Elimination of All Forms of Racial Discrimination (CERD) because, in the Court's view, Georgia was required, but had failed to, enter into negotiations with Russia over its claims under the CERD. The International Court practically split down the middle, with President Owada, Judges Simma, Abraham and Donoghue and Judge ad hoc Gaja disagreeing with the majority.

Serbia and Montenegro[94] of 2007 and *Belgium* v. *Senegal*[95] of 2012 the ICJ has held a defendant State liable for breach of a human rights treaty. The outcome of these developments will be the gradual strengthening of the ICJ's contentious jurisdiction. The immediate past President at the time of writing, Hisashi Owada, concluded his remarks to the UN group of government legal advisers in 2010, by underlining the importance of the recognition of the Court's compulsory jurisdiction: 'It is the interconnected web of optional clause declarations and compromissory clauses which create a foundation upon which the Court can develop a continuous jurisdiction that does not have to be re-established with each new dispute as does jurisdiction by special agreement.'[96]

Other features that we have discussed above are the ICJ's confirmation of customary international law in different areas of law, also outside the traditional core public international law discipline, as in *Diallo*, and the development of *erga omnes* and peremptory norms (*jus cogens*). In the core discipline of general public international law, the ICJ's jurisprudence on the binding character of provisional measures following *LaGrand (Germany* v. *United States of America)*[97] has been generally received by other international bodies with adjudicative functions, including the regional human rights courts and UN treaty bodies.

The citation of other courts and international bodies is another feature opening up for a dialogue across treaty regimes and other jurisdictions.[98] The 2012 *Diallo* judgment on compensation further developed the use of

94 *Case Concerning the Application of the Convention on the Prevention and Punishment of the Crime of Genocide (Bosnia and Herzegovina* v. *Serbia and Montenegro)*, Judgment of 26 February 2007, ICJ Reports 2007, 43.

95 *Questions Relating to the Obligation to Prosecute or Extradite (Belgium* v. *Senegal)*, 20 July 2012.

96 H. Owada, Remarks to the UN group of Government Legal Advisers at the Seminar on the Contentious Jurisdiction of the ICJ on 26 October 2010, available at www.icj-cij.org/presscom/files/5/16225.pdf?PHPSESSID=5c407.

97 *LaGrand (Germany* v. *United States of America)*, Judgment, ICJ Reports 2001, 46.

98 A former President of the ICJ at the time of writing, G. Guillaume, adds in 'The Use of Precedent by International Courts and Arbitrators' (2011) *Journal of International Dispute Settlement* 5–23, at 20, that 'the Court's policy of precedent essentially aims to assure a constructive dialogue with arbitration tribunals dealing with interstate disputes, primarily in border disputes. For their part, these tribunals are very attentive to the jurisprudence of the Court; by this method, coherence is satisfactorily assured in those matters'. This more narrow view of the role of the International Court otherwise taken in this article illustrates how radical the departure from previous doctrine is in the new case law to which *Diallo* contributes. This can be contrasted with the views of H. Owada, as President at the time of his writing of the articles cited in this chapter (see above).

judgments by other international courts and tribunals. Judge Greenwood placed this expansion into the context of the fragmentation discourse when he noted with approval:

> International law is not a series of fragmented specialist and self-contained bodies of law, each of which functions in isolation from the others; it is a single, unified system of law and each international court can, and should, draw on the jurisprudence of other international courts and tribunals, even though it is not bound necessarily to come to the same conclusions.[99]

The other courts and international bodies in this relationship may respond by taking a closer account of international law and its fundamental principles in applying the treaty base they may have for their activities. International courts and other bodies are increasingly provided with the tools of applying international law and securing coherence and unity, with the ICJ having this as its main business.

[99] Declaration, Greenwood, J, para. 8.

INDEX

For EU product safety concerns, contact us at Calle de José Abascal, 56–1°, 28003 Madrid, Spain or eugpsr@cambridge.org.

www.ingramcontent.com/pod-product-compliance
Lightning Source LLC
LaVergne TN
LVHW011533200926
848484LV00001B/255

* 9 7 8 1 1 0 7 0 8 2 0 9 0 *